W9-BMB-914

NORTHERN NORRLAND
See pp262–75

• Kiruna

LAPPLAND

NORR-
BOTTEN

NORTHERN NORRLAND

• Luleå

GULF OF BOTHNIA

VÄSTER-
BOTTEN

• Umeå

ÅNGERMAN-
LAND • Örnsköldsvik

nd

ERN
AND

EDELPAD

• Sundsvall

GULF OF BOTHNIA

LSING-
AND • Hudiksvall

GÄSTRIKLAND

un • Gävle

STOCKHOLM
See pp44–117

SOUTHERN NORRLAND
See pp246–61

UPPLAND

• Uppsala

IAN-
D **EASTERN SVEALAND**
• Västerås

SÖDER-
MANLAND **STOCKHOLM**

• Nyköping

Linköping
GÖTLAND

RN
AND

• Visby

GOTLAND

EASTERN SVEALAND
See pp122–39

GOTLAND
See pp158–69

mar • ÖLAND

BALTIC SEA

GE
• Karlskrona

RN GÖTALAND

EYEWITNESS TRAVEL

SWEDEN

EYEWITNESS TRAVEL

SWEDEN

DK

DK

LONDON, NEW YORK, MELBOURNE, MUNICH AND DELHI
www.dk.com

PRODUCED FOR DORLING KINDERSLEY BY
Streiffert Förlag AB, Stockholm

SENIOR EDITOR
Bo Streiffert

PROJECT AND PICTURE EDITOR
Guy Engström

ASSISTANT PICTURE EDITOR
Ebba Mörner

MAIN CONTRIBUTORS
Ulf Johansson, Mona Neppenström, Kaj Sandell

PHOTOGRAPHERS
Peter Hanneberg, Erik Svensson, Jeppe Wikström

CARTOGRAPHER
Stig Söderlind

ILLUSTRATORS
Stephen Conlin, Gary Cross, Urban Frank, Claire Littlejohn,
Jan Rojmar, John Woodcock

ENGLISH TRANSLATION
Kate Lambert, Stuart Tudball

EDITOR OF ENGLISH EDITION
Jane Hutchings

Reproduced by Colourscan, Singapore
Printed and bound by South China Printing Co Ltd, China
First American edition 1995

11 12 13 14 10 9 8 7 6 5 4 3 2 1

Published in the United States by DK Publishing,
375 Hudson Street, New York, NY 10014

Reprinted with revisions 2008, 2011

Copyright 2005, 2011 © Dorling Kindersley Limited, London
A Penguin Company

A CATALOG RECORD FOR THIS BOOK IS AVAILABLE FROM
THE LIBRARY OF CONGRESS.

ISSN 1542-1554

ISBN 978-0-7566-6935-5

FLOORS ARE REFERRED TO THROUGHOUT IN ACCORDANCE WITH EUROPEAN USAGE;
IE THE "FIRST FLOOR" IS THE FLOOR ABOVE GROUND LEVEL

Front cover main image: Skarhamn on island of Tjorn, Bohuslan.

MIX
Paper from
responsible sources
FSC™ C018179
www.fsc.org

**The information in this
DK Eyewitness Travel Guide is checked regularly.**

Every effort has been made to ensure that this book is as
up-to-date as possible at the time of going to press. Some details,
however, such as telephone numbers, opening hours, prices, gallery
hanging arrangements and travel information are liable to change.
The publishers cannot accept responsibility for any consequences
arising from the use of this book, nor for any material on third party
websites, and cannot guarantee that any website address in this
book will be a suitable source of travel information. We value the
views and suggestions of our readers very highly. Please write to:
Publisher, DK Eyewitness Travel Guides,
Dorling Kindersley, 80 Strand, London WC2R 0RL, Great Britain,
or email: travelguides@dk.com

Summer-flowering cottongrass in
the mountains of Sylarna

CONTENTS

INTRODUCING SWEDEN

STOCKHOLM AREA BY AREA

Erik XIV's crown in the Treasury
at Stockholm's Royal Palace

◁ Skogavik nature reserve on Bullerö in the Stockholm Archipelago

Inner courtyard of Läckö Slott,
Västergötland *(see p220)*

Cross-country skiers resting on
Åreskutan mountain *(see p259)*

Lingonberries, a much-loved
Swedish fruit

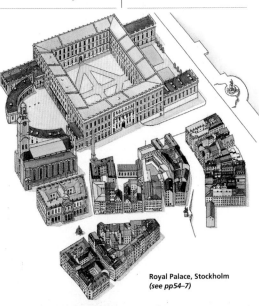

Royal Palace, Stockholm
(see pp54–7)

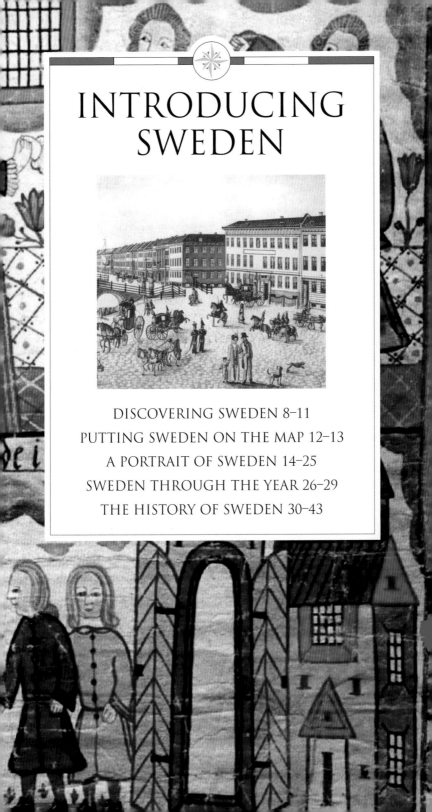

INTRODUCING
SWEDEN

DISCOVERING SWEDEN

Sweden is one of Europe's best kept secrets. As Scandinavia's largest country, it covers a vast range of landscapes, from rolling fields backed by glorious sandy beaches in the south, to dense pine forest and rocky mountains in the north. All over the country

Boathouse, Bohuslän, Western Gotaland

are charming towns and cities bursting with fascinating museums and great restaurants. To get the most out of a visit to Sweden, it is important to decide where to focus your visit. These pages offer a taste of what each region has to offer.

Stortorget's bustling café life in medieval Gamla Stan

STOCKHOLM

- **Medieval Gamla Stan**
- **Vasamuseet**
- **Old-time Skansen**
- **Stunning archipelago**

The Swedish capital, Stockholm, is one of the most delightful cities in Europe. Draped leisurely across 14 islands, it is an instantly likeable blend of medieval beauty set on water.

The heart of the city is the old town, **Gamla Stan** *(see pp49–61)*, a glorious jumble of narrow cobbled lanes and alleyways with some splendid Baroque architecture.

The city's top attraction, the **Vasamuseet** *(see pp90–91)*, is a perfectly preserved 17th-century warship which sank on her maiden voyage in Stockholm harbour.

Downtown Stockholm is predominantly modern in appearance, but there is a taste of old Sweden at **Skansen** *(see p92)*, an

outdoor museum with timber farmhouses and barns from across the country that provide a glimpse from generations back. In the summer actors dress in costume and give demonstrations of how country folk used to live.

While in Stockholm, try to get out onto the water. Just beyond the outer reaches of the harbour, there are 24,000 islands waiting to be discovered in the **archipelago** *(see p110–11)*. Regular boat departures head into a world of islands and skerries topped by pine forest, where visitors can relax in the sunshine, enjoy a picnic in the forest or take a stroll down quiet country lanes edged by wild roses.

EASTERN SVEALAND

- **Bustling Uppsala**
- **Medieval Sigtuna**
- **Viking-age Birka**
- **Majestic Gripsholms Slott**

One of the great things about the attractions of Eastern Svealand is that they are all

within easy distance of Stockholm. The scenery here is dominated by Lake Mälaren which makes a pleasant backdrop to many journeys.

Uppsala *(see pp128–9)* has a magnificent cathedral, and its many students give the place the feel of a Swedish Oxford. Much smaller and more picturesque is **Sigtuna** *(see p130)*, with its rows of neat wooden houses. In summer this quaint little town can be swamped by tourists, all drawn to the impressive medieval ruins of three churches.

There's a wonderful boat trip to **Birka** *(see pp130–31)*, which sits imposingly upon an island in Lake Mälaren, and takes the prize for Sweden's oldest town. This is the place to learn about Sweden's stirring Viking heritage, as it is rich with archaelogical remains.

If the imposing façade of **Gripsholms Slott** *(see p134)* looks familiar, it's because it features on the cover of ABBA's *Waterloo* album. Inside is one of Sweden's most engaging castles, full of Gustavian flourishes.

Canoeists paddling in Lake Mälaran by Gripsholms Slott

◁ **Wall-hanging depicting *The Wedding in Cana and Jesus's Entry into Jerusalem*, 1781**

EASTERN GOTALAND

- Vadstena Abbey
- Kolmårdens Djurpark
- Lake-side Gränna
- Kingdom of Crystal

This region is off-the-beaten-track Sweden. Eastern Götaland sees far fewer tourists than other areas, despite being home to one of the country's most historic towns. **Vadstena** *(see p145)*, with its double attractions of castle and medieval abbey, makes a good stop if heading south from Stockholm. It is a particularly pleasant spot in summer when the narrow, cobbled streets are bedecked with flowers.

Coffin which transported the holy Saint Bridget, Vadstena Abbey

Sweden is not associated with wild animals such as lions and crocodiles, but that's exactly what's waiting at **Kolmårdens Djurpark** *(see p144)*; this safari park comes complete with dolphinarium, tropicarium and ape house.

Gränna *(see p150)* is a low-key lake-side resort on the banks of the country's second largest lake, Vättern. It is a favourite with Swedes, who come here to enjoy the fantastic vistas and to sample the town's famous sweet peppermint flavoured rock.

Admirers of glassware will want to visit the **Kingdom of Crystal** *(see pp152–3)* in Sweden's deep south, where names like Kosta Boda and Orrefors have both sales outlets and production sites.

The unusual *raukar* (limestone stacks) off Gotland's northwest coast

GOTLAND

- Beautiful beaches
- Unspoilt Visby
- Fantastic cycling
- Medieval churches

The island of Gotland's main draw is golden, sandy beaches, which compare favourably with those of the Mediterranean.

At the heart of Gotland is **Visby** *(see pp163–7)*, Sweden's best preserved medieval city, ringed by walls and dominated at its cobbled heart by the impressive ruins of Sankta Karin's church.

Leave Visby and the island's charms unfold: rolling green countryside, quiet country lands edged by pine forest and charming fishing villages. One of the best ways to get around is to cycle since the island is predominantly flat. Along the way is another attraction – perfectly intact **medieval churches** standing proud against the backdrop of the Baltic Sea.

SOUTHERN GOTALAND

- Lund cathedral
- Gourmet eating in Lund and Malmö
- Karlskrona's Baroque architecture

The southern provinces are Sweden at its most continental. Forget the pine forests and reindeer of the north,

the scenery here is altogether more pastoral: undulating fields of bright yellow rapeseed backed by the deep blue of the Baltic Sea give Southern Götaland its distinctive character. There's a sophistication in the people, too, who enjoy sipping a cappuccino in an outdoor café and watching the world go by.

If there is one place that embodies this southern *joie de vivre*, it is handsome **Lund** *(see p177)*, a lively student city, whose impressive cathedral is the envy of the nation. Both Lund and Sweden's third city, **Malmö** *(see pp178–81)*, are great places to sample top-notch Swedish cuisine. This part of the country is renowned for its picture postcard coastlines. Alternatively, some of the country's best Baroque architecture is to be found at the heart of the city of **Karlskrona** *(see pp188–9)* with its rich maritime tradition.

The Baroque Fredrikskyrkan (see *p188*) on Stortorget, Karlskrona

GOTHENBURG

- Great views from GötheborgsUtkiken
- World-class amusement park, Liseberg
- Quaint Haga district
- Feskekörka fish market

With canals criss-crossing the city, Gothenburg bears more than a passing resemblance to its Dutch cousin, Amsterdam, and could not be more different from Stockholm. Whereas the capital is grand and imposing, Gothenburg, Sweden's second city, feels altogether warmer and more welcoming.

There is nowhere better to get a bird's eye view of Scandinavia's largest port than from the top of the bold red-and-white skyscraper **GötheborgsUtkiken**

Wooden cottage by the tranquil waters of Strömstad, Western Götaland

The tram from Central Station to Liseberg amusement park

(see p196). Gothenburgers are justifiably proud of their city and delighted, too, that the **Liseberg amusement park** *(see p200)* is acclaimed as Sweden's most popular tourist attraction, boasting the very latest stomach-churning rides and entertainment.

The **Haga** district *(see p201)*, with its narrow pedestrianized streets and craft stores is a quiet contrast to the bustle of the city centre. There is no greater pleasure here than browsing in the various stores and stopping to enjoy a coffee and a piece of apple and cinnamon pie. For something different,

visitors are spoilt for choice at the **Feskekörka fish market** *(see p201)* where there are two excellent restaurants at which to sample the wares.

WESTERN GOTALAND

- Island retreats
- Picturesque coastal villages
- Varberg fortress
- Laholm's sandy beaches

It is the dramatic coastline of this part of Sweden that makes a visit to Western Götaland appealing. If planning a visit to nearby Gothenburg, it's an easy journey north. From smooth granite rocks ideal for sun-bathing to sweeping bays of golden sands, there is sure to be a part of this popular coast to please.

The **Koster islands** *(see p211)* are found off the shores of Strömstad to the north and are perfect for long carefree days, either lazing in the sun or exploring by bicycle. The coastline south of this area is renowned for its picturesque villages. Perhaps the most charming is modest **Fjällbacka** *(see p212–3)*, whose narrow streets and wooden houses huddle around the harbour, which was once home to a vast herring fleet. Today, the town is popular for swimming and boating.

The pleasant seaside town of **Varberg** *(see p226)* with its fortress, once used for

repelling the Danish enemy, marks the beginning of the coast's sandy beaches, which are best enjoyed at **Laholm** *(see p227)*. Sea temperatures here in summer are really quite respectable, making swimming off this part of the Swedish coast a real pleasure. The beaches not only stretch for miles, but they are also clothing-optional.

WESTERN SVEALAND

- Rolling lakeland countryside
- Örebro Slott
- Folklore villages
- Fascinating bear park

For Swedes, Western Svealand is the most quintessentially Swedish part of the country: rolling hills, pastoral farmland and charming villages of typical wooden homes with red

The 13th-century Örebro Slott on the River Svartån

walls and white windows. This region is also dominated by water – there are lakes seemingly everywhere, including Sweden's largest lake, Vänern. Take a tour of the **Fryken lakes** *(see p232)*, north of Karlstad, to pass through some stunning lakeland countryside once home to Sweden's Nobel laureate and favourite children's author, Selma Lagerlöf *(see p233)*.

Water is also a key feature in Örebro, an engaging city between Karlstad and Stockholm. The 13th-century **Örebro Slott** *(see p238)* sits proudly on an island in the River Svartån which flows right through the heart of the city. The north of the region around Lake Siljan is characterized by quaint villages and undulating farmland where Sweden's **rich folklore** *(see pp240–41)* is still alive today. At Midsummer people don traditional dress and dance around the Maypole. Nearby, the interesting **Orsa Grönklitt** bear park *(see p244)* offers visitors a chance to come face to face with the king of the forest, as well as wolves, lynx and wolverine.

SOUTHERN NORRLAND

- **The High Coast's dramatic coastal scenery**
- **Jamtli open-air museum**
- **Åre ski resort**
- **Mountains of Härjedalen**

The region of Southern Norrland offers the first glimpse of Sweden's wild side: endless pine forests, remote mountain villages and highland pastures used for reindeer herding by the country's indigenous people, the Sámi. Arguably the best coastal scenery anywhere in the country can be found in this region, too. Stretching between Härnösand and Örnsköldsvik, the spectacular **High Coast** *(see p256–7)* with its fjords and islands resembles the indented coastline of neighbouring Norway.

Sámi herder tending to his reindeer

Inland, the delightful lakeside town of Östersund is home to one of the north's best museums, **Jamtli** *(see p258–9)*, an open-air exhibition of rural life during the last century.

The country's top ski resort, **Åre** *(see p259)*, lies close by and buzzes with life in the winter season. At any time of the year, however, a trip by cable car up the Åreskutan mountain, which rises to 1,420 m (4,659 ft), is an absolute must. **Härjedalen** province *(see pp260–61)*, just to the north, is one of Sweden's most mountainous and picturesque areas. It is also a good place to spot reindeer – there are large herds in the forests and hills around the provincial capital, **Sveg** *(see p261)*.

Picturesque farms and fjords in Ångermanland, Southern Norrland

Sledging in winter at Jukkasjärvi

NORTHERN NORRLAND

- **Sandy beaches and sunshine at Piteå**
- **World-famous Icehotel**
- **Arvidsjaur's Sámi life**
- **Fantastic mountain hiking**

This is Sweden at its most elemental: extensive pine forests and craggy mountains, but hardly any human habitation. Distances between the few settlements that do exist here are vast and the climate is at its most severe. However, one of the sunniest places in Sweden is also located here: **Piteå** *(see p268)* is renowned for its long hours of summer sunshine and superb sandy beaches. Now a world-famous attraction, the **Icehotel** *(see p272)* at Jukkasjärvi near Kiruna is rebuilt every winter of ice cut from the local river. For dog sledding or snow-mobiling, this region is one of the best places in Sweden to have a go and the **Kungsleden Trail** *(see p274–5)* is Sweden's longest hiking path at over 400 km (248 miles) long.

Arvidsjaur *(see p273)* is an excellent spot to get to grips with the history of the indigenous Sámi people, who have tended their reindeer in these parts of Swedish Lapland for centuries. Their characterful church village of wooden huts and traditional *kåtor* (similar to teepees) is a good starting point.

Putting Sweden on the Map

The kingdom of Sweden is one of the largest countries in Europe, covering 449,964 sq km (173,730 sq miles). The most southerly point, Smygehuk, lies at about the same latitude as Edinburgh in Scotland, and the northernmost tip, Treriksröset, is nearly 300 km (186 miles) north of the Arctic Circle. As the crow flies, Sweden is 1,572 km (977 miles) from south to north – the same distance as from Smygehuk to Rome. Sweden shares land borders with Norway to the west and Finland to the east, and water borders with Germany, Poland, Estonia, Latvia, Lithuania, Russia and Denmark, which lies across the Kattegat.

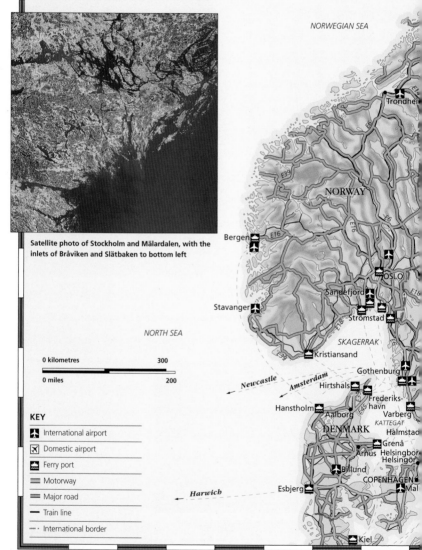

Satellite photo of Stockholm and Mälardalen, with the inlets of Bråviken and Slätbaken to bottom left

NORWEGIAN SEA

Trondhei

NORTH SEA

NORWAY

Bergen

OSLO

Sandefjord

Stavanger

Strömstad

SKAGERRAK

Kristiansand

0 kilometres	300
0 miles	200

← Newcastle   Amsterdam →

Gothenburg

Hirtshals

Hanstholm

Frederiks-havn

Aalborg

Varberg

KATTEGAT

DENMARK

Halmstad

Grenå

Århus

Helsingbor

Helsingör

Billund

COPENHAGEN

← *Harwich*

Esbjerg

Mal

Kiel

KEY

✈ International airport

🗙 Domestic airport

⚓ Ferry port

▬ Motorway

▬ Major road

▬ Train line

-·- International border

NORTHERN EUROPE

ICELAND

NORWAY
Stockholm
FINLAND
SWEDEN
ESTONIA
RUSSIA
LATVIA
DENMARK
LITHUANIA
RUSS. FED.
IRELAND
GREAT
BRITAIN
BELARUS
NETHERLANDS
BELGIUM
GERMANY
POLAND
LUXEMBOURG
UKRAINE
CZECH REP.
FRANCE
SLOVAKIA
SWITZERLAND
AUSTRIA
HUNGARY
MOLDOVA
SLOVENIA
CROATIA
ROMANIA
SPAIN
ITALY

GREATER STOCKHOLM

Uppsala
Norrtälje
Arlanda
Enköping
Sigtuna
Västerås
Vaxholm
Eskilstuna
Strängnäs
Mälaren
Bromma
Mariefred
Södertälje
Nynäshamn
Trosa
BALTIC SEA
Skavsta
Nyköping

0 kilometres 50

0 miles 30

RUSSIA

Narvik
Abisko
Torneträsk
Kiruna
Torneälven
Bodø
Gällivare
Pajala
Kalixälven
Mo i
Rana
Jokkmokk
Arjeplog
Boden
Haparanda
Hemavan
Arvidsjaur
Luleå
Skellefteälven
Piteå
Skellefteå
GULF OF BOTHNIA
Umeå
Storsjön
Östersund
Örnsköldsvik
Vaasa
Härnösand
FINLAND
Sundsvall
SWEDEN
Sveg
Hudiksvall
Ljungan
GULF OF BOTHNIA
Mora
Siljan
Falun
Gävle
Borlänge
Eckerö
Turku/Åbo
HELSINKI
Grisslehamn
Åland
Fagersta
Mariehamn
GULF OF FINLAND
Kapellskär
TALLINN
STOCKHOLM
Riga
BALTIC SEA
Nynäshamn
ESTONIA
Örebro
Norrköping
Ventspils
Linköping
Vättern
Västervik
Jönköping
Visby
Oskarshamn
Växjö
BALTIC SEA
Kalmar
Liepaja
Karlskrona
Klaipeda
Karlshamn
Åhus
Ystad
borg
Bornholm
Rönne
Sassnitz
Gdynia
Gdansk

A PORTRAIT OF SWEDEN

*S*wedes are passionate about nature and the outdoors, and
justly so since their country contains some of Europe's last
surviving areas of wilderness. As a nation, Sweden has built
its wealth on its natural resources and the ingenuity of its engineers.
It has a heritage rich in music, literature and folk traditions and its
people have a deep-rooted sense of peace and democracy.

Few nations in Europe offer
such an exceptionally
diverse landscape, rich in
flora and fauna, as
Sweden. From north of the
Arctic Circle the country stretches a
lengthy 1,572 km (977 miles) south,
a distance equal to almost half the
length of Europe.

Elk

The extreme north is the land of
the midnight sun, where daylight
lasts for 24 hours in high summer,
but is almost non-existent in midwinter. Moving southwards, the
forests and wetlands of Norrland
provide habitats for large numbers
of elk and a thriving birdlife.
In the far south, the rolling plains
of Skåne and the area around the
great lakes make good arable land.

To the east, the green islands of
the Stockholm archipelago
contrast with the bare rocky
outline of the west coast.

A COUNTRY SHAPED BY ICE

The mountain chain which runs
along part of Sweden's border with
northern Norway has several peaks
more than 2,000 m (6,500 ft) high. It
was formed when the ice which
covered the country until 10,000
years ago retreated northwards.
Several glaciers from this time still
linger in the north.

THE CLIMATE

Sweden has a relatively mild climate
for its northerly location. However,
because of the length of the

Start of the annual Vasaloppet race, which attracts more than 16,000 skiers

◁ Crown Princess Victoria and Princess Madeleine in national costume on Swedish Flag Day

Lars Magnus Ericsson, setting Sweden on the path to industrialization by founding Ericsson in 1876

country, the temperature in autumn and spring can vary by more than 20° C (68° F) from one end to the other. Northern Sweden holds the record for the coldest temperature of -53° C (-63° F), while Ultuna, near Uppsala, has recorded the highest temperature of 38° C (100° F). There are occasional green winters in southern Sweden, but the heaviest snow fell in 1998, with 150 cm (5 ft) accumulating on 4–5 December in Gävle in central Sweden.

SPACE FOR ALL

Sweden covers an area of 449,964 sq km (173,731 sq miles), and with just 9 million inhabitants Swedes have plenty of space. In the forested areas, towns can be few and far between.

Emblem of state

Towards the end of the 19th century and thanks largely to the coming of the railways, Sweden began to exploit her rich natural resources. Forestry and copper industries were established and the rivers were harnessed to produce hydroelectricity. Large manufacturing companies began to develop, such as Ericsson, Volvo and Scania, all of which are still in operation today. The needs of industry led to a massive shift in population. Today 85 per cent of the Swedish population

lives in the cities and less than 2 per cent is employed in agriculture.

In the post-war period the need for labour led to immigration. Flows of immigrants became even greater at the end of the 20th century with the arrival of refugees from the world's trouble spots.

GOVERNMENT AND POLITICS

Sweden is both a parliamentary democracy and a hereditary monarchy. As the head of state, the king has no political power, but he is considered to be an important representative of Sweden to the rest of the world. Carl XVI Gustaf is the descendant of one of Napoleon's marshals, Jean-Baptiste Bernadotte, who was chosen as the heir to the throne of the last of the Vasa kings, the childless Karl XIII. The Frenchman was crowned in 1818 as Carl XIV Johan, King of Sweden and Norway. Carl XVI Gustaf came to the throne in 1973 and married the German Silvia Sommerlath. Despite doubt over the king's choice of a commoner for his bride, Swedes soon took Queen Silvia to their hearts. The couple's eldest daughter, Crown Princess Victoria, is the heir to the throne.

Sweden's parliament, the Riksdag, has 349 members and is Sweden's legislative assembly. Elections are held every four years.

Since World War II, a balance has prevailed between the socialist and non-socialist parties in parliament. With only a few exceptions, the Social Democrats, as the largest group, have governed, either alone or with smaller supporting parties. Taxation has reached record levels, but the majority of Swedes tend to believe that they get value for money. However, an economic crisis in the 1990s led to cuts in health, education and social care. The environment is a key issue. Swedes have a deep-rooted love of nature, enshrined in the Right to Roam, which guarantees free access to the forests and countryside and the right to pick berries and mushrooms. There is widespread support for combating pollution.

LANGUAGES AND DIALECTS

While Swedish is the dominant language, Finnish, Tornedalsfinska (the dialect of Finnish spoken in the Torne Valley) and Sami are all official minority languages. The largest of these is Finnish with around 20,000 speakers, while Sami is spoken by about 10,000 people. Despite the general use of standard Swedish, dialects also flourish. The majority is multilingual and Swedes in general are often fluent in English.

RICH CULTURE

Besides the many specialist museums in the cities, there are more than 1,000 rural museums. Great interest is shown in art and handicrafts which can be seen in the galleries and shops.

Swedes are keen musicians, and many play in local orchestras or sing in choirs. Folk music and dancing enjoy a natural high season from Midsummer to the end of August.

The story of film culture also has a Swedish chapter, thanks to stars such as Greta Garbo and Ingrid Bergman.

Berry- and mushroom-picking in rural areas, with permission under Sweden's Right to Roam

A SPORTING NATION

Sweden's abundance of clean, unpolluted waters makes fishing a popular hobby, and the long coastline, glorious archipelagos and numerous waterways have made it a nation of sailors.

For a small nation Sweden has proud traditions, especially in winter sports. Skiing and ice hockey as well as football, handball, bandy (Russian hockey), tennis and golf, all set Swedish pulses racing, while swimming, athletics, boxing, water sports and motorsports also number several stars at international level *(see p25)*.

SWEDEN ON THE WORLD STAGE

The neutrality which protected Sweden from two world wars has remained a guiding principle. Sweden did not join NATO, choosing instead to focus on its own defence and related industry.

Sweden has been a member of the EU since 1995 and elections to the European Parliament are held every five years. The attitude towards the EU is divided and in 2003, the Swedes voted "no" to adopting the euro by a considerable majority.

Sweden is an enthusiastic advocate for the work of the UN. Its own Dag Hammarskjöld was a celebrated Secretary-General (1953–61), and Swedish troops have been involved in peace initiatives worldwide.

Ideal conditions for Sweden's sailing enthusiasts in sheltered archipelagos

Landscape and Wildlife

Sweden has a remarkably varied landscape. The flat arable land of Skåne in the south gives way to lakes and forests, rugged mountains, fast-flowing rivers and wild open moorland further north, leading to the Arctic tundra. Plant and animal species from both continental Europe and the Arctic thrive. Large areas of wilderness have become enclaves where endangered species such as bears and wolves, snakes and owls have been able to survive the pressure from civilization. The coastline, too, is immensely varied. Marine life is unique, as North Sea fish make their way into the brackish water of the Baltic and mix with species normally only found in fresh water.

Wolves *are a threatened species and, despite migration from neighbouring countries, there are only around 200 in Sweden.*

COASTS AND ISLANDS
Smooth rocks and sandy beaches dominate the west coast, where marine life includes saltwater fish such as cod and haddock. Freshwater pike and whitefish can be found off the northerly stretches of the east coast. On the limestone islands of Öland and Gotland orchid meadows flourish.

THE ARABLE SOUTH
The flat lands of Skåne with their fields of crops, willow windbreaks and half-timbered houses topped by storks' nests are a familiar image of Sweden. But just as typical are the stony pastures and juniper slopes of Småland surrounding red cottages, and the meadows and pasture lands of Mälardalen.

Seals *declined in number as a result of hunting, pollution and disease. But now populations of grey seals, ringed seals and harbour seals (pictured) are increasing, thanks to their protected status.*

Roe deer *were almost extinct in the early 19th century. Now they are so common in southern and central Sweden that they are known to raid local gardens in search of food.*

Sea eagles, *with a wing span of up to 250 cm (8 ft), are Sweden's largest birds of prey. They nest along the east coast and also on lakes in Lappland.*

Hedgehogs *rely on their 5,000 spines for protection and curl into a ball at the approach of danger. But this is of little effect against cars, and the popular doorstep guest is in decline.*

SWEDEN'S FLORA

Considering Sweden's unusually rich flora, it is not surprising that the father of botany, Carl von Linné *(see p128)*, was born here. There are more than 2,000 species of flowers alone. After a long cold winter, nature explodes into life with a profusion of blooms, as in the orchid meadows of Öland. Swedes' love of wild flowers is illustrated by the maypoles and garlands used to celebrate Midsummer.

Wood anemones *carpeting the forests signal the arrival of spring.*

The red water-lily *can only be found in some lakes in Tiveden National Park.*

King Karl's Spire *can grow 1 m (3 ft) tall – an impressive height for an orchid. It is most common in swampy mountain areas.*

FORESTS

More than half of Sweden's land area is covered by forests, with deciduous trees in the south, coniferous forests with pines and spruce further north. Here lingonberries, blueberries and chanterelles grow. This is the home of elk and beaver, and forest birds such as capercaillies and black grouse.

THE FAR NORTH

The mountains and moorlands are characterized by their proximity to the Arctic. With late spring come the migratory birds such as hooper swans and the lesser white-fronted goose, and the mountain flora bursts into flower. Wolves, bears, wolverine and lynx inhabit the national parks.

The elk *is the big game of the forest. Around 100,000 elk are killed in the annual hunting season and, despite the road warning signs, others die in accidents involving cars.*

Reindeer *live as domesticated animals in northern Sweden, farmed by Sami in the mountains and forests. In winter the herds move further south to graze.*

The brown bear *is the largest of Sweden's predators and can weigh up to 300 kg (660 lb). It may look slow, but it moves quickly and is dangerous if disturbed.*

The ptarmigan *lives above the tree line and is often encountered, as it is unafraid of mountain hikers. It follows the changing seasons with up to four changes of plumage.*

Sweden's Wooden Houses

The quintessential image of Sweden is the red-and-white painted wooden cottage. Originally, wooden houses were not considered attractive so they were painted red to make them look as though they were built of brick, or yellow to represent stone, and this tradition has continued. Every building from the humblest hut to the most majestic mansion was made of timber from the large tracts of forest. Wood triumphs in the grandiose manor houses of Hälsingland and the decoratively carved merchants' homes of the Stockholm Archipelago. Even today, architects are developing innovative ways of using this classic material.

Bell Tower
Many 18th-century churches had wooden bell towers: Delsbo's, with its elegant onion cupola, dates from 1742.

Hut in Härjedalen
This simple log-built hut in the mountain pasture of Ruändan incorporates the centuries-old tradition of a grass roof.

Interlocking posts bind together the external and interior walls, while the façades are often boarded.

Skogaholm Manor
Built in the 1680s, this Carolian timber house from Närke was originally painted red. In the 1790s, it was given a yellow plaster façade and large windows in line with Gustavian style. More recently it was moved to the museum at Skansen.

HALSINGLAND'S MANOR HOUSES
Reaping the benefits from the lucrative 19th-century timber industry, the forest-owning farmers of Hälsingland built themselves extravagant manor houses. The size of house and magnificence of the painted portico reflected the owner's wealth and status. The interiors were often decorated with wall paintings.

The façade is clad in pine and painted with a copper-vitriol paint, known as Falu red, to prevent rotting.

Swedenborg's Pavilion
The miniature manor house of philosopher Emanuel Swedenborg (1688–1772). It is now at Skansen (see p92).

Societetshuset
Decorative wooden buildings, such as this club house for wealthy visitors to the seaside town of Marstrand (see p216), were a feature of the fashionable west coast bathing resorts in the late 19th century.

Modern Wooden Architecture
The Nordic Watercolour Museum in Skärhamn on the west coast opened in 2000. The Danish architects Bruun/Corfitsen have clad the building's steel and concrete shell with vertical wooden panels in red, using this traditional material in a public setting.

Wooden Lighthouse
Dating from 1840, the wooden lighthouse at Bönan also served as a pilot station. It marked the shipping route into Gävle. The building is now a museum.

Two-storey houses are common in Hälsingland. The finest have an attic floor with half-windows.

Merchant's House in the Archipelago
In the late 19th century Stockholm's upper middle classes spent their summers in the archipelago, where they built magnificent wooden villas with verandas, summer houses, bathing huts and boat houses.

Foundations are a course of cobblestones.

Porticoes and outer doors are particularly richly ornamented and painted. Other details include turned pillars, intricate woodcarving and elegant roofs. The designs vary from parish to parish.

Fishing Cottages at Kungshamn
In fishing villages on the rocky islands of Bohuslän, where space is tight, timber-clad houses in pastel shades crowd in higgledy-piggledy fashion around the harbours.

Decorative Woodwork
More expensive wooden houses dating from around 1900 were often a riot of fretwork and rich ornamentation, known as "carpenter's joy", on verandas, entrances and gables.

Traditions, Customs and Folklore

Globalization and the gradual erosion of regional identity over the last 50 years have had a major impact on Swedish traditions and lifestyle. Much of the formerly rigid etiquette has been relaxed and today Swedes are more informal when it comes to dress and manners. However, despite this culture shift, Swedes still hold onto their roots, local customs, history and traditions. They are passionate about their little red cottages, the countryside, eating herring at Midsummer and enjoying the first fresh strawberries.

Folk musician

Sami in traditional costume for a celebratory occasion

FEASTS AND FESTIVITIES

Celebrating the high points of the year within the family has again become increasingly important, after a dismissive attitude towards tradition in the 1960s and 70s.

Many traditions have pagan origins, most of them related to the coming and going of seasons, and are an excuse to eat special treats and play games. The most important is Midsummer, the summer solstice feast. Along with dancing and games around the maypole, the light, short night (when all sorts of magic is in the air) can be marked by watching the sun set and rise a few hours apart (or hardly at all in the north). For those who go to bed it is the custom to pick seven different flowers in silence and place them under their pillow; their future partner will appear in their dreams. Walpurgis night, 30 April, is when the last day of winter is chased away with

huge bonfires, and songs and speeches welcome spring. Lucia Day, in December, is an intricate mix of pagan and Christian, a festival of light at the onslaught of darkness, which has adopted a Christian martyr as its symbol of hope and bringer of light. Every school, office and church has a Lucia, a girl dressed in white with a red ribbon around her waist symbolizing the martyr's blood, and a crown of candles on her head *(see p29)*.

Easter also has elements of old folk beliefs. Maundy Thursday is the day witches fly to Blåkulla *(see p154)* to dance with the devil. Today, children dress up, broomsticks and all, and give handmade Easter greetings cards in exchange for sweets. Christmas is preceded by the hectic run-up of Advent, when Swedes go partying and consume vast quantities of *glögg* (mulled wine usually mixed with cognac or vodka), *lussebullar* (saffron buns) and *pepparkakor* (ginger snaps).

DRESS AND ETIQUETTE

Those who own a folk costume take it out for midsummer, folk dances, weddings and other formal occasions. Each region has its own historic style and there is also a national dress *(see p14)*. The Sami have their own elaborate costumes.

At weddings people are expected to dress up, as specified on the invitation (white tie, black tie or suit). In everyday life, style is more casual, especially in summer.

Although Swedes are more easy-going these days, they are still fond of etiquette. It is important to know how to *"skål"*. Swedes first raise their glass to their female partner at the table, and then to the hostess. People look each other in the eye while raising their glass and saying *"skål"*, looking down as they drink and then re-establishing eye contact before putting down their glass. If the *skål* is communal, everyone has to look each person around the table in the eye before drinking.

Despite this interest in etiquette, Swedes tend not to observe minor courtesies such as holding open doors or apologizing when they bump into someone. They are very informal when addressing one another; everyone is on first name terms from the start, even when doing business.

SINGERS AND MUSICIANS

More than half a million Swedes sing in a choir, and their passion for song is reflected not just in singing

Midsummer celebrations with games and dancing round the maypole

at parties and the ever-increasing repertoire of drinking songs, but also in the popularity of singing together. There are few 50th birthday parties where each plate doesn't come with a songbook or where friends don't perform songs they have written themselves. Everyone is expected to know works by troubadour Carl Bellman and ballads by Evert Taube *(see p60)*.

Folk music is played at clubs and there are festivals dedicated to folk instruments such as the accordion and hurdy-gurdy. Pageants and history plays have also seen a huge upturn in popularity in recent years.

CLOSE TO NATURE

The Swedes' love of nature is deeply rooted. Many feel, subconsciously, an almost spiritual affinity with the forest, mountains or the sea. Legends and folklore are often linked to nature and many mythical beings are part of country lore. Trolls dwell in the forest, as does the Skogsrå or Huldra (siren), a beautiful young woman who lures men deeper and deeper into the woods and then, once they are lost, she turns around and all there is to be seen is a hollow tree. Women who stroll too far might hear a lovely tune drifting among the trees – that is Näcken, a handsome naked man, playing his fiddle in the middle of gushing streams

Painting depicting mythical beings in the forest

A tournament during Medieval Week, a popular pageant in Visby

and, needless to say, it is best to stay away from him. Giants and dwarfs roam the mountains while elves dance in the meadows and marsh-lands. Some beings have adopted modern guises. The Tomte, who traditionally is a stern, grey little man guarding farmers' barns and livestock, has been transformed into a kindly distributor of Christmas gifts. In the countryside, however, a plate of Christmas porridge is left for him on the doorstep, just to be safe.

There is a strong aware-ness of the changing seasons, linked to how deeply Swedes long for the bright summer. Spring is a slow affair, build-ing up with the blossoming of one flower at a time, each one eagerly awaited. People know when each bloom is due, hence expressions like "between bird cherry and lilac" (ie "at end of May").

Strawberry cream cake

On a more practical note, it is easy to be physically close to nature thanks to the Right to Roam. This grants everyone access to all land, apart from the immediate surroundings of a house or farm *(see p320)*. Many make the most of this resource, walking, camping, or going mushroom- or berry-picking.

A COUNTRY COTTAGE

The little red cottage is the symbol of paradise. Maybe it is the Swedes' farming roots combined with the

brief summer which makes having a holiday house in the countryside or out on an island such a major ambition.

When spring comes, people head out to tend their cottage gardens, and as the autumn nights draw in they are still at their cottages, curled up by the fire. Almost half the population have access to a summer cottage and 20 per cent own one of their own.

CULINARY TRADITIONS

People are rediscovering old Swedish dishes and there has been something of a revival in *husmanskost* ("home-cooking"). Few, however, have time to prepare these at home on a daily basis, so childhood favourites such as *kalops* (a slow-cooked meat stew), *köttbullar* (meatballs) and freshly cleaned and fried herring fillets are now often enjoyed in restaurants.

Swedes drink lots of coffee, and at work the *fika paus* (coffee break) is strictly observed. In fact, *fika* is something everyone does, as proven by the large number of cafés even in small towns. To accompany coffee there is a great variety of *bullar* (buns), cakes, gateaux and biscuits. Home-made sponge cake layered with lots of whipped cream and straw-berries is a summer favourite, especially for birthdays.

Swedish Design

Swedish design first attracted international attention at the 1925 World Exhibition in Paris, when glassware in particular took the world by storm and the concept of "Swedish Grace" was launched. The nation's design tradition is characterized by simplicity and functionality, with a major emphasis on natural materials. Swedish designers and architects are renowned for creating simple, attractive, "human" objects for everyday use. The 20th century marked the beginning of a new golden age, in which Swedish design has won worldwide acclaim.

Stoneware, Hans Hedberg
Swedish ceramics from the 1940s, 50s and 60s, such as stoneware egg, are popular u collectors around the world.

Armchair (1969), Bruno Mathsson
Bruno Mathsson, one of Sweden's most famous 20th-century furniture designers, is one of the creators of the style that became known as "Swedish Modern". He designed the first version of the Pernilla armchair in 1942.

Pale wood and simplicity is the concept most closely associated with Swedish style.

Cabinet (1952), Josef Frank
Frank was born in Austria, but worked in Sweden, and was another disciple of the "Swedish Modern" style. He is best known for his printed textiles, but he also designed furniture.

Rag rugs are an old Swedish weaving tradition adopted by Karin Larsson, whose skill as a textile designer is widely recognized.

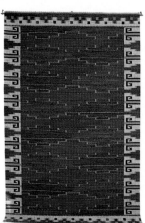

Carpet (1931), Märta Måås-Fjetterström
From 1919, Märta Måås-Fjetterström wove her famous rugs at her studio in Skåne. Her work was inspired by folklore and nature, and she created a design concept that was new but still firmly rooted in tradition.

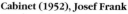

Silver jug (1953)
Sigurd Persson

Persson has an unrivalled ability to handle metal. He made his mark on the history of design with his everyday industrial pieces and exclusive artworks.

Flowers and plants on a windowsill and no curtains typifies the Larssons' ideas on interior decoration.

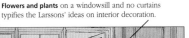

Chair (1981), Jonas Bohlin

The Concrete *chair was the most talked about piece of Swedish furniture in the 1980s. A graduation project, it represented an entirely new approach to furniture design.*

Bookshelf (1989),
John Kandell

The Pilaster *bookshelf stores books horizontally instead of vertically. The lines are simple and typically Scandinavian. The maker, Källemo, is one of Sweden's most unconventional furniture companies.*

Gustavian late 18th-century style elements have remained a strong feature in Swedish design through the centuries, but made an international comeback in the 1990s.

CARL LARSSON'S SUNDBORN

The home created by the artist Carl Larsson (1853–1919) and his wife Karin *(see p237)* became a inspiration around the world when it featured in his watercolours series *A Home.* The mixture of old and new, pure clear colours, light and space and lots of plants was a clear expression of the "Beauty for All" movement.

Vase, Ann Wåhlström
Wåhlström is one of Kosta Boda's new generation of glass designers. Organic, warm and beautiful, Cyklon *(1998) is an excellent example of contemporary Swedish glass.*

WHERE TO SEE SWEDISH DESIGN

Asplund
Sibyllegatan 31,
Stockholm. **Map** 2 E3.

Nationalmuseum
Södra Blasieholmshamnen,
Stockholm. **Map** 4 D2.

Nordiska Museet
Djurgårdsvägen 6–16,
Stockholm. **Map** 4 F1.

Svenskt Tenn
Strandvägen 5, Stockholm.
Map 2 E4.

Design Torget
Various major towns and
cities, including Vallgatan
14, Gothenburg.

Röhsska Museet
Vasagatan 37–39,
Gothenburg.

David Design
Skeppsbron 3, Malmö.

Glassworks shops
Various, Småland.
(See pp152–3).

SWEDEN THROUGH THE YEAR

Thanks to Sweden's geographical location, it experiences wide variations in seasons and climate. Winter retains its icy hold on the north until May, when in the south Skåne is often already basking in sunshine. Once spring gets going in the north and the days lengthen, nature soon catches up. Summers can be pleasantly warm throughout Sweden and that is when Swedes head off into the countryside to swim

The crocus, a sign of spring

and enjoy the outdoor life, often staying in a summer cottage. The holiday period from late June to August is the height of the tourist season, with the widest range of attractions on offer. In winter, Swedes make for the mountains, which see the first snowfall as early as November. They value festivals, and events such as Christmas, New Year, Easter, Midsummer's Eve and Walpurgis are celebrated with enthusiasm.

An April start for the salmon fly-fishing season in Mörrum

SPRING

After the long, dark Swedish winter, spring makes a welcome appearance. In Skåne the migratory birds return and spring flowers bloom in March, while in the north it's mid-May before winter releases its hold. Traditionally eaten before Lent, the *semla* cream bun is a tempting treat. Walpurgis Night, on the last day of April, marks a farewell to winter with folk dancing, torchlight processions, student choirs, bonfires and fireworks.

Semla bun

MARCH

Vasa Ski Race *(early Mar)*. World famous long-distance ski race *(see p245)*.
Stockholm International Boat Show *(early Mar)*. The spring's major boat exhibition at Stockholm International Fairs in Älvsjö.

Åselenappet *(end of Mar)*. Ice-fishing competition, which is the high point of the winter market in Åsele, Lapland.

APRIL

Start of Salmon Fishing Season, Mörrum *(1 Apr)*, Sweden's main salmon river *(see p187)*.
The "crane dance", Hornborgasjön *(mid-Apr)*. Several thousand cranes gather on the fields around this lake in Västergötland for their spectacular annual mating dance. Quite a sight to behold.
Walpurgis Night *(30 Apr)*. Around the country bonfires welcome in the new season, with students donning their white caps and making merry. In the student town of Uppsala, Walpurgis Night also includes fine student choirs, a fun river-rafting carnival and lots of other events.

MAY

May Day *(1 May)*. Workers' processions countrywide.
Linné's birthday, Stenbrohult *(23 May)*. The father of botany is commemorated at his childhood home in Småland.
Elite Race *(last weekend in May)*. International trotting competition at Solvalla.
"Tjejtrampet", Västerås *(last weekend in May)*. The 50-km (31-mile) women-only cycling competition.
Trollhättan waterfalls *(weekends in May)*. Magnificent falls, usually tamed by the power station, burst into life.
Gothenburg Jazz Festival *(late May)*. This three-day festival of swing, jazz, gospel and blues takes place at seven locations around the city.

Walpurgis Night bonfire, at Riddarholmen, Stockholm

Midsummer celebrations at Skansen open-air museum, Stockholm

SUMMER

The school year finishes in early June and summer comes into its own with Midsummer celebrations and dancing round the maypole. Evenings are often warm and the nights light, encouraging parties round the clock. In the far north the sun doesn't even set. July is traditionally the main holiday month and favourite spots can become crowded. But Sweden is big and there's room for everyone. The start of the school term at the end of August coincides with two popular culinary festivals celebrating crayfish and fermented Baltic herring.

JUNE

Stockholm Marathon (early Jun). One of the world's 10 biggest marathons with up to 17,500 runners.
Archipelago Boat Day, Stockholm (first Wed in Jun). Classic steamboats assemble at Strömkajen for a round trip to Vaxholm.
National Day (6 Jun). A public holiday since 2005, National Day is celebrated around the country as Swedish Flag Day. The royal family attend the celebrations at Skansen in Stockholm.
Postrodden Mail Boat Race, Grisslehamn (mid-Jun). Rowing race to the Åland islands following the old mail route.
"Vätternrundan" (mid-Jun). Classic cycling race 300 km (190 miles) round Lake Vättern with around 20,000 participants, starting and finishing in Motala.

Midsummer's Eve (penultimate Sat in Jun). A major Swedish festival celebrated by dancing around a flower-bedecked maypole. Midsummer in Dalarna, Rättvik and Mora is especially rich in tradition with folk music and the wearing of colourful national costumes.

JULY

Gotland Race (first week in Jul). Major international sailing race around Gotland, starting and finishing in Sandhamn in the Stockholm Archipelago.
Skule Song Festival (first weekend in Jul). One of Sweden's largest singing festivals, held at the foot of the Skule mountain on the High Coast.
HälsingeHambon (early Jul). Folk-dancing competition in Härga, Bollnäs and Arbrå.
Vansbro Swim (early Jul). Up to 5,000 people take part in the 3-km (2-mile) swim in the Vanån and Västerdal rivers, starting in Vansbro.
Stånga Games, Gotland (mid-Jul). Events featuring Gotland sports such as Square-and-border-ball, The Stone, Gotlandic Pole Throwing and "Hook the Bottom".
Gammelvala Brunskog, Värmland (end of Jul). Week-long festival celebrating the domestic skills of the past. Music, exhibitions, drama and local food.
Storsjöyran Festival (end of Jul). This week-long festival of pop and rock music in "the Republic of Jämtland" also includes drama, exhibitions and street artists.

Crayfish

Music in the Kingdom of Crystal, Småland's Glass-works (end of Jul). Folk music, choral singing, opera, wind bands and jazz in a charming setting.
Kukkolaforsen Whitefish Festival (last weekend in Jul). Celebrations in Sweden and Finland to mark the whitefish reaching the Torneälven river, which forms the border between the two countries. The fish are caught in large nets and eaten grilled or smoked.

AUGUST

Skänninge Market, Östergötland (Thu after first Wed in Aug). One of Sweden's most traditional markets, attracting 120,000 visitors to this medieval city.
Royal Philharmonic Orchestra Outdoor Concert, Stockholm (early Aug). This concert on the lawn outside Sjöhistoriska Museet is one of the highlights of the season.
Gotland Medieval Week (early Aug). Visby once more becomes a 14th-century Hanseatic city with tournaments, plays and music and participants in colourful medieval costumes.
Hjo Accordion Festival (mid-Aug). Accordion players from around the world meet in the small town of Hjo on the shores of Lake Vättern.
Crayfish and Fermented Herring (end of Aug). Although there is no longer a statutory start date for eating these national delicacies – accompanied by ice-cold schnapps, cheese and silly paper hats – this is when Swedes party the most.

Medieval Week tournament in Visby, Gotland

Beech forest in autumn at Söderåsen, Skåne

AUTUMN

The nights may be drawing in, but the mornings are light and the days often crisp and clear. In late autumn deciduous trees provide a stunning display of colours. It's harvest time in the forests and countryside, and a wide variety of delicious edible mushrooms, as well as blueberries, lingonberries and the red-gold cloudberries of the northern marshes are all ripe for the picking.

SEPTEMBER

Oxhälja Market, Filipstad *(early Sep)*. Traditional market in eastern Värmland.
Tjejmilen, Stockholm *(early Sep)*. In a lively atmosphere at Djurgården, Stockholm's royal park, 26,000 women take part in a 10 km run.

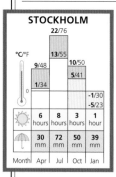

Chanterelles

Swedish Trotting Derby, Jägersro *(Sep)*. Sweden's top four year-olds compete for the derby title on the trotting track in Malmö.
Kivik Apple Market *(end Sep)*. Apples are the focus of this two-day festival, which attracts around 20,000 visitors. Giant art installations created with tons of apples are a particular highlight.

OCTOBER

LidingöLoppet *(first weekend in Oct)*. The world's largest cross-country race, with tens of thousands of competitors, including elite runners, senior citizens and children.
Harvest Festival, Öland (early Oct). Sweden's biggest harvest festival takes place over four days around Michaelmas, with around 900 events attracting 200,000 visitors to enjoy local food, concerts and exhibitions.
Umeå International Jazz Festival *(end Oct)*. Leading jazz festival, first staged in the 1960s.

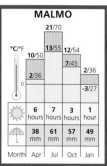

STOCKHOLM

Month	Apr	Jul	Oct	Jan
Average maximum temperature °C/°F	9/48	22/76 · 13/55	10/50	1/34
Average minimum temperature °C/°F			5/41	-1/30 / -5/23
Average daily hours of sunshine	6 hours	8 hours	3 hours	1 hour
Average monthly rainfall	30 mm	72 mm	50 mm	39 mm

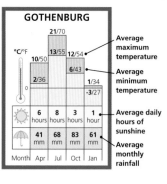

GOTHENBURG

Month	Apr	Jul	Oct	Jan
Average maximum temperature °C/°F	10/50	21/70 · 13/55	12/54	1/34
Average minimum temperature °C/°F	2/36		6/43	-3/27
Average daily hours of sunshine	6 hours	8 hours	3 hours	1 hour
Average monthly rainfall	41 mm	68 mm	83 mm	61 mm

CLIMATE

Considerable variations in climate from north to south sometimes result in southern Sweden having no snow and temperatures above freezing in winter, while the north is blanketed in thick snow. The differences are less extreme in summer. The effect of the North Atlantic and the Gulf Stream is felt on the west coast in mild damp winds and the highest rainfall.

MALMO

Month	Apr	Jul	Oct	Jan
°C/°F	10/50	21/70 · 13/55	12/54 / 7/45	2/36
	2/36			-3/27
hours sunshine	6 hours	7 hours	3 hours	1 hour
rainfall	38 mm	61 mm	57 mm	49 mm

OSTERSUND

Month	Apr	Jul	Oct	Jan
°C/°F	-5/41	19/66 · 10/50	6/43 / 1/34	-6/21 / -13/9
	-3/27			
hours sunshine	6 hours	7 hours	2 hours	1 hour
rainfall	32 mm	86 mm	45 mm	36 mm

LULEA

Month	Apr	Jul	Oct	Jan
°C/°F	-4/39	20/68 · 11/52	6/43 / 0/32	-7/19 / -16/3
	-4/25			
hours sunshine	7 hours	10 hours	3 hours	0.6 hour
rainfall	29 mm	50 mm	50 mm	40 mm

WINTER

While Christmas does not always go hand in hand with snow in southern Sweden, there are plenty of opportunities for ice-skating and there's always a chance of a white January. The mountains become a paradise for skiers, while snow cannons help out elsewhere if nature isn't up to the job. From the first day of Advent, the Christmas season is in full swing, culminating in present-giving on Christmas Eve. Restaurants enjoy their busiest time and Lucia processions brighten the winter darkness.

NOVEMBER

Gustav Adolf Day *(6 Nov)*. Gothenburg celebrates the royal founder of the city on the anniversary of his death *(see p195)*.
St Martin's Day *(10–11 Nov)*. Roast goose and "black soup" containing goose blood are served at parties for St Martin of Tours and Martin Luther.

DECEMBER

Nobel Day *(10 Dec)*. The year's Nobel Prize laureates are honoured in a ceremony at Konserthuset (Concert Hall) and a banquet in Stadshuset (City Hall) attended by the King and Queen.
Lucia Celebrations *(13 Dec)*. Sweden's chosen Lucia, with her girl attendants and "star boys", serves the Nobel laureates morning coffee with saffron buns and performs traditional songs. In the evening a Lucia procession winds through the capital to celebrations and fireworks at Skansen. Similar Lucia processions take place throughout Sweden and, on a smaller scale, in many homes and schools.
Christmas Markets throughout Sweden *(from early Dec)*. The markets at Skansen and Stortorget in Stockholm are particularly atmospheric.
Christmas *(24–26 Dec)*. Filled with traditions, Christmas is the most important Swedish holiday. The main

Lucia, the "Queen of Light", with her attendants at Skansen

event is Christmas Eve when an abundant *smörgåsbord* is followed by gifts. Christmas Day often begins with a church service.
New Year *(31 Dec–1 Jan)*. People go out on the town. Celebrations are televised from Skansen, including a traditional midnight reading of Tennyson's *"Ring out wild bells…"* Church bells peal and there are spectacular fireworks displays.

Northern Lights over Jokkmokk on a cold winter night

JANUARY

Hindersmässan *(end Jan)*. Market in Örebro dating back to medieval times.
Kiruna Snow Festival, *(last week in Jan)*. Renowned festival, especially for its reindeer racing.

FEBRUARY

Jokkmokks Winter Market *(first weekend in Feb)*. Colourful festival with market, reindeer sledding and races.
Gothenburg Boat Show *(early Feb)*. New boats on show at the Swedish Exhibition Centre in Gothenburg.
Vikingarännet *(as soon as the ice holds)*. Long-distance ice-skating race between Stockholm and Uppsala.
Globen Gala *(2nd half of Feb)*. Athletes compete at this top indoor competition.
Spring Salon *(Feb–Mar)*. Annual art exhibition of new talent at Liljevalchs, Stockholm.

PUBLIC HOLIDAYS

New Year's Day (1 Jan)
Epiphany (6 Jan)
Good Friday (Mar/Apr)
Easter Monday (Mar/Apr)
Ascension Day (6th Thu after Easter)
Labour Day (1 May)
National Day (6 Jun)
Midsummer (Jun)
Christmas Day (25 Dec)
Boxing Day (26 Dec)

Frozen Riddarfjärden in Stockholm as a winter park

THE HISTORY OF SWEDEN

*D*escribed in the 4th century BC as a land of frozen seas and midnight sun, this northerly nation of reindeer herders also produced the fearsome Viking traders of the 9th century. By the 17th century, Sweden, in its Age of Greatness, ruled supreme over the Baltic region. Vanquished by Russia in 1809, the country adopted a more peaceful role and today is heavily engaged in world affairs.

In the last 100,000 years, Sweden has been covered by thick inland ice on at least three occasions. As the ice retreated northwards for the last time in approximately 12,000 BC, nomadic reindeer hunters moved in to use the newly revealed land, but it was not until 6500 BC that Sweden was entirely free of ice.

Rune stone, 9th century

Farming was gradually adopted in southern Sweden from 4000 BC, while hunting continued to remain prevalent in the inland areas of Norrland for a long time to come. The first examples of domestic pottery date from this period and burial mounds appeared in the southern provinces.

Finds from the Bronze Age (1800–500 BC) bear witness to increased contact with the outside world. A chieftain society based on power and social alliances began to develop. Magnificent bronze objects, huge burial mounds and cairns with grave goods as well as rock carvings date from this period *(see p212)*.

The transition to the Iron Age in 500 BC saw the first written accounts about Scandinavia. In the 4th century BC the Greek explorer and trader, Phytheas of Massilia, described the journey to "Thule", with its frozen seas and midnight sun. In his *Germania* (AD 98), the Roman Tacitus refers to the *"sviones"* as a powerful people with strong men, weapons and fleets.

With the growth of the Roman Empire, links with the Continent increased and numerous finds show evidence of trade with Rome via the many German tribes in the area north of the Rhine. The fall of Rome and the subsequent period of population migrations saw the rise of small kingdoms across Europe. In Sweden there was a kingdom centred on Uppsala where large *kungshögar* (King's Mounds) can still be seen today *(see p129)*.

From 800 until Christianity reached Sweden in the mid-11th century, the Vikings took the world by storm. As traders, settlers and plunderers, they set sail in search of land, slaves and treasure. They carried out raids throughout Europe, sailed as far as Baghdad and even reached America. Christian monks wrote of attacks on rich monasteries and towns. But the Vikings were more than wild barbarians. They were also hard-working farmers, traders, experienced sailors, craftsmen and shipbuilders.

TIMELINE

c. 12,000 BC Thick ice covers the country. As the ice retreats, reindeer herders gradually move into the southernmost coastal area	1500 BC Regional provinces build barrows and cairns to powerful men and women	500 BC Early Iron Age; a worsening climate and a decline in agriculture	*Viking ship c. 980* 

12 000 BC	4000 BC	2000 BC	AD	500	1000
4000 BC Farming is gradually adopted in the south of the land	**3700 BC** Burials take place in chambered mounds, creating the first monuments in the Swedish countryside	**1800 BC** Bronze objects start to be made in Sweden along continental lines	**AD 98** Tacitus refers to the *sviones* in his writings	**800** The Viking period begins and the trading centre of Birka in Lake Mälaren is founded	

◁ *Gustav Vasa* (1523–60), painting by Cornelius Arendtz

CHRISTIANITY AND THE BIRTH OF A KINGDOM

During the 11th and 12th centuries several families from different provinces battled for power over the central part of what is known today as Sweden. The country was more like a federation of self-governing provinces, a number of which, for a limited time, had influence over those around them.

Little is known of the kings and chieftains in the early Middle Ages other than brief mentions in sagas. In the 11th century, King Olof Skötkonung (d. 1020) was converted to Christianity and was baptized in 1008, along with his sons Anund Jakob (d. 1050) and Edmund the Old (d. 1060). Thereafter power passed to the Stenkil family, which had strong links with Västergötland where the Christian church had gained the most influence.

Birger Jarl's seal

The church and the gradual transition to Christianity underway in the 12th century were vital to the growing power of the king. The priests brought with them an administrative tradition, a civil service and a rational system for regulating property. The church also

King Olof Skötkonung's baptism at Husaby well in Västergötland, 1008

reinforced the strength of the king ideologically through the idea that his power was derived from God.

Once the Stenkil dynasty came to an end around 1120, the royal houses of Västergötland (Erik) and Östergötland (Sverker) battled for supremacy. Both families died out in the first half of the 13th century at the time when the power of the *riksjarl* (earl) was at its height. The *riksjarl* was the king's most important statesman and the position gained greater influence through Birger Magnusson, known as Birger Jarl, who became *riksjarl* in 1248 under King Erik Eriksson. Until his death in 1266, Birger Jarl was the de facto wielder of power in Sweden, which by then had developed into a medieval kingdom similar to those elsewhere in Europe.

THE HANSEATIC LEAGUE AND THE BJÄLBO DYNASTY'S POWER STRUGGLE

The 13th century saw the founding of many of the medieval towns still standing today. Documents show that Stockholm existed as a town in 1252, four years after Birger Jarl became *riksjarl*. In 1289 it was described as the largest town in Sweden, but it was not yet a capital city. Its importance lay in its role as a trading centre, particularly for the German Hanseatic League, during the 14th century. The Hanseatic League had previously established a base in Visby on Gotland, which was one of its most important centres. In some places, the Hansa influence was so great that the king had to prevent Germans from holding more than half of the leading positions in the town.

Through Birger Jarl's son, Valdemar, elected king in 1250, power passed to

TIMELINE

Birger Jarl

1008	1100			1200	1250
1008 Olof Skötkonung is baptized a Christian in Västergötland	**1080** Pagan revolt replaces the Christian, Inge the Elder, by the Svea family, who choose Blot-Sven as king	**1143** Alvastra monastery in Östergötland is founded by Cistercians		**1248** Birger Jarl is *riksjarl*, the king's foremost statesman	
	1101 The meeting of the three kings in Kungahälla sets the borders of the Nordic countries	**1130** Östergötland chief Sverker the Elder elected king	**1222** The last of the Sverker dynasty, Johan Sverkersson, dies and is succeeded by Erik Eriksson	**1250** Erik Eriksson is succeeded by Valdemar Birgersson, son of Birger Jarl and first of the Folkung dynasty	

the Bjälbo dynasty. Valdemar was replaced after a revolt by his brother Magnus Ladulås who was elected king in 1275. During Magnus's reign, Swedish legislation was reformed and the Ordinance of Alsnö of 1280 granted the nobility and church far-reaching privileges and freedom from taxation.

The king's nickname, Ladulås (literally "lock barn"), is said to derive from his ban on nobles from helping themselves to sustenance from peasants' barns when travelling.

Beheading of 100 members of the Swedish nobility in the Stockholm Bloodbath, 1520

On Magnus' death in 1290, his son Birger was still a minor and Sweden was ruled by a regency. Once the king reached his majority in 1303, a power struggle broke out between Birger and his brothers, Dukes Erik and Valdemar. Sweden was divided between the brothers until in 1317 Birger invited Erik and Valdemar to a banquet at Nyköping Castle and had them both imprisoned and left to die. Soon, Birger himself was forced to flee the country after a revolt and Magnus Eriksson, the three year-old son of Duke Erik, was elected king of Sweden in 1319.

Magnus's rule was characterized by severe domestic opposition and financial problems. Sweden also suffered the Black Death in 1350 in which one-third of the population died. The crisis led to the Swedish nobles in 1363 appealing to the Duke of Mecklenburg, whose son Albrecht was hailed king of Sweden the following year.

THE KALMAR UNION

Albrecht of Mecklenburg came to the throne with the support of the nobility, who reacted with a revolt when he subsequently sought to wield his own power. The nobles were backed by Queen Margareta of Denmark-Norway and Albrecht was defeated at Fallköping in 1389, after which Denmark, Norway and Sweden came under the rule of Denmark. At a meeting in Kalmar in 1397, Margareta's nephew, Erik of Pomerania, was crowned king of Denmark, Norway and Sweden, thus establishing the Kalmar Union, which lasted until 1523.

The unification period was characterized by conflict in Sweden. Under Erik of Pomerania there was great dissatisfaction with newly-introduced taxes. A peasant revolt, known as the Engelbrekt revolt after its legendary leader, led to Erik being deposed in 1439. The Kalmar Union was unable to control the Council of State or the castles, and Sweden lacked a recognized supreme authority. Subsequent Danish kings were recognized as rulers in Sweden only for a few years and in between the country was controlled by representatives of the nobility.

At the Battle of Brunkeberg in Stockholm in 1471, the Danish King Christian I sought to enforce his power in Sweden, but was defeated by the viceroy, Sten Sture the Elder. A new Danish crusade under Christian II in 1520 culminated in the notorious Stockholm Bloodbath in which 100 Swedish nobles were executed.

1275 Magnus Ladulås elected king of Sweden at Mora Stones	**1349–50** Black Death rampages through Sweden	**1364** Albrecht of Mecklenburg elected king of Sweden	*Queen Margareta*	**1434** Engelbrekt leads revolt over the taxes and burdens imposed by the Kalmar Union
1300		**1350**	**1400**	**1450**
1280 Ordinance of Alsnö grants freedom from taxation to the nobility	**1350** Magnus Eriksson's law applies throughout the land, although cities have their own laws	**1397** The Kalmar Union unites the Nordic countries under Queen Margareta	**1471** Sten Sture the Elder defeats Danish King Christian I at Brunkeberg	**1520** Swedish nobles executed in the Stockholm Bloodbath

Gustav Vasa making his ceremonial entry into Stockholm, Midsummer Day, 1523

THE VASA ERA

Among the nobles fortunate to avoid execution in the Stockholm Bloodbath was the young Gustav Eriksson. At the end of 1520 Gustav organized an army to oust the Danish King Christian from Sweden. Gustav was successful and on 6 June 1523 – later to become Sweden's National Day – he was named king. On Midsummer Day the new monarch, Gustav Vasa, made his ceremonial entry into war-torn Stockholm.

When Gustav Vasa took the throne, he discovered a nation in financial crisis. He called on parliament to pass a controversial law transferring the property of the church to the state, which then became the country's most important source of economic power. Another important result of this policy was the gradual separation from Catholicism and the adoption of the Lutheran State Church, which was to remain tied to the state until 2000.

During his reign, Gustav Vasa implemented tough economic policies in

Portrait of Erik XIV (1561)

order to concentrate central power in Stockholm. This effective dictatorship also resulted in the Swedish parliament's decision in 1544 to make the monarchy hereditary.

Descendants of Gustav Vasa oversaw the rise of Sweden into one of Europe's great powers. During the reign of Gustav's eldest son Erik XIV (r. 1561–69), there were wars against Denmark, Lübeck and Poland. His brothers dethroned him. Erik died in prison, possibly by eating pea soup poisoned by his brother Johan III. During the reign of Karl IX, the third son, Sweden waged war against Denmark and Russia.

GUSTAV II ADOLF AND KRISTINA

When the next king, Gustav II Adolf, came to power in 1611, Sweden was involved in wars against Russia, Poland and Denmark. This reign came to be as remarkable as that of his grandfather and under his rule Sweden steadily increased its influence over the Baltic region. It was also in the 17th

TIMELINE

Vasa coat of arms

1523 Gustav Vasa is chosen as king and marches into Stockholm	**1542** Nils Dacke leads a peasants revolt in Småland	**1560** Gustav Vasa dies	**1568** Erik XIV imprisoned by his brothers at Gripsholms Slott	**1611** Gustav II Adolf becomes king
			1577 Erik XIV dies, probably poisoned	

1525	**1550**	**1575**	**1600**

| **1527** Reformation parliament confiscates church property | **1544** Hereditary monarchy established for Gustav Vasa's descendants | **1561** Eric XIV is crowned king and his brothers' powers curbed | **1570** Nordic Seven Years War ends
 1569 Johan III crowned in Stockholm | **1587** Johan III's son Sigismund chosen as king of Poland
 1612 Axel Oxenstierna made State Chancellor |

century that Stockholm started to develop into the country's political and administrative centre. In 1630 Gustav II Adolf, with his influential chancellor Axel Oxenstierna, decided to intervene in the Thirty Years War *(see p36)*, first on the side of the Protestants, then in an alliance with France. Sweden had some military successes during the war, but paid a heavy price for winning the bloody battle at Lützen in 1632, as the king was killed in action.

Gustav II Adolf's only child, Kristina, came to the throne at the age of six. During her reign (1633–54), life at court was influenced by the world of science and philosophy. Kristina's reluctance to marry resulted in her cousin, Karl Gustav, becoming Crown Prince. Kristina abdicated and left for Rome, where she converted to Catholicism, a sensation at the time.

Young Karl XII with the widowed queen on his arm leaving the burning Tre Kronor Palace, 1697

southernmost provinces. Karl XI (1660–97) secured the border and divided the land more evenly between crown, nobility and peasants.

While the body of Karl XI lay in state at Tre Kronor in 1697, a fire broke out which destroyed most of the building. The new monarch was the teenage Karl XII (1697–1718). He faced awesome problems when Denmark, Poland and Russia formed an alliance in 1700 with the aim of crushing the power of Sweden. Karl XII set off to battle.

Denmark and Poland were soon forced to plead for peace, but Russia was a harder nut to crack. A bold push towards Moscow was unsuccessful and the Swedish army suffered a devastating defeat at Poltava in Ukraine in 1709. This marked the beginning of the end of Sweden's Age of Greatness.

Queen Kristina corresponding with leading scientists and philosophers of the time

THE CAROLIAN ERA

Karl X Gustav (1654–60) was the first of three Karls to reign. At the height of Sweden's era as a great power, he defeated Denmark by leading his army across the frozen waters of the Great Belt *(see p36)*, thus gaining Sweden's

Karl XII, possibly the most written about and controversial Swedish monarch, returned to Sweden in 1715 after an absence of 15 years. His plans to regain Sweden's position of dominance never came to fruition and he was killed in Norway in 1718. Sweden was in crisis. Crop failures and epidemics had wiped out one third of the population and the state's finances were drained.

1617 Death penalty introduced for conversion to Catholicism

1632 Gustav II Adolf killed at Battle of Lützen

1633 Six-year-old Kristina becomes queen

1654 Kristina abdicates; Karl X Gustav is crowned

1655 Kristina converts to Catholicism and is ceremonially greeted in Rome

1697 Tre Kronor castle destroyed by fire; 15-year-old Karl XII crowned

1625	1650	1675	1700

1618 Thirty Years War starts in Germany

Gustav II Adolf

1648 Peace of Westphalia gives Sweden new territories

1658 Sweden acquires new territory, including Skåne, under Peace of Roskilde

1680 Karl XI starts the era of Carolian autocracy and limits powers of the nobility

1709 Swedish army defeated by Peter the Great at Poltava

1718 Karl XII dies during siege of Fredriksten, Norway

Sweden's Age of Greatness

For more than a century (1611–1721) Sweden was the dominant power in northern Europe, and the Baltic was effectively a Swedish inland sea. The country was at its most powerful after the Peace of Roskilde in 1658, when Sweden acquired seven new provinces. Outside today's frontiers, the Swedish Empire covered Finland, large parts of the Baltic states, and important areas of northern Germany. Over 111 years as a great power Sweden spent 72 of them at war, but the period also marked great cultural development and more efficient state administration. Treasures were brought back as trophies and grand palaces were built.

SWEDISH EMPIRE

☐ Sweden's empire after the Peace of Roskilde, 1658

The Tre Kronor Castle
Built as a defensive tower in the 1180s, the Tre Kronor castle was the seat of Swedish monarchs from the 1520s and became the administrative centre of the Swedish Empire. Named after the three crowns on the spire, it burned down in 1697.

The columns of troops ride out over the shifting ice towards Danish Lolland.

THE THIRTY YEARS WAR

A major European war raged from 1618–48, largely on German soil. Sweden entered the fray in 1630 and joined forces with France in 1631 against the Austrian Habsburgs. The Swedish army had been reorganized and rearmed by Gustav II Adolf and immediately had successes at the battles of Breitenfeld (1630) and Lützen (1632), where the king was killed in action.

Later the Swedes pressed into southern Germany and also captured Prague (1648). Rich cultural treasures were brought home from the war. In 1648 the Peace of Westphalia gave Sweden several important possessions in northern Germany.

The death of Gustav II Adolf at the Battle of Lützen in 1632

Stockholm in 1640
The city's transformation from a small medieval town into a capital city can be seen in the network of straight streets, similar to the present layout.

Karl XI's Triumphs

The ceiling painting in Karl XI's gallery at the Royal Palace (see p56) by the French artist Jacques Foucquet (1693) shows in allegoric form the king's victories at Halmstad, Lund and Landskrona.

Field Marshal Count Carl Gustav Wrangel *(see p127)*

Karl X Gustav himself leads the Swedish army of 17,000 men.

The Powerful Nobility

The nobility were very influential in the Empire era and many successful soldiers were ennobled. The Banér family coat of arms from 1651 is adorned by three helmets and barons' crowns.

Karl X Gustav

Portrait of Karl X Gustav (r. 1654–60) as a general. It was in this role that he became known throughout Europe during the final phase of the Thirty Years War.

CROSSING THE GREAT BELT

When Denmark declared war on Sweden in autumn 1657, the Swedish army was in Poland. Marching west, it captured the Danish mainland, but without the navy was unable to continue to Copenhagen. However, unusually severe weather froze the sea, making it possible for the soldiers to cross the ice of the Great Belt, and the Danes had to surrender.

Karl XII's Pocket Watch

The warrior king's watch-case dates from 1700. It shows the state coat of arms, as well as those of the 49 provinces that belonged to Sweden at that time.

Karl XII's Last Journey

After he was hit by a fatal bullet at Fredrikshald in Norway (1718), the king's body was taken first to Swedish territory then on to Uddevalla for embalming. Painting by Gustav Cederström (1878).

Gustav III with the white armband he wore when mounting his *coup d'etat* in 1772

THE AGE OF LIBERTY AND THE GUSTAVIAN ERA

A new constitution came into force in 1719 which transferred power from the monarch to parliament. As a result, Sweden developed a system of parliamentary democracy similar to that of Britain at the time.

The "Age of Liberty" coincided with the Enlightenment, with dramatic advances in culture, science and industry. The botanist Carl von Linné became one of the most famous Swedes of his time. Another was the scientist, philosopher and author Emanuel Swedenborg, who is thought to have influenced both Balzac and Baudelaire. The production of textiles expanded in Stockholm, and Sweden's first hospital was constructed on Kungsholmen.

Changes in the balance of power around 1770 gave the new king, Gustav III, an opportunity to strike in an attempt to regain his monarchical powers. On 19 August 1772 Gustav accompanied the guards' parade to the Royal Palace where, in front of his lifeguards, he declared his intention to mount a *coup d'etat*. The guards and other military units in Stockholm swore allegiance to the king, who tied a white handkerchief round his arm as a badge and rode out into the city to be acclaimed by his people. Absolute power had been restored.

Gustav III was influenced by the Age of Enlightenment and by French culture, which had a great effect on Swedish life *(see pp40–41)*. Over the years opposition grew to the king's powers, largely because of his costly war against Russia. In 1792 he was murdered by a nobleman during a masked ball at the Opera House.

Gustav III was succeeded by his son, Gustav IV Adolf. During his reign Sweden was dragged into the Napoleonic wars. After a war against Russia in 1808–9, Sweden lost Finland, which at the time accounted for one-third of Swedish territory. The king was deposed and went into exile.

THE ERA OF KARL JOHAN AND BOURGEOIS LIBERALISM

By the early 19th century the absolute powers of the monarch had been removed for all time, and the privileges

Napoleon's former marshal, Jean-Baptiste Bernadotte, as King Karl XIV Johan surrounded by his family

TIMELINE

1719 New constitution transfers power from the king to parliament

1741 Carl von Linné appointed professor at Uppsala

1754 Royal family moves into Royal Palace

1780s Immigrants given religious freedom

1790 Sweden defeats Russia at the Battle of Svenskund

1792 Gustav III is murdered

|1720|1740|1760|1780|1800|

1738 Parliamentary power is established in the Age of Liberty as the "Hat" party wins elections

Carl von Linné

1772 Gustav III crowned and mounts coup d'etat giving the king absolute power

1786 Swedish Academy founded

1778 National costume decreed. Death penalty removed for some crimes

Newspaper readers outside the *Aftonbladet* office in 1841

of the aristocracy were undermined even more in 1809 with a new constitution that divided power between the king, the government and parliament. With a new class structure and the effect of the French Revolution, a new middle class emerged which also wanted to be more influential. Altercations between middle-class liberals and the conservatives prevailed. One of the best-known newspapers founded at this time was the liberal mouthpiece, *Aftonbladet*.

Difficulties in finding a suitable new monarch led to the choice of one of Napoleon's marshals, Jean-Baptiste Bernadotte, who took on the Swedish name of Karl Johan. Founder of the present royal dynasty, Karl XIV Johan continued to speak French and never fully learned Swedish. His French wife, Desirée, found Stockholm a cultural backwater after Paris.

Swedes heading for a new life in North America

In 1813 a Swedish army, with Karl XIV Johan at its head, became involved in the final battle against Napoleon. The Battle of Leipzig ended in defeat for France, but more significantly for Sweden,

Denmark had to hand over Norway to Sweden. The Norwegians were reluctant to unite with Sweden, but after a display of military power in Norway, a union between the two countries was agreed which lasted from 1814 to 1905.

A long era of peace began, and with it came a dramatic increase in population, which grew by 1 million to 3.5 million by 1850. Many Swedes were driven into poverty because of the shortage of work. Mass emigration followed. From the 1850s to the 1930s about 1.5 million people left Sweden, mostly for North America.

SOCIAL MOVEMENTS AND INDUSTRIALIZATION

As Sweden was transformed from an agricultural society into an industrialized country, the problems posed by the population surplus were gradually tackled. Its industrial revolution started around 1850, gathering momentum in the late 19th century, and the textile, timber and iron industries provided the main sources of employment. Here the early and fast development of a coherent railway network played an important role.

Social movements sprang up in the 19th century which still play an important role in Swedish life. One of the first was the temperance movement, which emerged from a background of alcohol abuse – in the 1820s annual consumption of spirits was 46 litres (80 pints) per person.

809 Sweden loses Finland; Gustav IV Adolf deposed
1810 Parliament chooses Jean-Baptiste Bernadotte as Crown Prince

1842 Elementary schools established

1869 Emigration to North America increases due to crop failures

1876 L M Ericsson starts manufacture of telephones

August Strindberg

1905 Parliament dissolves union with Norway

| 1820 | 1840 | 1860 | 1880 | 1900 |

1818 Karl XIV Johan is crowned King of Sweden and Norway

1814 Sweden gains Norway in peace treaty with Denmark

1856 Sweden's first railway opens

1850 Sweden has 3.5 million inhabitants; 93,000 live in Stockholm

1879 August Strindberg's novel *The Red Room* is published

1908 Royal Dramatic Theatre opens in Stockholm

The Era of Gustav III

Gustav III (r. 1771–92) is one of the most colourful figures in Swedish history. The king's great interest in art, literature and the theatre made the late 18th century a golden age for Swedish culture, and several academies were founded at this time. After a bloodless revolution in 1772, Gustav III ruled with absolute power and initiated a wide-ranging programme of reform. But his attacks on the privileges of the nobility and his adventurous and costly foreign policy made him powerful enemies. In 1792 he was murdered during a masked ball at Stockholm's Opera House.

The Swedish Academy
The academy was founded by Gustav III in 1786 to preserve th Swedish language. Members received a token depicting the king's head at every meeting.

Gustav III's Coronation 1772
The coronation of the all-powerful monarch in Stockholm's cathedral was a magnificent ceremony, portrayed here by C G Pilo (1782). Every detail was overseen by Gustav himself, who used his flair for the dramatic in politics as well.

A courtier entertains by reading aloud.

Gustav III studies architectural designs.

COURT LIFE AT DROTTNINGHOLM

Hilleström's painting (1779) gives an insight int court life at Drottningholm, where the king reside between June and November. In what is now th Blue Salon, Gustav III and Queen Sofia Magdalen socialized with their inner circle. Behaviour wa modelled on the French court and etiquette wa even stricter at Drottningholm than at Versailles

The Battle of Svensksund
Gustav III was not known as a successful warrior king, but in 1790 he led the Swedish fleet to its greatest victory ever, when it defeated Russia in a major maritime battle in the Gulf of Finland.

Life in the Inns
Stockholm abounded with inns, frequently visited by the city's 70,000 inhabitants. J T Sergel's sketch shows a convivial dinner party.

Murder at the Masked Ball
In 1792 Gustav III fell victim to a conspiracy at the Opera House. He was surrounded by masked men and shot by Captain Anckarström on the crowded stage. He died of his wounds 14 days later.

Gustav III's Mask and Cocked Hat
Despite his mask, Gustav III was easy to recognize since he was wearing the badges of two orders of chivalry. The drama intrigued the whole of Europe and inspired Verdi's opera Un Ballo in Maschera.

Flogging of the King's Murderer
Among the conspirators, only Anckarström was condemned to death. Before he was taken to his execution in Södermalm, he was flogged on three successive days on the square in front of Riddarhuset.

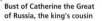
Bust of Catherine the Great of Russia, the king's cousin

Queen Sofia Magdalena does her needlework.

Swedish Court Costume
In 1778, Gustav III introduced a court costume, based on French lines, for daily wear at court, in order to restrain fashion excesses.

GUSTAVIAN STYLE
The mid-18th century saw the emergence of Neo-Classicism, with the focus on antiquities and Greek ideals. Gustav III embraced this trend with great enthusiasm and supported the country's talented artists and authors. He established his own Museum of Antiquities *(see p57)* with marble sculptures which he brought home from Italy. In handicrafts, the sweeping lines of Rococo elegance were replaced by the stricter forms of what has become known as Gustavian Style. Rooms at the Royal Palace were renovated with decoration and furnishings adapted to suit this style.

Chair designed in Gustavian style

UNIVERSAL SUFFRAGE

Sweden's population reached 5 million around 1900, despite mass emigration to America. Many people moved to the towns to work in industry, and by the early 20th century Stockholm's population was about 300,000, a fourfold increase since the year 1800.

Increasing social awareness and the rise of the Social Democrat and Liberal parties in the early 20th century gave impetus to the demands for universal suffrage. Authors such as August Strindberg became involved. A political battle ensued which was not resolved until 1921, when universal suffrage was introduced for both sexes.

Another question which was hotly debated in the 19th century was the role of the king and the extent of his powers. In his "courtyard speech" at the Royal Palace in 1914, King Gustav V called for military rearmament. This led to a constitutional crisis and the resignation of the Liberal government. After the 1917 election, the king had to accept a government which contained repub-

Branting and Gustav V in conversation, 1909

lican-friendly Social Democrats, including the future prime minister, Hjalmar Branting. By then it was parliament, not the king, that decided what sort of government Sweden should have.

THE GROWTH OF THE WELFARE STATE

In 1936 the Social Democrats and Farmers' Party formed a coalition which developed what was to become known as the welfare state. The Social Democrat prime minister, Per Albin Hansson (1885–1946), defined the welfare state as a socially conscious society with financial security for all. Reforms introduced under this policy included unemployment benefit, paid holidays and childcare. As a result, poverty in Sweden virtually disappeared during the 1930s and 1940s.

The right of everyone to good housing was also part of welfare state policy. Under the principle of "work-home-centre" a new Stockholm suburb, Vällingby, was built in the early 1950s. The idea was to transform the dormitory suburbs into thriving communities where people would both live and work. The concept was unsuccessful. It soon became apparent that the people who lived there still worked somewhere else, and vice versa. The great shortage of housing in the 1960s led to the "million" programme, which involved the building of a million homes in a very short time. These areas soon became known as the "new slums" despite high standards of construction.

Calls for democratic reforms in June 1917 led to riots like this one outside the parliament building in Stockholm

TIMELINE

	1930 Rise of Functionalist style in architecture, stimulated by the Stockholm Exhibition	1940 Swedish-German agreement on transit of German military personnel	1955 Obligatory national health insurance	1958 Women can be ordained as priests	1967 Driving on the right introduced
1921 Universal suffrage for men and women					
1920		**1940**		**1960**	

Selma Lagerlöf, winner of the Nobel Prize for Literature, 1909

	1939 Sweden's coalition government declares neutrality in World War II	1952 Stockholm's first underground railway is inaugurated	1964 Art exhibition at Moderna Museet shows works by Andy Warhol, Roy Lichtenstein and Claes Oldenburg
		1950 First public TV broadcast in Sweden	

THE WAR YEARS

Sweden declared its neutrality during both World Wars I and II. Its policy of continuing to trade with nations involved in the conflict during World War I provoked a number of countries into imposing a trade blockade on Sweden. The situation became so serious that hunger riots broke out in some towns.

World War II proved an even more difficult balancing exercise for Swedish neutrality, largely because its Nordic neighbours were at war. Through a combination of luck and skill, Sweden remained outside the conflict, but the concessions it had to make were strongly criticized both nationally and internationally.

Neutrality stamp issued in 1942

THE POST-WAR ERA

Although the Social Democrats dominated government from the 1930s to the 1970s, the socialist and non-socialist power blocs in Swedish politics have remained fairly evenly matched since World War II.

The policy of non-alignment has not proved an obstacle to Swedish involvement on the international scene, including the United Nations. The country has offered asylum to hundreds of thousands of refugees from wars and political oppression. Prime Minister Olof Palme (1927–86), probably the best-known Swedish politician abroad, was deeply involved in questions of democracy and disarmament, as well as the problems of the Third World. He was renowned for condemning undemocratic acts by right-wing and left-wing dictators. Palme's assassination on the streets of Stockholm in 1986 sent shock waves across the world. The murder has still not been solved.

Important changes took place during the closing decades of the 20th century. These included a new constitution in 1974 which removed the monarch's political powers. In 1995 Sweden joined the European Union after a referendum approved entry by a narrow majority. The start of the new millennium marked a change in the role of the church in Sweden, which severed its connections with the state after more than 400 years.

Sveavägen, the site of Palme's murder, 1986

Today, Sweden, like other developed countries shows signs of economic downturn, even though most people still lead a good, socially secure life. Rapid technical developments and globalization have given Sweden new job opportunities and new inhabitants, as well as a leading international role in technology and innovation.

The centre of Vällingby, which attracted attention among city planners worldwide in the 1950s

1974 The monarch loses all political powers

1980 New constitution gives women the right of succession to the throne

2000 Öresund Bridge opens between Denmark and Sweden

2003 Sweden rejects the euro

1980 | **2000** | **2020**

1986 Prime Minister Olof Palme murdered in Stockholm

1973 Gustav VI Adolf dies and is succeeded by his grandson, Carl XVI Gustaf

1995 Sweden joins European Union

2000 Swedish church separates from the state

2003 Foreign Minister Anna Lindh murdered in Stockholm

Crown Princess Victoria

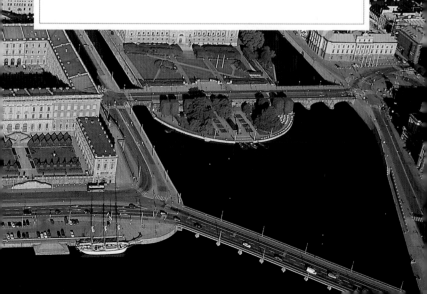

STOCKHOLM
AREA BY AREA

Stockholm at a Glance

Stockholm has around 100 museums covering every conceivable subject, as well as buildings of historic and architectural interest, such as Stadshuset (City Hall). The museum collections range from the treasures and antiquities of Kungliga Slottet (the Royal Palace) to the latest in contemporary art at Moderna Museet and the spectacular *Vasa* warship at Vasamuseet. Open spaces abound, and it is even possible to swim in the heart of the city.

Hallwylska Palatset
Thanks to a methical countess and her impeccable ta: this lavish 1890s' palace has becom a magnificent museum with 67,000 exhibits displayed in their original setting.

VASASTADEN

CITY

Stadshuset
This stunning building opened in 1923 is the seat of the capital's government and a symbol of Stockholm. It is also the venue for the annual Nobel Prize festivities.

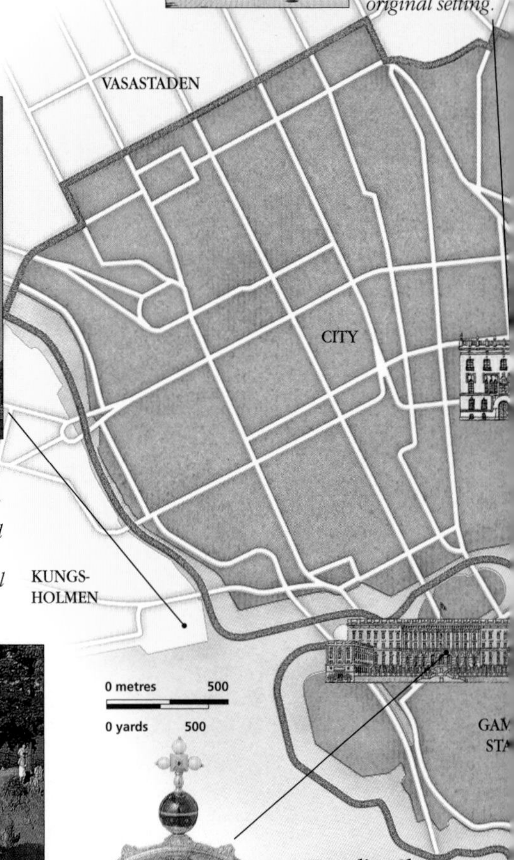

KUNGS-HOLMEN

0 metres   500
0 yards   500

GAM
STA

Swimming in the City
During the summer, swimmers bathe in the clean, warm water (about 20 °C/68 °F) in the city centre. Långholmen (see p102) has sandy beaches and smooth rocks – an ideal setting for a dip.

Kungliga Slottet
In addition to its own attractions, the Royal Palace has four specialis museums: the Treasury, featuring Erik XIV's orb (1561), the Royal Armoury, Gustav III's Museum of Antiquities, and Tre Kronor Museum

Nordiska Museet
A statue of Karl X Gustav greets visitors arriving at this enormous building. Opened in 1907, it houses many different artifacts illustrating Swedish life and customs.

Nationalmuseum
The Nationalmuseum, Sweden's largest art gallery, has superb collections of 18th- and 19th-century Swedish paintings, as well as applied arts and design, 18th-century French and 17th-century Dutch art. Rubens's Bacchanal on Andros dates from the 1630s.

Skansen
The world's first open-air museum, founded in 1891, shows the Sweden of bygone days with farms and manor houses, urban scenes and craftspeople at work. Nordic fauna and flora are also on display.

ÖSTERMALM

DJURGÅRDEN

SKEPPS-
HOLMEN

ER-
LM

Moderna Museet
Paradise (1966) by Tinguely/de Saint Phalle marks the way to Moderna Museet, which houses remarkable collections of international and Swedish modern art.

Vasamuseet
A fatal capsizal in 1628 and a successful salvage operation 333 years later gave Stockholm its most popular museum. The warship Vasa is 95 per cent intact after painstaking renovation.

GAMLA STAN

Relics of Stockholm's early history as a town in the 13th century can still be found on Stadsholmen, the largest island in Gamla Stan (Old Town). The island is a huge area of historical heritage, with the many sights just a few metres apart.

The Royal Palace is the symbol of Sweden's era as a great power in the 17th and early 18th centuries (see pp36–7), and its magnificent state rooms, apartments and artifacts are well matched to the Roman Baroque-style exterior. The historic buildings standing majestically

Anchor point on a palace façade

around Slottsbacken underline Stockholm's role as a capital city.

This area has a special atmosphere with much to offer: from the bustling streets of souvenir shops, bookstores and antique shops to elegant palaces, churches and museums. Many medieval cellars are now restaurants and cafés, while the narrow cobbled streets recall a bygone era.

Bridges lead to Riddarholmen, with its 17th-century palaces and royal crypt, and to Helgeandsholmen for the newer splendours of Riksdagshuset (the Parliament building).

SIGHTS AT A GLANCE

Palaces and Museums
Kungliga
  Myntkabinettet ❸
Livrustkammaren ❷
Medeltidsmuseet ⓰
Postmuseum ❿
*The Royal Palace
(Kungliga Slottet)
pp54–7* ❶

Public Buildings
Riddarhuset ⓮
Riksdagshuset ⓯

Historic Buildings
Tessinska Palatset ❹
Wrangelska Palatset ⓬

Streets and Squares
Evert Taubes Terrass ⓭
Mårten Trotzigs Gränd ❽
Stortorget ❻
Västerlånggatan ❾

Churches
Riddarholms-
  kyrkan ⓫
Storkyrkan ❺
Tyska Kyrkan ❼

KEY

▮ Street-by-Street map
  See pp50–51

▤ Ferry landing point

Ⓣ Tunnelbana station

▤ Bus stop

0 metres   250
0 yards   250

◁ **Prästgatan in Gamla Stan, with its yellow ochre plastering typical of the 18th century**

Street-by-Street: Slottsbacken

Slottsbacken is much more than just a steep hill
linking Skeppsbron and the highest part of Gamla
Stan (Old Town). It also provides the background for
ceremonial processions and the daily changing-of-the-
guard, and is the route for visiting heads of state and
foreign ambassadors when they have an audience with
the king at the Royal Palace. Alongside Slottsbacken the
palace displays its most attractive façade, with the
entrance to the Treasury (Skattkammaren), State Room
(Rikssalen) and Palace Church (Slottskyrkan). Architect
Nicodemus Tessin the Younger's ambition to make
Stockholm a leading European city in architectural terms
was realized in 1799 with the addition of the Obelisk.

The Olaus Petri statue by
Storkyrkan stands in front
of a tablet telling the
cathedral's history
since 1264.

**Outer
Courtyard**

**Axel Oxenstiernas
Palats** (1653) is, for
Stockholm, an
unusual example of
the style known as
Roman Mannerism.
For 30 years, Axel
Oxenstierna (1583–
1654) himself was a
dominant figure in
Swedish politics
(see p35).

TRÅNGSUND

The Obelisk by
Louis Jean Desprez
was erected in 1799
to thank the citizens
for supporting
Gustav III's Russian
war in 1788–90.

**Stock Exchange
*(see p54)***

STOR-
TORGET

★ **Storkyrkan**
*An impressive cathedral
with a late Gothic interior,
it is full of treasures from
many different eras* ❺

STAR SIGHTS

★ Storkyrkan

★ Livrustkammaren

★ The Royal Palace

Stortorget
*This square is the heart
of the "city between the
bridges", with a well
dating from 1778. It was
the scene of the Stockholm
Bloodbath in 1520* ❻

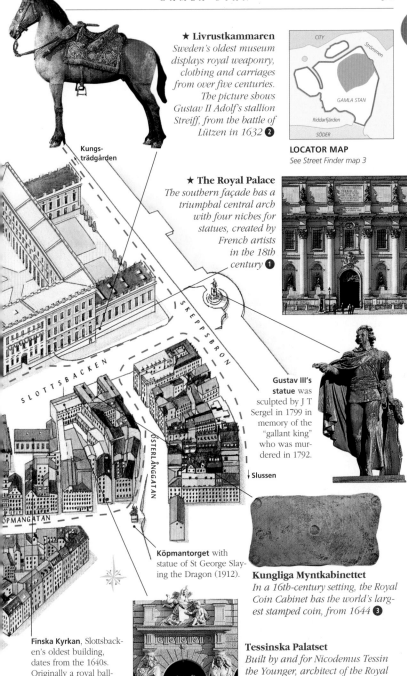

★ Livrustkammaren
Sweden's oldest museum displays royal weaponry, clothing and carriages from over five centuries. The picture shows Gustav II Adolf's stallion Streiff, from the battle of Lützen in 1632 ❷

LOCATOR MAP
See Street Finder map 3

★ The Royal Palace
The southern façade has a triumphal central arch with four niches for statues, created by French artists in the 18th century ❶

Gustav III's statue was sculpted by J T Sergel in 1799 in memory of the "gallant king" who was murdered in 1792.

↓ Slussen

Köpmantorget with statue of St George Slaying the Dragon (1912).

Kungliga Myntkabinettet
In a 16th-century setting, the Royal Coin Cabinet has the world's largest stamped coin, from 1644 ❸

Finska Kyrkan, Slottsbacken's oldest building, dates from the 1640s. Originally a royal ball-games court for the palace, since 1725 it has been the religious centre for the Finnish community.

Tessinska Palatset
Built by and for Nicodemus Tessin the Younger, architect of the Royal Palace, in 1694–7, this palace has been the residence of the Governor of Stockholm County since 1968 ❹

| 0 metres | 100 |
| 0 yards | 100 |

KEY

– – – Suggested route

The Royal Palace ❶

See pp54–7.

Livrust-kammaren ❷

Slottsbacken 3. **Map** 3 C2.
Tel 08-402 30 30. Ⓣ Gamla Stan.
🚌 2, 43, 55, 76. ☐ Jul–Aug:
10am–5pm daily; Sep–Jun: 11am–
5pm Tue–Sun (11am–8pm Thu).
🔊 📷 ⊘ ♿ ☐
www.livrustkammaren.se

Sweden's oldest museum,
Livrustkammaren (the Royal
Armoury) was founded in
1628 and is full of *objets d'art*
and everyday items used by
the Royal Family over the
past five centuries. The oldest
exhibit is Gustav Vasa's
crested helmet dating from
1542. The museum also
houses a variety of royal
items which illustrate
events in Swedish
history. Among
them are Gustav
II Adolf's stuffed
stallion, Streiff,
which he rode at
the Battle of Lützen
in 1632; Gustav
III's costume from
the notorious
masked ball at
which he was murdered in
1792; and Karl XII's blue
uniform with the still muddy
boots he was wearing when
he died at the siege of Fredrikshald in Norway in 1718.
  Coronation ceremonies are
illustrated by costumes such
as those worn by King Adolf
Fredrik and Queen Lovisa
Ulrika in 1751. The king's
attire alone was adorned with
some 2 kg (4 lb) of silver. The
coronation carriage, originally

**Sweden's first coin,
struck in about AD 995**

**The coronation carriage of King Adolf Fredrik and
Queen Lovisa Ulrika in Livrustkammaren**

built in the 17th century, was
modernized for this event. Its
renovation in the 1970s took
eight years and cost 700,000
kronor. The cellar vault, once
used for firewood, is skilfully
lit, providing an imaginative
setting for the exhibits.

Kungliga Myntkabinettet ❸

Slottsbacken 6. **Map** 3 C3.
Tel 08-519 553 04. Ⓣ Gamla Stan.
🚌 2, 43, 55, 76. ☐ 10am–4pm
daily. ● public hols. 📷 by
appointment. 🔊 📷 free Mon. ♿
🍴 🖥 ☐ www.myntkabinettet.se

The Royal Coin Cabinet is a
museum highlighting the
history of money from the
10th century to the present
day – from the little cowrie
shell via the drachma and
denarius to the current
cash card. The muse-
um also gives an
insight into the art
of medal design
over the past 600
years and shows
both traditional
portrait medals and
modern examples
such as those that
have been awarded
to Nobel laureates.
Visitors can also see the first
Swedish coin, struck in the
late 10th century by King Olof
Skötkonung. Other rarities
include Queen Kristina's coin
from 1644, weighing 19.7 kg
(43 lb) and reckoned to be
the world's heaviest coin.
From the island of Yap in
Micronesia the museum has
acquired the world's largest
means of payment, a so-
called "rai-stone" which greets
visitors in the foyer.
  The many
sections in the
museum include
"The World's
Money", "State
Finance" and
"Saving in a Piggy
Bank and Bank".
"Summa
Summarum" is a
section designed
for children and
illustrates the use
of money in play
and real life.

**The elegant Baroque garden in
Tessinska Palatset's courtyard**

Tessinska Palatset ❹

Slottsbacken 4. **Map** 3 C3.
Ⓣ Gamla Stan. 🚌 2, 43, 55, 71, 76.
● to the public.

The Tessin Palace at
Slottsbacken is considered to
be the most beautiful private
residence north of Paris. It is
the best-preserved palace
from Sweden's era as a great
power in the 17th century
and was designed by and for
Tessin the Younger (1654–
1728), the nation's most
renowned architect.
  Completed in 1697, the
building is located on a
narrow site which widens out
towards a courtyard with a
delightful Baroque garden.
The relatively discreet façade
with its beautiful porch was
inspired by the exterior
design of Roman palaces.
The decor and garden were
influenced by Tessin's time in
Paris and Versailles.
  Tessin, who became a count
and state councillor, spent
large sums on the building's
ornamentation. Sculptures and
paintings were provided by
the same French masters
whose work had graced the
Royal Palace. Later, however,
his son, Carl Gustaf, had to sell
the palace for financial reasons.
  The building was acquired
by the City of Stockholm as a
residence for its governor in
1773. In 1968 it became the
residence of the governor of
the County of Stockholm.

Storkyrkan ❺

Trångsund 1. **Map** 3 B3. **Tel** 08-723
30 16. 🚇 Gamla Stan. 🚌 2, 43, 55,
76. 🕐 10am–4pm daily. ✝ 11am
Sun. 📷 Jul–Aug: daily; Sep–Jun:
11am Tue. 🎫 ♿ 🏠
www.storkyrkan.nu

Stockholm's 700-year-old
cathedral is of great national
religious importance. It was
from here that the Swedish
reformer Olaus Petri
(1493–1552) spread his
Lutheran message around the
kingdom. It is also used for
royal ceremonies.

Originally, a small village
church was built on this site
in the 13th century, probably
by the city's founder Birger
Jarl. It was replaced in 1306
by a much bigger basilica, St
Nicholas, which was altered
over the centuries.

The Gothic character of the
interior, acquired in the 15th
century, was revealed in 1908
when, during restoration
work, plaster was removed
from the pillars, exposing the
characteristic red tiling. The
late Baroque period provided
the so-called "royal chairs"
and the pulpit, while the
façade was adapted to bring it
into keeping with the rest of
the area around the Royal
Palace. The 66-m (216-ft) high
tower, added in 1743, has four

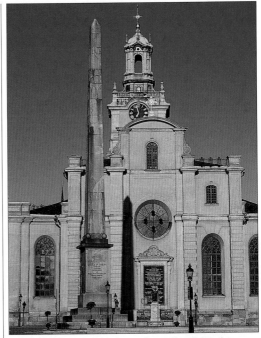

Storkyrkan's façade in Italian Baroque style, seen from Slottsbacken

bells, the largest of which
weighs about 6 tons.

The cathedral houses some
priceless artistic treasures,
including *St George and the
Dragon*, regarded as one of
the finest late Gothic works of
art in Northern Europe. The
sculpture, situated
to the left of the
altar, was carved
from oak and elk
horn by Lübeck
sculptor Bernt
Notke. Unveiled
in 1489, it com-
memorates Sten
Sture the Elder's
victory over the
Danes in 1471
(see p33).

The Last Judgment
(1696) is a massive
Baroque painting
by David Klöcker
von Ehrenstrahl.
The 3.7-m (12-ft)
high bronze can-
delabra before the
altar has adorned
the cathedral for
some 600 years.
One of the
cathedral's most
prized treasures is

the silver altar, which was a
gift from the diplomat Johan
Adler Salvius in the 1650s.

The pews nearest to the
chancel, the "royal chairs",
were designed by
Nicodemus
Tessin the
Younger in
1684 to be
used by royalty
on special
occasions. In
1705, the pulpit
was installed
above the grave
of Olaus Petri.

On 20 April
1535, a light
phenomenon
was observed
over Stockholm – six rings
with sparkling solar halos.
The Parhelion Painting,
recalling the event, hangs in
Storkyrkan and is thought to
be the oldest portrayal of the
capital. It shows the modest
skyline dominated by the
cathedral, at that time still the
basilica of St Nicholas.

In 2010, the cathedral underwent a large-scale renovation
ahead of the wedding of
Crown Princess Victoria.

**Storkyrkan's
silver altar
(detail)**

**The sculpture *St George and the Dragon* by
Bernt Notke (1489) in Storkyrkan**

The Royal Palace (Kungliga Slottet) ❶

Royal sceptre

Defensive installations or castles have stood on the island of Stadsholmen ever since the 11th century. The Tre Kronor (Three Crowns) fortress was completed in the mid-13th century, but became a royal residence only during the following century. The Vasa kings turned the fortress into a Renaissance palace which burned to the ground in 1697. In its place the architect Nicodemus Tessin the Younger created a new palace in Baroque style with an Italianate exterior and a French interior toned down to suit Swedish tastes. The palace's 608 rooms were decorated by Europe's foremost artists and craftsmen. Adolf Fredrik was the first king to move into the palace, in 1754. It is no longer the king's private residence, but remains one of the city's leading sights.

★ **Changing the Guard**
Stockholm's most popular tourist event is the daily changing of the guard at midday in the Outer Courtyard.

Entrance to the
Royal Apartments

The Western Staircase
Tessin was especially proud of the two stair-cases, made from Swedish marble and porphyry. On the western staircase stands a bust of the gifted architect.

★ **The Hall of State**
This opulent hall has an atmosphere of ceremonial splendour and forms an ideal setting for Queen Kristina's silver throne, probably the palace's most famous treasure.

The Guest
Apartments

Entrance to
Treasury and
Royal Chapel

OFFICIAL ROYAL RESIDENCE

The king and queen have their offices at the palace, where they hold audiences with visiting dignitaries,

King Carl XVI Gustaf and Queen Silvia

and official ceremonies. They travel around the country attending special events, official openings and anniversaries, and they make regular State visits abroad. The king is well known for his interest in the environment while the queen is heavily involved with her work for children, especially the disabled.

The Royal Chapel
This delightful little church has a rich interior decorated by many different artists. The pulpit is the work of J P Bouchardon.

For hotels and restaurants in this region see pp280–283 and pp298–300

STAR FEATURES

★ Karl XI's Gallery

★ The Hall of State

★ Changing the Guard

VISITORS' CHECKLIST

Gamla Stan. **Map** 3 B2. **Tel** 08-
402 61 30. Ⓣ Gamla Stan, Kungsträdgården. 🚌 2, 43, 55, 76.
**Royal Apartments, Treasury,
Tre Kronor Museum** ◻ mid-
May–mid-Sep: 10am–4pm daily
(Jun–Aug: to 5pm daily); mid-Sep–
mid-May: noon–3pm Tue–Sun.
● for official functions of Court.
📷 for tours in Eng, call 402 61
30. 🖼 🚫 ♿ 🛍 **Gustav III's
Museum of Antiquities** ◻
mid-May–mid-Sep: 10am–4pm
daily. **Royal Chapel** ◻ mid-
Jun–mid-Aug: noon–3pm Wed &
Fri. ✝ May–Aug: 11am Sun.
📷 www.royalcourt.se

Gustav III's State Bedchamber

*Sergel's bust of Gustav III (1779)
stands in the room where the
king died after being shot at the
Opera House. The 1770s
decor is by J E Rehn.*

The Bernadotte Apartments
are situated on the floor below
Karl XI's Gallery.

Tre Kronor Museum
entrance from
Lejonbacken
(see p57).

★ Karl XI's Gallery

*One of the most
magnificent rooms in
the palace, this fine
example of Swedish
Late Baroque is used
for banquets hosted by
the king and queen.
In the cabinet is this
priceless salt-cellar
dating from 1627–8.*

Carl Hårleman
played an
important role in
the design of the
palace. His bust
adorns this niche.

The Bernadotte Apartments

Logården
is the terrace
between the
palace's east
wings.

Livrustkammaren
(see p52)

Gustav III's Museum of Antiquities
*The museum's collection includes
antique statues brought home by
Gustav III from his journey to Rome.*

Exploring the Royal Palace

The public areas of the Royal Palace allow visitors to walk through grand rooms of sumptuous furnishings and priceless works of art and craftsmanship. The Hall of State and the Royal Chapel are both characterized by their magnificent lavish decor and Gustav III's Museum of Antiquities contains ancient marble sculptures from the king's journey to Italy. The palace also houses the Treasury with the State regalia; the Tre Kronor Museum, which depicts the palace before the 1697 fire; and the Livrustkammaren (see p52).

The Pillar Hall in the Bernadotte Apartments with original decor

Karl XI's Gallery, the finest example of the Late Baroque period in Sweden

THE STATE APARTMENTS

The Royal Family has lived at Drottningholm Palace (see pp106–9) since 1982, but official functions still take place in the State Apartments, including banquets hosted by the king during visits by foreign heads of state. Other official dinners are held here, as well as the annual festivities in December to honour the Nobel laureates.

The dinners are served in Karl XI's Gallery, the finest example of Swedish Late Baroque, modelled on the Hall of Mirrors at Versailles. Each window is matched with a niche on the inner wall where some of the palace's priceless works of arts and crafts are exhibited. Most remarkable is the salt-cellar made from ivory and gilded silver designed by the Flemish painter Rubens (1577–1640). The room known as "The

King Karl XIV Johan's egg cup

White Sea" serves as a drawing room. Gustav III's State Bedchamber, where the king died after being shot at the Opera House in 1792 (see pp40–41), is the height of Gustavian elegance. Along with Queen Sofia Magdalena's State Bedchamber, it was designed by the architect Jean Eric Rehn. The lintels on the doors to the Don Quixote Room, named after the theme of its tapestries, were made by François Boucher and are among the most treasured pieces.

THE GUEST APARTMENTS

An imposing part of the palace, these apartments are where visiting heads of state stay. The beautiful rooms include the Meleager Salon, where official gifts and decorations are exchanged, and a large bedroom with a sculpted and gilded bed. Other impressive rooms are the Inner Salon, whose decor was inspired by the excavations in Pompeii, and the Margareta Room, named after the present king's grandmother, which displays some pictures painted by her.

The apartments contain remarkable works of craftsmanship by such 18th-century masters as Georg Haupt, Ephraim Ståhle and Jean-Baptiste Masreliez.

THE BERNADOTTE APARTMENTS

This magnificent suite has earned its name from the gallery displaying portraits of the Bernadotte dynasty. The apartments have some notable ceiling paintings and mid-18th-century chandeliers, and are used for many a ceremonial occasion. The elegant Pillar Hall is the venue for investitures, and the East Octagonal Cabinet with probably the palace's best Rococo decor, is where the king receives foreign ambassadors. Along with the western cabinet, its interior has remained just as it was planned by Carl Hårleman more than 250 years ago.

Oscar II's very masculine Writing Room, dating from the 1870s, also looks much as it did in his day. However, the palace was kept up to date with the latest technical advances: electricity was installed in 1883, and the telephone only one year later.

THE HALL OF STATE

Rococo and Classicism were brought together in perfect harmony by the architects Nicodemus Tessin the Younger and Carl Hårleman when they designed the two-storey Hall of State.

The Hall provides a worthy framework for Queen Kristina's silver throne, a gift for the coronation in 1650 and one of the most valuable treasures in the palace. The throne was given to the queen by Magnus Gabriel de la Gardie and was made in Augsburg by the goldsmith

Abraham Drentwett. The canopy was added 100 years later for the coronation of King Adolf Fredrik and was designed by Jean Eric Rehn.

The room is lavishly decorated. The throne is flanked by colossal sculptures of Karl XIV Johan and Gustav II Adolf, while those on the cornice symbolize Peace, Strength, Religion and Justice.

Until 1975 the Hall of State was the scene of the ceremonial opening of the Swedish Parliament (Riksdagen), which included a march past of the royal bodyguard in full regalia. It is now used for official occasions and, like the Royal Chapel, is a venue for summer concerts.

The Hall of State, the most important ceremonial room in the palace

THE ROYAL CHAPEL

It took 50 years to build the Royal Palace, and a lot of effort went into the interior decoration of the Royal Chapel. The work was carried out largely by Carl Hårleman under the supervision of Tessin. As with the Hall of State, the co-operation between the two produced a magnificent result, enhanced by the contributions of several foreign artists.

A number of remarkable artifacts have been added over the centuries. The most recent was a group of six 17th-century-style bronze crowns, as well as two crystal crowns, given by the Court to King Carl XVI Gustaf and Queen Silvia to mark their marriage in 1976.

It also has some rare relics of the original Tre Kronor

fortress: new benches that had been ordered by Tessin. They had been rescued during the palace fire in 1697 and preserved, but not put in the chapel until the 19th century. The benches were made by Georg Haupt, grandfather of the Georg Haupt who was to create some of the palace's most prized furnishings *(see p80)*.

GUSTAV III'S MUSEUM OF ANTIQUITIES

Opened in 1794 in memory of the murdered king, the Museum of Antiquities initially housed more than 200 exhibits, mainly acquired during Gustav's Italian journey in 1783–4 and then supplemented with more purchases at a later date.

In 1866 the museum's collection was moved to the city's National Museum *(see pp80–81)*. During the 1950s the main gallery was renovated, followed by the smaller galleries 30 years later, which enabled the collection to be returned to its original setting.

The most prized exhibits are in the main gallery, the best known being the sculpture of Endymion, the eternally sleeping young shepherd and lover of the Moon Goddess Selene. The 18th-century sculptor Johan Tobias Sergel is represented by *The Priestess*, ranked as the collection's second most important piece. She is flanked by two large candelabras.

THE TREASURY

At the bottom of 56 well-worn steps, below the Hall of State on the south side of the palace, is the entrance to the Treasury (Skattkammaren) where the State regalia, the most potent symbols of the monarchy, are kept. Occasionally, for an important event, King Erik XIV's crown, sceptre, orb and the keys of the kingdom are taken out of their showcase and placed beside the uncrowned King

Erik XIV's crown, made by Cornelis ver Weiden in Stockholm in 1561

Carl XVI Gustaf. The 1-m (3 ft) high silver baptismal font, which took the French silversmith Jean François Cousinet 11 years to make, is over 200 years old and is still used for royal baptisms. Hanging in the Treasury is the only undamaged tapestry among six dating from the 1560s, salvaged from the 1697 fire.

TRE KRONOR MUSEUM

The newest attraction at the Royal Palace is the Tre Kronor (Three Crowns) Museum, which is housed in the oldest parts of the ruined Tre Kronor fortress, preserved under the north side of the palace. About half of a massive 12th-century defensive wall and brick vaults from the 16th and 17th centuries provide a dramatic setting for the museum which illustrates the palace's history over almost 1,000 years.

Two models of the Tre Kronor fortress show changes made during the second half of the 17th century and how it looked by the time of the fire. Among items rescued from the ashes are a schnapps glass, amber pots and bowls made from mountain crystal.

A glass bowl in the Tre Kronor Museum, saved from the 1697 fire

Stortorget, the former Stock Exchange, now home of the Nobelmuseet

Stortorget ❻

Map 3 B3. Ⓣ *Gamla Stan.* 🚌 *2, 3, 43, 53, 55, 76.* **Nobelmuseet** *Tel 08-23 25 06.* ⭕ *mid-May–mid-Sep: 10am–5pm daily, 10am–8pm Tue; mid-Sep–mid-May: 11am–5pm Wed–Sun, 11am–8pm Tue.* 🎭 🎫 🍴 📷 www.nobelmuseum.se

It was not until 1778, when the Stock Exchange (Börsen) was completed, that Stortorget ("the big square") in the heart of the Old Town, acquired a more uniform appearance. Its northern side had previously been taken up by several buildings that served as a town hall. Since the early Middle Ages the square had been a natural meeting point with a well and marketplace, lined with wooden stalls on market days.

A pillory belonging to the jail, which was once on nearby Kåkbrinken, used to stand on the square. It is now in the Town Hall on Kungsholmen.

The medieval layout is clear on Stortorget's west side, where the red Schantzska Huset (No. 20) and the narrow Seyfridtska Huset were built around 1650. The Schantzska Huset remains unchanged and has a lovely limestone porch adorned with figures of recumbent Roman warriors. The artist Johan Wendelstam was responsible for most of the notable porches in the Old Town. The 17th-century gable on Grilska Huset (No. 3) is also worth a closer study. Today there are cafés and restaurants in some of the vaulted cellars.

The decision to construct the Stock Exchange was taken in 1667, but the many wars delayed the start of the building by 100 years. The architect was the young and talented Erik Palmstedt (1741–1803), who also created the decorative cover for the old well. Trading on the floor of the Stock Exchange ceased in 1990. In 2001 the **Nobelmuseet** was opened here to mark the centenary of the Prize *(see p69)*. The exhibition explores the work and ideas of more than 700 creative minds by means of short films and original artifacts. On the upper floor, the Swedish Academy holds its ceremonial gatherings, a tradition maintained since Gustav III gave his inauguration speech here in 1786.

Tyska Kyrkan ❼

Svartmangatan 16. **Map** 3 B3. *Tel 08-411 11 88.* Ⓣ *Gamla Stan.* 🚌 *2, 3, 43, 53, 55, 71, 76.* ⭕ *May–Sep: noon–4pm daily; Oct–Apr: noon–4pm Sat & Sun.* ⛪ *11am Sun, German.* 🎫 *by arrangement in Swedish & German.* ♿

The German Church is an impressive reminder of the almost total influence that Germany had over Stockholm during the 18th century. The Hanseatic League trading organization was in control of the Baltic and its ports, which explains why the basic layout of Gamla Stan resembled that of Lübeck. Germany's political influence was only broken after the Stockholm Bloodbath and Gustav Vasa's accession to the throne in 1523 *(see p34)*, but its cultural and mercantile influence remained strong as German merchants and craftsmen settled in the city.

The church's congregation, which today has some 2,000 members, was founded in 1571. The present twin-aisle church was built in 1638–42, as an extension of a smaller church which the parish had used since 1576.

In German Late Renaissance and Baroque style, the interior has a royal gallery, added in 1672 for German members of

---

THE STOCKHOLM BLOODBATH

Detail of a painting of the Bloodbath (1524)

Stortorget is intimately linked with the Stockholm Bloodbath of November 1520. The Danish king, Christian II, besieged the Swedish Regent, Sten Sture the Younger, until he capitulated and the Swedes chose Christian as their king. The Dane promised an amnesty and ordered a three-day feast at Tre Kronor Fortress. Near the end of the festivities, the revellers were suddenly shut in and arrested for heresy. The next day more than 80 noblemen and Stockholm citizens were beheaded in the square.

The royal gallery in the 17th-century Tyska Kyrkan

the royal household. The pulpit (1660) in ebony and alabaster is unique in Sweden and the altar, from the 1640s, is covered with beautiful paintings surrounded by sculptures of the apostles and evangelists.

The sculptures on the south porch by Jobst Hennen date from 1643 and show Jesus, Moses and three figures portraying Faith, Hope and Love.

Mårten Trotzigs Gränd, the narrowest street in the city

Mårten Trotzigs Gränd ❽

Map 3 C4. 🚇 Gamla Stan. 🚌 2, 3, 43, 53, 55, 71, 76.

At only 90 cm (3 ft) wide, Mårten Trotzigs Gränd is the city's narrowest street. Climbing up the 36 steps gives a good impression of how the various parts of the Old Town differ in height and how tightly the houses are packed together.

Mårten Trotzigs Gränd is named after a German merchant called Traubzich who owned two houses here at the end of the 16th century. After being fenced off at both ends for 100 years, the street was reopened in 1945.

Västerlånggatan ❾

Map 3 B3. 🚇 Gamla Stan. 🚌 2, 3, 43, 53, 55, 71, 76.

Once a main road outside the city proper, built along parts of the original town wall, Västerlånggatan now runs through the heart of the

Old Town, and is usually thronging with people – tourists and locals – shopping or strolling. Starting at Mynttorget in the north, by the Chancery Office (Kanslihuset) and Lejonbacken, the lively and atmospheric street finishes at Järntorget in the south, where the export of iron was once controlled. On Järntorget is Bancohuset, which served as the headquarters of the State Bank from 1680 to 1906.

The building at No. 7 has been used by the Swedish Parliament since the mid-1990s. Its late 19th-century façade has a distinctive southern European influence.

No. 27 was built by and for Erik Palmstedt, who also designed the Stock Exchange and the well at Stortorget.

No. 29 is a truly venerable building, dating from the early 15th century. The original pointed Gothic arches were revealed during restoration in the 1940s.

No. 33 is a good example of how new materials and techniques in the late 19th century made it possible to fit large shop windows into old houses. The cast-iron columns which can be seen in many other places also date from this period.

No. 68, Von der Lindeska House, has a majestic 17th-century façade and a beautiful porch with sculptures of Neptune and Mercury.

Postmuseum ❿

Lilla Nygatan 6. Map 3 B3. Tel 08-781 17 55. 🚇 Gamla Stan. 🚌 3, 53. ◯ May–Aug: 11am–4pm Tue–Sun; Sep–Apr: 11am–4pm Tue–Sun (11am–7pm Wed). 🖋 by arrangement. ♿ 🛗 📷 🍴 🛍 www.postmuseum.posten.se

An attraction in itself, the Postmuseum building takes up a whole area bought by the Swedish Post Office in

Västerlånggatan, Gamla Stan's most popular shopping street

1720. About 100 years later the majestic-looking Post Office was built, incorporating parts of the 17th-century buildings. Stockholm's only Post Office until 1869, it was turned into a museum in 1906.

Letters have been sent in Sweden, in an organized way, since 1636, and the museum's permanent exhibits include a portrayal of early "peasant postmen" fighting the Åland Sea in their boat *Simpan*. Also on display is the first post bus which ran in northern Sweden in the early 1920s and a stagecoach used in eastern Sweden.

Mauritian stamp in the Postmuseum

The collection includes Sweden's first stamp-printing press and no less than four million stamps among which are the first Swedish stamps, produced in 1855. Also on show is "Penny Black", the world's first stamp dating from 1840, and some stamps issued by Mauritius in 1847.

There is a philatelic library holding 51,000 volumes and stamp collections, as well as computers and multimedia equipment for research. A special exhibition for children is on display in the basement.

Riddarholms-kyrkan ⓫

Birger Jarls Torg. **Map** 3 A3. **Tel** 08-402 61 30. Ⓣ Gamla Stan. 🚌 1, 3, 14, 53. ◯ mid-May–mid-Sep: 10am–4pm daily (Jun–Aug: to 5pm daily). 🎫 Eng: 11am daily. 📷 🚫 ♿

This church on the island of Riddarholmen is best known as a place for royal burials. Its interior is full of ornate sarcophagi and worn gravestones, and in front of the altar are the tombs of the medieval kings Karl Knutsson and Magnus Ladulås.

Built on the site of the late 13th-century Greyfriars abbey, founded by Magnus Ladulås, the majestic brick church was gradually enlarged over the centuries. After a serious fire in 1835, it acquired its present lattice-work cast-iron tower.

Inside, the church is surrounded by splendid burial vaults dating back to the 16th century. The coffins rest on a lower level with space for a memorial above. The most recent was built in 1858–60 for the Bernadotte dynasty.

The vaults contain the remains of all the Swedish monarchs from Gustav II Adolf in the 17th century to the present day with two exceptions: Queen Kristina was buried at St Peter's in Rome in 1689 and Gustav VI Adolf, who was interred at Haga in 1973 (see p96). The most magnificent sarcophagus is that of the 19th-century king, Karl XIV Johan, which had to be towed here by sledge from his porphyry workshops in northern Sweden.

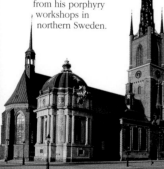

Riddarholmskyrkan and the external burial vault by Tessin and Hårleman

Wrangelska Palatset, a royal residence after the Tre Kronor fire of 1697

Particularly moving are the graves of royal children, including the many small tin coffins that surround the last resting place of Gustav II Adolf and his queen, Maria Eleonora.

Wrangelska Palatset ⓬

Birger Jarls Torg 16. **Map** 3 A3. Ⓣ Gamla Stan. 🚌 3, 53. ⬤ to the public.

Only two parts of Gustav Vasa's fortifications from 1530 remain – Birger Jarl's Tower and the southernmost tower of what became the Wrangel Palace. Built as a residence for the nobleman Lars Sparre in 1652–70, it was remodelled a few decades later by Carl Gustaf Wrangel. A field marshal in the Thirty Years War, Wrangel chose Nicodemus Tessin the Elder as his architect. The result was Stockholm's largest privately-owned palace.

In 1697 the royal family moved into the palace after the Tre Kronor fortress (see p54) was ravaged by fire. It became known as the King's House, and it was here in the same year that the 15-year-old Karl XII took the oath of office after the death of his father. Gustav III was born here in 1746 and in 1792 his assassin was incarcerated in the dungeons. The Court of Appeal now uses this building, as well as Rosenhane Palace

(Birger Jarls Torg 10) and Hessenstein House (Birger Jarls Torg 2), built in 1630 by Bengt Bengtsson Oxenstierna.

Evert Taubes Terrass ⓭

Norra Riddarholmshamnen. **Map** 3 A3. Ⓣ Gamla Stan. 🚌 3, 53.

A statue of Evert Taube, the much-loved troubadour and ballad writer, stands on the terrace below Wrangelska Palatset looking out over the waters of Riddarfjärden.

In an ideal position, given the poet's close links to the sea, the bronze sculpture was created by Willy Gordon in 1990. Close by stands Christer Berg's granite sculpture *Solbåten* (Sun Boat), unveiled in 1966. Inspired by the shape of a shell, from some angles it also resembles a sail.

Evert Taube (1890–1976)

Riddarhuset ⓮

Riddarhustorget 10. **Map** 3 A3. **Tel** 08-723 39 90. Ⓣ Gamla Stan. 🚌 3, 53. ◯ 11:30am–12:30pm Mon–Fri. ⬤ public hols. 📷 🎫 by appointment. **www**.riddarhuset.se

Often regarded as one of Stockholm's most beautiful buildings, Riddarhuset (House of Knights) stands on Riddarhustorget, the city's centre until the 19th century. Built in 1641–7 on the initiative of the State Chancellor, Riddarhuset provided the knights with a base for meetings and events. The building is a supreme example of Dutch Baroque design by the architects Simon and Jean de la Vallée, Heinrich Wilhelm and Justus Vingboons.

Riddarhuset, built in the 17th century in imposing Dutch Baroque style

Over the entrance on the northern façade is the knights' motto *Arte et Marte* (Art and War) with Minerva, Goddess of Art and Science, and Mars, God of War.

The sculptures on the vaulted roof symbolize the knightly virtues. On the south side is *Nobilitas* (Nobility) holding a small Minerva and spear. She is flanked by *Studium* (Diligence) and *Valor* (Bravery). Facing the north is the male equivalent, *Honor*, flanked by *Prudentia* (Prudence) and *Fortitudo* (Strength).

Inside, a magnificent double staircase leads up to the Knights' Room. This has a painted ceiling by David Klöcker Ehrenstrahl (1628–98) and Riddarhuset's foremost treasure, a sculpted ebony chair, 1623. The walls are covered with coats of arms.

Riksdagshuset **⑮**

Riksgatan 3 A. **Map** 3 B2. **Tel** 08-786 40 00. Ⓣ Kungsträdgården. 🚌 3, 43, 53, 62. ◯ tours & meetings in the Chamber. 🎫 daily in summer; weekends in winter; ring for details. ♿ ⛴ www.riksdagen.se

The Parliament building (Riksdagshuset) and Bank of Sweden (Riksbank) on Helgeandsholmen were inaugurated in 1905 and 1906 respectively. In the 1970s and

1980s the two buildings were combined and restored and a modern extension built to house a new, single debating chamber. The chamber is truly Nordic in its decoration with benches of Swedish birch and wall-panelling in Finnish birch. A large tapestry, *Memory of a Landscape* (1983), by Elisabeth Hasselberg-Olsson, covers 54 sq m (581 sq ft) of wall and took 3,500 hours to make. Parliamentary debates can be watched from the public gallery.

The original two-chamber Parliament is used for meetings of the majority party. The former First Chamber has three paintings by Otte Sköld (1894–1958); the other chamber contains works by Axel Törneman and Georg Pauli. Between the chambers is a 45 m (148 ft) long hall with an elegant display of coats of arms. The Finance Committee meets in the oak-panelled library surrounded by old prints and *Jugendstil* (Art Nouveau-style) lamps. Facing the Norrbro entrance is the original 1905 stairwell with columns, floor, steps and

Medieval stone head of Birger Jarl at Medeltidsmuseet

balusters in various marbles. The present entrance was the Bank of Sweden's main hall until 1976.

Medeltids-museet **⑯**

Strömparterren, Norrbro. **Map** 3 B2. **Tel** 08-508 317 90. Ⓣ Kungsträdgården. 🚌 43, 62. ◯ 11am–5pm Tue–Sun (noon–7pm Wed). 🎫 🔊 ♿ ⛴ 🏛 www.medeltids museet.stockholm.se

This fascinating museum of medieval Stockholm is built around some of the capital's archaeological remains, mainly parts of the city wall that date from the 1530s. They were discovered in 1978–80. Completely underground, the dimly-lit, atmospheric museum includes finds evoking Stockholm's early history. Among them is the 22 m (72 ft) long Riddarholm ship, dating from the 1520s, which was found off Riddarholmen in 1930.

The museum provides a good picture of Stockholm's early days. From the entrance, a 350-year-old tunnel leads into a reconstructed medieval world. There is a pillory in the square and gallows with the tools of the executioner's trade. The city has been recreated with a church, harbour and a square. Visitors can also see a 55 m (180 ft) long section of the original city wall, complete with a skeleton which was concealed there.

The new Parliament building, with the older building behind

CITY

The area known as City today was where, in the mid-18th century, the first stone-built houses and palaces outside Gamla Stan started to appear for the burghers and nobility. After World War II, the run-down buildings around Hötorget were demolished to form what is now Sergels Torg; many homes were replaced by rather dreary office blocks. In recent years, though, the area has livened up and become the true heart and commercial centre of Stockholm. A hub for public transport and banking, City is the place for the best department stores and shopping malls, exclusive boutiques and nightspots. The centre also has some beautiful parks and pleasant squares which serve as popular meeting places. The unique landscape surrounding Stockholm permeates even City, offering sudden unexpected glimpses of water complete with bustling boat life and a string of anglers along the embankments.

Street light near
Kungliga Operan

SIGHTS AT A GLANCE

Museums
Armémuseum ⑭
Dansmuseet ⑤
Hallwylska Palatset ⑱
Medelhavsmuseet ⑥
Musikmuseet ⑮
Strindbergsmuseet
 Blå Tornet ⑪

Churches
Adolf Fredriks
 Kyrka ⑫
Jacobs Kyrka ③
Klara Kyrka ⑧

Squares
Kungsträdgården ②

Public Buildings
Arvfurstens Palats ⑦
Hovstallet ⑯
Kungliga Biblioteket ⑬
Nordiska Kompaniet
 (NK) ①

**Theatres and
Musical Stages**
Konserthuset ⑩
Kulturhuset and
 Stadsteatern ⑨
Kungliga Dramatiska
 Teatern ⑰
Kungliga Operan ④

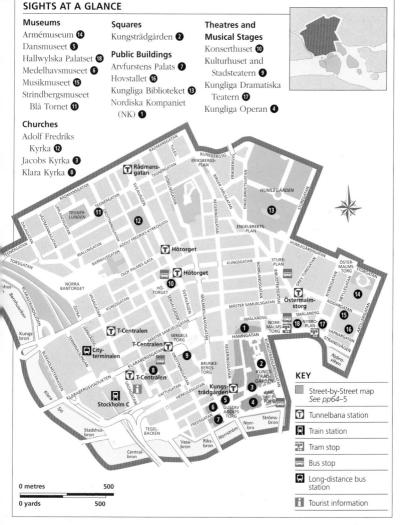

KEY

⬛ Street-by-Street map
 See pp64–5

Ⓣ Tunnelbana station

🚉 Train station

🚊 Tram stop

🚌 Bus stop

🚍 Long-distance bus
 station

ℹ Tourist information

0 metres ——— 500
0 yards ——— 500

◁ **Sagerska Palatset, official residence of the prime minister, between Rosenbad (left) and Arvfurstens Palats**

Street-by-Street: Around Kungsträdgården

With a history going back to the 15th century, the King's Garden (Kungsträdgården) has long been the city's most popular meeting place and recreational centre. Both visitors and Stockholmers gather here for summer concerts and festivals, or just to enjoy a stroll under the lime trees. Around the park is a wealth of shops, including the upmarket department store Nordiska Kompaniet, boutiques, churches, museums and restaurants. A short walk takes you to Gustav Adolfs Torg, flanked by the Royal Opera House and other stately buildings, including the Swedish Foreign Office.

★ Medelhavsmuseet
This museum near Gustav Adolfs Torg has vast collections from prehistoric cultures around the Mediterranean **6**

Dansmuseet
Anything connected with dance, such as costumes, stage-set sketches and posters for the famous Les Ballets Suédois, can be seen here **5**

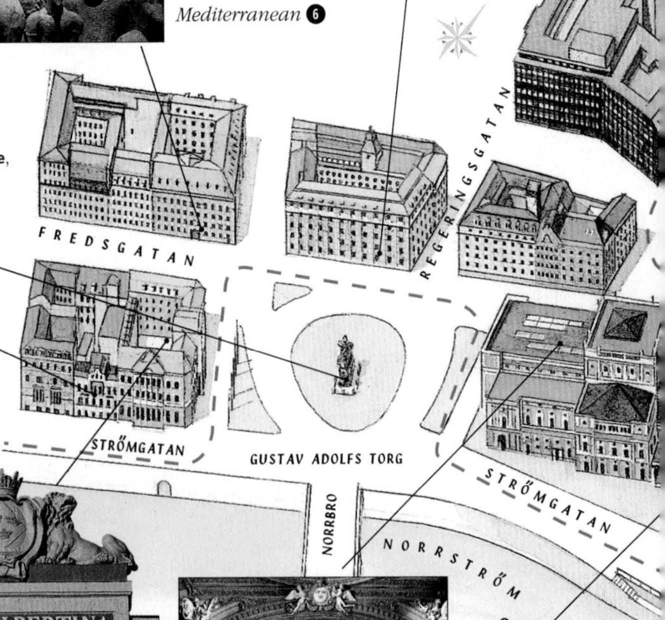

Gustav II Adolf's equestrian statue, designed by L'Archevêques, was unveiled in 1796.

FREDSGATAN

REGERINGSGATAN

Sagerska Palatset

STRÖMGATAN

GUSTAV ADOLFS TORG

NORRBRO

NORRSTRÖM

STRÖMGATAN

Arvfurstens Palats
The Swedish Foreign Office is based in this palace, built for Gustav III's sister Sofia Albertina in 1794 **7**

SOPHIA·ALBERTINA ÆDIFICAVIT·

Opera-källaren *(see p298)*

★ Kungliga Operan
Built in 1898 with a magnificently ornate auditorium, the Royal Opera House replaced an earlier one from the time of Gustav III **4**

KEY

– – – Suggested route

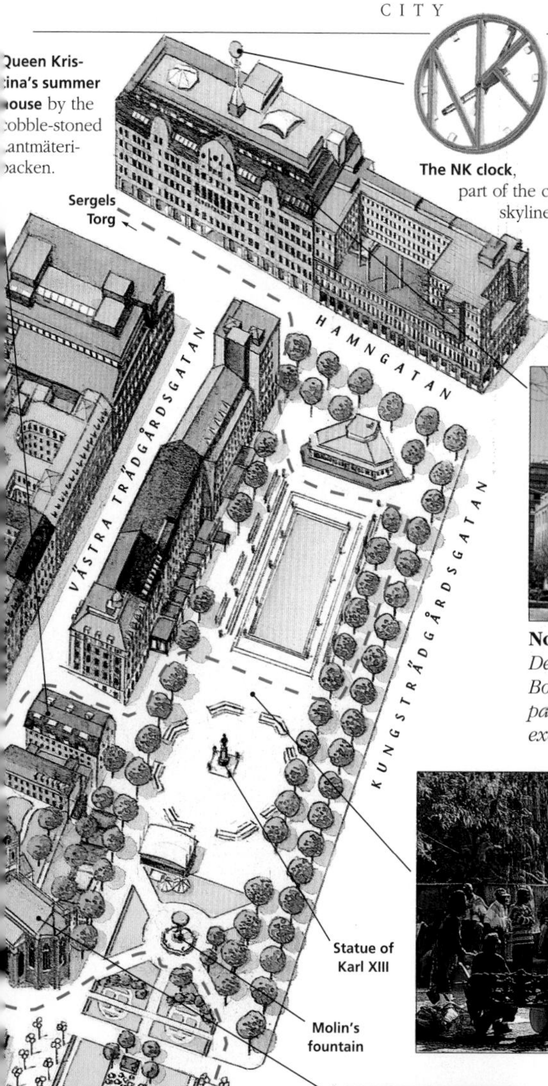

Queen Kristina's summer house by the cobble-stoned Lantmäteribacken.

The NK clock, part of the city skyline.

LOCATOR MAP
See Street Finder maps 1 & 2

Sergels Torg

HAMNGATAN

VÄSTRA TRÄDGÅRDSGATAN

KUNGSTRÄDGÅRDSGATAN

Nordiska Kompaniet (NK)
Designed by Ferdinand Boberg in 1915, the granite palace houses Sweden's most exclusive department store **1**

Statue of Karl XIII

Molin's fountain

Kungsträdgården
The king's kitchen garden was sited here in the 15th century. Today it is one of the most popular recreation centres in the city, both in summer and winter **2**

| 0 metres | 100 |
| 0 yards | 100 |

Karl XII's statue
by Molin was built in 1868 to mark the 150th anniversary of the king's death.

Jacobs Kyrka
Started in 1580, the church was consecrated in 1643. Its stone porches are beautifully crafted **3**

STAR SIGHTS

★ Medelhavsmuseet

★ Kungliga Operan

Nordiska Kompaniet (NK) ❶

Hamngatan 18–20. **Map** 2 D4. **Tel** 08-762 80 00. 🚇 *T-centralen.* 🚌 *47, 69, 76.* 🕐 *10am–8pm Mon–Fri, 10am–6pm Sat, noon–5pm Sun.*

Designed by Ferdinand Boberg, the granite palace on Hamngatan houses the department store Nordiska Kompaniet (NK). Opened in 1915, NK was – and still is – aimed at an exclusive clientele. It made its name as a showcase for Swedish arts and crafts, writing design history when the textiles department, Tetilkammaren, opened in 1937. The manager was the textile artist Astrid Sampe who commissioned leading contemporary artists and designers to supply work. Olle Baertling, Arne Jacobsen, Alvar Aalto and Viola Gråsten all contributed patterns. Sampe also introduced new fabric printing techniques.

Today at NK you can find almost everything from perfume, clothing and sporting equipment to glass, silver and porcelain, but above all, the store is, as its founder Josef Sachs once described it, a commercial and cultural theatre.

Kungsträdgården ❷

Map 3 B1. 🚇 *Kungsträdgården.* 🚌 *47, 69.*

The "King's Garden" is a popular meeting place for Stockholmers where there is something for everyone going on all year round. This open urban space is bordered by treelined promenades, with a modern fountain in the middle. At the Strömgatan end there is a square named after Karl XII with J P Molin's statue of the warrior king, unveiled in 1868, at its centre. In Kungsträdgården itself there is a statue of Karl XIII (1809–18) by Erik Göthe. During the summer, the park is the venue for food festivals, concerts, dancing and street theatre. In winter, the skating rink attracts children and grown-ups alike. Also to be seen is Molin's fountain, made from gypsum in 1866 and cast in bronze. It is the city's oldest park, starting as the royal kitchen garden in the 15th century. During Erik XIV's reign in the 16th century, it was transformed into a formal Renaissance garden. Queen Kristina built a stone summer house here in the 17th century, which stands at Västra Trädgårdsgatan 2, by the cobblestoned Lantmäteribacken.

Molin's fountain

Jacobs Kyrka ❸

Jakobs Torg 5. **Map** 3 B1. **Tel** 08-723 30 38. 🚇 *Kungsträdgården.* 🚌 *55.* 🕐 *11am–2pm Mon, 9am–4pm Tue & Wed, 8am–6pm Thu & Fri, 11am–4pm Sat, 2–8pm Sun.* 🕐 *In Eng 6pm Sun.* ♿

In medieval times there was a small chapel where Kungsträdgården now lies. Dedicated to St Jacob, the patron saint of wayfarers, the chapel and another modest-sized church were pulled down by King Gustav Vasa in the 16th century. His son, Johan III, wanted to provide two new churches in Norra Malmen, as the area was then called, and work to build the churches of St Jacob and St Klara *(see p68)* started in 1580. St Jacob's was consecrated first, in 1643. It has been restored several times since then, in some cases rather clumsily. However, several valuable items have been preserved, including a baptismal font from 1634 and some church silver, as well as porches by the stonemasons Henrik Blom and Hans Hebel.

The organ's façade was created by the architect Carl Härleman and the large painting on the west wall of the southern nave is by Fredrik Westin, Sweden's most distinguished historical painter of the early 19th century.

Altar in Jacobs Kyrka, dating in part from the 17th century

Kungliga Operan ❹

Gustav Adolfs Torg. **Map** 3 B1. **Tel** 08-791 43 00. 🚇 *Kungsträdgården.* 🚌 *2, 43, 55, 62, 65.* **Ticket Office** 🕐 *9am–6pm Mon–Fri, 10am–2pm Sat (open Sun for performances).* 🎭 *In Eng 1pm Sat.* ♿ 🍴 🖥 📷 **www**.operan.se

Opera has been staged in Sweden since 18 January 1773, when a performance took place at Bollhuset at Slottsbacken. Kungliga Operan (The Royal Opera House) on Gustav Adolfs Torg was inaugurated on 30 September 1782, but by the late 19th century it had become a fire hazard. The architect Axel Anderberg was commissioned to design a

View of Kungsträdgården, towards Hamngatan

For hotels and restaurants in this region see pp280–283 and pp298–300

The splendid golden foyer at Kungliga Operan

new opera house which was given to the State in 1898 by a consortium founded by the financier K A Wallenberg.

The colouring of the building in late-Renaissance style is in keeping with the Royal Palace and Parliament building, and some details of the architecture are common to all three. The beautiful staircase with ceiling paintings by Axel Jungstedt was inspired by the Paris Opera. The same artist's portrait of Oscar II hangs in the 28 m (92 ft) long golden foyer, where Carl Larsson was responsible for the decorative paintings. The wings at either side of the stage have been retained, as has the width of the proscenium arch (11.4 m/37 ft). Also saved was J T Sergel's group of angels above the stage. An angel in Vicke Andrén's ceiling painting is holding a sketch of the Opera House.

Dansmuseet ❺

Gustav Adolfs Torg 22–24. **Map** 3 B1.
Tel 08-441 76 50. Ⓣ Kungsträdgården. 🚌 43, 62, 65. 🕐 11am–4pm Tue–Fri (Mon–Fri Jun–Aug), noon–4pm Sat & Sun. 🎫 ♿ 🖥
📷 🏛 www.dansmuseet.se

In 1999 the Dance Museum moved into new premises on Gustav Adolfs Torg, in a former bank building opposite the Norrbro bridge. The museum was originally established in Paris in 1953 by the Swedish aristocrat Rolf de Maré (1888–1964). He was a noted art collector and founder of the renowned avant-garde company Les Ballets Suédois. The collection features all aspects of dance – costumes and masks, scenery sketches, art and posters, books and documents – and includes an archive on popular dance. Apart from the exhibition hall, there is also a data bank – the Rolf de Maré Study Centre –

Gold ceiling in Kungliga Operan

which contains video facilities, a library and archives. The museum shop stocks Sweden's largest collection of dance videos for sale.

Medelhavsmuseet ❻

Fredsgatan 2. **Map** 3 B1.
Tel 08-519 553 80. Ⓣ Kungsträdgården. 🚌 3, 43, 52, 62, 65. 🕐 noon–8pm Tue–Fri, noon–5pm Sat & Sun. 🎫 ♿ 🖥 📷 🏛
www.medelhavsmuseet.se

Gods and people from prehistoric cultures around the Mediterranean rub shoulders in Medelhavsmuseet (the Museum of Mediterranean and Near East Antiquities). Its many treasures include a large group of terracotta figures discovered by archaeologists on Cyprus in the 1930s. There is an extensive display covering ancient Egypt, with bronze weapons, tools and some remarkable mummies. Greek and Islamic culture, Roman and Etruscan art are all represented and complemented by temporary exhibitions.

Medelhavsmuseet is housed in a former bank, built in the 17th century for Gustav Horn, a general in the Thirty Years War. The stairwell, dating from 1905, and the peristyles and colonnade around the upper part of the hall are worth a visit in themselves.

Arvfurstens Palats ❼

Gustav Adolfs Torg 1. **Map** 3 B1.
Ⓣ Kungsträdgården. 🚌 43, 62.
● to the public.

Opposite the Royal Opera House, on the other side of Gustav Adolfs Torg, stands Arvfurstens Palats (Prince's Palace), built for Gustav III's sister Sofia Albertina and completed in 1794. She commissioned the architect Erik Palmstedt to carry out the work. He was a pupil of Carl Fredrik Adelcrantz, designer of the original opera house.

The palace and its decor are shining examples of the Gustavian style, thanks to the contributions of artists and craftsmen such as Louis Masreliez and Georg Haupt and their pupils Gustaf Adolf Ditzinger, J T Sergel and Gottlieb Iwersson. In 1906 the building was taken over by the Swedish Foreign Office.

Nearby is the elegant Sagerska Palatset (1894) in French Renaissance style, which is used by the prime minister as an official residence.

Arvfurstens Palats (1794), now the Swedish Foreign Office

Edvin Öhrström's obelisk in Sergels Torg, with Kulturhuset to the left

Klara Kyrka ❽

Klara Östra Kyrkogata. **Map** 1 C4.
Tel 08-723 30 31. 🇹 T-centralen.
🚌 47, 52, 59, 65. ⬜ 10am–5pm
daily. **Concert** noon Thu, 6pm Sat.
✝ 8am Thu, 11am & 2pm Sun
(Swahili). ♿ ▢

The convent of St Klara
stood on the site of the
present church and cemetery
until 1527, when it was pulled
down on the orders of Gustav
Vasa. Later, his son Johan III
commissioned a new church,
completed in 1590.

The church was ravaged by
fire in 1751. Its reconstruction
was planned by two of the
period's most outstanding
architects, Carl Hårleman and
Carl Fredrik Adelcrantz. The
pulpit was made in 1753 to
Hårleman's design, and J T
Sergel (see p81) created the
angelic figures in the northern
gallery. A pair of identical
angels adorn the chancel,
based on the gypsum originals.

In the 1880s, the 116 m (380
ft) tower was added. The
20th-century church artist, Olle
Hjortzberg, created the paintings in the vault in 1904.

Interior of Klara Kyrka with
decoration by Olle Hjortzberg

Kulturhuset and Stadsteatern ❾

Sergels Torg 3. **Map** 1 C4. **Kulturhuset**
Tel 08-508 315 08. **Stadsteatern**
Tel 08-506 202 00. 🇹 T-centralen.
🚌 47, 56, 59, 69. ⬜ 11am–7pm
Tue, Wed & Fri (to 9pm Thu, to 5pm
Sat & Sun). 🎦 some areas.
♿ 🍴 ▢ 🛍 www.kulturhuset.
stockholm.se; www.stadsteatern.
stockholm.se

The distinctive glass façade
of Kulturhuset (Cultural
Centre) fronts the southern
side of Sergels Torg. The
winning entry in a Nordic
architectural competition,
Kulturhuset has become a
symbol of Swedish Modern-
ism. It was designed by Peter
Celsing and opened in 1974.

Refurbished to meet the
needs of the new millennium,
the complex contains several
galleries which mount
regularly changing exhibitions. In the auditorium, a

varied programme of music,
dance, drama and lectures
is presented.

In the Children's Room,
youngsters can read books,
draw pictures, listen to stories
or watch films. "Lava" focuses
on youth culture nationwide.
There is a library for fans of
strip cartoons and reading
rooms providing computers,
newspapers and magazines.

Among the shops here is
Designtorget, selling items of
Swedish design. There are
two cafés: the top-floor Café
Panorama offers diners
fantastic city views, while
Café Ekoteket serves organic
and locally produced food and
also hosts tasting sessions.

Kulturhuset also houses
Stadsteatern (City Theatre),
whose main auditorium
opened in 1990. This part of
the building was formerly
occupied by Parliament while
its chamber on Helgeandsholmen was being rebuilt (see
p61). The theatre was
designed by architects Lars
Fahlsten and Per Ahrbom and
contains six stages of varying
size and style under one roof.

Konserthuset ❿

Hötorget. **Map** 1 C4.
Tel 08-786 02 00. 🇹 Hötorget. 🚌 1,
56. **Ticket Office** ⬜ 11am–6pm
Mon–Fri, 11am–3pm Sat, and 2 hours
before a concert. 🎦 ♿ ▢ 🛍
www.konserthuset.se

A Nordic version of a
Greek temple, Konserthuset
(the Concert Hall) is a masterpiece of the architect Ivar
Tengbom (1878–1968) and is

CITY'S TRANSFORMATION

During the 20th century Stockholm's population grew from
250,000 to more than 1.6 million. By the 1920s it was
obviously that the old heart of the
city would not meet the future
needs of business, public administration and the growth in traffic.
In 1951 a controversial 30-year
ongoing programme to transform
the lower Norrmalm city centre
was launched. Slums on 335 of
the 600 sites were pulled down
and 78 new buildings were built.
Two-thirds of the area's buildings
were added during this period.

The first steps towards a new
Hötorg City, 1958

The *Orpheus* sculpture group by
Carl Milles at Konserthuset

THE NOBEL PRIZES

Alfred Nobel (1833–96) was an outstanding chemist and
inventor. He left his fortune to endow the prestigious
Nobel Prizes – consisting of a monetary
award and a medal – which have been
presented every December since
1901. The ceremony takes place in
Konserthuset, where prizes are
awarded for physics, chemistry,
physiology or medicine, and
literature. Since 1969 the Bank of
Sweden has given a prize for
economic sciences in Nobel's memory. The Nobel Peace Prize is presented in Oslo on the same day. In 1901
each prize was worth 150,000 kr; in
2009 the figure was 10 million kr.

The Nobel Medal,
awarded annually

an outstanding example of the
1920s' Neo-Classical style.
Tengbom's tradition has been
carried on by his son Anders
(b. 1911), who was in charge
of its renovation in 1970–71,
and his grandson Svante
(b. 1942), who had a similar
task in 1993–6.

Constructed in 1923–6, the
main hall has undergone major
reconstruction and moderni-
zation to overcome acoustical
problems. Its interior is very
simple in contrast to the
Grünewald Hall, by the artist
Isaac Grünewald (1889–1946),
which is in the more lavish
style of an Italian Renaissance
palace. The four marble statues
in the main foyer are by Carl
Milles, creator of the *Orpheus*
sculpture group outside.

The Concert Hall is the
home of the Swedish Royal
Philharmonic Orchestra,
which gives some 70 concerts
every year, and international
star soloists perform regularly.
It is also the venue for the
Nobel Prize presentations.

Strindbergsmuseet
Blå Tornet ⓫

Drottninggatan 85. **Map** 1 C3.
Tel 08-411 53 54. Ⓣ *Rådmansgatan.*
🚌 *52, 65.* ◯ *Jul–Aug: 10am–4pm
Tue–Sun; Sep–Jun: noon–4pm Tue–
Sun.* 🎦 *1pm Thu–Sun (Swedish
only).* ⛹ 🖼 🛈 www.
strindbergsmuseet.se

The world-famous dramatist
August Strindberg (1849–
1912) lived at 24 different

addresses in Stockholm over
the years. He moved to the last
of these in 1908, and gave it
the name Blå Tornet (the Blue
Tower). By then he had gained
international recognition.

The apartment, now the
Strindbergsmuseet, was newly
built with central heating, toilet
and lift, but lacked a kitchen.
Instead he relied on Falkner's
Pension, in the same building,
for food and other services.
On his last few birthdays the
great man would stand on his
balcony and watch his
admirers stage a torchlight
procession in his honour.

Opened in 1973, the
museum shows the author's
home with his bedroom and
dining room and his study as it
was on his death, as well as
3,000 books, photographic
archives, press cuttings and
posters. In the adjoining
premises, a permanent
exhibition portrays Strindberg
as author, theatrical director,
artist and photographer. Temporary exhibitions and other
activities are often held here.

Strindberg's desk and writing
materials in his study

Adolf Fredriks
Kyrka ⓬

Holländargatan 16. **Map** 1 C3.
Tel 08-20 70 76. Ⓣ *Hötorget.* 🚌
52. ◯ *1–8pm Mon, 10am–4pm
Tue–Sun.* **Concert** *12.15pm Tue.*
✝ *7pm Mon, 12.15pm Wed & Thu,
11am Sun.* 🎦 *by appointment.* ⛹
🖳 🛈

King Adolf Fredrik laid the
foundation stone of this church
in 1768 on the site of an earlier
chapel dedicated to St Olof.
Designed by Carl Fredrik
Adelcrantz, in Neo-Classical
style with traces of
Rococo, the church
has been built in the
shape of a Greek
cross and has a
central dome.

The interior has
undergone a
number of
changes, but both
the altar and
pulpit have
remained intact.
The sculptor
Johan Tobias
Sergel created
the altarpiece
and the memorial

Memorial to
Descartes

to the French
philosopher Descartes who
died in Stockholm in 1650.
The paintings in the dome
were added in 1899–1900 by
Julius Kronberg. More recent
acquisitions include altar silver-
ware by Sigurd Persson.

The cemetery is the resting
place of the assassinated Prime
Minister Olof Palme (1927–86).
J T Sergel is also buried here.

Armémuseum, with the dome of Hedvig Eleonora Kyrka in the background

Kungliga Biblioteket ⑬

Humlegården. **Map** 2 D3.
Tel 08-463 40 00.
🚇 Östermalmstorg. 🚌 1, 2, 55, 56.
🕐 9am–8pm Mon–Thu, 9am–7pm Fri, 10am–5pm Sat; early Jun–mid-Aug: 9am–6pm Mon–Thu, 9am–5pm Fri, 11am–3pm Sat. 📷 by appointment. ♿ 🖥 www.kb.se

This is Sweden's national library and an autonomous Government department in its own right. Ever since 1661, when there were only nine printing presses in Sweden, copies of every piece of printed matter have had to be lodged with Kungliga Biblioteket (Royal Library). Since 1993 this requirement has also applied to electronic documents. As there are now some 3,000 printers and publishers in Sweden the volume of material is expanding rapidly. The stock of books is increasing at the rate of 35,000 volumes a year.

The imposing original building, dating from 1865–78, had to be expanded in the 1920s, and again in the 1990s.

The library is in a beautiful setting in Humlegården, created by Gustav II Adolf in 1619 to grow hops for the royal household. Ever since the 18th century, the park has been a favourite recreation area for Stockholmers.

The 13th-century "Devil's Bible" in Kungliga Biblioteket

Armémuseum ⑭

Riddargatan 13. **Map** 2 E4. **Tel** 08-519 563 00. 🚇 Östermalmstorg. 🚌 42, 69. 🕐 11am–8pm Tue, 11am–5pm Wed–Sun. 📷 📷 ♿ 🍴 🅿 www.armemuseum.se

The old armoury on Artillerigården has been the home of the Armémuseum (Royal Army Museum) since 1879. During the 1990s, the 250-year-old building and its displays underwent extensive renovation to create one of the capital's best-planned and most interesting museums.

Exhibits are arranged over three floors. Dramatic life-size settings have been made to portray Sweden's history of war and defence, showing not only what happened in battle but how the lives of the women and children at home were affected. Diaries, intelligence manuals, rifles, flags, banners and even cutlery add a note of reality.

During the summer guardsmen march from here to the Royal Palace at 11.45am daily for the changing of the guard.

Musikmuseet ⑮

Sibyllegatan 2. **Map** 2 E4.
Tel 08-519 554 90. 🚇 Östermalmstorg, Kungsträdgården. 🚌 47, 62, 69, 76. 🕐 noon–5pm Tue–Sun. 📷 by appointment only. 📷 📷 ♿ 🍴 🅿 www.musikmuseet.se

The Museum of Music opened in the old royal bakery in 1979. Bread was baked here for military personnel in Stockholm from 1640 right up to 1958. It is the capital's oldest preserved industrial building, in the city centre. Today the museum's collection includes about 6,000 instruments, and it also holds Sweden's national musical archive. With 20,000 manuscripts, it is a gold mine for anyone interested in Swedish folk music. The archive is open by appointment only. It hosts a regular programme of temporary exhibitions.

A Swedish cornet, part of the Musikmuseet's collection

Hovstallet ⑯

Väpnargatan 1. **Map** 2 E4. **Tel** 08-402 61 06. 🚇 Östermalmstorg. 🚌 2, 47, 62, 69, 71, 76. 🕐 for guided tours. 📷 2pm Sat & Sun; Jul–Aug: 2pm Mon–Fri. 📷

The Royal Mews looks after transport for the Royal Family and Royal Household. It maintains about 40 carriages, a dozen cars, carriage horses, and a few horses used for riding. The royal horses are Swedish half-breeds.

There are many treasures among the carriages, such as the glass-panelled State Coach known as a "Berliner". It was built in Sweden at the Adolf Freyschuss carriage works and made its debut at Oscar II's silver jubilee in 1897. It is still used today on ceremonial occasions.

Incoming foreign ambassadors travel to the Royal Palace for their formal audience with the monarch in Karl XV's coupé. Open horse-drawn carriages from the mid-19th century are normally used for processions.

INGMAR BERGMAN

The playwright and producer Ingmar Bergman was born at Östermalm in 1918. His long series of masterly films have made him world-famous, but he started his career in the theatre. From 1963–6 he was Director of Kungliga Dramatiska Teatern. His break-through as a film producer came with *Smiles of the Summer Night* (1955), and *The Seventh Seal* (1957) was a cinematic milestone. *Fanny and Alexander* (1982) was his last major film, after which he wrote screenplays and published his autobiography, *Magic Lantern*. Ingmar Bergman died in 2007.

Ingmar Bergman at a press conference, 1998

The Hallwylska Palatset courtyard, seen through the gateway arch

Kungliga Dramatiska Teatern ⑰

Nybroplan. **Map** 2 E4. **Tel** 08-667 06 80. 🚇 Östermalmstorg. 🚌 47, 62, 69, 76. **Ticket Office** 🕐 noon–7pm Tue–Sat, noon–4pm Sun (except Jun–Aug). 🎫 🚫 ♿ 🍴 www.dramaten.se

When plans were drawn up in the early 20th century to build the present Kungliga Dramatiska Teatern (Royal Dramatic Theatre) at Nybroplan, the State refused to give financial aid, so it was funded by lotteries instead. The results exceeded all expectations, giving the architect Fredrik Lilljekvist generous resources which he used to the full.

The new theatre, known as Dramaten, took six years to build and opened in 1908. The design was lavish, both in the choice of materials and in the contributions by leading Swedish artists.

The Jugendstil façade, inspired by Viennese architecture, is in expensive white marble. Christian Ericsson created the powerful relief frieze, Carl Milles the centre section and John Börjesson the bronze statues *Poetry* and *Drama*. These are comple-mented in the foyer by *Tragedy* and *Comedy* by Börjesson and Theodor Lundberg respectively.

The ceiling in the foyer is by Carl Larsson, while the upper lobby's back wall was painted by Oscar Björk, and the auditorium's ceiling and stage lintel by Julius Kronberg. Gustav Cederström provided the central painting in the marble foyer.

When Gustav III founded the Royal Dramatic Theatre in 1788 it performed in a building on Slottsbacken. The colour scheme there – blue, white and gold – was chosen for the new venue, but was changed to "theatre red" in the 1930s.

The original colours were reinstated in 1988.

Hallwylska Palatset ⑱

Hamngatan 4. **Map** 2 D4. **Tel** 08-519 555 99. 🚇 Östermalmstorg. 🚌 47, 62, 69, 76. 🕐 11.45am–4pm Tue–Sun, 11.45am–7pm Wed; Jul–Aug: 10.45am–4.30pm Tue–Sun. 🎫 3pm Sun (in Eng). 🎫 🚫 🅿 www.hallwylskamuseet.se

The impressive façade of Hamngatan 4 is nothing in comparison with what is concealed behind the heavy gates. The Hallwyl Palace was built from 1892–7 as a residence for the immensely wealthy Count and Countess Walther and Wilhelmina von Hallwyl. When the Countess died in 1930 the State was left a fantastic gift: an unbelievably ornate palace whose chatelaine had amassed a priceless collection of *objets d'art* over many decades. Eight years later the doors opened on a new museum with 67,000 catalogued items.

Wilhelmina left nothing to chance, often visiting the building site. The architect Isak Gustav Clason (1856–1930) had no worries about cost and nor did the decorative painter and artistic adviser Julius Kronberg. Every detail had to be perfect. A typical example is the billiards room which has gilt-leather wallpaper and walnut panelling, with billiard balls sculpted into the marble fireplace.

The paintings in the gallery, mostly 16th- and 17th-century Flemish, were bought over a period of only two years.

Kungliga Dramatiska Teatern's Jugendstil façade in white marble

BLASIEHOLMEN & SKEPPSHOLMEN

Opposite the Royal Palace on the eastern side of the Norrström channel lies Blasieholmen, a natural springboard to the islands of Skeppsholmen and Kastellholmen.

Several elegant palaces were built at Blasieholmen during Sweden's era as a great power in the 17th and early 18th centuries. But the area's present appearance was acquired in the period between the mid-19th century, when buildings such as Nationalmuseum were erected, and just before World War I. In the early 1900s, stately residences such as Bååtska Palatset became overshadowed by smart hotels, opulent bank buildings

Porthole in wooden boat

and entertainment venues. Blasieholmen is also the place for auction houses, art galleries, antiques shops and second-hand bookshops. And the quayside is the departure point for sightseeing and archipelago boats.

Skeppsholmen is reached by a wrought-iron bridge with old wooden boats moored next to it. In the middle of the 17th century the island became the base for the Swedish Navy and many of its old buildings were designed as barracks and stores. Today they house some of the city's major museums and cultural institutions, juxtaposed with the avant-garde construction of the Moderna Museet.

SIGHTS AT A GLANCE

Museums
Arkitekturmuseet ❸
Moderna Museet pp78–9 ❷
Nationalmuseum pp80–81 ❼
Östasiatiska Museet ❶

Islands and Squares
Blasieholmstorg ❾
Kastellholmen ❻
Raoul Wallenbergs Torg ⑫

Synagogues
Synagogan ❿

Hotels and Restaurants
af Chapman ❹
Berns' Salonger ⓫
Grand Hôtel ❽

Concert Halls
Nybrokajen 11 ⓭

Public Buildings
Kungliga
   Konsthögskolan ❺

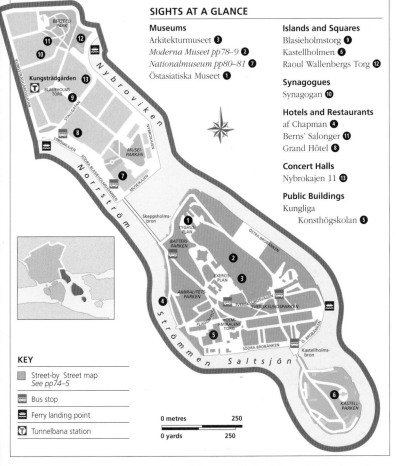

KEY

▨ Street-by Street map
See pp74–5

🚌 Bus stop

⛴ Ferry landing point

🚇 Tunnelbana station

| 0 metres | 250 |
| 0 yards | 250 |

◁ Skeppsholmsbron, linking Blasieholmen and Skeppsholmen, with the ship *af Chapman* in the background

Street-by-Street: Skeppsholmen

Skeppsholmen has long since lost its importance as a
naval base and has been transformed into a centre for
culture. Many of the naval buildings have been restored
and traditional wooden boats are moored here, but pride
of place now goes to the exciting Moderna Museet. The
island is ideal for a full-day visit, with its location between
the waters of Strömmen and Nybroviken acting as a
breathing space in the centre of Stockholm. The attractive
buildings, the richly wooded English-style park and the
view towards Skeppsbron and Strandvägen also make
Skeppsholmen a pleasant place for those who would
just prefer to have a quiet stroll.

Teater Galeasen is
Stockholm's avant-garde
theatre for new Swedish
and international drama.

Blasie-
holmen

Skepps-
holmsbron
(bridge)

★ Östasiatiska Museet
*Arts and crafts from China,
Japan, Korea and India, from
the Stone Age to the 19th century
are displayed here. This Song
Dynasty head is a highlight* ❶

**Skeppsholmen
Church** (1824–42)
in well-preserved
Empire style.

**Salute
battery**
(see p76)

Admiralty House

SVENSKSUNDSVÄGEN

ÖSTRA BROBÄNKEN

Paradise (1963), a
sculpture group by
Jean Tinguely and
Niki de Saint Phalle
for Montreal's World
Exposition, has stood
outside the site of
the Moderna Museet
since 1972.

Youth Hostel

**Swedish
Society of
Crafts & Design**

Kungliga Konsthögskolan
*The first part of the Royal College
of Fine Arts was completed in
the 1770s, but it acquired its
present appearance in
the mid-1990s. This
cast-iron boar
stands at the
entrance* ❺

af Chapman
*Built in 1888, the full-rigged former freighter
and school ship has served as a popular youth
hostel since 1949. Skeppsholmen Church (left)
and the Admiralty House (1647–50, rebuilt
1844–6) are in the background* ❹

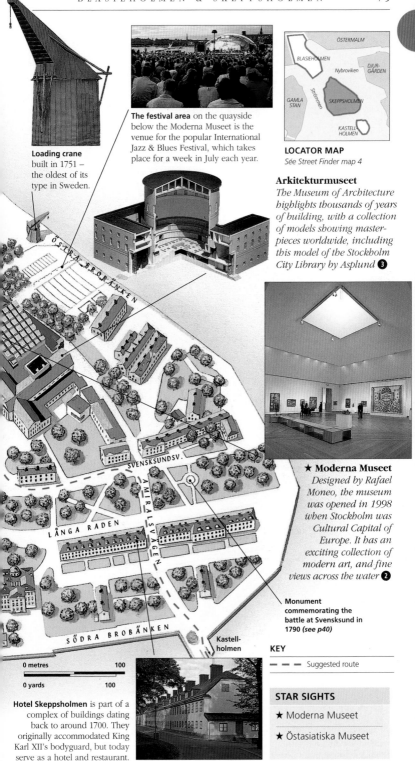

Loading crane built in 1751 – the oldest of its type in Sweden.

The festival area on the quayside below the Moderna Museet is the venue for the popular International Jazz & Blues Festival, which takes place for a week in July each year.

LOCATOR MAP
See Street Finder map 4

Arkitekturmuseet
The Museum of Architecture highlights thousands of years of building, with a collection of models showing master-pieces worldwide, including this model of the Stockholm City Library by Asplund **3**

★ Moderna Museet
Designed by Rafael Moneo, the museum was opened in 1998 when Stockholm was Cultural Capital of Europe. It has an exciting collection of modern art, and fine views across the water **2**

Monument commemorating the battle at Svensksund in 1790 *(see p40)*

KEY

– – – Suggested route

Hotel Skeppsholmen is part of a complex of buildings dating back to around 1700. They originally accommodated King Karl XII's bodyguard, but today serve as a hotel and restaurant.

0 metres   100
0 yards   100

STAR SIGHTS

★ Moderna Museet

★ Östasiatiska Museet

Arkitekturmuseet, housed in the Neo-Classical former naval drill hall

Östasiatiska Museet ❶

Tyghusplan. **Map** 4 D2. **Tel** 08-519 557 50. Ⓣ Kungsträdgården. 🚌 65. 🚢 Djurgårdsfärja. ◯ 11am–8pm Tue, 11am–5pm Wed–Sun. 📷 by appointment only. ♿ ▯ www.ostasiatiska.se

It is not unusual for Western capitals to have a museum devoted to art and archaeology from China, Japan, Korea and India. But it is not every Museum of Far Eastern Antiquities that, like Östasiatiska Museet, can claim one of the world's foremost collections of Chinese art outside Asia.

On a visit to the Yellow River valley in China in the early 1920s, the Swedish geologist Johan Gunnar Andersson discovered hitherto unknown dwellings and graves containing objects dating from the New Stone Age.

He was allowed to take a selection of items back to Sweden, and these formed the basis for the museum, founded in 1926. A key figure in its development was the then Crown Prince, later to become King Gustav VI Adolf,

who was both interested in and knowledgeable about archaeology. Later, he bequeathed to the museum his own large collection of ancient Chinese arts and crafts.

The museum has been on Skeppsholmen since 1963, when it was moved into a restored house which had been built in 1699–1700 as a depot for Karl XII's bodyguard.

Moderna Museet ❷

See pp78–9.

Arkitekturmuseet ❸

Exercisplan. **Map** 4 E3. **Tel** 08-587 270 00. Ⓣ Kungsträdgården. 🚌 65. 🚢 Djurgårdsfärja. ◯ 10am–8pm Tue, 10am–6pm Wed–Sun. 🎟 (free up to age 19; free for everyone 4–6pm Fri.) 📷 in English, by appointment only. 📷 ♿ ▯ 🍴 ▯ ▯www.arkitekturmuseet.se

The Swedish Museum of Architecture shares an entrance hall and restaurant with the Moderna Museet. It

has also reclaimed its earlier Neo-Classical home, a one-time naval drill hall.

In the permanent exhibition, more than 100 architectural models guide visitors through the history of Swedish building. They include the oldest and simplest of wooden houses to the highly sophisticated construction techniques and innovative styles of the present day.

It is fascinating to move from an almost 2,000-year-old longhouse to a modern supermarket, interspersed with examples of architecture in Gothenburg from the 17th century to the 1930s.

Models of historic architectural works worldwide, from 2000 BC up to the present day, are also on show.

The museum offers an ambitious programme – albeit only in Swedish – alongside the permanent and temporary exhibitions, including lectures, study days, city walks, guided tours, school visits and family events on Sunday afternoons, which involve model-building.

Chinese Bodhisattva in limestone (c.530), Östasiatiska Museet

THE SKEPPSHOLMEN CANNONS

A salute battery of four 57-mm rapid-fire cannons is sited on Skeppsholmen and is still in use. Salutes are fired to mark national and royal special occasions at 12 noon on weekdays and 1pm at weekends: 28 January – the King's name day; 30 April – the King's birthday; 6 June – Sweden's National Day; 14 July – Crown Princess Victoria's birthday; 8 August – the Queen's name day; 23 December – the Queen's birthday.

The salute battery on Skeppsholmen

af Chapman ❹

Västra Brobänken. **Map** 4 D3.
Tel 08-463 22 66. ⓣ *Kungsträd-gården.* 🚌 65. ⛴ *Djurgårdsfärja.*
🔟 ⬛ See **Where to Stay** p281.

The sailing ship *af Chapman*
is one of Sweden's most
attractive and unusual youth
hostels. The ship has 125
beds, and there are a further
155 beds in the hostel
building facing the gangway.

Visitors staying in more
conventional accommodation
can still go on board and
enjoy *af Chapman*'s special
atmosphere. The three-masted
ship was built in 1888 at the
English port of Whitehaven
and used as a freight vessel.
She came to Sweden in 1915
and saw service as a sail
training ship until 1934. The
City of Stockholm bought the
vessel after World War II and
she has been berthed here
since 1949. She is named after
Fredrik Henrik af Chapman, a
master shipbuilder who was
born in Gothenburg in 1721.

Kungliga Konst-högskolan ❺

Flaggmansvägen 1. **Map** 4 E3. *Tel*
08-614 40 00. ⓣ *Kungsträdgården.*
🚌 65. ⛴ *Djurgårdsfärja.* ⬭ *to the
public for special events.* ♿ ⬛

A stroll around Skepps-
holmen provides an
opportunity to have a closer
look at the beautifully
restored 18th-century naval
barracks which now houses
Kungliga Konsthögskolan (the
Royal Institute of Arts). At the
entrance there are two statues
depicting a lion and a boar.
"In like a lion and out like a
pig" is an old saying among
the lecturers and the 200 or
so students at this college, still
rich in tradition.

The college started out in
1735 as an academy for
painting and sculpture for the
decorators working on Tessin's
new Royal Palace. Gustav III
granted it a royal charter in
1773. Before it moved here in
1995, the college was located
on Fredsgatan as part of
Konstakademien, although
since 1978 it had been run

independently with departments for painting, sculpture,
graphics, computing and
video, as well as offering
courses for architects.

The college is not normally
open to the public, apart from
an "open house" once a year.
Then visitors can enjoy the
beautiful interiors, especially
the vaulted 18th-century cellars.

**The medieval-style castle on
Kastellholmen, built in 1846–8**

Kastellholmen ❻

Map 4 F4. ⓣ *Kungsträdgården.*
🚌 65. ⛴ *Djurgårdsfärja.*

Right in the middle of
Stockholm, Kastellholmen
is a typical archipelago island
with granite rocks and steep
cliffs. From Skeppsholmen it is
reached by a bridge built in
1880. Every morning since
1640 a sailor has hoisted the
three-tailed Swedish war flag
at the castle. Whenever a
visiting naval vessel arrives,
the battery's four cannons

fire a welcoming salute from
the castle terrace.

The charming brick pavilion
by the bridge was built in 1882
for the Royal Skating Club,
which used the water between
the two islands when it froze.

Nationalmuseum ❼

See pp80–81.

Grand Hôtel ❽

Södra Blasieholmshamnen 8. **Map** 3
C1. *Tel* 08-679 35 00. ⓣ *Kung-
strädgården.* 🚌 2, 55, 62, 65, 76. 🔟
⬛ See **Where to Stay** p281 and
Where to Eat p294. **www**.grand
hotel.se

Oscar II's head chef, Régis
Cadier, founded the Grand
Hôtel, Sweden's leading five-
star hotel, in 1874. Since 1901,
the hotel has accommodated
the Nobel Prize winners
each year.

Traditional Swedish
delicacies are served in an
abundant *smörgåsbord* in the
elegant Veranda. The hotel
also has two, Michelin-starred
restaurants and the Cadier
Bar, named after its founder.

The hotel has 24 banquet-
ing and conference suites, the
best known of which is the
lofty *Vinterträdgården*
(Winter Garden) which can
accommodate 800 people.
The *Spegelsalen* (Hall of
Mirrors) is a copy of the hall at
Versailles and was where the
Nobel Prize banquet was held
until 1929, when it became
too big and was moved to
City Hall *(see p100).*

The exclusive Grand Hôtel on Blasieholmen

Moderna Museet ❷

The Museum of Modern Art is an airy building, designed by the Catalan architect Rafael Moneo in 1998. The museum has a top-class collection of international and Swedish modern art, as well as photography and film. Built partly underground, the complex includes a cinema and auditorium; the photographic library is the most comprehensive collection of its type in northern Europe and there is also a collection of video art and art documentaries. A wide choice of books on art, photography, film and architecture can be found in the bookshop and the Restaurant MM Mat has attractive views over the water.

Breakfast Outdoors (1962)
This sculpture group by Picasso, executed in sandblasted concrete by Carl Nesjar, stands in the museum garden near the entrance

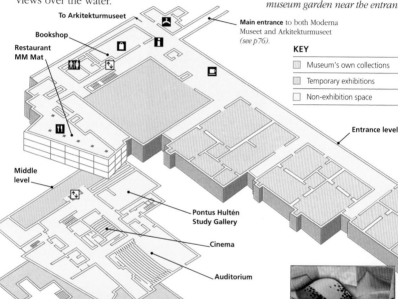

To Arkitekturmuseet

Bookshop

Restaurant MM Mat

Main entrance to both Moderna Museet and Arkitekturmuseet *(see p76)*.

KEY

Museum's own collections

Temporary exhibitions

Non-exhibition space

Entrance level

Middle level

Pontus Hultén Study Gallery

Cinema

Auditorium

Studio

★ **Marzella** (1909–10)
This boldly-coloured portrait by Ernst Ludwig Kirchner (1880–1938) highlights his desire to bring fresh ideas to art by refuting traditional artistic conventions.

RAFAEL MONEO

Rafael Moneo (b. 1937) is one of the leading contemporary architects. As a young architect, Moneo took part in the project to build the Sydney Opera House. His flair for adapting building design to sensitive surroundings was recognized in 1989 when his was chosen out of 211 entries as the winner of the competition to design the new Moderna Museet.

Moderna Museet's northern façade

★ **Landscape from Céret** (1913)
Inspired by Braque and Picasso, Spanish Cubist artist Juan Gris (1887–1927) developed his own unique take on the discipline, as seen in this vivid, geometric landscape painting.

VISITORS' CHECKLIST

Exercisplan. **Map** 4 E3.
Tel 08-519 552 00.
🚇 Kungsträdgården. 🚌 65.
⛴ Djurgårdsfärja. ⏱ 10am–
8pm Tue, 10am–6pm Wed–Sun.
⬤ 1 Jan, 24–25, 31 Dec
and some holidays.
📷 Eng: Jul–Sep. 🎫 free for children up to 18 years.
📷 ♿ 🍴 📷 💻 🎧
www.modernamuseet.se

GALLERY GUIDE

*The large room on the entrance
level is used for temporary
exhibitions. Three rooms on
the same level have an alternat-
ing selection of collections
from the eras 1900–45, 1946–
70 and 1971 to the present
day. The middle level has an
auditorium, cinema and
study gallery. Another
entrance is at the lowest level.*

★ **The Child's Brain** (1914)
*The surrealist Giorgio de
Chirico gave his work the
title* The Ghost, *but in the
irrational spirit of the movement Louis Aragon renamed
it in a pamphlet about the
artist's 1927 retrospective.*

STAR EXHIBITS

★ Marzella by Ernst
  Ludwig Kirchner

★ Landscape from Céret
  by Juan Gris

★ The Child's Brain
  by de Chirico

Blasieholmstorg ❾

Map 3 C1. 🚇 Kungsträdgården.
🚌 2, 55, 62, 65, 71, 76.

Two of the city's oldest
palaces are located in this
square, flanked by two bronze
horses. The palace at No. 8
was built in the mid-17th
century by Field Marshal
Gustaf Horn. It was rebuilt
100 years later, when it
acquired the character of an
18th-century French palace.
Foreign ambassadors and
ministers lodged here when
they visited the
capital, so it
became known
as the Ministers'
Palace. Later it
became a base for
overseas adminis-
tration and soon
earned its present
name of Utrike-
sministerhotellet
(Foreign Ministry
Hotel). Parts of the
building are now used as
offices by the Musical Academy
and the Swedish Institute.

Bååtska Palatset stands
nearby at No. 6. Its exterior
dates from 1669 and was
designed by Tessin the Elder.
In 1876–7 it was partly rebuilt
by F W Scholander for the
Freemasons, who still have
their lodge here.

Another interesting complex
of buildings can be found on
the square at No. 10. The
façade which faces on to
Nybrokajen, along the water's
edge, is an attractive example
of the Neo-Renaissance style
of the 1870s and 1880s.

**Bronze horse on
Blasieholmstorg**

Synagogan ❿

Wahrendoffsgatan 3B. **Map** 3 C1.
Tel 08-587 858 00. 🚇 Kungsträdgården. 🚌 2, 55, 62, 65, 71, 76.
📷 all year 9.15am Sat; Jun–Aug:
6.30pm Fri; Hebrew and partly
English. 🎫 summer and by
appointment. ♿

It took most of the 1860s
to build the Conservative
Jewish community's syna-
gogue on land reclaimed from
the sea. When it was inaugurated in 1870, the building
was standing on 1,300 piles

**Monument to the victims of the
Holocaust during World War II**

which had been driven down
to a depth of 15 m (50 ft). It
is built in what the architect,
F W Scholander, called
"ancient Eastern style". The
synagogue can be
visited on guided
tours during the
summer. Alongside
is the congrega-
tion's assembly
room and library.
Outside is a
monument erected
in 1998 in memory
of 8,000 victims
of the Holocaust whose
relations had been rescued
and taken to Sweden during
World War II.

There is also an Orthodox
synagogue in the city centre,
reached through the Jewish
Centre (Judiska Centret) on
Nybrogatan at No. 19.

Berns' Salonger ⓫

Berzelii Park. **Map** 2 D4. **Tel** 08-566
322 00. 🚇 Kungsträdgården,
Östermalmstorg. 🚌 2, 47, 55, 62,
65, 69, 71, 76. ♿ **Where to Eat** p294.

This has been one of Stockholm's most legendary
restaurants and entertainment
venues since 1863. Both
salons, with their stately
galleries, magnificent crystal
chandeliers and elegant
mirrors, were restored to their
original splendour by the
British designer and restaura-
teur Terence Conran to mark
the new millennium.

The new-look Berns' is one
of Stockholm's biggest
restaurants with seating for
400 diners. The gallery level,
with its beautifully decorated
dining rooms, was made
famous by August Strindberg's
novel *The Red Room* (1879).

Nationalmuseum 🌑

The Nationalmuseum is a landmark on the southern side of Blasieholmen. The location by the Strömmen channel inspired the 19th-century German architect August Stüler to design a building in the Venetian and Florentine Renaissance styles.

Completed in 1866, the museum houses Sweden's largest art collection, with some 16,000 classic paintings and sculptures. Drawings and graphics from the 15th century up to the early 20th century bring the total to 500,000. The applied art and design section has works spanning five centuries, including a 500-year-old tapestry, porcelain and examples of work by master furniture-makers, such as Georg Haupt. Space is devoted to the development of modern Swedish design *(see pp24–5)* from 1900 to today.

The Love Lesson (1716–17)
Antoine Watteau's speciality was the so-called fêtes galantes, *depicting young couples in playful mood.*

★ The Conspiracy of the Batavians under Claudius Civilis (1661–2)
Originally intended for Amsterdam, Rembrandt depicts the Batavians' conspiracy against the Romans, symbolizing the Dutch liberation campaign against Spain.

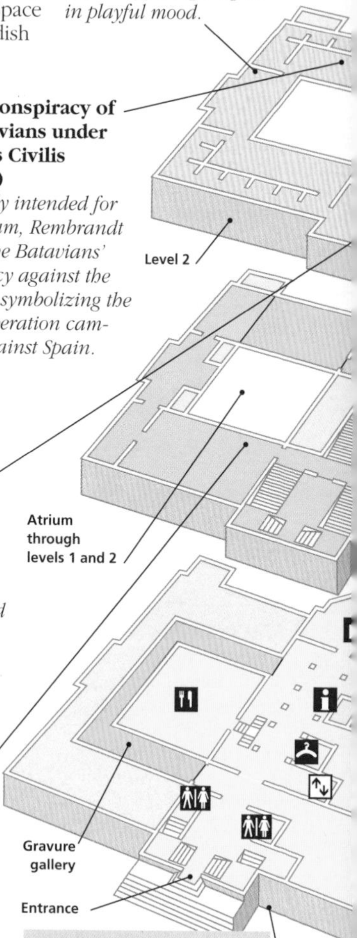

Level 2

Cupid and Psyche (1787)
Johan Tobias Sergel is considered the foremost sculptor of the Gustavian era. This piece is regarded as one of his most triumphant works. The sculpture refers to the victory of love over weakness.

Atrium through levels 1 and 2

Alhambra Vase
Discover the roots of European design development in furniture, embroidery, gold, glass and porcelain, featuring this late-14th Century Alhambra Vase, from Granada in Spain, on show in the permanent Design in Sweden (1500–1740) exhibition.

Gravure gallery

Entrance

STAR FEATURES

★ The Lady with the Veil by Roslin

★ The Conspiracy of the Batavians by Rembrandt

Entry for wheelchairs

★ **The Lady with the Veil**
*Alexander Roslin's elegant
portrait (1769) is often
considered to be a
glamorized symbol of
18th-century Sweden.*

VISITORS' CHECKLIST

Södra Blasieholmshamnen.
Map 4 D2. **Tel** 08-519 543 00.
🚇 Kungsträdgården. 🚌 65;
or 2, 55, 62, 76 to Karl XII's Torg.
⏰ 11am–8pm Tue & Thu
(Jun–Aug to 5pm Thu); 11am–
5pm Wed, Fri–Sun.
🔴 24, 25 & 31 Dec, 1 Jan,
some other hols. 🎫 📷 ♿ 🔎
in Eng. 🚻 🏠
www.nationalmuseum.se

The Upper Staircase
*At the back is Carl Larsson's
monumental mural* The Entry of
King Gustav Vasa of Sweden in
Stockholm 1523. *On the opposite
wall is his* Midwinter Sacrifice.

**Lamino Armchair
(1955)**
*Yngve Ekström's
beech and
laminated leather
armchair, produced
by Swedese Möbler,
features in the
Design in Sweden
(1900 to Present)
exhibition.*

GALLERY GUIDE
*Level 2 is devoted to painting
and sculpture. The accent is
on Swedish 18th- to early
20th-century art, but the 17th-
century Dutch and Flemish,
and 18th-century French
schools are also represented.
Exhibits may change. Level 1
shows mainly Swedish applied
art and design, particularly
furniture, porcelain, silver
and glass from the 15th
century up to modern Swedish
design. To the left of the
main entrance is the Gravure
Gallery with temporary
exhibitions of graphics etc.*

Level 1

Auditorium

Entrance
level

KEY

☐	Painting and sculpture
☐	Applied art and design
☐	Temporary exhibitions
☐	Non-exhibition space
☐	No admission

Raoul Wallenbergs Torg ⑫

Map 2 E4. 🚇 Östermalmstorg.
🚌 2, 47, 55, 62, 69, 71, 76.

This square is dedicated to
Raoul Wallenberg (1912–
unknown), who during World
War II worked as a diplomat
at the Swedish Embassy in
Budapest. By using Swedish
"protective passports" and
safe houses throughout the
city he helped a large number
of Hungarian Jews to escape
deportation to the Nazi
concentration camps.

In 1945, when Budapest
was liberated, Wallenberg was
imprisoned by the Soviet
Union and according to
Russian sources he died in
Moscow's Lubianka prison in
1947. His fate has never been
satisfactorily explained
despite strenuous efforts by
the Swedes to seek the truth.

The small square adjoins
Berzelii Park and Nybroplan
and faces the Nybrokajen
waterfront. The definitive
design of the square has been
hotly debated because it is
set in an architecturally sensitive area, but great efforts
have been made to ensure
that it remains a worthy
memorial to Raoul Wallenberg.

Nybrokajen 11 ⑬

Nybrokajen 11. **Map** 3 C1. **Tel** 08-
407 16 00. 🚇 Kungsträdgården,
Östermalmstorg. 🚌 47, 62, 69, 76.
🚢 Djurgårdsfärja. ⏰ for concerts
(phone for details). ♿
www.nybrokajen11.rikskonserter.se

Constructed in the 1870s,
this building facing the
waters of Nybroviken once
housed the Musical Academy.
Its concert hall, opened in
1878, was the first in the
country, and was used to
present the inaugural Nobel
Prize in 1901. Designed in
Neo-Renaissance style with
cast-iron pillars, the hall has a
royal box and galleries, and
can seat up to 600 people.

It is run by the state musical
organization, Rikskonserter,
and is a popular venue for
chamber and choral concerts,
jazz and folk music.

MALMARNA & FURTHER AFIELD

As Stockholm grew, the heart of the city, Gamla Stan, became cramped and building spread out to the surrounding areas, known as "Malmarna" (the "ore hills"). Parts of these now make up present-day Stockholm.

Old tram at Djurgården

Södermalm came into the ownership of the city in 1436. Much of Stockholm's old charm can still be found in the areas around Fjällgatan, Mosebacke and Maria-berget. To the north, the Norrmalm area expanded rapidly and became known as Stockholm's northern sub-urb in the 17th century. The once-rural Östermalm was transformed in the late 19th century into an affluent residential area with grand, wide boulevards, con-trasting with the 1930s Functionalist style of the adjoining Gärdet district.

To the west is Kungsholmen, the centre for local govern-ment, with distinguished build-ings such as Stadshuset (the City Hall) and Rådhuset (the Law Court). Nationalstadsparken (the National City Park), a green area of ecological and cultural interest sur-rounding the city and reaching into its central districts, offers lovely walking routes and many of the city's foremost museums.

SIGHTS AT A GLANCE

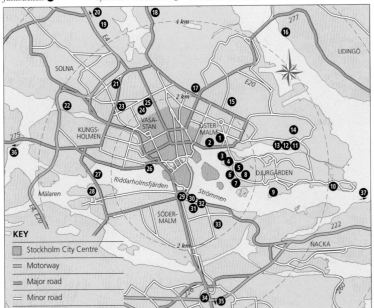

Historiska Museet ❶

The Museum of National Antiquities, Historiska Museet, was opened in 1943. It was designed by Bengt Romare and Georg Sherman. Bror Marklund (1907–77) was responsible for the decoration around the entrance and the richly detailed bronze gateways depicting events in early Swedish history. The museum originally made its name with its exhibits from the Viking era, as well as its outstanding collections from the early Middle Ages. Contemporary church textiles are also on show. Many of Historiska Museet's gold treasures have been gathered together to form one of Stockholm's most remarkable sights, Guldrummet (the Gold Room).

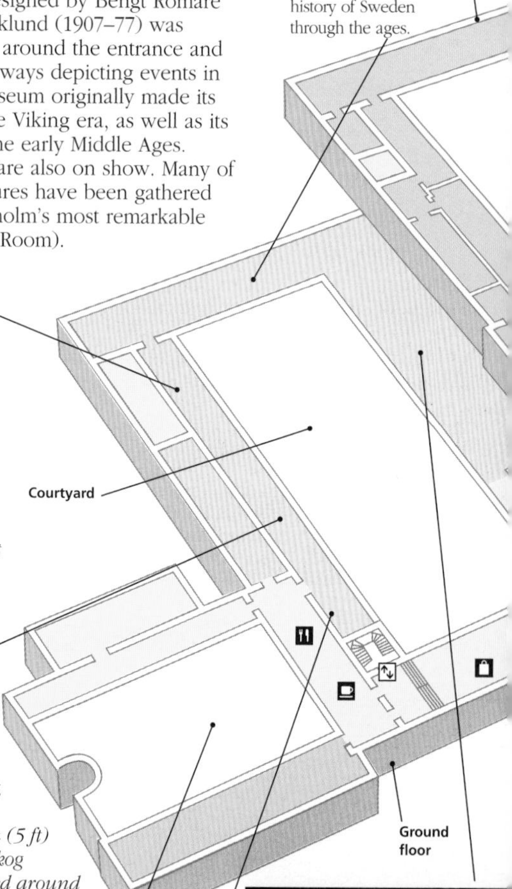

Upper floor
Exhibitions documenting the history of Sweden through the ages.
Courtyard
Ground floor
Rosen-gården

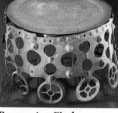

Bronze Age Find
This Bronze Age artifact, thought to be a percussion instrument, was discovered in a bog in southern Sweden in 1847.

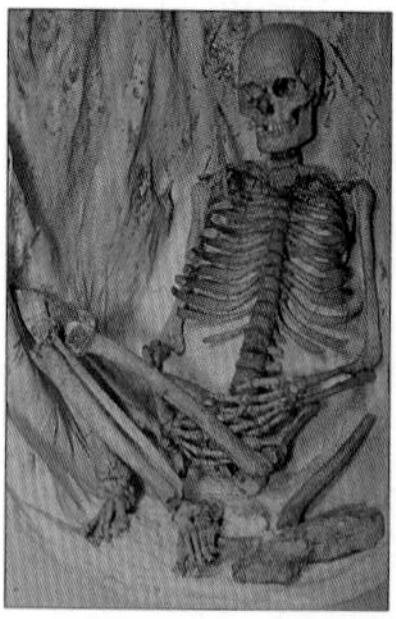

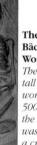

The Bäckaskog Woman
The 155 cm (5 ft) tall Bäckaskog woman lived around 5000 BC. She died at the age of 40–50 and was buried sitting in a cramped pit.

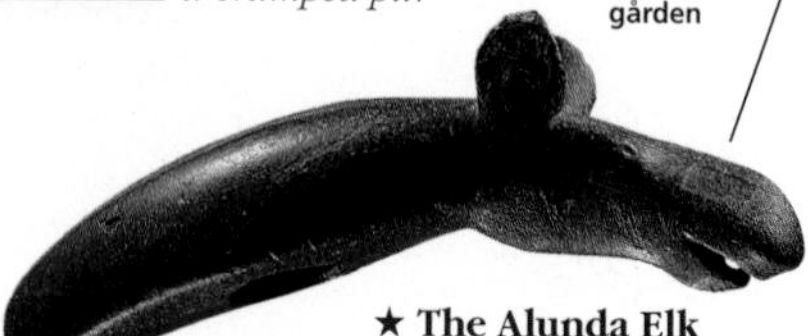

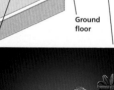

★ The Alunda Elk
This 21 cm (8 inch) stone axe, discovered in 1920 at Alunda in central Sweden, resembles an elk's head. It is a ceremonial axe, probably made in Finland or Karelia in around 2000 BC.

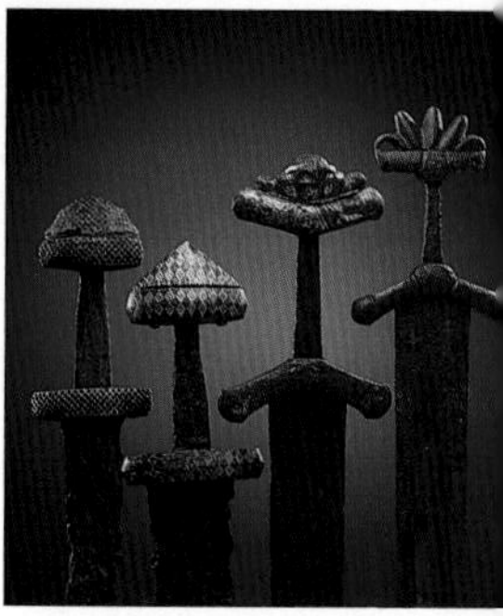

The Viking Era
This is the world's largest Viking exhibition, with more than 4,000 artifacts. The Vikings were most famous as warriors, but they were also keen traders.

STAR EXHIBITS

- ★ The Alunda Elk
- ★ Maria from Viklau
- ★ The Gold Room

For hotels and restaurants in this region see pp280–283 and pp298–300

The Skog Tapestry
This once hung in the wooden church at Skog in northern Sweden. It is one of the museum's oldest textile treasures.

Baroque Hall

Stairs descending to the Gold Room

Main entrance

★ **Maria from Viklau**
This Madonna figure without child is the best-preserved example from Sweden's early medieval period. The colourful wooden sculpture is richly gilded.

VISITORS' CHECKLIST

Narvavägen 13–17. **Map** 2 F4.
Tel 08-519 556 00. 📧 44, 56.
🚇 Karlaplan. ⏰ Oct–Apr:
11am–5pm Tue–Sun, also 5–8pm
Thu; May–Sep: 10am–5pm daily.
🔴 24, 25 & 31 Dec and some
holidays. 🎫 🖼 ♿ 🚫 📷 📖
www.historiska.se

GALLERY GUIDE

The exhibitions are divided chronologically on two floors with the prehistoric section on the ground floor and the Middle Ages on the upper floor, where there is also a Baroque Hall. In the basement, reached by a staircase from the entrance hall, is the Gold Room with stunning gold and silver objects.

KEY

🟦	Prehistoric Era
🟦	Middle Ages and Baroque
🟦	Temporary exhibitions
⬜	Non-exhibition space

★ THE GOLD ROOM

Since the early 1990s the museum's many priceless gold artifacts have been on show in Guldrummet (the Gold Room), a 700 sq m (7,500 sq ft) underground vault built with 250 tons of reinforced concrete to ensure security. The room is in two circular sections. The inner section houses the main collection, with 50 kg (110 lb) of gold treasures and 250 kg (550 lb) of silver from the Bronze Age to the Middle Ages.

The Elisabeth Reliquary was originally a drinking goblet which was mounted with gold and precious stones in the 11th century. In about 1230 a silver cover was added to enclose the skull of St Elisabeth. Sweden seized it in Wurzburg in 1631, as a trophy in the Thirty Years War.

The Gold Collars were found between 1827 and 1864; the three-ringed collar in a stone quarry in eastern Sweden, the five-ringed in a ditch on the island of Öland, and the seven-ringed hanging on a spike in a barn.

The underground Gold Room in Historiska Museet

Strandvägen with its stately houses and boats along the quayside

Strandvägen ❷

Map 4 E1. 🚌 47, 69, 76.
🚇 Östermalmstorg, Karlaplan. 🚋 7.

In the early 1900s Stockholm's 10 richest citizens – seven of whom were wholesale merchants – lived in palatial new houses along Strandvägen. Before 1897, when a major exhibition was held just across the water on Djurgården, this muddy, hilly stretch known as Ladugårdslands Strandgata aspired to becoming "a street, the like of which will not be found anywhere else in Europe". It was a long process. Even after all the grand buildings had been completed, the wooden quay erected in the 1860s was something of an eyesore. It was still used up to the 1940s by boats bringing firewood from the archipelago islands.

Nevertheless, the renamed Strandvägen, with its three rows of lime trees, soon became the elegant boulevard envisaged and, then as now, it was a popular place for a stroll, to admire the elegant façades, watch the boats and to see and be seen.

The financiers behind this and other housing projects in the early 1900s were wealthy and could call on the best architects, including I G Clason (1856–1930). Clason was influenced by Italian and French Renaissance styles for his work on No. 19–21 (Thaveniuska Huset) and No. 29–35 (Bünszowska Huset), where he designed gateways made of ships' timbers. No. 55 (Von Rosenska Palatset) is also by Clason.

Junibacken ❸

Galärvarvsvägen. **Map** 4 F1. **Tel** 08-587 230 00. 🚌 44, 47, 69. 🚋 7. 🚢 Djurgårdsfärja. 🕙 Sep–May: 10am–5pm Tue–Sun; Jun & Aug: 10am–5pm daily; Jul: 9am–6pm daily. 🎦 ♿ 🍴 📷 🛍 www.junibacken.se

They are all here – Pippi Longstocking, Mardie, Karlsson on the Roof, Emil, Nils Karlsson Pyssling, Ronja the robber's daughter, the Lionheart Brothers and many more favourite characters

A colourful scene from one of Astrid Lindgren's stories

from Astrid Lindgren's children's books. In accordance with the popular novelist's wishes, visitors can also meet the creations of other Swedish children's authors. When she heard about Staffan Götesam's project for a children's cultural centre she was adamant it should not be just an Astrid Lindgren museum.

Nevertheless Junibacken is still something of a tribute to the much-loved author. It was officially opened by the Royal Family in the summer of 1996 and has become one of the city's most popular tourist attractions. A mini-train takes visitors from a mock-up of the station at Vimmerby (the author's home town) to meet some of her characters, finishing with a visit to Pippi's home in Villekulla Cottage, where children can play in the different rooms.

There is also a well-stocked children's bookshop and a restaurant.

WOODEN BOATS ALONG STRANDVAGEN

Until the 1940s sailing vessels used to carry firewood from Roslagen on the Baltic coast to the quayside at Strandvägen. This trade had lost its importance by the 1950s and boating enthusiasts started buying up these old vessels. Some were renovated and sailed to the Caribbean, others became illegal drinking or gambling clubs on Strandvägen. New harbour regulations led to the formation of two associations to administer the boats. The wooden boats moored along Strandvägen today are owned by people who want to preserve a piece of the area's cultural heritage.

Old wooden boats along the Strandvägen quay

For hotels and restaurants in this region see pp280–283 and pp298–300

Gröna Lund funfair seen from
Kastellholmen

ASTRID LINDGREN AND PIPPI LONGSTOCKING

Astrid Lindgren has written around 100 children's books which have been translated into 74 languages, making her

one of the world's most-read children's authors. Publishers turned down her first book about Pippi Longstocking, but she went on to win a children's book competition two years later, in 1945. Her headstrong and tough character Pippi soon won the hearts of children worldwide.

Born on 14 November 1907 in Vimmerby in southern Sweden, Astrid stopped writing books at 85, but her characters live on at Junibacken.

**Astrid Lindgren
(1907–2002)**

Nordiska Museet ➍

See pp88–9.

Biologiska Museet ➎

Lejonslätten. *Tel* 08-442 82 15. 🚌 44, 47. 🚋 7. ◯ Apr–Sep: 11am–4pm daily; Oct–Mar: noon–3pm Tue–Fri, 10am–3pm Sat–Sun. 🎟 by appt. 📷
🌐 www.skansen.se

The National Romantic influences of the late 19th century inspired the architect Agi Lindegren when he was commissioned to design Biologiska Museet (Museum of Biology) in the 1890s. He based his plans on the simple lines of the medieval Norwegian stave churches.

The man behind the museum was the zoologist, hunter and conservationist Gustaf Kolthoff (1845–1913). In 1892, he persuaded the industrialist C F Liljevalch – who later financed the nearby art gallery – to form a company with the aim "to develop and maintain a biological museum to include all the Scandinavian mammals and birds as stuffed specimens in natural surroundings". Within a few months of opening in autumn 1893, Gustaf Kolthoff had delivered a couple of thousand stuffed animals, as well as birds' nests, young and eggs, to the museum. Many of the creatures are

shown against a diorama background, with about 250 species of Scandinavian birds and land mammals in their respective biotypes. Kolthoff's friend, the artist Bruno Liljefors, was responsible for the paintings.

Since 1970 the Museum of Biology has belonged to the Skansen Foundation. During the 1990s it underwent extensive renovation and was reopened on 13 November 1993 – exactly 100 years after its original inauguration.

Vasamuseet ➏

See pp90–91.

Gröna Lund ➐

Lilla Allmänna Gränd 9. *Tel* 08-587 501 00. 🚌 44, 47. 🚋 7. 🚢 Djurgårdsfärja. ◯ late Apr–mid-Sep: opening hours vary. 📷 ♿ 🍴
📺 🌐 www.gronalund.com

A tavern called Gröna Lund (Green Grove) existed on this site in the 18th century, and it was one of the haunts

Biologiska Museet's wooden façade, inspired by Nordic medieval design

of the renowned troubadour Carl Michael Bellman *(see p93).*

Jakob Schultheis used the tavern's name for the modest-sized funfair which he opened here in 1883 with a two-level horse-drawn roundabout as the main attraction. Today Gröna Lund is Sweden's oldest amusement park.

The 130-day season, starting around the end of April, is short but hectic. Gröna Lund draws up to 18,000 visitors a day to its attractions, which include a thrilling roller-coaster and haunted house. Popular attraction "Insane", is a vertical roller-coaster that can reach speeds of 60 km per hour (47 miles per hour), and it is considered to be one of the highest and longest of its kind in the world.

The park also has restaurants and cafés, two stages, a cabaret restaurant, a theatre and beautiful gardens.

Nearby is Liljevalchs Konsthall, a gallery featuring collections of Swedish, Nordic and international art. It also holds temporary exhibitions, including the annual Spring Salon.

Nordiska Museet ❹

Resembling an extravagant Renaissance castle, Nordiska Museet portrays everyday life in Sweden from the 1520s to the present day. It was created by Artur Hazelius (1833–1901), who was also the founder of Skansen *(see p92)*. In 1872, he started to collect objects which would remind future generations of the old Nordic farming culture.

The present museum, designed by Isak Gustav Clason, was opened in 1907. Today it has more than 1.5 million exhibits, with everything from luxury clothing and priceless jewellery to everyday items, furniture and children's toys, and replicas of period homes.

Doll's Houses
The doll's houses show typical homes from the 17th century to modern times. This example illustrates one from 1860.

Level 3

Corridor to staircase

Level 2 (Main Hall)

Ground floor

State Bedchamber from Ulvsunda Castle
At the end of the 17th century, the lord of the manor at Ulvsunda accommodated prominent guests in this prestigious bedchamber.

STAR FEATURES

★ Table Settings

★ Strindberg Collection

★ Main Hall

GALLERY GUIDE

The museum is arranged over four floors. From the entrance, stairs lead up to the temporary exhibitions in the Main Hall on Level 2. Floor 3 houses the Strindberg Collection, Doll's Houses, Table Settings, Traditions and the Fashion and Textile Galleries. On the fourth floor are sections dealing with Folk Art, Interiors, Swedish Homes, Small Objects and a section covering the Sami People and Culture.

Obelisk with the inscription: "The day may dawn when not even all our gold is enough to form a picture of a bygone era."

Equestrian statue of Karl X Gustav

Main entrance

★ **Table Settings**
In the mid-17th century table settings were a feast for the eyes. A swan is the centrepiece at this meal.

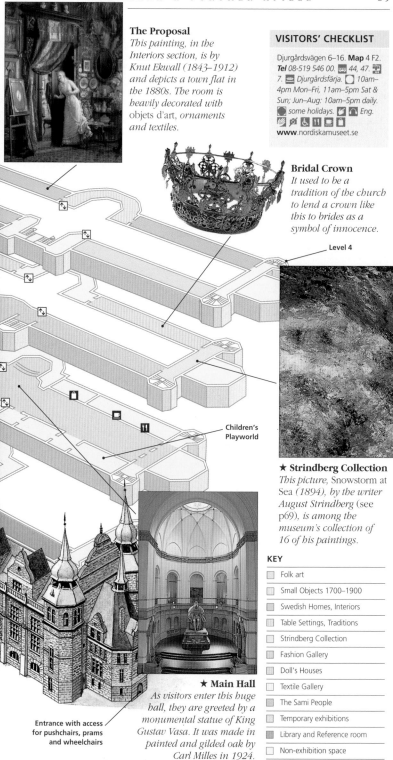

The Proposal
This painting, in the Interiors section, is by Knut Ekwall (1843–1912) and depicts a town flat in the 1880s. The room is heavily decorated with objets d'art, *ornaments and textiles.*

VISITORS' CHECKLIST

Djurgårdsvägen 6–16. **Map** 4 F2.
Tel 08-519 546 00. 📧 44, 47. 🚋
7. 🚢 Djurgårdsfärja. ◐ 10am–
4pm Mon–Fri, 11am–5pm Sat &
Sun; Jun–Aug: 10am–5pm daily.
◐ some holidays. 🎟 🎧 Eng.
📷 🚫 👶 🍴 🛍 ♿
www.nordiskamuseet.se

Bridal Crown
It used to be a tradition of the church to lend a crown like this to brides as a symbol of innocence.

Level 4

Children's Playworld

★ Strindberg Collection
This picture, Snowstorm at Sea (1894), by the writer August Strindberg (see p69), is among the museum's collection of 16 of his paintings.

KEY

☐	Folk art
☐	Small Objects 1700–1900
☐	Swedish Homes, Interiors
☐	Table Settings, Traditions
☐	Strindberg Collection
☐	Fashion Gallery
☐	Doll's Houses
☐	Textile Gallery
☐	The Sami People
☐	Temporary exhibitions
☐	Library and Reference room
☐	Non-exhibition space

★ Main Hall
As visitors enter this huge hall, they are greeted by a monumental statue of King Gustav Vasa. It was made in painted and gilded oak by Carl Milles in 1924.

Entrance with access for pushchairs, prams and wheelchairs

Vasamuseet ❻

After a maiden voyage of just 1,300 m (1,422 yd) in calm weather, the warship *Vasa* capsized in Stockholm's harbour on 10 August 1628. About 50 people went down with what was supposed to be the pride of the navy, only 100 m (109 yd) off the southern tip of Djurgården. Guns were all that were salvaged from the vessel in the 17th century and it was not until 1956 that a private researcher's persistent search led to the rediscovery of *Vasa*. A complex operation began to salvage the wreck, followed by a 17-year conservation programme. The city's most popular museum opened in 1990, less than a nautical mile from the scene of the disaster.

Gun-port Lion
More than 200 carved ornaments and 500 sculpted figures decorate Vasa.

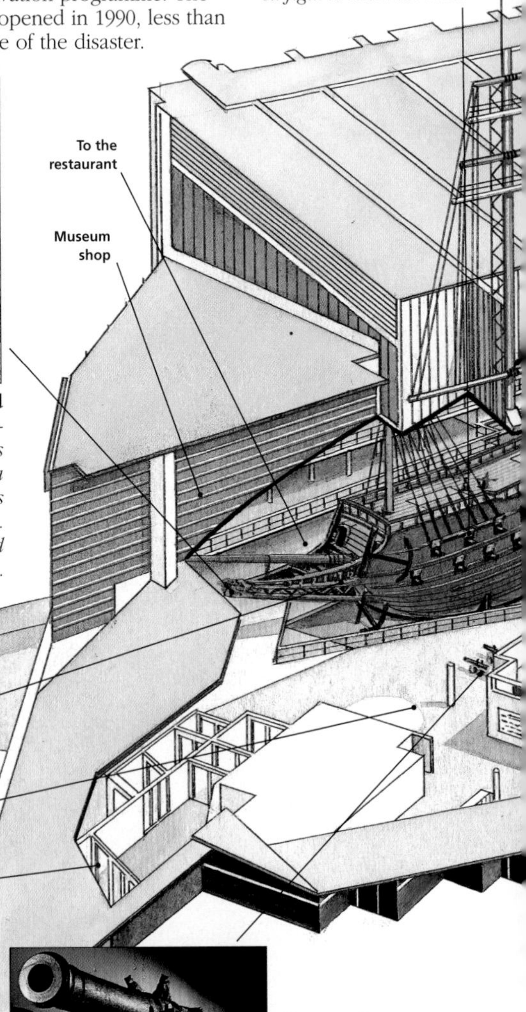

★ Lion Figurehead
King Gustav II Adolf, who commissioned Vasa, *was known as the Lion of the North. So a springing lion was the obvious choice for the figurehead. It is 4 m (13 ft) long and weighs 450 kg (990 lb).*

To the restaurant

Museum shop

Information desk

Entrance

Emperor Titus
Carvings of 20 Roman emperors stand on parade on Vasa.

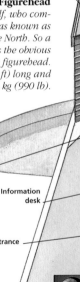

Bronze Cannon
More than 50 of Vasa's *64 original cannons were salvaged in the 17th century. Three bronze cannons are on display in the museum.*

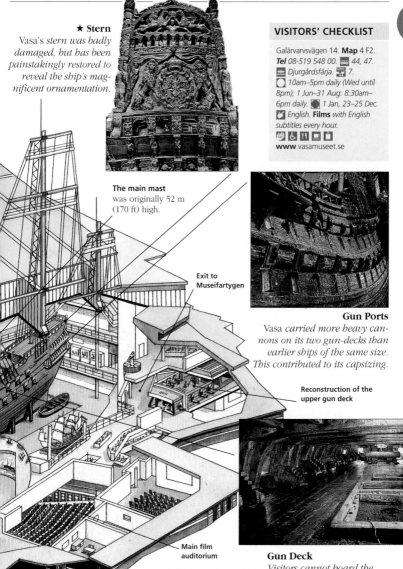

★ Stern
Vasa's *stern was badly damaged, but has been painstakingly restored to reveal the ship's magnificent ornamentation.*

VISITORS' CHECKLIST

Galärvarvsvägen 14. **Map** 4 F2.
Tel 08-519 548 00. 44, 47.
Djurgårdsfärja. 7.
10am–5pm daily (Wed until 8pm); 1 Jun–31 Aug: 8:30am–6pm daily. 1 Jan, 23–25 Dec.
English. **Films** with English subtitles every hour.
www.vasamuseet.se

The main mast
was originally 52 m (170 ft) high.

Exit to Museifartygen

Gun Ports
Vasa *carried more heavy cannons on its two gun-decks than earlier ships of the same size. This contributed to its capsizing.*

Reconstruction of the upper gun deck

Main film auditorium

Gun Deck
Visitors cannot board the ship, but there is a full-size replica of a part of the upper gun deck with carved wooden dummies of sailors, which gives a good idea of conditions on board.

THE SALVAGE OPERATION

The marine archaeologist Anders Franzén had been looking for *Vasa* for many years. On 25 August 1956 his patience was rewarded when he brought up a piece of blackened oak on his plumb line. From the autumn of 1957, it took divers two years to clear space beneath the hull for the lifting cables. The first lift using six cables was a success, after which *Vasa* was raised in 16 stages into shallow water. Plugs were inserted into holes left by rusted iron bolts, then the final lift began and on 4 May 1961 *Vasa* was towed into dry dock.

Vasa in dry dock after being salvaged in 1961

STAR FEATURES

★ Lion Figurehead

★ Stern

Hornborgastugan, a 19th-century timber cottage at Skansen

Skansen ⓪

Djurgårdsslätten 49. **Tel** 08-442 80 00.
🚌 44, 47. 🚋 7. 🚤 Djurgårdsfärja.
⏰ daily. Mar–Apr & Oct: 10am–4pm;
May–Jun & Sep: 10am–8pm; Jul–Aug:
10am–10pm; Nov–Dec: 10am–3pm.
📷 Jun–Aug. ⬤ 24 Dec. 🎫 ♿ 🖥
🍴 🎁 **Seglora Kyrka** 🔔 call for
details. **www**.skansen.se

The world's first open-air
museum, Skansen was
established in 1891 to
show an increasingly
industrialized society
how people once
lived. It comprises
around 150 houses
and farm buildings
from all over Swe-
den. But it is not
just a museum, Skansen
also plays an important
role in nurturing the country's
folklore and traditions.
Sweden's National Day,
Walpurgis Night, Midsummer,
Christmas and New Year's Eve
celebrations take place here
(see pp26–9).

In the Town Quarter,
complete with 19th-century
wooden town houses, glassblowers, bookbinders and
other craftspeople demon-
strate their skills. The 300-year-
old Älvros farmhouse, from
the Härjedalen region,
represents rural life with an
intriguing collection of everyday tools. At the other end of
the scale, Skogaholms
Herrgård (see p20), a Carolian
manor from 1680, shows how
the wealthy lived. The shingle-
roofed Seglora Church (1729)
is popular for weddings.

Nordic animals such as elk,
wolves and bears, can seen in
the zoo, and exotic snakes
in the aquarium.

**Brown bear
at Skansen**

Waldemarsudde ⓪

Prins Eugens Väg 6.
Tel 08-545 837 00. 🚌 47. 🚋 7.
⏰ 11am–5pm Tue–Sun, 11am–8pm
Thu. 📷 🎫 ♿ 🍴 🖥 🎁
www.waldemarsudde.com

Prince Eugen's Waldemar-
sudde, which passed
into State ownership after
his death in 1947, is one
of Sweden's most visited
art galleries. The prince was
trained as a military
officer, but became
a successful artist
and was one of the
leading landscape
painters of his
generation. He
produced monu-
mental paintings for
several of the city's
important buildings, including
Kungliga Operan and
Stadshuset. Among his own
works hanging in Waldemarsudde, his former palace, are
three of his most prized
paintings: *Spring* (1891), *The
Old Castle* (1893) and *The
Cloud* (1896).

Together with works by his
contemporaries, the gallery
holds an impressive collection
of early 20th-century Swedish
art. Oscar Björck, Carl Fredrik
Hill, Richard Bergh, Nils
Kreuger, Eugène Jansson,
Bruno Liljefors and Anders
Zorn are all featured.

Prince Eugen was a
generous patron to the next
generation – the group known
as "The Young Ones" – so
works by younger artists,
including Isaac Grünewald,
Einar Jolin, Sigrid Hjertén and
Leander Engström are also in
the collection. Sculptors of the
same era are well represented,
particularly Per Hasselberg,
whose works can be seen in
both the gallery and the park.

Prince Eugen and his
architect, Ferdinand Boberg,
drew up the sketches for the
palace, completed in 1905.
The same architect was called
in later to design the gallery,
which was finished in 1913.
This now includes parts of the
collection of some 2,000
works, as well as the Prince's
own paintings.

The guest apartments remain
largely unchanged, and the

Prince Eugen's Waldemarsudde, seen from the water

Hornsgatan (1902) by Eugène Jansson, in Thielska Galleriet

two upper floors with the Prince's studio at the top are used for temporary exhibitions. The buildings are surrounded by beautiful gardens.

Thielska Galleriet ❿

Sjötullsbacken 6–8. *Tel 08-662 58 84.* 🚌 69. ⏰ noon–4pm daily. 🎫 *by appointment.* 📷 📹
www.thielska-galleriet.se

When the magnificent apartments of the banker Ernest Thiel (1860–1947) on Strandvägen started to over-flow with his comprehensive collection of Nordic art from the late 19th and early 20th centuries, he commissioned the architect Ferdinand Boberg to design a dignified villa on Djurgården.

However, during World War I Thiel lost most of his fortune. His collection was bought by the State, which opened Thielska Galleriet in his villa in 1926.

Thiel was regarded as something of a rebel in the banking world. He was particularly fond of works by painters belonging to the Artists' Union, which had been formed in 1886 to counter the influence of the traditionalist Konstakademien (Royal Academy of the Arts).

There are paintings by all the major Swedish artists who formed an artists' colony at Grèz-sur-Loing, south of Paris, including Carl Larsson, Bruno

Liljefors, Karl Nordström and August Strindberg.

In additon, the gallery features works by Eugène Jansson, Anders Zorn and Prince Eugen, as well as wooden figures by Axel Petersson and sculptures by Christian Eriksson. Thiel also acquired pieces by foreign artists, not least his good friend Edvard Munch.

Etnografiska Museet ⓫

Djurgårdsbrunnsvägen 34.
Tel 08-519 550 00. 🚌 69. ⏰ 10am–5pm Mon–Fri (11am Sat–Sun). 🎫
♿ 🍴 📷 📹 **www**.etnografiska.se

The National Museum of Ethnography is a show-case for the collections brought home to Sweden by enterprising travellers and

scientists from the 18th century to the present day. All are arranged in imaginative displays designed to provide a better understanding of the unknown or unfamiliar from around the world.

Another aspect of the museum's work is to reflect the multicultural influences on Sweden brought about by the large-scale immigration into the country during the late 20th century.

The explorer Sven Hedin (1865–1952), who was the last Swede to be ennobled (in 1902), contributed many exhibits to the museum, including Buddha figures and Chinese costumes, as well as Mongolian temple tents donated by leaders of the Kalmuck people in western China to King Gustav V.

Another section of interest shows masks and totem poles from western Canada.

A Japanese tea house was opened in 1990, which is a work of art in itself. Here, visitors to the museum can take part in traditional tea ceremonies during the summer.

Religious mask from British Columbia

The museum runs an extensive educational programme with lectures, courses and workshops. In addition to the permanent exhibitions, the museum also displays themed temporary exhibits.

The MatMekka restaurant offers a menu of Swedish and international dishes made with organic and locally produced ingredients.

AN IMMORTAL TROUBADOUR

Carl Michael Bellman (1740–95) was a much-loved trouba-dour. Gustav III gave him a job as secretary of a lottery, but he was best known around Stockholm's many taverns – particu-larly on Djurgården. His works about the drunken watchmaker Jean Fredman and his contemporaries (*Fredman's Epistles* and *Fredman's Songs*) have never lost their popu-larity and form part of Sweden's musical heritage. A bust of Bellman was unveiled on Djurgården in 1829 in the presence of Queen Desideria.

Bust of Bellman by J N Byström (1829)

Kaknästornet with the buildings of Sjöhistoriska Museet, Tekniska Museet and Folkens Museum Etnografiska in the foreground

Tekniska Museet ⑫

Museivägen 7. **Tel** 08-450 56 00. ▦
69. ⬜ 10am–5pm Mon–Tue, Thu–Fri,
10am–8pm Wed, 11am–5pm Sat &
Sun. ⬤ 1 Jan, Midsummer, 24, 25 &
31 Dec. ⬛ by appointment. ▦ ⬛
⬛ ▮▮ ⬛ www.tekniskamuseet.se

The Museum of Science
and Technology contains a
wealth of exhibits connected
with Sweden's technical and
industrial history. It also
houses the science centre,
Teknorama, with hands-on
experiments designed for
children and young people.

The machinery hall features
the country's oldest preserved
steam engine. Built in 1832, it
was used in a coal mine in
southern Sweden. The classic
model T-Ford and early
Swedish cars from Volvo,
Scania and Saab are also on
display. Swinging from above
is Sweden's first commercial
aircraft, built in 1924. There is
another rarity – the scientist
Emanuel Swedenborg's model
of a "flying machine" (1716).

The museum also has
sections on electric power,
computing, technology in the
home, and the Swedish
forestry, mining, iron and
steel industries.

Tekniska Museet's machinery hall
with historic aircraft

Sjöhistoriska Museet ⑬

Djurgårdsbrunnsvägen 24.
Tel 08- 519 549 00. ▦ 69.
⬜ 10am–5pm daily. ⬛ ▦ ⬛ ⬛
⬛ www.sjohistoriska.se

The National Maritime
Museum focuses on
shipping, shipbuilding and
naval defence. It is housed
in an attractive building,
designed by the archi-
tect Ragnar Östberg in
1938, in a beautiful
location by the calm
waters of
Djurgårdsbrunnsviken.

There are some
100,000 exhibits,
including more
than 1,500 model
ships. The oldest
Swedish model is
a reproduction of
the "Cathedral ship"
from the early 1600s.
The model collection
comprises every conceivable
type of ship from small
coasters to oil tankers, coal
vessels, dinghies, full-riggers
and submarines. A series of
models on a scale of 1:200
shows the development of
ships in Scandinavia since
the Iron Age.

Life-size settings provide a
good idea of life on board the
various ships. Among them
are the exquisite original
cabin and elegant stern from
the royal schooner Amphion.
Designed by the leading
shipbuilder F H af Chapman
and built at the Djurgården
shipyard, Amphion was
Gustav III's flagship in the
1788–90 war with Russia.

Figurehead,
about 1850

The museum has some
notable examples of ship
decoration from the late 17th
century. They include part of
the national coat of arms
recovered by divers in the
1920s from the stern of the
Riksäpplet, which sank at
Dalarö in 1676. A large relief
portrayal of Karl XI on
horseback from the stern of
Carolus XI – an 82-cannon
ship launched from the
shipyard in 1678 – is also on
show. It is thought that the
relief was removed some
years later when the ship was
renamed Sverige. There are
many fine figureheads in the
collection, including one
depicting Amphion, the son
of Zeus, playing his lyre,
which adorned the schooner
of the same name.

The museum often hosts
temporary exhibitions
focusing on themes such
as piracy, shipping and
treasure recovered
from shipwrecks.

Linked to the
museum is the
Swedish Marine
Archaeology
Archive, containing
an extensive collec-
tion of maritime
documents and
photographs. There
is a special children's
section with a work-
shop which is open on
Saturdays and in
school holidays. On
the gable facing
Djurgårdsbrunnsviken is
The Sailor, a monument
to the victims of naval
warfare by Nils Sjögren.

Kaknästornet ⑭

Ladugårdsgärdet. **Tel** 08-667 21 05.
▦ 69. ⬜ 10am–9pm Mon–Sat;
10am–6pm Sun. ⬛ by appointment.
▦ ⬛ ▮▮ ⬛ ⬛
www.kaknastornet.se

Anchored by 72 steel poles,
driven 8 m (26 ft) into
the rock, the 34-storey
Kaknästornet soars to a
height of 155 m (508 ft). The
tower, designed by the
architects Bengt Lindroos and
Hans Borgström, was opened
in 1967. It was erected as a

centre for the country's television and radio broadcasting and also contains technical equipment to conduct conferences by satellite between European cities. Five dishes to the left of the tower – the largest of which has a diameter of 13 m (43 ft) – relay signals to and from satellites. The main hall containing the transmitters and receivers has been blasted out of the rock below the dishes.

The observation points on levels 30 and 31 provide a spectacular view of the city, and the restaurant on the 28th floor has panoramic windows. It is reached by two lifts, travelling at 18 km/h (11 mph). There is a tourist information office at the entrance, selling souvenirs, maps and the Stockholm Card (see p327). Decorative features include a wall relief by Walter Bengtsson, which was inspired by the tower's daunting technology.

Functionalist style, Tessinparken

Tessinparken & Nedre Gärdet ⑮

Map 2 F2. Ⓣ Karlaplan, Gärdet. 🚌 1, 4, 62, 72.

Three generations of the Tessin family of architects have given their name to this park which opened at Lower Gärdet in 1931. Tessinparken runs from north to south and is attractively designed with lawns, play areas, paths and ponds. The adjoining houses, built between 1932 and 1937,

Millesgården, home of the sculptor Carl Milles in the early 20th century

have their own gardens and blend in such a way that they give the impression of being part of the park itself.

The earliest houses, nearest to Valhallavägen, still show signs of 1920s Classicism, although Gärdet's real hallmark is Functionalism. The lower white houses along Askrikegatan, marking the northern boundary of the park, are Functionalist in style and noticeably different from other buildings in Gärdet. Some 60 different architects were involved in designing the Gärdet development, including Sture Frölén.

A granite statue of a woman with a suitcase, *Housewife's Holiday*, stands in the part of Tessin Park adjoining Valhallavägen. It was made by Olof Thorwald Ohlsson in the 1970s. At the other end of the park is a colourful concrete statue, *The Egg*, by Egon Möller-Nielsen.

Millesgården ⑯

Herserudsvägen 32, Lidingö. Ⓣ Ropsten, then bus 201, 202, 204, 206, 208, 212, or train to Torsvik. **Tel** 08-446 75 90. 🕙 mid-May–Sep: 11am–5pm daily; Oct–mid-May: noon–5pm Tue–Sun. 🎟 by appointment. ♿ 🎁 🍴 💻 www.millesgarden.se

Carl Milles (1875–1955) was one of the 20th century's greatest Swedish sculptors and the best known internationally. From 1931 he lived for 20 years in the USA, where he became a prolific monumental sculptor with works such as the *Meeting of the Waters* fountain in St Louis and the *Resurrection* fountain in the National Memorial Park outside Washington DC. In Stockholm visitors can see 15 of his public works, including the *Orpheus* fountain in front of Konserthuset (see p69).

In 1906 Milles purchased land on the island of Lidingö on which he built a house, completed in 1908. He lived here with his wife until 1931, and also after his return from the USA. In 1936 he and his wife donated the property to the people of Sweden. Millesgården extends over a series of terraces filled with sculptures and includes Milles' studios with originals and replicas of his work. There is a magnificent garden – a work of art in itself – and a fine view over the water.

Tessinparken, surrounded by Functionalist-style housing dating from the late 1930s

Running track at Stadion, 1912

Stadion ⑰

Lidingövägen 1–3. **Map** 2 E2.
Tel 08-508 284 06. ⊤ Stadion.
🚌 4, 55, 72, 73. ⏲ 8am–4pm daily.
🎟 during events. ♿

A new main arena was built for the 1912 Olympic Games in Stockholm, the towers of which have become a familiar landmark on the capital's skyline. The architect of Stadion, Torben Grut (1871–1945), followed the National Romantic influences of the day. The complex is richly decorated. The clock tower has two figures by Carl Fagerberg, *Ask and Embla*, the counterparts of Adam and Eve in Nordic mythology. There are also busts of Victor Balck, the man behind the 1912 Olympics, and P H Ling, the father of Swedish gymnastics.

Four notable sculptures were added in the 1930s. The painter and gymnast Bruno Liljefors created *Play* at the main entrance, Carl Eldh made *The Runners*, and Carl Fagerberg provided *Relay Runners* and *The Shot-Putter*.

Stadion has continued to be an important venue for athletics events and can hold up to 35,000 spectators. The European Athletics Championships were held here in 1958, and an international athletics gala is staged every summer. In 1990 it hosted the World Equestrian Championships.

The arena is also used as a venue for concerts by internationally renowned bands.

Naturhistoriska Riksmuseet ⑱

5 km (3 miles) N of city centre along road 264. **Tel** 08-519 540 00.
⊤ Universitetet. 🚌 40, 540.
⏲ 10am–8pm Tue, 10am–7pm Wed–Fri, 11am–7pm Sat & Sun. 🎟 by appointment. ♿ 🅿 📷 🖥 🍴
🏠 **www**.nrm.se

Completed in 1916, the vast Naturhistoriska Riksmuseet (Swedish Museum of Natural History) was designed by Axel Anderberg and decorated by Carl Fagerberg. The museum is a venerable institution, founded in 1739 by Carl von Linné *(see p128)* as part of Vetenskapsakademien (the Academy of Science). It is one of the 10 largest museums of its kind in the world. Over the centuries, the number of exhibits has risen to 17 million.

Polar bear, Naturhistoriska Riksmuseet

During the 1990s it was modernized and there are both permanent and temporary exhibitions on a wide range of themes from dinosaurs and sea creatures to the "Marvels of the Human Body". The hugely popular Cosmonova opened at the same time. Both a plane-

tarium and an IMAX cinema, its screen is 25 times the size of a conventional one. The *Vega Monument* was erected in front of the museum in 1930 to mark the 50th anniversary of explorer Adolf Erik Nordenskiöld's return from the first voyage through the Northeast Passage in his ship *Vega*. Designed by Ivar Johnsson, it is an obelisk in granite topped with a copper ship.

Hagaparken ⑲

4 km (2.5 miles) N of city centre, along E4. 🚌 515. **Haga Parkmuseum Tel** 08-27 42 52. ⏲ Oct–May: 10am–3pm daily. **Gustav III's Paviljong Tel** 08-402 61 30. 🎟 every hour Jun–Sep: noon–3pm Tue–Sun. **Fjärils- & Fågelhuset Tel** 08-730 39 81. ⏲ Apr–Sep: 10am–5pm daily; Oct–Mar: 10am–4pm daily.
◑ Midsummer's Eve. 🅿 🍴 in Koppartälten and Fjärils- & Fågelhuset and Café Vasaslätten.

King Gustav Vasa decided to create a royal park in the popular Haga area in the mid-18th century. The king's vision was realized by the architect of the moment, Fredrik Magnus Piper. The result was an English-style park with some very unusual buildings, including the Chinese Pagoda and the Roman battle tent, Koppartälten. A royal palace inspired by Versailles in France was also planned, but construction came to a halt after the king's death and it remained unfinished.

Gustav III's Pavilion, a Gustavian masterpiece designed by Olof Tempelman, with an interior by Louis Masreliéz, is the park's greatest architectural attraction, while Fjärils- & Fågelhuset has colourful,

Hagaparken's Roman battle tent, designed by Louis Jean Desprez (1790)

exotic butterflies and birds flying freely around a tropical greenhouse.

Haga Slott, built in 1802–04 for Gustav IV Adolf, was the childhood home of the present monarch, Carl XVI Gustaf, and his sisters. Now it is used for government receptions and to accommodate visiting heads of state.

Hagaparken is very popular with Stockholmers, who come all year round. The park is part of Ekoparken, an oasis of nature and culture close to the city centre *(see box)*.

Exotic butterflies in the greenhouses at Hagaparken

Ulriksdal ⑳

7 km (4 miles) N of Stockholm.
Tel 08-402 61 30. 🚌 503.
Palace ⬜ *Jun–mid-Sep: Tue–Sun for guided tours only.* 🕐 *noon, 1pm, 2pm & 3pm.* **Orangery** ⬜ *Jun–Aug: noon–4pm Tue–Sun.* 🅿 🖼 ♿ 🚻
🔼 🖥 www.kungahuset.se

Situated on a headland in the bay of Edsviken, Ulriksdal's attractive buildings and leafy surroundings are well worth a visit. At the entrance to the grounds is one of Stockholm's best-known restaurants, Ulriksdals Wärdshus *(see p300)*.

The original palace was built in the 1640s and designed by Hans Jakob Kristler in German/Dutch Renaissance style. The owner, Marshal of the Realm Jakob de la Gardie, named the palace Jakobsdal. It was bought in 1669 by the Dowager Queen Hedvig Eleonora. Fifteen years later, she donated the palace to her grandson Ulrik as a christening gift, and it was renamed Ulriksdal.

Around this time the architect Tessin the Elder suggested some rebuilding

Ulriksdal with its magnificent 18th-century Baroque exterior

work, but only a few of his proposals saw the light of day. In the 18th century the palace acquired its Baroque exterior.

After being a popular place for festivities in the time of Gustav III (1746–92), it began to lose its glamour. Interest was revived under Karl XV (1826–72), and furnishings and handicrafts many hundreds of years old are on show in his rooms.

The park was laid out in the mid-17th century. It has 300-year-old lime trees, as well as one of Europe's most northerly beechwoods. Carl Milles's two sculptures of wild boars stand by the pool in front of the palace. A stream

is crossed by a footbridge, which is supported by Per Lundgren's *Moors Dragging the Nets*.

More art can be seen in the Orangery, designed by Tessin the Elder in the 1660s for Queen Hedvig Eleonora. It now houses a sculpture museum.

The palace chapel, a popular place for weddings, was designed by F W Scholander and built in 1865 in Dutch Neo-Renaissance style. The riding school, built in 1671, was converted into a theatre by Carl Hårleman and C F Adelcrantz in the 1750s, and performances continue to be staged in the theatre every summer.

EKOPARKEN – THE ROYAL NATIONAL URBAN PARK

Ekoparken – the world's first National City Park – was established by the Swedish Parliament in 1995. Its creation has enabled the capital to safeguard the ecology of its "green lung", a 27 sq km (10.5 sq miles) area for recreation and outdoor activities.

The park threads through Stockholm's central districts, including Skeppsholmen and the southern part of Djurgården, and continues northwest to northern Djurgården, Hagaparken, Brunnsviken and Ulriksdal. It also encompasses the tiny islands of Fjäderholmarna *(see p110)*. Much of the park was a royal hunting ground as early as the 16th century, scattered with beautiful palaces and other sights.

Haga Forum, at the southern entrance to Hagaparken, provides plenty of information about Ekoparken.

There are also boat tours on Brunnsviken, with stops at some of the sights. For further details, telephone 08-587 140 40 or visit www.ekoparken.com.

Breeding herons at Isbladskärret, part of Ekoparken's rich bird-life

Karlbergs Slott, a palace dating from the 1630s – now one of Sweden's military academies

Vin- & Sprithisto-riska Museet ㉑

Dalagatan 100. **Map** 1 A1.
Tel 08-519 186 50. Ⓣ Odenplan.
🚌 65, 73. ⃝ 10am–7pm Tue,
10am–4pm Wed–Sun. ♿ 🎞 📷 📷
💻 📷 www.vinosprithistoriska.se

Swedish punsch and schnapps
are the themes of Vin- &
Sprithistoriska (Wine and
Spirits Historical Museum),
located in a former wine
warehouse. The building was
designed by
Cyrillus Johansson
and completed in
1923, but as the
trade of wine in
barrels decreased,
the warehouse
began to be
used for other
purposes until
1967, when the
first exhibition was staged.

Schnapps label, Vin- &
Sprithistoriska Museet

Today's museum dates from
1989. It shows how a wine
shop would have looked
around 1900. From the same
era is a typical southern
Swedish distillery in which
potatoes were used to make
schnapps. There is also a collection of spices added to
schnapps and liqueurs, and
50,000 labels are on show.
Visitors can also listen to
some 200 "schnapps songs".

In 2012, the museum
moves to Djurgården, close
to the Vasamuseet.

Karlbergs Slott ㉒

Karlbergs Slottsväg. Ⓣ St Eriksplan.
🚌 42, 72 to Karlberg station, then 15-
min walk. **Park** ⃝ 6am–10pm daily.

Admiral Karl Karlsson
Gyllenhielm started to build
Karlbergs Slott in the 1630s,
during the Thirty Years War.
From 1670 the palace was
extended and rebuilt by
Magnus Gabriel de la Gardie,
an important political and
military figure at the time,
with Jean de la Vallée as his
architect. When Karlberg became royal
property in 1688,
it was one of
Sweden's most
majestic palaces.
It was where the
"hero King" Karl
XII (1682–1718)
grew up, and it
was here that he
lay in state after his death at
the Battle of Fredrikshald (see
p35). In 1792 the architect C C
Gjörwell converted the
property into the Royal
War Academy, which later
became the Karlberg
Military School, and since
1999 it has been the site
for one of the country's
military academies.

The interior decorations
include Carl Carove's
magnificent stucco-work
which can be seen in the
grand hall. The palace
church has been renovated

several times, but the 17th-
century lanterns are original.
De la Gardie's wood-panelled
"rarities room" is now the
sacristy, but once it housed
his collection of valuables.

Judiska Museet ㉓

Hälsingegatan 2. **Map** 1 A2. **Tel** 08-
31 01 43. Ⓣ Odenplan. 🚌 2, 4,
47, 72. ⃝ noon–4pm Mon–Fri &
Sun. 📷 in English by appointment.
🎞 ♿ 💻 📷 www.judiska-
museet.a.se

In 1774 Aaron Isaac became
the first Jewish immigrant
to settle in Stockholm and
practise his religion. Today,
half of Sweden's Jewish
population of around 18,000
live in the Stockholm area.
Judiska Museet depicts the
history of the Swedish Jews
from Isaac's time to the
present. It focuses on Judaism
as a religion, its integration
into Swedish society and the

An eight-stemmed *chanuki*
(candlestick) at Judiska Museet

Holocaust. A comprehensive collection of pictures and other items provide an insight into Jewish life in Sweden with its traditions and customs. The beautiful *Torah* (the five books of Moses), the bridal canopy, and the collection of eight-stemmed *chanukis* (candlesticks) are just some of the museum's treasured spiritual artifacts.

The old observatory (1748–53) at the top of the Observatory hill

Observatorie-museet ㉔

Drottninggatan 120. **Map** 1 B2.
Tel 08-545 483 90. Ⓣ Odenplan.
🚌 40, 42, 65, 72. ⬜ Oct–Mar:
6–9pm Tue & Thu, noon–3pm Sun.
◐ Jul. ▣ 6pm Tue includes
telescope observation if sky is clear; in Eng by appointment. ▣ ▣ ⑪ ▣
www.observatoriet.kva.se

A number of institutions connected with science and education can be found on and around the hill of Brunkeberg. The oldest is the former observatory designed by Carl Hårleman for the Royal Scientific Academy and opened in 1753. In 1931, astronomical research was moved to Saltsjöbaden in the Stockholm archipelago and replaced by Observatoriemuseet (the Observatory Museum). Here visitors can see the observation room with its instruments, the two median rooms and the weather room. There is a great view of Stockholm from the hilltop and it is sometimes possible to view the stars.

The grove which surrounds the old observatory began to take shape in the 18th century. It is an idyllic enclosed area,

first opened to the public in the 20th century. On top of Brunkeberg is Sigrid Fridman's statue *The Centaur*.

A park stretches down to Sveavägen, where a pond is fed by a hillside stream. The statue *Dancing Youth* is by Ivar Johnsson. At the southern entrance of the park is Nils Möllerberg's sculpture *Youth*.

Stadsbiblioteket ㉕

Sveavägen 73. **Map** 1 B2.
Tel 08-508 311 00. Ⓣ Odenplan,
Rådmansgatan. 🚌 2, 4, 42, 53, 59,
72. ⬜ 9am–9pm Mon–Thu, 9am–
7pm Fri, noon–4pm Sat & Sun. ♿
www.biblioteket.stockholm.se

Gunnar Asplund's masterpiece, Stadsbiblioteket (City Library), is one of the capital's most architecturally important buildings. Asplund, the champion of the Functionalist

style prevalent in the 1930s, designed a public library which was dominated by Classical ideals. It was opened in 1928.

Internally, the furnishings and many of the light fittings were designed by Asplund himself. The work of Swedish artists is well represented: in the entrance hall are Ivar Johnsson's stucco reliefs with themes from Homer's *Iliad*; the sparkling mural painting in the children's section, *John Blund*, is by Nils Dardel; and the depiction of the stars in the heavens by Ulf Munthe. The door lintels, door handles and drinking fountains are by Nils Sjögren. Hilding Linnquist was responsible for the giant-sized tapestry, and also for four mural paintings using ancient fresco techniques.

The library lends more than a million books every year and also organizes author sessions and other events.

GUNNAR ASPLUND

Gunnar Asplund (1885–1940) was a dominant figure among Swedish and internationally renowned architects in the 1930s. His first major commission was the chapel at the Skogskyrkogården Cemetery, designed in National Romantic style. His last work was Heliga Korsets Kapell, the cemetery's crematorium (1935–40). Regarded as a masterpiece in the Functionalist style, it has earned a place on the UNESCO World Heritage list *(see p105)*. Asplund designed Stadsbiblioteket (City Library, 1920–28). He pioneered the Functionalist style as chief architect for the Stockholm Exhibition in 1930.

Stockholm Exhibition, by Gunnar Asplund, 1930

Stadsbiblioteket, in Neo-Classical style, designed by Gunnar Asplund

Stadshuset ㉖

Probably Sweden's biggest architectural project of the 20th century, the City Hall was completed in 1923 and has become a symbol of Stockholm. It was designed by Ragnar Östberg (1866–1945), the leading architect of the Swedish National Romantic style, and displays influences of both the Nordic Gothic and Northern Italian schools. Several leading Swedish artists contributed to the rich interior design. The building contains the Council Chamber and 250 offices for city admin-istrative staff. The annual Nobel Prize festivities take place in the Blue Hall.

Engel-brekt

★ The Golden Hall
The Byzantine-inspired wall mosa by Einar Forseth (1892–1988) ar made up of 18.6 million pieces of glass and gold. The northern wa theme is Queen of Lake Mälaren.

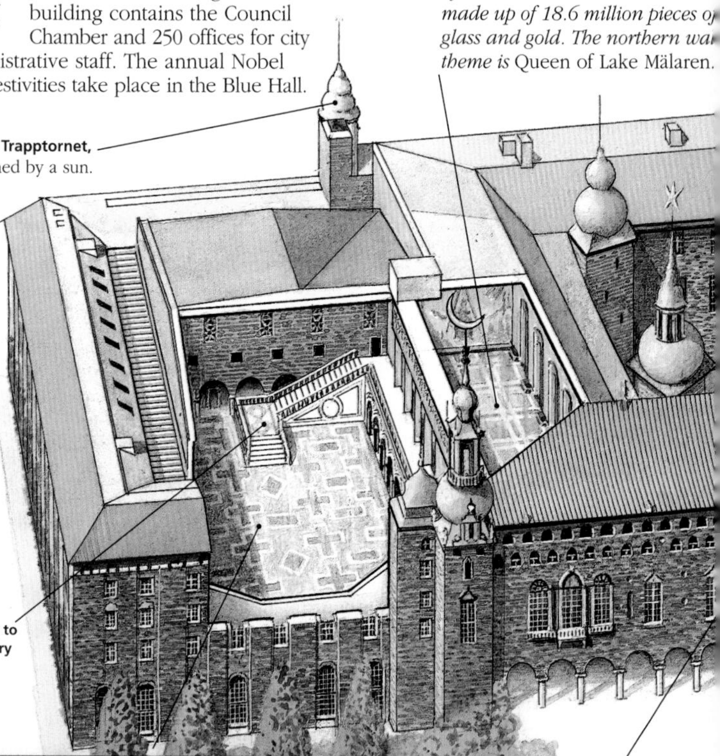

Norra Trapptornet, crowned by a sun.

Stairway to the gallery

★ The Blue Hall
The banqueting room is made from handmade bricks. The name is from the initial plan to paint the bricks blue, but the architect changed his mind.

★ The Prince's Gallery
A fresco, The City on the Water, in the Prince's Gallery, was painted by Prince Eugen (see p92), who donated it to the City Hall.

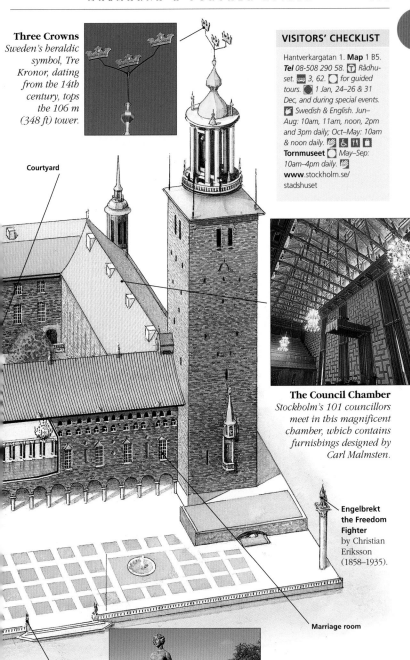

Three Crowns
Sweden's heraldic symbol, Tre Kronor, dating from the 14th century, tops the 106 m (348 ft) tower.

Courtyard

VISITORS' CHECKLIST

Hantverkargatan 1. **Map** 1 B5.
Tel 08-508 290 58. Rådhuset. 3, 62. for guided tours. 1 Jan, 24–26 & 31 Dec, and during special events. Swedish & English. Jun–Aug: 10am, 11am, noon, 2pm and 3pm daily; Oct–May: 10am & noon daily. **Tornmuseet** May–Sep: 10am–4pm daily. www.stockholm.se/stadshuset

The Council Chamber
Stockholm's 101 councillors meet in this magnificent chamber, which contains furnishings designed by Carl Malmsten.

Engelbrekt the Freedom Fighter by Christian Eriksson (1858–1935).

Marriage room

The Dance
The steps leading to Riddarfjärden are flanked by two statues by Carl Eldh. Dansen is the figure of a woman, Sången *(The Song) of a man.*

STAR FEATURES

★ The Golden Hall

★ The Blue Hall

★ The Prince's Gallery

Västerbron bridge, opened in 1935, linking Kungsholmen with Södermalm across Lake Mälaren

Västerbron ㉗

🚌 4, 40, 77.

As Stockholm expanded and car-use increased in the 1920s, it became necessary to build an additional bridge between the northern and southern shores of Lake Mälaren. German experts dominated the architectural competition launched in 1930, but their plans were implemented by Swedish architects and engineers and Västerbron bridge was completed in 1935.

The attractive design blends well with the landscape. The bridge is built in two spans of 168 m (551 ft) and 204 m (669 ft) with a vertical clearance of 26 m (85 ft). There are footpaths and cycle lanes on each side and a walk to the centre of Västerbron is rewarded with a magnificent view of central Stockholm.

Exercise yard in the former royal prison on Långholmen

Långholmen ㉘

🚇 Hornstull, then 10 min walk.
🚌 4, 40, 66. 🅗 🖵

Below the majestic Västerbron bridge is the island of Långholmen, which is linked to Södermalm by two bridges.

Långholmen is best known for the various prisons which have been located here since 1724. During the 20th century it was the site of the largest prison in Sweden, housing 620 inmates. The prison closed in 1975, since when the island has become a popular recreational area.

The prison buildings have been demolished, but the former royal jail dating from 1835 remains. The one-time cells now form both a hotel and a prison museum. There is also a youth hostel and an excellent restaurant, as well as a museum to the poet C M Bellman *(see p93)* with a café in the gardens which run down towards Riddarfjärden.

Långholmen's park has an open-air theatre, and offers excellent swimming both from the beaches and the rocks.

Stockholms Stadsmuseum ㉙

Ryssgården. **Map** 3 B5. *Tel* 08-508 316 00. 🚇 Slussen. 🚌 2, 3, 43, 53, 55, 76. ◯ 11am–5pm Tue–Sun (to 8pm Thu). 🎫 🚫 ♿ 🛍 🖵 🎧
www.stadsmuseum.stockholm.se

Hemmed in between the traffic roundabouts of Slussen and the steep hill up to Mosebacke Torg is Stockholms Stadsmuseum (City Museum). It is housed in a late-17th-century building originally designed by Tessin the Elder as Södra Stadshuset (Southern City Hall). After a fire, it was completed by Tessin the Younger in 1685. It has been used for various purposes over the centuries,

including law courts and dungeons, schools and city-hall cellars, theatres and churches, until in the 1930s it became the city museum.

The museum documents the history of Stockholm. The city's main stages of development are described in a slide-show and a series of four permanent exhibitions. The first starts with the Stockholm Bloodbath of 1520 *(see p58)* and continues through the 17th century. The eventful 18th century is illustrated with exhibits that include the Lohe Treasure – 20 kg (44 lb) of silver discovered in Gamla Stan in 1937. The other sections depict industrialization in the 19th century and the tremendous growth in the 20th century with the emergence of a new city centre and new suburbs. The museum also organizes tours that take in the locations mentioned in writer Stieg Larsson's popular *Millennium* trilogy.

The library has a large picture archive and a Stockholm reference room. There are children's activities, concerts and lectures.

The 18th-century Lohe Treasure at Stockholms Stadsmuseum

For hotels and restaurants in this region see pp280–283 and pp298–300

Katarinahissen ㉚

Stadsgården. **Map** 3 C5. *Tel 08-642
47 85.* ⊤ *Slussen.* 🚌 *2, 3, 43, 53,
55, 59.* ◯ *7.30am–10pm Mon–Sat,
10am–10pm Sun.* 🎫 🛗 🍴 ✳

Katarinahissen is the oldest
of Stockholm's "high-rise"
attractions. The 38 m (125 ft)
high lift was opened to the
public in March 1883 and is
still a prominent silhouette on
the Söder skyline. The first
Swedish neon sign was
erected here in 1909 – a
legendary advertisement for
Stomatol toothpaste. Since the
1930s, the sign has been
placed on a nearby rooftop.

The original lift was driven
by steam, but it switched to
electricity in 1915.

In the 1930s it was replaced
by a new lift when the
Cooperative Association (KF)
built its large office complex at
Slussen. In its first year of
operation, the lift was used

**Stomatol sign,
Katarinahissen**

by more
than a
million
passengers,
but its
record year
was 1945,
when it
carried a
total of 1.8 million people
between Slussen and
Mosebacke Torg.

At the top there is a bar
and a gourmet restaurant,
Gondolen. The views from
here are spectacular.

**Katarina Kyrka (1695) after its extensive
restoration due to a devastating fire in 1990**

Katarina Kyrka ㉛

Högbergsgatan 13. *Tel 08-743 68 00.*
⊤ *Slussen, Medborgarplatsen.* 🚌 *2,
3, 53, 71, 76.* ◯ *11am–5pm Mon–
Fri, 10am–5pm Sat & Sun.* 🎫 *by
appointment.* 🎵 *12.15pm Tue & Thu
(organ music), 11am Wed & Sun.* 🛗
📷 📱 *www.svenskakyrkan.se*

The buildings surrounding
the hilltop on Katarinaberget
date partly from the 18th
century, although there have
been churches on the site since
the late 14th century. The most
impressive of all the buildings
is the 17th-century Katarina
Kyrka, designed by one of the
era's greatest architects, Jean

de la Vallée
(1620–96). King
Karl X Gustaf
was also deeply
involved in the
project, and
specified that
the church
should have a
central nave with
the altar and pul-
pit positioned
right in the mid-
dle. Construction
began in 1656
and the church
was finally
completed in
1695. In 1723 it
was badly dam-
aged by fire,
along with large
parts of the
surrounding
area, but it was restored over
the next couple of decades.
The architect Göran Josua
Adelcranz designed a larger,
octagonal tower.

Major restoration was carried out in the 20th century,
and a new copper roof was
added in 1988. Then two
years later, on the night of 16
May 1990, there was another
fire and the interior and virtually all its fittings were
destroyed. Only the outer
walls survived.

The architectural practice of
Ove Hidemark was commis-
sioned to design a new
church which, as far as possible, was to be a faithful
reconstruction of the original.

In order to carry out such a
detailed reconstruction, the
architects resorted to the use
of 17th-century building techniques. Experts and craftsmen
skilfully joined heavy timber-
ing on to the central dome in
the traditional way, and the
church's central arch was
rebuilt with bricks specially
made in 17th-century style.

In 1995, Katarina Kyrka was
reconsecrated and, in the
eyes of many people, looked
more beautiful than ever. The
altar was sited exactly where
it was originally planned.

The reconstruction cost
270 million kronor, of which
145 million kronor was covered by insurance. The
remainder was raised through
public donations.

Katarinahissen with Stockholms Stadsmuseum in the background

Fjällgatan ㉜

Street light

Per Anders Fogelström (1917–98), pro bably Söder's best-known author, wrote: "Fjällgatan must be the city's most beautiful street. It's an old-fashioned narrow street which runs along the hilltop with well-maintained cobblestones … and with street lights jutting out from the houses. Then the street opens up and gives a fantastic view of the city and the water…" This area offers an experience of the authentic Söder and its unique atmosphere.

The Heights of Söder
With its 300-year-old houses and terraced gardens, the Söder hilltop stands like a giant stage-set behind Stadsgården harbour.

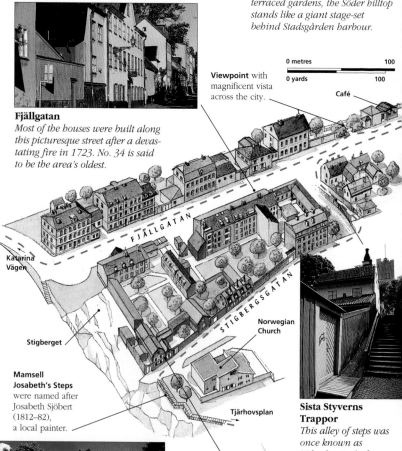

Fjällgatan
Most of the houses were built along this picturesque street after a devastating fire in 1723. No. 34 is said to be the area's oldest.

Viewpoint with magnificent vista across the city.

| 0 metres | 100 |
| 0 yards | 100 |

Café

FJÄLLGATAN

Katarina Vägen

STIGBERGSGATAN

Norwegian Church

Stigberget

Mamsell Josabeth's Steps
were named after Josabeth Sjöbert (1812–82), a local painter.

Tjärhovsplan

Sista Styverns Trappor
This alley of steps was once known as Mikaelsgränd after a 17th-century executioner. Later it was named after the inn on the harbour, Sista Styvern ("The Last Penny").

Söder Cottages
Typical well-preserved cottages can be found along Stigbergsgatan. One of them is No. 17, the house of the blockmaker Olof Krok during the 1730s.

KEY

– – – Suggested route

Vita Bergen ㉝

Södermalm. 2, 3, 55, 66, 76.

Today famous for its popular open-air theatre performances, this park is also an opportunity to see houses originally built for workers at Söder's harbours and factories. They were simple homes, often with a small garden and surrounded by a fence. In 1736 the building of new wooden houses was forbidden because of the fire risk, but slum districts, as this was then, were exempted.

Around 1900, when Sofia Kyrka was built, the area was turned into a leafy hillside park with allotment-garden cottages to the east. The park has a bronze statue, *Elsa Borg*, by Astri Bergman Taube (1972), wife of the great troubadour Evert Taube (*see p60*).

Globen ㉞

3 km (2 miles) S of Stockholm. Globen. 4, 164, 150, 807. Tel 08-508 353 00. during events. gondola ride. by appt. www.globearenas.se

In 1989 Stockholm acquired a new symbol in the shape of the indoor arena Globen, which has a circumference of 690 m (2,260 ft) and a height of 85 m (279 ft). The arena offers a wide programme of events, from international sports to performances by musicians and bands from around the world.

The spectacular Skyview ride enables visitors to travel up the outside wall of the arena in glass gondolas.

Chapel of the Holy Cross by Gunnar Asplund at Skogskyrkogården

Skogskyrko-gården ⑲

6 km (3.5 miles) S of Stockholm. Tel 08-508 301 00. Skogskyrkogården. Jun–Aug by appt (call 08-508 316 59).

Nature and architecture have combined to give the Skogskyrkogården Cemetery a place on the UNESCO World Heritage list. The cemetery is the creation of architects Gunnar Asplund (*see p99*) and Sigurd Lewerentz, winners of a design competition for the site in 1915. It is set amid pinewoods which provide a sombre framework for the various chapels and crematorium, all of which are important examples of Sweden's National Romantic and Functionalist styles.

Asplund's first work, Skogskapellet (Woodland Chapel),

Epitaph to Gunnar Asplund

featuring a steep shingled roof, was opened at the same time as the cemetery in 1920, and was decorated by Carl Milles. This was followed five years later by Uppståndelsekapellet (the Resurrection Chapel), designed by Lewerentz.

In 1940 Asplund's last masterpiece, Skogskrematoriet (Woodland Crematorium), was completed, along with its three chapels representing Faith, Hope and the Holy Cross. John Lundqvist's *The Resurrection* stands in the pillared hall of Heliga Korsets Kapell, the largest of the chapels, where there is also a mural painted by Sven Erixson. Adjoining the chapel is Asplund's black granite cross. The Hill of Meditation lies to the west. Skogskyrkogården is the final resting place of Greta Garbo.

GRETA GARBO

The legendary Greta Garbo, one of the 20th century's outstanding film stars, was born in 1905 in a humble part of Södermalm. At the age of 17 she joined the theatre academy of Dramaten and made her film debut in *Peter the Tramp*. Her breakthrough came in 1924 in Mauritz Stiller's film of Selma Lagerlöf's book *The Atonement of Gösta Berling*. The following year she moved to Hollywood, where she soon became the reigning star. Garbo appeared in 24 films, including *Anna Karenina* (1935) and *Camille* (1936). She never married and lived a solitary life until her death in 1990. Her ashes were interred at the Skogskyrkogården Cemetery in 1999.

Garbo in *As You Desire Me* (1932)

The silhouette of Globen arena dominating the surrounding area

Drottningholm 36

The unique Baroque and Rococo environment of Drottningholm – its palace, theatre, park and Chinese Pavilion – have been perfectly preserved. This royal palace emerged in its present form towards the end of the 17th century, and was one of the most lavish buildings of its era. Contemporary Italian and French architecture inspired Tessin the Elder (1615–81) in his design, which was also intended to glorify royal power. The project was completed by Tessin the Younger, while architects such as Carl Hårleman and Jean Eric Rehn finished the interiors. The Royal Family uses parts of the palace as their private residence. Drottningholm was designated a UNESCO World Heritage Site in 1991.

Baroque Garden
The bronze statue of Hercules (1680s) by the Dutch Renaissance sculptor Adrian de Vries adorns the parterre in the palace's Baroque Gardens.

Upper South Bodyguard Room
This ante-room to the State Room, used for ceremonial occasions, was decorated with stucco works by Giovanni and Carlo Carove, and ceiling paintings by Johan Sylvius.

Apartments of the Royal Family

STAR FEATURES

★ Staircase

★ Queen Lovisa Ulrika's Library

★ Queen Hedvig Eleonora's State Bedroom

Writing Table by Georg Haupt
Standing in the Queen's Room is this masterpiece (1770) commissioned by King Adolf Fredrik as a gift to Queen Lovisa Ulrika. Textiles for the walls and furnishings date from the 1970s.

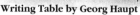

★ Queen Lovisa Ulrika's Library
The Queen commissioned Jean Eric Rehn (1717–93) to decorate this splendid library, which illustrates her influence on art and science in Sweden in the 18th century.

VISITORS' CHECKLIST

10 km (6 miles) W of Stockholm.
Brommaplan, then bus 177, 178. May–Sep.
Palace Tel 08-402 62 80.
May–Aug: 10am–4.30pm daily; Sep: noon–3.30pm daily; Oct–Apr: noon–3.30pm Sat & Sun. public hols.
Chinese Pavilion May–Sep. Theatre Museum May–Sep.
www.royalcourt.se

The Palace Church in the northern cupola was completed by Hårleman in the 1720s.

★ Queen Hedvig Eleonora's State Bedroom
Morning receptions ("levées") were held in this lavish Baroque room designed by Tessin the Elder. It took about 15 years for Sweden's foremost artists and craftsmen to decorate the room, which was completed in 1683.

Entrance

★ Staircase
Trompe-l'oeil paintings by Johan Sylvius adorn the walls, giving the impression that the already spacious interior stretches further into the palace.

Exploring Drottningholm

The Palace of Drottningholm, a UNESCO World Heritage Site, is complemented by the Court Theatre (Slottsteatern), the world's oldest theatre still in active use, the Theatre Museum (Teatermuseum) and the elegant Chinese Pavilion (Kina Slott). The complex is situated on the shores of Lake Mälaren, surrounded by Baroque and Rococo gardens, and lush English-style parkland. In summer there are jousting tournaments, and the theatre stages opera and ballet.

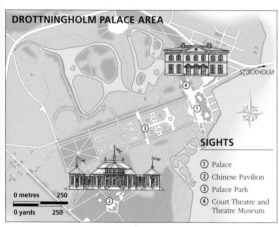

DROTTNINGHOLM PALACE AREA

STOCKHOLM

0 metres 250
0 yards 250

SIGHTS

① Palace
② Chinese Pavilion
③ Palace Park
④ Court Theatre and Theatre Museum

Karl XI's gallery at Drottningholm, featuring the victory at Lund, 1667

THE PALACE APARTMENTS

The first thing that meets the eye on entering the apartments is a Baroque corridor with a view that frames part of the gardens in all their splendour. The central part of the palace is dominated by the staircase, crowned by a lantern with ceiling paintings by Ehrenstrahl. There are examples of Baroque stucco work by Giovanni and Carlo Carove. Marble statues of the nine muses and their protector, Apollo, are placed at the corners of the balustrades.

Medallion symbolizing life and death

The Green Salon is reached from the lower vestibule via the Lower Northern Bodyguard Room. This is the beginning of the main ceremonial suite, which continues with Karl X's Gallery where paintings illustrate his major military exploit, the crossing of the iced-over Store Bælt (Great Belt) by the Swedish army in 1658. Queen Hedvig Eleonora (1636–1715) held audiences in the Ehrenstrahl Salon, named after the artist whose paintings dominate the walls. More prominent guests were received in the State Bedroom which later in Queen Lovisa Ulrika's time was in fact used for sleeping. Her Meissen porcelain can be seen in the Blue Cabinet; the Library has her collection of more than 2,000 books. Behind the Upper Northern Bodyguard Room, with a ceiling by Johan Sylvius, is a Gustavian drawing room with a bureau by Johan Niklas Eckstein. In 1777, following Gustav III's assumption of power, the Blue Salon was decorated in the Neo-Classical style.

The Chinese Salon was used as a private bedroom by King Adolf Fredrik. It is directly above the Queen's State Bedroom and there is a hidden staircase linking the two floors. The "bureau"

opposite the tiled stove is also a sofa bed. The Oscar Room was refurbished by Oscar I (1799–1859) and is adorned by a tapestry dating from the 1630s. After the General's Room, Karl XI's Gallery commemorating the victory at Lund (1667), and the Golden Salon, comes the Queen's Salon. Just as the adjoining State Room has portraits of all the European monarchs, the portraits in the Queen's Salon are of European queens. This floor finishes with the Upper South Bodyguard Room, an ante-room to the State Room and lavishly decorated by the Carove stucco artists and the ceiling painter Johan Sylvius.

THE CHINESE PAVILION

On her 33rd birthday in 1753 Queen Lovisa Ulrika was given a Chinese pavilion by her husband, King Adolf Fredrik. It had been manufactured in Stockholm and the previous night it was shipped to Drottningholm and assembled a short distance from the palace. It had to be taken down after 10 years because rot had set in, and was

The Chinese Pavilion, an extravaganza in blue and gold

replaced by the Chinese Pavilion (Kina Slott) which is still one of the major attractions at Drottningholm. The polished-tile building was designed by D F Adelcrantz (1716–96).

At this time there was great European interest in all things Chinese. In 1733 the newly formed East India Company made its first journey to China. After Lovisa Ulrika's death in 1782 this interest waned, but it was rekindled in the 1840s. The Chinese Pavilion is a mixture of what was considered 250 years ago to be typical Chinese style along with artifacts from China and Japan. Efforts have been made to restore the interior to its original state with the help of a 1777 inventory.

Four smaller pavilions belong to the building. In the northeastern pavilion the king had his lathe and a carpenter's bench. Alongside is the Confidencen pavilion, where meals were taken if he wished to be left undisturbed. The food was prepared in the basement, the floor opened and the dining table hauled up. The adjoining Turkish-style "watch tent" was built as a barracks for Gustav III's dragoons. It now houses a museum about the estate.

Tiled stove in a cabinet in the Chinese Pavilion

THE PALACE PARK

The palace's three gardens are each of a completely different character but still combine to provide a unified whole. The symmetrical formal garden started to take shape in 1640. The garden was designed to stimulate all senses with sights, sounds and smells. It starts by the palace terrace with its "embroidery" parterre and continues as far as the Hercules statue. The water parterre is situated on slightly higher ground and is broken up with waterfalls and topiaries. The sculptures, mainly carved by the Flemish

sculptor Adrian de Vries (1560–1626) were war trophies from Prague in 1648 and from Fredriksborg Castle in Denmark in 1659.

The avenues of chestnut trees were laid out when the Chinese Pavilion was completed, as well as the Rococo-inspired garden area – a cross between the formal main garden and the freer composition of the English park. The English park has natural paths and a stream with small islands, along with trees and bushes at "natural" irregular intervals. Gustav III is reputed to have been responsible for its design and also planned several buildings. Not all his plans were realized, but he added four statues which he had bought during his travels in Italy.

The first 300 of a total of 846 lime trees were planted in the avenues flanking the Baroque garden as early as 1684.

THE COURT THEATRE AND THEATRE MUSEUM

The designer of the Chinese Pavilion, Carl Fredrik Adelcrantz, was also responsible for the Drottningholm Court Theatre (Slottsteatern), which dates from 1766. The theatre was commissioned by Queen

Court Theatre stage machinery dating from 1766

The magnificent 18th-century stage in the Drottningholm Court Theatre

Lovisa Ulrika, but Adelcrantz did not have the same resources as the architects of the palace itself. This simple wooden building with a plaster façade is now the world's oldest theatre still preserved in its original condition. The interior and fittings are masterpieces of simple functionality. The pilasters, for example, are made from gypsum and the supports from papier mâché. The scenery, with its wooden hand-driven machinery, is still in working order.

After Gustav III's death in 1792 the theatre fell into disuse until the 1920s, when the machinery ropes were replaced, electric lighting was installed, and the original wings were refurbished.

The scenery is adapted to 18th-century plays. It can be changed in just a few seconds with the help of up to 30 scene-shifters. The sound effects are simple but authentic: a wooden box filled with stones creates realistic thunder, a wooden cylinder covered in tent cloth produces a howling wind. Every summer there are about 30 performances, mainly opera and ballet from the 18th century. The theatre is open daily for visitors to the palace.

A Theatre Museum and shop are housed in Duke Carl's pavilion, built in the 1780s. The museum focuses on 18th-century theatre, with decoration sketches, paintings, scenery models and costumes. A *Commedia dell'arte* room contains paintings by Pehr Hilleström and sketches for Gustav III's dramatic productions by Louis Jean Desprez.

The Stockholm Archipelago ㊲

Extending 80 km (50 miles) east from the sheltered waters of Stockholm to the open sea, the archipelago encompasses tens of thousands of islands of all shapes and sizes, some inhabited, others not. Many of the inner archipelago's larger islands, such as Värmdö, Ingarö and Ljusterö, are linked to the mainland by bridges and car ferries, making them in parts little more than city suburbs. But the majority of the archipelago islands, with their traditional wooden houses, cosy hotels and youth hostels, and summer sailing regattas, can be reached by an extensive network of scheduled ferries departing from Stockholm, Vaxholm, Stavsnäs and Dalarö.

Huvudskär in Stockholm's outer archipelago

ARCHIPELAGO HIGHLIGHTS

① Fjäderholmarna
② Vaxholm
③ Grinda
④ Finnhamn
⑤ Möja
⑥ Sandhamn
⑦ Utö

✴ Fjäderholmarna

6 km (4 miles) E of Stockholm.
🛈 08-718 01 00. 🚢 May–Sep from Nybrokajen and Slussen.

With the inclusion of the Fjäderholmarna islands in Ekoparken (see p97), the city's "green lung" has acquired a small part of the archipelago. The main island, Stora Fjäderholmen, is only 25 minutes by boat from Nybrokajen or Slussen.

There was an inn here as long ago as the 17th century, conveniently sited for islanders on their way to the city to sell their wares. Today there is an attractive harbour, restaurants, an art gallery and museums devoted to boating and angling as well as the Baltic Sea Museum, home to virtually every type of aquatic creature from Stockholm to Landsort. Local handicrafts include metal-work, weaving, wood-carving and glassmaking. The other three islands have a rich birdlife and one, Libertas, has Sweden's last remaining gas-powered lighthouse.

♙ Vaxholm

25 km (16 miles) NE of Stockholm.
🛈 08-541 314 80. 🚌 670. 🚢 from Strömkajen and Nybrokajen. **Vaxholm Fortress** and **Vaxholm Fortress Museum Tel** 08-541 721 56/57. ◯ mid-Jun–Sep: 11.30am–5.30pm daily.

The archipelago's main community, Vaxholm, is easily reached by boat from Stockholm on a delightful one-hour journey through the archipelago. Vaxholm Fortress, on the nearby island of Vaxholmen, guards this busy port. First fortified in 1548 by Gustav Vasa, the more recent 19th-century citadel houses a military museum.

Two of Stockholm's best-known architects have left their mark on Vaxholm. The law courts were given their present appearance in 1925 by Cyrillus Johansson, and the

The Fjäderholmarna islands, a popular summer excursion just 25 minutes by boat from the city

Vaxholm Fortress, strategically sited on the approach to Vaxholm

hotel on the headland, by Erik Lallerstedt (1899), has Jugendstil ornamentation.

The wooden buildings and shops around the square and along Hamngatan provide a pleasant stroll.

♙ Grinda

30 km (19 miles) E of Stockholm.
🛈 08-542 490 72. 🚌 670 from Östra station to Vaxholm, then boat. 🚢 from Strömkajen and Nybrokajen.
◯ 🍴 (summer only).

Grinda is a leafy island, typical of the inner archipelago, about one and a half hours by boat from the city. It has some excellent beaches and rocks for swimming, as well as good fishing. The architect Ernst Stenhammar, who designed the Grand Hôtel in Stockholm (see p77), built a large Jugendstil villa here, which is now a pub and

Sandhamn, the yachting centre in Stockholm's outer archipelago

restaurant with guest rooms. There are chalets to rent, a campsite and a youth hostel in a former barracks. Boats can be hired.

Finnhamn
40 km (25 miles) NE of Stockholm. 08-542 462 12. from Strömkajen and Nybrokajen.

Finnish ships used to moor at Finnhamn on their way to and from Stockholm. This attractive group of islands lies two and a half hours by boat from Stockholm at the point where the softer scenery of the inner archipelago gives way to the harsher landscape of the outer islands. As on Grinda, the main island has a wooden villa designed by Ernst Stenhammar (1912). Today it is the largest youth hostel in the archipelago. There is a restaurant, chalets to rent and a campsite. Smaller islands nearby are accessible by rowing boat.

Möja
50 km (31 miles) E of Stockholm. 08-571 640 53. 670 to Vaxholm, then boat. from Strömkajen and Nybrokajen.

Fishing and strawberry-growing were the mainstays of this idyllic corner of the archipelago. Now there are few Möja strawberry growers and only one professional fisherman among the island's 300 inhabitants. Instead, picturesque harbours attract the sailing fraternity in particular. Nature reserves on and around Möja shelter a rich abundance of wildlife. Services on the island are good in the summer, with cottages, boats and kayaks for hire, and guest houses.

Sandhamn
50 km (31 miles) E of Stockholm. 08-571 530 00. 433, 434 from Slussen to Stavsnäs, then boat. from Nybrokajen.

Over the past 200 years Sandhamn has been a meeting point for sailors. The Royal Swedish Yacht Club is based in Seglarrestaurangen (Sailors' Restaurant), and every year the world's yachting elite arrive to take part in the Round Gotland Race.

Sandhamn is a pretty village with narrow alleys and houses adorned with decorative carvings. There are shops, crafts centres and a swimming pool. About 100 people live here permanently. The Customs House, built in 1752, is a listed heritage building and former home of poet and artist Elias Sehlstedt (1808–74).

Camping is not permitted, but hotel, bed-and-breakfast and chalet accommodation are available and there are great sandy beaches.

Utö
50 km (31 miles) SE of Stockholm. 08-501 574 10. in summer, from Strömkajen. www.utoturistbyra.se

No other island in the archipelago has as rich a history as Utö, which was inhabited before the Viking era. In the 12th century the islanders started to mine iron ore, and this activity continued until 1879. Their story is told in the Mining Museum adjoining the hotel. Today's holiday homes along Lurgatan were built as miners' cottages in the 18th century. A windmill, built in 1791, provides an unrivalled view of the island.

Utö is one of the best seaside resorts in the Stockholm area, and is ideal for a weekend or full-day excursion.

Hotel, youth hostel, camping, chalet and bed-and-breakfast accommodation are available. Bicycles, rowing boats and canoes can be hired. The bakery is renowned for its delicious "Utölimpa" bread.

EXCURSIONS BY STEAMBOAT

Traditional steamboats are a familiar feature on the waters around Stockholm. Both in the archipelago and on Lake Mälaren visitors can still enjoy the tranquil atmosphere of a steamboat voyage. One of the veterans, *SS Blidösund*, built in 1911, is operated by voluntary organizations and serves mostly the northern archipelago. Some routes, for example Stockholm–Mariefred, are operated partly or completely by steamers. Most of the other passenger boats from the early 20th century have been fitted with oil-fired engines, but still provide a nostalgic journey back in time.

SS Blidösund, one of the oldest in Stockholm's fleet of steamboats

STOCKHOLM STREET FINDER

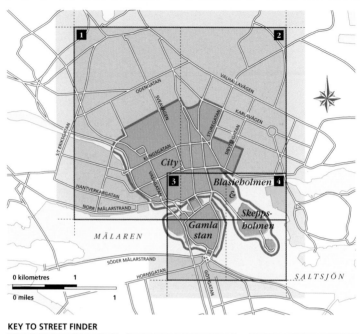

KEY TO STREET FINDER

▢ Major sight	🅿 Car park	⬚ Pedestrian street
▢ Place of interest	🛈 Tourist information office	
▢ Other building	✚ Hospital	**SCALE OF MAP PAGES 1–2**
🚉 Train station	🚓 Police station	0 metres 200
Ⓣ Tunnelbana station	✝ Church	0 yards 200
🚌 Main bus stop	✡ Synagogue	
🚍 Long-distance bus station	⊠ Post office	**SCALE OF MAP PAGES 3–4**
⛴ Ferry boarding point	☀ Viewpoint	0 metres 200
🚊 Tram stop	Railway line	0 yards 200

A

Adolf Fredriks Kyrkogata	1 C3
Akademigränd	1 C5, 3 A1
Ankargränd	3 B3
Apelbergsgatan	1 C4
Arkivgatan	3 A2
Armfeltsgatan	2 F1
Arsenalsgatan	3 C1
Artillerigatan	2 F2
Atlasgatan	1 A3
Atlasmuren	1 A3

B

Baggensgatan	3 C3
Baldersgatan	2 D2
Banérgatan	2 F4
Barnhusbron	1 B4
Barnhusgatan	1 B4
Bastugatan	3 A5
Bedoirsgränd	3 B3
Bellmansgatan	3 A5
Bergsgatan	1 A5
Biblioteksgatan	2 D4
Bigarråvägen	1 C1
Birger Jarls Torg	3 A3
Birger Jarlsgatan	1 C2, 2 D3

Blasieholms-gatan	2 E5, 4C1
Blasieholmstorg	2 D5, 3 C1
Blecktornsgränd	3 A5
Blekholmsterrassen	1 B4
Bo Bergmans gata	2 F2
Bolinders plan	1 B5
Bollhusgränd	3 C3
Bragevägen	1 C2
Brahegatan	2 E2
Bredgränd	3 C3
Brinellvägen	2 D1
Brunkebergsgatan	3 A1
Brunkebergstorg	3 A1
Brunnsgatan	2 D3
Brunnsgränd	3 C3
Bryggargatan	1 C4
Brännkyrkagatan	3 A5
Bältgatan	2 F3

C

Cardellgatan	2 E3
Carl-Gustaf Lindstedts gata	1 A4
Cederdalsgatan	1 B1
Celsiusgatan	1 A4
Centralbron	1 C5, 3 B4

D

Dalagatan	1 A2
Danderydsgatan	2 D2
Danderydsplan	2 D2
Dannemoragatan	1 A1
David Bagares gata	2 D3
Didrik Ficks gränd	3 B3
Drakens gränd	3 C3
Drottning Kristinas väg	2 D1
Drottning Sofias väg	2 E1
Drottninggatan	1 C3, 3 A1
Drottninghusgränd	2 D3
Döbelnsgatan	1 C2

E

Engelbrekts Kyrkogata	2 D2
Engelbrektsgatan	2 D2
Engelbrektsplan	2 D3
Erik Dahlbergsallén	2 F3
Erik Dahlbergsgatan	2 F2
Eriksbergsgatan	2 D3
Eriksbergsplan	2 D3
Evert Taubes Terrass	3 A3
Exercisplan	4 E3

F

Ferkens gränd	3 C3

Finska Kyrkogränd	3 C3
Fiskargränd	3 C5
Fiskartorpsvägen	2 E1
Flaggmansvägen	4 E3
Fleminggatan	1 A4
Floragatan	2 E2
Fredsgatan	2 D5, 3 B1
Frejgatan	1 A2
Friggagatan	2 D2
Fryxellsgatan	1 C2
Funckens Gränd	3 B4

G

Gaffelgränd	3 C3
Gambrinusgatan	1 A3
Gamla Brogatan	1 C4
Garvar Lundins gränd	1 A5
Garvargatan	1 A5
Glasbruksgatan	3 C5
Grev Magnigatan	2 F4
Grev Turegatan	2 E2
Grevgatan	2 F3
Grevgränd	3 C1
Grubbens gata	1 A4
Grubbensringen	1 A4
Guldfjärdplan	3 B4

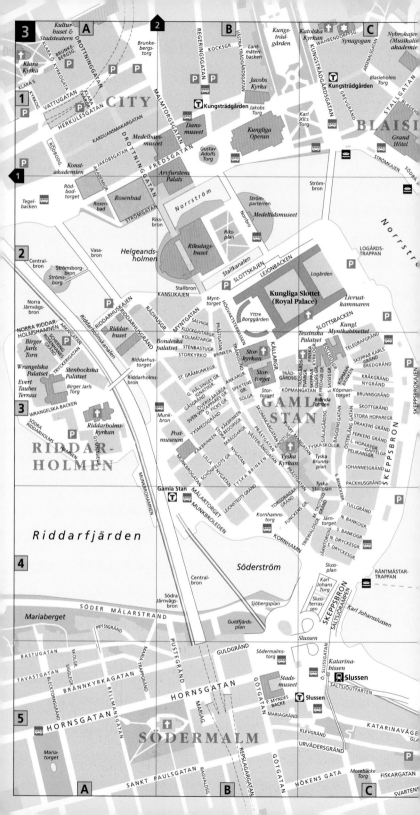

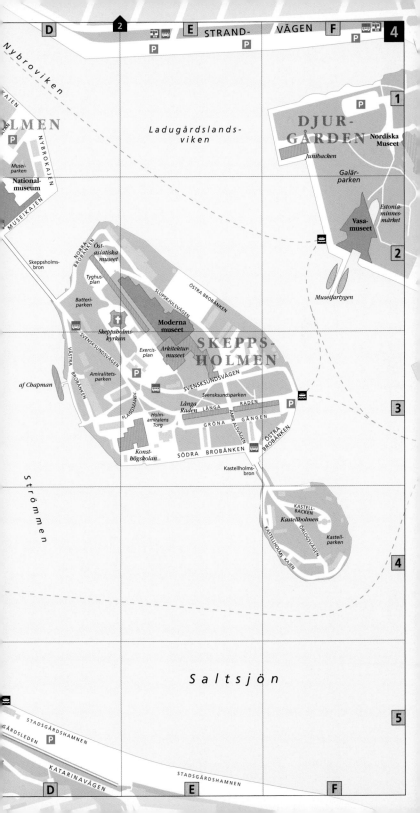

SWEDEN
AREA BY AREA

Sweden at a Glance

Sweden is a long country, traditionally divided into
Norrland, Svealand and Götaland. In Norrland the
landscape is characterized by its proximity to the
Arctic, with mountains in the west, rivers running east
towards the coast, and an interior of forest or
marshland. With the exception of the larger towns
along the coast, the area is sparsely populated. In
Svealand the countryside is hilly, with lakes and
rivers interspersed with farmland. Island archipelagos
lie offshore. The population is concentrated in
Mälardalen, centring on Stockholm. Götaland,
comprising the southern part of the country, offers
the most variation with differing landscapes and a
high urban and rural population.

The Mountains of Härjedalen *are a
haven for outdoor activities in both
summer and winter* (see pp260–6

The Fryken Lakes
*in Värmland are
edged by superb
manor houses such
as Rottneros, whose
park overlooking
Mellanfryken
contains an out-
standing collection
of statues, including
works by Carl Milles*
(see p232).

Götaplatsen, *Gothenburg's finest
square, features Carl Milles' statue*
Poseidon *with Konstmuseet in the
background* (see p200).

Fiskebäckskil, *with its red fishermen's
huts and white wooden houses, is
typical of the coastal villages of
Bohuslän* (see p215).

Österlen, *on the
southeastern coast
of Skåne, is
characterized by
rolling agricultural
land and the
half-timbered
farmhouses typical
of the area*
(see p183).

WESTER
SVEALA.
(See pp228

WESTERN
GÖTALAND
(See pp206–27)

GOTHENBURG
(See pp190–205)

K A T T E G A T T

SOUTHE
GÖTALA
(See pp170

NORTHERN
NORRLAND
(See pp262–75)

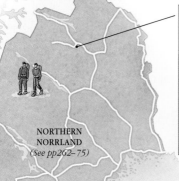

The Ice Hotel *in Jukkasjärvi is an extraordinary creation built entirely of ice and snow. It melts in the spring each year and is recreated in November* (see p272).

Uppsala, *the seat of Sweden's archbishop, has a High Gothic cathedral founded in 1455 – although parts of it date from the 13th century – and the oldest university in the Nordic countries, established in 1477* (see pp128–9).

SOUTHERN
NORRLAND
(See pp246–61)

GULF OF BOTHNIA

EASTERN
SVEALAND
(pp122–39)

STOCKHOLM
(See pp44–117)

BALTIC SEA

Visby, *"the town of roses and ruins", with its medieval perimeter wall and half-timbered houses, is a UNESCO World Heritage Site* (see pp164–7).

EASTERN
GÖTALAND
(pp140–57)

GOTLAND
(See pp158–69)

The Kingdom of Crystal *is the part of Småland known for its glassware, both artistic and practical. The plate, Amber, was designed by Göran Wärff at Kosta Glasbruk in 2003* (see pp152–3).

| 0 kilometres | 200 |
| 0 miles | 100 |

EASTERN SVEALAND

he waterways of Lake Mälaren and the vast archipelago extending to the Baltic both divide and unite the provinces of Uppland, Södermanland and Västmanland. This is a land of verdant islands and glittering bays, splendid castles and little wooden towns, and a cultural heritage that predates the Vikings. With Stockholm at the centre, the region is home to one-third of Sweden's population.

This area was the cradle of ancient Svea, as can be seen in the rock carvings, burial mounds and standing stones in the shapes of ships that dot the landscape. It was from the town of Birka on Lake Mälaren and from Roslagen in Uppland that the Vikings headed east on plundering raids and trading missions around Europe and beyond *(see p31)*. The centre of the ancient pagan Æsir cult in Uppsala held out against Christianity until the 12th century. Many beautiful, small medieval churches testify to the fact that Christianity finally dominated. They are richly decorated with paintings depicting biblical scenes for the benefit of the local congregations. Uppsala itself became a cathedral city and the seat of the archbishop in 1258.

The many castles and fortresses which guard the waterways are an eye-catching sight. Several of these date back to the Middle Ages, but the most important, such as Skokloster, are the result of the great wealth which flooded into the country after Sweden's victories in the various European wars of the 17th century *(see pp35–7)*. Shipping brought further prosperity to the region, with centres such as Arboga lying on the iron route between Bergslagen, Stockholm and the Uppland harbours. There are well-preserved ironworks in all three provinces, including Engelsbergs Bruk, a UNESCO World Heritage Site.

The extensive archipelago straddles the coasts of Uppland and Södermanland, and Lake Mälaren itself is so full of islands that the archipelago appears to continue uninterrupted.

All the architectural sights and natural attractions of Eastern Svealand are best enjoyed at a slow pace by bicycle or boat, or on foot.

The flat skerries of the outer archipelago

◁ Gripsholms Slott at Mariefred on Lake Mälaren, established by Gustav Vasa in 1540

Exploring Eastern Svealand

This, the heartland of Sweden, offers as many
tempting treats as the most well-stocked Swedish
smörgåsbord. Whether travelling by car, bus, train,
bicycle or on foot, visitors will enjoy frequent
glimpses of lakes and bays, as water is a constant
presence. This makes travelling by boat an
unbeatable way of discovering Eastern Svealand's
history and culture and enjoying the area's natural
beauty. There are hundreds of canoe trails, and
canoes and boats can be hired all over the region. For
walkers, Sörmlandsleden, Upplandsleden
and Bruksleden in Västmanland offer more than
1,500 km (940 miles) of stunning trails.

**Botanist Carl von Linné's Hammarby,
outside Uppsala *(see p129)***

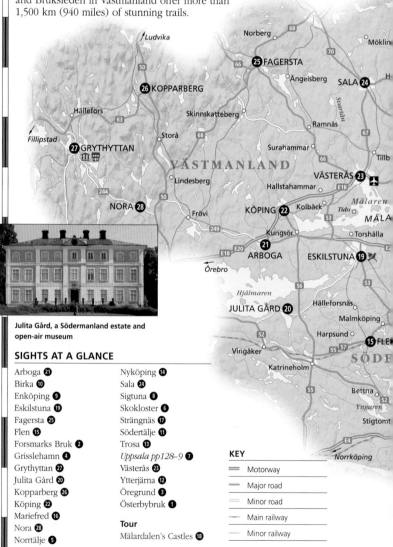

**Julita Gård, a Södermanland estate and
open-air museum**

SIGHTS AT A GLANCE

KEY

═══	Motorway
───	Major road
⋯⋯	Minor road
⚊⚊	Main railway
────	Minor railway

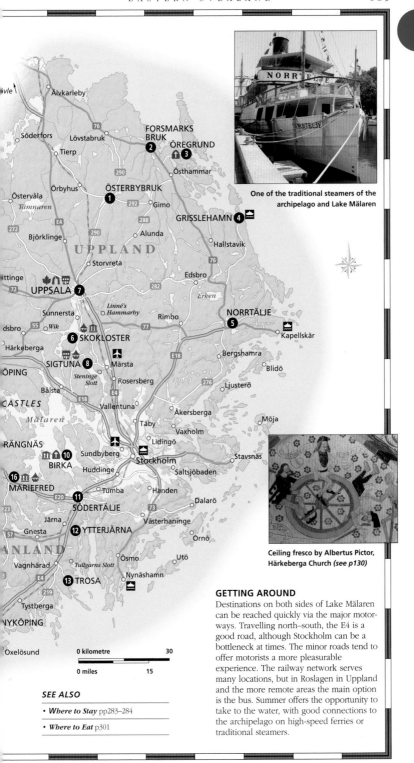

One of the traditional steamers of the
archipelago and Lake Mälaren

Ceiling fresco by Albertus Pictor,
Härkeberga Church *(see p130)*

GETTING AROUND

Destinations on both sides of Lake Mälaren
can be reached quickly via the major motorways. Travelling north–south, the E4 is a
good road, although Stockholm can be a
bottleneck at times. The minor roads tend to
offer motorists a more pleasurable
experience. The railway network serves
many locations, but in Roslagen in Uppland
and the more remote areas the main option
is the bus. Summer offers the opportunity to
take to the water, with good connections to
the archipelago on high-speed ferries or
traditional steamers.

SEE ALSO

0 kilometre   30

0 miles   15

Österbybruk's English gardens with estate offices and clock tower

Österbybruk ❶

Uppland. ⚶ 2,100. 🚌 1 Jun–31 Aug: Ånghammaren 0295-214 92. 🚍 817, 823 from Uppsala. 🚻 📷 Vallonsmedjan ☐ Jun–Aug: daily. 🎫 by appointment, 0295-200 72. Liljeforsateljén ☐ May–mid-Jun, mid-Aug–Sep: noon–4pm Sat & Sun; mid-Jun–mid-Aug: noon–5pm daily. 🎪 Hurdy-Gurdy Festival (weekend before Midsummer), Fire Festival (2nd weekend Aug).

Iron played a key role in the region and nowhere is this more apparent than at Österbybruk. It is the area's oldest ironworks, dating back to the 15th century, but things only really took off when Dutchman Louis de Geer bought the foundry in 1643. With the help of migrant Walloon blacksmiths, he developed the iron industry so crucial to Sweden's position as a great power.

As the world's only fully preserved Walloon forge, the 15th-century **Vallonsmedjan** uses puppets, sound and light to recreate life in the hammer mills. Around it are charming 18th- and 19th-century streets.

The 18th-century manor house was home to wildlife painter Bruno Liljefors in the early 20th century. In summer, his popular animal paintings are exhibited in **Liljefor-sateljén** in the gardens.

Dannemora Gruva was the mine on which local iron-working was built. Gaping opencast pits such as Storrym-ningen are relics of an industry that has gone on here since the Middle Ages. Above the mine is the building in which Mårten

Triewald built Sweden's first steam engine in 1726.

🚇 **Dannemora Gruva**
2 km (1 mile) west of Österbybruk. **Tel** 0295-214 92. ☐ Jun–Sep: daily. 🎫 📷

Forsmarks Bruk ❷

Uppland. 🚍 826, 832, 851 from Uppsala. 🚹 next to Brukscaféet, Jun–Aug: 0173-500 15. ☐ 10am–4.30pm Mon–Fri, 10am–3pm Sat & Sun. 📷 mid-Jun–mid-Aug: 10am (call to book). 🚻 🛏 🎫 ♿

The historic ironworks of Forsmarks Bruk retains its well-preserved streets with their beautiful, whitewashed rows of houses and a manor house built in 1767–74. The manor is set in English-style gardens.

The nuclear power station of **Forsmarks Kärnkraftverk** lies on the coast, 3 km (2 miles) from the ironworks. It provides one-seventh of Sweden's electricity. Guided tours include such features as the vast biotest lake where the environmental impact of the cooling water is studied.

Louis de Geer's Walloon ironworks empire also included the impressively preserved **Lövstabruk**.

🏛 **Forsmarks Kärnkraftverk**
3 km (2 miles) north of Forsmark. 🚹 0173-812 68. ☐ Mon–Fri. 📷 mid-May–mid-Aug: tours from Forsmarks Bruk; other times by appointment. ♿

🚇 **Lövstabruk**
16 km (10 miles) north from Forsmark. 🚹 summer: 0173-500 15. ☐ summer: daily (manor). 🎫 ♿ 📷 🚻

Öregrund ❸

Uppland. ⚶ 1,600. 🚌 639 from Stockholm. 🚹 Jun–Aug: Harbour Office 0173–305 55; all year round: Östhammar Tourist Office, Rådhusgatan 6, Östhammar, 0173–178 50. 🎪 🎪 Östhammar Music Festival (early Jul), Roslagsloppet speedboat race (mid-Aug). **www**.roslagen.se

The twin towns of Öregrund and Östhammar are closely linked geographically and historically. At the end of the 15th century, the citizens of Östhammar founded Öregrund in order to obtain a better harbour. Seafaring and iron-exporting became vital to the town. In 1719, Öregrund was burned by the Russians, but the wooden buildings were rebuilt according to a town plan from 1744. The Town Hall is from 1829. At the end of the 19th century, the sleepy area became a seaside resort and continues to attract visitors to this day.

The Öregrund and Östhammar region is home to many well-preserved old ironworking communities, including **Harg** and **Gimo**. Built in 1763–70, Gimo Manor was the first in Sweden to be designed in Gustavian style by Jean Eric Rehn.

Outside Gimo lies **Skäfthammars Kyrka**, a medieval church particularly renowned for its lectern, which was built for the Gimo smiths.

🔒 **Skäfthammars Kyrka**
Gimo, 16 km (10 miles) southeast of Östhammar. **Tel** 0173-404 27. ☐ call for info.

Öregrund Church's shingle-clad, free-standing bell tower (1719)

Albert Engström's studio on the granite cliffs outside Grisslehamn

Grisslehamn ❹

Uppland. 🏠 4,700. 🚌 637 from Norrtälje. 🛈 Engströmsgården 0175-331 02. 🎭 Postrodden boat race to Åland (Jun).

The choppy Åland Sea constantly batters the red granite cliffs of northern Väddö at Grisslehamn. This is the closest point in Sweden to Finland and the reason for the town's existence. Today's ferry crossing to Eckerö takes only two hours, but things were much tougher in the 17th and 18th centuries when this was the main link with the eastern outposts of the Swedish empire. Until 1876, the post was rowed across the water by local fishermen in open boats. To commemorate the "post rowers", a race is held across the Åland Sea every year in similar boats.

Today, apart from those making the ferry crossing, the sleepy fishing port of Grisslehamn attracts Väddö's many holidaymakers. Delicious fresh fish can be bought from the red sheds on the harbourside.

In 1902, painter and writer Albert Engström (d. 1940) moved to Grisslehamn. He became much loved for his priceless characters such as the tramp, Kolingen, and the Roslagen figure, Österman. The **Albert Engströmsmuseet**, a reconstruction of his home containing Engström's art and memorabilia, was moved to Augustberg in 2006.

🏛 **Albert Engströmsmuseet**
Augustberg. **Tel** 0175-331 02.
🕒 late Jun–Aug; rest of year by appointment only. 🈂 🎦 🖭

Norrtälje ❺

Uppland. 🏠 16,400. 🚌 676 from Stockholm. 🛈 Danskes Gränd 4, 0176-719 90. 🎭 🎵 Norrtälje Jazz Festival (late Jun/early Jul).
www.norrtalje.se

An idyllic town, built of wood, Norrtälje is the natural hub of Roslagen, the area which covers large parts of the Uppland coast. Norrtälje received its town charter from Gustav II Adolf in 1622, when an important armaments factory was established here. In the second half of the 19th century, the town became a seaside resort, not least due to the health-giving properties of the mud found in Norrtälje Bay.

Thousands of summer residents from Stockholm still head for Norrtälje. The town centre and the buildings along the Norrtäljeån river retain their 18th-century features. The church was built in 1726 and the Town Hall dates from 1792. Attractions include **Roslags-museet** in the old armaments factory, focusing on seafaring and coastal life. **Pythagoras** is an unusual museum in a former diesel engine factory and one of Sweden's best preserved industrial relics.

Viking ship in Norrtälje

🏛 **Roslagsmuseet**
Hantverkargatan 23. **Tel** 0176-576 30.
🕒 for renovations to late 2011. ♿

🏛 **Pythagoras**
Verkstadsgatan 6. **Tel** 0176-100 50.
🕒 mid-Jun–mid-Aug: daily. 🈂 🎦 🖭

Skokloster ❻

Uppland. **Tel** 08-402 30 60. 🚆 SL train from Stockholm to Bålsta, then bus 894. 🚢 from Sigtuna. 🕒 May–mid-Jun & Sep: noon–4pm weekends; mid-Jun–Aug: 11am–5pm daily. 🈂 🎦 🖭 🛗

One of the best preserved Baroque castles in Europe, Skokloster, on Lake Mälaren, contains a unique collection of furniture, art, weapons, textiles and books. Construction was started in 1654 for army commander Carl Gustav Wrangel, who accumulated incredible treasures during the Thirty Years War (1618–48). This magnificent building was a way for Wrangel to show off his success, but he only ever lived here for a few weeks. Time seems to have stood still at the castle: the Banquet Hall, for example, remains incomplete, with all the tools lying where the craftsmen left them. The most sumptuous rooms are the armoury and library.

Next to the castle is Sweden's second oldest brick church. Built in the 13th century for nuns of the Cistercian order, it still contains a 13th-century triumphal cross. In the 17th century, it became the Wrangel family church. The churchyard contains several runestones, some of which are signed by the Viking runemaster, Fot, who was active in the mid-11th century.

The Baroque Skokloster Castle, beautifully situated on Lake Mälaren

Uppsala ❼

The city of learning on the idyllic Fyrisån river long remained a small town despite becoming the seat of the archbishop in 1258, having the first university in Scandinavia in 1477 and being the venue for parliaments and coronations. Scientists such as Carl von Linné and Anders Celsius gained the university worldwide glory, but as late as 1800 the town had only 4,000 inhabitants. It wasn't until 20th-century industrialization and the expansion in education that Uppsala grew into Sweden's fourth largest city. The Gothic cathedral, castle, historic university buildings, botanical gardens and ancient Gamla (Old) Uppsala make this one of Sweden's foremost sights.

The cathedral's twin spires, restored in the 19th century

🔒 Domkyrkan

Domkyrkoplan 2. **Tel** 018-430 36 30. ⬭ daily. ⬭ & ♿ 🔔 📷 🖼 🛍 daily. **Skattkammaren** ⬭ daily. 🖼

The first sight on approaching Uppsala is the 119 m (390 ft) high twin spires of the largest cathedral in the Nordic region. The building, with its impressive, colonnaded Gothic nave, was consecrated in 1435. Many monarchs have been crowned here and kings Gustav Vasa and Johan III, as well as botanist Carl von Linné and theosophist Emanuel Swedenborg (1688–1772), are buried here. The chapel contains the remains of St Erik, patron saint of Sweden, in a golden shrine.

The cathedral treasury, Skattkammaren, in the north tower has a superb collection of textiles and silver.

🏛 Gustavianum

Akademigatan 3. **Tel** 018-471 75 71. ⬭ Tue–Sun. ⬭ public holidays. 📷 Sat & Sun (also Eng). 🖼 Ø & 🛍

Sweden's oldest university building takes its name from Gustav II Adolf who, in 1620, donated a number of medieval buildings from which this one was created. The unusual dome was built in 1662 for Olof Rudbeck's Theatrum Anatomicum. This is an amphitheatre with standing room for 200 spectators – students and paying members of the public – who would gather here to watch dissections of executed criminals. The room which visitors see today is largely a faithful reconstruction.

The Gustavianum mounts exhibitions connected with the work of the university since its foundation in 1477. One of the gems on show is the Augsburg Art Cabinet from the early 17th century. It is a kind of universal museum showing the world view of the time in miniature. Various

archaeological collections from Egypt and the Classical world are also on display.

🏛 Universitetshuset

St Olofsgatan/Övre Slottsgatan. **Tel** 018-471 17 15. ⬭ Mon–Fri and for events. &

The university's imposing main building was constructed in 1887 in Neo-Renaissance style. It contains an attractive auditorium and is home to part of the university's art collection.

🏛 Carolina Rediviva

Dag Hammarskjölds Väg 1. **Tel** 018-471 39 00. ⬭ Mon–Sat (mid-May–mid-Sep also Sun). ⬭ public holidays. 🖼 mid-May–mid-Sep. &

In 1841, the 200-year-old university library moved into this specially designed building which houses 5 million printed books and 4 km (2 miles) of shelving holding handwritten manuscripts. Rarities include the Silver Bible from the 6th century and Olaus Magnus's *Carta Marina* (1539).

🏛 Uppsala Slott

Slottsbacken. **Tel** 018-727 24 85. 📷 phone for info. **Konstmuseet** ⬭ Tue–Sun. 🖼 📷 🖼 🛍 ♿

Standing on a glacial ridge, this Vasa castle competes with the cathedral for domination of the city. Established as a fortress in 1549, it was added to several times, but never finished. A disastrous city fire in 1702 destroyed much of the castle and restoration work was started by Carl Hårleman. The castle now houses Uppsala's art museum and the governor's residence.

CARL VON LINNÉ

"God created, Linné organized," goes the saying about the Swedish king of plants. It is thanks to Linné's groundbreaking *Systema Naturae*, first published in 1735, that the

world has the familiar system of binomial nomenclature, giving all plants and animals two Latin names. In 1741, Linné, also known as Linnaeus, became professor of medicine at Uppsala and his spirit has suffused the city ever since. At his country house in Hammarby, Linné tutored students. It was not unknown for him to greet them dressed only in his nightshirt, for the morning's nature walk. According to Linné "nature does not wait for powder and wigs".

Bust of Carl von Linné, 1707–78

Burial mounds next to Gamla Uppsala church and Disagården

VISITORS' CHECKLIST

Uppsala. 🏘 195,000. ✈ 25 km
(16 miles) south of the centre. 🚌
🚆 Kungsgatan. ℹ Fyristorg 8,
018-727 48 00.
🛒 Vaksala market (Sat).
🎭 Walpurgis Night celebrations
(30 Apr), Uppsala Reggae Festival
(late Aug), Culture Night (2nd Sat
in Sep). www.uppsala.to

✿ Botaniska Trädgården

Villavägen 8. **Tel** 018-471 28 38.
◻ daily. ◼ public holidays.
▨ greenhouse.

The botanical gardens have had an educational function since the end of the 18th century. They hold more than 130,000 plants, many exotic, in a beautiful setting that includes several greenhouses, one of which is tropical. The first garden was established on the banks of the Fyrisån river by Olof Rudbeck in 1655. In 1741, Carl von Linné took it over and made it one of the leading gardens of its time. Lovingly restored, it is now known as the Linné garden. After a donation from Gustav III in the late 18th century, teaching was switched to the castle garden, where the Linneanum, housing the orangery, opened in 1807.

⛪ Gamla Uppsala

Route 290 or E4, 5 km north of the centre. **Disagården Tel** 018-16 91 30. ◻ mid-May–Aug: daily. ▨ ◻ Sun.

Gamla Uppsala and its museum are like a time capsule. Royal burial mounds rise up from the plain as they have done for 1,500 years. This was a centre for worshipping the Norse gods long into the 11th century, with a temple which, according to Adam of Bremen's description from 1070, was clad entirely in gold and contained images of Odin, Thor and Frey. Every nine years, a bloody festival was celebrated with men, stallions and dogs sacrificed around the temple. In the early 12th century, the heathen temple gave way to a Christian church, then a cathedral. But in 1273,

the seat of the diocese moved to Uppsala and the cathedral became a parish church of which only small parts remain. Nearby is Disagården, an open-air museum focusing on the life of local farmers in the 19th century.

🏛 Linné's Hammarby

13 km (8 miles) southeast of Uppsala.
Tel 018-32 60 94. ◻ May–Sep:
Gardens daily. **Museum** Tue–Sun.
◼ Whitsun, Midsummer's Eve. ▨ ◻

Linné bought Hammarby farm in 1758, because he thought the air in Uppsala was bad for his health. The estate was his rural retreat, where he was able to cultivate plants that could not tolerate the moist soil in the botanical gardens. The farm is now owned by the state and run by Uppsala University.

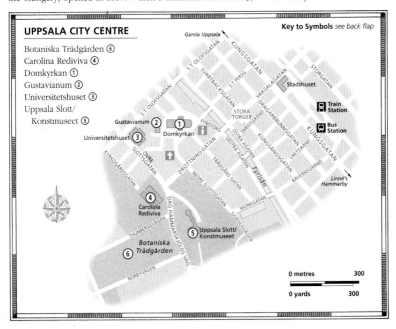

UPPSALA CITY CENTRE

Botaniska Trädgården ⑥
Carolina Rediviva ④
Domkyrkan ①
Gustavianum ②
Universitetshuset ③
Uppsala Slott/
   Konstmuseet ⑤

Key to Symbols see back flap

0 metres   300
0 yards   300

Steninge Slott near Sigtuna, one of the best examples of a 17th-century Carolian country house

Sigtuna 8

Uppland. 🏠 7,700. ✈️ 🚌 to Märsta C, then bus. 🚌 🚆 🛈 Stora Gatan 33, 08-594 806 50. 📷 Sigtuna Meeting (last Sat & Sun in Aug). **www**.sigtuna.se

Sweden's second oldest town after Birka was founded in 980 and soon became a centre of Christianity. Ruins of three of the original seven churches in medieval Sigtuna, St Per, St Lars and St Olof, still remain. The attractive main street, Stora Gatan, is lined with colourful wooden buildings and follows the original route. Still in use today is the 13th-century church of St Maria, with its medieval paintings. It is the oldest brick-built church in Mälardalen.

Sigtuna has Sweden's smallest town hall, built in 1744, and Lundströmska Gården, an early 20th-century home furnished in the style of the period. There are around 150 11th-century rune stones in the surrounding region.

The area is also well-endowed with stately homes. These include Skokloster *(see p127)* and the royal palace of **Rosersberg**, with some of Europe's best-kept interiors from the period 1795–1825.

East of Sigtuna is **Steninge Slott**, architect Tessin the Younger's Italianate Baroque masterpiece built in the 1690s. The attractive gardens contain a monument to Count Axel von Fersen, renowned not least for his romance with the French queen Marie Antoinette, and a cultural centre and art gallery.

🏛 Rosersbergs Slott
15 km (9 miles) from Sigtuna. **Tel** 08-590 350 39. 🕐 Jun–Aug: 11am–4pm daily. 📷 📷 11am & 1pm in Eng. 🍴 📷

🏛 Steninge Slott
7 km (4 miles) east of Sigtuna. **Tel** 08-592 595 00. **Palace** 🕐 Jun–Aug daily. 📷 ✔️ 📷 🍴

Enköping 9

Uppland. 🏠 39,000. 🚌 🚆 🚌 🛈 Gustav Adolfs Plan, 0171-625 040. **www**.enkoping.se

This centrally located town on Lake Mälaren calls itself Sweden's "nearest town". Another name is "Horseradish Town" from the vegetable production which made the town known in the 19th century. And Enköping remains a city of greenery with its inviting parks.

Enköping was granted a town charter in 1300. It was a spiritual centre with three churches and a monastery. Of these, only the largely remodelled Vårfrukyrkan remains.

Northeast of the town, the medieval church of **Härkeberga** is a real gem. At the end of the 15th century, its star chamber was decorated by the master painter Albertus Pictor with colourful representations of biblical stories *(see p125)*.

Triumphal cross, Härkeberga Kyrka

🛈 Härkeberga Kyrka
10 km (6 miles) northeast of Enköping. 🕐 Mar–Oct: daily.

Birka 🔟

Uppland. 🚤 from Stockholm during summer season only. **Birkamuseet Tel** 08-120 040 30. 🕐 May–Sep: 10am–5pm daily. 📷 📷 🍴 🛈 📷

The trading post of Birka on the island of Björkö in Lake Mälaren was established in the 8th century and is thought to be the oldest town in Scandinavia. The founder was the Svea king, who had his royal residence on nearby Adelsö. About 100 years later, Birka is described by a writer as having "many rich merchants and an abundance of all types of goods and a great deal of money and valuables". It was thought to have had 1,000 inhabitants, including craftsmen of every kind, whose products attracted merchants from distant countries. The town was planned on uncomplicated lines. People lived in modest houses which stood in rows overlooking the long jetties. At these lay the ships which took the Vikings out on trading missions and war expeditions. In 830 the arrival of a monk named Ansgar marked the start of Sweden's conversion to Christianity. But Birka's moment of greatness soon passed. In the 10th century,

Iron Age burial ground at Birka on the island of Björkö in Lake Mälaren

the town was abandoned in favour of Sigtuna, on the nearby mainland.

Today, Björkö is a green island with meadows and juniper-covered slopes. It has a fascinating museum and ongoing archaeological digs. The museum shows how Birka would have looked in its heyday, along with some of the finds. Visitors can also share in the day's discoveries when digs are in progress.

In summer, services are held in the Ansgar Chapel. There is a harbour, restaurant, and good places to swim.

Neat wooden houses lining the harbour canal in Trosa

Testing the laws of nature at Tom Tits Experiment, Södertälje

Södertälje ⓫

Södermanland. 🏠 85,000. 🚗 🚆 🛥 🛈 Järnagatan 11, 08-503 803 70. www.sodertalje.nu

Good communications are the key to the economic success of Södertälje, one of Sweden's oldest towns. In the 9th century, a rise in land levels rendered the sound between the Baltic Sea and Lake Mälaren unnavigable and so Tälje became a reloading point. The small town flourished in the Middle Ages but fires, war and plague almost eradicated it in the 17th and 18th centuries. Fortunes improved with the construction of the canal pin 1819, and with the arrival of the railway in 1860 indus-trialization took off. The town grew quickly. Today, major companies such as vehicle-maker Scania and pharmaceu-ticals giant AstraZeneca form the basis of a booming commercial life.

Södertälje's history is the focus of **Torekällbergets Museum**, an open-air museum with animals, historic buildings and a craft quarter. **Marcus Wallenberg-hallen** contains a large collection of veteran vehicles from Scania's 100-year production history.

At **Tom Tits Experiment**, inquisitive children discover how the laws of nature work through experiments with sound, light, air and water.

🏛 **Torekällbergets Museum**
Tel 08-550 214 22. ☐ daily.
🖼 🍴

🏛 **Marcus Wallenberg-hallen**
Tel 08-553 825 00. ☐ Mon–Thu.
🌑 public holidays.

🏛 **Tom Tits Experiment**
Storgatan 33. **Tel** 08-522 525 00.
☐ 10am–5pm daily. 🌑 1 Jan, 23–26 Dec & 31 Dec. 🖼 🖼 🍴 🛍 🅿

Ytterjärna ⓬

Södermanland. 🚆 to Järna, then bus.
🛈 Kulturhuset, 08-554 302 00.
☐ 10am–5pm daily. 🌑 public holidays. 🖼 ♿ 🖼 🍴

Since the 1960s, Ytterjärna has become the centre for Swedish anthroposophists, followers of the teachings of Austrian philosopher Rudolf Steiner (1861–1925). Anthroposophists focus on the development of the whole human being, particularly in the fields of art, music, farm-ing and medicine. There are a number of Steiner organiza-tions here, including schools, the Vidar-kliniken hospital, bio-dynamic farms and market gardens. The Kulturhuset is renowned as a centre for art, music and thea-tre, and for the build-ing's audacious design by architect Erik Asmussen, with its intertwined dialogue of colour and shape inside and out.

Trosa ⓭

Södermanland. 🏠 5,500. 🚆 to Vagnhärad or Södertälje, then bus. 🛈 Rådstugan Torget, 0156-522 22. 🛥 🎭 Trosa Market (2nd Sat in Jun). 🎭 Dance at the harbour (Wed in Jul–1st week in Aug). www.trosa.com

Known as the end of the World, idyllic Trosa is something of a geographical dead end if you are not venturing into the wonderful Trosa archipelago beyond. Like so many coastal towns, it was burned to the ground by the Russians in 1719, although the church dating from 1711 was spared. Pretty groups of red wooden buildings can be found mainly in Kåkstan, where Garvaregården is an arts and crafts museum. The main square, with its minia-ture town hall and market, is a focal point for the town.

Nearby, **Tullgarns Slott** was the favourite summer residence of Gustav V (1858–1950). The beautiful 18th-century palace has magnificent interiors and English-style gardens.

♠ **Tullgarns Slott**
On E4, 10 km (6 miles) north of Trosa.
Tel 08-551 720 11. ☐ Jun–Aug: daily, for guided tours only. 🖼 🖼

Kulturhuset by Erik Asmussen, in the anthroposophists' Ytterjärna

Nyköpingshus, site of the fatal Nyköping Banquet in 1317

Nyköping ⑭

Södermanland. 🏰 33,000. 🚂 🚌 📧
ℹ️ Rådhuset, Stora Torget, 0155-24
82 00. 🔼 🎭 Nyköping Banquet
(Jul). **www**.nykoping.se

Södermanland's county town
is probably best-known for the
notorious Nyköping Banquet
in 1317. King Birger invited the
Dukes Erik and Valdemar to a
banquet at which the disputes
between the brothers were to
be resolved. Instead, Birger
had the dukes thrown into
Nyköpinghus's dungeon,
where they were left to die.
The story is retold in summer
in a colourful pageant at the
castle. A fire in 1665 destroyed
the original castle and only the
tower remains. In the adjoining
county governor's residence,
the **Sörmlands Museum**
contains a lively mix of
historical exhibitions.

A pleasant way to see the
sights in the summer is to take
the Tuffis tourist train which
departs from Stora Torget. On
the coast north of the town,
Nynäs Slott nature reserve is
also worth a visit.

🏛️ **Sörmlands Museum**
Nyköpingshus. **Tel** 0155-24 57 00.
⭕ Jun–Aug: daily (call ahead for
opening hours). 🎫 🏠

Flen ⑮

Södermanland. 🏰 6,200. 🚌 🚂 ℹ️
Sveavägen 1, 0157-190 15; Malm-
köping (summer) 0157-202 04. 🛍️
Malma Market (last Sat & Sun in Jul).
🎭 Flen Festival (2nd weekend in Jun).

One of the youngest towns in
Sweden, Flen only gained its
town charter in 1949. Although
the town itself has little to
offer, it is a good starting point
for the attractions in the area.

Environs
On Lake Valdemaren, just east
of the town, lies Stenhammar's
beautiful castle, renowned as
the residence of Prince Vilhelm
in the early 1900s. The castle is
now used by Carl XVI Gustav
and is not open to the public.
Northeast of Flen is the prime
minister's summer residence,
Harpsund, where the gardens
are open to visitors. The old
regimental town of
Malmköping has
Malmahed, a former
military site, now a
museum and
nature centre.
There are
several military
museums, as
well as
Museispårvägen,
displaying veteran
trams and other public
transport vehicles. Visitors can
enjoy a short tram ride
through the countryside.

**Volvo taxi (1950),
Museispårvägen**

🏛️ **Museispårvägen**
Malmköping, 17 km (11 miles)
north of Flen, road 55. **Tel** 0157-
204 30. ⭕ late May–end Jun:
weekends only; end Jun–mid-Aug:
daily (call for opening hours). 🎫

Mariefred ⑯

Södermanland. 🏰 4,700. 🚌 📧
ℹ️ Rådhuset, 0159-297 90. 🔼
🎭 Steam Day (1st Sat & Sun in Jun),
Medieval Festival (3rd Sat & Sun in
Jul). **www**.mariefred.nu

The town of Mariefred should
ideally be approached from
the water to get the best view
of the splendid **Gripsholms
Slott**. The first fortress on this
site was built in the 1380s by
the Lord High Chancellor, Bo
Jonsson Grip, who gave the
castle its name. Work on the
present building, initiated by
Gustav Vasa, started in 1537,
but extensive alterations were
made by Gustav III in the late
18th century. It was during
this period that the National
Portrait Gallery was set up. It
now contains 4,000 portraits,
representing the celebrities of
the past 500 years.

Gripsholms Slott has a
number of well-preserved
interiors from various periods,
with highlights
including Gustav III's
theatre and the White
Salon. The town of
Mariefred, which
grew up in the
shadow of the
castle, derives its
name from a
medieval
Carthusian
monastery. An inn
has stood on the site of the
monastery since the early
17th century.

The peaceful old streets of
Mariefred with their delightful
wooden buildings are a
pleasure to stroll around. Art
enthusiasts should head for
Grafikens Hus on a hill
leading up to the former royal
farm, where stables and

Mariefred Town Hall (1784), site of the town's tourist office

◁ Strömsholms Slott, the centre of Sweden's equestrian sport (see p136)

haylofts have been converted into attractive galleries.

One of the best ways to visit Mariefred is by boat. The 1903 steamer *S/S Mariefred* plies the three-and-a-half-hour voyage from Stockholm. There is a Railway Museum in the town and **ÖSLJ**, the Östra Södermanlands Järnväg museum society, operates narrow-gauge steam trains from the harbour on a 40-minute trip to Läggesta.

Red-painted, 18th-century wooden buildings in central Strängnäs

♟ Gripsholms Slott
1 km (half a mile) south of the centre.
Tel 0159-101 94. ☐ early May–Sep:
daily; other times: by appt only.
● 21 Dec–1 Jan. 🖼 🎥 🚻

🏛 ÖSLJ
500 m (546 yd) west of the centre.
Tel 0159-210 01. ☐ 1 May–Sep:
varies so call ahead for days and
times. 🖼 🚻

Bedchamber of Duke Karl (Karl IX, 1550–1611), Gripsholms Slott

Strängnäs ⓗ

Södermanland. 🏘 15,000. 🚉 🚌
ℹ Storgatan 38, 0152-296 299
(summer), otherwise 0159-297 90.
🛍 Strängnäs market (2nd Sat in Oct).
www.strangnas.se

As keeper of the keys of the Kingdom, Strängnäs was an important centre in the Middle Ages. It was mentioned as an episcopal see as early as 1120 and is dominated by the imposing tower of its Gothic cathedral, **Domkyrkan**, completed in 1280. It was here that Gustav Vasa was chosen as king on 6 June 1523, the date which was to become Sweden's National Day. Quaint wooden buildings surround the cathedral. To its east is Roggeborgen, the bishop's palace from the 1480s. Strängnäs Municipality includes the largest island in

Lake Mälaren, **Selaön**. There are more rune stones here than in any other part of Södermanland, indicating that this was an ancient cultural centre. Selaön is also the location of the former summer residence of the Strängnäs bishops, Tynnelsö Slott, which was transformed by Karl IX in the 17th century into a Renaissance palace.

The newly renovated Mälsåkers Palace dating from the 17th century is another of Selaön's attractions.

🏛 Domkyrkan
Stora Torget. **Tel** 0152-245 00.
☐ daily. 🎥 by appointment.
🎵 Wed & Sun.

Mälardalen's Castles ⓘ

See pp136–7.

Eskilstuna ⓙ

Södermanland. 🏘 95,000. 🚉 🚌
ℹ Tullgatan 4, 016-710 7000.
www.eskilstuna.se

The town is named after St Eskil, the Englishman who became Svealand's first Christian bishop and built his church on the riverbank along

A Sumatran tiger, one of many exotic animals at Eskilstuna's Parken Zoo

Eskilstunaån at the end of the 10th century. During Sweden's Age of Greatness in the 17th century, Eskilstuna flourished after Karl X Gustav gave master smith Reinhold Rademacher a 20-year monopoly on the manufacture of items such as cannons, knives and scissors. Rademachergatan still has a few forges kept as they were in the 1650s, where visitors can try their hand at being a blacksmith.

Today's modern industrial town and centre of learning features more than 200 items of public art, including Carl Milles's *Hand of God (see p95)* in Stadsparken.

Parken Zoo is one of Sweden's leading zoos, as well as a popular amusement park with a heated outdoor pool. The entrance is guarded by the Phantom, whose Skull Cave is a magnet for youngsters and comic fans alike.

Environs
North of Eskilstuna is **Torshälla**, a small town of cobbled streets and well-kept wooden houses. The magnificent 12th-century church dominates the old quarter. Northeast of Torshälla is **Sunbyholms Slott** *(see p136)* from where a 10-minute walk leads to **Sigurdsristningen**, Sweden's finest rock carving, which is thought to date back to 1040.

🐾 Parken Zoo
1 km (half a mile) west of the
centre. **Tel** 016-100 100. **Zoo**
☐ early May–mid-Sep: 10am–
5pm daily (Jun–mid-Aug: to 6pm).
Amusement Park ☐ May: Sat &
Sun; Jun–mid-Aug: daily; mid-Aug–
mid-Sep: Fri–Sun. 🖼 🎥 ♿ 🚻
🍴 🛍

A Tour of Mälardalen's Castles ⑱

There are more than 100 sturdy castles, opulent palaces and ravishing country houses around Lake Mälaren. Often strategically located near Iron Age and Viking settlements, they highlight the significance of this extensive waterway. Wik's 15th-century castle and the Vasa kings' solid, 16th-century fortress of Gripsholm show how long the need for defences lasted. From the mid-17th century, the grand palaces of Sweden's Age of Greatness, such as Skokloster, predominated, as manifestations of their owners' wealth and power. Many have excellent museums.

Engsö
The medieval castle was rework in French Rococo style in the 174 It has many beautiful interiors fr various periods and a major collection. The castle grounds a a nature reserve full of wildl

Tidö ⑥
Lord Chancellor Axel Oxenstierna's country house, built in 1642, is a fine example of a Baroque manor. It is noted for its handsome state apartment and 43 inlaid wooden doors. A museum displays 30,000 antique toys.

Grönsöö ④
The grand manor from the early 17th century stands guard high above Lake Mälaren. It is still occupied by the von Ehrenheim family, and its grounds represent 400 years of garden history.

Strömsholm ⑦
Equestrianism dates from the 16th century at Strömsholm, with its beautiful pastureland and bridle paths. The palace was built in the 1670s in Carolian Baroque style.

KEY

- ▬ Suggested route
- ═ Other roads
- ♣ Other castles open to the public

TIPS FOR DRIVERS

This tour, taking in the ten suggested palaces, involves a trip of more than 500 km (300 miles), lasting three days, despite the generally good roads. An option is to select a group of palaces close to each other. For more information, see **www**.malarslott.nu *Tel Mälarslott, 016-48 06 80.*

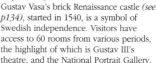

Gripsholm ⑧
Gustav Vasa's brick Renaissance castle *(see p134)*, started in 1540, is a symbol of Swedish independence. Visitors have access to 60 rooms from various periods, the highlight of which is Gustav III's theatre, and the National Portrait Gallery.

0 kilometres

0 miles

(Map labels) LUDVIKA · SALA · Enköping · E18 · Västerås · Hallsta-hammar · E18 · Köping · ⑦ Strömsholm · Engsö ⑤ · Tidö ⑥ · MÄLAREN · Grönsöö · Sundbyholm · Fiholm · Arboga · Eskilstuna · E20 · Mälsåk · Mariefred · Grips[holm]

Wik ③

This 15th-century castle is Sveland's best-preserved late-medieval fortress. With its solid walls and moat, Wik was considered impregnable. It was remodelled in 1656–60. Today, Wik is a hotel and conference centre.

Skokloster ②

Field Marshal Carl Gustaf Wrangel's 17th-century showpiece contains treasures from his campaigns, as well as exceptional collections of art, furniture, textiles, weapons and books *(see p127).*

Steninge ①

Built in the 1690s, the palace was designed by Nicodemus Tessin the Younger in the style of an Italian villa *(see p130).*

Drottningholm ⑩

This royal palace, built in the 17th century, was one of the most lavish undertakings in Sweden. With its theatre, gardens and Chinese Pavilion, Drottningholm is a UNESCO World Heritage Site *(see pp106–9).*

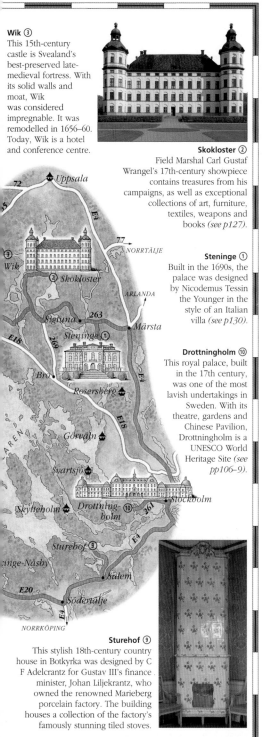

Sturehof ⑨

This stylish 18th-century country house in Botkyrka was designed by C F Adelcrantz for Gustav III's finance minister, Johan Liljekrantz, who owned the renowned Marieberg porcelain factory. The building houses a collection of the factory's famously stunning tiled stoves.

Julita Gård ⑳

Södermanland. **Tel** 0150-48 75 00. 🚆 🚌 Mälarbanan to Eskilstuna, then bus 404, 405. ⬜ May–Sep daily.

This extensive Södermanland estate on Lake Öljaren is said to be the world's largest open-air museum. It was created in the first half of the 20th century by the romantic Lieutenant Arthur Bäckström and in 1941 was donated to Stockholm's Nordiska Museet. Julita is a working estate farm with parks and gardens, and an 18th-century manor house built on the site of a medieval Cistercian monastery.

The estate has a collection of buildings reflecting rural life in Södermanland. Threatened national species of cow, pig, sheep, hen and duck are cared for at the Swedish agricultural museum. There is also a dairy museum. Children are welcome to pop into the house of the much-loved children's literary character, Pettson, and his cat Findus.

Julita Gård's buildings representing rural life in Södermanland

Arboga ㉑

Västmanland. 🏘 11,000 ✕ 🚆 🚌 ⛴ ℹ 🎨 Medieval Festival (Aug).

Red-painted iron warehouses, Ladbron quay and the railway line recall Arboga's great age as the chief shipping port for iron from Bergslagen. Fahlströmska Gården is a typical 16th-century warehouse with a huge loft.

Arboga was an important town in medieval times and the site of Sweden's first parliament in 1435. Churches from the period include the hospital chapel on Stortorget, which has been preserved as a town hall. The 14th-century **Heliga Trefaldighets Kyrka** on Järn-torget has a splendid Baroque pulpit by Burchardt Precht.

Anundshögen, the 7th-century burial mound of King Bröt-Anund, with a stone ship in the foreground

Köping ②

Västmanland. 👥 18,100. 🚌 🚃 ℹ️
Barnhemsgatan 2, 0221-256 55.
🎫 *Köpingsfesten Festival (28–30 May).*

The port of Köping on Lake
Mälaren has been a vital link
for transporting products to
and from the mines and
forests of Bergslagen since
medieval times. The city
burned down in 1889, but
buildings to the west of the
river were saved, including
the 17th-century **Nyströmska
Gården**, a joiner's yard where
visitors can see how the town's
special tilt-top table was made.
Other attractions include the
motor museum, **Bil och
Teknikhistoriska Samlingarna**.

East of Köping is the 11th-
century church of Munktorp.

🏛 **Bil och Teknikhistoriska
Samlingarna**
Glasgatan 19. **Tel** 0221-206 00.
⏰ *May–Sep: 10am–6pm Tue–Sun.
Pre-booked groups all year round.*
🌐 *Midsummer.* 🎫 🖼 📷

Västerås ㉓

Västmanland. 👥 132,000. 🚌 🚃
🚉 ℹ️ *Kopparbergsvägen 1, 021-39
01 00.* 🎫 *City Festival (1st week Jul),
Power meet (Jul).*

Strategically situated at the
point where the Svartån river
runs into Lake Mälaren, the
county town of Västerås has
been an important trading
centre since Viking times.
Construction of the castle and
cathedral began in the 13th
century and in 1527 Parliament was convened here.
The cathedral, **Domkyrkan**,
contains the sarcophagus of
Erik XIV (r.1561–69), the
unfortunate king who was
allegedly poisoned by his

brother Johan III, by pea
soup laced with arsenic.

Around the cathedral lies
the town's old centre of
learning, where Johannes
Rudbeckius opened Sweden's
first upper secondary school
in 1623.

In the 17th and 18th
centuries Västerås became a
major port for the Bergslagen
region. Today it is an industrial centre and headquarters
of the engineering giant Asea-
Brown-Boveri (ABB).

To the east of the town lies
the 7th-century Anundshögen
mound where Bröt-Anund,
the king who settled Bergslagen, is said to be buried.
Standing stones in the shapes
of ships 50 m (164 ft) long can
be seen around the mound.
The area was an important
Viking meeting place.

Northwest of the town is
Skultuna Messingsbruk,
Europe's oldest active brass-
works, founded in 1607 and
renowned for its cannons and
stylish candlesticks.

🏰 **Domkyrkan**
Västra Kyrkogatan 6.
Tel 021-81 46 11. ⏰ *daily.* 🎫

🏛 **Skultuna Messingsbruk**
16 km (10 miles) NW of Västerås.
Tel 021-783 01. ⏰ *Tue–Sun.*
tel for info. 📷 📷

Sala ㉔

Västmanland. 👥 12,100. 🚌 🚃
ℹ️ *Stora Torget, 0224-552 02.*
🎫 *Autumn market (last Fri & Sat in
Sep).* **www**.sala.se/turism

During the 16th century,
the silver mine in Sala was
one of the richest in the
world; 200,000 kg (440,000
lb) were mined up to 1570,
providing valuable funds for
the state coffers. The former

Silvergruvan mine is open to
the public down to a level of
60 m (200 ft). There are beautiful walks around the old pits
and canals, and silver treasure
hunts are organized in the
mine for children.

Aguélimuseet showcases
the work of Sala's own artist,
Orientalist Ivan Aguéli (1869–
1917), and other Modernists.

🏛 **Silvergruvan**
Drottning Christinas Väg. **Tel** 0224-
677 250. ⏰ *11am–4pm Thu–Sun
(May–Sep: 10am–5pm daily), call to
book other times.* 🎫 📷 📷 📷 🏛

🏛 **Aguélimuseet**
Vasagatan 17. **Tel** 0224-138 20. ⏰
11am–4pm Wed–Sat. 🎫 📷 📷

Hauling plant at the Sala silver
mine, in use until 1908

Fagersta ㉕

Västmanland. 👥 11,000. 🚌
ℹ️ *Norbergsvägen 19, 0223-131 00.*
🎫 *Spring Fever (late May), Autumn
Festival (27–28 Aug).*

Iron-working has shaped
Fagersta since the outset. In
Dunshammer, just south of
the town, Iron Age blast
furnaces show how iron used
to be extracted from bog ore.
Today Fagersta is home to
metal-manufacturing and
stainless steel industries.

At the UNESCO World
Heritage Site of **Engelsbergs
Bruk**, the historic blast
furnace and ironworks have
been preserved in working

For hotels and restaurants in this region see pp283–284 and p301

order and give a remarkable impression of how the site operated between the 17th and 19th centuries.

Oljeön, the world's oldest preserved oil refinery (1875–1902), lies 1.5 km (1 mile) from the ironworks.

Running through Fagersta is the 200-year-old Strömsholm canal from Lake Mälaren to Smedjebacken in Dalarna. It was a vital transport link for the Bergslagen foundries. Twenty-six locks, six of them in Fagersta, raise boats a total of 100 m (330 ft). Passenger ferries operate on the canal.

🏛 **Engelsbergs Bruk.**
15 km (10 miles) E of Fagersta. *Tel* 0223-131 00. ⬜ early May–mid-Jun: Sat & Sun; mid-Jun–Aug: daily; Sep: Sat & Sun.

The mansion at the Engelsberg ironworks, dating from the 1740s

Kopparberg ㉖

Västmanland. 🏘 3,300. 🚉 Gruvstugutorget, 0580-805 55. Gold panning competitions (end Jun). **www.**ljusnarsberg.se

The discovery of copper in the early 17th century attracted miners from Falun, who brought with them the name of their old mine and called the place Nya Kopparberget (New Copper Hill). The 2.5 km (2 mile) Kopparstigen (Copper Trail) takes in 28 places of interest, and provides a good view of the many mine buildings.

Along the way is **Kopparbergs Miljömuseer**, a complex including a goldsmiths' museum, postal museum and 1880s photography studio. The 17th-century courthouse and unusually large and impressive wooden church from 1635 are also worth looking at.

🏛 **Kopparbergs Miljömuseer**
Gruvstugutorget. *Tel* 0580-805 55. ⬜ Jun–Aug: daily.

Grythyttan ㉗

Västmanland. 🏘 1,700. *Tel* 0591-340 60. 🚉 to Örebro, then bus. 🍴

A local vein of silver brought prosperity and town status to Grythyttan in 1649, but when the silver ran out 33 years later, the town charter was withdrawn. In recent years, Grythyttan has awakened from its long slumber and is now a gastronomic centre.

It all started when the inn, built in 1640, was given a new lease of life in the 1970s, thanks to inspired innkeeper Carl Jan Granqvist. Now, in addition to Grythyttan's wooden houses and red-painted church, there is a catering college centred on **Måltidens Hus i Norden**. It occupies Sweden's spectacular pavilion built for EXPO 1992 in Seville. A varied range of activities offers something for everyone interested in food and cooking, alongside exhibitions and a cookery book museum.

South of Grythyttan lies **Loka Brunn**, a classic Swedish spa founded in the 1720s.

Grythyttan's inn with its beautifully renovated 17th-century interior

The site has state-of-the-art facilities, but the old spa, with its gardens and spring, has been preserved in the Swedish spa museum. You can sample the spring water and view the restored bathhouse, pharmacy, clinic and royal kitchen built in 1761.

🏛 **Måltidens Hus i Norden**
Sörälgsvägen 4. *Tel* 0591-340 60. ⬜ end of Jun–mid-Aug: daily; other times: Mon–Fri. exhibition.

🏛 **Loka Brunn**
15 km (9 miles) S of Grythyttan. *Tel* 0591-631 00. **Pool** ⬜ daily. **Museum** ⬜ summer only. museum.

Nora ㉘

Västmanland. 🏘 6,400. 🚉 to Örebro, then bus. 🚉 Station House on Norasjön side, 0587-811 20. Nora Festival (1st week in Jul), Noramarken fair (4th weekend in Aug). **www.**nora.se

This idyllic wooden town is an ideal place to stroll around, with its cobbled streets and charming shops, many in 18th-century buildings. **Göthlinska Gården** (1793) is an interesting museum furnished in the style of a middle-class family home from around 1900.

The highlight of the Nora mining area's monuments is **Pershyttan**, 3 km (2 miles) west of the centre, where the charcoal blast furnace dates from 1856. In summer, a steam train operates from Nora on the Nora Bergslags Veteranjärnväg, Sweden's first normal-gauge railway. Nora's train sheds house historic steam trains, diesel engines and carriages.

Kopparberg's old mining community, now an idyllic wooden village

EASTERN GOTALAND

he three provinces of Östergötland, Småland and Öland, which make up Eastern Götaland, each retain their own distinctive character. Östergötland is the agricultural heart of Sweden, Småland is the centre of glassmaking and Öland attracts sun-seekers and nature lovers. They are all popular tourist areas typified by their little red cottages and historical sights, quiet lakes and great coastlines.

In north Östergötland, the major towns of Norrköping and Linköping are almost part of Greater Stockholm. Once beyond the steep hills of Kolmården, which form the northern border, flat agricultural land extends as far as the eye can see. Besides being the granary of Sweden, this is historical soil – it was here that the royal Folkung dynasty had its roots and it was here that Birgitta Gudmarsson (St Bridget) advised the political and religious leaders of the 14th century.

The hills north of Gränna and the ruins of Brahehus castle mark the beginning of Småland. For a long time Småland formed the border with Denmark and it was from this region that Nils Dacke led a peasants' revolt in the 16th century. The land is poorer and stonier than Östergötland with small farms and crofters. Mass emigration drained the area of thousands of people during the famine of the 19th century.

However, Småland has had its success stories: it is the ideal location for one of its major industries, glassworking, which relies on timber and water. The landscape has also been immortalized in the books of Astrid Lindgren, who was born in the province and turned the place where she grew up into a playground for her popular children's characters, Emil and Pippi Longstocking.

The region's archipelago is a favourite with boat-lovers, stretching south from the Sankta Annas islands in Östergötland through the Kalmarsund between Småland and Öland. Thanks to Ölandsbron bridge, the long narrow island of Öland is easily accessible. Holiday-makers are drawn to its sandy beaches, while botanists head for the Alvar plain and ornithologists for Ottenby bird station.

The crew of a sailing boat preparing to pass through the lock at Berg on the Göta Canal

◁ The ruins of Brahehus castle with views over Lake Vättern and the island of Visingö

Exploring Eastern Götaland

This is too big an area to explore in just a few days, but by leaving the major roads and heading cross-country it is possible to have a taste of the different provinces. The Royal Route, or Eriksgatan, created in 2005, has a historical theme and is marked on maps of the region available in any service station or tourist office. Cycling is also an excellent way to see the region, and cruising in comfort on the Göta Canal *(see pp146–7)* offers an unforgettable experience. For a tour of the Kingdom of Crystal *(see p152)* a car is almost essential, but otherwise Småland has countless canoeing routes, lakes for swimming and sights along small forested roads ideally explored by bike.

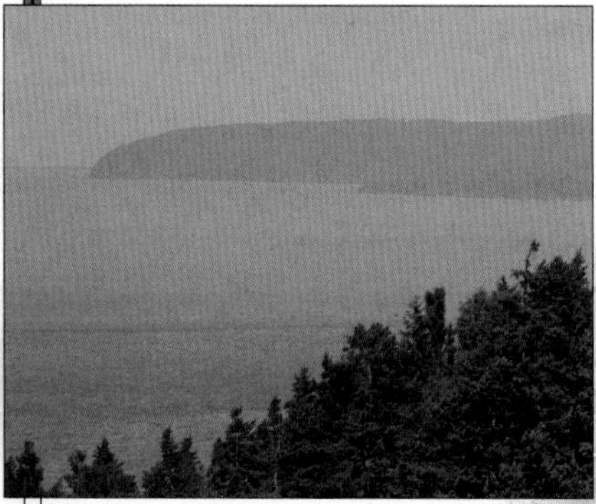

The mythical Omberg on Lake Vättern seen from Brahehus castle *(see p150)*

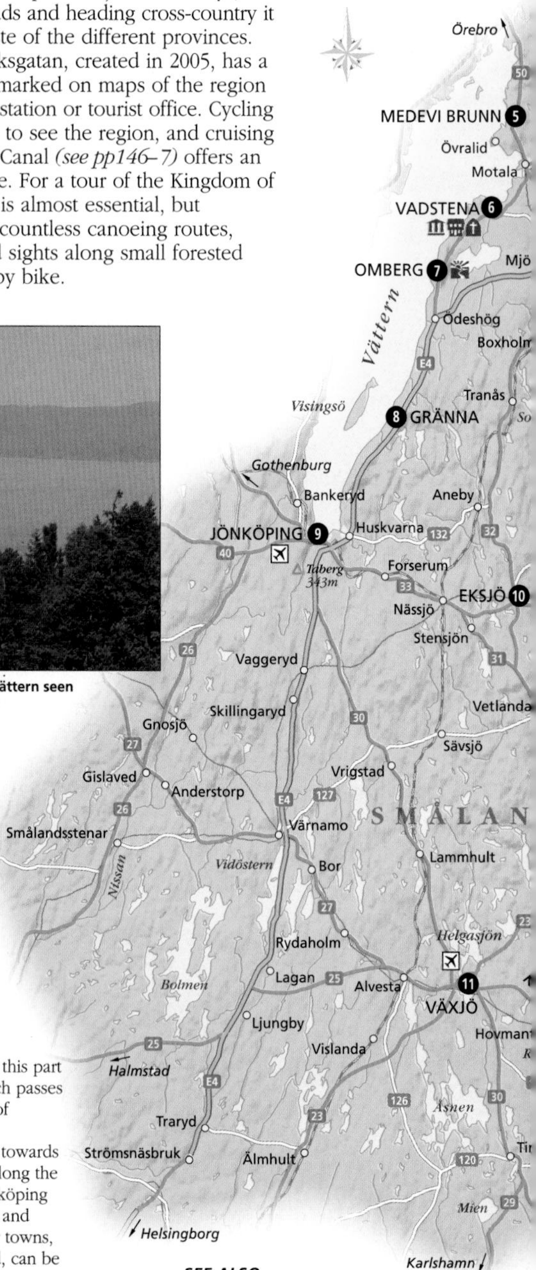
Örebro
50
MEDEVI BRUNN 5
Övralid
Motala
VADSTENA 6
OMBERG 7
Mjö
Vättern
Ödeshög
Boxholm
E4
Tranås
Visingsö
8 GRÄNNA
So
Gothenburg
Bankeryd
Aneby
JÖNKÖPING 9
Huskvarna
132
32
40
Taberg 343m
Forserum
33
EKSJÖ 10
Nässjö
Stensjön
26
Vaggeryd
31
Skillingaryd
Vetlanda
30
Gnosjö
Sävsjö
27
Gislaved
Vrigstad
Anderstorp
127
26
SMÅLAN
Smålandsstenar
Värnamo
Nissan
Vidöstern
Bor
Lammhult
27
23
Helgasjön
Rydaholm
Bolmen
Lagan
25
Alvesta
11
VÄXJÖ
Ljungby
Hovmant
Vislanda
25
Halmstad
E4
126
30
Åsnen
23
Traryd
Strömsnäsbruk
Älmhult
120
Tin
Mien
29
Helsingborg
Karlshamn

KEY

- Motorway
- Major road
- Minor road
- Main railway
- Minor railway
- Summit

GETTING AROUND

The main artery for traffic in this part of the country is the E4 which passes west of Växjö, via the cities of Norrköping, Linköping and Jönköping, on its way south towards Helsingborg. The E22 runs along the coast, leaving the E4 at Norrköping and continuing via Västervik and Kalmar to Malmö. The larger towns, both on the coast and inland, can be reached by train, but local buses or a car will be needed to visit places in the countryside. There are domestic flights to all major cities.

SEE ALSO

- ***Where to Stay*** pp284–285
- ***Where to Eat*** pp301–302

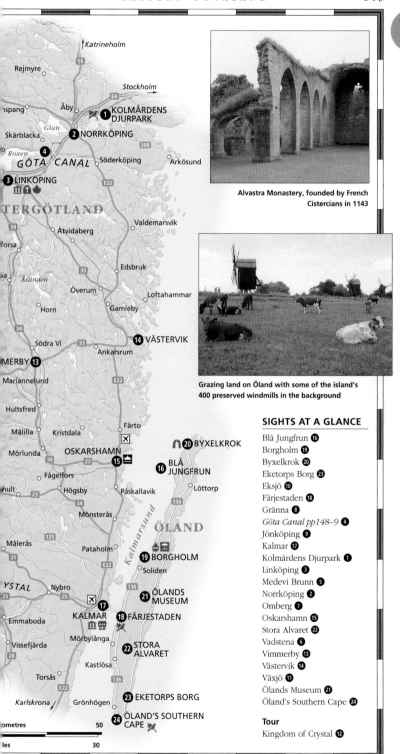

Alvastra Monastery, founded by French
Cistercians in 1143

Grazing land on Öland with some of the island's
400 preserved windmills in the background

SIGHTS AT A GLANCE

Blå Jungfrun **16**
Borgholm **19**
Byxelkrok **20**
Eketorps Borg **23**
Eksjö **10**
Färjestaden **18**
Gränna **8**
Göta Canal pp148–9 **4**
Jönköping **9**
Kalmar **17**
Kolmårdens Djurpark **1**
Linköping **3**
Medevi Brunn **5**
Norrköping **2**
Omberg **7**
Oskarshamn **15**
Stora Alvaret **22**
Vadstena **6**
Vimmerby **13**
Västervik **14**
Växjö **11**
Ölands Museum **21**
Öland's Southern Cape **24**

Tour
Kingdom of Crystal **12**

Lion on the prowl in the Safari Park at Kolmårdens Djurpark

Kolmårdens Djurpark ❶

Östergötland. Junction from E4, 12 km (7 miles) N of Norrköping. 🚗 ℹ 011-24 90 00. ⬜ May: 10am–5pm daily; Jun–Aug: 10am–6pm daily; Sep: 10am–5pm Sat–Sun. 🎫 ✂ 🍴 🖥 ♿ 🛍 www.kolmarden.com

Kolmårdens Djurpark is no ordinary zoo, even the animal enclosures are large and attractively landscaped.

There is a drive-through Safari Park which brings visitors close to the creatures of the savannah who live here alongside Nordic species such as brown bears and wolves.

A Dolphinarium offers spectacular shows with trained dolphins. Snakes and crocodiles inhabit the outdoor Tropicarium, while the Aparium is designed so that the apes can be viewed indoors and out. Tiger World, offers a unique walk-through experience in close proximity to the big cats. A cable-car ride provides a bird's-eye view of the grounds.

There are a variety of accomodation options available for visitors including African tents on the savannah.

Norrköping ❷

Östergötland. E4. 🏠 128,000. 🚗 🚉 ℹ Dalsgatan 9, 011-15 50 00. 🎉 Norrköping International Horse Show (4th week in May), National Day Festival (first week in Jun). www.destination.norrkoping.se

In the 17th century the skills of entrepreneur Louis de Geer, combined with water power from the Motala Ström river

system, transformed Norrköping into Sweden's first industrial town. Norrköping and neighbouring Linköping make up Sweden's fourth largest urban region.

Although Norrköping is an industrial town, the mix of old and new buildings, parks and trams make it an attractive place to visit. On a small island in Motala Ström sits **Arbetets Museum** (Museum of Labour), in an old spinning mill known as Strykjärnet (the Iron).

Environs
The area has a long history of habitation - around 1,650 carvings, some dating back to 1000 BC, can be seen at **Himmelstalund** on the edge of town. About 10 km (6 miles) south of Norrköping on the E4 is the 17th-century **Löfstad Slott** with its beautiful English-style park. The castle remains as it was in 1926 on the death of the owner, Emelie Piper.

🏛 **Arbetets Museum**
Laxholmen. *Tel 011-18 98 00.* ⬜ daily. ⬛ public hols. 🎫 🍴 🛍 🖥

🏯 **Löfstad Slott**
10 km (6 miles) S of Norrköping. *Tel 011-33 50 67.* ⬜ Jun–Aug: daily; May: Sat, Sun, public holidays; Apr, Sep, Oct: Sun; Nov–Mar: phone for info. 🎫 🖥 🍴 🛍

Strykjärnet (the Iron) in Norrköping, housing Arbetets Museum

Linköping ❸

Östergötland. E4. 🏠 142,000. 🚉 🚗 ✈ ℹ Storgatan 15, 013-190 00 70. 🎉 Ekenäs Castle Tournament (Whitsun), Handicraft Festival and Folk Festival (4th week in Aug). www.visitlinkoping.se

The county capital and cathedral city of Linköping lies in the middle of the Östgöta plain. First populated 3,000 years ago, it is now Sweden's fifth largest city, and is known for its university and high-tech industry.

Construction of the **Domkyrkan** (Cathedral) started in the mid-13th century. The interior contains superb medieval stone carvings. The Renaissance altarpiece is by the Dutch painter M J Van Heemskerck (1498–1574).

The old town open-air museum, **Gamla Linköping**, is a collection of 80 buildings from the city and surrounding area. This charming setting, complete with picturesque wooden buildings, cobbled streets and gardens, is a window on a past way of life.

Malmen, site of Sweden's first military flying school (1911), is now home to the **Flygvapen-museum** (Swedish Air Force Museum). Exhibits include examples of Swedish military aircraft.

Environs
Kaga Kyrka, one of the region's best-preserved medieval churches, is located on the Svartån river south of Linköping. Dating from the 12th century, its walls are decorated with frescoes.

On Erlången lake, 10 km (6 miles) southeast of the centre, lies the castle of **Sturefors**, which is renowned for its 18th-century interiors and beautiful grounds. The castle is a private residence, but parts of the grounds are open to the public.

🔒 **Domkyrkan**
St Persgatan. *Tel 013-20 50 50, 20 50 57.* ⬜ daily. 🎫 phone for info. ♿ 🛍

🏠 **Gamla Linköping**
2 km (3 miles) west of the centre. *Tel 013-12 11 10.* ⬜ daily. 🖥 🛍 🍴

🏛 **Flygvapenmuseum**
4 km (3 miles) west of the centre.
Tel 013-28 35 67. ◻ *Sep–May:
Tue–Sun; Jun–Aug: daily.* 🅰
🅱 *phone for details.* 📷 🅱

Göta Canal ❹

See pp146–7.

Medevi Brunn ❺

Östergötland. Road 50. 🚃 🚌
🅸 *0141-911 00.* 🎺 *Grötlunken
marching band processions (Jun/Jul).*

In the 17th-century the
scientist and doctor Urban
Hjärne analyzed water from
the Medevi spring and
declared it to be "superior to
other medication". Thus began
the transformation of Medevi
Brunn into a health spa.
Today, the season at Medevi
starts at Midsummer and lasts
for seven weeks, during
which time the traditional
brass sextet Brunnsorkester
performs daily concerts.

South of Medevi, on the
edge of Lake Vättern, lies
Övralid, the former home of
poet and Nobel laureate
Verner von Heidenstam
(1859–1940). Designed by
Heidenstam himself, the
house has stunning views
across the lake.

🏯 **Övralid**
10 km (6 miles) N of Motala, Road
50. *Tel* 0141-22 05 56, 22 00 36.
◻ *15 May–31 Aug: daily.* 🅰
🅱 *10am–5pm on the hour.* 📷

**Medevi Brunn, the first health spa
in the Nordic countries**

Vadstena Slott, built in 1545 for protection against the Danes

Vadstena ❻

Östergötland. Road 50. 🏯 *5,700.*
🚃 🚌 🅸 *Castle, 0143-31571.* 🎪
*St Bridget Festival (3rd week in May),
Vadstena Academy Opera performances
(Jul).* **www**.vadstena.com

Situated on Lake Vättern,
Vadstena is dominated by the
abbey, which dates back to the
14th century and St Bridget,
and the mid-16th-century castle of the Vasa kings. Cobbled
streets, wooden buildings and
glorious gardens add to the
town's character.

The stately **Vadstena Slott**
was built in 1545 as a fortress
against the Danes and is
surrounded by a moat. As well
as being a museum, the castle
also hosts opera, theatre
performances and concerts.

The abbey area encompasses
the original abbey, Vadstena
Kloster, established in 1384 and
dissolved after the Reformation

in 1595, and **Vadstena
Klosterkyrka** (1430). This
abbey church houses the relics
of St Bridget and a life-like
wooden sculpture of the saint.
It is also the site of the Pax
Mariae convent, which was
founded in the 1980s and is
home to around ten nuns.

Environs
Less than 20 km (12 miles)
south of Vadstena towards
Skänninge is **Bjälbo Kyrka**, a
late-12th-century church.
Bjälbo is said to be the
birth-place of the founder of
Stockholm, Birger Jarl.

🏯 **Vadstena Slott**
100 m (110 yd) SW of the centre.
Tel 0143-31571. ◻ *Sep–May:
Mon–Fri; Jun–Aug: daily.* 🅱 *Jun–
Aug.* 📷 🅰

🛐 **Vadstena Klosterkyrka**
◻ *daily.* *Tel* 0143-31570, 0143-
298 50. 🅱 *Sun.* 🅱 *Jun–Aug.* 🅰

ST BRIDGET, SWEDEN'S PATRON SAINT

At the age of only 13, Bridget (c.1303–73) was married to
local dignitary Ulf Gudmarsson. She became lady of the
manor of Ulvåsa in Östergötland and the mother of eight
children. Even as a child, she had religious visions and as an
adult made pilgrimages to Santiago de Compostela in Spain
in 1341–2, Rome in 1349 and
Jerusalem in 1372–3.
Some of her visions also had
political themes and Bridget
became influential in the political
arena. In 1370 she gained the
Pope's permission to found a
monastic order, the Brigittine
Order. The first nuns were
ordained in 1384. Bridget died
on returning to Rome following
her pilgrimage to Jerusalem. Her
remains were taken to Vadstena
in 1374. Canonized in 1391,
Bridget is the patron saint of
Sweden, and in 1999 became the
patron saint of Europe.

**Sculpture of St Bridget in
Vadstena Klosterkyrka**

Göta Canal ❹

Opened in 1832, the Göta Canal provided a vital link for
transporting timber and iron between Stockholm
and Gothenburg. But it was another 100 years before
leisure traffic took off on the waterway. Today in
summer, the canal bustles with small craft and passenger
boats and it is possible to cruise the entire length on the
classic *M/S Diana* (1931), *Wilhelm Tham* (1912) and
Juno (1874). Other boats take passengers along shorter
stretches and there are numerous special packages
available, such as combining cycling holidays with canal
trips. There are guest marinas offering services along the
entire length of the canal. Motala is regarded as the
"capital" of the canal, and the man behind its construction, Baltzar von Platen (1766–1829), is buried here.

Building the Canal
*Karl XIV Johan inspects
construction near Berg in
Östergötland with Crown
Prince Oscar. Baltzar von
Platen is standing bare-
headed to the left of the king.*

Sjötorp on Lake Vänern
marks the end point of the
canal in Västergötland.

Karlskoga

Örebro

Örebro

Mariestad

202

E20

50

49

VÄTTERN

36

Boren

•Motala

32

50

**Karlsborgs
Fästning** *(see
p221)*, towers
above the canal.

Lock-keeper
*Several of the lock gates along the stretch
of canal which lies in Västergötland are
still worked by hand by friendly and
patient lock-keepers.*

KEY

▦	Motorway
▦	Other road
⌑⌑⌑	Canal

Borensberg
*The long-established Göta Hotell is an
idyllic summer spot on the canal.
Built in 1894, it offers food and
accommodation to passers-by.*

Bergs Slussar

The staircase of seven locks at Berg raises boats a total of 18 m (59 ft). The spectacle of opening the lock gates always attracts an audience.

The lake of Roxen is home to some 260 species of birds, including wetland species, as well as some rarer varieties.

Canal Boats

From May to August traditional white boats such as M/S Juno *ply the canal. Built in 1874,* Juno *is one of the oldest boats afloat with sleeping accommodation still in use.*

Mem is the first lock in the canal system on the journey west.

CLIMBING FROM THE BALTIC TO LAKE VÄNERN

"The Blue Band of Sweden" as the Göta Canal is known, is the high point of Swedish engineering history. It took 58,000 men, mainly soldiers, and 22 years to build a waterway across Sweden from the Baltic Sea to join the already completed Trollhättan Canal *(see p217)*, and provide a route through to the Kattegatt. The problem was not simply digging the canal, but coping with a difference in height of around 92 m (301 ft). Completing this mammoth project took more than just spades and advantage was taken of the latest technological innovations – dredgers, hoists, cranes, pile drivers, mortar mills and optical instruments. Most of the machinery was imported from England, but as the project grew, and with it the need for mechanical equipment, Baltzar von Platen eventually took the initiative to set up a factory in Motala where the mechanical equipment could be made or modified. The canal has 58 locks between Mem on the Baltic and Sjötorp on Lake Vänern.

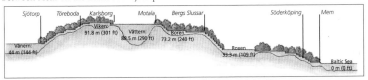

From Mem the canal begins its climb to reach the highest point between Lakes Vättern and Vänern

View over Lake Vättern from Hjässan, the highest point of Omberg

Omberg ❼

Östergötland. 20 km (12 miles) S of Vadstena. 🚗 🛈 *Naturum, Stocklycke, 0144-332 45.* ⬭ *call to check opening times.* 🎫 🚻
www.ostergotland.info

Rising mountain-like from the wide Östgöta plains is Omberg. Its highest point is 175 m (574 ft) above Lake Vättern. It is the legendary home of Queen Omma, whose name means "steam" and indeed the fog that often surrounds the hill gives it a mythical quality. Orchid marshes, beech woodlands and ancient forest flourish on the limestone-rich rock. Walking trails cross the area. To the south lies author Ellen Key's home, **Strand**, and the nature reserves of Bokskogen and Stora Lund. On the plains southeast of Omberg is the ruin of **Alvastra Kloster** where St Bridget *(see p145)* once stayed.

To the east, Omberg slopes down to Lake **Tåkern**, barely 1 m (3 ft) deep and favoured by flocks of geese and cranes in spring and autumn. The **Rökstenen** at Röks Kyrka is a large 9th-century runestone.

🏛 **Strand**
10 km (6 miles) N of Ödeshög. *Tel 0144-330 30.* ⬭ *15 Apr–Midsummer, mid-Aug–mid-Sep: Tue–Sun.* 🎫

Gränna ❽

Småland. E4. 👥 *2,600.* 🚌
🛈 *Brahegatan 38, 0390-410 10.*
🎭 *Andrée Festival (2nd week in Jul), County Festival (3rd week in Jul).*
www.grm.se

Gränna was at its height in the 17th century in the days of Count Per Brahe, who founded the town and whose plan is still evident today. On the square in the centre of town, **Grenna Museum** has fascinating tales to tell of the tragic expedition to the North Pole headed by the town's famous son Salomon August Andrée in the hot-air balloon *Örnen*. Inspired by Andrée, Gränna has become a centre for balloon flights. The town is also known for its *polkagris* (peppermint rock), an ideal souvenir. The red and white sweet originated in 1859 when widow Amalia Eriksson started a rock factory in the town.

Along the beautiful stretch of the E4 beside Lake Vättern, just north of Gränna, lies the ruined **Brahehus** castle, built for Count Per Brahe in the 1640s. On a clear day Brahehus offers magnificent views over Vättern towards Västergötland on the other side of the lake and **Visingsö**. This flat island can be reached by boat from Gränna. It is the largest island in Lake Vättern, 14 km (9 miles) long and 3 km (2 miles) wide with a population of 800. In the 12th and 13th

Polka-gris

centuries the island was the seat of Sweden's first kings, including Magnus Ladulås. Per Brahe built the castle, Visingsborgs Slott, now a ruin, and a church on the island in the 17th century. The boat trip from Gränna takes about 25 minutes and the service is frequent in the summer months.

🏛 **Grenna Museum**
Brahegatan 38–40. *Tel 0390-41015.* ⬭ *daily.* ⬤ *1 Jan, 24, 25, 31 Dec.* 🎫 🚻 ♿ 🅿 ♿

Jönköping ❾

Småland. E4. 👥 *125,000.* 🚗 🚌
🚄 🛈 *Railway station, 036-10 50 50.* 🎭 *Jönköping Market (end of May).* **www**.jonkoping.se/turist

King Magnus Ladulås granted Jönköping its charter in 1284, by which time the town was already an important trading centre. For a long time Småland formed Sweden's southern border with Denmark, but when the Danes invaded in 1612 the people set fire to their town and fled to Visingsö.

In the 19th century Jönköping became synonymous with matchstick production; the Lundström brothers opened their first factory in the 1840s. In the old part of town, **Tändsticksmuseet** (the Match Museum) is set in a former match factory (1848). The historic Västra Storgatan 37 houses **Viktor Rydbergs Museum**. Local history comes

The ruins of Brahehus Castle on Lake Vättern looking towards Visingsö

◁ **Kapelludden on the east of Öland, and the 13th-century ruins of St Bridget's chapel** under the spotlight at **Jönköpings Läns Museum**. The museum also has a display of work by the local artist John Bauer, as well as contemporary art.

Environs
Just outside Jönköping, **Hakarps Kyrka** is famous for its paintings by Edvard Orm. **Taberg**, south of Jönköping, is known as "the Alps of Småland" and is 343 m (1,125 ft) above sea level. The countryside is stunning, with extensive views over Lake Vättern. Sights include a mine and an industrial museum and there are hiking trails and overnight accommodation.

🏛 **Tändsticksmuseet**
Tändsticksgränd 27. **Tel** *036-10 55 43.* ⭘ *daily (Sep–May: Tue–Sat).* ⬤ *public hols & eves of public hols.* 🖼🎞🏛

🏛 **Jönköpings Läns Museum**
Dag Hammarskjölds Plats 2. **Tel** *036-30 18 00.* ⭘ *Tue–Sun.* 🖼 🎞🏛

Eksjö ⑩

Småland. Road 32/33. 🏛 *16,000.* 🚍 🚌 🚕 *Norra Storgatan 29, 0381-361 70.* 🏁 *Ränneslättsloppet Motocross Race (end Sep), Hussar Festival (mid-Jun).* **www**.eksjo.se

The small town of Eksjö, in the highlands of southern Sweden, is the country's most genuine wooden town. This was border country until the 17th century and Eksjö was burned down by its own people in conjunction with a Danish retreat. In the 1560s Erik XIV drew up a new town plan for Eksjö, which largely remains today. Gamla Stan (the Old Town) escaped the fire and its buildings remain intact and have been sympathetically renovated.

Environs
About 13 km (8 miles) east of Eksjö, the **Skurugata** nature reserve encompasses an impressive canyon in porphyritic rock, 800 m (2,625 ft) long and 35 m (115 ft) deep. From Eksjö to the neighbouring town of **Nässjö** is just over 20 km (12 miles). Nässjö owes its existence to

the coming of the railway in the 1860s. At that time the village had 57 inhabitants; today it has nearly 30,000 and the railway companies Statens Järnvägar and Banverket are still the main employers. Sights in Nässjö include **Järnvägsmuseum** (the Railway Museum) and Hembygds-parken with its woodlands and collection of 18th- and 19th-century buildings.

🏛 **Järnvägsmuseum**
Brogatan 10, Nässjö. **Tel** *0380-722 07.* ⭘ *Jun–Aug: 11am–3pm Tue–Sun.* 🖼

Växjö ⑪

Småland. Road 23/25/30. 🏛 *56,000.* 🚍 🚌 🚕 🚕 *Stadsbiblioteket Västra Esplanaden 7, 0470-414 10.* **www**.vaxjo.se

A bishopric as early as the 12th century, Växjö was granted its town charter by King Magnus Erikson in 1342. For some time the town lay on the border with Denmark and it was from here that Nils Dacke led his peasant revolt against the King of Sweden in the 16th century. Devastating fires, the most recent in 1843, destroyed the town, which has since been rebuilt. The cathedral dates originally from the end of the 12th century, but has been remodelled over

The twin steeples of Växjö's 12th-century cathedral

the centuries. It contains an altar-piece in glass and wood made in 2002 by the glass artist Bertil Vallien.

Smålands Museum, with Sveriges Glasmuseum (Glass Museum), depicts the history of the county of Kronoberg and the development of the glassworks. Next to it is **Utvandrarnas Hus**, which focuses on the mass emigration in the 19th century.

🏛 **Smålands Museum**
Södra Järnvägsgatan 2. **Tel** *0470-70 42 00.* ⭘ *Jun–Aug: daily; Sep–May: Tue–Sun.* ⬤ *public holidays.* 🖼 🎞🏛 🖥 ⬤

🏛 **Utvandrarnas Hus**
Vilhelm Mobergs Gata 4. **Tel** *0470-201 20.* ⭘ *Sep–Apr: Tue–Sat; May–Aug: daily.* 🖼 🎞🏛 🖥 ♿

EMIGRATION TO AMERICA
Disillusioned by poverty, religious intolerance and political discontent, many Swedes in the late 1860s dreamed of a better life in North America. Famine in Sweden, combined with the end of the Civil War in the fast expanding USA, prompted around 100,000 Swedes to emigrate in 1868–71, the majority from southern Sweden, particularly the barren lands of Småland. Another major wave followed in the 1880s when 350,000 people left Sweden.

Nobel Prize-winner Vilhelm Moberg's epic trilogy *The Emigrants* describes the tough life Swedish emigrants faced in their new land.

Emigration to the USA tailed off with the Depression of the 1930s, but by then 1.2 million Swedes had already left their homeland.

Emigrants on the Way to Gothen-burg, Geskel Saloman (1821–1902)

A Tour through the Kingdom of Crystal ⑫

Växjö, home to the Swedish Glass Museum, is an ideal starting point for a tour of at least nine of the famous glassworks set in the beautiful countryside between Växjö and Nybro. Access to timber and water accounts for the concentration of glassworks in this area of Småland, where forest, lakes and waterways dominate the landscape. The glassworks are mostly only 20–30 km (12–20 miles) apart, and many have shops offering discounted items and displays of the designers' latest creations.

Bergdala ①
Bergdala's signature is blue-edged glass, but designers are pushing the boundaries when it comes to colour and shape. The temperature of the smelting oven is a constant 1,150° C (2,102° F).

Kosta ③
The oldest glassworks, Kosta (1742), like Boda and Åfors, has attracted some of Sweden's foremost contemporary designers. Shown here is the entrance to the original office.

Strömbergshyttan ②
Studioglas was established in 1987 by three master glassblowers, who work with young designers to create groundbreaking works of art.

KEY

▬ Suggested route

═ Other roads

TIPS FOR DRIVERS

Length: Växjö–Nybro, road 25, approx. 85 km (53 miles). Well signposted.
Places to eat: Many glassworks have a café/restaurant and some of the larger ones hold herring evenings. Check opening times.

Åfors ④
Bertil Vallien, Ulrica Hydman-Vallien and upcoming artist Ludvig Löfgren work for the glassworks in Fina Stugan, one of the area's most exciting galleries. Glass eggs are by Ulrica Hydman-Vallien.

0 kilometres   10

0 miles   5

Orrefors ⑧
The glassworks was founded in 1898 and has become the flagship of Swedish glass-making, producing functional, decorative items and *objets d'art*. The work of Orrefors over the years is on show in its museum.

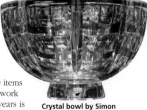

Crystal bowl by Simon Gate (1883–1945)

Målerås ⑨
The employees bought this glassworks from Kosta in 1981. It is famous for its crystal animal reliefs by glass artist and master etcher Mats Jonasson.

Pukeberg ⑦
The glassworks was founded in 1871. Extensive production in this beautiful old setting has mainly been focused on lighting and domestic glassware using traditional methods.

① Målerås
③¹
Hälleberga
Orrefors ⑧
³¹
Hermanstorp
⑥ Boda
²⁵
Nybro
²⁵
Örsjö
⑦ Pukeberg
KALMAR
hansfors
¹²⁰
mmaboda
KARLSKRONA

Johansfors ⑤
This glassworks is known as the Eden of the Kingdom of Crystal, symbolized by Christopher Ramsey's *Astrakhan Apple*. Glass-blowing is demonstrated daily and there is a museum.

Boda ⑥
The traditional Boda glassworks has been converted into a Kosta Boda factory shop, museum and exhibition area with a special focus on local artist Erik Höglund.

Vimmerby ⑬

Småland. Road 33/34. 🚶 *9,000.* 🚌
🚉 ⓘ *Rådhuset 1, 0492-310 10.*
🎭 *Holiday Race (2nd week in Jul).*

The small town of Vimmerby began as a marketplace on the "King's Road" between Stockholm and Kalmar. It was strategically important and constantly fought over by the Danes, who burned it to the ground on many occasions. Few old buildings remain, but along Storgatan there is the austere Neo-Classical-style Rådhuset (Town Hall) from the 1820s. Like the houses of Tenngjutar-gården and Grankvistgården, it is one of Vimmerby's historical monuments.

For many years Vimmerby has been associated with Astrid Lindgren *(see p87)*, who was born in Näs and set many of her popular children's books in this area. All her beloved characters can be encountered in **Astrid Lindgrens Värld** (Astrid Lindgren's World). The park also includes the Astrid Lindgren Centre with an exhibition about the author's life and work.

Environs
Norra Kvill National Park, 20 km (12 miles) northwest of Vimmerby, is an area of virgin forest in the highlands of Småland containing pine trees over 350 years old. The park slopes down to a small lake, Stora Idegölen, with waterlilies and bogbean.

🎭 **Astrid Lindgrens Värld**
Fabriksgatan. *Tel 0492-798 00.*
🕐 *15 May– end of Aug: daily.*
🅿️ 🚻 🛝 🍴 🎁 🍽️
www.alv.se

Miniature house in Astrid Lindgrens Värld, Vimmerby

Picturesque red cottages on Båtsmansgränd in Västervik

Västervik ⑭

Småland. E22. 👥 21,000. 🚊 🚌
✕ 🛈 Strömsholmen, 0490-254
040. 🎵 Song Festival (Jul).
www.vastervik.com

Strategically sited at the
mouth of Gamlebyviken Bay,
Västervik was the subject of
frequent Danish attacks,
despite protection from the
once mighty fortress of
Stegeholm. The last attack in
1677 destroyed the town.
Rebuilt, it became a major
seafaring centre. The area
known as Gamla Norr
contains the oldest preserved
houses in Västervik, including
Aspagården and the former
poor-house, Cederflychtska
Huset. **Kulbackens Museum**
outlines the history of the
town. Part of the museum is
in the open air with a nature
exhibition and traditional
buildings. The railway line
was closed in 1984, but train
enthusiasts have reopened the
70-km (43-mile) stretch from
Västervik to Hultfred, to preserve it as part of Sweden's
industrial heritage.

The annual Folk Festival
first took place in 1966 and
has since grown to become a
major event. It is held in the
ruins of Stegeholm fortress.

Lunds By, just outside
Västervik, is the region's
oldest and best preserved
village, comprising eight small
red cottages around a square.
It was chosen as a location to
film Astrid Lindgren's book
The Bullerby Children.

🏛 **Västerviks Museum**
Kulbacken. **Tel** 0490-211 77.
🕐 Jun–Aug: daily; Sep–May:
Mon–Fri, Sun. 🗐 🎟 🖼

Oskarshamn ⑮

Småland. E22. 👥 18,000. 🚊 🚌
🛈 Hantverksgatan 18, 0491-881 88.
🎟 Oskarshamn Harbour Festival (end
Jul). www.oskarshamn.se

King Oskar I gave his name
to this town, previously
known as Döderhultsvik,
which gained its charter in
1856. It grew up around the
harbour and today is still an
important place with a lively
seafaring industry. The old
areas of Besväret and Fnyket
have wooden 19th-century
houses and are ideal for
exploring on foot. There are
great views over the water
and the island Blå Jungfrun
from Långa Soffan, an extra-
ordinarily long 72-m (79-yd)
bench built close to the
harbour in 1867.

Oskarshamn has several
museums. On show at
Döderhultarmuseet are the
original wooden figures by
sculptor Axel Petersson, also
known as "Döderhultarn",
together with a description of
his life in late-19th-century
Småland. **Oskarshamns
Sjöfartsmuseum** (Maritime
Museum) has a
superb collection
of local mari-
time history.

An expressive carved wooden figure by
"Döderhultarn" Axel Petersson (1865–1925)

Environs
Stensjö By is a cultural
museum showing how a
village looked in the 18th
century. Just under 40 km (25
miles) west of Oskarshamn at
Högsby there is the **Bråbygden**
nature reserve and a permanent exhibition about film star
Greta Garbo, whose mother
came from here. Children and
adults enjoy the toy museum,
Nostalgia, in Fågelfors, where
visitors can see but not touch
2,000 toys from the past.

🏛 **Döderhultarmuseet**
Hantverksgatan 18. **Tel** 0491-880
40. 🕐 Jun–Aug: daily; Sep–May:
Mon–Sat. 🌑 until Jun 2011. 🖼
pre-book. 🗐 🗐 🖼 🛗

🏛 **Oskarshamns
Sjöfartsmuseum**
Hantverksgatan 18. **Tel** 0491-880
45. 🕐 Tue–Sun. 🎟 pre-book. 🗐
🗐 🖼 🛗

🏛 **Nostalgia**
Bruksgatan 43, Fågelfors, 40 km (25
miles) W of Oskarshamn. **Tel** 070-
304 18 63. 🕐 end Jun–first week
in Sep: Tue–Sun. 🖼

Blå Jungfrun ⑯

Småland. 20 km (12 miles) E of
Oskarshamn. 🚢 from Oskarshamn
& Byxelkrok. 🛈 Oskarshamn Tourist
Office, 0491-881 88.

In the northern part of
Kalmarsund, the sound
separating the mainland from
the island of Öland, the
national park Blå Jungfrun
(the Blue Maiden) encom-
passes an island about 800 m
(875 yd) in diameter and the
waters surrounding it. Blå
Jungfrun's highest point is
86 m (282 ft) above sea level,
making it easily visible from
the mainland and from Öland.

According to legend, the
island is the site of Blåkulla,
home of the witches, and is
the subject of many a dark
tale. Carl von Linné
(see p128) described it
as "horrible". Others
have found it romantic,
including the poet Verner
von Heidenstam, who
was married here in
1896. The island is
mainly bare pink
granite, polished
smooth by ice and

Medieval Kalmar Slott, a beautifully preserved castle rebuilt in Renaissance style in the 16th century

water, with deciduous forest in the south and a population of black guillemots. It is unlikely that it was inhabited, although a stone labyrinth was built here and there are caves. Boats run from Oskarshamn or Byxelkrok (see p156) to Blå Jungfrun, once a day, weather permitting. The journey takes 90 minutes from Oskarshamn with a three-and-a-half-hour stay on the island.

Kalmar ⑰

Småland. E22. 🚶 35,000. 🚌 🚗 🛩
ℹ️ Ölandskajen 9, 0480-41 77 00.
🎭 Kalmar Market (3rd week in Jul),
Medieval Market in Salvestaden (3rd
week in Jul). www.kalmar.se

Founded in the 12th century, Kalmar's key position on Kalmarsund made it a flourishing trading post as well as a target for Danish attack. To prevent the latter, **Kalmar Slott** was built in 1200 and it was here in the castle that the Kalmar Union was formed in 1397, binding the Scandinavian kingdoms for 130 years (see p33). In 1523 Gustav Vasa gained control of Kalmar and fortified the town.

Today, the magnificent Renaissance castle has been restored and contains furnished apartments and exhibitions. With its twisting streets and 17th and 18th-century buildings, the area around the castle, Gamla Stan (Old Town), is made for walking. Next to the castle is **Kalmar Konstmuseum** (Art Museum) showing Swedish art.

The Italian Baroque **Domkyrkan** (cathedral) on the island of Kvarnholmen dates from the second half of the 17th century and was

designed by Tessin the Elder. In front of it is the square Stortorget, restored to its original austere appearance. Kvarnholmen is also home to **Kalmar Läns Museum** with the man-of-war *Kronan* and out on "Kattrumpan" **Kalmar Sjöfartsmuseum**, featuring 5,000 maritime exhibits.

Environs
Ölandsbron, the bridge across Kalmarsund, opened in 1972 and provided a major boost for tourism to Öland. The bridge is 6,072 m (19,921 ft) long, 13 m (43 ft) wide and a sight in its own right. Nearly 35 km (22 miles) north of Kalmar on the coast is the idyllic village of **Pataholm**, a shipbuilding and seafaring community dating from the Middle Ages, with well-preserved historic buildings and cobbled streets.

🏰 Kalmar Slott
Kungsgatan 1. **Tel** 0480-45 14 90
⏰ Apr–Sep: daily; other times: 2nd
weekend in the month. 🎫 🏛 📷 🍴

🏛 Kalmar Konstmuseum
Slottsvägen 1D. **Tel** 0480-42 62 82.
⏰ daily. ⏰ some public hols.
🎫 pre-book. 🏛 📷

🏛 Kalmar Läns Museum
Skeppsbrogatan 51. **Tel** 0480-45 13
00. ⏰ daily. ⏰ some public hols.
🎫 pre-book. 🏛 📷 📹

Färjestaden ⑱

Öland. Road 136. 🚶 4,500. 🚌 ℹ️
Turistvägen, 0485-56 06 00.
🎭 Victoria Day (14 Jul).

The Ölandsbron Bridge connects Färjestaden on Öland with the mainland. Since the bridge's arrival in the 1970s, Färjestaden has more or less become a suburb of Kalmar. The first turning to

the north in Färjestaden leads to **Ölands Djurpark**, a popular destination for families. The zoo has 200 species of animals, a water world and amusement park, circus and theatre performances.

Beijershamn, south of Färjestaden, is an interesting reed-covered birdwatching area with wetland and archipelago species. Not far from here is **Karlevistenen**, a remarkable 11th-century runestone dedicated to a hero named Sibbe the Wise.

Vickleby village street, on road 136 to the south, is the epitome of idyllic Öland. Next to the church is Capellagården School of Craft and Design, founded by furniture designer Carl Malmsten in the 1950s and currently a centre for various design-related courses. The school exhibits and sells students' work.

East of Färjestaden, in the forest, is the Iron Age fort of **Gråborg** with the medieval ruins of St Knut's chapel just outside it.

🎠 Ölands Djurpark
3 km (2 miles) N of Färjestaden.
Tel 0485-392 22, info 0485-308
73. ⏰ early May–Sep: 10am–4pm
daily. 🎫 📷 🏛 📹 🍴

A gigantic clown at the entrance to Ölands Djurpark

Solliden, the king's summer residence, whose park is open to the public

Borgholm ⑲

Öland. Road 136. 🏛 *3,200.* 🚌
ℹ️ *Sandgatan 25, 0485-890 00.*
🎪 *Victoria Day 14 Jul.*

In summer Borgholm town
centre bustles with shoppers
and boats fill the guest
harbour. Borgholm became a
seaside resort at the end of
the 19th century and some of
the older buildings still have
their ornamented wooden
verandas where gentlemen
enjoyed their coffee and
punsch at the beginning of
the last century.

Dominating the town is
Borgholms Slottsruin, a
vast ruined medieval castle
with an eventful historical
past. There is a museum
inside. Guides recount
the history of the ruins
and offer special tours for
children in summer.
Also in summer, the castle
stage is a popular venue for
concerts.

Environs
Just south of the centre lies
Sollidens Slott, the summer
residence of the Swedish
royal family, completed in
1906. On 14 July each year,
the birthday of Crown Princess
Victoria is celebrated here with
various events. Exhibitions
are held in the pavilion and
there is a palace gift shop.

Störlinge Kvarnrad, a row
of seven windmills on the
eastern coast road, is just a
sample of the 400 windmills
still standing on the island.
There are around 150 km (93
miles) of beaches around
Borgholm, two of the best
being Köpingsvik and Böda.

🏛 **Borgholms Slottsruin**
1 km (half a mile) S of Borgholm.
Tel *0485-123 33.* ⏰ *Apr–Sep:
daily; Oct–Mar: by appointment.* 🎫
🔲 🚻 🛍️ 🅿️ 🔓

🏰 **Solliden**
1.5 km (1 mile) S of Borgholm.
Tel *0485-153 56.* ⏰ *mid-May–
mid-Sep: daily.* 🎫 🚻 🛍️ 🔲

Byxelkrok ⑳

Öland. Road 136. 🏛 *200.* 🚌
ℹ️ *Öland Tourist Information, 0485-
560 600.*

Almost at the northernmost
end of Öland's west coast on
Kalmarsund is the popular
old fishing village of Byxelkrok. Boats to Blå Jungfrun
(see p154) depart from here.

About 5 km (3 miles) to the
north is **Neptuni Åkrar**, an
area of ridged stones resembling ploughed fields with
several ancient monuments,
including the Iron Age stone
ship Forgalla-skeppet.

Löttorp, the largest town in
northern Öland, is home to a
paradise for car-mad children
– **Lådbilslandet** (Boxcar
Country), Glabo Gocart. Here
youngsters can race round

the 6-km (4-mile) course in
motorized vehicles, attend
driving school or enjoy
the playground.

Böda, 10 km (6 miles)
north of Löttorp, has wonderful sandy beaches. It is also
the site of **Skäftekärr
Järnåldersby**, a reconstructed
Iron Age village. Complete
with goods, animals, houses
and people, it provides a
fascinating insight into Iron
Age life.

The village also has an
arboretum featuring a
collection of *Thuja
occidentalis* planted in the
late 19th century.

🚗 **Lådbilslandet**
40 km (25 miles) N of Borgholm.
Tel *0485-203 35.* ⏰ *mid-Jun–mid
Aug: daily.* 🎫 📷 🔲 🔓

🏛 **Skäftekärr Järnåldersby**
50 km (31 miles) N of Borgholm.
Tel *0485-221 11.* ⏰ *end Jun–Aug:
daily; other times: call to check.* 🎫
🔲 📷 🔓

Ölands Museum ㉑

Öland. 20 km (12 miles) NE of Färjestaden. 🚌 ℹ️ *0485-56 10 22.* ⏰
*May–Aug: 10am–5.30pm daily; Sep:
11am–5pm weekends.* 🎫 🔲 📷 🔓

Himmelsberga, in the centre
of the island, is home to
Ölands Museum, an open-air
museum of art and cultural
history. It centres around a
well-preserved linear village
with 18th- and 19th-century
farms. The interiors of the
houses show how life was
once lived, and pigs, chickens
and sheep are kept in the
grounds. A shop sells crafts
and books about Öland. Next
to the museum is a gallery
showing work by local artists.

North of Himmelsberga,
Gärdslösa Kyrka is one
of the most interesting
churches on Öland. It
dates from the mid-13th
century and has
excellent limestone
murals, a beautiful
votive ship and a 17th-
century pulpit.

The fort of
Ismantorps Borg in
Långlöt has been dated
to the 5th century.
Archaeological finds

The island Blå Jungfrun *(see p154)* seen
from Byxelkrok harbour

show that it was probably an important marketplace and cult site. It is encircled by a wall up to 6 m (19 ft) thick and 3 m (10 ft) high with nine gates.

Öland's best preserved row of windmills can be seen in Lerkaka, just to the south of Himmelsberga. The interesting **Lerkaka Linmuseum** shows how linen is made.

🏛 **Lerkaka Linmuseum**
25 km (16 miles) NE of Färjestaden.
Tel 0485-56 20 90.
◯ Midsummer–Aug: daily.

Stora Alvaret ㉒

Öland. 🚌 ℹ️ *Ölands Turist,*
0485-56 06 00.

The extraordinary limestone plain of Stora Alvaret dominates southern Öland. Here, the bedrock is around 400 million years old and is covered in a thin layer of soil that was used from prehistoric times as grazing land. In the year 2000 the area was declared a UNESCO World Heritage Site.

In spring the ground is covered in pasque flowers (*Pulsatilla pratensis*). The dominant species include meadow oat-grass (*Helictotrichon pratense*), sheep's fescue (*Festuca ovina*) and a moss species, *kalkbackmossa* (*Homalothecium lutescens*). Juniper bushes are common and lichen inches over bare rock.

The extreme climate has created almost desert-like conditions to which the flora and fauna have had to adapt. Mountain and Mediterranean plants grow here as well as a unique species of rock-rose (*Helianthemum oelandicum*). The island is a resting place for cranes, but conditions on the plain are so harsh that only a few birds, such as the skylark and wheatear, have succeeded in adapting to the environment.

Eketorps Borg ㉓

Öland. 🚌 ℹ️ 0485-66 20 00.
◯ May–Sep: 11am–5pm daily (late Jun–mid-Aug: 10am–6pm daily).
🎭 Midsummer's Eve. 🎪 Iron Age Festival (first week in Aug). 📷
www.kalmarlansmuseum.se/eketorp

The only one of Öland's ancient forts to have been completely excavated, Eketorps Borg was built in three stages. It originated in the 4th century to protect the population and was later converted into a fortified farming village with military functions, but was abandoned in the 7th century. It was thrust into use again at the end of the 12th century in the war between the royal houses of Erik and Sverker.

The fort has been partly reconstructed to show how people lived and worked in the Iron Age. In the museum the numerous artifacts uncovered on the site are on display, including jewellery and weapons.

Around 10 km (6 miles) north of Eketorp lies **Seby Gravfält** with no fewer than 285 visible ancient monuments in the form of different kinds of burial sites, mainly dating from the Iron Age.

Look out for hedgehogs, a threatened species

Långe Jan at Öland's Southern Cape, Sweden's tallest lighthouse

Öland's Southern Cape ㉔

Öland. 🚌 ℹ️ *Ottenby Naturum,*
0485-66 12 00 (Jun–Aug: daily). 📷

In the mid-16th century the area around Öland's southern cape became a royal hunting ground and even today descendants of the fallow deer introduced by Johan III in 1569 can be spotted. The northern boundary of his land is marked by Karl X's wall, built in the 1650s to prevent local people and their animals from entering the grounds. To the south, Sweden's oldest and tallest lighthouse, **Långe Jan**, stands to attention, 41.6 m (136 ft) high, and offers amazing views.

At the southernmost tip of the island is a nature reserve, Ottenby Naturum, and **Ottenby Fågelstation** (the bird station). Ornithologists come here to study migratory birds close up and conduct research. The station has several bird-related exhibitions and offers guided tours around the nature reserve.

🦅 **Ottenby Fågelstation**
Öland's Southern Cape. *Tel* 0485-66 10 93. ◯ Mar–Oct: daily. 📷
Set guided bird tours mid-Mar–mid-Nov. 📷 🖥

The mighty walls of Eketorps Borg, a partly reconstructed Iron Age fort

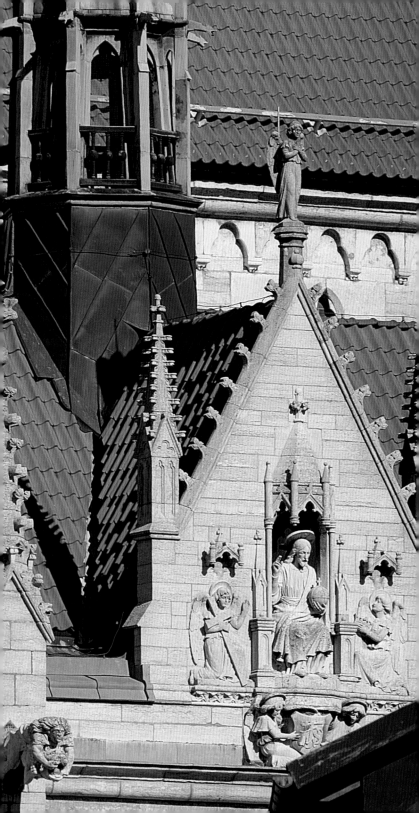

GOTLAND

*S*weden's largest island, Gotland is a popular holiday destination, favoured for its mild climate, sandy beaches, distinctive landscape and beautiful walled town of Visby. It is known as the "Pearl of the Baltic". The island's strategic position made it an important trading centre especially in the Middle Ages. Gotland celebrates its heritage with enthusiasm in the annual Visby Medieval Week.

In geological terms, Gotland is fairly old. It consists of layers of rocks which were deposited in a tropical sea during the Silurian period around 400 million years ago. Fossils can still be found washed up along the shore. At the northern and southernmost tips of the island, the limestone comes to the surface and plant life is sparse. In the centre of the island forest dominates. The high limestone cliffs with their large bird population are broken by sandy beaches beloved by sun-worshippers, and standing offshore are numerous extraordinary sea stacks, known as *raukar*.

The long, warm autumns and mild winters allow trees such as walnut and apricot to survive in sheltered spots. No less than 35 different orchids can be found on the island and the flower meadows which blossom at Midsummer are typical of Gotland. The island's fauna lacks the large mammals of the mainland. The odd fallow deer is probably an escapee from an enclosure, but there is a herd of *russ*, Gotland's little wild ponies, as well as foxes and wild rabbits.

A wealth of archaeological finds have been uncovered on the island, from the ship burials of the Bronze Age to the silver treasure of the Viking period. More than 90 medieval churches dot the landscape and the museums have numerous artifacts from the Hanseatic period and the Danish King Valdemar Atterdag's capture of Visby in 1361. Visby itself is a UNESCO World Heritage Site.

Gotlanders have their own dialect, *Gutamål*, and their own traditions. These are especially reflected in the games of the annual Gotland Olympics and in the Medieval Week in Visby *(see p27)*, a 21st-century recreation of the Middle Ages with tournaments, jesters and fair maidens.

Hoburgen in southern Gotland, a 35-m (115-ft) high limestone cliff containing red "Hoburg" marble

◁ Domkyrkan Sta Maria dating from 1225, the only one of Visby's ancient churches which is not in ruins

Exploring Gotland

A visit to Gotland naturally begins in Visby, where the ferry terminal and airport are located. To experience this unusual part of Sweden it is best to strike out into the countryside and discover the exceptional landscape with its distinctive flora, long sandy beaches, curious limestone sea stacks and multitude of medieval churches. Hiring a bike and cycling round Gotland is a popular way of seeing the island. There are almost no hills and car-free country lanes constantly lead to new hideaways. There is plenty of bed-and-breakfast accommodation and the island has many good campsites for those with tents or caravans. Bookings should be made well in advance for the month of July.

A ruined medieval church towering above the Visby rooftops

SIGHTS AT A GLANCE

Bro Kyrka ⑥
Bunge ②
Fårö ①
Fröjel Kyrka ⑪
Gotska Sandön ⑮
Hoburgen ⑭
Karlsöarna ⑫
Ljugarn ⑨
Lojsta ⑩
Lummelundagrottan ⑤
Petes ⑬
Roma ⑧
Slite ③
Tingstäde ④
Visby pp164–7 ⑦

KEY

═══ Motorway

──── Major road

═══ Minor road

Kappelshamn

Irevik 149

Lärbro

LUMMELUNDA-GROTTAN ⑤

TINGSTÄDE ④

149   148

SLITE

⑥ BRO KYRKA

147

⑦ VISBY   ○ *Vatlings Gård*

Hogklint   Åminne

143

Gnisvard 140   ⑧ ROMA   146

Tofta Strand   Ang

GOTLAND   Katthamma

Klintehamn   *Torshurgen*

143

Lojsta Hed

Lilla Karlsö

KARLSÖARNA ⑫   FRÖJEL KYRKA ⑪ 141   ⑩ LOJSTA ⑨ LJUGARN

144

Stora Karlsö   ○ Stånga

142

Hemse ○   När ○

140

PETES ⑬   ○ Ronehamn

○ Havdhemn

○ Kattlunds

142

Burgsvik

○ Faludden

○ Vändburg

⑭ HOBURGEN

0 kilometres

0 miles   10

Fårö ①

Gotland. 🏠 600. 🚌 📋 Mar–Sep: at Fårö church 0498-22 40 22; Oct–Feb: Visby Tourist Office, 0498-20 17 00. **www**.gotland.info

A summer paradise for visitors from the mainland and further afield, Fårö appears exotic even to a Gotlander from the main island. Lying at the northern tip of Gotland, the little island of Fårö has a language and traditions all of its own. During the summer car ferries shuttle back and forth on the 15-minute trip from Fårösund to Broa. At other times of year the service is more limited.

Sparse, low pine forest and moorland with swamp and marshland cover the island. There are sheep everywhere. Off the main road between Broa and Fårö lighthouse there are plenty of cattle grids, which prevent the sheep from straying.

Off the northwest coast are the spectacular limestone stacks, known as *raukar*, of Langhammars and Diger-huvud. The sand dune of Ullahau is at the northern end of the island, and Sudersand's long sandy beach is popular with holiday-makers. The easternmost cape of Holmudden is topped by the 30-m (98-ft) high lighthouse, Fårö Fyr. Roughly in the centre of the island, **Fårö Kyrka** offers stunning views over the inlet of Kyrkviken. The church contains votive paintings dating from 1618 and 1767, depicting seal hunters miraculously being rescued from the sea.

Sheep in front of a typical Gotland farmhouse, today a tempting renovation project for incomers from the mainland

GETTING AROUND

The most common way to get to Gotland is by ferry or fast catamaran, either from Nynäshamn or Oskarshamn. In summer there are several crossings a day to Visby. Another option is to arrive by air on one of the daily flights from Stockholm, Norrköping or Nyköping. On Gotland, the only means of public transport is the bus. Services outside Visby are infrequent with perhaps just one morning and one afternoon bus, making a car or a bike a necessity for getting around. Bicycles can be hired at the ferry terminal and elsewhere around the island.

🏛 **Fårö Kyrka**
5 km (3 miles) N of Broa. **Tel** 0498-22 10 74. ◻ Jun–Aug: daily; Sep–May: Sat & Sun. 🏛 🎫 by appointment.

"The coffee pot", an eroded limestone stack on Fårö's coast

…he of Gotland's many long sandy beaches attracting hundreds of …ousands of visitors to the island every summer

Bunge ❷

Gotland. Road 148. 🏛 *900.* 🚍
🛈 *Fårösund, 0498-22 11 12.*
🎪 *Tournament (2nd week in Jul).*

The village of Bunge is renowned for its 14th-century church **Bunge Kyrka**, built in Gothic style. Its tower was constructed in the 13th century to defend an earlier church – holes from pikes and arrows in the north wall bear witness to past battles.

Inside are beautiful limestone paintings dating from around 1400, which are thought to depict the Teutonic Knights fighting the Vitalien brothers, pirates of Mecklenburg who occupied Gotland in the 1390s. In the chancel is a poor box in limestone signed by stone-mason Lafrans Botvidarson. Like the font, it dates from the 13th century.

8th-century picture stone, Bungemuseet

Next to the church is **Bungemuseet**, one of Sweden's largest rural museums. It was created in 1917 by Bunge schoolteacher Theodor Erlandsson, who wanted to show how the people of Gotland used to live. In the fields next to the school he gathered together cottages, buildings and cultural objects from different parts of Gotland covering the 17th, 18th and 19th centuries as well as four carved stones from the 8th century. The museum hosts many events in the summer, including medieval tournaments, markets and handicraft festivals. In Snäckersstugan cottage, with the date 1700 carved into the gable, visitors can enjoy a cup of coffee and attempt to make out the Gotland proverbs painted on the ceiling.

Just north of Bunge is the busy **Fårösund**, one of the larger towns in northern Gotland with around 1,000 inhabitants. For many years the area was dominated by the military and countless young men were drilled here in defence of the island. Since the coastal artillery unit was disbanded in 2000 with the loss of many jobs, the area risks going into decline.

🏛 **Bunge Kyrka**
60 km (37 miles) N of Visby.
***Tel** 0498-22 10 74 (Tue & Fri).* 🕐 *mid-Jun–Aug: daily.* 🕇 *every other Sun.*

🏛 **Bungemuseet**
2 km (1 mile) E of Bunge. ***Tel** 0498-22 10 18.* 🕐 *Jun–Sep: daily.* 🖼 *ring for appointment.* 📷 🅿 🛈

Slite ❸

Gotland. Road 147 🏛 *1,500.* 🚍
🚢 🛈 *Gotlands Tourist Information Centre, 0498-20 17 00.* 🎪 *Golf round Gotland (2nd week in May).*

Occupying a stunning setting in a bay facing its own archipelago is the town of Slite. It is the second largest community in Gotland. Slite had a long and troubled history from the Viking

Majestic limestone stack at Kyllaj, Slite Bay

period onwards, and development only really took off in the late 19th century with an upturn in seafaring. Today the town is dominated by a cement factory.

In summer, the fine sandy beaches, harbour, tennis courts, stunning stone stacks and lime kiln attract holiday-makers. The islands offshore are perfect for short trips, including Enholmen with Karlsvärd fortress, which dates from 1853–6.

Environs
On the opposite side of the bay is Hellvi, with the delightful old harbour of **Kyllaj**. The quiet beach is in a beautiful setting overlooking weathered sea stacks. Strandridaregården, the 18th-century coastguard's house, now belongs to Bungemuseet.

Northwest of Slite is **Lärbro Kyrka**, a mid-13th century church with an 11th-century watch tower next to it. In the churchyard are buried 44 of the former prisoners of war who came from the German concentration camps to the hospital at Lärbro in 1945.

St Olofsholm, nearby, is dedicated to Olav the Holy who visited Gotland in 1029 to convert the island to Christianity. In medieval times it was a place of pilgrimage. This is also the site of Ytterholmen's large group of limestone stacks and a glorious pebble beach.

🏛 **Lärbro Kyrka**
10 km (6 miles) N of Slite. ***Tel** 0498-22 51 25.* 🕐 *15 May–30 Sep: daily.* 🕇 *every other Sun.* 📷 🅿 🛈 ♿

Buildings at Bungemuseet with thatched roofs of Gotland sedge

Tingstäde ❹

23 km (14 miles) N of Visby. 🚶 280.
🚌 🏛 Gotland Tourist Information
Centre, 0498-20 17 00.
🌿 Nature trail with lady's slipper in
flower (early Jun).

Halfway between Visby and
Fårösund on road 148 lies
Tingstäde, a community
best-known for its sea rescue
radio station and its marsh.
The church dating from the
13th and 14th centuries has
one of the highest towers
on the island.

Tingstäde marsh is, in fact,
a shallow lake and popular,
child-friendly bathing spot.
Submerged in the centre of
the lake is Bulverket, a
10th–11th-century fortress
surrounded by a palisade of
1,500 stakes.

Lummelunda-
grottan ❺

Road 149, 13 km (8 miles) N of Visby.
🚌 🏛 1 May–Sep: 0498-27 30 50,
other times ring to book.
📷 obligatory. Cave adventure must
be pre-booked. ♿ 🎒 🅿 🛒

In 1948 two local school
boys discovered an opening
in the ground in Martebo
marsh and crawled in. They
had explored upon the
entrance to a giant network of
caves and passageways, now
Gotland's main tourist
attraction. Today the entrance
is at Lummelundas Bruk.
Exploration of the caves
continues, but the part which
is open for viewing provides
a fantastic show of stalactites
and stalagmites, magic mirrors
of water and spine-tinglingly
tight openings. The geological

museum, Silurum, is
located at the entrance.

Immediately to the
south of the caves is
Krusmyntagården, a
herb garden designed
in traditional monastic
style with wonderful
views over the sea.

🌿 **Krusmyntagården**
Road 149, 10 km (6 miles)
N of Visby. **Tel** 0498-29 69
00. 🕐 Jun–Aug: daily. 📷
🅿 🍴 🛒

Bro Kyrka ❻

Road 148, 11 km (7 miles) NE of
Visby. 🚌 **Tel** 0498-27 27 55,
070-25 92 070. 🕐 Apr–Oct: 8.30am–
7pm daily. ✝ every other Sun.

Tradition has it that Bro
Kyrka is built over a votive
well and in medieval times it
was a famous votive church,
particularly among sailors. The
building dates from the 13th
and 14th centuries. Inside, the
prayer chamber contains
5th-century picture stones.

About 1 km (half a mile)
north of Bro Kyrka, on road
148, are two picture stones
known as "Bro Stajnkällingar".
According to legend, two
elderly women were turned to
stone for arguing on the way
to the Christmas Mass.

From Bro, a turning leads to
Fole church on road 147, and
a short detour takes you to
Vatlings Gård. The estate has
Gotland's best-preserved
medieval stone house outside
Visby and is well worth a visit.

🏠 **Vatlings Gård**
Road 147, 18 km 18 km (11 miles)
E of Visby.
🕐 daily. **Tel** 0498-29 27 00.

**Roma Kungsgård, built in 1733 using
materials from Roma Kloster**

Visby ❼

See pp164–7.

Roma ❽

18 km (11 miles) SE of Visby. 🚌
🏛 Roma Kungsgård: 0498-500 43.
🕐 10am–4pm daily.

Cistercian monks from
Nydala monastery in
Småland founded **Roma
Kloster** in 1164. The
monastery was built on the
pattern of the French mother
monastery and became a
religious centre for the entire
Baltic region. The three-aisle
church in the Fontenay style
was completed in the 13th
century. The monastery was
abandoned during the
Reformation in 1530 and
ended up in the ownership of
the Danish crown as a royal
manor under Visborg Castle.

When Gotland came under
Swedish rule in 1645, the
monastery was practically in
ruins. The county governor
used materials from the site to
build his residence, **Roma
Kungsgård**, in 1733. Only the
church remained intact, and
that was used as a stable. In
1822, Roma Kungsgård was
rented to the crown and
served as an army store.

The ruins of Roma
monastery are a popular
tourist attraction. Even today
they bear witness to the
monks' skill in construction
techniques. The beautiful
vaulted ceilings are reminiscent of Roman aqueducts.

In the summer, Romateatern
performs Shakespearian plays
on an open-air stage set
among the ruins.

A painting on wood in Bro Kyrka showing Adam and Eve in paradise

Street-by-Street: Visby ⑦

Sign for Gamla Apoteket

A town of roses and ruins, the walled city of Visby is a UNESCO World Heritage Site as well as a popular party town in summer, when it fills up with holiday-makers from the mainland. Its cobbled streets are lined with picturesque cottages, haunting medieval ruins and a multitude of cafés and bars. Away from the busy, more touristy parts of Strandgatan, Stora Torget and around the pleasure boat harbour, the evocative ambience recalls the town's medieval history *(see p167)*. This is also evident from the imposing town wall and its many towers, including Kruttornet (the Gunpowder Tower).

Konstmuseet
Visby Town Wall *by Hanna Pauli (1864–1940) is on display in the Museum of Art.*

★ Gotlands Museum
The Historical Museum is devoted to Gotland's past from ancient times to modern day. The Science Centre and Natural History Museum are in the same building.

Burmeisterska Huset
Hans Burmeister, a wealthy merchant from Lübeck, built this house in the 17th century. It is one of the best-preserved examples of its kind in Visby.

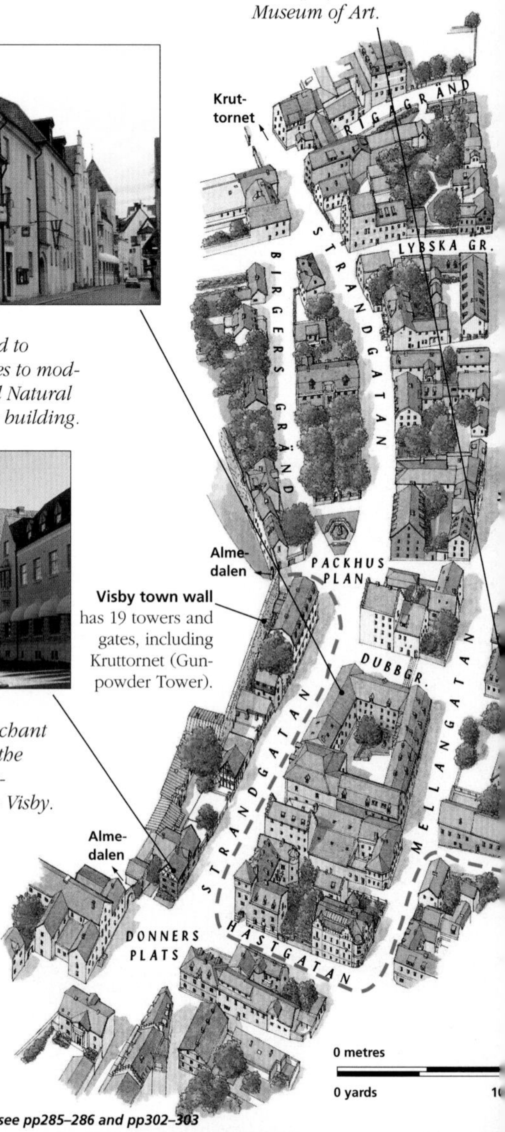

Visby town wall has 19 towers and gates, including Kruttornet (Gunpowder Tower).

KEY

– – – Suggested route

STAR SIGHTS

★ Domkyrkan Sta Maria

★ Gotlands Museum

0 metres

0 yards

Kapitelhusgården
In this leafy medieval courtyard setting, the public can try their hand at medieval crafts. During the summer, it can become busy, especially during Medieval Week.

aniska
lgården

St Drotten, the sister church to St Lars.

VISITORS' CHECKLIST

Gotland. 🏘 22,000. ✈ 🚢 ✕
🛥 ℹ Gotlands Tourist Information Centre, Skeppsbron 4–6, 0498-20 17 00. 🎭 Midsummer Week (Jun), Medieval Week (early Aug), Gotland Chamber Music Festival (Jul), Visby Day (first Sat in Oct), Gotland Grand National (first weekend in Nov).
www.gotland.info

★ Domkyrkan Sta Maria
Completed in 1225, the cathedral was the church of the German merchants. It is the only one of Visby's 17 medieval churches which is not in ruins.

St Lars, also known as the church of Sta Anna after the mother of the Virgin Mary.

STORA TORGET

Söderport

Around Stora Torget
Entertainment focuses on the main square, Stora Torget. Munkkällaren, with a terrace on the square, is one of the many restaurants and bars here.

Ruins of Sta Karin (St Catherine's) Church
Franciscan monks built the church and monastery of Sta Karin in 1233. Dominicans rebuilt it in the 14th century. But in 1525 was destroyed by an army from Lübeck.

Exploring Visby

Within the walls, Visby is relatively small and all the sights are within easy walking distance. The main streets run north to south: Strandgatan with historic sights and nightlife spots, St Hansgatan with its many churches, and Adelsgatan, the shopping street leading from Söderport (South Gate) to Stora Torget, the main square. North of here are quieter residential streets and alleyways, making for a lovely stroll. Near Norderport (North Gate) it is possible to climb up on the ramparts and admire the magnificent wall.

VISBY TOWN CENTRE

☐ Street-by-Street: Visby, see pp164–5

Medieval vaulted street in Visby, a UNESCO World Heritage Site

The Heart of the Town

The medieval inner town of Visby is shaped by its mighty town wall, almost 3.5 km (2 miles) in length. Construction of the wall began at the end of the 13th century. It was originally 5.5 m (18 ft) high and designed to protect against attack from the sea. On the inland side, the wall was surrounded by a deep moat. Within the ramparts, narrow cobbled streets are lined with tightly-packed houses, wealthy merchants' homes and the ruins of historic churches. UNESCO described the town as the "best fortified commercial city in northern Europe" and declared it a World Heritage Site in 1995.

Just outside the wall is Almedalen, the former site of the Hanseatic harbour. Today the area is a park. South of Almedalen is Visby marina, which throngs with boats, especially during Medieval Week in August.

🏛 Around Stora Torget

At the heart of Visby lies Stora Torget (Big Square) from which the roads to the town gates radiate. This is still a focal point for visitors to Visby, despite the development of a modern town centre outside Österport, and there is a lively market here in summer. Several medieval houses surround the square, including the restaurants of Gutekällaren, with its characteristic stepped gable, and Munkkällaren, with its deep vaulted cellars and inner courtyard.

The ruins of the church of Sta Karin (St Catherine), dating from the 1230s, form a dramatic backdrop on the southern side of Stora Torget. In the shadow of the ruins is Rosengård, a café where generations have ordered coffee and delicious pastries.

🏛 Gotlands Museum

Strandgatan 14. **Tel** 0498-29 27 00. ☐ 15 May–14 Sep: daily; 15 Sep–14 May: Tue–Sun. 🅿 📷 🖵 🏛 ⛔ www.lansmuseetgotland.se
Gotland's long history going back to prehistoric times has made this collection one of Sweden's richest regional museums. It is housed in a former royal distillery, built in the 1770s.

The Hall of Picture Stones contains an impressive array of carved stones from the 5th–11th centuries, some of which feature runic inscriptions. Next door, the Gravkammaren (Grave Room) shows burial customs from ancient times to the Vikings. Several skeletons are on display, including the 8,000-years-old Stenkyrkamannen (Stenkyrka Man). One of the most remarkable sights is the collection of Viking silver treasure – no fewer than 700 items have been recovered from sites around the island.

Church art is well represented. The museum holds the original, Gothic Öja Madonna (Öja church in southern Gotland has to make do with a copy). A large gallery displays medieval furniture, as well as collections from later periods.

The museum also houses Fenomenalen, a hands-on science centre.

Picture stones from the 5th–11th centuries in Gotlands Museum

Visby's medieval town wall, approximately 3.5 km (2 miles) long and up to 5.5 m (18 ft) high

🏛 Ruins of St Nicolai

St Nicolaigatan. **Tel** *Visby Tourist Office 0498-20 17 00.*

The ruins of St Nicolai are all that remains of a Dominican monastery founded in Visby in 1228. The Black Friars expanded it and built a Gothic cathedral which they dedicated to the patron saint of sailors and merchants, St Nicholas. When the people of Lübeck stormed Visby in 1525 much of the cathedral was destroyed.

Between 1929 and 1990 a pageant, *Petrus de Dacia*, was performed here every summer. This Gotlander was a famous mystic and author, and prior of the Dominican monastery at the end of the 13th century. Today, musical and theatrical events are staged in the ruins and the Gotland Chamber Music Festival is usually held here each summer. The audience sit protected from wind and weather by the remaining part of the roof.

🏛 Ruins of Helge And

Helge Ands Plan. 🛈 *Gotlands Länsmuseum 0498-29 27 00.*

Helgeandstiftelserna was a religious order founded during the early 13th century to take care of the poor and the sick. The ruin of Helge And (Church of the Holy Spirit) is one of Visby's most remarkable church ruins and dates from this period. The octagonal building has two floors opening onto a choir. Two large staircases lead up to the first floor. It was designed in this way to allow patients from the hospital to reach the church via a passage from the upper floor. Today the ruins are used for cultural events and are open to visitors during the summer.

🦋 Botaniska Trädgården

Visby. **Tel** *0498-21 83 87.* ⬜ *24 hrs daily.* ◉ *Nights in Medieval Week.*

Gotland's Botanical Garden was founded in 1856 by the Badande Wännerna (Society of the Bathing Friends), a gentlemen's club formed in 1814 to work for the benefit of the public. The society also established Gotland's first school and set up its first bank. To reach the garden, follow the promenade along the shore from the harbour and go through Kärleksporten (Gate of Love) in the north-west corner of the town wall.

Inside the gate, the lush park offers a spice-scented herb garden and a pretty rose garden (at its peak Jul–Aug). There are over 16,000 species including many plants and trees that are exotic to the Nordic countries, such as walnut, mulberry and ginkgo. In its midst stand the ivy-clad ruins of St Olof's church and there is a water-lily pond and a small pavilion making an ideal resting place.

VISBY'S EARLY HISTORY

Archaeological finds, including Roman, Arabic and Russian coins, show that Gotland had a lively foreign trade already in Viking times. At the end of the 12th century, trade with Germany took off and the Hanseatic League was formed – a mercantile and political association between German merchants and towns around the North Sea and the Baltic. The League was centred on Visby and the town enjoyed a boom in the 13th century with people coming from all around to settle here. Towards the end of the century a trading-political power struggle on Gotland led to internal strife and the gradual decline of Visby. Poor harvests and the Black Death contributed to the decline, as did the introduction of large ships capable of travelling longer distances. In 1361 Visby was captured by Valdemar Atterdag and Gotland succumbed to Danish rule. Then in 1525 Visby was plundered by its rival Hanseatic town, Lübeck, and buildings were destroyed or abandoned.

Valdemar Atterdag pillaging Visby in 1361

The small community of Ljugarn with typical Gotland limestone houses close to the sea

flourishing port and limeworks. In the early 1800s lime baron Axel Hägg bought Katthamra manor, which he had rebuilt and decorated in Empire style. Today there is a hotel and youth hostel here, but the manor house itself is a private home.

Ljugarn ❾

40 km (25 miles) SW of Visby.
🚶 295. 🚌 🛈 Visby Tourist Office, 0498-20 17 00.

This cheerful resort was Gotland's first and makes a good centre for touring the southeast of the island. There was a harbour here long before Russian forces raided Ljugarn on their way to laying waste to the east coast of Sweden in 1714–18. By 1900, the small community, with its long sandy beach, limestone sea stacks and guesthouse, had become a popular bathing spot.

South of Ljugarn is the 13th–14th century **Lau Kyrka**. One of Gotland's largest churches, it has a triumphal crucifix from the 13th century and excellent acoustics for the concerts held there.

Northwest of Ljugarn, **Torsburgen** fortress was built in the 3rd or 4th century and is one of the largest of its kind in Scandinavia. It is protected by naturally steep slopes and a wall 7 m (23 ft) high and up to 24 m (79 ft) wide. To reach it, take the forest road from the 146 towards Östergarn, 2 km (1 mile) east of Kräklingbo church.

About 6 km (4 miles) south of Ljugarn, at **Guffride**, are seven Bronze Age stone-settings, in the form of ships, and are the largest on Gotland. Open to tourists is the 11th Century Church of Garde, southwest of Ljugarn. The Church features paintings in the Byzantine style.

The idyllic **Katthammarsvik**, north of Ljugarn, was once a

Lojsta ❿

15 km (9 miles) S of Visby.
🚶 120. 🚌 🛈 Visby Tourist Office, 0498-20 17 00. 🐴 Gotland pony judging (4th week in Jul).

Like so many of Gotland's churches, **Lojsta Kyrka** dates from the mid-13th century. The choir and the nave have ornamental paintings and the figures above the triumphal arch are by the master known as "Egypticus" in the mid-14th century.

On **Lojsta Hed**, an area of forest and heath north of the church, lives a herd of semi-wild Gotland ponies *(russ)*, the stubborn little horse native to the island. The animals are owned by local farmers and by Gotlands Läns Hushållningssällskap. Several annual events are organized, such as the release of the stallion in early June, and the high point of the year, the Gotland pony judging at the end of July.

About 2.5 km (2 miles) from Lojsta towards Etelhem is a large building with a sedge roof, **Lojstahallen**. This is an excellent reconstruction of a late-Iron Age hall building. Next to it is a medieval fortress, Lojsta Slott.

Fröjel Kyrka ⓫

40 km (25 miles) S of Visby. 🚌
Tel 0498-24 00 05, 070-51 71 38.
🕐 daily. 🕆 every 3rd Sun. 🎨 ♿

In a stunning location, high up overlooking the sea, is the saddle-roof church of Fröjel Kyrka, built in the 12th and 13th centuries. Inside is an impressive triumphal crucifix by the craftsman who created the rood screen of Öja church. The churchyard has an ancient maze which shows that the site was used long before the arrival of Christianity.

North of the church lies the magnificent **Gannarve Skeppssättning** (Gannarve Ship Barrow), which is considered to be one of the best in Gotland. This has been dated to the late Bronze Age (1000–300 BC) and is 30 m (98 ft) long and 5 m (16 ft) wide.

The splendid Gannarve Bronze Age stone ship barrow

Karlsöarna ⓬

Gotland. **Stora Karlsö** ⛴ from Klintehamn. 🛈 Visby Tourist Office, 0498-20 17 00. 🎨 🚌 ⅋ **Lilla Karlsö** ⛴ from Klintehamn. 🛈 0498-48 52 48, summer: 0498-24 11 39. 🎨

Many myths have been spun around Stora and Lilla Karlsö, the rocky islands 6.5 km (4 miles) off the west coast of Gotland.

Stora Karlsö covers 2.5 sq km (1 sq mile) and is a nature reserve with steep cliffs, caves such as "Stora Förvar",

Bird islands Lilla Karlsön (left) and Stora Karlsön seen from Gotland

moorland, leafy groves, and rare flowers and birds. Here, between the bare rocks in May and June, the orchids *Adam och Eva (Dactylorhiza sambucina)* and *Sankt Pers nycklar (Orchis mascula)* form carpets of blooms. Sea birds such as auks, gulls and eider duck can be seen. Razorbills lay their eggs among the stones on the beach, while guillemots prefer the shelves of the steep cliffs.

A guided tour takes a couple of hours and is included in the price of the boat crossing. There is also a museum in Norderhamn.

Like Stora Karlsö, **Lilla Karlsö** is also a nature reserve. The island has been grazed by sheep since the Bronze Age. It is home to guillemots, razorbills, cormorants and gulls. Eider duck, little terns, Sandwich terns and velvet scoters nest on the flat land. The Swedish Society for Nature Conservation organizes guided tours. There is a youth hostel on the island – book in advance.

Petes Museigård, typical 18th- and 19th-century Gotland houses

Petes ⑬

Gotland. 🖼 🛈 *Länsmuseet på Gotland, 0498-29 27 00.* ⬜ *Mid-Jun–Aug: 11am–5pm, daily.*

To the southwest of Gotland, just before Hablingbo church on coastal road 140, there is a turning to the seaside community of Petes. Here, the well-preserved houses show Gotland's architecture from the 18th and 19th centuries.

For younger visitors, **Barnens Petes** displays classic toys such as stilts, hobby horses, hoops, wooden rifles and wooden dolls.

The unbroken sandy beaches of Gotska Sandön

Hoburgen ⑭

80 km (50 miles) S of Visby. 🚌

Far to the south lies Hoburgen, a 35-m (115-ft) high steep cliff of fossil-rich limestone with seams of the local red Hoburgen marble. On the clifftop is a lighthouse built in 1846. From here it is 176 km (97 miles) to the northernmost lighthouse on the island of Fårö.

Below the lighthouse is Sweden's most famous sea stack, Hoburgsgubben (the Old Man of Hoburg), guarding the caves of Skattkammaren (the Treasure Chamber) and Sängkammaren (the Bed Chamber).

Hoburgen is a favourite spot for ornithologists who come to study the multitude of birds which swoop over Gotland's southernmost outpost all year round. In summer there is a restaurant nearby.

Profile of Hoburgsgubben, the "Old Man of Hoburg"

Gotska Sandön ⑮

🛈 *Visby Tourist Office, 0498-20 17 00; booking: 0498-24 04 50.* ⬜ *from Nynäshamn and Fårösund.*

Just 40 km (25 miles) north of Fårö lies the most isolated island in the Baltic, Gotska Sandön. It is one of Sweden's national parks and features a unique landscape of deserted, constantly changing sandy beaches and dunes, pine forests and a rich flora. There are migratory birds, unusual beetles, but only one mammal, the hare. The island became a national park in 1909.

Gotska Sandön has been inhabited since the dawn of civilization, although the population has never been large. Colonies of grey seals led seal hunters to settle on the island and the dangerous waters offshore attracted wreck plunderers. In the 17th and 18th centuries sheep were grazed here and later crops were grown. As recently as the 1950s a few lighthouse keepers and their families (and one female teacher) lived here, but now the lighthouse is automated and the only permanent resident is a caretaker.

There is no harbour and boat traffic from Fårösund or Nynäshamn is infrequent and dependent on the weather. It is possible to camp or stay in a shared sleeping hut or cottage. Accommodation must be booked before arrival.

SOUTHERN GOTALAND

*S*weden's two southernmost provinces, Skåne and Blekinge, together form Southern Götaland, with the country's third largest city, Malmö, as the region's main town and gateway to Europe. The gentle, undulating landscape retains its Danish atmosphere from times past. Castles and medieval and Viking sites abound, and the historic naval port of Karlskrona is a UNESCO World Heritage Site.

The province of Skåne has an undeserved reputation for being completely flat, but apart from the plain of Söderslätt the countryside is surprisingly hilly with the rocky ridges of Söderåsen, Linderödsåsen and Romeleåsen dividing the region. To the northwest, the area is bounded by the imposing Hallandsåsen ridge.

The province of Blekinge, crisscrossed by rivers and lakes, is known as the Garden of Sweden. It has its own island archipelago with sheltered harbours beloved by sailors. North, towards the border with Småland, the slightly wild forest landscape predominates.

Throughout Southern Götaland the Danish influence prior to 1645 *(see p35)* is still evident, not least in the architecture, which differs greatly from elsewhere in Sweden. A common sight in rural Skåne is the traditional, often half-timbered farmhouse with a thatched roof, built around a cobbled courtyard. Castles and manor houses, in many cases built by the Danish nobility, are a feature of the countryside. In the coastal communities, former fishing huts are today cherished by their summer residents.

Southern Götaland differs from the rest of Sweden in atmosphere, too. The people of Skåne are known for being relaxed and for loving good food – and in large quantities – something which has lent this part of the country its inn culture, which has its equivalent in the Danish *kroen* just across Öresund.

Having been sparring partners in the long-distant past, Sweden and Denmark are now linked by the Öresund Bridge from Malmö to Copehhagen. Both sides of the sound are now collaborating over the creation of a visionary new Swedish-Danish region, Örestad.

Ales Stenar, a stone ship on Skåne's south coast, thought to be a late Viking grave or cult site

◁ Traditional thatched-roof farmhouse in Östarp, built in 1811 and set around a courtyard

Exploring Southern Götaland

As well as arable fields and willow windbreaks, this southernmost part of Sweden has its share of gently rolling hills, forests and lakes. The region is ideal for cycling through the country from village to village, discovering manor houses and castles along the way, walking through nature reserves or along the Skåneleden trail, canoeing, fishing, swimming in the many small lakes and rivers, driving, or sailing along the coast and putting into shore at fishing harbours on tiny islands. Towns such as Lund and Malmö offer a wealth of history, best discovered on foot, Karlskrona is renowned for its naval port and maritime past, and Trelleborg has a reconstructed Viking fortress.

Spiral beech trees in Trollskogen forest, Torna Hällestad

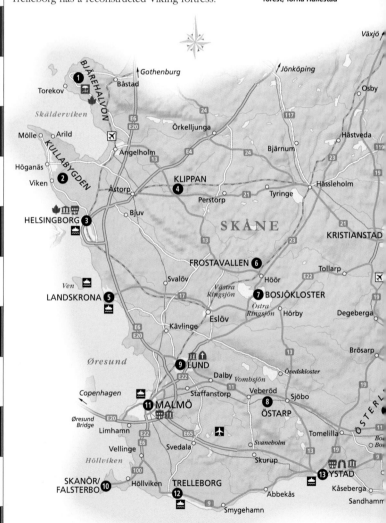

IGHTS AT A GLANCE

järehalvön 1
osjökloster 7
rostavallen 6
Ielsingborg 3
arlshamn 17
arlskrona pp188–9 20
lippan 4
ristianopel 19
ristianstad 15
ullabygden 2
andskrona 5
Lund 9
Malmö pp178–81 11
Ronneby 18
Skanör/Falsterbo 10
Sölvesborg 16
Trelleborg 12
Ystad 13
Östarp 8

Tour

Österlen 14

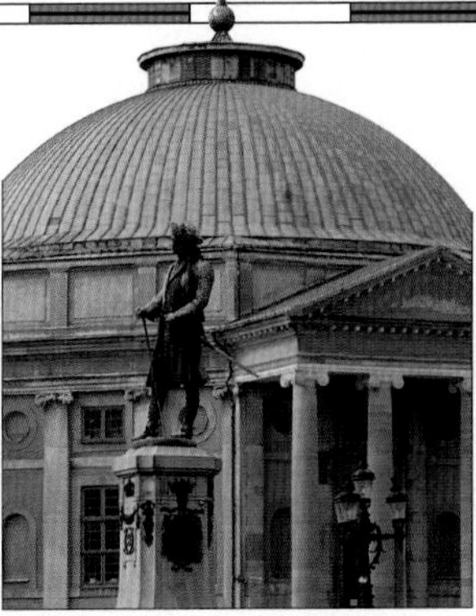

Statue of the founder of Karlskrona, Karl XI, in front of Trefaldighetskyrkan

0 kilometres 30

0 miles 20

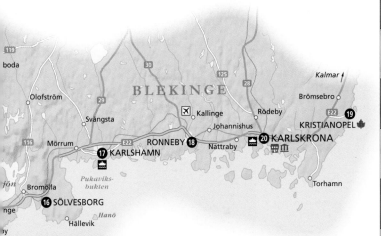

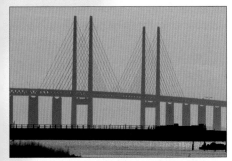

The 8-km (5-mile) long Öresund Bridge, completed in 2000, linking Sweden with Denmark and Continental Europe

KEY

- Motorway
- Major road
- Minor road
- Main railway
- Minor railway

GETTING AROUND

The E20 motorway across the Öresund Bridge from Continental Europe joins the E6, E22 and E65 south of Malmö and continues north to Helsingborg where it meets the E4 to Stockholm. The region has several airports and there are train connections to the large towns. Local commuter trains serve districts around the major cities. Ferries from Germany operate to Trelleborg and Ystad and there are frequent ferries from Denmark to Helsingborg.

SEE ALSO

- ***Where to Stay*** pp286–287
- ***Where to Eat*** pp303–304

Hovs Hallar, a nature reserve on the bay of Laholmsbukten

Bjärehalvön ❶

Skåne. Road 105. 🚗 🚌 ✕ 🛈
Båstad Tourist Office 0431-750 45,
Torekov Tourist Office 0431-36 31 80.
🎵 *Båstad Chamber Music Festival*
(4th week in Jun), Båstad tennis
(Jun/Jul). **www**.bastad.com

Several popular resorts
surround the peninsula of
Bjärehalvön, between the bays
of Skälderviken and Laholmsbukten. The medieval town
of **Båstad** is now best known
for hosting the annual Swedish
Open tennis tournament, but it
also has beautiful old houses
and glorious beaches. Just
over 10 km (6 miles) to the
west is the old fishing village
of **Torekov**. Boat trips run
from Torekov to the nature
reserve **Hallands Väderö**, a
remnant of the Hallandsåsen
ridge now left 3 km (2 miles)
out to sea. Of special note is
the alder marsh.

On the northern cape of the
peninsula is **Hovs Hallar**, a
geologically interesting area
with dramatic rocks and caves.
The area is a nature reserve
popular with birdwatchers and
walkers. Hovs Hallar is the
westernmost end of the
Hallandsåsen ridge, which
forms the border between the
Bjärehalvön peninsula and
Halland *(see p207)*. With its
meadows and varied flora, the
ridge is ideal for walking.

West of Båstad along the
coast is **Norrvikens
Trädgårdar**, a paradise for
garden lovers created by
architect Rudolf Abelin in the
early 20th century. There are

Fruit trees in blossom at Norrvikens
Trädgårdar gardens

several different gardens,
including a Baroque garden
and a Japanese garden.

The town of **Ängelholm**,
nestling between the
Bjärehalvön and Kullahalvön
peninsulas at the end of the
bay of Skälderviken, has a
sandy beach 6 km (4 miles)
long. Historically, Ängelholm
was known for its pottery
industry and today clay
cuckoos, the town's symbol,
are made here.

♣ **Norrvikens Trädgårdar**
5 km (3 miles) W of Båstad.
Tel 0431-36 90 40. ◯ *May–Aug:*
daily. 🅿️ 🎁 🛈

Kullabygden ❷

Skåne. Road 111/112. 🚌 🚍 🛈
Centralgatan 20, Höganäs, 042-33 77
74. 🎵 *Music in Kullabygden (2nd*
week in Jul), Kulla Market in Jonstorp
(first week in Jul).

The beautiful Kullen Peninsula has been inhabited
since the Iron and Bronze
Ages. Today, the pretty
medieval fishing villages of
Arild, Mölle, Höganäs and
Viken have become popular
seaside resorts. Höganäs is
best known for its ceramics.

Just outside Arild lies
Brunnby Kyrka, parts of
which are 12th-century. The
church contains impressive
ceiling paintings. **Krapperups
Slott**, north of Höganäs, dates
from the mid-16th century; the
castle houses an art gallery
and museum.

🏰 **Krapperups Slott**
7 km (4 miles) N of Höganäs. *Tel 042-*
34 41 90. **Castle** ◯ *by appointment.*
Gallery & museum ◯ *late-Apr–May:*
Fri–Sun; Jun–Jul: daily; Aug: Tue–Sun;
selected days in Dec. 🎁 🛈 🅿️

Helsingborg ❸

Skåne. E4. 🏘 *128,000.* ✕ 🚌 🚍
🚢 🛈 *Kungsgatan 11, 042-10 43*
50. 🎵 *Helsingborg Festival (late Jul),*
Horse Festival (last weekend in Jul);
Antiques Fair (end of Jul).
www.helsingborg.se

Known as the "Pearl of the
Sound", Helsingborg is a
lively town, spectacularly

TYCHO BRAHE

Astronomer Tycho Brahe was born in Skåne in 1546 into a
Danish noble family. At the age of 13 he was sent to
university in Copenhagen to study philosophy and went on
to study at several German universities. Inspired by an
eclipse of the sun in 1560, he took up astronomy. He
believed that the old methods of measurement to determine
the position of the planets were not sufficiently exact and
designed a new system. In 1572 he observed
a new bright star in the constellation
Cassiopeia. His discoveries in astronomy
paved the way for a new view of the
universe. In recognition, the Danish
king granted Brahe the island of Ven,
where he had an observatory built
(see p175) which became the finest
in Europe. Following a difference
of opinion with the Danish court,
Brahe went into exile and settled
in Prague where he died in
Prague in 1601.

Statue of Tycho Brahe in
St Ibbs Kyrka on Ven island

located on the shores of the Öresund within sight of the Danish coast. The town's strategic position at the narrowest point of the sound led to a stormy history, and the 34-m (111-ft) tower **Kärnan** is all that remains of its 12th-century fortress. The brick tower of the town hall (1897) also features on the skyline. It was designed by architect Alfred Hellerström and contains glass paintings by Gustav Cederström.

Jacob Hansen's half-timbered house, built in 1641, is the oldest house in Helsingborg. The new **Dunkers Kulturhus**, by Danish architect Kim Utzon, encompasses a museum, art gallery and theatre under one roof.

The open-air **Fredriksdal Friluftsmuseum** displays historical buildings from the region and has a botanical garden containing the wild plants of Skåne.

Environs
Ramlösa Brunn, 5 km (3 miles) southeast of Helsingborg, is known for its spring water, discovered in the late 19th century and now on offer in the Water Pavilion.

The castle of **Sofiero** was bequeathed to Helsingborg municipality by Gustav VI Adolf. The park is particularly famous for its Royal Gardens containing more than 300 varieties of rhododendron.

🏰 **Kärnan**
Slottshagen. *Tel 042-10 59 91.*
🕐 *Jun–Aug: daily.* 🎫

Helsingborg's recently renovated tower, Kärnan

Tycho Brahe's underground observatory on the island of Ven

🏛 **Dunkers Kulturhus**
Kungsgatan 11. *Tel 042-10 74 00.*
🕐 *Tue–Sun.* 🎫 💻 📷

🏛 **Fredriksdals Friluftsmuseum**
Gisela Trapps Vag. *Tel 042-10 45 00.* 🕐 *daily.* 🎫 💻 ♿

🌷 **Sofiero**
Sofierovägen, 5 km (3 miles) N of the centre. *Tel 042-10 25 00.* **Parken** 🕐 *Apr– Sep: daily.* 🎫 🍴 **Slottet** 🕐 *Jun–Aug: guided tours only.* 🎫 📷

Klippan ❹

Skåne. Road 21. 🚗 *8,000.* 🚌 🚆
🛈 *Storgatan 46, 0435-282 00.*
🎭 *Åby Market (3rd Tue–Wed in Jun), Ljungbyhed old-time market (3rd Fri–Sat in Aug).*

Located on the Söderåsen ridge, 30 km (19 miles) east of Helsingborg, Klippan is known for having Sweden's oldest operating paper mill, built in the 16th century.

There are many churches in the area worth a visit. Today only the sacristy remains of **Herrevadskloster**, a former Cistercian monastery founded in the 12th century. This has been restored and is used as a chapel. Art exhibitions are held here in the summer.

Söderåsen National Park offers leafy forests, dramatic screes, babbling brooks and breathtaking views from Kopparhatten and Hjortsprånget. The Skåneleden trail runs through the park.

The 17th-century mansion **Vrams Gunnarstorp**, 10 km (6 miles) west of Klippan, is built in the Dutch Renaissance style. The stunning park with its acclaimed hornbeam avenue is open to the public.

🏠 **Herrevadskloster**
10 km (6 miles) E of Klippan, road 13. *Tel 0435-44 19 90.* **Museum** 🕐 *daily.* 📷 *pre-book.* 🍴 💻 ♿ 📷

Landskrona ❺

Skåne. 🚗 *27,000.* 🚌 🚆 🛈 *Storgatan 36, 0418-47 30 00.* 🎭 *Vallåkraträffen Customized Car Festival (mid-Aug), Gardening Festival (Aug).*

The shipbuilding town of Landskrona was granted its charter in the 15th century. In 1549, the Danish king Christian III built the Citadel as protection against the Swedes. This substantial fortress surrounded by a moat dominates the town. Most of the sights can be found in the area around it, including **Landskrona Museum**, with its local history collection, and Konsthallen (Art Gallery) surrounded by a sculpture park.

Environs
In the sound between Sweden and Denmark lies the island of **Ven**, where Tycho Brahe set up his underground observatory, Stjärneborg, in the 1580s. The Tycho Brahe Museum features multimedia shows about the observatory.

There is a ruined castle on Ven, Uraniborg, and at the highest point of the island stands the medieval church of St Ibb. Steep Backafallen is the place for the most spectacular views.

The island can be reached by regular ferries from Landskrona all year round and by fishing boat from Råå during the summer.

🏛 **Landskrona Museum**
Slottsgatan. *Tel 0418-47 31 20.*
🕐 *noon–5pm daily.* ⚫ *Easter Saturday, Saturday before Whitsun, Midsummer Eve, 24, 25 & 31 Dec.*

🏝 **Ven**
In Öresund 7 km (4 miles) W of Landskrona. 🚢 *from Landskrona. Tel 0418-47 30 00, 0418-724 20.* **Tycho Brahe Museum** 🕐 *11 Apr–30 Sep: daily.* 📷 *pre-book.* 🎫 💻 ♿ 📷

Bosjökloster, originally an 11th-century Benedictine convent

Frostavallen ❻

Skåne. 3 km (2 miles) N of Höör on road 21. 🚉 to Höör. 🚌 🛈 *Höör Tourist Office, 0413-275 75.*

The beautiful countryside around Höör in central Skåne offers something for everyone, from hiking, canoeing and swimming to fishing from the shore or by boat on Vaxsjön lake. The availability of restaurants, cafés, hotels, cottages and campsites makes Frostavallen ideal for a day trip or a longer stay. There are playgrounds and all kinds of leisure equipment are available for hire.

Nearby is **Skånes Djurpark**, a zoo specializing in Nordic animals, which makes a popular excursion for children. It has more than 1,000 wild and domesticated Nordic animals. Watch lynx being fed or enjoy a pony ride.

A very different kind of experience is offered at **Höörs Stenåldersby**, where visitors can see for themselves what life was like in a Stone Age village. Flint-knapping and bow-making can be tried.

🐾 **Skånes Djurpark**
Frostavallen. *Tel 0413-55 30 60.* ⬜ *daily.* 🎫 🚻 🍴 ⬜ *summertime.* ♿

🏛 **Höörs Stenåldersby**
Next to Skånes Djurpark. *Tel 0413-55 32 70.* ⬜ *Jul by appointment.*

Bosjökloster ❼

Skåne. Road 23. *Tel 0413-250 48.* 🚌 ⬜ *May–1 Oct: 10.30am–5.30pm daily.* 🎫 🎫 ⬜ 🍴 **Park** ⬜ *May–Oct: 8am–8pm; other times: 10am–5pm.* 🎪 *Game Fair (last weekend in Aug).*

On a peninsula between the lakes of Östra and Västra Ringsjön lies one of Sweden's most remarkable houses. Bosjökloster was built around 1080 as a convent and soon became one of the wealthiest in Skåne. Rich families paid a great deal to secure a place for their daughters, often donating goods and land. This all came to an end with the Danish Reformation in 1536 and its possessions were transferred into private ownership.

In 1875–9 Bosjökloster was reconstructed to a design by architect Helgo Zettervall and became the prime example of his skill for renovating Swedish manors and palaces. In the early 20th century the property was bought by Count Philip Bonde and today it is owned by his grandson.

The family opened the house to the public in 1962 and is now it is one of the most popular stately homes in Skåne with parks and gardens, a restaurant, café, mini-zoo, boats for hire and fishing, too. The park features a 1,000-year-old oak tree. The oldest room in the house, Stensalen, is devoted to exhibitions of arts and crafts.

Östarp ❽

Skåne. Near road 11. 🚌 **Kulturens Östarp** *Tel 046-350 400.* ⬜ *May–Aug: 10am–5pm daily; Sep–Apr: noon–4pm Tue–Sun.* 🎫 🚻 🍴 **www**.kulturen.com

In the Middle Ages the town of Östarp was owned by a monastery. But it fell to the crown during the Reformation in the 16th century and was subsequently destroyed to make way for a manor house, which itself burned down. All that remained of the town was Östarps Gamlegård, built in 1812. This farmhouse was bought in 1923 by Kulturen in Lund, and today forms the centrepiece of the open-air Kulturens Östarp. It is a living museum using horses rather than machinery to farm the land. There is an excellent inn.

The countryside around Östarp is dotted with castles and stately homes, and Lake Vombsjön is a paradise for birdwatchers and fishermen alike. On the eastern shore of the lake is **Övedskloster**, a beautiful 18th-century manor house set in an elegant park. The property has been owned by the Ramel family since 1753. The main house, "Stora huset", is one of the most stunning Rococo-style houses in Sweden. It was designed by Carl Hårleman and completed in 1776. The park, modelled on Versailles, is open to the public in the summer. Surrounding the estate are woods and

The 18th-century windmill at Kulturens Östarp museum

Old buildings of Lund preserved by the open-air museum of Kulturen

meadows, as well as a village of fine half-timbered houses.

🏛 **Övedskloster**
Road 11 from Lund towards Sjöbo. **Tel** 046-630 63. ◯ daily (park only). 🏇 Horse trials (early Sep).

Lund ❾

Skåne. E 22. 👥 60,000. ✈ Sturup. 🚉 🚌 � Kyrkogatan 11, 046-35 50 40. 🎭 Walpurgis Night (30 Apr & 1 May), Cultural Evening (3rd Sat in Sep). **www**.lund.se

Founded by King Sven Tveskägg more than 1,000 years ago, the university town of Lund was once Denmark's capital. In the Middle Ages it was a religious, political and cultural centre and site of a cathedral, **Lund Domkyrka**, which was consecrated in 1145. Over the centuries it has been rebuilt, most recently by Helgo Zettervall, 1860–80. Look out for the 14th-century astronomical clock and a sculpture in the crypt of the giant Finn supporting the cathedral's vaulting.

Lund University was established in 1666, in the grounds of the bishop's palace, Lundagård. A new main building was completed in 1882, and now the university is the second largest seat of learning in Sweden with around 40,000 students.

In the heart of the partly medieval city centre lies **Kulturen**, an open-air museum with perfectly preserved streets, cottages and town houses. Kulturen also has extensive historical collections. The 14th-century chapel of Laurentiikapellet, in central Lund, is thought to have been the library of the monastery of St Laurence.

Of Lund's many museums, **Historiska Museet**, containing Domkyrkomuseet, is one of Sweden's largest museums of archaeology, and includes an exhibition devoted to the history of the cathedral. **Lunds Konsthall**, designed by Klas Anshelm, displays contemporary art.

Environs
The spring flowers are magnificent at **Dalby Söderskog**, a national park 10 km (6 miles) southeast of Lund, where there is a forest of elm, ash and oak trees.

Gårdstånga Kyrka, 10 km (6 miles) north of Lund, is a 12th-century Romanesque church. The impressive carvings inside were crafted by local wood-carver Jacob Kremberg in the 17th century.

⛪ **Lunds Domkyrka**
Kyrkogatan. **Tel** 046-35 87 00. ◯ daily. 📷 🚻 ♿

🏛 **Kulturen**
Tegnerplatsen. **Tel** 046-35 04 00. ◯ May–Sep: daily; Oct–Apr: Tue–Sun. 🎫 📷 🚻 📕 ♿

🏛 **Historiska Museet**
Krafts Torg 1. **Tel** 046-222 79 44. ◯ Tue–Fri. 📷

🏛 **Lunds Konsthall**
Mårtenstorget 3. **Tel** 046-35 52 95. ◯ Tue–Sun. 📷 Thu & Sun. 🚻 ♿ 📕

Skanör/Falsterbo ❿

Skåne. Road 100. 👥 7,000. ✈ Sturup. 🚌 ❶ Östra Hamnplan 2, 040-42 54 54. 🎭 Falsterbo Horse Show (Jul), Sandcastle Competition (last Sun in Jul). **www**.vellinge.se/turism

Today the twin towns at the far end of Skåne's south-western cape are idyllic seaside resorts, but they owe their development to the lucrative herring industry in the Middle Ages.

Sights include the ruins of the 14th-century fort of **Falsterbohus**, **Falsterbo Museum** with its local history collection, and **Falsterbo Konsthall**, an art gallery in the old railway station. On the headland is **Falsterbo Lighthouse**, built in 1793. It is now a historical monument although it is still in working order. Skanör Town Hall dates from 1777 and the church is 13th-century.

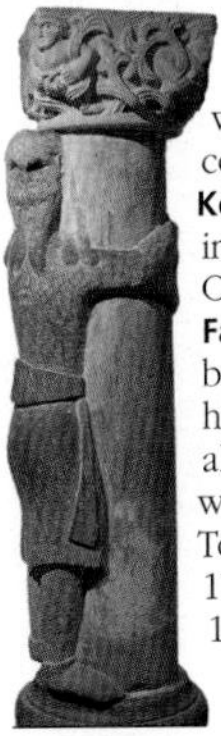

Bärnstensmuseet, the Amber Museum in Höllviken, near the Viking earthworks of Kämpinge Vall, is worth visiting to see both the amber and archaeological finds.

Giant Finn in the cathedral

🏛 **Bärnstensmuseet**
Kämpinge, 10 km (6 miles) E of Falsterbo. 🚌 **Tel** 040-45 45 04. ◯ Tue–Sun. 📷 📷

The low, single-storey houses in the small town of Skanör

Malmö ⓫

Sweden's gateway to Europe, Malmö is the country's third largest city. It was founded in the mid-13th century. Under Danish rule from 1397 to 1658, Malmö was an important town, but once it was returned to Sweden its position waned until an upturn in its fortunes at the end of the 18th century. Today, thanks largely to the Öresund Bridge and associated development, Malmö is once more in the spotlight. The city has a lively, distinctly European atmosphere and has become a centre for contemporary art and design. The old town is centred on Stortorget with its historic Town Hall and governor's residence.

Stortorget with Residenset (left) and Rådhuset (right)

🏛 Rådhuset

Stortorget. ⬤ *to the public.*
🗓 *by special arrangement, phone 040-12 19 83.*

The centre of Malmö is the square Stortorget, laid out in the 1530s by the town's mayor Jörgen Kock. Stortorget is dominated by Rådhuset, the town hall, originally built in Renaissance Dutch style in 1546. The cellar remains of the medieval building, which served both as a prison and an inn. In 1860 architect Helgo Zettervall renovated the town hall, giving it a completely new look. A number of changes were made in the cellars, (including the removal of the prisoners). The inn is still standing today and is one of the most popular bars in Malmö.

🏛 Jörgen Kocks Hus

Stortorget. ⬤ *to the public.*

Stortorget also contains Jörgen Kocks Hus, a large six-storey building with a stepped gable roof, constructed in 1525. Jörgen Kock, appointed mint-master for Denmark in 1518. Four years later he was elected mayor of the city becoming one of the most powerful men in Malmö. He was involved in the rebellion over the Danish succession and was captured and sentenced to death, but escaped and was reinstated as mayor of Malmö in 1540.

🏛 Residenset

Stortorget. ⬤ *to the public.*

In the mid-18th century two buildings Kungshuset and Gyllenpalmska Huset were combined to form the new governor's residence. Around 100 years later the building was given a new façade by architect F W Scholander, to which Helgo Zettervall adapted his extensive redesign of the town hall. Today the building is the home of the county governor.

🔒 St Petri Kyrka

Göran Olsgatan 1. *Tel 040-35 90 56.*
◯ *daily.* 🔒 🗓 *by appointment, phone 040-35 90 49 to book.* 🛆

In a street behind Stortorget is Malmö's cathedral, St Petri Kyrka. Built in the 12th century, the church, modelled on St Mary's in Lübeck, is made from red brick. The high tower, constructed in the late 19th century, after two 15th-century towers collapsed, is prominant in Malmö's skyline. The church used to contain limestone paintings, removed during renovation in the mid-19th century. Only the paintings in Krämarkapellet (the Tradesman's Chapel) are preserved.

The cathedral has treasures from the 16th and 17th centuries when Malmö's prosperity was high. The magnificent 15-m (49-ft) high altar in Renaissance style is beautifully ornamented, painted and gilded. The pulpit dating from 1599 is in sandstone and black limestone. Later additions include the organ front, a masterpiece created to a design approved by Gustav III in 1785. The original medieval organ is said to be the oldest working organ in the world and is now in Malmö Museum.

🏛 Moderna Museet

Gasverksgatan 22. *Tel 040-685 79 37.* ◯ *10am–8pm Tue, 10am–6pm Wed–Sun.* ⬤ *some public holidays.*
🖼 ◻ 🛆

Moderna Museet is one of Europe's leading museums of modern and contemporary art, and the only one north of Amsterdam with an international collection covering the entire 20th century.

In autumn 2009, the Moderna Museet opened second a branch in an old power station, which was built in 1900 and once housed the Rooseum. The building was converted by architect Johan Smedberg, who has worked on other well known buildings in southern Sweden.

Malmö's Moderna Museet occupying an old power station

For hotels and restaurants in this region see pp286–287 and pp303–304

City library Stadsbiblioteket

⛪ Malmö Konsthall

St Johannesgatan 7. **Tel** 040-34 12 93. ☐ daily. ● Midsummer Eve, Midsummer, 24, 25 & 31 Dec.
☐ ⚓ ⛫ ☐ daily. ♿

The Art Hall holds around ten exhibitions a year, with an international focus spanning the entire spectrum from modern classics to experimental art. The sculptures of Tony Cragg and an installation by Peter Greenaway are among those featured. A cornerstone of the gallery's collection is the bequest to the city by private donors Jules and Karin Shyl. During the 20th century they brought together a collection of more than 100 works, including drawings by contemporary artists Per Kirkeby, Richard Serra and Miroslav Balka.

The Konsthall was designed by architect Klas Anshelm and opened in 1975.

🏛 Stadsbiblioteket

Kung Oscars Väg. **Tel** 040-660 85 00.
☐ May–Aug: Mon–Sat; Sep–Apr: daily. ● public holidays.
⚓ ☐ ♿

The City Library moved into the "castle" on Kung Oscars Väg in 1946, but by the 1960s there was talk of expansion. Finally, in 1999, the new state-of-the-art library opened. Architect, Henning Larsen, renovated and extended the old building, introducing large, modern glass panels. He also created the bright and airy Calendar of Light hall.

The library is fitted with the latest modern technology. Electronic, telephone and data connections can be accessed throughout the building and visitors can use the library's databases, internet and CD-ROM network on 40 computers. In Malmö eight out of ten residents have visited it, borrowing an estimated 1,500,000 items a year.

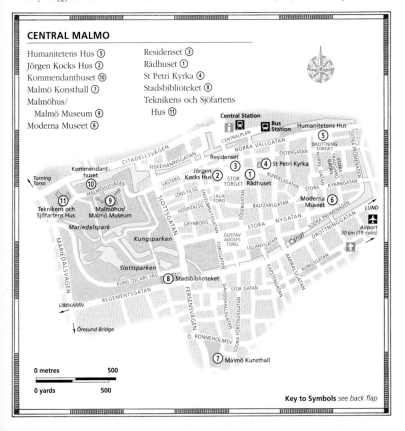

CENTRAL MALMÖ

Humanitetens Hus ⑤
Jörgen Kocks Hus ②
Kommendanthuset ⑩
Malmö Konsthall ⑦
Malmöhus/
  Malmö Museum ⑨
Moderna Museet ⑥
Residenset ③
Rådhuset ①
St Petri Kyrka ④
Stadsbiblioteket ⑧
Teknikens och Sjöfartens
  Hus ⑪

Key to Symbols see back flap

0 metres 500
0 yards 500

Exploring Malmö

The centre of Malmö, where most of the sights are located, is compact and easy to explore on foot. Start at Västra Hamnen, near the fortress of Malmöhus, and walk towards the centre, in the direction of the tower of St Petri Kyrka on Stortorget. Lilla Torg and Möllevångstorget are lively market squares, and the beautiful parks, such as Slottsparken or Pildammsparken, are a delight to wander through. While the centre retains its old-town atmosphere, futuristic projects are taking shape on the outskirts as part of the visionary new Öresund region.

Malmöhus fortress, built in 1537 and now the home of Malmö Museum

⚏ Malmöhus/Malmö Museum

Malmöhusvägen. **Tel** 040-34 44 00. ⬚ daily. ● 1 Jan, 1 May, Midsummer Eve, Midsummer, 24, 25 & 31 Dec. 🎫 🎫 by appointment. ▢ 🏠 & partly.
Originally built by Erik of Pomerania in 1434, the fortress of Malmöhus was largely destroyed as a result of the war. It was rebuilt by Christian III in 1537. Today it is the oldest preserved Scandinavian Renaissance castle in the Nordic region. Originally, it was a fortified royal manor and mint. After the 17th century the fortress was reinforced with bastions, but it fell into disrepair and through most of the 18th and 19th centuries served as a prison. The solid brick fort is

Calendar of Light hall in Malmö's award-winning library

surrounded by a deep moat. Extensive restoration work was carried out in 1932, after which Malmö Museum moved into the building. The museum's collections cover archaeology, ethnography, the history of art and handicrafts, and zoology.

Stadsmuseet (the City Museum) illustrates the history of Malmö and surrounding Skåne with tools, weapons and domestic objects. It contains models, a large textiles collection and an ethnographical collection.

Some of the rooms in the fortress can also be seen. Another popular attraction is the 18th-century tower with its 7.5-m (25-ft) thick walls and original cannons.

Malmö Museer runs Teknikens och Sjöfartens Hus, Kommendanthuset, Ebbas Hus, Malmö Konstmuseum, which can all be visited on a single ticket.

⚏ Kommendanthuset

Malmöhusvägen. **Tel** 040-34 44 39. ⬚ daily. ● 1 Jan, 1 May, Midsummer Eve, Midsummer, 24, 25 & 31 Dec. 🎫 🎫 by appointment. ▢ 🏠 &
In the latter part of the 18th century the storage buildings in the Malmöhus courtyard

had fallen into disrepair and Gustav III ordered the construction of a new armoury. It was built outside the fortress in the Banér bastion and was completed in 1794. By 1814 the fortress's military days were over and it had become a prison. Kommendanthuset (the Governor's House) became the quarters first for the prison's doctor and priest and later the prison governor.

In the 20th century the city of Malmö took over the building and restored it to its original appearance, incorporating it into Malmö Museer. Its collections feature military history and the history of weaponry. Temporary exhibitions are also held here.

⚏ Teknikens och Sjöfartens Hus

Malmöhusvägen. **Tel** 040-34 44 38. ⬚ daily. ● 1 Jan, 1 May, Midsummer Eve, Midsummer, 24, 25 & 31 Dec. 🎫 🎫 by appointment. ▢ 🏠 &
The Museum of Technology and Seafaring is also part of Malmö Museer. Its exhibits cover virtually everything to do with technological development and seafaring, as well as the history of roadbuilding and aviation, engines, and steam engines in particular, just to name a few examples on display. Among the exhibits is the delta-winged fighter plane J35 Draken from the 1960s. The technically curious can satisfy their urge to experiment in the *kunskapstivoli* interactive test lab.

The museum also covers the industrial and seafaring history of Skåne. Here, the star exhibits include experiencing the *U3* submarine and the steam launch *Schebo*. For those who have never been in a submarine, it is an opportunity not to be missed. This exhibit is very popular with children.

The shipbuilding and shipping industry and the development of the ports from the 17th century onwards are highlighted, as is ferry traffic, so vital to Skåne. There is also an interactive knowledge park, where you can do your own science experiments.

The 8-km (5-mile) long Öresund Bridge between Sweden and Denmark, carrying a motorway and railway line

🏛 Koggmuseet

Skeppsbron 10, Malmö hamn.
Tel 040-330 820. ⬜ Jun–Aug,
11am–4pm Tue-Sun.
⬜ 29 Dec– 3 Jan. 🗷 🔢
Koggmuseet is an experience centre built around two full-scale replica medieval cog ships (one of which is the largest in the world), representing the real trading ships that navigated the Baltic Sea in the 14th century. Visitors are able to learn about the unique history surrounding the ships and can even climb onboard.

Medieval cog ship at Koggmuseet

🏛 Limhamn

5 km (3 miles) SW of the centre. 🛈
Malmö Tourist Office, 040-34 12 00. ⬛
On the southern edge of Malmö lies Limhamn, a shipping port for lime since the 16th century. Limhamn-Bunkeflo is one of ten districts which make up the city of Malmö.

One of Limhamn's sights is the early-19th century small, blue Soldat-torpet (soldier's house), which shows how soldiers used to live. The

cottage was inhabited until 1956. The Limhamn Museum Society runs various events at Midsummer and Christmas.

🏛 The Öresund Bridge

E20. 6 km (3 miles) SW of the centre.
The idea of a bridge between Sweden and Denmark had been discussed for over 100 years, but in 1991 both countries agreed on how and where this dream could be realized.

Opened in July 2000, the Öresund Bridge is 8-km (5-mile) long linking Lernacken in Sweden, southwest of Malmö, and the 4-km (2.5-mile) long Danish artificial

island of Peberholm, south of Saltholm. The highest part rests on four pylons, 204 m (670 ft) tall and the roadway is around 30 m (100 ft) wide. The E20 runs along the upper level with a railway along the lower level. It is the longest cable-stayed bridge to carry both a railway and motorway.

On the west side of Peberholm the link plunges into a 4-km (2.5-mile) long tunnel leading to Copenhagen's international airport. The journey by train from Malmö to Copenhagen takes 35 minutes. The link is due to be augmented by a railway tunnel to central Malmö in 2011.

THE ORESUND REGION

As part of the EU's vision for a Europe without borders, the Öresund Region project aims to integrate southern Skåne in Sweden with the area around Copenhagen in Denmark, allowing people to cross from one country to another without restrictions. The construction of the Öresund Bridge and tunnel has brought with it enormous benefits for the city of Malmö. It has made the region considerably more attractive to business, the new suburb of Brostaden (Bridge City) has sprung up, cultural exchanges between the two countries are easier and the improved communications have brought more visitors. Architect Santiago Calatrava's stunning Turning Torso tower, located in the Western Harbour, is a bold creation that can be seen as an expression of the region's faith in the future. Completed in 2005, the 190 m (623 ft) sculptural high rise consists of nine cubes twisting skyward. The Western Harbour waterfront has developed into a residential area.

The Turning Torso building soaring 190 m (623 ft) high

Trelleborgen, a reconstructed Viking fortress

Trelleborg

Skåne. E22. 24,850. 🏛 🚌 ⛴
ℹ Hamngatan 9, 0410-733 320.
🎷 Smygehuk Jazz Festival (mid-Jul),
Michaelmas Market.
www.trelleborg.se

The centrepiece of modern-day Trelleborg is **Trelleborgen**, a remarkable re-creation of a Viking fortress. It is based on the original fortress, thought to have been built by King Harald Blue Tooth in the 10th century and excavated 1,000 years later. The reconstruction opened in 1995.

The town was at its most prosperous in the Middle Ages when German merchants came to trade salt for herring. Some of the old Skåne houses still remain in the quarter around Gamla Torg (Old Square) and in Kloster-gränden, where the ruins of a 13th-century Franciscan monastery still stand. The monastery itself was closed during the Reformation, but its garden is a recreated oasis with a herb, hop and pleasure garden. Stadsparken, the town park with a g orgeous rose garden, is well worth a visit.

Among the other sights is **Trelleborgs Museum**, focusing on local history, **Sjöfartsmuseet** (the Seafaring Museum) and **Axel Ebbehal-len**, which has a large collection of sculptures by Skåne artist Axel Ebbe.

Environs
A short distance west of Trelleborg lies the village of Skegrie and beside the E6 is **Skegriedösen**, a Stone Age burial mound. The rectangular grave chamber is formed from four stone blocks with a giant pointed block as a roof, surrounded by 17 foot-stones. This type of Stone Age burial site is only found in southern and western Sweden.

⋔ Trelleborgen
Bryggaregatan. **Tel** 0410-460 77.
☐ daily. 🎫 🛒 🔲

🏛 Trelleborgs Museum
Östergatan 58. **Tel** 0410-733 045.
☐ Tue–Sun. 🎫 🛒 🔲 🔲

🏛 Axel Ebbehallen
Mesekillgatan 1. **Tel** 0410-733 056.
☐ Jun–Aug: Tue–Sun. 🎫 🛒 🔲

Ystad

Skåne. E65. 16,850. 🏛 🚌 ⛴
ℹ St Knuts Torg, 0411-57 76 81.
www.ystad.se

In Ystad the impact of Danish rule and contact with the German Hanseatic League is apparent and the medieval church and monastery communities have also left their mark on the town. Among the many old buildings is the 13th-century

Apoteksgården, one of Ystad's many fine half-timbered houses

Sta Mariakyrkan, where every night the watchman in the tower declares that all is well by blowing his horn. In **Karl XII's Hus** on Stora Västergatan the warrior king is said to have spent the night in 1715 following his return from Turkey (see p35).

Ystad has a number of museums, including **Ystads Konstmuseum** (Art Museum), **Charlotta Berlins Museum** (an intact home of a 17th-century nobleman) and a military museum. There is a fine theatre on the harbourside, the home of the Ystad opera company.

Environs
High above the fishing community of Kåseberga lies the stone ship **Ales Stenar**. The 67-m (220-ft) monument comprises 59 stones and is a mystical and beautiful place that is well worth a visit.

Bollerups Borg, 20 km (12 miles) east of Ystad, is a 13th-century fortress which has been rebuilt several times. The fort is owned by an agricultural college, but is open to the public.

Sandhammaren is best known for its sandy beaches, but in the past was feared by sailors as new reefs were constantly forming around the cape. The lighthouse dates from 1862.

Marsvinsholms Slott is an estate dating back to the 14th century. The castle is not open to the public, but during the summer visitors can enjoy the sculpture park within the castle's grounds or see a play at the open-air theatre.

Valleberga Kyrka lies 17 km (11 miles) east of Ystad and is the only round church in Skåne. It has a 12th-century font by Majestatis.

🏛 Ystads Konstmuseum
St Knuts Torg. **Tel** 0411-577 285. ☐
Tue–Sun. ⬤ public holidays. 🎫 🔲 🔲

⋔ Ales Stenar
Kåseberga. Road 9, 15 km (9 miles)
E of Ystad. **Tel** 0411-57 76 81.
☐ daily.

🏰 Marsvinsholms Slott
On E65, 12 km (8 miles) NW of
Ystad. **Tel** 0411-577 681. **House**
⬤ to the public. **Park** ☐ daily.
☐ in summer.

A Tour of Österlen ⑭

The name Österlen means "the land to the east"
and refers to the southeast corner of Skåne from
Ravlunda south to Ystad and west to the
Linderödsåsen ridge. The land is the most fertile in
Sweden and across the rolling plains are many of
the country's most treasured ancient monuments,
grandest castles and forts and oldest churches.
Along the coast, idyllic fishing villages are dotted
like pearls on a string and the entire region has
become a haven for painters and writers.

**Apple orchard in
spring, Kivik**

Kivik ②
Kivik is best known
for its annual market
and apple orchards,
but it is also a
charming fishing
village with winding
streets and half-
timbered houses.

Brösarps Backar ①
This nature reserve is
awash with rare flowers.
The sight of anemones
and cowslips blooming
in spring is particularly
spectactular. The area
has lots of walking
trails.

KRISTIANSTAD

① Brösarps Backar
Ravlunda

② *Kivik*

Fågeltofta

St Olof

Rörum

Vik

*Baske-
mölla*

LUND

Smedstorp

Tomelilla ⑤
YSTAD

Simrishamn ③

BALTIC SEA

Tomelilla ⑤
Tomelilla is an ideal
starting point for a
tour of Skåne's rolling
countryside. Byagården,
the town's Tudor-style
farmstead, is considered
one of the best examples
of its kind in the region.

Hammenhög

④

Glimmingehus

*Brante-
vik*

Skillinge

*Glemminge-
bro*

Löderup

YSTAD

Simrishamn ③
Old low-rise houses
give the town its
character. Craftsmen
lived around the
square, Lilla Torg, and
fishermen made their
home by the harbour.

KEY

▦ Suggested route

═ Other roads

Ales Stenar

Sandhammaren

TIPS FOR DRIVERS

Length: around 55 km (34 miles).
*Major roads are of a good
standard, but country roads can
be in poorer condition.*
Places to eat: cafés and/or
restaurants are found in most
towns. Hammenhög has a typical
Skåne inn, ideal for a lunch break.
Äpplets Hus, Kivik, is worth a look.

0 kilometres   10

0 miles   5

Glimmingehus ④
The evocative 16th-
century knight's manor
offers exciting ghost
trails and a taste
of medieval cooking.

Heliga Trefaldighetskyrkan, a Renaissance church, Kristianstad

Kristianstad ⓯

Skåne. E22. 🏛 *31,600.* ✈ 🚂 🚌
🛈 *Stora Torg, 044-12 19 88.*
🎭 *Christianstad Festival (10 days in Jul).* **www**.kristianstad.se

The Danish King Christian IV built the town of Kristianstad in the early 17th century and the original street layout with two gates can still be seen today. The town's main sight is **Heliga Trefaldighetskyrkan** (the Church of the Holy Trinity) from the same period, an excellent example of Renaissance architecture. A more recent attraction is the eco-museum **Vattenriket**, a 35-km (22-mile) stretch of wetlands on the Helgeån river. It is best seen on a guided river tour. Fishing permits can be bought at the tourist office.

Environs
About 15 km (9 miles) to the northeast is **Bäckaskog Slott**, a former monastery dating from the 13th century, which was rented by the Swedish royal family during the 19th century. The castle is set in beautiful parkland with a herb garden.
   Rinkaby Kyrka lies halfway between Kristianstad and Åhus. The 13th-century church

contains paintings from the 15th century depicting the seasons and farming life.
   Among the most idiosyncratic objects to be seen at the castle of **Trolle-Ljungby**, 10 km (6 miles) east of Kristianstad, are the Ljungby drinking horn and pipe, which feature in a local legend. On Wednesdays and Saturdays in summer they are exhibited in a window facing the courtyard.
   The park of **Wanås Slott**, 20 km (12 miles) northwest of Kristianstad, is a setting for international contemporary art.
   Åhus, 14 km (9 miles) southeast of Kristianstad, is a coastal community with half-timbered houses and sandy beaches. There are 20 golf courses in a 50-km (30-mile) radius.

⚒ Vattenriket
Tel *Kristianstads Tourist Office, 044-12 19 88.* 🗓 *daily.* 🎫 ♿ *(some parts)*
www.vattenriket.kristianstad.se

🏰 Bäckaskog Slott
Fjälkinge, 15 km (9 miles) NE of Kristianstad. **Tel** *044-532 20.*
🗓 *Apr–Sep: daily.* 🎫 ▢ 🍴 ♿

🏰 Trolle-Ljungby
Fjälkinge, 10 km (6 miles) NE of Kristianstad. **Tel** *044-550 43.* 🗓 *(park & courtyard only) Jun–Sep: Wed & Sat.*

Sölvesborg ⓰

Blekinge. E22. 🏛 *16,500.* 🚂 🚌 🛈
Repslagaregatan 1, 0456-100 88. 🎭
Nogersund Harbour Festival (early Jul).
www.solvesborg.se

In the Middle Ages, Sölvesborg, on the cape of Listerlandet, was an important trading centre protected by a castle. The town has a Danish feel to it and still retains its medieval charm.
   In a former granary and distillery, **Sölvesborgs Museum** traces the history of Lister. The town's oldest building is St **Nicolai Kyrka**,

a church with parts dating from the 13th century.

Environs
West of Sölvesborg and at the far end of the cape lies the old town of **Hällevik** with its traditional wooden houses, fishing harbour, smokery and guest harbour. It also has a great little fishing museum and is well worth a visit.
   Ferries run from Nogersund to the island of **Hanö** in Hanöbukten bay. It's an attractive place and a popular destination for sailors. The island served as an English naval base in the Napoleonic Wars in the early 19th century and there is a graveyard here for British seamen.

🏛 Sölvesborgs Museum
Skeppsbrogatan. **Tel** *0456-161 57.*
🗓 *May–Aug: daily; Sep–Apr: by arrangement.*

Karlshamn ⓱

Blekinge. E22. 🏛 *18,900.* ✈ 🚂 🚌
🛈 *Pirgatan 2, 0454-812 03* 🎭
Baltic Festival (3rd week in Jul).

The town of Karlshamn was founded in 1664. It was planned as a naval base and **Kastellet**, on the island of Frisholmen, was built to defend it. However, the naval port role went to Karlskrona *(see pp188–9)* and Karlshamn became a trading centre with a reputation for the production of punsch. A reconstruction of Punschfabriken, the factory which produced the delectable alcoholic drink "Flaggpunsch", forms part of **Karlshamns Museum**. Next to the punsch factory is **Karlshamns Konsthall** (Art Gallery).
   Other places of interest include **Skottsbergska Gården**, a merchant's house built in 1763 where both the living

Kastellet on the island of Frisholmen, Karlshamn

◁ **A carpet of white and yellow anemones on a spring day in Stenshuvud National Park**

quarters and tobacco shop can be seen as they were in the 18th century. **Asschierska Huset** on Stortorget was Karlshamn's first town hall. The celebrated **Mörrumsån** salmon fishing river runs through the municipality.

Environs
Around 15 km (9 miles) east of Karlshamn is **Eriksbergs Vilt- och Naturpark**, one of the largest wildlife and nature sanctuaries in Europe and home to golden eagles, sea eagles and deer.

Tjärö, in the idyllic Blekinge archipelago, is a 15-minute boat trip away.

🏛 **Karlshamns Museum**
Vinkelgatan 8. *Tel* 0454-148 68. ⭘
mid-Jun–mid-Aug: Tue–Sun. 📷

Ronneby ⑱

Blekinge. E22. 🚶 18,500. ✈ 🚃 🚌
🛈 Västra Torggatan 1, 0457-61 75 70. 🏛 Tosia Bonnadan Market (2nd week in Jul). **www**.visitronneby.se

Founded in the 13th century, Ronneby did not become Swedish until 1658. Prior to that, it was the main town of Blekinge and a busy trading centre. In 1564, during the Seven Years War with the Danes, it was overrun by the army of Erik XIV and burned. About 3,000 inhabitants – the majority of the population –

Renovated spa pavilions at Brunnsparken in Ronneby

were slaughtered in what became known as the Ronneby Bloodbath. In the early 19th century the town gained a new lease of life thanks to the Kockums foundry and enamel works in Kallinge and the Ronneby Brunn spa.

There are a few old buildings in Bergslagen and around Brunnskällan, and the beautiful 18th-century spa park has been restored.

Environs
Just east of Ronneby is the 13th-century church **Edestads Kyrka**, which once served as a defensive fort. A remarkable 4-m (13-ft) high, 8th-century runestone, **Björketorpsstenen**, lies 7 km (4 miles) east of the town. The text inscribed on the stone is a curse.

Hjortsberga Grave Field on the Johannishus ridge contains 120 ancient burial mounds. About 12 km

(7 miles) northeast of Ronneby is **Johannishus Åsar**, a nature reserve set in beautiful pasture land.

Kristianopel ⑲

Blekinge. E22. 🚶 1,500. 🚌 🚌
🛈 Stortorget 2, 0455-30 34 90. 🏛 Medieval Market (4th week in Aug).

Enjoying a beautiful location on a peninsula in Kalmarsund, the little fortified town of Kristianopel has become a popular summer haunt with a guest harbour and tourist facilities. It was built by the Danish King Christian IV and gained its town charter in 1600. At the Peace of Roskilde in 1658 it became Swedish. Garden lovers head for **Rosengården**, a private garden filled with more than 500 different varieties of old roses.

Environs
Brömsebro lies 8 km (5 miles) north of Kristianopel, just inland from the coast. Here on the border between Blekinge and Småland is where peace with Denmark was declared in 1645, when Jämtland, Härjedalen and Gotland once more became Swedish provinces. The negotiations were held on an islet in Brömsebäcken river and a commemorative stone was raised here in 1915. At the mouth of the river are the ruins of Brömsehus, a fortress which was captured in 1436 by Swedish rebel hero Engelbrekt (*see p33*).

🌹 **Rosengården**
Tel 0455-36 62 36. ⭘ mid-May–mid-Sep: daily; other times: by appointment. 🏠

SALMON FISHING IN MORRUMSAN

Every year the salmon fishing in the Mörrumsån river attracts enthusiasts from all over the world. Fishing here dates back to the 13th century when the king held all the rights. The river flows through a beautiful landscape from

Fly-fishing for salmon in Mörrumsån

Lake Vrången in the north to the sea at Elleholm via the lakes of Helgasjön and Åsnen.

A fishing permit is required and these cost between 300 and 500 kr per day. During the 2003 season 1,160 salmon were caught here, the record catch weighing in at 17.98 kg (39.6 lbs).

Laxens Hus (Salmon World) in Mörrum gathers together everything to do with fishing and mounts a variety of exhibitions on, for example, the animal life of the river, and the history of the sport.

Karlskrona ⑳

The naval town of Karlskrona is built over several islands in the Blekinge archipelago. Granted a town charter in 1680, it was planned by Erik Dahlbergh and is said to have been inspired by both Versailles and Rome. It centres around the two squares, Stortorget on the island of Trossö, and Amiralitetstorget. The decision to locate Sweden's main naval base in Karlskrona was taken because in winter the fleet was often ice-bound in Stockholm, and an ice-free port was needed further south. Karlskrona has a number of outstanding sights from Sweden's Age of Greatness *(see pp36–7)*. In 1998 the town was declared a UNESCO World Heritage Site on account of its naval architecture.

Karl XI, the town's founder

Fredrikskyrkan on Stortorget, designed by Tessin the Younger in Baroque style, 1744

🏛 Grevagården/Blekinge Museum

Fisktorget 2. **Tel** 0455-30 49 60.
◯ Jun–Aug: daily; rest of the year: Tue–Sun. ◯ some public holidays.
🈯 ♿ ▯ ▯ 🔟 www.blekingemuseum.se

Grevagården on Fisktorget is the main building of Blekinge Museum. The building dates from the early 18th century and was the home of Admiral-General Hans Wachtmeister – the café is set in what was once his kitchen and store room. The museum focuses on the history of Blekinge and Karlskrona's heyday. There is a small Baroque garden reached via a double staircase flanked by two yew trees, believed to

date from 1704. Outside on the square stands Erik Höglund's statue of the *Fisherwoman*.

♖ Stortorget

The imposing square is said to be the largest in northern Europe. It is flanked, in the Baroque tradition, by two impressive churches, both designed by the architect Nicodemus Tessin the Younger.

Fredrikskyrkan is a large basilica consecrated in 1744, but characterized by the 17th-century taste for Baroque lines. The southern tower has 35 bells which ring three times a day. The other church, Heliga Trefaldighet-skyrkan (Holy Trinity), is also known as the German Church after Admiral-General Hans Wachtmeister who inspired it and is buried in the crypt. It was completed in 1709. After a fire in 1790 the church was rebuilt with a lower dome than its predecessor.

The town hall, completed in 1798, has been rebuilt several times. Today it serves as the seat of Karlskrona district court.

Vattenborgen, the now protected water tower, was built in 1863 to supply Trossö with fresh water. It was replaced by a water tower outside the town in 1939.

🏛 Marinmuseum

Stumholmen. **Tel** 0455-359 302.
◯ May–Sep: daily; Oct–Apr: Tue–Sun. 🈯 🈺 ♿ ▯ ▯ 🔟
www.marinmuseum.se

The fascinating naval museum, opened in 1997, stands on the harbour on Stumholmen, an island which for almost 300 years has been part of the main base of the Swedish navy. The museum was founded originally in 1752 by King Adolf Fredrik to collect and document naval objects in what was known as Modellkammaren (the Model Room).

Marinmuseum covers every imaginable aspect of maritime activity. It holds a particularly impressive collection of figureheads, weapons and uniforms. From an under-water glass corridor it is possible to see the wreck of an 18th-century ship lying on the bottom of the sea.

One of the world's smallest full-rigged ships, *Jarramas*, a training ship for naval ratings, is moored on the quay outside the museum, along with the minesweeper *Bremön* and the torpedo boat *T38*. The Sloop and Long-Boat Shed contains an exhibition of working boats and often allows visitors the opportunity to see how old wooden boats are restored.

Marinmuseum, showcase for Karlskrona's naval heritage

♖ Gamla Örlogsvarvet

Högvakten, Amiralitetstorget 1.
Tel 0455-30 34 90. ◯ Jun–Aug: daily. 🈯 🈺 compulsory.

The Karlskrona shipyard, founded in 1679, became over time one of the country's foremost military shipyards, a position it still holds today. Fortifications and buildings were constructed to build, equip and repair warships. Additional buildings went up on the islands of Lindholmen,

The **"Old Man" Rosenbom poor-box**
outside Amiralitetskyrkan

Söderstjärna and Stumholmen.
The only way to see this vast
naval harbour and its many
18th-century buildings and
workshops is to take a guided
tour. Among the most
interesting sights in Gamla
Örlogsvarvet are the 300-m
(984-ft) long Rope Walk,
where the rigging for the fleet
was manufactured, the Wasa
Shed and Polhem Dock on
Lindholmen and Five-finger
Dock and the Old Mast Crane
in the western part of the
shipyard. It is the existence of
buildings such as these, and

the fact that Karlskrona is such
a well-preserved example of a
late-17th-century planned
naval base, that has earned the
town World Heritage Site
status. Karlskrona was a model
for other naval bases throughout Europe in the 18th century.

Close to the entrance to the
old shipyard, Högvakten, is
Amiralitetskyrkan (the Admiralty church). Consecrated in
1685, it is Sweden's largest
wooden church. In front
of the church is a replica of
the Gubben "Old Man"
Rosenbom poor-box.

Today's high-tech shipyard,
Karlskronavarvet, run by
Kockums, is not open to the
public, but new vessels can
often be seen along the quay.

🏛 Skärfva Herrgård
5 km (3 miles) W of centre, E 22.
Tel 0455-490 03. ◻ daily in
summer (park). ◻ ◪
In 1785 the ship designer
Fredrik Henrik af Chapman
built a summer house on the
shore between Karlskrona and
Nättraby. The building is an
unusual mix of a traditional

VISITORS' CHECKLIST

Blekinge. 🏠 62,000. ✈ 25 km W
of centre. 🚉 🚌 Järnvägsstation-
sgatan. 🚢 Verkö (Gdynia).
ℹ Stortorget 2, 0455-30 34 90.
🎪 Leaf Market (Thu before Midsummer). 🎉 Sail Karlskrona (2nd
week in Aug), VIVA Karlskrona Food
& Music Festival (last week in Jul).
www.visitkarlskrona.se

Blekinge cottage open to
the roof space and other
architectural styles, including
an entrance reminiscent of a
Doric temple in front of an
octagonal cupola.

Inside, several rooms are
preserved in their original
state, including af Chapman's
workroom in the form of a
ship's cabin. The house is set
in an English-style park with a
temple-like summer house.

The surroundings are part of
Skärfva Nature Reserve which
protects the flora and fauna of
the manor house estate.

During the summer boats
run daily from Karlskrona
to Skärfva.

KARLSKRONA TOWN
CENTRE

Gamla Örlogsvarvet ④
Grevagården/Blekinge
Museum ①
Karlskronavarvet ⑤
Marinmuseum ③
Stortorget ②

0 metres   500
0 yards   500

Key to Symbols see back flap

GOTHENBURG

The people of Gothenburg have nicknamed their city "the face of Sweden". This maritime metropolis has for centuries been one of Sweden's gateways to the outside world. Historically, the Göta Älv river was the country's only outlet to the west, as can be seen by the remains of fortresses and earthworks that once protected it. Gothenburg is still Sweden's most important port and holds fast to its maritime past.

With its great harbour and seafaring traditions, it is perhaps only natural that Sweden's second largest city is also its most outward looking. Visitors are always welcome and it is not for nothing that the entertainment on offer and the atmosphere have led to Gothenburg being called "Little London".

Today's Gothenburg (Göteborg in Swedish) was preceded by four earlier towns along the Göta Älv river. These were pawns in a period of constant conflict between Sweden and Denmark. The first town was built by Dutch settlers on the island of Hisingen in the early 17th century. It was hardly established before Gustav II Adolf decided in 1619 that it should be moved to the area where the suburbs of Vallgraven and Nordstaden now stand. The inhabitants still came from Holland and the grid of canals is reminiscent of Amsterdam. Gothenburg's 17th-century incarnation was as a fortified town created by the architect and field marshal Erik Dahlbergh. The 18th century saw Gothenburg become even more cosmopolitan thanks to German, English and Scottish immigration. With the advent of steam power, the shipping industry flourished in the mid-19th century, and the city became a prominent shipbuilding centre. The shipyards have mostly gone, but Gothenburg is still a major industrial city and home of the car manufacturer Volvo.

This vibrant little metropolis of 500,000 people (famous for their particular wittiness) is ideal for sightseeing, and is peppered with green spaces, such as the Botanical Gardens and the amusement park, Liseberg. It is a good starting point for excursions to the west coast islands with their pretty fishing villages and smooth rocks for bathing.

Gothenburg's Botanical Gardens, a green oasis not far from the centre of the city

◁ An old windjammer, the barque *Viking*, at Lilla Bommen in Gothenburg's inner harbour

Exploring Gothenburg

A good quick way to get an overview of Gothenburg is to see the city from one of the many excellent observation points such as GötheborgsUtkiken, Sjömanstornet or LisebergsTornet. The central parts of the town lie south of the Göta Älv river, but it is easy to cross to the large island of Hisingen by ferry, or by car via the Götaälvbron or Älvsborgsbron bridges, or the Tingstad tunnel. Gothenburg has retained its excellent tram network which provides an ideal way to tour the town, especially on the vintage carriages of the Ringlinjen line. Paddan's white tour boats *(see p205)* operate trips along the 17th-century canals and out into the lively harbour.

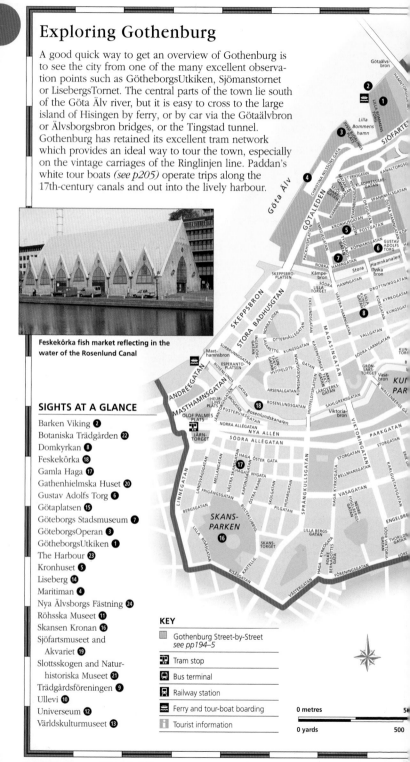

Feskekôrka fish market reflecting in the water of the Rosenlund Canal

SIGHTS AT A GLANCE

Barken Viking ❷
Botaniska Trädgården ㉒
Domkyrkan ❽
Feskekôrka ⓲
Gamla Haga ⓱
Gathenhielmska Huset ⓴
Gustav Adolfs Torg ❻
Götaplatsen ⓯
Göteborgs Stadsmuseum ❼
GöteborgsOperan ❸
GötheborgsUtkiken ❶
The Harbour ㉓
Kronhuset ❺
Liseberg ⓮
Maritiman ❹
Nya Älvsborgs Fästning ㉔
Röhsska Museet ⓫
Skansen Kronan ⓰
Sjöfartsmuseet and Akvariet ⓳
Slottsskogen and Natur-historiska Museet ㉑
Trädgårdsföreningen ❾
Ullevi ❿
Universeum ⓬
Världskulturmuseet ⓭

KEY

▢ Gothenburg Street-by-Street *see pp194–5*

🚊 Tram stop

🚌 Bus terminal

🚉 Railway station

⛴ Ferry and tour-boat boarding

ℹ Tourist information

0 metres   5[0]

0 yards   500

GETTING TO GOTHENBURG

The sea has always been the key to Gothenburg and ferries run daily from Norway, Denmark, Germany and the UK. Fast trains whisk travellers from Stockholm or Malmö in three hours. A well-developed commuter train network and express bus lines ease regional trips. The E6 along the west coast and the E20 from Stockholm meet at the Göta Älv river. Landvetter international airport is Sweden's second largest airport with direct flights to many domestic and international destinations. Gothenburg City Airport is a 20 minute drive from the city centre.

VISITORS' CHECKLIST

🚶 500,000. 🚉 🚌 ⛴ 🚶
Landvetter 45 km (28 miles) E of the centre. 🛈 Gothenburg Tourist Information Centre, Kungsportsplatsen 2 & Nordstan, 031-368 4200. 🎬 Gothenburg Film Festival (Jan/Feb); Science Festival (early May); Gothenburg Cultural Festival (Aug); Jazz Festival (Aug); International Book Fair (end of Sep); Gothenburg Horse Show (spring); Culture Night (Oct). **www**.goteborg.com

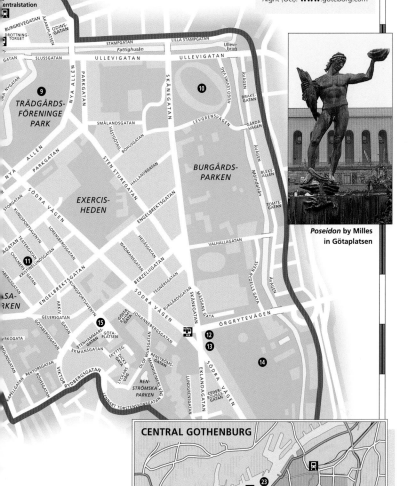

Poseidon by Milles in Götaplatsen

CENTRAL GOTHENBURG

| 0 kilometres | 2 |
| 0 miles | 1 |

Street-by-Street: Västra Nordstan

This part of Gothenburg is the pulse of the seafaring
city, encapsulating almost 400 years of history. On the
quayside along the Göta Älv river the maritime world
is ever present, with museum ships at anchor and
the constant to-ing and fro-ing of boats and ferries.
Spectacular new buildings, such as GöteborgsOperan
and GötheborgsUtkiken, contrast with the city's
historic monuments. These include the East India
Company building on Stora Hamnkanalen, a reminder
of the Dutch influence on Gothenburg's design, and
Kronhuset, the city's oldest secular building. Shoppers
should head for nearby Östra Nordstan and its
department stores and galleries.

★ **GöteborgsOperan**
*Generous donations
enabled the building of the
long-awaited Opera House,
which opened in 1994* ❸

★ **Maritiman**
*In the harbour is one of the world's largest
floating ship museums. Both the destroyer
Småland, launched 1952 (in the background), and the submarine Nordkaparen, 1962, can be boarded* ❹

**Ture
Rinman
footbridge**

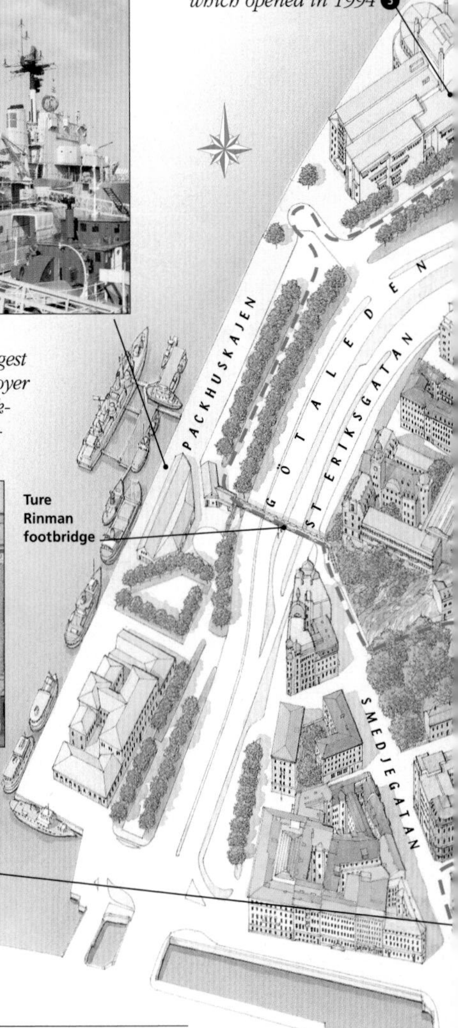

Göteborgs Stadsmuseum
*The former East India Company's
classical 18th-century headquarters
building is now the setting for
Göteborgs Stadsmuseum* ❼

STAR SIGHTS

★ Maritiman

★ Barken Viking

★ GöteborgsOperan

KEY

▬ ▬ ▬ Suggested route

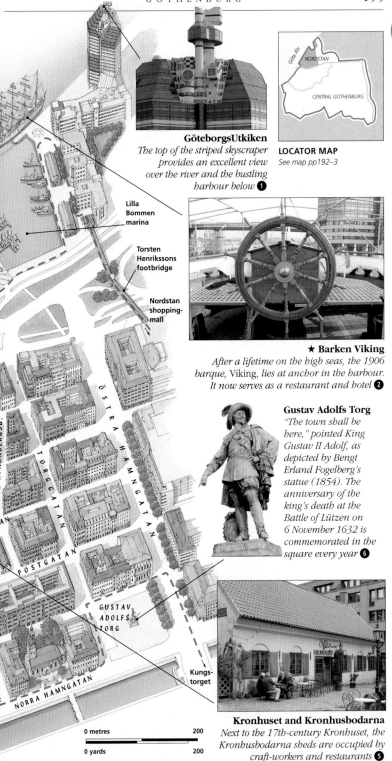

GöteborgsUtkiken
The top of the striped skyscraper provides an excellent view over the river and the bustling harbour below ❶

LOCATOR MAP
See map pp192–3

Lilla Bommen marina

Torsten Henrikssons footbridge

Nordstan shopping-mall

★ **Barken Viking**
After a lifetime on the high seas, the 1906 barque, Viking, lies at anchor in the harbour. It now serves as a restaurant and hotel ❷

Gustav Adolfs Torg
"The town shall be here," pointed King Gustav II Adolf, as depicted by Bengt Erland Fogelberg's statue (1854). The anniversary of the king's death at the Battle of Lützen on 6 November 1632 is commemorated in the square every year ❻

GUSTAV ADOLFS TORG

Kungstorget

Kronhuset and Kronhusbodarna
Next to the 17th-century Kronhuset, the Kronhusbodarna sheds are occupied by craft-workers and restaurants ❺

| 0 metres | 200 |
| 0 yards | 200 |

GötheborgsUtkiken (the "Lipstick"), and the sailing ship *Viking*

Götheborgs-Utkiken ❶

Lilla Bommen 2. *Tel* 031-368 42 00.
🚋 5, 10. 🚌 40, 42, 52, 99. ⬜ mid-May–mid-Aug: 11am–4pm daily; other times: 11am–3pm Mon–Fri. The lift goes up every hour. 🖥 ♿

The cheeky red and white GötheborgsUtkiken office building has dominated the Lilla Bommen harbour area since 1989. Architects Ralph Erskine and Heikki Särg's daring design was soon christened the "Lipstick" by Gothenburg wits. Standing 86 m (282 ft) above sea level, it offers incredible views over the harbour and the city centre from the top floor.

Barken Viking ❷

Gullbergskajen. *Tel* 031-63 58 00.
🚋 5, 10. 🚌 40, 42, 52, 99.
⬜ daily. ● 22–31 Dec. ⬛ summer.
🍴 ♿ limited access.

One of the world's few preserved four-masted barques from the great age of sail is permanently moored in Gothenburg. The *Viking* was built in 1906 by the Copenhagen shipyard Burmeister & Wain. She sailed the wheat route to Australia and shipped guano from Chile in South America. A fast and beautiful vessel, she logged a record speed of 15.5 knots in 1909. Her days as a merchant ship ended in 1948. In 1950 she

became a training centre for sailors and chefs.

Today, the *Viking* is an unusual setting for an hotel and conference centre. In summer the 97 m (318 ft) deck becomes a popular harbourside café, restaurant and bar, with a very lively, bustling atmosphere.

Göteborgs-Operan ❸

Christina Nilssons Gata. *Tel* 031-13 13 00. 🚋 5, 10. 🚌 40, 42, 52, 80, 99. ⬜ mid Aug–Jun: in conjunction with performances; other times: phone for info. ● 1 May, Good Friday, 24, 25, Dec. 🖥 ♿ 🎫 book. 🖥 🍴 ⬛ **www**.opera.se

The 1994 opening of the impressive Opera House reflected in the water of the Göta Älv river had been eagerly anticipated by western Sweden's music lovers. This is shown by the vast donation wall listing the names of the 6,000 people who helped to fund the new building.

The theatre is designed on a grand scale in every sense. The octagonal auditorium has the capacity for an audience of 1,300, all able to enjoy the excellent acoustics. The main stage covering 500 sq m (5,380 sq ft) is complemented by a further four equally large

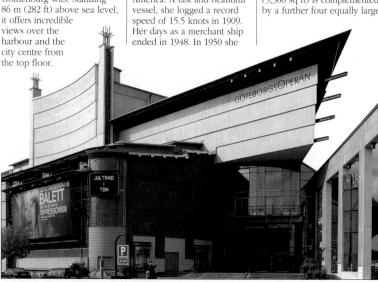

The striking exterior of the riverside GöteborgsOperan, the city's main venue for opera, musicals and ballet

For hotels and restaurants in this region see pp287–288 and p305

areas for storing sets. Using advanced technology, it is possible to switch quickly between productions, thus enabling the Opera House to stage a repertoire of opera, musicals and ballet.

Architect Jan Izikowitz was inspired by Gothenburg's harbourside location, the aim of his design being for the "building to be possessed by a lightness which encourages thoughts to soar like seagulls' wings over the mighty river landscape".

Gustav Adolfs Torg flanked on its north side by Börsen, built in 1859

The destroyer *Småland*, 1952, in Maritiman

Maritiman ❹

Packhuskajen 8. **Tel** 031-10 59 50. 🚋 5, 10. 🚌 40, 42, 52, 80, 99. 🕐 May–Aug: 10am–6pm daily; Oct: 10am–6pm Fri–Sun; other times: 10am–4pm daily. 📷 www.maritiman.se

As the city's new port facilities moved further out towards the sea, Gothenburg's inner harbour became denuded of ships. Fortunately, the situation was rectified in 1987 when Göteborgs Maritima Centrum was set up on the harbour. The museum, now has 19 vessels at anchor, comprising what is said to be the world's largest floating ship museum.

Vessels include the destroyer *Småland*, built in 1952 at Eriksbergs shipyard on the other side of the river, the submarine *Nordkaparen* (1962), and the monitor *Sölve* (1875), as well as lightships, fireboats and tugs.

Kronhuset ❺

Postgatan 6–8. 🚋 1, 2, 3, 4, 5, 6, 7, 9, 10, 11, 13. 🚌 16, 40, 42, 50, 52, 58, 60, 86, 90, 91, 99, 771. 🚻 📷 ♿

A grand brick building in Dutch style, Kronhuset was constructed in 1643–55 and is Gothenburg's oldest preserved secular building. This part of town was originally a storage area for the artillery. The ground floor was converted into a chamber for the parliament of 1660.

Today, the building is used regularly for concerts and exhibitions.

Around the square are Kronhusbodarna (the Kronhus sheds), which create a pleasant setting for crafts people whose wares include pottery, glass, clocks and

Mid-17th-century Kronhuset, one of Gothenburg's oldest buildings

homemade sweets. There is also an old-fashioned country store with a café.

Gustav Adolfs Torg ❻

🚋 1, 2, 3, 4, 5, 6, 7, 9, 10, 11, 13. 🚌 16, 40, 42, 50, 52, 58, 60, 86, 90, 91, 99, 771. **Rådhuset** 🕐 8am–4.30pm daily. 🔵 public holidays. **Stadshuset** 🔵 to the public. **Börsen** 🔵 to the public.

Gothenburg's founder, Gustav II Adolf, gave his name to the city's central square. Since 1854 Bengt Erland Fogelberg's statue of the "hero king" has gazed imperiously over the square and Rådhuset (the Town Hall), Börsen (the Stock Exchange) and Stadshuset (the City Hall).

On 6 November, the date on which the king died at the Battle of Lützen in 1632, a special marzipan cake is made in his honor. It is topped with a piece of chocolate in the shape of the king's head.

Rådhuset, closest to Norra Hamngatan, was designed by Nicodemus Tessin the Elder and completed in 1673. It has a Functionalist extension designed in 1937 by Gunnar Asplund *(see p99)*.

The 18th-century **Stadshuset** and Wenngrenska Villa on the north side of the square are used by the city administration. **Börsen**, designed by P J Ekman in 1849, is the city's main venue for receptions and council meetings.

Ostindiska Huset (East India House) housing Göteborgs Stadsmuseum

Göteborgs Stadsmuseum ⑦

Norra Hamngatan 12. *Tel* 031-368 36 00. 🚋 1–11. 🚌 60, 86, 90. ⏰ 10am–5pm Tue–Sun (10am–8pm Wed). 🌐 public holidays. 📷 🎫 pre-book. 🛒 🍴 ♿

The city museum is aptly located in the historic Ostindiska Huset (East India House). The building, designed by Bengt Wilhelm Carlberg and Carl Hårleman, was constructed in 1747–62 as management premises, auction rooms and a warehouse for the East India Company. When trading

Chinese plate in the collection of Göteborgs Stadsmuseum

ceased in the early 19th century the building became a natural history museum, and in 1861 the City Museum was founded.

The permanent exhibitions show the early history of Western Sweden and the importance of the Göta Älv river as a route to Europe from the Viking period onwards. Displays focus on the history of the first inhabitants of Gothenburg and the industrialization and social upheavals of the 20th century. The work of the East India Company and its trade in exotic goods such as Chinese porcelain, silk and lacquer work, is also featured.

Domkyrkan ⑧

Västra Hamngatan. *Tel* 031-731 61 30. 🚋 1, 2, 6, 9, 11, 13. 🚌 16, 40, 60. ⏰ daily. 🎫 pre-book. 🛒 ♿ 🕐 daily.

Gothenburg's cathedral, Gustavi Domkyrka, was designed by C W Carlberg in

Neo-Classical style in 1815–25. It stands on the ruins of its two predecessors, which were both destroyed by fire.

In front of the cathedral in Domkyrkoplan is one of the city's preserved watering places: from the late 18th century water was transported here in hollowed-out oak logs from the well of Gustafs Källa to the south of the city.

Gustavi Domkyrka's impressive gilded altarpiece

Trädgårds-föreningen ⑨

Slussgatan. *Tel* 031-365 58 58. 🚋 1–5, 7, 9–11, 13. 🚌 21, 25, 28, 29, 43, 58, 59, 60, 514. **Park** ⏰ 7am–6pm Mon–Fri, 9am–6pm Sat & Sun; extended opening hours May–Sep. 📷 🎫 🛒 🍴 ♿ **Palm House** *Tel* 031-365 58 58. May–Aug: 10am–5pm daily; Sep–Apr: 10am–4pm daily. 24, 25 & 31 Dec. 📷 ♿

Gothenburg has many parks, but Trädgårdsföreningen is in a class of its own. In 1842 work began to transform a marshland south of Vallgraven into beautiful parkland for the benefit of the city's residents.

The flora of five continents are represented in the magnificent Palmhuset (Palm House) built in 1878. The building is filled with flowering camellias, giant bamboo, exotic orchids and plenty of palm trees.

Vattenhuset (the Water House) is carpeted by the twisting roots of mangrove trees and the 2-m (6-ft) wide petals of the giant water-lily.

The Rosarium is not to be missed, especially by rose lovers. It has become a leading world collection with more than 1,900 varieties.

There are cafés in the park and Trägår'n, a restaurant and

THE EAST INDIA COMPANY

Attracted by goods such as tea, silk and porcelain, Sweden was one of the countries which invested in trade with China in the 18th century and Gothenburg became a natural centre for this highly lucrative industry. The Swedish East India Company received its charter in 1731 and operated for 82 years, based in Ostindiska Huset (*see above*). In total, 132 expeditions were made to China in 38 different ships. In recent years interest in the work of the Company has resulted in the building of the East Indiaman *Götheborg*. This exact replica of the ship, which sank off Nya Älvsborgs Fästning (*see p205*) on its homeward voyage 250 years ago, set out to sail the traditional trade route to Canton in 2005. Since its return in 2007, the ship has been moored in the harbour.

The East Indiaman *Wasa* at Nya Älvsborgs Fästning

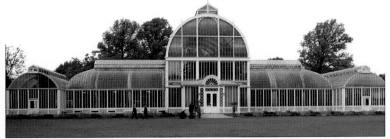

Trädgårdsföreningen's Palmhuset, containing plants and trees from five continents in various climatic zones

nightclub which has been entertaining pleasure-seeking locals since the 19th century. It is now housed in a new building with a large open-air terrace for partying.

Ullevi ⑩

Skånegatan. **Tel** 031- 81 10 20. 🚋 1, 3, 6. 🚌 2, 8, 60. ◯ during events. 🍴 ♿

Sweden's largest sporting arena, Ullevi, opened for the 1958 football World Cup and over the years has hosted numerous international events. Architect Fritz Jaenecke's elegant wave-shaped ellipse has been renovated and modernized several times. The arena seats 43,000 spectators for sporting events and can accommodate an audience of 60,000 for concerts.

In front of the arena, a statue has been erected in honour of Gunnar Gren (1920–91), one of Sweden's greatest-ever footballers.

Röhsska Museet ⑪

Vasagatan 37–39. **Tel** 031-61 38 50. 🚋 3, 4, 5, 7, 10. 🚌 42, 45, 49, 58, 753, 760, 764, 765. ◯ 11am–5pm Sat & Sun. ⬤ 24, 25, 31 Dec. 📷 📸 pre-book. 🖥 🎧 ♿ www. designmuseum.se

The country's leading museum of applied art and design, Röhsska Museet contains a marvellous collection of 20th-century Nordic domestic and decorative items. Other parts of the museum are devoted to European applied art, and antiquities from the ancient world, Japan and China. A

mere fraction of the total of 50,000 objects can be displayed at any one time. Specialist temporary exhibitions are also mounted.

The museum was founded with donations from financiers Wilhelm and August Röhss. It opened in 1916 as the Röhss Museum of Handicrafts in the beautiful brick building designed by architect Carl Westman.

Next to the museum is the University College for Arts and Crafts Design.

Chinese sculpture, Röhsska Museet

Universeum ⑫

Korsvägen. **Tel** 031-335 64 50. 🚋 4 5, 6, 8, 13. 🚌 49, 50, 52, 91, 330, 513, 761, 771. ◯ 10am–6pm daily (Jul–Aug: 9am–9pm). 📷 📸 🖥 🍴 🎧 ♿ www.universeum.se

Along the Mölndalsån river, not far from Kungsportsavenyn, spreads an area containing several of Gothenburg's major sights and venues, including Liseberg (see p200), Ullevi and Scandinavium sporting arenas and the conference

Universeum, designed by Gert Wingårdh and built in 2001

centre Svenska Mässan. The Universeum science centre is the latest addition, and provides an educational and fun experience for all the family. Opened in 2001, the environmentally friendly building was designed by Gothenburg architect Gert Wingårdh and was voted Sweden's best contemporary building in the same year. The centre aims to stimulate the interest of children and young people in science and technology. Here, they can come face-to-face with exotic creatures such as sting-rays, anacondas and monkeys, study galaxies, use forensic evidence to solve crimes, and conduct ingenious experiments.

Världskultur-museet ⑬

Södra Vägen 54. **Tel** 031-63 27 00. 🚋 2, 4, 5, 6, 8, 13. 🚌 50, 52, 91. ◯ noon–5pm Tue, Fri–Sun, noon–9pm Wed–Thu. 📷 📸 🖥 🍴 🎧 ♿ www.varldskulturmuseet.se

Designed by the London-based architects Cécile Brisac and Edgar Gonzalez, the icecube-like Världskultur-museet is a museum of world cultures, completed in 2005. The exhibitions, like the building, are far from traditional; they are intended to surprise, provoke and question stereotyped attitudes towards culture and subculture, and are complemented by a programme of concerts, films, dance and poetry.

Konstmuseet on Götaplatsen, the city's main square, with Carl Milles' statue of Poseidon in the foreground

Liseberg ⑭

Örgrytevägen 1. 🚋 2, 4, 5, 6, 8, 13.
🚌 50, 49, 52, 91, 513, 761, 771.
Tel 031-400 100. ⬜ *last week in Apr–
last week in Sep: opening times vary.
Christmas opening: mid-Nov–23 Dec.*
🖼 🏠 🍴 ♿ 🍴 www.liseberg.se

The people of Gothenburg
are rightly proud of their
amusement park which
attracts huge numbers
of visitors. Apart from
the latest rides, this is
the place for dancing
and entertain-
ment, shows
and theatre
performances. It
is also a beautiful
green park where
garden design has
always played a
major role.

The park's history
began in the 18th
century when financier
Johan Anders Lamberg
bought the land and built
the first magnificent house,

Flower Girl by
Gerhard Henning in
Liseberg park

Landeriet, in 1753. He had
two passions in life – gardening and his wife Lisa, after
whom the new house on the
hill was named, Liseberg.

The City of Gothenburg
bought the site for the Gothenburg Exhibition in 1923 and
founded the amusement park
with the installation of an
impressive wooden roller-
coaster. Other rides
followed, attracting 140
million visitors over the
past 80 years. "Balder" is
the biggest roller-coaster
in the Nordic
countries. It reaches
a speed of 90 km/h
(56 mph) from a
top height of 36 m
(118 ft). This
wooden roller-
coaster is
reminiscent of the
park's first one.
"Kanonen" offers
another extreme experience,
with its rapid acceleration,
sharp loops and turns and
360-degree rotation.

Götaplatsen ⑮

🚋 4, 5. 🚌 42, 58, 158.
Konstmuseet *Tel* 031-368 35 00.
⬜ *11am–6pm Tue, Thu; 11am–9pm
Wed; 11am–5pm Fri–Sun.* ● *1 Jan,
Good Friday, 1 May, Midsummer,
6 Jun, 24, 25 & 31 Dec.* 🖼 ♿ 🏠
🖥 **Konsthallen** *Tel* 031-368 34 50.
⬜ *11am–6pm Tue, Thu; 11am–8pm
Wed; 11am–5pm Fri–Sun.* 🖼 ♿ 🏠
🖥 **Konserthuset** ⬜ *for concerts.*
Tel 031-726 53 10. **Stadsteatern** *Tel*
031-708 71 00. ⬜ *for performances.*

The focal point of the city
is Götaplatsen, the square at
the southwestern end of
Kungsportsavenyn. Here
Gothenburg's bastions of
culture, Konstmuseet (the
Art Museum), Konsthallen
(the Art Hall), Konserthuset
(the Concert Hall), Stadsteatern
(the City Theatre) and Stadsbiblioteket (the City Library) sit
in state. In the centre of this
grand square, the water plays
around Carl Milles' giant statue
Poseidon, which has become
the symbol of Gothenburg.

Götaplatsen was built for
the city's 300th anniversary
and the Gothenburg Exhibition in 1923, which is why
many of the buildings were
exhibition premises from the
start. Wide steps lead up from
the southeastern side of the
square to **Konstmuseet**,
designed by Sigfrid Ericson,
which became a museum in
1925. It contains a rich
collection of Nordic art, with
key works by Carl Larsson,
Ernst Josephson and the
Gothenburg Colourists. The

Liseberg's main stage and venue for shows, bands, acrobats and more

For hotels and restaurants in this region see pp287–288 and p305

Danish golden age, Dutch and Flemish painting and French Modernists are also represented. Pride of place is taken by Furstenbergska Galleriet, a copy of the gallery which the great patron of the arts had in his private palace in the late 19th century. The neighbouring **Konsthallen** shows temporary exhibitions. The bronze lion on the façade is by Palle Pernevi.

Konserthuset on the south-western side of the square was designed by Nils Einar Eriksson and opened in 1935. The foyer is decorated with murals by Prince Eugen (*Grove of Memories*) and Otte Sköld (*Folk Song*) as well as a large tapestry by Sven X-et Erixson (*Melodies in the Square*).

Stadsteatern, built in 1934, reopened in 2002 after extensive renovation to highlight the best of Carl Bergsten's elegant 1930's architecture.

Skansen Kronan fortress (1687) on guard high above Gothenburg

Skansen Kronan

Skansberget. 🚃 1, 6. 🚌 60, 80, 760, 764, 765. **Tel** 031-711 30 33. 🕐 noon–3pm Fri. ⬤ public holidays. 📷 pre-book. ♿ limited access.

Topped by a golden crown, the octagonal Skansen Kronan fortress dates from Sweden's Age of Greatness (*see pp36–7*). It sits enthroned on the peak of Skansberget. Like its counterpart Skansen Lejonet, near the station area, Kronan is one of the most striking survivors of Erik Dahlbergh's fortifications. It was built in 1687 to protect the city from attack from the south. During the 1850s it was used as a shelter for homeless citizens and has also been a prison.

The fortress is surrounded by Skansberget, a leafy park offering excellent views from the top, up steep steps.

Walkers and shoppers in Haga with its pleasant wooden houses

Haga ⓱

🚃 1, 3, 6, 9, 11. 🚌 60, 80, 760, 764, 765.

The former working-class area of the city south of Vallgraven is one of the few places to experience old Gothenburg. The cobbled streets, courtyards and wooden houses of Gamla Haga are home to craftspeople and lined with small shops, cafés and restaurants.

Haga was Gothenburg's first suburb as early as the 17th century and was mainly populated by harbour workers. During the industrialization of the 19th century a shanty town grew up here and tenements filled with people thronging in from the countryside to seek work.

In the 1960s and 70s Haga was fast becoming a slum and threatened with demolition. Widespread public opposition to the plans ensured that important parts were saved and the houses renovated. Some of the *landshövdinge-husen* ("county governor's houses") typical of the area can be seen. These were built in the 1880s, when rules set in 1854 banning wooden houses in the centre more than two storeys high were circumvented – with the governor's approval. Providing the building had a ground floor in brick, as these do, it could have two wooden floors above and not constitute a fire risk.

Feskekôrka ⓲

Rosenlundsgatan. 🚃 1, 3, 6, 9, 11. 🚌 50, 60, 91, 80, 760, 764, 765. 🕐 9am–5pm Tue–Thu; 9am–6pm Fri; 10am–3pm Sat. ⬤ public hols. 📷 🍴 ♿

It is easy to see why the wits of Gothenburg nicknamed the fish market Feskekôrka (the fish church). Victor von Gegerfelt borrowed from Gothic church architecture when he designed this market hall in 1874, incorporating a steeply pitched roof and large oriel windows.

The catch from the North Sea is brought here directly, guaranteeing the freshest mackerel and the most delicious shellfish. These days there is more to the market than simply selling fish over the counter – the hall provides a colourful setting for restaurant tables at which seafood specialities can be sampled.

Feskekôrka fish market, a paradise for lovers of fish and seafood

Sjöfartsmuseet and Akvariet ⑲

Karl Johansgatan 1–3. *Tel 031-61 29 00.* 🚃 3, 9 and 11. ◐ 10am–5pm Tue–Sun (10am–8pm Wed). ● some public holidays. 📷 phone for info. ♿ 🏠 📷 📷
Sjömanstornet *Tel 0731-81 56 00.* ◐ groups only, phone for info. 📷
www.sjofartsmuseum.goteborg.se

The maritime history of Gothenburg and Bohuslän is the subject of Sjöfartsmuseet (the Maritime Museum). Set up in 1933, it was funded by the Broström shipping family and is situated on Stigberget, high above the Göta Älv river.

The work of Sweden's largest port, changes in the shipbuilding industry over the centuries and the history of Gothenburg's many shipping lines come under the spotlight. Fishing from the medieval herring period to today also features prominently.

Akvariet (the Aquarium) is dedicated to the marine life of the west coast. Here, it is possible to see how crabs, starfish and sea anemones live 40 m (130 ft) below the surface. A touch-pool allows visitors to come into close contact with some creatures.

Gamla Varvsparken contains various busts including one of the shipbuilder F H af Chapman (1721–1808) (see p77). **Sjömanstornet** tower outside the museum is topped by Ivar Johansson's bronze sculpture *Woman by the Sea*, 1933, in memory of the sailors from western Sweden who died in World War I.

The sculpture *Woman by the Sea* topping the "sailors' tower"

Gathenhielmska Huset, once the home of Privateer Captain Lars Gathenhielm

Gathenhielmska Huset ⑳

Allmänna Vägen. 🚃 3, 9, 11. ● to the public apart from the café. 📷

The western side of the Stigberget hill was formerly the site of the Amiralitetsvarvet shipyard and it was here in the early 1700s that Privateer Captain Lars Gathenhielm was granted land by Karl XII. His widow built a two-storey manor house here in 1740. It is one of Sweden's best examples of a Carolian wooden house designed to imitate stone.

Next to the house is an open-air museum of small wooden houses showing what a suburb looked like in 1800.

Slottsskogen and Naturhistoriska Museet ㉑

Linnéplatsen. 🚃 49. 🚃 1, 2, 6, 13.
Naturhistoriska museet
Tel 031-775 24 00. ◐ 11am–5pm Tue–Sun. ● some public holidays. 📷 📷 phone to book. 🏠 📷 ♿
www.gnm.se

Since the 1870s, Slottsskogen has been one of the city's finest green spaces. Crisscrossed by paths, it features dazzling planting, ponds, a zoo and various activities. In spring the azalea valley is ablaze with colour. In 1999, what was then the world's longest border, with over 90,000 flowering bulbs, was created. There are a number of old cottages from western Sweden to be seen in the park. Areas for sport and outdoor activities include Slottsskogsvallen. The park has several cafés and a restaurant.

Gothenburg's oldest museum, **Naturhistoriska Museet** (the Museum of Natural History), lies in the northern part of the park. Dating from 1833, it moved to Slottsskogen in 1923. Its vast collection of more than 10 million exhibits incorporates animals of all sizes from all around the world, including brightly coloured insects and an African elephant.

The most famous of its stuffed animals is Malmska Valen, a blue whale measuring more than 16 m (52 ft) long, which was beached in Askimsviken in 1865. It was stuffed and mounted on a treetrunk. The upper jaw opens, and inside the whale there is a room with benches and wall hangings where it is said coffee used to be served. Now the whale is only open for visits on special occasions.

Botaniska Trädgården ㉒

Carl Skottsbergs Gata 22 A. *Tel 031-741 11.* 🚃 58. 🚃 1, 2, 7, 8, 13. ◐ 9am–sunset daily. 📷 voluntary. ♿ 📷 🏠 📷 **www**.gotbot.se

Covering 1,750,000 sq m (432 acres) and containing 16,000 species, Gothenburg's Botanical Garden is one of the largest of its kind in Europe. Just under a fifth of the area has been developed into gardens, while the remainder forms a nature reserve partly consisting of primeval forest.

The gardens began to be designed in 1916 and have been expanded continually ever since. The Rhododendron Valley offers a rich tapestry

◁ **Haga's "county governor's buildings" with a stone ground floor and two wooden storeys above**

of dazzling flowers in late spring each year.

The Rock Garden, in a former quarry, contains 5,000 alpine plants from around the world. In early summer the Japanese Glade with its scented magnolias is a delight while autumn sees an oriental riot of colour.

Large greenhouses shelter the plants from the sometimes bitter climate. The controlled environments within recreate a variety of conditions from desert to steaming rain forest. In the tropical house, bamboo and banana plants stretch more than 10 m (33 ft) up to the ceiling and there are 1,500 orchids in the most amazing colours and shapes.

Eriksbergs shipyard with Sjömanstornet and Älvsborgsbron bridge

Botaniska Trädgården, a blossoming oasis in the city

The Harbour ㉓

N of the centre between Götaälvbron and Älvsborgsbron bridges. *Tel* 031-60 96 60. 🚊 to Lilla Bommen. 🚢 from Lilla Bommen or Padden sightseeing boat from Kungsportsbron, up to 4 times an hour. **www**.borjessons.co

Seafaring has been of immense importance to Gothenburg and the harbour and shipyard have long dominated the area along the Göta Älv river. Now the shipbuilding industry is a shadow of its former self and apart from ferry traffic, the major shipping activities have moved down to the mouth of the river. Yet, although there is little loading and unloading to be seen in the centre of the city these days, three times more goods are shipped today than in the 1960s.

The inner harbour and shipyard area bordered by the imposing **Älvsborgsbron** bridge have been transformed to provide housing, offices and centres for research and education. Nevertheless, the pulse of seafaring can still be experienced either on a regular ferry from Lilla Bommen to **Eriksbergsvarvet** shipyard, or on the white, flat-bottomed **Padden Boats** which run from Kunsportsbron bridge (about a 10-minute walk away) via 17th-century Vallgraven down the river to the inner harbour. The round trip takes about 50 minutes.

GöteborgsOperan is best viewed from the water *(see p196)*, as are **Barken Viking** *(see p196)* and **Göteborgs Maritima Centrum** *(see p197)*.

Eriksbergs shipyard on Hisingen is the home port of the spectacular East Indiaman *Götheborg (see p198)*. Tours also operate around the island of Hisingen and the outer harbour, and to the Gothenburg archipelago. The **Fishing Harbour** holds an auction Tuesdays to Fridays at 6.30am.

Nya Älvsborgs Fästning ㉔

8 km (3 miles) W of the centre. *Tel* 031-60 96 70. 🚢 from Lilla Bommen. ☐ May– Aug. 🖼 🍴 ✦

In 1660 a new fortress on Kyrkogårdsholmen, at the mouth of the Göta Älv river, replaced the dilapidated, centrally located Älvsborg castle to defend Sweden's precious gateway to the North Sea. It was besieged by the Danes in 1717 and 1719, but never captured. In the late 18th century it became a prison which closed in 1869.

Today the fortress is a popular tourist destination in summer; it even has a wedding chapel.

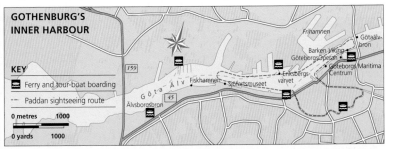

GOTHENBURG'S INNER HARBOUR

KEY

🚢 Ferry and tour-boat boarding

--- Paddan sightseeing route

0 metres   1000

0 yards   1000

Frihamnen · Götaälv-bron
Barken Viking ·
GöteborgsOperan ·
· Göteborgs Maritima Centrum
159
Fiskhamnen · Sjöfartsmuseet · Eriksbergs-varvet
Göta Älv
45
Älvsborgsbron

WESTERN GOTALAND

*S*panning four provinces – Dalsland, Bohuslän, Västergötland and Halland – this attractive and immensely diverse part of Sweden borders Norway to the west, touches on the great forests in the north and reaches to Lake Vättern in the east. Sweden's largest lake, Vänern, lies at its heart. The waters of the Kattegat and Skagerrak wash the rocky shores and sandy beaches along the coast.

Dalsland in the northwest of Western Götaland is one of Sweden's smallest provinces and is relatively unknown even among Swedes. The landscape is hilly and it is often said that the border with Norrland starts here with the mountain area of Kroppefjäll as its southwestern outpost. From the plains of agricultural Dalsland this border can be seen rearing up like a dark forest-clad wall to the west, while the blue expanse of Lake Vänern glistens to the east. The area is sparsely populated, but campaigns are in hand to attract Norwegians over the border to swell the numbers.

In the southwest, Dalsland borders Bohuslän, a coastal province where the smooth bare rocks are dotted with brightly-painted little wooden houses. Here fishing and the stone industry have been the backbone of the economy since the Middle Ages, but today tourism is the chief money earner; the population of many coastal communities doubles in summer. Bohuslän's main city is Gothenburg, Sweden's second largest metropolis *(see pp190–205)*.

Västergötland lies between lakes Vänern and Vättern. The area has been inhabited since ancient times and has many prehistoric remains. It was the first region in Sweden to be converted to Christianity and has an abundance of early churches. The country's first Christian king, Olof Skötkonung, is thought to have been baptised at Husaby in 1008 *(see p32)* and two of the medieval royal dynasties had their roots in Västergötland. Some claim that this was indeed the cradle of Sweden.

Halland, the coastal region south of Gothenburg, is also a summer paradise, with its long sandy beaches. There are several towns for shopping and some of southern Sweden's most interesting castles and manor houses.

Gunnebo, a wealthy merchant's 18th-century manor house near Gothenburg, now a museum

◁ Tjärnö in Bohuslän, a typical west-coast settlement with fishermen's huts, boats and lobster pots

Exploring Western Götaland

Driving is one of the best ways to explore Western Götaland and experience Dalsand's landscape of lakes, mountain plateaus and rural flatlands, and still have time to spend on the sandy beaches of Halland in the south. Boat trips are a popular way of seeing the small islands and fishing hamlets off the coast of Bohuslän, while the scenery around lakes Vänern and Vättern can be enjoyed from aboard a ferry. Between the lakes, the great forest of Tiveden offers opportunities for hiking. The region as a whole is one in which the ancient past is always present, especially at the UNESCO World Heritage Site of Tanum, where Bronze Age people carved pictures in the rock.

Oslo

3 STRÖMSTAD   Kornsjö

4 KOSTER ISLANDS

Tanumshede

5   Högs

6 FJÄLLBACKA

Gerlesborg   Munkeda

NORDENS ARK **7**

Hunnebostrand   UDDEVALL

SMÖGEN **8**

LYSEKIL **10**

SKAFTÖ **12** **11** BASSHOLM

GULLHOLMEN **13**   **14** ORUST

Stenungsund

Mollösund

Skärhamn   **15** TJÖRN

BOHUSLÄN

MARSTRAND **16** KUNGÄLV

Surt

Götheborg
(See pp190–205)

GUNNEBO S

KUNGSB

Ry

Kattega

The former lighthouse-keeper's cottage on the approach to Marstrand, now an exclusive summer residence

GETTING AROUND

For drivers, two major roads cross through Western Götaland: the E20, which comes from the northeast via Örebro across the plains to Gothenburg on the west coast, and the E6, which follows the coast northwards towards Norway. Road 45 from Värmland runs south through Dalsland. There are bus and train links between the large towns and populated areas. Regular ferries operate to the majority of inhabited islands along the coast.

KEY

▬▬▬	Motorway
▬▬	Major road
▭▭▭	Minor road
▬▭▬	Railway line
▭▭	Minor railway
▬▬▬	International border
△	Summit

Tylösand outside Halmstad, one of the many glorious, long sandy beaches of Halland

SEE ALSO

- **Where to Stay** pp288–290
- **Where to Eat** p306

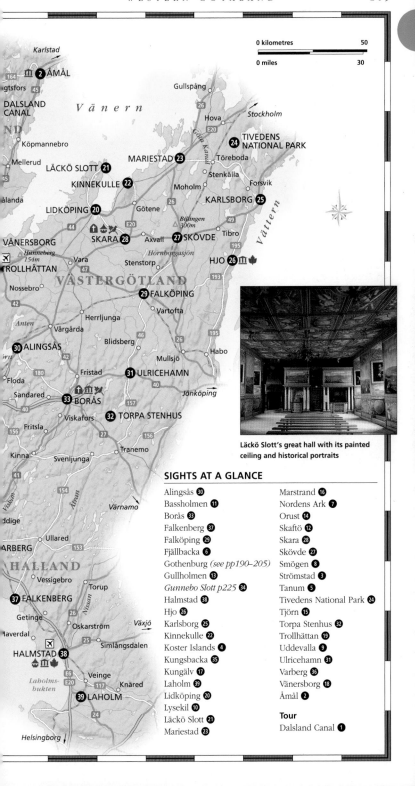

| 0 kilometres | 50 |
| 0 miles | 30 |

Karlstad

2 ÅMÅL

gtsfors

**DALSLAND
CANAL**

ND

Köpmannebro

Mellerud

LÄCKÖ SLOTT **21**

KINNEKULLE **22**

LIDKÖPING **20**

ålanda

VÄNERSBORG

TROLLHÄTTAN

Hunneberg
154m

Vara

SKARA **28**

VÄSTERGÖTLAND

Nossebro

Anten

Vårgårda

30 ALINGSÅS

Floda

Sandared

33 BORÅS

Fritsla

Kinna

Svenljunga

Viskafors

31 ULRICEHAMN

32 TORPA STENHUS

Tranemo

Värnamo

ddige

Ullared

ARBERG

HALLAND

Vessigebro

Torup

37 FALKENBERG

Getinge

Oskarström

Växjö

Maverdal

HALMSTAD **38**

Veinge

Laholms-
bukten

Knäred

39 LAHOLM

Helsingborg

Gullspång

Hova

Stockholm

24 TIVEDENS
NATIONAL PARK

MARIESTAD **23**

Töreboda

Stenkälla

Moholm

Forsvik

KARLSBORG **25**

Götene

Billingen
△ 300m

Axvall

27 SKÖVDE

Tibro

Stenstorp

Hornborgasjön

HJO **26**

29 FALKÖPING

Vartofta

Herrljunga

Blidsberg

Mullsjö

Habo

Fristad

Jönköping

Vänern

Göta Kanal

Vättern

Vreten

Simlångsdalen

Läckö Slott's great hall with its painted
ceiling and historical portraits

SIGHTS AT A GLANCE

A Tour on the Dalsland Canal ●

From Bengtsfors the Dalsland Canal carves its way south towards Köpmannebro on Lake Vänern, passing through 19 locks and dropping 45 m (148 ft) to the lake. The scenery varies from beautiful, almost untouched countryside to modern communities, from old ironworks to historic manor houses. The spectacular aqueduct at Håverud is formed from a series of steel plates joined by 33,000 rivets. Both a rail and a road bridge traverse the deep gorge. The canal was designed by Nils Ericsson in the 1860s.

One of the canal's 19 locks making navigation possible

Baldersnäs Herrgård ②
The manor house stands on a promontory in Lake Laxsjö, on the Dalsland Canal. It is set in a romantic park with paths, caves and artificial islands.

Bengtsfors ①
The canal trip begins or ends here. Don't miss Gammelgården open-air museum with its wooden cottages and storehouses.

KEY

▬ Suggested route by car

-- Route by boat

= Other roads

— Railway line

Högsbyn Rock Carvings ③
Pictures of ships, people and footprints carved in stone 3,000 years ago can be reached by special boat from Håverud, or by car.

Håverud Aqueduct ④
A solution to the problem of crossing a gorge and a 9-m (30-ft) high waterfall was to build four locks and a long steel aqueduct over the waterfall, followed by another lock.

TIPS FOR THE TRIP

Length: 5½ hours by boat.
Boat route: from Bengtsfors to Köpmannabro or reverse. The boat stops at several points along the way. Return by bus or train, around 1 hour.

0 kilometres 5

0 miles 3

Hotell Skagerack on the harbourfront in Strömstad

Åmål ②

Dalsland. Road 45. 🏠 *9,400.* 🚌
🚌 🚆 *Karlstad.* ⛴ 🛈 *Marinan,
Hamngatan 1, 0532-170 98.* 🎫 *Åmål
Blues Festival (2nd week in Jul).*
www.dalsland.se

Dalslands only town, Åmål,
was founded in 1643. Thanks
to its strategic location on
Lake Vänern, Åmål soon
became an important market
place, controlling timber
exports to Norway and later
acting as a transit port for
timber and iron to Gothenburg.
After several fires in the 17th
century and a major fire in
1901, a new town was built
on the north side of the
Åmålsån river. Little remains
of the original buildings apart
from a few 18th-century
houses around the town park,
Plantaget. The local history
museum, **Åmåls Hembygds-
museum**, whose three floors
house a dentist's clinic and a
flat furnished in 1920s style,
can be found in Snarhögs-
gården. The Railway Museum
is located in former engine
sheds at Åmål Östra.

At **Forsbacka** on the
Åmålsån river, 7 km (4 miles)
from Åmål towards
Bengtsfors, a mechanical
hammer for producing iron
bars was built at the end of
the 17th century. It was used
until the end of the 19th
century. Today the 18th-
century house at Forsbacka
ironworks is a hotel and the
old buildings are protected. A
golf course is on the land.

🏛 **Åmåls Hembygdsmuseum**
Hamngatan 4. **Tel** *0532-158 20.*
⭘ *mid-Jun–Aug: daily.* 🎫
🔖 *partly.*

Strömstad ③

Bohuslän. E6. 🏠 *6,000.* 🚌 🚌
⛴ *from Sandefjord, Norway.* ⛴
🛈 *Norra Hamnen, 0526-623 30.*
🎫 *Winter World Festival (1st week in
Mar), Strömstad Festival (2nd Sat in
Jul). Summer music (Jul), Man Must
Dance (last weekend in Jul).*

When Strömstad became
Swedish in 1658 it was just a
small fishing village, but by
1676 it had become a town,
acting as a strategic counter
to the Norwegian towns of
Halden and Fredrikstad. In
the mid-19th century sea-
bathing became the
fashion and ever since,
Strömstad, with its
glorious island archi-
pelago and many hours
of sunshine, has been
one of Sweden's major
holiday resorts.

After a fire in the
1870s Strömstad was
rebuilt. Today it is a
modern town and its
proximity to Norway is
evident from the
number of Norwegian
cars and boats.

The **Strömstads Museum**
focuses on local history, while
Friluftsmuseet Fiskartorpet is

an open-air museum
featuring fishermen's cottages.

The harbour with bars and
shops is in the centre of the
town and boats from here
serve the islands, including
Kosteröarna. Seal safaris
operate to waters around the
Ursholmarna islands south of
Sydkoster. The nature
reserves on Rossö and Saltö
can be reached by car.

🏛 **Strömstad Museum**
Södra Hamngatan 22. **Tel** *0526-102
75.* ⭘ *Mon–Sat.* ⬤ *public holidays.*
🏛 **Friluftsmuseet
Fiskartorpet**
Karlsgatan 45. **Tel** *0526-617 53.*
⭘ *summer: daily.* 🔖

Koster Islands ④

Bohuslän. 🏠 *300.* 🚢 *from Strömstad.*
⛴ 🛈 *Strömstad Tourist,
0526-623 30.*

The islands of Koster are
renowned for their beauty
and their flora. Together they
form a nature reserve. These
are the westernmost
Swedish islands to be
inhabited: Nordkoster
has a permanent
population of around 40
people. Sydkoster is the
largest island in the
group. It is greener than
Nordkoster and is best
explored by bike. In
contrast, Nordkoster is
much more barren and
can easily be explored
on foot.

The highlights of
the Koster Islands'
calendar include the annual
rowing race across the sound
between the islands in August
and the lobster festival in
the autumn.

**Boiled Koster
lobster**

Made for sunbathing, the polished granite rocks on Nordkoster

Tanum ❺

Bohuslän. E6. 🏠 12,000. 🚉 🚌
ℹ️ Tourist Office, Tanumshede, 0525-
183 80. **www.**tanumturist.se

The municipality of Tanum
has an extraordinary 525 km
(326 miles) of coastline
indented with fjords and bays.
It stretches from Gerlesborg in
the south to Galtö in the
north, and is sheltered by a
mass of islets and skerries
offshore. Inland, farms nestle
between rocky outcrops.

Above all, Tanum is
renowned for its Bronze Age
rock carvings, with the earliest
dating from around 1000 BC.
Indeed, the concentration of
these pictorial images and
their contribution to the
understanding of Bronze Age
culture is such that they were
designated a UNESCO World
Heritage Site in 1994. Subjects
include human life, animals,
boats and weapons carved
onto smooth rock.

The largest carving, covering
200 sq m (2,150 sq ft), can be
seen at Vitlycke. **Vitlycke
Museum** is well worth a visit
for a fascinating insight into
this form of rock art. The
museum contains exhibitions
and a reconstructed Bronze
Age farm. Guided tours by
night, when carvings that are

Fjällbacka's painted wooden houses in the shadow of Vetteberget

not visible by day emerge in
the light of a torch, are
especially enthralling for any
age group.

Around the region, carvings
featuring hunting scenes can
be seen at **Fossum**, east of
Tanumshede; **Tegneby** has
images of ships; and at
Asberget scenes containing
animals, ploughs and axes can
be found.

🏛️ **Vitlycke Museum**
3 km (2 miles) S of Tanumshede. **Tel**
0525-209 50. ⬜ May–Sep. 📷 🔒
🚻 🍴 🛍️ 📷 by arrangement. ♿

Fjällbacka ❻

Bohuslän. E6/road 163. 🏠 850.
🚌 to Tanum, then bus. 🚌 ℹ️
Torget, 0525-321 20. 🎣 Mackerel
Fishing World Championships (last Sat
in Aug).

On the coast between
Strömstad and Uddevalla lies
the picturesque village of
Fjällbacka. There has been a
settlement here since the 17th
century and like many other
villages along this coast the
community made a living
from herring fishing and
seafaring. Today, holidaymakers come for the
swimming and boating.

Attractive low-rise wooden
houses and shops line the
narrow streets, but it is the
harbour which is the heart of
the community. This is where
the fishing huts, bars and
tourist services are located.
Fjällbacka has a stunning

BRONZE AGE ROCK CARVINGS

The rock carvings at Tanum represent a high point in the
artistic language of pictures and symbols used by Bronze
Age people more than 3,000 years ago. Images reflect daily
life and hardships, battles won and lost, weapons and
hunting scenes. Mating scenes, fertility symbols and the
afterlife are also common. The importance of the sea is
reflected in the proliferation of ships and fishing scenes. It
is thought that the rock paintings were primarily of ritual

significance, but the depiction
of animals could have acted as
a calendar to show when various creatures could be hunted.
Hands and feet as motifs are
thought to be associated with a
godly being too holy to have
his whole body depicted.

Rock carvings can be found
all over the world, with the
oldest dating from 20,000 BC.
Those in Sweden are younger,
since it wasn't completely free
of ice until 6,500 BC. The
carvings at Tanum date from
1000–500 BC.

Bronze Age warrior in a state
of sexual arousal, Tanum

Bust of actress Ingrid Bergman
(1915–82) in Fjällbacka

location with islands offshore and the 70-m (230-ft) high mountain, Vetteberget, creating a precipitous backdrop to the village centre and square known as Ingrid Bergmans Torg. Actress Ingrid Bergman spent many summers in Fjällbacka and after her death her name was given to the square and a bust made by Gudmar Olovson (1983).

Vetteberget is divided by a huge gorge, known as Kungsklyfta, named after King Oscar II who visited Fjällbacka in 1887 and had his name carved at the entrance to the chasm. This dramatic setting was also used as a location for the film of Astrid Lindgren's children's book *Ronja Rövardotter* (Ronja the Robber's Daughter).

Nordens Ark ❼

Bohuslän. Road 17, 20 km (12 miles) N of Smögen. 🚍 *Tel* 0523-795 90. ⏰ *10am–5pm daily (to 7pm mid-Jun–mid-Aug, to 4pm Oct–Apr).* 📷 🚻 ♿
www.nordensark.se

The nature park and zoo, Nordens Ark, caters specifically for endangered species. Located in Åby Säteri, it contains animals from every corner of the world, including ancient Swedish breeds such as Gotland sheep and mountain cows, Nordic wild animals such as wolves and

Red panda one of the many endangered species at Nordens Ark

wolverine, and exotic species such as the Amur leopard and a variety of parrots. Many of the creatures are part of special programmes to protect them from extinction.

To see the animals at close quarters, follow the 3-km (2-mile) walk around the park – and bring binoculars to spot the wide variety of birds. The route takes you between the enclosures via wooden bridges and along gravel paths. Admission in the summer includes a guided tour. The breeding and quarantine areas are not open to the public.

Nordens Ark is a particularly enjoyable outing for families as there are special children's activities throughout the park. Youngsters can find out how animals adapt in relation to their food, enemies and the environment by being active

themselves, trying things out and playing – even adults find these activities entertaining.

Overnight accommodation is also available.

Smögen ❽

Bohuslän. E6/Road 174. 🚩 *1,500.* 🚌 *from Gothenburg.* ♿ 🚻 ℹ️ *Sotenäs Tourist Office, Kungshamn, 0523-66 55 50.* 🎭 *Herring and Shellfish Festival (3rd weekend in Jul), Tradjazz (first weekend in Aug).* **www**.sotenasturism.se

One of Sweden's largest fishing communities, Smögen today is a delightful holiday resort with shrimp trawlers and the daily fish auction providing popular entertainment. Commerce is particularly lively along the wooden quayside.

Ferries operate to the island of Hållö, a nature reserve south of Smögen where there is a lighthouse, **Hållö Fyr**, which has guided seafarers since 1842.

The **Sotenkanalen** links Smögen and Hunnebostrand. Built in the 1930s, the canal is 6 km (4 miles) long and a popular tourist route. **Hunnebostrand** is a typical west coast holiday destination and home to Svenska Hummerakademien (the Swedish Lobster Academy). The village's development was based on stonemasonry.

Wooden houses lining the quays of Smögen's well-protected harbour

Uddevalla ❾

Bohuslän. E6, road 44. 🏃 *36,000.*
🚊 🚌 ✈ *Trollhättan.*
ℹ️ *Kungstorget, 0522-997 20.*
🎭 *Motocross World Championships
(first weekend in Jul), West Coast
Dance Festival (mid-Jul), Fjord Festival
(last weekend in Jul).*
www.uddevalla.com

The town of Uddevalla was
famous for shipbuilding on
a grand scale until the 1980s
when an economic crisis
forced the closure of its shipyard. Uddevalla's history dates
from 1498 when it gained its
town charter. Its strategic
location helped trade to
flourish, but also left it open
to attack. It became Swedish
in the Peace of Roskilde in
1658, as the statues of Karl X
Gustav and Erik Dahlbergh in
front of the old town hall
testify. Among the town's
attractions, the collections at
Bohusläns Museum focus on
the cultural and natural
heritage of the region. The
museum is by the harbour,
and includes **Konstgalleriet**, a
gallery for contemporary art.
Sveriges Sjömanshusmuseum
concentrates on the history of
seafaring. **Bohusläns Försvars-
museum** (Defence Museum)
has a soldier's cottage among
its exhibits.

Environs
Nature lovers will enjoy the
unusual shellbanks and
museum devoted to them,
Skalbanksmuseet, in Kuröd,
outside Uddevalla.
  The old church of **Bokenäs**
is originally from the 12th
century. The tower and the
church's restored ceiling
paintings date from the 18th
century. The church is on

**Bohusläns Museum in Uddevalla with a
display of old working boats**

Ornate carving on the façade of Restaurang Havsbadet, Lysekil

road 161, 23 km (14 miles)
west of Uddevalla.

🏛 **Bohusläns Museum**
Museigatan 1. **Tel** *0522-65 65 00.*
⬜ *Aug: daily; Sep: Fri–Sun.* 🎟 *by
arrangement.* 🖼 🍴 📷

🏛 **Skalbanksmuseet**
5 km (3 miles) E of Uddevalla.
Tel *0522-65 65 00.* ⬜ *Aug: daily;
Sep: Fri–Sun.* 📷

Lysekil ❿

Bohuslän. E6/road 162. 🏃 *7,300.*
🚊 *to Uddevalla, then bus.* 🚌 🚢
from Fiskebäckskil. ℹ️ *Södra Hamngatan 6, 0523-130 50.* 🎭 *Hot Bulb
Engine Festival (3rd weekend in Aug).*
www.lysekil.se

When Lysekil gained its
town charter in 1903 the town
was already an established
seaside resort. Buildings in
the old part of Lysekil,
Gamlestan, are more than
200 years old. A walk along
Strandgatan reveals the charm
of this old quarter.
  The 19th-century sea-bathing
area has been beautifully
restored. There is a cold bath
house, Oscars Festsal, and the
Nordic-style Curmanska
Villas. The rest of the town is
dominated by the
large, Neo-Gothic
granite church dating
from 1901.
  Lysekil lies at the far
end of the Stångenäset
peninsula, with
Gullmarsfjorden –
Sweden's only real
"fjord" in a Norwegian
sense – to the south
and Brofjorden to the
north, and here the
sea has always played
a major role. The

town's aquarium, **Havets Hus**,
is devoted to the marine and
plant life found off the
Bohuslän coast. Around 100
different species of fish can
be viewed in their natural
habitats. There is a walk-
through aquarium and a multimedia centre. The town's
fishing traditions can also be
experienced at the Hot Bulb
Engine Festival.

🏛 **Havets Hus**
Strandvägen 9. **Tel** *0523-66 81 61.*
⬜ *Feb–Dec: daily.*
🎟 📷 🍴 📷 ♿ 📷

Bassholmen ⓫

Bohuslän. Road 161 towards
Fiskebäckskil. 🚌 *to Källeviken, then 2
km (1 mile) walk and boat.* 🚢 *from
Uddevalla Tue–Sat.* ♿ ℹ️ *Uddevalla
Tourist Office, 0522-997 20.*
Youth Hostel Tel *0522-65 13 08.*

The nature reserve on the
island of Bassholmen,
between Orust and Skaftö, is
one of the highlights of the
Bohuslän archipelago. The
landscape is one of narrow
valleys, leafy meadows and
pine forest, with grazing
horses and sheep. It is a
particularly attractive area for
walking. In the centre of the
island an old farm stands
amid parkland and trees. The
former farm building, with its
many courtyards, is now a
youth hostel.
  Bassholmen is also home to
a number of traditional
shipbuilder's yards, which
come under the care of the
Föreningen Allmoge Båtar,
a society which works to
preserve and renovate the
traditional wooden boats of

Bohuslän. Many of these boats can be seen in the museum.

Every summer boating enthusiasts converge on the island for a nostalgic feast to study the craftsmanship involved in greater detail and experience the life of a boatman at the end of the 19th century.

There is a guest jetty in the former shipyard for visiting craft. In summer boats run to Bassholmen from Uddevalla.

Grundsund harbour, edged with original fishermen's huts

Fiskebäckskil, a summer paradise on Skaftö in Gullmarsfjorden

Skaftö ⑫

Bohuslän. Road 161 towards Fiskebäckskil. 🚍 from Uddevalla. 🛈 *Lysekil Tourist Office, 0523-130 50.*

The best way to see the island of Skaftö is to walk or cycle around it. The scenery varies between fertile agricultural land, pine forests and bare hills. Skaftö's potatoes and strawberries are justifiably famous. In the centre of the island is Gunnesbo, a favourite spot for children where pony rides and a mini-zoo can be found.

In the far south on the slopes running down towards the sea lies **Rågårdsvik**, a small community overlooking the wide Ellösefjorden and the village of Ellöse, site of the internationally successful Hallberg Rassy shipyard. Rågårdsvik Pensionat provides excellent west-coast cuisine.

Between Skaftölandet and Orust are the winding, narrow Malö straits, made famous by the songs of troubadour Evert Taube, while the beautiful Snäckedjupet separates Skaftö

from the mainland. **Fiskebäckskil** in Gullmarsfjorden is a seafaring community established at the end of the 19th century, featuring a captain's house, richly decorated wooden cottages and romantic gardens. It is also the site of Kristineberg Marine Research Station.

The village of **Grundsund** dates from the 17th century. A canal runs through it past the closely packed red fishermen's huts on the lively quayside, so typical of the west coast. The small **Weathervane,** wooden church, built in **Fiskebäckskil** 1799, is well worth a look. Delicious fresh seafood is served in the harbourside inn.

Gullholmen ⑬

Bohuslän. 🏠 150. 🚢 from Tuvesvik, Orust. 🛈 *Henåns Tourist Office, 0304-33 44 94.* **www**.bastkusten.se

Dating from 1585, Gullholmen is one of the oldest fishing communities in Bohuslän. In the mid-19th century one of Sweden's early canning factories was set up here. Line fishing on the Dogger Bank in the North Sea

produced good catches and in 1910 Gullholmen had a fishing fleet of more than 50 cutters. As the fishing industry declined, so did the population and summer residents have taken over many of the houses. Gullholmen is a typical west-coast summer paradise.

Sights include the church, inaugurated in 1799, and the pilot's lookout which was dismantled in 1916, but is now being rebuilt. **Skepparhuset**, a late 19th-century captain's home with original interiors, is well worth a look. South of Gullhomen, as if thrown out to sea, lies the completely barren **Käringön**. The island is so bare that in the past earth for its small churchyard had to be transported from Orust. The charming tightly-packed houses are almost entirely used by summer visitors and in the season the popular guest harbour is bursting with life. A fishing cottage houses a small museum. The island can be reached by boat from Hällevikstrand on Orust.

🏛 Skepparhuset
Tel 0304-570 70. ☐ *3rd week of Jun–first week of Aug: Tue & Sun. Other times by arrangement.*

Sailing past the picturesque houses of Gullholmen

Mollösund, a typical fishing village on Orust

Orust ⑭

Bohuslän. 🏠 *15,100.* 🚢 *from Kulturhuset, Kajutan.* 🛈 *Henån Tourist Office, Strandvägen 3, 0304-311 40.* 🎭 *Taube Festival on Flatön (mid-Jul), Boatyard open days (last weekend in Aug).* www.bastkusten.se

One of Sweden's largest islands, Orust's fortunes over the centuries have been tied to the rise and fall of herring fishing. On the southwest coast, the village of **Mollösund** dates from the 16th century when herring fishing was at its height. A decline in stocks brought poverty, but with the herring's reappearance in the 1750s the population increased, inns opened and refineries for making train oil from herring developed. The bare rocks of Bohuslän are a reminder of this time; the train oil refineries needed lots of wood and the coastline was practically deforested.

Most homes had a fisherman's hut on the harbour and even today the houses and huts are closely packed together. There is a strong smell of stockfish hanging out to dry to produce *Lutfisk* for the Swedish Christmas table.

Today Orust is a centre for the manufacture of superior leisure boats. Half the boats exported from Sweden come from here. The boatyards display their craft in the "Öppna Varv" open days.

Tjörn ⑮

Bohuslän. 🏠 *15,000.* 🚢 *from Stenungsund.* 🛈 *Skärhamn Tourist Office, 0304-67 10 40.* 🎭 *Round Tjörn Yacht Race (3rd Sat in Aug).* www.bastkusten.se

The municipality of Tjörn comprises six inhabited islands. Fishing, boat-building and small businesses are the cornerstones of the economy and in summer the population doubles with the arrival of holidaymakers.

Opened in 1960, the **Tjörn Bridges** offer fantastic views over land and water. Tjörnbroleden, the road linking the islands of Tjörn and Orust to the mainland at Stenungsund, crosses the bridges of Stenungsöbron, Källosundsbron and Tjörnbron over Askeröfjorden. In 1980 Tjörnbron collapsed when a ship collided with it in thick fog; a new bridge opened the following year. At its northern end is an ideal site for camping with great views.

Skärhamn, on the west side of Tjörn, is the island's main town. It has a guest harbour, restaurants and hotel. Sights include **Sjöfartsmuseum** (the Seafaring Museum), Smedja Volund smithy and the popular **Nordiska Akvarellmuseet** (Nordic Watercolour Museum), a stunning building

Fishing net float

Tjörn Bridge, 664 m (726 yd) long, and 45 m (147 ft) high

hosting exhibitions and courses for amateur painters.

Pilane Gravfält, a burial site with more than 100 Iron Age mounds, stone circles, rings and standing stones, is on northwest Tjörn. Take the road towards Kyrkesund, turn left to Hällene and after 1 km (half a mile) there is a car park.

🏛 **Nordiska Akvarellmuseet**
Skärhamn. Södra Hamnen. **Tel** 0304-60 00 80. ☐ *Jun–Sep: daily; Oct–May: Tue–Sun.* ● *some public holidays.* 🎟 🖥 🍴 🛍 ♿

The Watercolour Museum, Tjörn, resting on piles in the water

Marstrand ⑯

Bohuslän. Road 168. 🏠 *1,400.* 🚢 ☐ 🚠 🛈 *0303-109 70.* 🎭 *Fortress Re-enactments, Swedish Match Cup (one week in early Jul), Marstrand Regatta (last week in Jul).* www.kungalv.se

Sun, sailing and the smell of the sea are what Marstrand is all about. The little town of pastel-coloured wooden houses has its roots in the herring boom of the mid-16th century, which attracted fortune-hunters. But it really took off in the mid-19th century as a fashionable seaside resort. Marstrand built its baths and society arrived.

The town is crowned by the impressive **Carlstens Fästning**, a fortress built in 1666–73 and redesigned in the 1680s by architect Erik Dahlbergh. At one time it was a notorious prison. Tours provide a glimpse into the life and times of the fortress and its inmates in the 18th century. Plays are staged here and feasts held during the summer.

Northwards into the wide waters of Marstrandsfjorden is the rocky island of **Åstol**, almost entirely covered by characteristic white houses and fishing huts. The island can be reached by a 10-minute ferry ride from Rönnäng on Tjörn.

Ⓦ Carlstens Fästning
Tel 0303-602 65. ◯ daily. 🎥 📷
📷 ♿ partly.

Kungälv ⓱

Bohuslän. E6. 🚶 20,500. 🚃 to Ytterby then bus. 🚌 ✈ Landvetter. ℹ 0303-109 00. 🎄 Medieval Festival (mid-Jul). www.kungalv.se

Strategically located between the Nordre Älv and Göta Älv rivers, Kungälv occupies the site of the 10th-century Viking settlement of Kongahälla. It is dominated by the ruins of **Bohus Fästning**, a fortress built by the Norwegian King Håkon Magnusson in 1308. Constructed first in wood and later in stone, the fortress was at the frontline in the constant wars between Sweden, Norway and Denmark. At the Peace of Roskilde in 1658 it became Swedish, but it went on to be besieged no less than 14 times without being captured.

In 1678, 900 Swedish defenders faced 9,000 Norwegians and 7,000 German mercenaries, but still the castle didn't fall. In the 18th century it became a prison and in 1789 all the towers were destroyed apart from the main one known as "Fars Hatt" (Father's Hat).

Red-roofed Gungälv church, situated in the market square, dates from 1679.

Ⓦ Bohus Fästning
Tel 0303-109 00. ◯ May–Sep: daily. 🌙 Midsummer's Eve. 🎥
🎥 by arrangement.

Bohus Fästning, the impregnable 14th-century fortress at Kungälv

Vänersborg ⓲

Västergötland. Road 45. 🚶 4,700.
🚃 🚌 ✈ ℹ Railway Station, 0521-27 14 00. 🎄 Christmas market (Dec). www.vanersborg.se

Vänersborg is otherwise known as "Little Paris" after the poems of Birger Sjöberg (1885–1929). A statue of the local poet's muse, Frida, can be seen in the beautiful Skräckleparken on the lake shore, and a reconstruction of his home is in **Vänersborgs Museum**. Other museums focus on medical history, dolls and sport. The town was founded in 1644 and its Neo-Classical church completed in 1784.

Environs
Just over 5 km (3 miles) east of the town, the steeply-sided hills of Halleberg and Hunneberg rise up over the landscape. The hillside forests are a nature reserve featuring a large elk population, which is the focus of an annual royal hunt.

On top of Hunneberg is **Kungajaktmuseet Älgens Berg** where the "king of the forest" is presented in interactive displays. The intricacies of elk hunting are explained and visitors can try their hand at shooting an elk themselves, virtually of course.

🏛 Vänersborgs Museum
Tel 0521-72 14 08. ◯ Tue, Thu, Sat & Sun (also Wed Jul–Aug). 📷 ♿

🏛 Kungajaktmuseet Älgens Berg
Hunneberg. On road 44. *Tel* 0521-27 79 91. ◯ Feb–May & Sep–Nov: 11am–4pm Tue–Sun; Jun–Aug: 10am–6pm daily; Dec–Jan: 11am–4pm Tue–Fri. ● eves of public hols. 🎥 🎥 by appt. 📷 💻 🍴 ♿

Staircase of locks on the Trollhättan Canal, rising 32 m (105 ft)

Trollhättan ⓳

Västergötland. Road 45. 🚶 44,000.
🚃 🚌 ✈ ⛴ ℹ Innovatum, Åkersjövägen 10, 0520-135 09.
🎄 Fallens Dagar (3rd weekend in Jul). www.trollhattan.se

The opening of the Trollhättan Canal in 1800, linking Lake Vänern and the North Sea, marked the birth of Trollhättan as an industrial town. Today, Trollhättan successfully combines high-tech industries such as SAAB and Volvo Aero with a burgeoning film industry that has earned the town its local nickname, "Trollywood".

The town's main sight is the waterfall area where four locks regulate the once wild 32-m (105-ft) high falls. In summer the sluices are opened several times a week to let the mass of water rush freely down river.

The technology centre **Innovatum Kunskapens Hus** (IKH) features multi-media exhibits on the history and development of Trollhättan. From the centre, a cable car transports visitors 30 m (98 ft) above the canal to the opposite bank. A short walk leads to the Canal Museum.

🏛 Innovatum (IKH)
Åkersjövägen 10. *Tel* 0520-28 94 00. ◯ mid-Jun–mid-Aug: daily; other times: Tue–Sun.
🎥 📷 💻 🍴 ♿

Lidköping ⑳

Västergötland. Road 44. 🏘 24,500.
✕ 🚉 🚌 ℹ Stationshuset,
Bangatan 3, 0510-200 20. 🎭
Arnspelen Pageant (2nd & 3rd weeks
in Jul), GladJazz Festival (4th weekend
in Jul). www.lidkoping.se

The town of Lidköping lies
at the heart of the area of
Västergötland that is considered to be the cradle of the
Svea Kingdom. Like so many
of Sweden's wooden towns,
Lidköping suffered a devastating fire in 1849, though
some of the 17th-century
buildings around the square
of Limtorget survived.

The Lidan river divides the
town into old and new, and
the two main squares (1446
and 1671 respectively) face
each other across the water.
Nya Stadens Torg (New Town
Square) is the site of a former
hunting lodge, which the
founder of the new town,
Magnus Gabriel de la Gardie,
brought here to serve as a
town hall.

Lidköping is known for the
Rörstrands Porcelain Factory
and **Rörstrands Museum**
attracts visitors in search of
bargain dinner services or
simply to enjoy the showpiec-
es in the museum.

Vänermuseet with the Paleo
Geology Centre is an
interactive science museum.

Rörstrand ceramic stove, now in the
porcelain factory museum

Environs

Husaby, 10 km (6 miles) east
of Lidköping, encapsulates
Swedish history. It was here
at Husaby well that King Olof
Skötkonung was baptised by
the English monk Sigfrid in
1008. A 12th-century church
now stands at the site.
Gösslunda Kyrka, just west of
the town, also dates from the
12th century. Outside is a
rune stone that was originally
part of the church wall.

Jan Guillou's popular novels
about the fictional knight Arn
have attracted unexpected
attention to the Lidköping
region. Guided coach tours
are organised in summer.

🏛 **Rörstrands Museum**
Fabriksgatan 4. **Tel** 0510-823 48.
◯ daily. ⬤ some public holidays.
🚻 ♿ ℹ

🏛 **Vänermuseet**
10 min walk from the centre. **Tel** 0510-
77 00 65. ◯ Jun–Aug: daily; Sep–May:
Tue–Sun. ⬤ some public holidays.
📷 by arrangement. 🏪 ♿ ℹ 🚻

Läckö Slott ㉑

Västergötland. 20 km (12 miles) N of
Lidköping. 🚌 from Lidköping.
Tel 0510-103 20. ◯ May–Sep:
11am–6pm daily. 🏪 📷 ♿ ℹ ⛪
🎭 Medieval Market 3rd week in Jun.
www.lackoslott.se

Jakob de la Gardie was the
first to make his mark on
Läckö Slott after it was
assigned to him in 1615. In
2001 Läckö was named the
most beautiful castle in

Läckö Slott, a splendid castle on the shore of Lake Vänern

Sweden. It is surrounded by
water on three sides. Originally built in the 13th century
by Bishop Brynolf Algotsson,
it became the seat of the
bishops of Skara. Count Jakob
and his son, Magnus de la
Gardie, embarked on
remodelling the castle in the
17th century. But in 1681
Läckö was claimed by Karl XI
in his recovery of crown
lands from the nobility and its
contents were scattered.

Restoration work in the
20th century has revealed
more than 200 rooms,
including the richly decorated
apartment of Princess Marie
Euphrosyne, wife of Marcus
de la Gardie, and the King's
Hall with its paintings of the
Thirty Years' War.

Läckö is the setting for art
exhibitions and summer
opera performances are held
in the courtyard. The garden
is also open to the public.

Kinnekulle ㉒

Västergötland. Road 44. ℹ Götene-
Lidköping Tourist Office, Bangatan 3,
Lidköping, 0510-200 20.

The 306-m (1,000-ft) high
plateau of Kinnekulle,
known as "the flowering
mountain", rises from the
Västergötland landscape,
providing habitats for wild
flowers, deciduous woods,
pine forests, meadows and
pastures. It is topped with bare
limestone and a 20-m (66-ft)
high lookout tower. Those not

up to the climb can enjoy the views from the restaurant at Högkullen. Limestone has been quarried here since the 12th century. In summer demonstrations at the remaining quarry show how the work used to be carried out.

The area is peppered with ancient Stone Age and Bronze Age sites.

Forshems Kyrka, just to the east, dates from the 12th century and is known for its stone reliefs. The churchyard of the 12th-century church at **Kinne-Vedum**, 2 km (1 mile) north of Götene, has several lily stones, typical of this area.

Mariestad ㉓

Västergötland. E20. 🏠 15,000. 🚉
🚌 ✈ Lidköping. 🚢 🛈 Kyrkogatan 2, 0501-75 58 50. 🐎 Göta Canal Swim (4th week in Jul).
www.vastsverige.com

Duke Karl founded the pretty town of Mariestad in 1583, naming it after his wife, Maria of Pfalz. He built the cathedral and lavishly decorated it in the Baroque style. It is well worth exploring the interesting little streets surrounding the cathedral, lined with buildings from the 18th and 19th centuries.

In 1660 Mariestad became the county town of Skaraborg. The former royal manor of Marieholm, on an island where the River Tidan flows into Lake Vänern, was the governor's residence. It now houses **Vadsmo Museum** and **Mariestads Industrimuseum** (Industrial Museum).

Mariestad's location on Lake Vänern and the River Tidan makes it an idyllic summer town. The Göta Canal (see pp146–7) runs through it and

Kanalmuseet (the Canal Museum) is located in Sjötorp just north of the town.

Those keen on rural life should head for **Klockarbolet** in Odensåker, a reconstructed village dating from the 17th and 18th centuries.

🏛 **Vadsbo Museum and Mariestads Industri-museum**
Marieholm. **Tel** 0501-75 58 31.
🕐 Sep–May: Sat & Sun; Jun–Aug: Tue–Sun. 🎥 📷 🖥 🍴 🛍 ♿

🏛 **Kanalmuseet**
Sjötorp, off road Rv 26. **Tel** 0141-20 20 50. 🕐 Jun–Aug: daily. 📷

Tivedens National Park ㉔

Västergötland. Road 49. 🚌 from Karlsborg. 🛈 Karlsborgs Tourist Office, 0505-173 50.

On the border between Närke and Västergötland lies Tiveden national park, an untouched area of rugged wilderness. It was established in 1983 to protect the remaining primeval forest and lakes, of which Fagertärn is the original habitat of the large red water-lily (see p19).

The area is very hilly and demanding for walkers. There is a visitor centre at Stenkälla with information on trails, parking and things to see inside the park.

Giant Ice Age boulders, some up to 10 m (33 ft) high, litter the forest around **Trollkyrka**, the hill east of the road by the visitor centre. The mountain's name is thought to be derived from the fact that the site was used by local people who came here to worship after the ban in 1726 on holding religious services outside churches.

Karlsborgs Fästning, a 19th-century wartime hideaway

Karlsborg ㉕

Västergötland. Road 49. 🏠 7,000.
🚌 🚢 🛈 Karlsborgs Tourist Office, Ankarvägen 2, 0505-173 50. **Fortress** 🕐 10am–3pm Mon–Fri. 🎥 📷 Eng by appointment 📷

In 1819 King Karl XIV Johan decided that a fortress should be built at Vanäs on the shore of Lake Vättern. It was named Karlsborg and was to act as an emergency capital in the event of war; a place of safety for the royal family, the national bank and the government. The 90 years it took to build meant that by the time it was finally finished the fortress was out of date and it never had any real significance. Today, however, it is a major tourist attraction. The "town" enclosed within the 5-km (3-mile) long walls is best viewed on one of the hour-long guided adventure tours that run daily in the summer. Action fans can watch Fästningsäventyret, an adventure depicting life in the fortress in the 1860s complete with stunt men and special effects.

Outside the fortress, the Göta Canal wends its way towards Lake Vänern, passing **Forsviks Bruk**, which offers an interesting glimpse into Sweden's industrial heritage, with a blacksmith's forge, saw-mill and working flour mill.

🏛 **Forsviks Bruk**
8 km (5 miles) north of the centre.
Tel Karlsborgs Tourist Office, 0505-173 50. 🕐 Jun–Aug: daily. 🎥

Marieholm, the former governor's residence in Mariestad

For hotels and restaurants in this region see pp288–290 and p306

Hjo's wooden buildings, awarded the Europa Nostra medal in 1990

Hjo 🐼

Västergötland. Road 193/194.
🏛 6,000. 🚌 to Skövde then bus.
🚲 ℹ Floragatan 1, 0503-352 55.
🎭 Craft Fair (2nd weekend in Jul),
Round Vättern cycle race (3rd
weekend in Jun). www.hjo.se

Mention Hjo and Swedes immediately think of the exquisite little wooden houses dating from the end of the 19th century with their ornately carved verandas. Hjo is a delightful town to visit. On the shore of Lake Vättern is Stadsparken, a park created when Hjo Spa was founded in the late 19th century. Villa Svea, one of the former spa buildings in the park, houses **Hjo Stadsmuseum** (the Town Museum). It is worth a look for its remarkable calendar clock *Hjouret*, and recreated rooms from the heyday of the spa. The park also contains Fjärilsmuseum (the Butterfly Museum) and Vätternak-varium, an aquarium.

Just like the town, the harbour has medieval origins, but the present one was built in the mid-19th century after the construction of the Göta Canal. In summer, the *Lok-Hjo-Motivet* train takes guided tours (daily except Monday) through the town starting from the harbour. The steamer *S/S Trafik* (1892) runs Sunday tours to Visingö, and jazz cruises to Vadstena across the lake.

The Hjoån river valley, stretching from Lake Vättern to Mullsjön lake 4 km (2.5 miles) west of Hjo has several spectacular waterfalls.

🏛 **Hjo Stadsmuseum**
Villa Svea, Stadsparken. *Tel 0503-352 55.* ⭕ May–Aug. ♿ partly.

Skövde 🐼

Västergötland. Road 48/49.
🏛 32,500 🚌 🚉 ℹ Sandtorget,
0500-44 66 88. 🎭 Food Festival (last
weekend in Aug), Skövde Film Festival
(Nov). www.skovde.se

The modern industrial town of Skövde celebrated its 600th anniversary in 2001. Skövde has been destroyed by fire several times, but after a devastating fire in 1715 little remained other than a single 17th-century house, **Helénsstugan**. Today the house is part of Skövde Stadsmuseum (the Town Museum), along with Gamla Rådhuset (the Old Town Hall), 1776, and the neighbouring Gamla Kanslihuset (the Old Government Building), 1915. The museum also holds exhibitions in Hertig Johans Torg.

Kulturhuset, designed by Hans-Erland Heineman in 1964, houses the library, art museum and an art gallery exhibiting Swedish modern art. The library contains Siri Derkert's relief *The Mustard Tree*. In the square in front of Kulturhuset are the sculptures *Monument of an Axeman* by Eric Grate (1965) and *La Mano* by Liss Eriksson. The latter was raised in 1986 in memory of murdered Prime Minister Olof Palme.

Environs
Rising to the west of Skövde is the 300-m (984-ft) high **Billingen** plateau, with views stretching as far as Lake Vättern. The area

is a popular recreation spot with hiking trails, holiday cottages and campsites. The exclusive Billingehus Hotel contains a sports museum.

West of Skövde, on road 49, is the 12th-century church **Våmbs Kyrka**. The church was restored to its original appearance in the 1940s. On the same road, slightly nearer to Skövde, is **Varnhems Klosterkyrka**, a 13th-century three-aisle basilica.

🏛 **Helénsstugan**
Helénsparken. *Tel 0500-49 80 69.*
⭕ summer. 🎭 📷 by arrangement.
🏛 **Kulturhuset**
Trädgårdsgatan. *Tel 0500-49 85 60.*
Konsthallen & Konstmuseet ⭕
Sep–May: Tue–Sun; Jun–Aug: Tue–Sat.
⭕ eves of public holidays. 🎭 📷 📶 🍴

Skara 🐼

Västergötland. E20. 🏛 11,400. 🚌 ℹ
Bladska Huset, Skolgatan 1, 0511-325
80. 🎭 Naturum Crane Dance (end
Mar–Apr). www.skara.se/turism

Traditionally an important seat of learning and a bishopric, Skara is one of Sweden's oldest towns. The 11th-century cathedral lies at its heart, surrounded by a network of streets following a pattern set out in the Middle Ages. On Stora Torget stands Krönikebrunnen, a well which

The nave of Skara's Gothic cathedral, founded in the 12th century

on its exterior chronicles important events in the history of Skara and of Sweden. **Stadsparken** is the site of Västergötlands Museum with its local history collection, and Fornbyn, an open-air museum complete with cottages showing how people lived in the past.

Environs
Axvall, 8 km (5 miles) from Skara on road 49, is the location of **Skara Sommarland**, a large amusement park with a water park, campsite and holiday cottages.

Around 20 km (12 miles) east of Skara, Lake **Hornborgasjön** is a popular resting place for birds, especially dancing cranes in April–May. There is an observation tower and two information centres.

🛶 Skara Sommarland
Axvall, road 49 towards Skövde. **Tel** 0511-770 300. 🕐 29 May–22 Aug. 📷 **www**.sommarland.se

🦋 Hornborgasjön
Naturum Hornborgasjön, road 189. **Tel** 0500-49 14 50. 🕐 daily in season.

Falköping 29

Västergötland. Road 46. 🏠 15,400. 🚇 🛈 Odengatan 24, 0515-77 70 55. **www**.falkoping.nu

Between the hills of Mösseberget and Ålleberg lies the old town of Falköping. Of particular interest are the 12th-century church, St Olofs Kyrka, the medieval wooden houses and the town square, Stora Torget, with Ivar Tengbom's statue *Venus Rising from the Waves* (1931). **Falbygdens Museum** describes the local history.

Environs
Ekornavallen, 15 km (9 miles) north of Falköping, is an important historic burial site from the Stone, Iron and Bronze Ages.

Dalénmuseet in Stenstorp uses sound-and-light shows to illustrate the life and work of the 1912 Swedish Nobel laureate Gustaf Dalén, who invented the AGA oven and was an innovator in the the field of lighting technology.

Gökhems Kyrka, west of the town, is a small Romanesque apse church without a tower. It dates from the early 12th century. Inside, limestone paintings depict *The Creation*.

Gudhems Klosterruin and **Klostermuseum** north of the town are the ruins of a convent founded in 1160. Today it is a museum. **Karleby**, to the east, is one of three villages along a road which probably existed in the Stone Age. Each farm had its burial site and there are 13 passage tumuli here, including one with a burial chamber 17 m (56 ft) long.

🏛 Falbygdens Museum
St Olofsgatan 23. **Tel** 0515-850 50. 🕐 Tue–Fri & Sun. 🌑 some public holidays.

🏛 Dalénmuseet
Stenstorp, 10 km (6 miles) N of centre. **Tel** 0500-45 71 65. 🕐 Mar–Sep: Tue–Sun, Jul also Mon; Oct: Sat & Sun. Dec–Feb, Midsummer Eve. 📷

Alingsås 30

Västergötland. E20. 🏠 25,000. 🚇 🛈 Stora Torget 1, 0322-61 62 00. 🎉 Potato Festival (3rd weekend in Jun); Ljus i Alingsås (Oct). **www**.alingsas.se

Jonas Alströmer and the textile industry have, between them, left their mark on Alingsås. In the early 18th century, Ahlströmer founded his textile factory and on the proceeds he built **Nolhaga Slott**, a manor which today

Skulls of Stone Age inhabitants from the Falköping area in Falbygdens Museum

has a zoo and bird park. **Alingsås Museum** is housed in the 1730s Ahlströmerska Magazinet.

Alingsås Kulturhus contains an art gallery and library, and organizes regular events.

Environs
Gräfsnäs Slottsruin and Park is a ruined castle and park on Lake Anten, 20 km (12 miles) north of Alingsås. An exhibition describes its history. On the road towards Gothenburg lies **Nääs Slott**, a 17th-century castle with an impressive 19th-century interior. Here, the handicraft tradition of western Sweden is cultivated through events and exhibitions. The Midsummer celebrations here are fantastic.

🏛 Alingsås Museum
Lilla Torget 1. **Tel** 0322-61 65 96. 🕐 Tue–Sat.

🏛 Alingsås Kulturhus
S. Ringgatan 3. **Tel** 0322-61 65 98. 🕐 Tue–Sat. 🌑 some public holidays. 📷 (free on Fri). ♿

🏯 Nääs Slott
Floda, E20, 30 km (19 miles) N of Gothenburg. **Tel** 0302-318 39. 🕐 winter: Mon–Fri; summer: daily. 📷 🎫 🖥 🍴 🛍

Nolhaga Slott, home of the textile magnate Jonas Ahlströmer, 1727

Ulricehamn Town Hall, 1799, housing the town's tourist office

Ulricehamn ③

Västergötland. Road 40. 🚗 9,100.
🚌 🚆 ℹ️ *Rådhuset, 0321-595 959.*
🎭 *Kärringrallyt (all year round: Thu).*
www.ulricehamnsturistbyra.se

The town of Ulricehamn occupies a beautiful setting on Lake Åsunden in an area rich in historic monuments. Originally known as Bogesund, there has been a settlement here since the 14th century. The old coaching road across Västergötland to Halland ran through the town along Storgatan. The local history museum, **Ulricehamns Museum**, is located in an 1868 schoolhouse, while Ulricehamns Konst- och Östasiatiska Museum, with its fine collection of Chinese ceramics, is in the old railway station.

Textile enterprises dominate the local economy and in Gällstad the knitwear factories south of the town open their gates to bargain hunters every Thursday afternoon for what is known as *Kärringrallyt* (the "old women's race").

Environs
Bystad, a farmstead 30 km (19 miles) south of Ulricehamn, has one of Sweden's oldest animal traps, a pit measuring about 5 m (16 ft) in diameter and more than 3.5 m (11 ft) deep.

Along the road between Ulricehamn and Mullsjö lies

Näs Gård. The manor's six historic red-painted buildings date from the 17th, 18th and 19th centuries and now form a regional cultural centre and art gallery. Concerts and other cultural events are held here.

Södra Vings Kyrka is a medieval gem of a church, dating in part from the 12th century. The artistic decoration is unusually lavish and includes 15th-century limestone paintings in the nave. The stately lectern was carved in Rococo style in 1748.

🏛 **Ulricehamns Museum**
Järnvägstorget. *Tel 0321-59 50 00.*
⏰ *Jan–Dec: Sun.* 🎭 💰 by arrangement. 🔲 📷

Torpa Stenhus ③

Västergötland. 30 km (19 miles) SE of Borås. *Tel 033-28 13 24.* ⏰ *May–mid-Sep: Sat–Sun (mid-Jun–mid-Aug: daily).* 🎭 💰 *Eng 11am; eve in Eng: phone Tourist Office in advance.* 🔲

Standing on a promontory at the southern end of Lake Åsunden is the medieval castle Torpa Stenhus. It belonged to the Stenbock family and from the 14th–mid-17th century was an important stronghold for defence against the Danes. The evening guided tour includes thrilling ghost stories from the castle's past.

Theatre performances, known as *Torpaspelen*, are staged here in summer.

Painting of Saturn at Torpa Stenhus

Borås ③

Västergötland. Road 40. 🚗 62,000.
🚆 🚌 🚕 ℹ️ *Österlånggatan 1–3, 033-35 70 90.* 🎭 *Culture Night (first week in May), Harvest Festival (first week in Sep).* **www**.boras.se.

In 1620 King Gustav II Adolf decided that the textile pedlars of the Knallebygden area should have a town of

their own and Borås was founded. Textile factories still line the Viskan river, which winds through the town, although the industry has lost ground in recent years.

Borås is a green town with beautiful parks: Stadsparken in the centre is popular, as is Ramnaparken where the open-air Borås Museum is located. Also in the town centre is **Borås Djurpark**, a zoo with more than 80 species from all corners of the world. Large enclosures and attractive grounds make this zoo a pleasant family park.

Environs
On the road between Borås and Alingsås lies **Hedareds Kapell**, Sweden's only preserved stave church. Apart from its windows and shingled roof, the little, wooden 16th-century church remains as it was when it was built, complete with original 16th-century paintings.

Textilmuseet (the Textile Museum) is a living museum housed in a late-19th-century spinning shed. The history of the textile industry is brought to life with recreated scenes and art and textile exhibitions.

🦁 **Borås Djurpark**
Boråsparken, bus line 1 from Södra Torget. *Tel 033-35 32 70.* ⏰ *May–mid-Sep: daily; Oct & Apr: Sat & Sun; school holidays: daily* 🎭 🔲 📷

🏛 **Textilmuseet**
Druverforsvägen 8, road 40.
Tel 033-35 89 50. ⏰ *Tue–Sun.*
⚫ *some public holidays.* 🎭 💰 by arrangement. 🔲 📷

Pink flamingo, one of the many exotic species at Borås Djurpark

Gunnebo Slott ❹

In the 1780s, John Hall, one of the richest men in Sweden at the time, commissioned city architect Carl Wilhelm Carlberg of Gothenburg to design a summer villa and park at Gunnebo. On completion in 1796, Carlberg had created one of the most beautiful and stylistically pure examples of Neo-Classical Swedish architecture. Hall is said to have paid the bill with 38 barrels of gold, but that included everything: the interiors, servants' quarters, orangery, park, kitchen gardens and greenhouse. An adjoining farm made the estate virtually self-sufficient.

VISITORS' CHECKLIST

15 km (9 miles) SE of Gothenburg. E6/E20, then Gunnebogatan. **Tel** 031-334 16 00. **Mansion** ◻ (tours only) Oct–Aug: phone for times. 🎟 🚻 ◻ ◻ ◻ ◻ ⊘ **Garden** ◻ all year. 🎟 mid-Jul–mid-Aug: Sun & public hols 2pm. 🎟 🅿 1 Jan, Midsummer's Eve 24, 25 Dec, 31 Dec. www.gunneboslott.se

The Hall
Three magnificent French windows let in the sunlight, which is reflected on the beautiful parquet floor.

Northern Façade
Ionian columns frame the sheltered terrace which opens onto the garden with its neatly clipped trees.

Oval vestibule

The frieze on the southern gable is made from lead painted to imitate marble.

The staircase leads to the park with its parterres and gravel paths.

The entrance is through the cellar, the starting point for tours.

Ceramic Stoves
The interior design, including exquisite ceramic stoves, is by Carlberg who adopted the light Gustavian style which pervades the entire house.

Park and Gardens
The French-inspired formal garden surrounding the house was also designed by Carlberg, as was the English park, which makes an ideal setting for a walk.

Varberg Fästning, a fortress on the shores of the Kattegat housing a local history museum

Kungsbacka ㉟

Halland. E6/E20. 👥 17,200. 🚌 🚉
ℹ Storgatan 41, 0300-83 45 95. 🎭
Kungsbacka Chamber Music Festival
(first weekend in Aug).
www.kungsbacka.se

Although Kungsbacka was
an important trading centre
in the 13th century, almost
nothing remains of the old
wooden town. All but two of
the houses were destroyed in
a devastating fire in 1846. The
two survivors are the red
cottage in Norra Torggatan
and the mayor's house at
Östergatan 10. The pretty
pastel-painted wooden houses
that replaced the old at the
end of the 19th century can be
seen around the square. Today,
Kungsbacka is almost a southern suburb of Gothenburg.

Environs
Around 10 km (6 miles)
outside Kungsbacka at Rydet
is **Mårtagården**, a typical
18th-century sea captain's
house. The house is open to
the public in the summer.
Tjolöholms Slott, one
of Sweden's more unusual
buildings, lies 15 km (9 miles)
south of Kungsbacka. This
magnificent English Tudor-
style mansion was built for a
Scottish merchant and completed in 1904. It contained
state-of-the-art features such as

Tjolöholms Slott, an eccentric English Tudor-
style mansion with Art Nouveau interiors

vacuum cleaners, showers and
hot-air heating. The house is
surrounded by lovely parkland.

🏯 Tjolöholms Slott
10 km (6 miles) S of the centre, E6/E20
to Fjärås exit, then road 939.
Tel 0300-54 42 00. ◯ Mar–May &
Sep–Nov: Sat & Sun; mid-Jun–Aug:
daily. **Park** ◯ daily. 🍴

Varberg ㊱

Halland. E6/E20. 👥 25,000. 🚌 🚉
🚢 from Grenå. ℹ Brunnsparken,
0340-868 00. 🎭 Wheels & Wings
motor exhibition (mid-Jul).
www.turist.varberg.se

The coastal town of Varberg
has, since the 19th century,
been famous for its bathing,
whether the cold curative
baths fashionable of the period
or swimming from the rocks
and sandy beaches. The town
was founded in the 13th century, but little from that time
remains after several fires.
   The harbour area is worth a
look and, in particular,
Kallbadhuset, the renovated
cold bath house in Moorish
style with separate sections for
men and women. The oriental
touch is repeated in **Societetshuset**, built in the 1880s when
the town's popularity as a spa
was at its height. Today it
houses a café, restaurant, pub
and disco, playground and
mini-golf. On
summer evenings
concerts are held on
the stage in the park.
   Guarding the
approach from the
sea is the mighty
Varbergs Fästning.
Most of the fortress
was built in the 17th
century with parts
dating from the 13th
century. Today it
houses a museum,

**Länsmuseet Varbergs
Fästning**, focusing on the
history of Halland. The
museum's biggest attraction is
the 14th-century Bocksten
Man whose body was discovered in a bog still dressed in a
complete outfit from the
Middle Ages. The notorious
bullet which killed King Karl
XII in 1718 is also on show.
An outpost of the museum is
Båtmuseet, the boat museum
in Galtabäck, 10 km (6 miles)
south of Varberg, displaying
traditional boats and models.

🏛 Länsmuseet Varbergs
Fästning
Varbergs Fästning. *Tel* 0340-828 30.
◯ daily. 🎭 by arrangement. 🍴

Falkenberg ㊲

Halland. E6/E20. 👥 18,600. 🚌 🚉
ℹ Holgersgatan 11, 0346-88 61 00.
🎭 Song festival (first week in Jul).
www.visitfalkenberg.se

A town with medieval roots,
Falkenberg stands at the
mouth of the River Ätran.
The oldest areas of the town
still have their wooden buildings, including St Laurentii
Kyrka (St Laurence's church),
parts of which date from the
14th century.
   The pottery **Törngrens
Krukmakeri** (1789) is still in
operation, run by the seventh
generation of potters.
   Falkenbergs Museum is
housed in a half-timbered
granary at Söderbron. The
grain dryer is a lofty landmark
in the old town. The museum
features a faithful reproduction
of an apartment from the
1950s and the café has a
working jukebox.
   Falkenberg has several
interesting smaller museums,
including **Falkenbergs
Hembygdsmuseum** (Rural

Museum) in St Lars Kyrkogata, a rural museum with a section on salmon fishing. The **Fotomuseet Olympia** in Sandgatan is housed in the town's first cinema (1912) and displays cameras and photos.

Environs
North of the town is **Morups Tånge**, known for its lighthouse built in the mid-19th century. The beach below is a nature reserve, a wetland area of international interest and a home for waders.

The former training ship *Najaden* against a backdrop of Halmstad Slott

🦐 Törngrens Krukmakeri
Krukmakaregatan 4. **Tel** 0346-103 54 ◯ daily. 🏠 Nygatan 34.

🏛 Falkenbergs Museum
Skepparesträtet 2. **Tel** 0346-88 61 25. ◯ Sep–May: Tue, Fri & Sun; Jun–Aug: Tue–Sun. 🏠

Fly-fishing in the salmon-rich River Ätran in Falkenberg

Halmstad ㊳

Halland. E6/E20. 🚶 53,500. 🚃 🚌 ✈ 🚢 from Grenå. 🚶 Tourist Office, Halmstad Slott, 035-13 23 20. 🎭 Street Theatre Festival (Aug). **www**.halmstad.se

At the point where the River Nissan flows into Laholmsbukten bay lies Halmstad. In the Middle Ages it was the largest town on the west coast. Today, the medieval inner city with its half-timbered architecture is classified as being of national interest. Kirsten Munk's house on Storgatan is an exceptional 17th-century building in green-glazed Dutch brick. Local craftsmen can be seen at work in **Fattighuset**, Lilla Torg, a former poorhouse dated 1859.

Several modern artists have left their mark on the town and Carl Milles' fountain

Europa and the Bull in Stora Torg and Picasso's *Woman's Head*, which stands between the bridges over the river Nissan, are easily encountered on a stroll.

Halmstad Slott, a 17th-century castle, was built by the Danish King Christian IV. The former training ship *Najaden* is moored on the quayside in front of the castle.

Länsmuseet (the County Museum) has a wide collection of art and cultural history. **Tropikcenter** in Strandgatan is exciting for children with more than 100 species of tropical animals set in their natural habitats. Another hit for children is **Miniland**, a park with models of famous Swedish buildings on a scale of 1:25 and several kids' play attractions such as a BMX track and motorized lorries.

Environs
To the north, the popular summer resorts of Tylösand, Haverdal and Frösakull spread out along the coast. **Simlångs-dalen**, around 20 km (12 miles) from Halmstad on road 25, has several natural attractions including Danska Fall in the River Assman, a 36-m (118-ft) high waterfall.

🦐 Fattighuset
Lilla Torg. **Tel** 035-21 15 15. ◯ Mon–Sat. 🏠

🦋 Tropikcenter
Strandgatan. **Tel** 035-12 33 33. ◯ daily. 🖼 🏠 🅿 🏠

🅤 Miniland
Ga Tylösandsvägen 1. **Tel** 035-10 84 60. ◯ 4 Jun–29 Aug: daily. 🖼 🏠

Laholm ㊴

Halland. Road 24. 🚶 6,000. 🚃 🚌 🚶 Rådhuset, Stortorget, 0430-154 50. 🎣 Waterfall Day (2nd Sun in Aug), Salmon Festival (3rd Sun in Aug).

Halland's oldest and smallest town, Laholm is primarily associated with the long sandy beaches around the bay of Laholmsbukten. Mellbystrand, on the bay 6 km (4 miles) to the west of the town, throngs with holiday-makers in summer. The River Lagan also attracts visitors for the salmon fishing.

Laholm itself is characterized by its winding streets and low houses, reminiscent of Danish rule before 1645. Of the buildings around the square, the 200-year-old **Rådhuset** (Town Hall) is particularly beautiful. Open year round, it houses the Tourist Office, Laholms Teckningsmuseum (the Drawing Museum), a small exhibition on the history of the town and a cell from the time when the building served as a police station. On the western gable there is an automaton symbolizing the meeting in Laholm in 1278 between the Swedish King Magnus Ladulås and Danish King Erik Klipping.

Laholm's tidy rows of houses bearing the hallmarks of the town's Danish past

WESTERN SVEALAND

V*ärmland, Närke and Dalarna, with their rich rural heritage, colourful folk costumes, red-painted wooden houses and pastoral scenes, attracted visitors long before the onset of tourism. Stretching from the flatlands of Närke to the mountains of Dalarna, this region is known for its annual ski race and Midsummer festivities, as well as its industrial heritage based on mining and forestry.*

Large expanses of water dominate all three provinces. Southern Värmland encompasses the huge Lake Vänern, which is also the end of the line for the arterial Klarälven river. The beautiful Fryken lakes provided inspiration for one of the province's well-known authors, Selma Lagerlöf *(see p233)*. Her home, Mårbacka, was in this region where so many of her adventures are set. There is plenty of scope for outdoor activities in Värmland, including boating, canoeing, rafting on the Klarälven river and fishing. The forests have exciting trails where walkers are unlucky if they don't see an elk, and on wildlife safaris there is even the chance of glimpsing one of the big four predators – bear, wolf, lynx or wolverine.

Närke, one of Sweden's smallest provinces, is sandwiched between two large lakes, Hjälmaren and Vättern. The centre of the province is dominated by the fertile Närke flatlands, encircled by forest, including the once infamous haunt of bandits, Tiveden, in the south. Örebro, Western Svealand's largest metropolis and Närke's county town, has all the charm of a small town.

Dalarna has the beautiful Siljan lake and the Dalälven river with its arms stretching into the mountains. The province offers more contrasts than most – from the gentle farmland around Siljan to the mountainous north. Every March, these are linked by the Vasaloppet race *(see p245)*, when some 10,000 skiers head from Sälen down to Mora. Midsummer celebrations on Siljan are emblematic of Dalarna. Villages compete to see who has the most stylish maypole, the most accomplished musicians and the best folk dancers.

Rustic interior of Gammelgården in Mora, Dalarna

◁ **Stora Kils church on Nedre Fryken lake, Värmland**

Exploring Western Svealand

Fertile agricultural land spreads out around the major lakes, Vänern, Vättern, Hjälmaren and Siljan, and along the river valleys, giving way to a predominantly forested landscape. The region provides ample opportunities for nature lovers, with its abundance of wildlife, and for anglers, who will easily find a good catch. The mountains in Dalarna are the setting for some of the country's most popular ski resorts, walking trails and national parks. Motorists have many attractive small roads to choose from, while the Fryksdalsbanan and Inlandsbanan railway lines guarantee spectacular sights from the train window and leisurely boat trips provide glorious views from the water.

Author and Nobel laureate Selma Lagerlöf's Mårbacka, one of Värmland's many stately homes

GETTING AROUND

Passing through Örebro and Karlstad, the E18 motorway crossing from Stockholm to Oslo is the main artery for traffic to this region. Travelling up into Värmland and Dalarna, the roads follow the river valleys, where the local population is also concentrated. Rail links are good to the southern parts of the provinces, but the northern areas can only be reached by car or bus. Between towns and popular tourist areas the bus services are quite frequent, but they can be patchy in rural areas. In summer, boats ply the major lakes of Vänern, Hjälmaren and Siljan.

KEY

▬▬▬	Motorway
▬▬▬	Major road
▭▭▭	Minor road
▬▪▬	Main railway
▭▭▭	Minor railway
▬▬▬	International border
△	Summit

Map labels

Städjan 1131m
311
IDRE 21
SÄRNA 21
Storbön 1035m
Granfjället 949m
Elverum
20 SÄL
71
Lir
Höljes
62
Malungsfors
Ma
Klarälven
Stölle
Östmark
62
Ekshärad
239
Kongsvinger
Torsby
HAGFOR
61
VÄRMLAN
Charlottenberg
Torsby
Åmotfors
Sunne
2 ARVIKA
1
Glafsfjorden
61
Töcksfors
Stora Gla
Kil
62
Oslo
Årjäng
175
Valberg
45
Foxen
5
BORGVIKS BRUK 3
KARLS
E18
Lelång
Svanskog
Vä
Säffle
4
Uddevalla
VÄRMLANDSNÄS
Eken

SEE ALSO

• **Where to Stay** pp290–291

• **Where to Eat** p307

```
0 kilometres        50
0 miles          30
```

The 16th-century Ornässtugan (in foreground), one of the places associated with Gustav Vasa's adventures in Dalarna

Engelbrekt, champion of liberty, in Örebro, by C G Qvarnström, 1866

Sveg
Tandsjöborg
Hamra
45
Djurberga
Älvdalen   Mässbacken   Amungen
296   Norrboda
Våmhus   **19** ORSA   301
Orsasjön   Boda
MORA 18   Nusnäs
70
nsjön   Siljan   **17** RÄTTVIK
Gesunda   Tällberg
DALARNA   Linghed
80
LEKSAND 16   Grycksbo
Insjön   **14** SUNDBORN
FALUN **15**
Djura   Runn   Gävle
BORLÄNGE **13**   270   Stjärnsund
Björbo   Sater   Husby
274   68
Nyhammar   Horndal
50   HEDEMORA **12**
Skattlösberg   70
245   LUDVIKA **11**   Smedjebacken   Avesta
Grängesberg   66   68
Lesjöfors   Stockholm
50
Långban
7 FILIPSTAD
ors
26   205
Västerås
8 KARLSKOGA   E20
Kristinehamn   E18   **10** ÖREBRO   Hjälmaren
egerfors   Kumla
26   Hallsberg   52
Skagern   Pålsboda
pång   Laxå   NÄRKE
E20   205   51
9 ASKERSUND
Unden
riestad   49   50
Vättern

SIGHTS AT A GLANCE

Arvika **2**
Askersund **9**
Borgviks Bruk **3**
Borlänge **13**
Falun **15**
Filipstad **7**
Hagfors **6**
Hedemora **12**
Idre and Särna **21**
Karlskoga **8**
Karlstad **5**
Leksand **16**
Ludvika **11**
Mora **18**
Orsa **19**
Rättvik **17**
Sundborn **14**
Sälen **20**
Värmlandsnäs **4**
Örebro (pp238–9) **10**

Tour
Around the Fryken Lakes **1**

A Tour around the Fryken Lakes ❶

Author Selma Lagerlöf called the Fryken lakes the
"smiling leaves", and it is the natural surroundings, the
glittering waters, the flowering meadows and the dark
forests on the horizon that strike visitors most. The
author's spirit is a constant presence, and no more so
than at the Rottneros estate, which is Ekeby in *Gösta
Berling's Saga*, and the author's home, Mårbacka,
across the water. The best ways to experience the lakes
are aboard the vintage steamer *Freja af Fryken*, or by
bicycle or car from Sunne, the main centre of the area.

**View across Övre Fryken
from Tossebergsklätten**

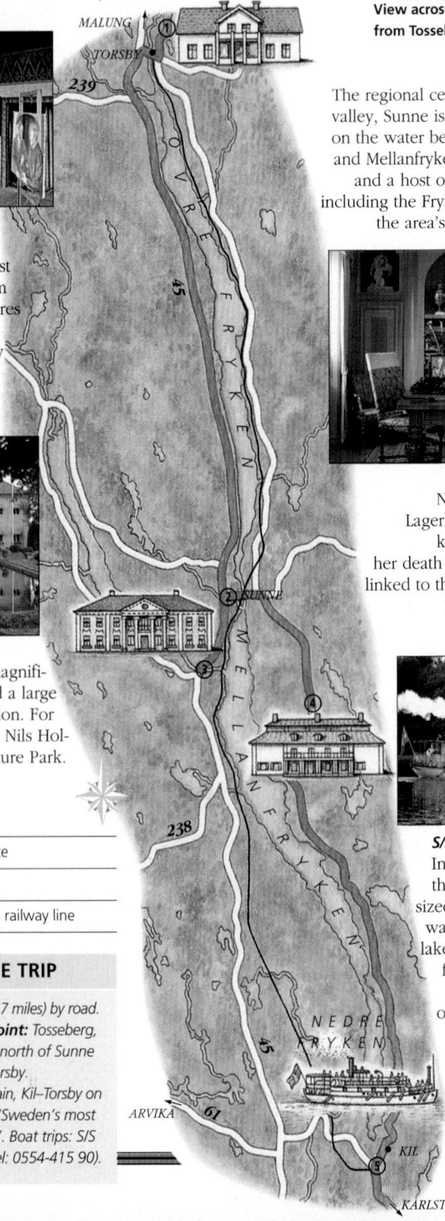

Sunne ②

The regional centre of the Fryksdal
valley, Sunne is beautifully situated
on the water between Övre Fryken
and Mellanfryken. Heritage centres
and a host of events in summer,
including the Fryksdal Dance, reflect
the area's rich folk traditions.

Sahlströmska
Gården ①

The home of artist
siblings Sahlström
in Utterbyn features
mementoes of
some of the early
20th century's
most colourful
Swedish artists.

Mårbacka ④

Nobel laureate Selma
Lagerlöf's home has been
kept just as it was on
her death in 1940. Exhibitions
linked to the author's work are
held in the summer.

Rottneros ③

The estate has magnifi-
cent gardens and a large
sculpture collection. For
children, there is Nils Hol-
gersson's Adventure Park.

KEY

▬ Suggested route

═ Other roads

— Fryksdalsbanan railway line

S/S Freja av Fryken ⑤

In 1896, the queen of
the Fryken lakes cap-
sized; 98 years later she
was salvaged from the
lake bed and now sails
from the port of Kil,
powered by her
original 1868 engine.

TIPS FOR THE TRIP

Length: 75 km (47 miles) by road.
Stopping-off point: Tosseberg,
20 km (12 miles) north of Sunne
on the road to Torsby.
Other routes: train, Kil–Torsby on
Fryksdalsbanan, "Sweden's most
beautiful railway". Boat trips: S/S
Freja av Fryken (tel: 0554-415 90).

0 kilometres   8

0 miles   5

Arvika ❷

Värmland. Road 61. 🏛 14,000.
🚌 🚕 ✈ ⛴ ℹ Storgatan 22,
0570-817 90. 📷 Arvika Festival (mid-Jul), Harbour Festival (Jun).
www.arvika.se

The people of Värmland are known for their wit and ability to tell funny stories, particularly in Jösse, where Arvika is the main town. It is situated on a hill above the bay of Kyrkviken, which is linked to the lake of Glafsfjorden by a narrow strait.

Arvika Fordonsmuseum, centrally located next to the fire station, has an exciting collection of veteran vehicles, including hundreds of cars, motorcycles and carriages.

The area has long been home to craftworkers and artists, as can be seen in the **Rackstadmuseet** in Taserud just outside the town. This is where sculptor Christian Eriksson set up his studio, Oppstuhage, in the mid-1890s. For many years it was a magnet for artists attracted by the pristine Värmland countryside, such as the painter Gustaf Fjaestad, renowned for his winter scenes.

Klässbols Linneväveri, 20 km (12 miles) south of Arvika, is the Nordic region's only damask weaving mill and a rewarding destination for those who want to see how the linen tablecloths for the Nobel Prize banquets, or fabric for the Royal Family, are made.

A 1903 Humber in Arvika Fordonsmuseum

🏛 **Arvika Fordonsmuseum**
Thermiavägen 2. **Tel** 0570-803 90.
🕐 Sep–May: Sat–Sun; Jun–Aug: daily. Group bookings: by appointment. 📷 🚻 🛍 📷 ♿

🏛 **Rackstadmuseet**
Taserud. **Tel** 0570 809 90. 🕐 Oct–Mar: Thu, Sat, Sun; Apr, May & Sep: Tue–Sun; Jun–Aug: daily; other times by appointment. 📷 🚻 🛍

🧵 **Klässbols Linneväveri**
Damastvägen 5. 20 km (16 miles) S of Arvika. **Tel** 0570-46 01 85. 🕐 Oct–Apr: Mon–Fri & Sat; May–Sep: daily. 🛍 only pre-booked. 🚻 🛍 ♿

century church make Borgvik one of the leading monuments to a bygone industrial age in Värmland. Near Västra Smedbyn is **von Echstedtska Gården**. This impressive 1760s' Carolian manor is known for its murals. Even the privy has burlesque and, to say the least, educational paintings.

🧵 **von Echstedtska Gården**
Västra Smedbyn. 20 km (12 miles) NW of Säffle. **Tel** 0533-630 74. 🕐 May–Sep. 📷 🛍 only pre-booked. 🚻 🛍

Borgviks Bruk ❸

Värmland. 35 km (22 miles) W of Karlstad. Road 45. 🏛 400. 🚌
Borgvik Byggnadsvård Tel 0555-743 80, winter: 054-14 31 00.
🕐 Jun–Aug.

The ironworks in Borgvik operated from 1600 to 1925. The foundry ruins and works buildings along with the striking manor and 18th-

Värmlandsnäs ❹

Värmland. 5 km (2 miles) S of Säffle.

Jutting out into Lake Vänern is a large peninsula noted for its excellent agricultural land and the medieval churches of **Botilsäter** and **Millesvik**.

From the southernmost tip in Ekenäs it is possible to head out to **Lurö**, Sweden's largest inland archipelago. This is the ideal spot to enjoy countryside well off the beaten track. The boat trip to the main island of Lurö takes an hour.

SELMA LAGERLOF

In 1909, Selma Lagerlöf (1858–1940) became the first woman to receive the Nobel prize for literature. And despite the passing of a century since she wrote her first masterpiece, interest in the author's captivating adventures continues unabated. Numerous film and TV versions of her works have been produced, including *The Treasure, Thy Soul Shall Bear Witness!, The Emperor of Portugallia* and *Jerusalem*. When she made her debut in 1891 with the imaginative novel *Gösta Berling's Saga*, she put the Värmland countryside around the Fryken lakes and the family estate of Mårbacka on the literary map. Even more remarkable was the success of *The Wonderful Adventures of Nils*. The tale of the tiny boy's epic journey with wild geese was translated around the world.

Selma Lagerlöf, sculpture by Carl Eldh, Rottneros

Perfect bathing spots along the shore at Värmlandsnäs

For hotels and restaurants in this region see pp290–291 and p307

The Almen quarter, a heritage centre in Karlstad on the Klarälven river

Karlstad ❺

Värmland. E18. 🏘 *57,000.* ✈ 🚆
🚌 ❂ *Västra Torggaton 26, 054-29
84 00.* 🎪 *Swedish Rally (1st
weekend in Feb), Harbour Festival
(Jul/Aug), Round Vänern Race (Jul/
Aug).* www.karlstad.se

The phrase *"Sola i Karlsta"*
(Enjoy the sun in Karlstad)
has been used to attract visitors
to the Värmland metropolis.
Yet the truth is that this is no
sunnier a place than any other
in the province. It was, in fact,
a jovial hostess at the town's
inn who brought sunshine into
people's lives in the early 19th
century – her statue now
stands outside the Stadshotell.
But Karlstad has plenty of
other attractions. It was built
on the delta formed by the
Klarälven river before it flows
into Lake Vänern, and was a
market town in medieval
times. It received its charter in
1584 along with its name from
the then king, Karl IX.

Karlstad has been devastated
by fire on many occasions,
most recently in 1865. The
Almen quarter on Västra
Älvgrenen is a heritage centre
comprising traditional wooden
houses which survived the
blaze. Thanks to its large
garden, another survivor was
the bishop's palace, built in
1781. The cathedral was less
fortunate, having to have its
exterior rebuilt along with
its tower. Parts of the early
18th-century interior were
preserved. A well-known
feature of the town is the 12-
arched Östra Bron bridge,
built in 1811. A good insight
into Värmland's history and

folk culture can be gained at
Värmlands Museum down by
the river. The museum also
runs the beautifully situated
Alsters Herrgård, 8 km (5
miles) east of Karlstad, birthplace of poet Gustaf Fröding
in 1860. The manor is a
memorial to him and
other local poets.

The open-air
museum in **Marie-
bergsskogen** has
several historic
buildings, including a
sauna and smoking
hut built by Finnish
immigrants to the
manor of Marieberg.
In the grounds lies
Värmlands Naturum,
featuring the flora and fauna
of the province.

🏛 **Värmlands Museum**
Sandgrundsudden. 400 m (440 yd)
N of the centre. *Tel 054-701 19 00.*
◯ *daily.* 🎫 ⭗ 🖵 🍴 📷 ♿

🏛 **Alsters Herrgård**
8 km (5 miles) E of Karlstad. *Tel
054-83 40 81.* ◯ *May–Aug: daily;
Sep: weekends only.* ⭗ 🖵 📷 📷

**Gustaf Fröding
(1860–1911)**

Hagfors ❻

Värmland. Road 62. 🏘 *6,500.*
🚌 ❂ *Folkets Väg 1, 0563-187 50.*
🎪 *Swedish Rally (early Feb), Klar-Hålja
Festival (early Jul), Klarälvsmässan Fair
(3rd week in Aug).*

In the heart of Värmland
on the Klarälven river lies
Hagfors, which has long been
a centre for the steel and
forestry industries. Today,
steel is still manufactured in
Uddeholm just to the west of
the town.

Hagfors is a good starting
point for trips up the Klarälven
valley and out into the forest.
Various places upriver offer raft
and small boat launch areas,
providing the opportunity to
spend a few relaxing days
drifting at 1–2 knots, watching
the world go by. **Ekshärad**, 20
km (12 miles) north of
Hagfors, has a red
shingled church built
in 1686 with superb
views of the river.
The churchyard is
known for around 300
iron crosses with
"leaves" which play
in the wind.

West of the
town is the
Rovdjurscenter,
which specializes in
the big four predators: lynx,
bear, wolf and wolverine. In
addition to its permanent
exhibits, the centre offers
guided tours of the habitats
of these animals.

🐾 **Rovdjurscenter, Räda**
13 km (8 miles) W of Hagfors.
Tel 0563-54 05 90. ◯ *Apr–May:
Sun; Jun–Aug: daily.* ⭗ 🖵 📷
🎫 ♿

Alsters Herrgård, near Karlstad, birthplace of poet Gustaf Fröding

Filipstad 7

Värmland. Road 63. 🚶 6,500. 🚐 🚆
ℹ️ Stora Torget 3 D, 0590-613 54.
🎪 Oxhälja Market (1st Sat in Sep).

Karl IX founded Filipstad in 1611, naming it after his son Karl Filip. Mining, iron-working and blacksmithing were the mainstay of the town, but today it is known for a very different type of industry – it is home to the world's largest crispbread bakery, owned by Wasabröd. A bread museum is combined with the bakery – both are open on weekdays.

Two of the town's great sons have contrasting memorials. A life-size sculpture by K G Bejemark of the popular poet and songwriter Nils Ferlin (1898–1961) in top hat and tails has been placed on a park bench. Next to Daglösen lake stands inventor John Ericsson's imposing mausoleum. He was a locomotive and warship pioneer and inventor of the screw propeller. Two *Monitor*-type cannons stand next to the monument.

John Ericsson grew up along with his equally illustrious brother Nils in the mining community of **Långban**, 20 km (12 miles) north of Filipstad. Here an entire community built around iron has been

Alfred Nobel's laboratory in the Nobelmuseet, as it was when he died

preserved, including a foundry, now renovated, gaming house and pithead buildings. Mineral hunters investigating the slag heaps of Långban have unearthed an exceptionally diverse collection of no less than 312 minerals.

🏛 Långban
20 km (12 miles) N of Filipstad.
Tel 0590-221 81. 🕐 mid-Jun–mid-Aug: daily. 🎫 🅿 🍽 📷

Poet Nils Ferlin on his park bench in Filipstad

Karlskoga 8

Värmland. E18. 🚶 29,000. 🚐
ℹ️ Kyrkbacken 9, 0586-614 74.
🎪 Swedish Touring Car Championship (end May & mid-Aug).
www.karlskoga.se

Iron ore has been mined and processed in this area since the 13th century, but it was not until Alfred Nobel (*see p69*) bought the Bofors ironworks and cannon factory in 1894 that the foundation was laid for Karlskoga's expansion. During the 20th century, Bofors grew to become one of the world's leading arms manufacturers.

The **Nobelmuseet** in Björkborns manor, Nobel's last home, shows developments at Bofors and offers an insight into the life of the inventor. Nobel's laboratory is just as he left it when he died. The stable where he kept his Russian stallions is now an industrial museum displaying the history of the ironworks.

Karlskoga's only preserved blast furnace can be found at **Granbergsdals Hytta**, 10 km (6 miles) north of the town.

At the end of the Ice Age water poured out from a lake at **Sveafallen** near Degerfors, 15 km (9 miles) south of Karlskoga. The landscape it created can be seen in the Domedagsdalen (Doomsday valley) and from walking trails through the nature reserve.

Kristinehamn is an idyllic town 25 km (16 miles) west of Karlskoga. Its claim to fame is Picasso's 15-m (50-ft) high sculpture of a Native American head to the south of the town.

🏛 Nobelmuseet
2 km (1 mile) N of the centre. **Tel** 0586-834 94. 🕐 Jun–Aug: Tue–Sun; other times: phone to book. 🎫 🅿 📷

THE INVENTOR JOHN ERICSSON

The multi-talented Swedish-American inventor John Ericsson (1803–89) was born in Långban, Värmland, where his father was mine captain. At the age of 13, he was employed in the construction of the Göta Canal (*see p146*), together with his brother, Nils (1802–70), the father of the Swedish railway. He wrestled with the development of a steam engine and in his early twenties went to England to exploit his invention. He constructed a groundbreaking engine (1829) which, in the locomotive *Novelty*, took part in the Manchester-Liverpool race and was narrowly beaten by George Stephenson's *Rocket*. In the USA, Ericsson designed the frigate *Princeton*, and fitted his newly created screw propeller. In competition, the ship claimed victory over the fastest paddle-steamer of the day, the *Great Western*. Ericsson's ultimate triumph came in the American Civil War with the design of the armour-plated warship *Monitor*, with

John Ericsson's mausoleum

a rotating cannon tower. She overcame the Southern States' *Merrimac* in 1862.

Stjärnsunds Slott, home of Gustaf, the 19th-century "singing prince"

Askersund ❾

Närke. 🏛 *4,000.* 🚌 🚉 🛈 *Rådhuset, 0583-810 88.* 🎷 *Trad Jazz Festival (2nd week in Jun), Golf Week (2nd week in Jul), All Car and Bike Meet (end of Jul).* **www**.tiveden.se

On the north shore of Lake Vättern lies Askersund, the main town of southern Närke, offering easy access to the forests of Tiveden and islands on the lake. Askersund received a mention in a Papal letter dated 1314. A devastating fire struck the town in 1776, but many wooden buildings constructed since then have been preserved.

The brick-built church, **Landskyrkan**, designed by Jean de la Vallé in 1670, survived the fire. It is one of the most splendid religious buildings from Sweden's Age of Greatness (*see pp36–7*), with its magnificent Baroque pulpit and altar-piece. The Oxenstierna-Soopska chapel designed by Erik Dahlbergh contains a tin sarcophagus.

Environs
Lake Vättern's northern archipelago comprises around 50 islands, most of which are a nature reserve. The islands can be reached by boat from Askersund. Plying the route is the *S/S Motala Express*, which entered service in 1895 and is known as "the prisoner of Vättern" as she is too large to leave the lake via the Göta Canal.
Stjernsunds Slott 4 km (2 miles) south of Askersund was the home of the "singing prince" Gustaf (1827–52), the song-writing son of Oscar I. It was so lavishly decorated that today it is considered to

contain Sweden's finest mid-19th-century interiors.

🏛 **Stjernsunds Slott**
4 km (2 miles) S of Askersund. **Tel** *0583-100 04.* **House** ☐ *15 May–31 Aug: daily; other times: by appt.* 📷 📹 *oblig.* 🅿 **Park** ☐ *daily.*

Örebro ❿

See pp238–9.

Ludvika ⓫

Dalarna. Road 50. 🏛 *14,000.* 🚌 🚉 ✈ 🛈 *Fredsgatan 10, 0240-860 50.* 🎷 *Dan Andersson Week (last week in Jul), Dragon Boat Festival (May/Jun), Ludvika Festival (1st week in Jul).* **www**.visitludvika.se

The western part of Bergslagen has foundries, mines and mining magnates' estates around every corner. The industry has also left its mark on the main town, Ludvika. **Ludvika Gammelgård och Gruvmuseum** offers a good impression of mining as it was in bygone times as does the surrounding countryside.

Environs
For many years Grängesberg, 16 km (10 miles) southwest of Ludvika, was central Sweden's

largest iron ore mine. It was closed in 1989. Ore deposits extended beneath the settlement, and in places buildings had to be abandoned to allow mining to continue. The ore was taken by railway to Oxelösund on the Baltic coast.

Grängesbergs Lokmuseum (the Locomotive Museum) contains the world's only operational steam turbine locomotive.

Skattlösberg 35 km (22 miles) northwest of Ludvika, is where Dan Andersson, "poet of the forests", was born in 1888. It is typical of the villages created by immigrant Finns in the 17th and 18th centuries. **Luossa-stugan**, where Andersson used to write, is now a memorial to the much loved poet.

🏛 **Ludvika Gammelgård och Gruvmuseum**
Ludvika. **Tel** *0240-100 19.* ☐ *16 Jun–17 Aug: daily; 1–15 Jun & 18–31 Aug: Mon–Fri.* 📷 📹 ☐

🏛 **Grängesbergs Lokmuseum**
Grängesberg. **Tel** *0240-207 35.* ☐ *10 Jun–10 Jul: daily.* 📷 *Midsummer's Eve.* 📷 📹 🅿 ☐

🏛 **Luossa-stugan**
Skattlösberg. **Tel** *0240-860 50.* ☐ *15 May–Aug: daily.* 📷 📹

Hedemora ⓬

Dalarna. Road 70. 🏛 *15,500.* 🚌 🚉 🛈 *Långgatan 1, 0225-343 48.* 🎷 *TT-Race Anniversary Day (early Jun), Hedemora Market (mid-May).*

This small Dalarna town is the oldest in the province with a charter dating from 1459. The 13th-century church and the pharmacy built in 1779 are among the few buildings which survived a major fire in

Hedemora, Dalarna's oldest town, granted a town charter in 1459

1849. Another survivor is **Theaterladan** from the 1820s. It was built by a theatre-loving merchant above a granary. Performances take place here in the spirit of the early 19th century and the grain has made way for a museum.

Environs
Husbyringen, north of Hedemora, is the location for a 60-km (37-mile) circular tour, taking in the countryside and local culture. There are mining centres en route and Kloster has the ruins of an abbey. The star feature is Stjärnsund's 18th-century mining settlement, where the father of Swedish mechanics, Christopher Polhem, worked. **Polhemsmuseet** exhibits the work of this inventive genius, including the Stjärnsund clock and ingenious Polhem lock.

Christopher Polhem (1661–1751)

🏠 Theaterladan
Gussarvsgatan 10. **Tel** 0225-151 15.
⏰ 15 May–Sep. 📷 phone for tour.

🏛 Polhemsmuseet
Stjärnsund, 15 km (9 miles) S of Hedemora. **Tel** 0225-800 90, winter 0225-80131. ⏰ Jun: Sat & Sun; Jul–Aug: daily. 📷 🎫 pre-book. 🚻 🅿 ♿

Borlänge ⑬

Dalarna. Road 50. 🏘 45,000. 🚉
🚌 ℹ Sveagatan 1, 0243-25 74 90.
🎵 Peace & Love Music Festival (end Jun–early Jul); Dalecarlia Cup (early Jul). **www**.borlange.com

Dalarna's second largest town, Borlänge came to prominence in the 1870s when the Domnarvets Jernverk ironworks was established and several railway lines came together here. But it only received its town charter in 1944. In recent years it has gained a university college to add to its iron and paper industries. **Jussi Björlingmuseet** celebrates the town's greatest son, the internationally renowned tenor Jussi Björling (1911–60). All his recordings can be enjoyed here.

Carl Larssongården, a place of pilgrimage for interior designers

Environs
Stora Tuna, 4 km (2 miles) southeast of Borlänge, is the traditional centre of the flatlands. The medieval church was built at the end of the 15th century with the aim of becoming Dalarna's cathedral, but the province never became a diocese. Its treasures include a 15th-century crucifix.

At **Ornässtugan**, it is said that in the 16th century the future king, Gustav Vasa, fled from Danish knights via the privy.

🏛 Jussi Björlingmuseet
Borganäsvägen 25. **Tel** 0243-742 40. ⏰ Sep–May: Tue–Fri; Jun–Aug: daily. ● some public holidays. 📷 🎫 🅿 ♿

🏛 Ornässtugan
8 km (5 miles) NE of Borlänge. **Tel** 0243-22 30 72, 745 49. ⏰ May: pre-book; Jun–Aug: daily. 📷 🎫 obligatory. 🚻 🅿

Sundborn ⑭

Dalarna. 12 km (7 miles) NE of Falun.
🏘 800. 🚉 ℹ 023-600 53.

Situated in the village of Sundborn is **Carl Larssongården**, Lilla Hyttnäs, home of the artist Carl Larsson (1853–1919). The interior, containing wooden furniture and traditional Swedish textiles, along with influences from the Arts and Crafts movement and Art Nouveau, has been carefully preserved. Sundborn's shingled wooden church, built in 1755, features paintings by Larsson (1905) and the graveyard contains the artist's family plot.

Nearby, **Stora Hyttnäs** manor is a complete home from the start of the last century with an interesting textile collection and garden.

🏛 Carl Larssongården
Tel 023-600 53. ⏰ May–Sep: daily; Oct–Apr: Tue. 📷 🎫 🚻 🅿 limited access.

CARL AND KARIN LARSSON
Through his book *A Home* (1899), the interior design of artist Carl Larsson and particularly his wife, Karin, as expressed in their house in Sundborn, attracted attention worldwide. The couple had lived around Europe before settling with their children in a wooden farmhouse in Sundborn. Here they were able to develop their ideas for home interiors, producing a decorative scheme in traditional rural Swedish style using rustic furniture, home-woven textiles and colourful country patterns combined with a touch of the Arts and Crafts and Art Nouveau movements. This was in strong contrast to the stifled, bourgeois tastes which prevailed at the end of the 19th century. The joy and happiness in the Larsson home can be traced in every brushstroke and line of his book illustrations, which perhaps explains why Carl and Karin's Swedish idyll continues to inspire interior designers (*see pp24–5*).

Karin and Kersti by Carl Larsson

Örebro ⑩

There has been a town on this site for 750 years, but in 1854 a major fire destroyed the centre of Örebro. This gave scope for a new, more spacious layout on both sides of the Svartån river and elegant buildings coupled with the castle and St Nicolai Kyrka created a particularly fine townscape. A local newspaper described it as "a magnificent 19th-century salon, extravagantly furnished with buildings which proclaim growth and success". But there is also a greener side to Örebro with the promenade that follows the Svartån river to the delights of Wadköping and Karlslund. The river can be explored on foot, by bicycle or in a rowing boat. The free salmon fishing should not be missed.

Örebro Slott on the Svartån river, now the county governor's residence

♛ Örebro Slott

Kansligatan. **Tel** 019-21 21 21.
◯ daily. ☑ obligatory. 🖪 🔲 🗖
🖪 limited access. **Northwest Tower**
◯ daily, admission free.

Örebro Slott has dominated the town since Örebro received its charter in the 13th century. In 1347, King Magnus Eriksson gathered the great and the good at Örebro House, as the castle was then called, to adopt a common law for Sweden. At the end of the 16th century, King Karl IX remodelled the castle to create a Renaissance palace. Today's appearance, however, with its mighty round towers, is the result of major rebuilding in the 1890s.

The castle has been the scene of a number of historical events, including the adoption of the first Swedish Parliament Act in 1617 and the election of the French Marshal Jean-Baptiste Bernadotte as heir to the Swedish throne in 1810. Now it is the official residence of the county governor and also houses Örebro Tourist Office. An exhibition in the Northwest Tower highlights the castle's history.

🏛 Örebro Läns Museum

Engelbrektsgatan 3. **Tel** 019-602 87 00. ◯ daily. ◉ public holidays ☑ phone to book. 🔲 🖪

With its roots in the 1850s, the county museum is Sweden's oldest, although the main collection of more than 100,000 objects from across the county is on show in a 1960s' building in Slottsparken. A permanent exhibition focuses on farming since the Stone Age. The museum's most valuable artifacts, including the Viking silver from Eketorp (*see p157*), are housed in the Treasury. The museum also runs **Landstingsmuseet** in north Örebro, which is set in an 18th-century hospital building and covers healthcare and mental health through the centuries.

♛ Rådhuset

Stora Torget. ◉ closed to the public.
Built in 1858–63, the magnificent Neo-Gothic Town Hall was something of a showpiece in its time. King Karl XV didn't think the castle-like building befitted a provincial town, calling it: "…sparkling wine not weak beer!" Today only a fraction of Örebro's administration fits into the Town Hall, although it remains the seat of the Municipal Executive Board. When the clock chimes, automatons from Örebro's history appear, such as reformer Olaus Petri (*see p53*).

⛪ St Nicolai Kyrka

Nikolaigatan 8. **Tel** 019-20 95 30.
◯ daily. ☑ phone for info.
🖪 ⛪ Sun.

The church on Stortorget has origins from the 13th century, but has been restyled many times. The north and south entrances are from the original church and were carved from Närke limestone. The rest is an example of English-inspired Neo-Gothic style, with the tower added at the end of the 19th century.

🏛 Wadköping

On the Svartån river, 1 km (half a mile) from the centre. **Tel** Tourist Office, 019-21 21 21. ◯ daily. 🔲 🗖 🗖

The beautiful promenade along the Svartån river through Stadsparken leads to the idyllic wooden houses of Wadköping. This is a cultural centre to which old buildings have been moved to make way for the modern town. It is a vibrant community with craftworkers and small shops, and many people live here.

The oldest building is the early 16th-century Kungsstugan (King's Cabin), named after its use by the then Duke Karl on his visits to Örebro in

Wadköping, an open-air museum with traditional wooden houses

the 1580s. His bedchamber has murals painted by his personal artist.

Other buildings include Hamiltonska Huset (1844), moved here from the south of the town, are the grandest building of its era, and Cajsa Warg's Hus (17th century), the childhood home of the well-known cookery writer Casja Warg. In summer there are concerts and theatre performances.

⚜ Svampen

Dalbygatan 3. *Tel 019-611 37 35.* ◯ *May–Aug: daily; Sep–Apr: Sat & Sun.* 🅿 ▢ 🍴 ♿

The mushroom-shaped water tower, which offers a superb view of the town, the flatlands of Närke and Lake Hjälmaren, has become a symbol of Örebro. Since its opening in 1958, 8 million visitors have enjoyed the panorama from a height of 55 m (180 ft). Its construction has set something of a trend – there is a copy in Riyadh in Saudi Arabia.

The tower contains the science centre **Aqua Nova**, where the public has the opportunity to conduct practical experiments with water in all its forms.

⚜ Karlslunds Herrgård

5 km (3 miles) W of Örebro. Diedens Allé 11. *Tel 019-27 07 88.* ◯ *by appointment.* 📷 *pre-book.*

Owned by Örebro town, the royal estate of Karlslunds Herregård dates from the 16th century and brings together nature and culture in perfect harmony. The Gustavian manor house, built in 1804–1809, incorporates wings from the 18th century.

The estate was once a self-sufficient community with around 80 buildings. Craftspeople and artists work here and there are several museums and shops, as well

Karlslunds Herrgård's Gustavian manor house dating from 1804–1809

VISITORS' CHECKLIST

Närke. 🏠 132,000. ✈ 12 km (7 miles) W of Örebro, E18. 🚌 🚉 ℹ Destination Örebro, Örebro Slott, 019-21 21 21. 🎭 Hjalmars Revue (spring and autumn), Craft Fair (Apr, Dec), Cheese and Wine Fair (Apr, Oct), Crayfish Fishing on Svartån (Aug), Christmas Markets in Wadköping and Karlslund (Dec). **www**.orebro.se

as nature trails. Carlslunds Kraftstation, built in 1897, is the country's oldest working power station. There is a restored mill housing technological exhibits and an experiment workshop. In the dairy, a museum shows the harsh life of the agricultural labourer in the early 20th century.

Originally, the gardens at Karlslund were remarkably grand and over the past 30 years work has been ongoing to restore them to their former glory, partly in the form of an ecopark.

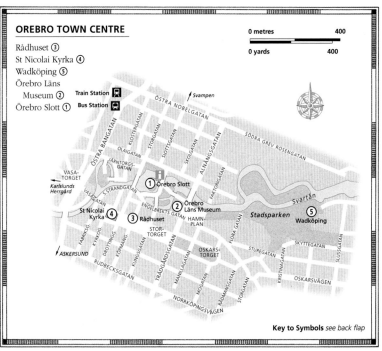

ÖREBRO TOWN CENTRE

Rådhuset ③
St Nicolai Kyrka ④
Wadköping ⑤
Örebro Läns
　Museum ② Train Station 🚉
Örebro Slott ① Bus Station 🚌

0 metres　　400
0 yards　　400

Key to Symbols *see back flap*

The huge Stora Stöten (Great Pit) in the old Falu copper mine outside Falun

Falun ⓯

Dalarna. Road 50. 🏠 35,000. 🚌
🚗 ✕ ℹ Ttotzgatan 10–12, 023-
830 50. 🎭 Falukalaset (start of Jun),
Falun Då – festival at World Heritage
Site (start of Jul). www.visitfalun.se

It goes without saying that
Falun has had a colourful
impact on Sweden. Wooden
buildings painted in the
distinctive Falu red can be
seen everywhere. The paint
has been made since the 17th
century from powdered ore
containing ferrous sulphate
from the Falu mine, on the
back of which the town was
founded. Stora Kopparberget
(Copper Mountain) was the
country's treasure chest – at
its peak, two-thirds of the
world's copper was mined
here. The entire area, including Stora Stöten (the Great
Pit, formed by a collapse in
1687), Falun's historic
buildings and industrial
remains, outlying settlements
and the **Gruvmuseet** (the
Mining Museum), was
designated a UNESCO World
Heritage Site in 2001.

Dalarnas Museum gives a
broad insight into the cultural
history of Dalarna with
extensive collections of folk
costumes, local paintings and
traditional craftwork.

🏛 Gruvmuseet
1 km (half a mile) S of the centre.
Tel 023-78 20 30. ☐ May–Sep:
10am–5pm daily; Oct–Apr: 11am–
5pm Mon–Fri (to 4pm Sat & Sun).
● 1 Jan, Good Friday, Midsummer,
24 & 25 Dec. 🎫 🎫 ▢ 🔟 🔐

🏛 Dalarnas Museum
Tel 023-76 55 00. ☐ daily. ● Good
Friday, Midsummer, 24 & 25 Dec.
🎫 🎫 ▢ ♿

Leksand ⓰

Dalarna. Road 70. 🏠 15,500. 🚌
🚗 ℹ Norsgatan, 0247-79 61 30.
🎭 Music by Siljan Lake (1st week in
Jul), Rowing race in church boats (1st
Sun Jul). www.siljan.se

The landscape around Siljan
lake is especially beautiful,
but the Leksand area is the
most striking. One of the best
times to see the lake is during
the annual rowing race in
church boats in early July.

Another event worth
seeing is Himlaspelet, one
of Sweden's oldest rural
pageants. First performed in
1941, Rune Lindström's play
about a path which leads to
heaven depicts the witch trials
of the 1670s.

The onion dome of
Leksand's 18th-century Baroque
church can be seen from far
and wide. Parts of the church
date from the 13th century.

Environs
**Karlfeldtsgården – Sångs i
Sjugare** was the summer
retreat of author and Nobel
prize-winner Erik Axel Karlfeldt

The folk sculpture *Dalecarlian
Couple* in Leksand

(1864–1931). It lies on
Opplimen lake just north of
Leksand. Here it is possible to
follow in the footsteps of the
author's heroine, who came
wandering over the meadows
of Sjugare. Also worth a visit is
the garden on the poet's estate.

Younger visitors to Leksand
will be attracted by **Äventyret
Sommarland**, comprising
three amusement parks on the
banks of Siljan lake: Waterland,
Motorland and Summerland.

Insjön, 8 km (5 miles) south
of Leksand was the birthplace
in 1899 of the Swedish mail
order business run by Åhlén &
Holms. The mail order
tradition lives on with Clas
Ohlson, whose store attracts
so many DIY enthusiasts that
Insjön has become Dalarna's
most visited tourist destination.

**🏛 Karlfeldtsgården – Sångs
i Sjugare**
7 km (4 miles) N of the centre. Road
Rv 70. **Tel** 0247-600 28. ☐
16 Jun–8 Aug: Tue, Thu & Sat. 🎫

🎢 Äventyret Sommarland
Tel 0247-13375. ☐ 26 Jun–22 Aug
daily. ● Midsummer's Eve. 🎫
🎫 ▢ 🔟

Rättvik ⓱

Dalarna. Road 70. 🏠 4,500. 🚌 🚗
ℹ Stationshuset, 0248-79 72 10.
🎭 Music on Siljan Lake (Jul), Classic
Car Week (late Jul). www.siljan.se

No one can fail to notice
Rättvik's landmark, Lång-
bryggan pier. After docking at
the pier on the *M/S Gustaf
Wasa*, passengers have a 628-
m (690-yd) walk to reach the
mainland. The pier with all its
fine carpentry was built in 1895
to allow steam boats to moor

near the shallow shore. Rättvik also has a medieval church, beautifully situated on a promontory surrounded by former church stables – the oldest dating from the 1470s.

Environs
A search for older Dalarna buildings, rural communities and paintings will be rewarded at **Gammelstan** in Norrboda, 35 km (22 miles) north of Rättvik. The village street is lined with old buildings, some of which date back to the 17th century.

Tällberg, 12 km (7 miles) south on the shore of Lake Siljan, has many preserved timber houses in the classic Dalarna style. It is also known for its top-class hotels and guest houses, including the renowned Åkerblads *(see p291)* with its excellent restaurant. At the top of the village, Holens Gammelgård features workshops selling traditional handicrafts.

At **Dalhalla**, 7 km (4 miles) north of Rättvik, a limestone quarry has been converted into an auditorium. The quarry forms an amphitheatre with unique acoustics which have been praised by the world's top opera singers. Concerts are held in summer, and Dalhalla can also be toured in the day. The area was formed 360 million years ago when a meteor landed here, creating a crater which encompasses the whole of the Siljan region.

Bedroom in Zorngården, Anders Zorn's home and studio

Dalhalla
7 km (4 miles) NW of the centre. Road 70. *Tel* 0248-79 79 50. ☐ for performances and tours. 🖼 🖭 🖸
🍴 🖸 🖳

Mora ⑱

Dalarna. Road 70. 🚉 *11,000.* 🚉
🚌 ✈ 🚻 *Siljan Tourism Mora, Strandgatan 14, 0250-59 20 20.*
🎿 *Vasaloppet Ski Race (1st Sun in Mar), Stora Daldansen Dance Festival (3rd week in May).* **www**.siljan.se

The municipality of Mora and the town itself – beautifully situated between Orsasjön and Siljan lakes – offers a wide range of

attractions. Mora is particularly associated with King Gustav Vasa (1496–1560) and artist Anders Zorn (1860–1920). Gustav Vasa's travels in Dalarna in 1520 to mobilize local men against the Danish occupation have left many traces. Near Mora, the Utmeland monument (1860) shows several romanticized paintings chronicling Gustav's adventures. It was built over the cellar where he is said to have hidden from Danish scouts. The annual Vasaloppet ski race *(see p245)* is another memorial to the king. At the finishing line in Mora stands Anders Zorn's statue of Gustav Vasa and the nearby **Vasaloppsmuseet** recounts the history of the famous ski race.

Anders Zorn became known internationally not least for his portraits of plump, naked local women. He was genuinely interested in peasant culture and an ardent collector of local handicrafts. In **Zorngården**, which he built himself, he revelled in a world of National Romanticism. On the estate there are a number of older buildings which have been moved here, such as the 12th-century bakehouse which was used as a studio. The nearby Zornmuseet displays Zorn's own art and private collections.

Zorn's statue of Gustav Vasa in Mora

Environs
Nusnäs, 8 km (5 miles) south of Mora, is where the national symbol of Sweden, the Dala horse, is manufactured. Originally a 19th-century toy, the horses are carved with a

knife and colourfully decorated. It is possible to watch them being made on weekdays.

On the island of **Sollerön** on Lake Siljan is the boatyard where the traditional church boats used on church outings and rowing races between the lakeside villages are made. There is also a pretty church dating from 1785.

Tomteland in Gesunda is the home of Father Christmas and his workshop, which is busy all summer making presents for children. The huge park offers various activities, including the witch's school – strictly for youngsters who want to learn about magic and how to help friends and protect the environment.

🏛 Vasaloppsmuseet
Vasaloppets Hus. *Tel* 0250-392 25.
☐ *16 Jun–15 Aug: daily; 16 Aug–15 Jun: Mon–Fri.* ● *public holidays.*
🖼 🖸 🖸 🖳

🏛 Zorngården
Vasagatan 36. *Tel* 0250-59 23 10, 0250-59 23 16. ☐ *daily.* ● *Good Friday, 24 & 25 Dec.* 🖼 🖸

🏛 Tomteland
Gesunda. 12 km (7.5 miles) S of Mora. *Tel* 0250-287 70. ☐ *varies, phone for info.* 🖼 🖸

A giant-sized Dala horse, manufactured in Nusnäs

Horse-riding in Dalafjällen, one of the many outdoor activities on offer

Orsa 🔞

Dalarna. Road Rv 45. 🏘 *5,200.* 🚌
🚉 *Dalagatan 1, 0250-55 25 50.*
🎭 *Orsayran Music Festival (Weds in Jul).*

The Orsa region extends from the gentle agricultural landscape around Lake Orsasjön to the desolate lands of Finnmark in the north.

In the past many of the local inhabitants made grindstones as a sideline, a skill which can now be studied at **Slipstensmuseet** in Mässbacken, 12 km (7 miles) northeast of Orsa.

In this part of Sweden animals are still taken to the mountains for summer grazing. Around Djurberga, Fryksås and Hallberg it is possible to see how dairymaids used to live, far from their villages, churning butter and making cheese from the milk of hornless mountain cattle and goats.

In **Våmhus**, on the western side of Orsasjön, two crafts are practised which in the past were a major source of income locally: basket weaving and making jewellery out of hair. The women used to walk as far afield as St Petersburg in Russia, and Germany, to sell their work.

Orsa Grönklitt, 14 km (9 miles) north of Orsa, is the main area for outdoor activities. At Orsa Björnpark (Orsa Bear Park) special paths and ramps allow a close-up view of the bears, wolves, lynx and wolverine which live here in large enclosures.

🏛 Slipstensmuseet
Mässbacken. *Tel 0250-55 02 55.*
⭕ *summer.* 🅿 🎫 *pre-book.* 🚻 🍴

🎿 Orsa Grönklitt
Grönklitt. 15 km (9 miles) NW of Orsa. 🚉 *0250-462 00.* ⭕ *daily.*
🚻 🍴 📷 🚻

Sälen 🔟

Dalarna. Road 71. 🏘 *1,200.* 🚌 🚉
Centrumhuset, 0280-187 00. 🎿
Snowboarding World Cup, Speed Skiing World Cup (May), Vasaloppet Ski Race (1st Sun in Mar).

Like the majority of Dalarna's mountains, Transtrandsfjällen, with Sälen at their heart, are rounded and undulating and less dramatic than the those further to the north. The highest peak, Östra Granfjället, is 949 m (3,114 ft) above sea level. However, the terrain is excellent for both downhill and cross-country skiing and this, combined with its relative proximity to Sweden's cities, has made the area one of the country's leading destinations for winter sports enthusiasts.

Whether it's black runs for advanced skiers, velodrome curves, spines or jumps for snowboarders, or family slopes for children, there is plenty to choose from in Sälen. Around 200 km

(124 miles) of trails are marked for cross-country skiers and summer hikers alike.

Sälen is the starting point of the 90-km (56-mile) Vasaloppet ski race to Mora.

Idre and Särna 🔳

Dalarna. Road 70. 🏘 *1,500.* 🚌 🚉
Framgårdsvägen 1, Idre; Särnavägen 6, Särna; 0253-200 00. 🎿 *Mountain Orienteering (4th week in Jun), Mountain Festival (2nd week in Jul), Festival Week (3rd week in Jul).*

Northernmost Dalarna, with the towns of Idre and Särna, belonged to Norway until 1644 and the local dialects still sound Norwegian. This is a mountainous region and the views from the peaks are impressive. In the Nipfjället mountains it is possible to drive up to a height of 1,000 m (3,280 ft) for a good view of Städjan, a peak 1,131 m (3,710 ft) high. The STF mountain station at **Grövelsjön** on Långfjället, to the north, is an ideal starting point for mountain tours.

Idrefjäll is a modern tourist resort on Idresjön lake with excellent slopes and lifts. Särna has a beautiful wooden church dating from the late 17th century and the rural museum of Buskgården. **Fulufjället National Park** contains Sweden's highest waterfall, Njupeskär, with a drop of 90 m (295 ft). The effects of a violent storm in August 1997 can still be seen here when 400 mm (16 in) of rain fell in 24 hours. Streams became torrents and fallen trees dammed the water, ploughing wide furrows through the forest.

The distinctive peak of Städjan in the Nipfjället mountains

◁ **Interior of a traditional mountain pasture hut at Balungen in eastern Dalarna**

The Vasaloppet Ski Race

The world's longest and oldest ski race was first held in 1922 when 136 competitors skied the 90 km (56 miles) from Sälen to Mora. Today more than 14,000 skiers take on the challenge on the first Sunday in March. Many more prefer the calmer Open Track race held the previous weekend or special races such as *Tjejvasan* for women. A staff of 3,000 support the skiers by providing blueberry soup, ski waxing and blister plasters. And all

Wreath bearer

because in 1520 Gustav Vasa could not get the men of Dalarna to rise up against the Danes. Disheartened, he fled on skis from the Danish troops towards Norway, but when the local men heard about the Stockholm Bloodbath *(see p58)*, they changed their minds and their two best skiers raced to intercept their future king near Sälen.

In summer, a hiking trail follows the course from Berga in Sälen to the finish at Zorn's statue of Gustav Vasa in Mora.

Berga, *just south of the village of Sälen, is the starting point for the 14,000 skiers who are let loose in the early dawn in several stages, top skiers first.*

Evertsberg *lies halfway between Sälen and Mora. Here, as in many places along the route, the competitors fortify themselves with blueberry soup. Those only skiing half the race can leave the track at this point.*

The first steep hills are succeeded by flat marshland.

VÄSTERDALÄLVEN

• Sälen

Smågan
11 km (7 miles)

• Berga

• Transtrand

VÄNAN

Mångsbodarna
24 km (15 miles)

Risberg
35 km (22 miles)

Evertsberg
47 km (29 miles)

ÖSTERDALÄLVEN

Oxberg
61 km (38 miles)

Hökberg
70 km (43 miles)

Eldris
80 km (50 miles)

Mora
90 km (56 miles)

| 0 kilometres | 20 |
| 0 miles | 10 |

THE FIRST VASALOPPET

At Christmas 1520 Gustav Vasa fled on skis from Mora towards Norway to escape Danish troops. At Lima, near Sälen, local men caught up with him and persuaded the future king to turn back. Since 1922 almost 750,000 skiers have repeated the achievement, albeit skiing in the opposite direction.

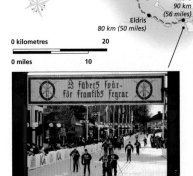

Mora *marks the end of the race. The winning time is usually just over four hours, but some entrants can take ten hours. The text on the finishing line reads: "In the footsteps of our forefathers for the victories of tomorrow."*

For hotels and restaurants in this region see pp290–291 and p307

SOUTHERN NORRLAND

The six provinces of Southern Norrland cover almost a quarter of the country. The character shifts noticeably from the coast with its industry and fishing to the farming communities up along the river valleys, then westwards through forests to the mountains of Härjedalen and Jämtland. Natural resources such as timber and waterpower have had a visible impact on the region.

In the Middle Ages, the southeasterly province of Gästrikland belonged to Svealand and its gently rolling landscape is more akin to that of neighbouring Uppland than Norrland. An offshoot of the Bergslagen mining district extends into this area and iron-working formed the basis of today's manufacturing industry. The trading port of Gävle has long been a gateway to Norrland.

The pass between Kölberget and Digerberget in the province of Hälsingland is another gateway to the north, beyond which the mountainous Norrland landscape becomes more evident. Huge wooden mansions stand proud with their ornate porches and exquisitely decorated interiors. These houses are evidence of the successful trade in the green gold of the local forests in a landscape of which 80 per cent is covered with productive woodland.

Exploitation of the forests had an even bigger impact on the provinces of Medelpad and Ångermanland. At the end of the 19th century, the timber barons of Sundsvall and Ådalen made themselves a fortune. Today, processing wood into pulp and paper is still a key industry. The smell of sulphur can be quite striking – or could it be the herring dish *surströmming*, best sampled by those who dare at one of the fishing villages along the High Coast, a UNESCO World Heritage Site *(see p256)*.

The provinces of Jämtland and Härjedalen only became part of Sweden in 1645. There is often talk of the "Republic of Jämtland" among diehard locals who seek self-rule. The mountains stretch out to the west, attracting visitors both to the ski resorts and to the upland areas where the wildlife and countryside can still be enjoyed undisturbed.

A reindeer herd round-up for division according to owner, by use of lassos and ear tags

◁ The mighty Tännforsen Falls on the Åreälven river, with a drop of 26 m (85 ft)

Exploring Southern Norrland

In this region of immense contrasts, the coastal provinces of Gästrikland and Hälsingland are home to a colourful rural culture enlivened with traditional folk music and dancing. The High Coast, with its dramatic island archipelago accessible by bridges and ferries, is Ångermanland's contribution to UNESCO's list of World Heritage Sites. Inland, the mountainous provinces of Jämtland and Härjedalen offer wide open spaces for skiing and hiking.

One of the best ways to experience Norrland's varied landscape is to start from the coast and follow one of the river valleys which cut across the country. As the roads wind up-river, they pass through dense forests and on up into the mountains.

The heather and rushing streams of Helag, with the mountain of Helagsfjället in the distance

GETTING AROUND

The E4 along the coast and the E14 from Sundsvall across the country to Trondheim in Norway are the main arteries for motorists. The inland roads running north-south are of a generally good standard. The roads east-west tend to follow the courses of the rivers. The main railway line runs north-south. Along the coast, the railway goes as far north as Härnösand before heading inland. The Jämtland mountains can be reached by train, but in Härjedalen transport is by car or bus. The Inlandsbanan railway operates in summer. Air travel is an option and the range of domestic flights is good.

KEY

═══	Motorway
───	Major road
∷∷∷	Minor road
┈┉	Main railway
──	Minor railway
▬▬	International border
△	Summit

A wooden mansion in Arbro, Hälsingland, typical of the area's traditional architecture

SEE ALSO

Map labels:
Storjorm
Kvarnbergsvattne
Gädde
Fågelbe
Sösjöfjällen 1246m
340
336
Kallsjön
Lillho
Tännforsen
Åreskutan 1420m
JÄMTLAN
Trondheim
E14
16
Järpen
Hägger
Krokom
17
ÅRE
STORLIEN   Handöl
Storsjön
ÖSTERSUND
Helagsfjället 1797m
Myrviken
Bru
Röros Mittådalen
Ljungan
Svens
45
18
Funäsdalen
Tännäs
84
Vemdalen
Rat
Rogen
Hede
HÄRJEDALEN
311
Ytterhoga
Lofsdalen
Duvberg
SVEG **19**
Lillhärdal
45
Lillhamra
Mora

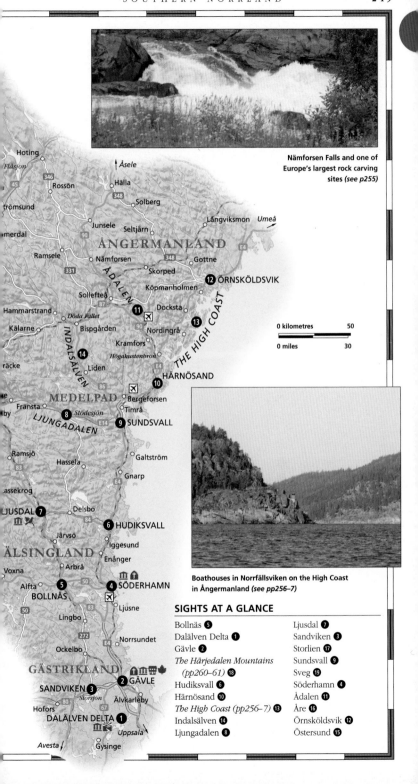

Nämforsen Falls and one of
Europe's largest rock carving
sites *(see p255)*

Boathouses in Norrfällsviken on the High Coast
in Ångermanland *(see pp256–7)*

SIGHTS AT A GLANCE

The Dalälven delta, one of the top ten fishing spots in Sweden

Dalälven Delta ❶

Gästrikland, Uppland. ℹ️ *Gysinge Tourist Office, 0291-210 00.* 🔧 *Weir Day in Älvkarleby (first Sun before Midsummer).*

Before the mighty Dalälven river empties into the bay at Gävle, it forms an expansive delta with hundreds of small islands. The flora and fauna are particularly abundant and the area offers some of the best sport fishing in Sweden.

Least affected by forestry and farming is the area around Färnebofjärden, part of which was declared a national park in 1998. The birdlife is incredibly diverse, with more than 100 breeding species, including several different endangered woodpeckers and owls.

A good place to start exploring the area is Gysinge on road Rv 67, 38 km (24 miles) south of Gävle. The falls between Färnebofjärden and Hedesundafjärden attracted ironworking here at the end of the 17th century. The well-preserved industrial community has a main street dating from the 1770s and a magnificent manor from 1840. Gysinge is also home to **Dalälvarnas Flottnings-museum**, which shows just how important the river once was for timber transportation.

Another important feature of the Dalälven river is hydro-electric power, which manifests itself in **Älvkarleby**, further down-river. The imposing power station, built in 1915, is an attraction in itself, but the most impressive sight is when the water is released at full-flow on Weir Day. Älvkarleby attracts many anglers, who annually land as

much as 20 tonnes of salmon and sea trout.

In **Österfärnebo**, Koversta rural heritage centre is an 18th-century village, offering an insight into local rural life.

🏛 **Dalälvarnas Flottningsmuseum**
Gysinge Bruk. ***Tel** 0291-210 00.* ⏰ *mid-May–mid-Aug: daily.* 🏷 ♿

Gävle ❷

Gästrikland. 🏘 *68,000.* 🚂 🚌 ℹ️ *Gallerian Nian Stortorget, 026-14 74 30.* 🔧 *City Festival (1st week in Aug, Wed–Sat), Country Festival (1st weekend in Aug).* www.gastrikland.com

Gästrikland's main town has been the gateway to Norrland since the Middle Ages. The mouth of the Gävlean river made an ideal port and traders set up base here to conduct business in the north. The harbourside warehouses along Skeppsbron bear witness to this. Gävle remains one of Sweden's larger ports, although operations have moved further out into the bay. A fire in 1869

destroyed the buildings north of the river, with the exception of the town hall built in 1790 and **Heliga Trefaldighets-kyrkan**, a three-aisle Baroque church dating from 1654. As a result, Gävle has attractive 19th-century buildings and broad tree-lined esplanades as protection against fires. The jewel is the splendid theatre on Rådhusesplanaden, built in 1878. The city park, **Boulog-nerskogen**, which features Carl Milles's famous sculpture, *Five Playing Geniuses,* is the most popular of Gävle's parks.

South of the Gävlean river lies **Gävle Slott**, Sweden's northernmost royal fortification, dating from the 16th century. This is also the location of the old town, "Gamla Gefle", with fine streets of wooden houses from the 18th century which have attracted many artists and craftsmen. **Joe Hill Gården** on N Bergsgatan, the birthplace of the Swedish-American union agitator, is now a museum. Other museums include **Länsmuseet Gävleborg** with extensive collections relating to the history of Gästrikland.

Sveriges Järnvägsmuseum offers a delightful selection of old locomotives and carriages,

The oldest Swedish locomotive (1855) in Sveriges Järnvägsmuseum

from mining titans to neat little narrow-gauge carriages.

Fängelsemuseet is a small but fascinating museum housed in 17th-century prison cells. It gives an insight into prison life at the time.

Furuviksparken attracts families who come to enjoy its Nordic and exotic animals, and live performances, and to swim in a beautiful setting.

🏛 **Länsmuseet Gävleborg**
S. Strandgatan 20. *Tel* 026-65 56 00. ⏰ *Tue–Sun.* ● *public holidays.*
📷 🔲 📷

🏛 **Sveriges Järnvägsmuseum**
Rälsgatan 1. *Tel* 026-14 46 15. ⏰ *Jun–Aug: daily; Sep–May: Tue–Sun.* ● *public holidays.*
📷 🔲 📷

🏛 **Fängelsemuseet**
Hamiltongatan 1. *Tel* 026-65 44 30. ⏰ *Wed–Sun.* ● *public holidays.* 📷

🎿 **Furuviksparken**
10 km (6 miles) E of the centre. Road Rv 76. 📷 *Tel* 026-17 73 00. ⏰ *end May–Aug: daily.*
📷 🔲 🍴 ♿

Sandviken ❸

Gästrikland. 🏙 *23,000.* 📷 📷
ℹ *Folkets Hus, Köpmangatan 5–7, 026-24 13 80.* 🎵 *Bangen Jazz Festival (end Jun), Chamber Music Festival (end Jul).* **www**.gastrikland.com

The town of Sandviken grew up with the establishment of an ironworks on the shore of Storsjön lake in 1860. The new railway line to Gävle was one of the factors in its location. Using the groundbreaking Bessemer production process, Sandviken soon gained a reputation for its steel. In the 1920s it began making stainless steel and by the 1940s it was the world's leading producer of steel for tools and drill bits.

Environs
Evidence of Sandviken's iron-working roots can be seen in Högbo. Today the community is a centre for recreation and adventure sports. Located nearby in Kungsgården is **Rosenlöfs Tryckerimuseum**, which has on display a still-functioning printing press from the 1890s.

Opposite Sandviken, on the southern shores of Storsjön, lies the medieval church of

Årsunda, with paintings by the master Eghil. Just south of the church is a Viking burial ground, which inspired the Årsunda Viking centre, offering activities with a Viking slant.

🏛 **Rosenlöfs Tryckerimuseum**
Kungsgården, 10 km (6 miles) W of Sandviken. *Tel 0290-376 18.*
⏰ *Jun–Aug: Sat & Sun; Jul: Tue–Sun.* 📷 *Midsummer.* 📷 📷 📷

Söderhamn ❹

Hälsingland. 🏙 *12,700.* 📷 📷
ℹ *Resecentrum, railway station, 0270-753 53.* 🎵 *Family fun evenings at Östra Berget (Thu in Jul), Herring Games (mid-Aug).*

Sweden's ambitions for power and the need for armaments lead to the foundation of Söderhamn in 1620. Hälsingland's weapon makers were brought together from around the region to work in the town. The gun and rifle-making factory, built in 1748, now houses the town museum, **Söderhamns Stadsmuseum.** Russian attacks in 1721 and four disastrous fires have meant that the only remaining building of significance is

Oscarsborg lookout tower, offering a superb view of Söderhamn

Part of an old furnace in the town of Sandviken, famous for its steel production

Ulrika Eleonora Kyrka. The pink cruciform church was designed by Tessin the Younger in 1693. The upside of the fires is that a series of parks now creates a green patchwork around the city. Söderhamn's landmark is the **Oscarsborg** tower, which rises proudly on Östra Berget. Anyone braving the 125 steps is rewarded with a breathtaking view of the town and archipelago.

Environs
The 10 km (6 miles) of the Söderhamnsfjärden inlet were lined with 11 steam-powered sawmills during the industrial boom of the late 19th century. The industrial museum in Ljusne and **Bergviks Industrimuseum** tell the story. A museum featuring more modern technology is **Söderhamns/ F15 Flygmuseum**, which exhibits military aircraft.

The 13th-century church **Tronö Kyrka**, 17 km (11 miles) northwest of Söderhamn, complete with walls, gates and bell tower, is unusually redolent of the Middle Ages. The archbishop and Nobel prize-winner Nathan Söder-blom (1866–1931) was born in the rectory, which now houses his memorabilia.

🏛 **Söderhamns Stadsmuseum**
Oxtorgsgatan 5. *Tel* 0270-157 91. ⏰ *by appt or for temporary exhibitions.*

🏛 **Bergviks Industrimuseum**
15 km (9 miles) west of the centre. *Tel* 0270-42 32 80. ⏰ *by appointment.* 📷 📷 *voluntary.*

🏛 **Söderhamns/F15 Flyg-museum**
Flygstaden, 4 km (2 miles) east of the centre. *Tel* 0270-142 84. ⏰ *Jun–Aug: daily; Sep–May: Sun.* 📷 🍴 📷 *by appointment.*

Kämpen rural heritage centre at a 16th-century farm in Bollnäs

Bollnäs **⑤**

Hälsingland. 🏛 13,000. 🚉 🚌
ℹ Stadshustorget, 0278-258 80.
🎭 Hälsingehambo Festival (1st Sat
after 1st Sun in Jul), Flax Week (1st
week Aug). **www**.bollnas.se

Located in the heart of
Hälsingland's rich farming
land, Bollnäs is the gateway to
the valleys of the Voxnan and
Ljusnan rivers. The town itself
has a semi-modern centre,
with some wooden
mansions. The church,
built in the 1460s,
contains ornate medieval
sculpture work. In the
Classical-style **Bollnäs
Museum** (1929),
there is a room
devoted to
Onbacken, an Iron
Age settlement just
a stone's throw from
the museum. Also
worth visiting is **Kämpen** rural
heritage centre, a 16th-
century farm displaying a
wealth of local culture.
Bollnäs is on the route of the
lively Hälsingehambo
marathon dance from Hårga
to Bollnäs in early July.

Log-floater by Per
Nilsson Öst (1972)

Environs
Hälsingland was a major flax-
growing area in the 18th
century, and local landowners
displayed their wealth in
lavishly decorated wooden
mansions *(see p18)*. Some of
Hälsingland's finest estates
and farms can be seen around
Alfta, about 20 km (12 km)
into the Voxnadalen valley.
Alfta rural heritage centre,
Löka, in Gundbo, comprises
three farm buildings, some
with beautiful murals. **Hansers**
farm has wall hangings from
the 15th century. In **Arbrå**,

16 km (10 miles) north of Bollnäs, there is an 18th-century
wooden mansion on the Hans-
Andersgården estate where
journalist Willy Maria Lundberg
(b.1909) created a centre for
the preservation of old
buildings. As well as being an
attraction in its own right, the
manor also has exhibitions
and specialist gardens. In
summer, the tourist office runs
guided tours of Hälsingland's
farms and manor houses.

Växbo, east of Bollnäs, has
the only flax-spinning
works in Sweden,
which produces and
sells items such as
tablecloths and napkins.

🏛 **Bollnäs Museum**
Odengatan 17. **Tel** 0278-
253 26. ◯ during exhi-
bitions Tue–Sun. 🅿 ♿

Hudiksvall **⑥**

Hälsingland. 🏛 15,000. 🚉 🚌 ⛴
ℹ Storgatan 33, 0650-191 00.
🎭 Delsbo Festival (1st Sun Jul), Music
at Dellen (1st week in Jul),
www.hudiksvall.se

Fishing, seafaring and trade
have been the mainstay of
Hudiksvall throughout its 400-
year history. In the late 19th

century the timber industry
boomed and the town
became known for its high
living, giving rise to the
phrase "Happy Hudik".

Despite attacks by Russian
forces in the 18th century and
numerous fires, a number of
older buildings remain, giving
the town charm and
character. The Sundskanal in
the centre, a canal linking
Lillfjärden and Hudiksvalls-
fjärden inlets, is lined with
red huts and merchants'
warehouses from the mid-
19th century.

East of the inlet is Fiskarstan
(Fishermen's Town), with its
partly-preserved wooden
houses from the early 19th
century. Along Hamngatan
there are several fine old
merchants' yards featuring the
elegant wood-panelled
architecture of the time. They
have terraces on the water-
side and shops on the parallel
street of Storgatan. An
example is the **Bruns Gård**
pharmacy, which has an
ornate pharmacy entrance on
Storgatan and a winged house
on the terraces of Hamngatan.

Dominating the skyline is
St Jakobs Kyrka, a church
built in the 17th and 18th
centuries, although its onion
dome dates from 1888.

Hälsinglands Museum,
in an imposing former bank
building, provides a good
picture of the colourful
history of the area.

Environs
Hudiksvall municipality covers
a large area of northern
Hälsingland, including **Delsbo**
and the beautiful Dellensjö
lakes to the west. South of the
town is **Iggesund**, with its 400
years of ironworking history,
and **Enånger**, where the

Picturesque warehouses and quay on Sundskanalen in Hudiksvall

Torpsjön, a typical lake on the mighty Ljungan river, with Fränsta Kyrka on its shore

15th-century church contains exquisite medieval ceiling paintings by Andreas Erici and wooden sculptures by master sculptor Håkon Gullesson.

🏛 **Hälsinglands Museum**
Storgatan 31. *Tel 0650-196 01.*
◯ Mon–Sat. ◉ public holidays & eves of public holidays. 📷 by appointment. ◻ ◻ &

Ljusdal ⓸

Hälsingland. 🚊 🚌
🛈 Stationsgatan 2, Järvsö, 0651-820 40. 🏒 Bandy World Cup (end Oct).
www.ljusdal.se

In the heart of northwest Hälsingland on the Ljusnan river is Ljusdal. Settlers have long been attracted to this fertile valley and their history is explored at **Ljusdalsbygdens Museum**. Christianity came early to the area; parts of the church of **St Olovs Kyrka** are 12th-century.

The Swedish national sport of bandy – similar to ice hockey – is enormously popular in Ljusdal, where teams of bandy players assemble for three days in October to compete for the World Cup.

Environs
Opportunities for fishing and walking present themselves at every turn. From **Lassekrog**, 40 km (25 miles) upstream from Ljusdal, those who dare can run the rapids on the Ljusnan river. Lassekrog has been an inn since the 17th century. Here, author Albert Viksten's forest camp is a monument to the foresters of old.

South of Ljusdal, at **Järvsö**, wildlife from the north, including predators such

as bear, wolf, wolverine and lynx and their prey, can be seen at **Järvzoo Djurpark** and the adjacent Rovdjurscentret (Predator Centre). Järvsö village itself is known for having Sweden's largest provincial church; when it was completed in 1838 it had space for 2,400 parishioners. On the opposite bank lies **Stenegård**, a 19th-century trading post, now a centre for arts and crafts, with a theatre in the wooden barn.

Stenegård is also the end point for the annual Hälsinge-hambo Polka Festival, which starts in Hårga, 65 km (40 miles) to the south.

🏛 **Ljusdalsbygdens Museum**
Museivägen 5, Ljusdal.
Tel 0651-71 16 65. ◯ Tue–Sat.
◉ public holidays. 📷 by appointment. ◻

🐾 **Järvzoo Djurpark**
1 km (half a mile) south of Järvsö centre. *Tel 0651-411 25.* ◯ daily.
📷 📷 by appointment. ◻

Ljusdalsbygdens Museum, in a wooden Hälsingland building

Ljungadalen ⓼

Medelpad. E14. 🛈 Sundsvalls Tourist Office, 060-61 04 50.

The 350-km (220-mile) Ljungan river rises at Helagsfjällen mountain and flows into the Gulf of Bothnia just south of the town of Sundsvall. In Medelpad, the river forms an often wide valley with a series of lakes. The E14 follows long stretches of the river, offering spectacular views. The great Norrland forests loom on the horizon and the river was an important timber route.

Stöde Kyrkby on Stödesjön lake, 40 km (25 miles) west of Sundsvall, has a long history, which is illustrated at the Huberget rural heritage centre. The church was built in the 1750s, but contains medieval artifacts from an older, now demolished church.

Borgsjö, 40 km (25 miles) further upriver, has a fine Rococo church built in 1768, with a superb wooden bell tower from 1782. Next to the church is Borgsjö rural heritage centre featuring Jämtkrogen Inn, which was relocated here from the Jämtland border.

Ånge, a railway junction 100 km (60 miles) west of Sundsvall, is an ideal starting point for exploring the area. To the west, the countryside of Haverö spreads out around the Havern and Holmsjön lakes, which are good for canoeing. **Haverö Strömmar** is an 8-km (5-mile) stretch of at times wild rapids with three streams where former dams, mills and fishing huts have been preserved. **Alby**, just off route 83, has a restored eel house showing a fishing meth-od used in the 16th century.

The carefully restored Hotell Knaust's marble staircase

Sundsvall **❾**

Medelpad. 🏠 *50,000.* 🚇 🚌
✈ *Midlanda.* 🚏 🛈 *Stora Torget,
060-658 58 00.* 🎭 *Sundsvall Street
Festival (1st or 2nd weekend Jul),
Dragonboat Festival (1st week in Aug),
Selånger market (2nd weekend in
Aug).* **www**.visitsundsvall.se

The view from Norra and
Södra Stadsberget hills
shows Sundsvall sandwiched
between the mouths of the
Ljungan and Indalsälven
rivers. The sheltered inlets
attracted traders to this spot
in the 6th century, as can be
seen from the Högom burial
ground near Selånger. Alongside Selånger's 12th-century
church lay St Olofs Hamn,
the starting point for
trading missions and
pilgrimages to
Norway's
Nidaros
(Trondheim).
Sundsvall
was founded in
1624. It took off in
the mid-1800s
with the advent of
the steam-powered sawmill.
Sweden's first such sawmill
was built in 1849 in Tunadal;
when the industry was at its
height there were 19 sawmills
on the island of Alnön alone.
In 1888, fire destroyed large
parts of the town centre. The
railway station survived, and
the attractive wooden
building is now a casino. A
grand "stone town" rose from

the ashes. In Stora Torget
stands the statue of the
founder King Gustav II Adolf.
The square is flanked by the
Town Hall and the **Hirschska
Huset** with its extravagant
pinnacles and towers. A
notable building on Storgatan
is the newly renovated **Hotell
Knaust**, built in 1890, with its
superb marble staircase. The
cultural centre, Kulturmagasinet, near the harbour,
contains the town library and
Sundsvalls Museum. On
Norra Stadsberget lies
Sundsvalls Stadspark, which
has a collection of buildings
from Medelpad, as well as
animal enclosures and
lookout towers. Södra
Stadsberget's outdoor
recreation
centre has
adventure
trails for
children.

**Statues on the roof of
Sundsvall town hall**

Environs
Linked to
Sundsvall by the
Alnöbron bridge,
Alnön has many
monuments to the timber
industry. The 13th-century
church is interesting for its
wooden interior and medieval
paintings and sculptures, and
the fishing village of **Spikarna**
is well worth a visit.
Around 26 km (16 miles)
southeast of Sundsvall lies
Galtström, Medelpad's first
ironworks, built in 1695. The
works have been restored.

🏛 **Sundsvalls Museum**
Kulturmagasinet. **Tel** *060-19 18 03.*
⭕ *daily.* ⚫ *Easter Mon, Whit Mon,
Midsummer's Eve.* 🎫 *by
appointment.* 📷 🔲 ♿

🏛 **Sundsvalls Stadspark**
Norra Stadsberget. **Tel** *060-15 40
40.* ⭕ *daily.* ⚫ *eves of public
holidays.* 🎫 *by appointment.* 🖼
(by Stadsparken). 🔲 🍴 📷 ♿

Härnösand **❿**

Ångermanland. 🏠 *18,000.* 🚌
🚆 🚏 🛈 *Spiran, Järnvägsg 2, 0611-
881 40.* 🎭 *Midsummer celebrations
at Murberget, Härnösandskalaset (Jul),
Park Festival (2nd–3rd week in Jul).*

The county town of west-
ern Norrland has a proud
history. It received its town
charter from Johan III in 1585,
became diocesan capital in
1647 and had an upper
secondary school by 1650.
Härnösand's rich history,
combined with the fact that,
in contrast to other Norrland
coastal towns, it was spared
major fires for almost 300
years, makes it an interesting
place to stroll around. The
Russians plundered
Härnösand in 1721. A new
wooden town replaced the
old and charming districts
such as Östanbäcken and
Norrstan still remain. Standing
out among the many public
buildings are the town hall
from the 1790s on Stora
Torget, the old upper
secondary school and the
county governor's residence.
At Murbergets Frilufts-
museum, which is part of
Länsmuseet Västernorrland,
18th-century buildings have
been preserved, including the
town hall built in 1727. This
large open-air museum also
reflects farming culture, with
crofts and farms, a blacksmith's and sawmill, and a
Norrland church village.
Skeppsbron fills with yachts
in July when the town's maritime history is celebrated at
the Härnösandskalaset festival.

🏛 **Länsmuseet
Västernorrland**
Murberget. **Tel** *0611-886 00.*
⭕ *Tue–Sun.* ⚫ *1 Jan, Easter,
1 May, 24, 25, 31 Dec.* 🎫 *by
appointment.* 📷 🔲 ♿

Ådalen ⓫

Ångermanland. Road 90. 🚗 *from Örnsköldsvik.* 🚉 *Kramfors Tourist Office, 0612-801 20.* 🎪 *Kramfors Town Festival (weekend before Midsummer).*

As the forestry industry flourished, Ådalen, the river valley leading to Junsele, became a hotbed of trade unionism and earned the nickname "Red Ådalen". In 1931, the year of the Great Depression, a most unlikely event occurred: the military shot indiscriminately into a peaceful strikers' march in Lunde, killing five people. Lenny Clarhäll's powerful sculpture depicting the drama stands on Sandöbron bridge.

Already in the mid-18th century, Livonian Johan Kramm set up a water-powered sawmill on the site which in 1947 became the town of Kramfors. Cargo ships were able to navigate 50 km (31 miles) up the river and the lower valley became a magnet for the forestry industry. The line of factories

One of the many rock carvings in Nämforsen from around 4000 BC

is now almost entirely gone. Further up river, however, there are numerous power stations – the Faxälven tributary is home to 36 alone. Particularly worth visiting is **Nämforsen**, where in summer visitors can view the large power station and occasionally see the mighty waterfall burst into life. The islands in the falls are an outstanding site for rock carvings. From 4000–2500 BC, hunters carved out over 2,500 figures.

Örnsköldsvik ⓬

Ångermanland. 🚉 *to Sundsvall or Mellansel, then bus/taxi.* 🚉 ✈ 🚢 🚉 *Strrardgatan 24, 0660-881 00.* 🎪 *Harbour Festival (1st weekend in Jul), Dragonboat Festival (mid-Aug).* **www**.ornskoldsvik.se/turism

Nolaskogs is one of the names by which this part of northern Ångermanland is known. It means "north of the forest" – the wild frontier forest of Skule *(see p256).*

Its main town, Örnsköldsvik, or Ö-vik as it is often called, was founded in 1842. Unusually for the time, it was named after a non-royal figure, the county governor Per Abraham Örnsköld. There are good views of the town from Varvsberget and from the top of the ski-jumping tower on Paradiskullen. Many of the town's older buildings have

Arken, designed by architect Per Eddi Byggstam, 1991

been lost to modern developments. A few exceptions include the delightful town hall which, thankfully for Ö-vik's remarkably large artists' colony, was saved as an exhibition space. The beautifully restored junior secondary school houses **Örnsköldsviks Museum**, which displays the history of Nolaskogs.

Attractive new architecture can be seen in the development of the inner harbour, where **Arken** – a centre for offices, university buildings and a library – forms an exciting backdrop. One of its glass-roofed courtyards houses the **Hans Hedbergs Museum** dedicated to the Swedish sculptor *(see p24).*

Environs

Next to an excavation site in **Gene fornby**, 5 km (3 miles) south of the town, a 6th-century farm has been reconstructed, where people come to live and work as they did in the Iron Age.

The most striking medieval church in the area is the octagonal **Själevads Kyrka** from 1880, which was voted Sweden's most beautiful church in a nationwide poll.

🏛 **Örnsköldsviks Museum**
Läroverksgatan 1. **Tel** 0660-886 01. ◐ *Midsummer–Aug: daily; other times: Tue–Sat.* ◑ *public holidays.* 📷 🚻

🏛 **Arken**
Strandgatan 21. **Tel** 0660-785 00. **Public areas** ◐ *daily.* **Hans Hedbergs Museum** ◐ *ring Tourist Office 0660-881 00 for info.* ◑ *public holidays.* 📷 🚻

SURSTRUMMING, A FISHY DELICACY

The coast of Southern Norrland has a speciality which many Swedes, not only the people of Norrland, consider to be the ultimate delicacy, although the majority probably detest it. This treat is fermented herring, known as *surströmming,* which, after around eight weeks of fermenting, is canned. When the can is opened it produces what is, to say the least, a characteristic aroma, which aficionados consider absolutely divine. The fishing villages along the High Coast *(see pp256–7),* such as Ulvöhamn, are the centre of production, and a market is now opening up as far afield as Japan. The fermented herring is eaten reverentially, almost ritually, in early autumn, accompanied by small almond-shaped potatoes and chopped onion. It is best washed down with copious amounts of beer and schnapps.

Can of Surströmming

The High Coast

Sweden's spectacular high coast is best experienced on a light summer evening, when the wooded hills are reflected in the calm waters of the bays, or on the quay in Ulvöhamn during the *surströmming* season (*see p255*), when the peculiar speciality of fermented herring is enjoyed with flat bread, tiny potatoes and schnapps. A boat is ideal for getting around, but the new Höga-kustenbron bridge provides easy access and ferries sail regularly from several ports. The dramatic landscape is the main attraction. Declared a UNESCO World Heritage Site in 2000, it is the result of the land rising 300 m (984 ft) since the ice receded around 9,600 years ago. At that time Skuleberget hill, north of Docksta, was a tiny island.

Skuleskogens National Park
Watched over by Skuleberget hill, the park covers 30 sq km (12 sq miles) of wilderness, with walking trails through magical ancient forest and over the clifftops along the coast.

Ullångersfjärden
Motorists on the E4 rejoin the Gulf of Bothnia at Ullångersfjärden bay which, with its high, sheer cliffs, is almost fjord-like.

Nordingrå
"Fair Nordingrå" was a tourist destination long before the term High Coast was coined. Beautiful roads lined with steep hills pass through stunning scenery.

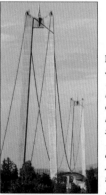

Högakustenbron
Since 1997, the 1,800-m (6,000-ft) bridge, suspended on 180-m (600-ft) high pylons, has saved travellers the 13-km (8-mile) detour up the Ångermanälven valley to the Sandöbron bridge.

VISITORS' CHECKLIST

Ångermanland. E4.
🛈 Örnsköldsvik Tourist Office,
0660-881 00. Kramfors Tourist
Office, 0612-801 20. 🚢 from
Örnsköldsvik.
Skule National Park Skule
Naturum, 0613-70 02 09.
🎵 Skule Song Festival (1st
weekend in Jul).
www.hogakusten.com

Skagsudde

The High Coast walking
trail stretches 127 km (79
miles) from the mouth of
the Ångermanälven
to Örnsköldsvik.

● Köpmanholmen

Trysunda

N. ULVÖN

MJÄLTÖN   Ulvöhamn   *GULF OF
BOTHNIA*

S. ULVÖN

llom   ● Norrfällsviken

mnefjärden

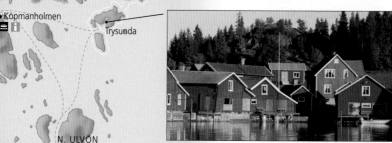

Trysunda
*One of the best-preserved villages,
Trysunda has a richly-decorated,
17th-century fishermen's chapel.
Part of the island is a nature reserve.*

Ulvöhamn
*This is the spiritual
home of the herring
speciality,* surström-
ming. *Norrland's
largest fishing fleet
made its home in the
sheltered harbour
lying between Norra
and Södra Ulvön.
The chapel dates
from 1622.*

● Bönhamn

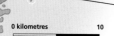
| 0 kilometres | 10 |
| 0 miles | 5 |

KEY

━━ Major road

═══ Minor road

- - Ferry route

- - High Coast walking trail

▪▪ National Park

▪▪ Nature Reserve

Högbonden
*The 100-year-old light-
house on the island of
Högbonden warned
shipping of the rocky
coastline. Today it is a
youth hostel, reached by
boat from Bönhamn, the
most authentic fishing
village on the mainland,
and the place to savour
local specialities such
as fresh river salmon,
whitefish and, of
course,* surströmming.

Thai monument in Utanede, commemorating the King of Siam's royal visit in 1897

Indalsälven ⑭

Jämtland/Medelpad. Road 86. 🚉 to Sundsvall, then bus. 🛈 Ragunda Tourist Office, 0696-68 20 90. 🎪 Vildhussen Festival (1st and 2nd weeks in Jul). **www**.ragunda.se

The 430-km (270-mile) long Indalsälven river rises in the mountains of Norway and flows into Klingerfjärden, north of Sundsvall. The lower stretch of the river from Ragunda in Jämtland includes **Döda Fallet** (the Dead Falls) caused by a disastrous attempt by Vildhussen *(see box)* to control the river in 1796.

Döda Fallet is now a nature reserve where it is possible to walk around the rocky landscape and see the giant basins carved out by stones in the falls. An extraordinary revolving open-air theatre has been created next to the falls,

with a stand for an audience of 420. A stage in the round is set against breathtaking natural scenery.

Utanede features an exotic Thai pavilion, the **King Chulalongkorn Memorial**, erected in memory of the King of Siam's trip along the river in 1897 as a guest of King Oscar II. The decorative elements of the golden pavilion were built by Thai craftsmen and seven million parts were shipped to Sweden and assembled. The interior holds a life-sized bronze statue of the king.

Among the churches along the river, **Lidens Kyrka**, dating from 1510, has the most attractive location (road 86, 37 km/23 miles northwest of Sundsvall) and contains medieval sculptures, with a Madonna from the 13th century. Vildhussen is buried in the cemetery here.

Bergeforsen on the coast is the last of the river's many power stations. There is an aquarium where Baltic fish such as salmon, sea trout and eel are raised.

🏛 **King Chulalongkorn Memorial**

Utanede. Road 86, 7 km (4 miles) south of Bispgården. **Tel** 0696-321 06. 🕐 mid-May–mid-Sep: daily. 🎫 hourly. 🅿 🚻 🛃 some facilities.

VILDHUSSEN AND THE DEAD FALLS

A drama which was to have a lasting impact unfolded on 6 June 1796 in Ragunda on the Indalsälven river. Magnus Huss, known as Vildhussen (Wild Huss), a merchant in Sundsvall, had been building a log flume to bypass the 38-m (125-ft) high Storforsen waterfall when an unusually high spring flood put pressure on the lake above the falls. The log flume burst and the river forged a new route, emptying the 27-km (17-mile) long lake in just four hours and sending so much soil and debris downstream that it formed Sweden's largest delta at the river mouth. The Storforsen waterfall had become Döda Fallet (the Dead Falls). Local people were sceptical of Huss's scheme from the start and despite the now navigable river and fertile land on the old lake bed, discontent brewed. A year later Huss died when his boat capsized. Rumour has it that the oars had been hidden and his boat pushed out into the fast-flowing river.

Döda Fallet, Vildhussen's creation

Östersund ⑮

Jämtland. 👥 44,000. 🚉 🚌 🚐 ⊠ 🛈 Rådhusgatan 44, 063-14 40 01. 🎪 Storsjöyran Festival (last weekend in Jul), Arnljot Games (Jul). **www**.turist.ostersund.se

Established on the shores of Storsjön lake in 1786, the county town of Östersund lies opposite Jämtland's ancient centre of Frösön. Before coming under Norwegian rule in 1178, the people of Jämtland had ruled themselves and would be happy to do so again if the Republic of Jämtland movement had its way. In a fairly lighthearted manner, the movement protects local culture – the highpoint is the Storsjöyran Festival at the end of July.

The county museum, **Jamtli**, with its highly praised Historieland feature, offers an exciting picture of life around Storsjön. This time machine transports visitors to scenes from the 18th and 19th centuries, where history can be felt, heard and even tasted. The museum's showpiece are the oldest preserved Viking *Överhogdal* tapestries.

A short bridge leads to the rolling, green island of Frösön. Its eastern parts are more like a part of town, but the views across Storsjön to the peak of Oviksfjällen inspired the composer Wilhelm Peterson-Berger to create his distinctive home, **Sommarhagen**, in 1914. The house is now a museum and the rich interior with decorative paintings by Paul Jonze is something of a companion to Carl Larsson's Sundborn *(see p240)*. Every

Old stone fireplace in Jamtli Museum, Östersund

summer *Arnljot*, Peterson-Berger's drama about the Viking from 11th-century Frösö, is performed in a field a short distance away.

The 12th-century **Frösö Kyrka** is one of Sweden's most popular churches in which to get married. **Frösö Zoo** has 700 animal species from around the world.

Environs
Storsjön lake is best explored on a steamer, such as the 1875 *S/S Thomeé*, Sweden's oldest steamer still in regular use. Many enthusiasts try to spot the elusive Storsjö Monster, the so-called sister of Scotland's Loch Ness monster.

Brunflo, 15 km (9 miles) south of Östersund, has an 18th-century church with a 12th-century lookout tower.

🏛 **Jamtli**
Museiplan. **Tel** 063-15 01 10. ⬜ mid-Jun–Aug: daily; Sep–mid-Jun: Tue–Sun. ⬤ 24, 25, 31 Dec. 🖼🅿🅿 summer. ⬜ 🍴 🅿 ♿

🏨 **Sommarhagen**
Frösön, 9 km (6 miles from the centre). **Tel** 063-430 41. ⬜ end Jun–end Aug: daily; other times by arrange-ment. 🖼 by appointment. 🖼 🅿 🅿

🦌 **Frösö Zoo**
3 km (2 miles) south of the centre. **Tel** 063-51 47 53. ⬜ mid-Jun–mid-Aug: daily. 🖼 🅿 🍴 🅿 ♿

Åre 🔟

Jämtland. E14. 🏔 1,000. 🚉 🚌 🛫 Östersund. 🛈 St Olofs Väg, 0647-177 20. 🎿 Alpine World Cup (Feb), Country Festival (2nd week in Jul). www.are360.com

Åreskutan is Sweden's most visited mountain peak. The cable car lifts passengers from the village of Åre to within 150 m (490 ft) of the summit at 1,420 m (4,658 ft). At this altitude, the skiing season lasts into June. Facilities are plentiful in what has become Sweden's leading ski destination. There are 40 lifts and 100 pistes, some of which are the longest and steepest in the country. Hotels and conference centres rise

The 1,700-m (5,600-ft) high Syl, just over a day's walk south of Storlien

up into the sky. This is in contrast to how the resort looked at the end of the 19th century with hotels such as Åregården and the Grand. Still here is the Bergbanan run, which has attracted tobogganists of all ages. Prominent visitors have included Winston Churchill, who came to hunt elk. Today's range of activities includes scooter safaris, dog sledding, paraskiing, ice-climbing, surfing rapids and mountain biking on Åreskutan.

Environs
The **Tännforsen** waterfall, 20 km (12 miles) west of Åre, is one of the most impressive in Jämtland, with a drop of 37 m (120 ft).

Narke Sameläger, on an island on Häggsjön lake, has a Sami camp where visitors can learn how to lasso, or taste delicacies such as reindeer heart. On Åreskutan's eastern spur, 10 km (6 miles) from Åre, lies **Fröå Gruva**, where copper was mined from 1752 to 1916. The countryside is beautiful to wander through, with buildings from various eras. At **Huså Bruk**, another centre for copper mining further to the north, is Huså Herrgård, a manor built in 1838.

Skiers resting at a hut on Åreskutan, Sweden's top ski resort

Storlien 🔟

Jämtland. E14. 🚉 🚌 🛫 Östersund. 🛈 Åre Tourist Office, 0647-177 20. www.storlien.nu

The arrival of the railway in Trondheim in the 1880s opened up new opportunities for Storlien, which is located near the border with Norway. It is only 60 km (37 miles) to the Trondheim Fjord, and the broad pass between Stenfjället and Skurdalshöjden allows mild Atlantic winds to sweep through. The healthy air attracted spa guests to a mountain sanatorium, and with the dawn of the 20th century tourists began arriving.

Today, Storlien is one of Sweden's leading ski centres for both cross-country and downhill. It is also a starting point for walks in the Jämtland mountains, such as via the STF stations of Blåhammaren, Storulvån, Sylarna and Vålådalen. The mountains can also be reached from Enafors on the E14 and by train.

Popular with birdwatchers, nearby **Ånnsjön** lake has a bird station and sanctuary. **Handöl**, on the western shore, has been a site for soapstone mining since the late Middle Ages. It was also where the surviving Carolian forces gathered in 1799 after Carl Gustaf Armfelt's catastrophic retreat from Norway. The Carolian monument on the waterfront is a memorial to the 3,700 men who froze to death in the mountains. Today accommodation and better equipment have prompted more and more people to take up the challenge of completing the 75-km (47-mile) long Carolian March.

The Härjedalen Mountains ⑱

The tree line in Härjedalen is at 900 m (2,950 ft) and
even in the forested lowlands in the east there are
mountains with bare summits such as Sånfjället and
Vemdalsfjällen. But the mightiest mountains loom
large in the west towards Norway and the province
of Jämtland, with Helagsfjället the highest peak at
1,797 m (5,900 ft). Funäsdalen is the local hub, from
where in summer Sweden's highest road runs via the
Sami village of Mittådalen and the plateau of Flatruet
to Ljungdalen. There are many opportunities for ski-
touring and downhill skiing, fishing in summer and
hiking along the southern part of the Kungsleden trail.

Helags
*STF (see p320) has a
mountain station at the base of
Helagsfjället, Sweden's highest
peak south of the Arctic Circle.*

Ramundberget
*In the summer, this popular
winter sports venue, known for its
early snowfalls, is a good starting
point for mountain hikes to
Helags, Ljungdalen and Fjällnäs.*

The road over the Flatruet
Plateau is only open in summer.

Røros
(Norway)

Fjällnäs 🎿

Tänndalen 🎿 84

Bruksvallarna 🎿

Mittådalen

Ljungda

Tännäs

Funäsdalen
*This lively town in the Härjedalen mountains
has the award-winning Härjedalens Fjäll-
museum, which shows how the Sami and upland
farmers survived the challenges of past times.*

KEY

▬▬	Major road
▭▭	Minor road
– –	Walking trail
🎿	Ski resort

Högvålen

Idre

Rogen
*The nature reserve
around Härjedalen's
largest lake system has
unusual flora and
fauna. It is great for
canoeing. The Sami village
of Ruvhten offers ice-fishing
for grayling and char.*

For hotels and restaurants in this region see pp291–292 and pp308–309

Reindeer Pastures

The Sami villages of Mittådalen and Ruvhten (Tännäs) have summer pastures in the western mountains. The winter pastures stretch as far as the forests of Sveg and into Dalarna.

VISITORS' CHECKLIST

Härjedalen. Road 84. 🚉 to Ljusdal or Östersund, then bus. 🚌 from Stockholm and Gothenburg. ✈ Sveg or Östersund. 🛈 Lofsdalen, 0680-412 33. Funäsdalen 0684-155 80. Vemdalen, 0684-302 70. 🛍 Funäsdalen Mountain Market (Wed). **www**.herjedalen.se

---

Vemdalsfjällen

This skiers' paradise has a joint lift system for the main resorts: Vemdalskalet, Björnrike, Klövsjö and Storhågna, as well as great facilities for cross-country skiing.

Klövsjö 🎿

Vemdalsskalet 🎿

315

Storhågna
Ånge

Vemdalen 🎿

Björnrike 🎿

Sveg

Sånfjället

Parts of this mountain in the forest were declared a national park in 1909, partly to protect the bear population. Wolves, lynx and wolverine also live here.

84 — Hede

Tärsjövålen 🎿

84

🎿 Lofsdalen

Sveg

0 kilometres	20
0 miles	10

Sveg ⑲

Härjedalen. 👥 2,700. 🚉 Inlandsbanan (summer), or to Mora or Ljusdal then bus. 🚌 ✈ 🛈 Ljusnegatan 1, 0680-107 75. 🎭 Olsmäss Festival (last weekend in Jul), Bear Festival (Jul).

Härjedalen's central town is Sveg, the gateway to the mountains. The municipality of the same name covers an area larger than many counties, and with just 11,000 inhabitants it has a population density of less than one person per sq km. Forest stretches in every direction. Winding waterways provide opportunities for fishing, canoeing and beaver safaris. The nearest mountain for skiing is a 30-minute drive away.

Around Sveg, small villages such as Duvberg, Ytterberg, Överberg and Äggen are well-preserved, with 18th-century features. **Gammel-Remsgården**, 15 km (9 miles) north of Sveg, is a typical early-18th-century Härjedalen manor house with richly decorated interiors. About 15 km (9 miles) east of Sveg lies the village of **Älvros**, whose church has a beautifully painted bell tower.

Lillhärdal, 30 km (19 miles) south of Sveg, is said to have been founded in the 9th century by the Viking Härjulf Hornbrytare. Bildhöst has one of the last working crofts, complete with cattle and milkmaids, while Hamre Skans is a timbered fortification from the 18th century.

Älvros church near Sveg, with a free-standing, painted bell tower

NORTHERN NORRLAND

*S*tretching from the populated Baltic coast through wild forests
and marshes to the open expanses of the mountains, Northern
Norrland is a vast, almost untouched region. The biting chill
and eternal darkness of the long northern winter are compensated
for by summer's midnight sun, when nature seizes its short window
of opportunity to flourish and the reindeer are moved to new pastures.

The three provinces of Västerbotten, Norrbotten and Lappland make up Sweden's most northerly region. Västerbotten, on the Gulf of Bothnia, is the most southerly. Its coast and river valleys had booming settlements for many centuries. But today commercial activity is concentrated in towns such as Umeå, with its university and youthful population, and Skellefteå, known as the "Town of Gold" because of its proximity to two of Europe's largest gold deposits. Inland, the wilderness takes hold with vast tracts of forest and marsh. After a journey between Lycksele and Sorsele, Carl von Linné wrote: "A priest could never make Hell sound worse than this." But with modern transport, today's traveller can look forward to outdoor adventures and wildlife in this unspoilt landscape.

North of Västerbotten, Norrbotten's coastline harbours features of rural culture such as the church village in Gammelstad, a UNESCO World Heritage Site. The Norrbotten archipelago is renowned for being the sunniest place in the country and its beach resorts lure holiday-makers. The border with Finland lies along the Torne river, but here the phrase "two countries, one people" is the most applicable.

Lappland borders Norway in the west and Finland in the northeast, but for the Sami (Lapp) people their land extends beyond official boundaries, across the mountains and forests and down to the coast, where their thriving culture of reindeer herding, hunting and fishing prevail. Known as Laponia, this area is also a UNESCO World Heritage Site. National parks such as Sarek protect the alpine landscape with its glaciers and waterfalls. The main towns of Kiruna and Gällivare in northern Lappland owe their existence to the mining industry.

Dog sledding in Jukkasjärvi, Lapland

◁ Kaitumsjön Lake, Lapland

Exploring Northern Norrland

An area covering more than one-third of Sweden cannot be explored in a hurry. And things are not made easier by the large areas of wilderness north of the Arctic Circle without roads, in Europe's most sparsely populated region. Despite their northerly latitude, the coastal areas combine a captivating archipelago landscape with rich cultural sights. Spectacular roads lead up into the mountains with romantic names such as "Saga Vägen" (the Saga Highway) and "Blå Vägen" (the Blue Highway). Skiers are tempted by the record-length season, while for hikers, the northernmost section of the 440-km (275-mile) long Kungsleden trail *(see p274)* between Abisko and Hemavan crosses the mountainous UNESCO World Heritage Site of Laponia.

Lake Saggat seen from the Kvikkjokk road in northwestern Lappland

GETTING AROUND

Flying is the most comfortable means of transport. Around a dozen airports offer scheduled flights. Only a few trains travel on the Vännäs–Luleå line and the Malmbanan line running Luleå–Kiruna–Riksgränsen. The Inlandsbanan line through Lappland from Gällivare provides a summer tourist route. The major roads E4, E10 and E12 (the Blue Highway) are of a high standard, but road conditions are variable elsewhere. Bus services between the main towns are usually good, but almost non-existent in the wilder areas. Ferries operate across some mountain lakes in summer, saving time for hikers.

KEY

▬	Major road
▭	Minor road
▬	Main railway
—	Minor railway
▬	International border

SEE ALSO

- *Where to Stay* pp292–293

- *Where to Eat* p309

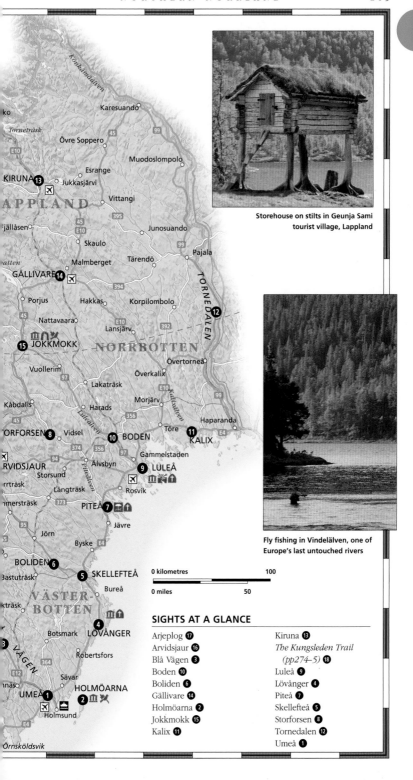

**Storehouse on stilts in Geunja Sami
tourist village, Lappland**

**Fly fishing in Vindelälven, one of
Europe's last untouched rivers**

SIGHTS AT A GLANCE

Birch avenue in Umeå, with the Town Hall in the background

Umeå **❶**

Västerbotten. 🏠 110,000. 🚊
🚊 ✈ ⛴ from Vasa, Finland.
ℹ Renmarkstorget 15, 090-16 16
16. 🎭 Jazzfestival (4th week in Oct),
Film Festival (2nd weekend in Sep).
www.visitumea.se

With 3,000 birch trees lining the streets, it is not surprising that Umeå is known as "The City of Birches". After a major fire in 1888, a new city was built with broad, tree-lined esplanades and parks to prevent fires spreading. Post-fire buildings of interest include the **Scharinska villa** on Storgatan, designed by Ragnar Östberg, and **Moritska Gården**, Umeå's grandest residence for a local timber baron. The city's Neo-Gothic church was completed in 1894.

Umeå dates back to the 16th century and became a county town in 1622. It was an important trading and administrative centre. The opening of a new university in 1965 prompted an expansion that transformed Umeå into a city – Norrland's only one. With 30,000 students and lecturers, it is very much a young persons' place (average age 36), which is reflected in the wide range of entertainment on offer.

In Gammlia, a 10-minute walk from the centre, the **Västerbottens Museum** is one of Sweden's most rewarding county museums, focusing on the history of Umeå and Västerbotten. It includes Svenska Skidmuseet, which covers the history of skiing, and the fishing and maritime museum Fiske- och Sjöfartsmuseet. In the summer, the open-air museum **Gammlia Friluftsmuseum** shows off its historic farm buildings, complete with pets, and there are activities for children.

Gammlia is also the location of **Bildmuseet**, a museum for contemporary visual arts.

🏛 **Västerbottens Museum**
Gammlia. **Tel** 090-17 18 00. 🚊
🕐 mid-May–mid-Aug: daily; other times: Tue–Sun. ● 24, 31 Dec. 📷
🅿 ♿ **Gammlia Friluftsmuseum**
🕐 mid-May–mid-Aug: daily. ♿

🏛 **Bildmuseet**
Gammlia. **Tel** 090-786 52 27. 🕐 mid-Jun–mid-Aug: daily; other times: Tue–Sun. 📷 by appointment. 🖥 🅿 ♿

SWEDEN'S 200-YEAR PEACE

Sweden has enjoyed almost 200 years of peace. The last battles on Swedish soil took place in Sävar and Ratan north of Umeå in August 1809. Russian troops had been plundering the coast and a Swedish expeditionary force landed at the port of Ratan to attack the Russians from the rear. The troops marched south towards Sävar and clashed with the Russians on 19 August. The Swedes were defeated and withdrew to Ratan, where another battle was fought the next day. This time the Swedish troops stood their ground, but 1,000 men died in the conflict. A memorial in Sävar honours the fallen. As a result of the war, Finland was lost to Russia.

Infantryman, model, 1807

Holmöarna **❷**

Västerbotten. 🏠 90. ⛴ to
Norrfjärden 30 km (19 miles) N of
Umeå, then ferry. ℹ Umeå Tourist
Office, 090-16 16 16. 🎭 Seajazz
Festival (2nd weekend in July).

A 45-minute free ferry trip from Norrfjärden leads to the Holmö archipelago. There are four main islands – Holmön, Grossgrundet, Angesön and Holmögadd – and several smaller ones. The majority of the group forms part of Sweden's largest archipelago nature reserve. It is an area of exciting geological formations and extensive fields of rubble stones. The forest and shorelines provide habitats for 130 species of birds and a variety of flora.

The islands have been inhabited since the 14th century and **Holmöns Båtmuseum** focuses on the lives of the local fishermen, seal hunters and farmers.

The archipelago is ideal for cycling, bathing and fishing.

🏛 **Holmöns Båtmuseum**
At the ferry quay. **Tel** 090-552 20
(summer). 🕐 mid-Jun–mid-Aug:
daily. 📷 🅿

Encountering a reindeer on the Blue Highway

Blå Vägen **❸**

Västerbotten, Lappland. E12. 🚊 ℹ
Umeå Tourist Office, 090-16 16 16.

From Lake Onega in Russia to Träna on Norway's Atlantic coast, the Blå Vägen (Blue Highway, E12) stretches 1,700 km (1,050 miles). The Swedish section follows the Umeälven river from Umeå through the towns of Lycksele, Storuman and

Hemavan. Klabböle, near Umeå, is the site of the river's first power station, built in 1899. It now houses the museum of **Umeå Energicentrum**, and is well worth a visit. Children enjoy the "Playing with Energy" exhibit and trying to balance on logs like a log driver. **Stornorrfors**, 6 km (4 miles) upstream, is one of Europe's largest hydroelectric power stations. The immense turbine hall, 90 m (295 ft) underground, is open to the public.

At **Vännäs**, 26 km (16 miles) from Umeå, the unspoilt Vindelälven river joins the Umeälven, and a detour can be made to the mighty **Mårdsele falls** to ride the rapids or fish for salmon, salmon trout and grayling.

Lycksele, the only town in southern Lappland, lies 123 km (76 miles) from Umeå. The local zoo, **Lycksele Djurpark**, specializes in Nordic wildlife.

🏛 **Umeå Energicentrum**
10 km (6 miles) W of Umeå.
Tel 090-480 28. ◯ 2nd week in Jun–3rd week in Aug: daily. ☑ ☐

🦌 **Lycksele Djurpark**
Brännbergsvägen. **Tel** 0950-167 10.
◯ 3rd week in May–Aug: daily. ☑
☐ ☐ ☑ ☐ ☐

Lövånger ❹

Västerbotten. E4. 🏠 2,400. ☐ ☐
Lövångers Kyrkstad, 0913-103 95.

The church village at Lövånger is one of the largest in the country with 117 cabins. It dates from the Middle Ages, although the oldest surviving cabin is from 1746. The village was built to accommodate churchgoers from remote outlying areas during church festivals. A number of cabins have been converted into hotel rooms. The 16th-century granite church of St Anne is decorated with medieval sculptures.

Sockenmuseet, just north of the church, illustrates how the people of Lövånger lived in the 19th century.

🏛 **Sockenmuseet**
Tel 0913-100 40. ◯ daily in summer (call for opening times). ☑

The church village in Lövånger with accommodation for churchgoers

Skellefteå ❺

Västerbotten. E4. 🏠 34,800. ☐ to Bastuträsk, then bus. ☐ ☒ ☐ Trädgårdsgatan 7, 0910-45 25 00. ☑ Skellefteå Festival (4th weekend in Jun); Woodstock Music Festival (Jul). **www**.destinationskelleftea.se

Northern Västerbotten had to wait until 1845 for its first town, but there had long been a marketplace alongside Skellefteå church. In order to accommodate the large congregation, an impressive Neo-Classical cruciform church was built in 1800 on the site of a 15th-century church. Worshippers came from far afield, staying in Bonnstan, Skellefteå's church village built in the mid-19th century.

It was with the boom in the mining industry in the 1920s that Skellefteå's development took off, fuelled by the huge smelting plant at the mouth of the Skellefteälven river.

The town's green lung is the Nordanå Centrum of Culture, a park on the northern bank of the river. It houses an art gallery, **Skellefteå Museum** and historic buildings.

🏛 **Skellefteå Museum**
1.5 km (1 mile) W of the centre.
Tel 0910-73 55 10. ◯ daily. ◯ some public holidays. ☑ ☐ ☐ ☐ ☐

Boliden ❻

Västerbotten. E4/road 95. ☐ ☒ Skellefteå, then bus. ☐ Skellefteå Tourist Office, 0910-73 60 20. ☑ Geology Festival (end Aug/early Sep).

The Kingdom of Gold is the name given to Skellefteå's ore field which, with Boliden

at its heart, stretches from Bottenviken through northern Västerbotten towards the mountains of Lappland. Europe's two largest gold deposits are mined here, in addition to zinc, copper, silver and tungsten.

Bergrum Boliden, in the old mining office, traces the history of the formation of the sulphide ores more than 4,600 million years ago to their extraction today.

In World War II, the world's longest cable car system was constructed to transport the ore 96 km (60 miles) from the mines in Kristineberg. It is possible to travel along a 13-km (8-mile) long stretch from Örträsk to Mensträsk, swinging over the beautiful countryside at a sedate 10 km/h (6 mph).

🏛 **Bergrum Boliden**
1 km (half a mile) NW of the centre.
Tel 0910-58 00 60. ◯ Jun–Aug: daily. ◯ Midsummer. ☑ ☐ ☐
☐ ☐

The Kristineberg cable car system, once used to transport ore

Piteå's sandy beach, and Sweden's best chance of sun

Piteå ❼

Norrbotten. E4. 🏠 22,000. 🚗
✈ Kallax. 🚌 🚢 ⓘ Bryggargatan
14, 0911-933 90. 🎭 Piteå Dances
and Smiles Festival (last week Jul).
www.pitea.se

Originally situated next to
Öjebyn, Piteå was moved after
a fire to the mouth of the
Piteälven river. The new town
was burned by the Russians in
1721 and rebuilt. Picturesque
wooden buildings from the
19th century can be found on
the square of Rådhustorget,
where the attractive Town Hall
dates from 1830. But it is the
coast that is the main attraction.
The **"Nordic Riviera"** offers
extensive sandy beaches and
Sweden's best chance of sun.
If the weather turns, there is
an indoor fun pool.
   Öjebyn has a well-preserved
15th-century church and village.

Environs
Jävre, off the E4 south of Piteå,
has traces of Norrbotten's first
settlers from the Bronze Age.
The archaeology trail takes in
graves, sacrificial stones and
labyrinths.

Storforsen ❽

Norrbotten. 80 km (50 miles) NW of
Piteå, road 374. 🚌 ⓘ Älvsbyn
Tourist Office, 0929-17 00. 🍴

Europe's mightiest untamed
stretch of whitewater
can be found on the Piteälven
river, 40 km (25 miles) north
of Älvsbyn. The rapids drop
82 m (270 ft) over 5 km
(3 miles), at speeds of over

800 cubic metres (176,000
gallons) per second. Efforts to
channel the rapids into a
single course created Döda
Fallet (the Dead Falls), where
giant basins can be seen. Log
floating has ceased, but a visit
to the **Skogs- och Flottningsmuseet** will reveal how things
looked when Storforsen's
huge log jams were formed.

🏛 **Skogs- och
Flottningsmuseet**
Storforsen. **Tel** 0929-17 00.
◯ May–Aug: daily. 🎟 📷
obligatory. 🖥 🍴

**Storforsen in the Piteälven river, a
vast expanse of whitewater rapids**

Luleå ❾

Norrbotten. E4. 🏠 45,000.
✈ 🚌 🚗 🚢 ⓘ Järnvägsstationen,
0920-45 70 00. 🎭 Luleå Party
(1st week in Aug).
www.lulea.se

The county town of Luleå is
surrounded by water as the
Luleälven river flows into
glittering bays with a lush
archipelago beyond. A good
harbour was the reason for
the town's location here in
the mid-17th century, when
the original site upstream
became too shallow.
   The church village,
Gammelstads Kyrkstad, and

its church, Nederluleå Kyrka,
form a unique monument to
the old trading centre and in
1996 were designated a UNESCO
World Heritage Site. The 15th-
century granite building with
its perimeter wall is upper
Norrland's largest medieval
church. The white steeple
towers over a group of 408
small red cabins. This is
where churchgoers from
remote villages would stay
overnight and stable their
horses. The church's star vaulting is decorated with paintings
from the Albert Pictor school
of the 1480s. The magnificent
altar-screen from Antwerp
dates from 1520.
   The cathedral in the new
Luleå was built in 1893.
Norrbottens Museum
concentrates on the history
of Luleå and Norrbotten.
   The ore-loading harbour
and SSAB's steelworks are the
cornerstones of Luleå. They
also influence the science
museum, **Teknikens Hus**,
where technical experiments
can be attempted, such as
drilling in a mine and
launching a space rocket.

Environs
Luleå archipelago, comprising
more than 700 islands and
islets, is a favourite place for
boat owners. Ferries provide
access to places of interest,
such as the fishing villages on
Rödkallen and Brändöskär.

🔒 **Gammelstads Kyrkstad**
10 km (6 miles) NW of the centre.
🚌 **Tel** 0920-45 70 10. ◯ 2nd
week in Jun–mid-Aug: daily; other
times: Tue–Thu. 🎟 🎮 🍴 🖥 ♿

🏛 **Norrbottens Museum**
Storgatan 2. **Tel** 0920-24 35 02.
◯ Tue–Sun. ⬤ public holidays.
📷 🖥 ♿

🏛 **Teknikens Hus**
University district, 5 km (3 miles) N
of the centre. **Tel** 0920-49 22 02.
◯ Tue–Sun. 🎟 🖥 🍴 📷 ♿

**Norrbottens Museum with a Sami
summer tent and hut**

Boden ⑩

Norrbotten. 35 km NW of Luleå, Road 97. 🚉 ✈ Kallax. 🚌 ℹ Kungsgatan 40, 0921-624 10. 🎭 Boden Alive Festival (early Jul), Harvest Festival (Aug). **www**.experienceboden.nu

Its strategic location on the Luleälven river, at the intersection of two main train lines, has made Boden a centre for Sweden's northerly defences. It became the country's largest garrison town at the beginning of the last century and countless young men from across the country have completed their military service here. Five artillery forts circled the town. The nuclear bunker deep in the rock was top secret until only a few years ago. Now **Rödbergsfortet** is a national monument open to the public who can experience life in the fort and even stay in rooms carved out of the rock.

The central Björknäs area is also worth a visit for its open-air heated swimming pool and to see historic Norrbotten farms.

About 3 km (2 miles) north of the centre, a Wild West ranch has been built which offers a taste of pioneering life in the 19th century.

🏛 Rödbergsfortet
5 km (3 miles) W of the centre. **Tel** 070-266 31 62. ⭕ 3rd week in Jun–1st week in Aug; other times by appointment. 🎫 📷 🖥 🔲 limited access.

Kalixälven river, one of Europe's few entirely unregulated large rivers

Russians. During the 1809 war, it served as a stable for Russian horses. Englundsgården Cultural Heritage Centre is a good example of Norrland's beautiful wooden architecture.

Environs
The **Kalixälven** is one of Sweden's few unregulated rivers, ensuring good catches of salmon trout and salmon. The archipelago offers pike and whitefish and the opportunity for seine fishing. Of the islands which can be reached by tour boat, Malören has a timber chapel dating from 1769, an old lighthouse and a pilot station.

Cannon from Boden fort

Tornedalen ⑫

Norrbotten. Road 99. 🚌 ℹ Haparanda-Tornio Tourist Office, 0922-120 10. 🎭 Pajala Market (end Jun), Whitefish Festival in Kukkola (last weekend in Jul).

The Torne river and its tributary, Muonio, form the border with Finland, but culturally the areas along both shores are united. Place names are in Finnish, and many of the inhabitants speak a local form of Finnish.

Haparanda, at the mouth of the river, was created as a border town when Torneå became part of Finland in the peace treaty of 1809. A bridge links the sister towns and they share a tourist office.

The disproportionately large train station, which has both normal and Russian wider gauge tracks, is a legacy from its time as a Russian border town.

Fishing is an important part of life on the Torne. Whitefish has been caught in the Kukkola rapids 15 km (9 miles) upstream since the 13th century, using large nets fixed to piers. The best fishing is to be had in late July, when the whitefish festival is held.

Övertorneå, 70 km (43 miles) north of Haparanda, is a fertile horticultural area. The long light summer nights help berries, fruit and vegetables to develop an exceptional flavour. There is a church dating from the 17th century and a good view from the top of the mountain, Luppioberget, where Father Christmas is said to live.

Pajala is the centre of northern Tornedalen. The area is popular for fishing and wilderness camps and it is possible to shoot the rapids on the Torne and Tärendö rivers. The latter is a 50-km (31-mile) long natural link between the Torne and Kalix rivers. **Laestadius Pörte** and museum attract Laestadian Lutherans on a pilgrimage to the simple cabin of the revivalist preacher and botanist Lars Levi Laestadius (1800–61).

🏛 Laestadius Pörte
Pajala. **Tel** 0978-120 00. ⭕ May–Aug: daily. 🎫 📷 🔲

Kalix ⑪

Norrbotten. E4, 50 km (31 miles) W of Haparanda. 🚉 🚌 ✈ Kallax. 🚢 ℹ Strandgatan 10, 0923-129 79. 🎭 Grayling Day (end Jul), National River Festival (mid-Aug). **www**.kalix.se

The Kalix area to the north of the Gulf of Bothnia has been inhabited since Stone Age times. **Nederkalix** became a parish in the 15th century, but its church has a turbulent history, with devastating fires and plundering by the

Octagonal church in Övertorneå, the Tornedalen valley's main town

Strikingly shaped church in Kiruna, inspired by a Sami hut

Kiruna ⓭

Lappland. E10. 👥 19,100. 🚉 🚌 ✈
🛈 Folkets Hus, Lars Janssonsgatan 17, 0980-188 80. 🎿 Snow Festival (last weekend in Jan), Kiruna Festival (4th weekend in Jun).
www.kirunalappland.se

In terms of area, Kiruna is one of the world's largest municipalities. It is the site of Sweden's highest mountain, Kebnekaise, 2,016 m (6,614 ft), from where, on a clear day, one can see one-eleventh of the country. For 50 days in summer the sun never sets, and for 20 winter days it never rises. But even in the dark and cold, the people make the best of things. In January they hold a snow festival with exciting activities such as a scooter jump show, kick-sled racing and reindeer racing.

Kiruna's development is due largely to the local iron ore deposits. In 1899 the first ore train rolled out from the mine on the newly laid railway line to Luleå. Ten years later, Kiruna had grown to a town of 7,000 inhabitants. Older buildings include the church, a gift of the mining company LKAB in 1912, whose shape was inspired by a Sami hut, and which is richly decorated by artists of the time, including Prince Eugen, Christian Eriksson and Ossian Elgström.

The Kirunavaara mine is open for guided tours. **LKAB InfoMine** lies 540 m (1,772 ft) below ground and paints a vivid picture of mining in the region. Shiitake mushrooms are grown in some of the mine's disused tunnels.

Environs
The space centre **Esrange**, 40 km (25 miles) east of Kiruna has, since the first rocket was launched in 1966, been a vital link in the European space programme. Guided tours can be arranged.

The former Sami village of **Jukkasjärvi**, 17 km (11 miles) east of Kiruna, has Lappland's oldest chapel, dating from 1607. It houses Bror Hjorth's altar-screen in wood depicting the charismatic 19th-century preacher Lars Levi Laestadius' missionary work among the Sami and Swedish pioneers.

Jukkasjärvi has achieved renown more recently with the creation of the **Icehotel** in 1992. In mid-November each year, a team of builders constructs a hotel with ice blocks and snow. Drinks are served in the cool Icebar and guests sleep on ice beds, wrapped in furs, even though it is -40°C outside. As spring arrives, the structure slowly thaws. During the summer, guided tours take in the process involved in making the ice blocks used to construct the hotel and show how the blocks are stored until work begins on the next hotel. A restaurant stays open all year.

Kiruna's vast mountain landscape is traversed by the **Kungsleden** trail (see p274).

Altar-screen by Bror Hjorth, Jukkasjärvi church

🏛 **LKAB InfoMine**
Tel Kiruna Tourist Office, 0980-188 80 for bookings. ⬜ daily. 🎿 📷
🏨 **Icehotel Jukkasjärvi**
40 km (25 miles) E of Kiruna. 🚌 from Kiruna. **Tel** 0980-668 00.
Icehotel ⬜ Dec–Apr. 🎿 📷 🍴 📷

Gällivare ⓮

Lappland. E10. 👥 8,400. ✈ 🚉 🚌
🛈 Centralplan 3, 0970-166 60.
🎿 Winter Market (mid-Mar), Laponia Festival (1st weekend in Jul). **www**.visitgallivare.se

The twin communities of Gällivare and Malmberget grew rapidly from the late-19th century as the mining industry developed. But there was a settlement here long before that time: a chapel was built for the Sami in the 17th century and the Sami church on the Vassaraälven river opened in 1751. The arrival of the railway in 1888 sparked an iron ore rush which can be relived at **Kåkstan** in Malmberget and experienced from 1,000 m (3,280 ft) down in the LKAB iron ore mine. **LKAB's Gruvmuseum** focuses on 250 years of mining history.

The Gällivare municipality stretches to the Norwegian border, covering parts of the Laponia UNESCO World Heritage Site (see p275). The Dun-

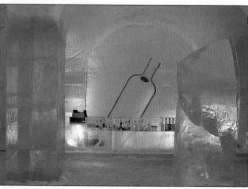

Icebar in the 60-room Icehotel, Jukkasjärvi, a creation of ice and snow

◁ **Kebnekaise massif, Lappland, with Sydtoppen, Sweden's highest peak, in the foreground**

dret nature reserve has good cross-country skiing facilities. Dug into the rock here, the adventure centre **Boda Borg** runs activities for families.

Boda Borg
Dundret. *Tel 0970-660 68.*
phone for info.

Jokkmokk ⑮

Lappland. Road 97 & 45. 3,500.
Stortorget 4, 0971-222 50.
Jokkmokk Market (1st Thu–Sat Feb), Music week in Saltoluokta (early Aug). **www**.turism.jokkmokk.se

The town of Jokkmokk is best-known for its winter market. For a few days in February, snow, darkness and cold give way to light, warmth and sparkling colours, when more than 30,000 people arrive to browse among the 500 market stalls and join in the festivities. The annual reindeer race through the town often causes chaos, but things are even faster at the reindeer race on the frozen Lake Talvatissjön.

The life of the Sami and the pioneering Swedish settlers is depicted in **Ájtte Suenskt Fjäll- och Samemuseum**. Unfortunately in 1972 the Sami church built in 1753 burned down. The exterior of the new church replicates the original, but it has a modern interior.

Environs
The municipality includes the magnificent national parks of Padjelanta, Sarek, Stora Sjöfallet and a section of Muddus, which is part of the Laponia UNESCO World Heritage Site *(see p275)*.

Porjus, 40 km (25 miles) north of Jokkmokk, was Sweden's first major hydro-electric power station (1910–15). Its story is related in **Porjus Expo** which has a power station museum 50 m (164 ft) underground.

In Vuollerim, 43 km (26 miles) south of Jokkmokk, Stone Age settlements have been uncovered on the Stora Luleälv river. The museum **Vuollerim 6000 År** gives visitors the chance to experience Stone Age life.

Muddus National Park, part of the Laponia UNESCO World Heritage Site

Ájtte Suenskt fjäll- och Samemuseum
Kyrkogatan 3. *Tel 0971-170 70.*
Jun–Aug: daily; other times: Mon–Fri.

Porjus Expo
Porjus. 40 km (25 miles) N of Jokkmokk, road 45. *Tel 0973-776 00.* Jun–Aug: daily; other times by appointment.

Vuollerim 6000 År
Vuollerim. 42 km (26 miles) SW of Jokkmokk, road 97. *Tel 0976-101 65.* Jun–Aug: daily; other times: Tue & Wed.

Arvidsjaur ⑯

Lappland. Road 94 & 45. 4,700.
to Jörn, then bus. Östra Skolgatan 18C, 0960-175 00.
Julikalaset (mid-Jul), Sami Festival (last weekend in Aug). **www**.arvidsjaur.se

This community in central Lapland was founded in the early 17th century when King Karl IX set up a church here to bring Christianity to the Sami. **Arvidsjaur's Sami church village** contains 80 huts and cabins from the 18th century.

Located in Glommersträsk, a small village southeast of Arvidsjaur, is **Hängengården**, a homestead dating from the

Traditional huts and log cabins in Arvidsjaur's 18th-century Sami church village

1800s. It is now a museum with 12 old buildings and around 3,000 items of interest.

In the summer a steam train operates on the Inlandsbanan line to the **Rallarmuseet** in Moskosel, which tells of the pioneers who built the railway.

Rallarmuseet
Moskosel, 40 km (25 miles) N of Arvidsjaur, road Rv 45. *Tel 0960-175 00.* mid-Jun–mid-Aug: daily. limited access.

Hängengården
Glommersträsk, 45 km (28 miles) SE of Arvidsjaur, road Rv 95. *Tel 0960-202 91.* early Jun–mid-Aug: call for opening times.

Arjeplog ⑰

Lappland. Road 95. 4,700.
Arvidsjaur. Torget 1, 0961-222 30. Marknan (1st week Mar), Silveryran Festival (Jul).
www.polcirkeln.nu

On the "Silver Road" between Hornavan and Uddjaur lies Arjeplog, home to the **Silvermuseet**. It was created by the "Lappland doctor" Einar Wallquist, whose home Doktorsgården is open to the public in July. In addition to 16th-century Sami silverwork, the museum looks at the life of the Sami and the pioneering incomers.

The area has much to offer hunting and fishing enthusiasts.

Silvermuseeet
Torget. *Tel Tourist Office, 0961-612 90.*
Jun–mid-Aug: daily; other times: Mon–Sat. limited access.

For hotels and restaurants in this region see pp292–293 and p309

The Kungsleden Trail ⑱

The best way to experience the magnificence of the Swedish mountains is to hike along a few stages of the Kungsleden Trail. In 1900, the Swedish tourism organisation, Svenska Turistföreningen (STF), drew up plans for a network of marked walking trails and huts for overnight stays through the mountains from Lappland south to Grövelsjön lake in Dalarna. Today, the 440-km (275-mile) long stretch between Abisko mountain station on the Malmbanan railway line in the north and Hemavan in southern Lappland forms the Kungsleden Trail. The simple huts have given way to mountain stations and rest cabins which offer hikers shelter in bad weather and overnight accommodation. Some also have a ferry service to help people on their way.

Mountain walkers on the well-marked Kungsleden Trail

Sarek

Perhaps the most spectacular of Sweden's national parks, Sarek has 200 lofty peaks, more than 100 glaciers, wild waterfalls and valleys such as Rapadalen. It is home to elk, lynx and wolverine.

Ammarnäs

The village is located in the Vindelfjällen nature reserve, created in 1976 and known for its fauna. Its 200 inhabitants mostly live off tourism and reindeer herding.

Hemavan is the final point for the Kungsleden Trail's northern section. With the ski town of Tärnaby close by, it is a mecca for alpine skiers.

KEY

– –	Kungsleden Trail
- - -	Other walking trails
▦	Major road
▨	Minor road
—	Railway line
⌂	Mountain stations and cabins

Padjelanta National Park

Vaisa
Kutjaure
Låddejåkka
Araslu
Stáloluokta
Tuottar
Sårjåsjaure · Staddajåkkå
Tarraluo
Sämmärla
Vaimok
Pieskehaure · Tarreka

Vuonatjvik
Jål
Pieljekaise
Båverholmen · Adolfström
Dalovardo · Sinjultje
Vitnjul
Råvfallsstugan
Skidbäcksstugan
Tärnasjö
Viterskalet · Serve
Syter · Ammarnäs
Hemavan · Aigert
Tärnaby

0 kilometres   30
0 miles   2

Riksgränsen is the last station on the Malmbanan line and a skier's paradise with lifts often operating until as late as Midsummer.

VISITORS' CHECKLIST

Lappland. E12 to Hemavan, E10 to Kiruna and Abisko. *Kiruna Tourist Office, 0980-188 80, Abisko Tourist Station, 0980-402 00, Tärnaby Tourist Office, 0954-104 50.* Storuman or Kiruna, then bus. to Kiruna and Abisko. guided tours in some parts. www.stfturist.se

Nikkaluokta is the end of the road. It is a 19-km (12-mile) walk to the STF mountain station at Kebnekaise; 7 km (4 miles) can be cut by catching the lake ferry.

Abisko
Thanks to the E10 and its own train station, the STF tourist facility at Torneträsk in Abisko national park is a natural starting point for mountain walkers.

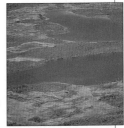

Kebnekaise
Topping the Kebnekaise massif is Sweden's highest peak at 2,016 m (6,614 ft). Below the summit, the STF station in Ladtjodalen, 690 m (2,264 ft), is a good starting point for tackling the range.

Stora Sjöfallet
This area is impressive for the mountains and glaciers of Akka and the primeval pine forests, but the waterfall is dry due to hydro-electric schemes.

LAPONIA WORLD HERITAGE SITE

The mountainous region of Lappland was designated a UNESCO World Heritage Site in 1996. Laponia has been home to the Sami since prehistoric times and provides the ideal conditions for their traditional nomadic reindeer herding, governed by the seasons. It is also Europe's largest single wilderness area, home to brown bears and alpine flora, as well as being geologically important. These factors contributed to its inclusion on UNESCO's list. The region includes the four national parks Padjelanta, Sarek, Stora Sjöfallet and Muddus, as well as the wetlands of Sjaunja with their rich birdlife.

Sjaunja National Park's extensive wetlands

For hotels and restaurants in this region see pp292–293 and p309

TRAVELLERS' NEEDS

WHERE TO STAY

S weden has thousands of hotels and guesthouses to suit all tastes and budgets, from small family-run establishments to large luxury hotels. In addition, there are almost 500 youth hostels which offer great value accommodation for all ages and will normally provide breakfast for a small charge. There is also a range of bed-and-breakfast accommodation, some-

Hotel doorman

times advertised by a discreet sign outside saying *"RUM"* ("room"). In the mountains large ski resorts offer both hotels and small cottages to rent. Cottages are also plentiful elsewhere in Sweden, often on sites which also offer camping. Pages 280–93 have details of 125 places to stay throughout the country, covering a wide selection from cosy youth hostels to grand hotels.

The elegant Hotel Diplomat on Stockholm's Strandvägen *(see p282)*

CHOOSING A HOTEL

When you stay at a beautifully-located classic hotel, you pay for the privilege. But there are plenty of cheaper options which provide good accommodation and many hotels have a star rating as a guide. There are 500 youth hostels (*"Vandrarhem"*) for the budget traveller and these are normally of a high standard. A self-catering cottage may provide ideal family accommodation at a reasonable price.

The larger hotels cater mainly for business travellers and conference-goers, and are often fully-booked during the week. Most hotels offer attractive weekend packages.

It is highly recommended that you book a room in advance, particularly during the week in cities. Hotels in Stockholm tend to be busy from May to November and, when events or trade fairs are on, it can be hard to find a hotel room in the capital. To

find out when the busiest times are likely to be, check the **Stockholm Visitor Board's** events calendar on the Internet *(see p327)*.

HOW TO BOOK

If you do not book a hotel through a travel agent, you can easily make your own reservation on the Internet. One excellent site is **Visit Sweden** *(see p327)*, operated by Sveriges Rese-och Turistråd. The site allows you to search for all kinds of accommodation, such as hotels, youth hostels and B&Bs, and provides contact information so you can make a booking. If you find yourself in Stockholm looking for a room, pay a visit to **Hotellcentralen** at the city's Central Station for a friendly booking service which charges a small fee.

HOTEL CHAINS

There are several chains with hotels across Sweden. Many of these have at least one hotel in every major town, although the main

The spectacular Icehotel in Jukkasjärvi, built entirely from ice

focus is on the largest cities. These hotels cater mainly for business travellers, but often offer good deals for tourists off-season and at weekends. All the chains offer central booking facilities, either by phone or online. Of course, you can always contact your chosen hotel direct to make a reservation.

Choice Hotels Scandinavia has around 60 hotels in Sweden in three categories: Comfort, Quality and the premium Clarion.

Elite has centrally-located hotels in Swedish towns, often in classic buildings.

First is a Nordic chain with an environmentally-friendly ethos and hotels in three categories: First Hotel, First Express and First Resort.

Radisson SAS has a number of larger hotels at the higher end of the price range in around ten Swedish cities.

Best Western is an international chain with about 62 hotels from Malmö in the south to Luleå in the north.

Rica City Hotels has 20 or so hotels in Sweden, including some in the mountains.

Romantik Hotels has, as its name implies, some particularly romantic hotels.

Scandic Hotels is the leading chain in the Nordic region, with nearly 70 hotels across Sweden.

PRICES AND PAYMENT

Prices in the hotel listing are for the cheapest double room, including breakfast, service and VAT. However, most hotels offer rooms at greatly reduced rates at weekends

◁ **Östermalmshallen, offering an abundance of delicacies in a well-preserved 1880s setting**

The lobby of the pleasant Clarion Hotel Wisby on Gotland

and in low season. For cheaper hotels this means a price reduction of 100–300 Kr per night; for medium-priced hotels around 500 Kr and for top hotels up to l,000 Kr.

Nearly all hotels accept the major credit cards. Larger hotels will also change foreign currency, but the easiest and cheapest way of changing money is to use a bureau de change *(see p330)*.

YOUTH HOSTELS

There are almost 500 youth hostels in Sweden, of which more than 300 are affiliated to the **Svenska Turistföreningen (STF)**. The flagship is the tall ship *af Chapman*, in Stockholm – floating proof that a youth hostel can be just as spectacular as a top-class hotel. **Sveriges Vandrarhem i Förening (SVIF)** has more than 195 youth hostels throughout the country. Both STF and SVIF are members of the International Youth Hostel Federation (IYHF).

The standard of youth hostels is generally high, particularly at those affiliated to the STF, and they are popular with people of all ages. Expect to pay around 200 Kr per

person in a double room; 100 Kr in a larger room or dormitory, with a discount of around 50 Kr for STF members. Prices usually exclude breakfast and bed linen hire.

It is always wise to book ahead, and the simplest way is to phone or e-mail the hostel direct. You can book online for some hostels by visiting the STF or SVIF website. Many youth hostels close in winter.

BED & BREAKFAST

Bed and breakfasts can be a good alternative to staying in a hotel or youth hostel. There is usually a reasonable range of B&B accommodation in large towns and close to major roads. You can choose between single or double rooms or an apartment, and breakfast, bed linen and towels are generally provided. Expect to pay 300–500 Kr per person per night at a town B&B; an apartment will cost from 600 Kr per night. In the capital, rooms can be booked through **Bed & Breakfast Service Stockholm** (a small booking fee is charged).

COTTAGES AND CAMPING

Sweden's right to roam allows freedom to camp in forests and on open land (but not in view of houses on private land), but staying at a campsite will ensure a more comfortable stay. Campsites often offer cottages to rent. Visit the **Sveriges Camping- och Stugföretagares Riksorganisation** website for details. Campsites are graded on a scale of one to five stars.

The Svenska Turistföreningen (STF) youth hostel in Motala

DIRECTORY

CENTRAL BOOKING

Hotellcentralen
(For reservations in Stockholm.)
Centralstationen, Vasagatan.
Tel 08-508 285 08.
www.stockholmtown.com

Göteborg & Co
(For reservations in Gothenborg.)
Tel 020-83 84 85.
www.goteborg.com/co

HOTEL CHAINS

Best Western
Tel 020-792 752.
www.bestwestern.se

Choice Hotels
Tel 020-666 000.
www.choicehotels.se

Elite Hotels
Tel 0771-788 789.
www.elite.se

First Hotels
Tel 020-41 11 11.
www.firsthotels.com

Radisson SAS
Tel 020-238 238.
www.radissonsas.se

Rica Hotels
Tel 08-723 72 72.
www.rica.se

Romantik Hotels
www.romantikhotels.com

Scandic Hotels
Tel 08-517 517 00.
www.scandic-hotels.se

YOUTH HOSTELS

STF
Tel 08-58 63 86.
www.stfturist.se

SVIF
Tel 0413-55 34 50.
www.svif.se

COTTAGES, CAMPING, BED & BREAKFAST

Sveriges Camping- och Stugföretagare
www.camping.se

Bed & Breakfast Service Stockholm
Tel 08-660 55 65.
www.bedbreakfast.a.se

Choosing a Hotel

Hotels have been selected across a wide price range for facilities, good value and location. All rooms have private bath, TV, air conditioning, and are wheelchair accessible unless otherwise indicated. Most have internet access, and in some cases, fitness facilities may be offsite. The hotels are listed by area. For map references, *see pp112–17.*

PRICE CATEGORIES
The following price ranges are for a standard double room and taxes per night during the high season. Breakfast is not included, unless specified.
Ⓚ Under 850 Kr
ⓀⓀ 850–1,800Kr
ⓀⓀⓀ 1,800–2,500Kr
ⓀⓀⓀⓀ Over 2,500Kr

STOCKHOLM

GAMLA STAN First Hotel Reisen   ⓀⓀⓀ
Skeppsbron 12, 111 30 **Tel** *08-22 32 60* **Fax** *08-20 15 59* **Rooms** *144*   **Map** *3 C3*

Housed in three 18th-century buildings and perched on the waterfront, the Reisen is a lively hotel that attracts locals and tourists alike. Rooms are comfortably furnished in classic style and have modern amenities. There's a French-Swedish style bistro and the bar is a popular meeting place. **www.firsthotels.com/reisen**

GAMLA STAN Rica City Hotel Gamla Stan   ⓀⓀⓀ
Lilla Nygatan 25, 111 28 **Tel** *08-723 72 50* **Fax** *08-723 72 59* **Rooms** *51*   **Map** *3 B4*

Charming winding streets lead to the doorstep of this cosy establishment. Located close to the Royal Palace, portraits of Swedish royalty dating from the 1650s adorn the walls of the rooms. Here guests will find all the modern amenities they could wish for, including conference facilities in the historic wine cellars **www.rica.se**

GAMLA STAN Lord Nelson Hotel   ⓀⓀⓀⓀ
Västerlånggatan 22, 111 29 **Tel** *08-50 64 01 20* **Fax** *08-50 64 01 30* **Rooms** *29*   **Map** *3 B3*

Built in 1350 and filled with nautical antiques, this is the narrowest hotel in Stockholm as well as being a fascinating museum. The main floor and lobby resemble the inside of a ship, with the rooms decorated along the same lines. Guests can relax on the roof terrace, which is a unique experience in Gamla Stan. **www.lordnelsonhotel.se**

GAMLA STAN Victory Hotel   ⓀⓀⓀⓀ
Lilla Nygatan 5, 111 28 **Tel** *08-50 64 00 00* **Fax** *08-50 64 00 10* **Rooms** *45*   **Map** *3 B3*

The flagship of the Collector's Hotel chain, and housed in a beautifully maintained townhouse, this boutique hotel is ideally located in the heart of Gamla Stan. The service is exceptional and the maritime design timeless. The Michelin-star Leijontornet Restaurant is also part of the Victory. **www.victoryhotel.se**

CITY Comfort Hotel Stockholm   ⓀⓀ
Kungsbron 1, 111 22 **Tel** *08-56 62 22 00* **Fax** *08-56 62 24 44* **Rooms** *163*   **Map** *1 B4*

Modern business hotel located in the World Trade Center and close to the central train station. The rooms are small, clean and simply furnished. The Comfort does not have a restaurant, but does serve a buffet breakfast. Well-equipped for business travellers with a 24-hour front desk. **www.choicehotels.se**

CITY Clarion Hotel Sign   ⓀⓀⓀ
Östra Järnvägsgatan 35, 101 26 **Tel** *08-676 98 00* **Fax** *08-676 98 99* **Rooms** *558*   **Map** *1 B4*

This hotel offers crisp, clean-cut Scandinavian style in a central location. With furnishings by key Nordic designers such as Arne Jacobsen and Bruno Mathsson from the lobby to the breakfast room and the bedrooms, it is like taking a walk through a design museum. The stylish theme continues in the Aquavit Grill & Raw Bar. **www.clarionsign.com**

CITY Hotel Crystal Plaza   ⓀⓀⓀ
Birger Jarlsgatan 35, 111 45 **Tel** *08-406 88 00* **Fax** *08-24 15 11* **Rooms** *111*   **Map** *1 C4*

Built in 1895 and situated close to Stureplan, all the rooms at the Crystal Plaza have been renovated in a variety of styles, including speciality rooms in the bell tower (one of which even includes a Finnish spa). The hotel offers the Plaza Studios for travellers looking for long-term stay options. **www.crystalplazahotel.se**

CITY Hotel Riddargatan   ⓀⓀⓀ
Riddargatan 14, 114 35 **Tel** *08-55 57 30 00* **Fax** *08-55 57 30 11* **Rooms** *78*   **Map** *2 E4*

This 1930s Art Deco-styled hotel has a good location in Stockholm's "golden triangle", just behind the Royal Dramatic Theatre. Convenient for shopping and the city's department stores. Close to restaurants, bars and nightlife – sometimes visiting world-famous jazz musicians stay and perform here. **www.profilhotels.se**

CITY Rica City Hotel Kungsgatan   ⓀⓀⓀ
Kungsgatan 47, 111 56 **Tel** *08-723 72 20* **Fax** *08-723 72 99* **Rooms** *270*   **Map** *1 C4*

Located on the upper stories of the PUB department store, the Kungsgatan is one of the largest hotels in Scandinavia and has views of Hötorget, Stockholm's oldest marketplace. There is no restaurant but breakfast is served in the rooms, which are medium-sized. An ideal location for travellers wishing to shop. **www.rica.se**

Key to Symbols *see back cover flap*

CITY Berns' Hotel

🛗 P ⅋   ⊗⊗⊗⊗

Näckströmsgatan 8, 111 47 **Tel** *08-56 63 22 00* **Fax** *08-56 63 22 01* **Rooms** *82*   **Map** *2 D4*

Located in the heart of bustling central Stockholm, this lively boutique hotel first opened in 1863. Fine dining is available in its restaurant or on the terrace, as well as world-class nightlife with five bars and a popular night club in the basement. A favourite venue for international singers and musicians. **www.berns.se**

CITY Hotel Rival

🛗 P ⅋   ⊗⊗⊗⊗

Mariatorget 3. **Tel** *08-545 789 00* **Fax** *08-545 789 24* **Rooms** *99*   **Map** *3 A5*

This trendy boutique hotel comes equipped with its own cinema and has a great location in the heart of Stockholm. Built in the 1930s, the owner, Benny Andersson (of Abba fame) has recaptured the glamour of the era in the hotel's design. Each of the 99 guest rooms are individually designed. **www.rival.se**

CITY Nordic Hotel

🍴 🛗 P ⅋   ⊗⊗⊗⊗

Vasaplan 7, 101 37 **Tel** *08-50 56 30 00* **Fax** *08-50 56 30 30* **Rooms** *542*   **Map** *1 B4*

Two hotels in one – Nordic Light and Nordic Sea – both with award-winning rooms. Nordic Sea rooms are individually decorated in Scandinavian style; Nordic Light rooms are decorated in black and white with unique lighting designs. The famous Ice Bar, completely constructed of ice, is a must-see. **www.nordichotels.se**

CITY Radisson Blu Royal Viking Hotel

🍴 🛗 P ⅋   ⊗⊗⊗⊗

Vasagatan 1, 101 24 **Tel** *08-50 65 40 00* **Fax** *08-50 65 40 01* **Rooms** *359*   **Map** *1 C5*

One of Stockholm's best-known hotels, the Royal Viking offers two bars, one in the ground floor atrium and the exciting Sky Bar on the top floor, as well as the excellent Stockholm Fisk Restaurant. This hotel maintains high standards suited to both business and leisure travellers. **www.radissonblu.com**

CITY Scandic Hotel Sergel Plaza

🍴 🛗 P ⅋   ⊗⊗⊗⊗

Brunkebergstorg 9, 103 27 **Tel** *08-51 72 63 00* **Fax** *08-51 72 63 11* **Rooms** *403*   **Map** *3 A1*

This centrally located hotel offers a full range of services for tourists and business travellers. The rooms are compact and the decor a little bland, but this is more than made up for by the convenient location. The hotel's restaurant serves buffet and à la carte dining options. **www.scandichotels.se**

CITY Sheraton Stockholm Hotel

🍴 🛗 P ⅋   ⊗⊗⊗⊗

Tegelbacken 6, 101 23 **Tel** *08-414 34 00* **Fax** *08-412 34 09* **Rooms** *465*   **Map** *1 C5*

In a central location within the business district, close to shops and just a short walk from transport links, the Sheraton is an excellent hotel for both business travellers and tourists alike. Rooms are comfortable, modern and well equipped. The breakfast buffet costs extra but is generous and offers many choices. **www.sheratonstockholm.com**

BLASIEHOLMEN & SKEPPSHOLMEN Af Chapman & Skeppsholmen

P ⅋   ⊗

Flaggmansvägen 8, 111 49 **Tel** *08-463 22 66* **Fax** *08-611 71 55* **Rooms** *76*   **Map** *4 E3*

One of the most beautiful youth hostels in the world, offering beds on board a classic ship permanently moored across from the Royal Palace, on Skeppsholmen island. The ship has been renovated but retains its charm. The hostel offers 76 rooms with a total of 280 beds. Book early – it fills up quickly. **www.stfchapman.com**

BLASIEHOLMEN & SKEPPSHOLMEN Grand Hôtel Stockholm

🍴 🛗 P ⅋   ⊗⊗⊗⊗

Södra Blasieholmshamnen 8, 103 27 **Tel** *08-679 35 60* **Fax** *08-611 86 86* **Rooms** *368*   **Map** *3 C1*

Magnificently located just a stone's throw from the Nationalmuseum and Kungsträdgården, the Grand is often considered to be Sweden's best hotel. Now part of the InterContinental Hotel chain, it has two Michelin-star restaurants and the popular Cadier Bar. **www.grandhotel.se**

BLASIEHOLMEN & SKEPPSHOLMEN Hotel Skeppsholmen

🍴 🛗 P ⅋   ⊗⊗⊗⊗

Skeppsholmen, 111 86 **Tel** *08-407 23 00* **Rooms** *81*   **Map** *4 E3*

Located on the peaceful island of Skeppsholmen, and just a ten-minute walk from the city centre, is this boutique hotel in an historic 16th-century building. Inside, the original wooden floors remain, but the decor is modern and stylish. Food and drinks reflect Swedish traditions, but with a quirky twist. **www.hotelskeppsholmen.com**

BLASIEHOLMEN & SKEPPSHOLMEN Radisson Blu Strand Hotel

🛗 P ⅋   ⊗⊗⊗⊗

Nybrokajen 9, 103 27 **Tel** *08-506 640 00* **Fax** *08-506 640 01* **Rooms** *152*   **Map** *2 E5*

Exceptional waterfront location, with views over Nybroviken from the lounge and restaurant, the Strand offers wireless Internet throughout and many other amenities for the business traveller. Discount entry for guests to the nearby Sturebadet spa is a bonus. Excellent buffet breakfast. **www.radissonblu.com**

FURTHER AFIELD ARLANDA Jumbo Hostel

P   ⊗

Jumbovägen 4, 190 47 **Tel** *08-593 604 00* **Fax** *08-593 604 11* **Rooms** *27*

For aviation fans and anyone looking for a unique place to stay, this hostel offers a selection of rooms in a converted jumbo jet parked on the edge of an airport runway. The most coveted room is the cockpit suite with its panoramic view. Breakfast is freshly made and served in in-flight meal boxes by the friendly cabin crew. **www.jumbohostel.com**

FURTHER AFIELD DJURGÅRDEN Scandic Hotel Hasselbacken

🛗 P ⅋   ⊗⊗⊗

Hazeliusbacken 20, 100 55 **Tel** *08-51 73 43 00* **Fax** *08-51 73 43 11* **Rooms** *112*   **Map** *4 D3*

A beautifully restored traditional hotel dating from 1765 and adjoining Skansen, the Hasselbacken is close to the city centre, but surrounded by woodland in a peaceful location. Medium-sized rooms are a mixture of Swedish design with wooden features. Excellent restaurant, terrace grill and summerhouse bar. **www.scandic-hotels.se**

FURTHER AFIELD SÖDERMALM The Red Boat Mälaren   P   Ⓚ
Söder Mälarstrand 6, 117 20 **Tel** *08-644 43 85* **Fax** *08-641 37 33* **Rooms** *97*

Two converted boats moored where Lake Mälaren meets the Baltic Sea make up this youth hostel and hotel. The rooms and lobby are decorated to resemble a ship and have been well maintained. The Red Boat is within walking distance of all parts of downtown Stockholm. **www.theredboat.com**

FURTHER AFIELD SÖDERMALM Tre Små Rum Hotel   Ⓚ
Högbergsgatan 81, 118 54 **Tel** *08-641 23 71* **Fax** *08-642 88 08* **Rooms** *7*

This inexpensive but cosy modern hotel was started by a traveller hoping to offer an economical and friendly hotel option with a central location. All the rooms are non-smoking, and none en suite. Healthy breakfasts are created to guests' individual order. Early booking is essential. Bicycles are available for hire. **www.tresmarum.se**

FURTHER AFIELD SÖDERMALM Columbus Hotel   P   ⓀⓀ
Tjärhovsgatan 11, 116 21 **Tel** *08-50 31 12 00* **Fax** *08-50 31 12 01* **Rooms** *40*   **Map** *3 C5*

This building from 1780 had been used as a brewery, a barracks and a hospital before becoming a hotel in 1976. The Columbus is in the popular Södermalm area near restaurants, shopping and nightlife. Enjoy breakfast in the courtyard in the summer at this hidden treasure. **www.columbus.se**

FURTHER AFIELD SÖDERMALM Långholmen Hotel   P 🍴   ⓀⓀⓀ
Långholmsmuren 20, 102 72 **Tel** *08-720 85 00* **Fax** *08-720 85 75* **Rooms** *102*

A converted prison, the Långholmen offers accommodation in modernised "cells" in the city centre. There is a restaurant in the warden's residence and also a pub, wine cellar, prison museum, and even a private bathing beach. Youth hostel available all year round too. **www.langholmen.com**

FURTHER AFIELD SÖDERMALM Hilton Hotel Slussen   🛏 🍴 P 🍴   ⓀⓀⓀⓀ
Guldgränd 8, 104 65 **Tel** *08-51 73 53 00* **Fax** *08-51 73 53 11* **Rooms** *289*

Well-equipped modern international hotel with two restaurants and two bars. High on a hill overlooking Gamla Stan and Riddarfjärden, the Slussen has magnificent views from the summertime terrace bar. There's free Wi-Fi, 24-hour room service and excellent gym facilities. **www.hilton.com**

FURTHER AFIELD VASASTAN Hotel Tegnerlunden   P   ⓀⓀⓀ
Tegnerlunden 8, 113 59 **Tel** *08-54 54 55 50* **Fax** *08-54 54 55 51* **Rooms** *102*   **Map** *1 B3*

Near to the August Strindberg museum on Drottninggatan, the Tegnerlunden offers a family atmosphere and a quiet location. Breakfast buffet is served on the roof with spectacular views over the city centre. This hotel is superbly situated for exploring all parts of the city. **www.hoteltegnerlunden.se**

FURTHER AFIELD ÖSTERMALM Esplanade, Hotel   ⓀⓀⓀ
Strandvägen 7A, 114 55 **Tel** *08-663 07 40* **Fax** *08-662 59 92* **Rooms** *34*   **Map** *2 E4*

Frequented by representatives of nearby embassies and others who enjoy its traditional charm, the Esplanade is a cosy tourist hotel set in a majestic patrician house. It is located on fashionable Strandvägen, close to Stockholm's best boutique shopping, and has individually decorated rooms. **www.hotelesplanade.se**

FURTHER AFIELD ÖSTERMALM Mornington Hotel   🛏 🍴 P 🍴   ⓀⓀⓀ
Nybrogatan 53, 102 44 **Tel** *08-50 73 30 00* **Fax** *08-50 73 30 39* **Rooms** *220*   **Map** *2 E3*

A modern hotel in the upmarket Östermalm part of town, the Mornington is located across from Stockholm's largest auction house and many antique shops. There's a popular bar which sometimes has live music and the Library Bar where more than 4,000 books line the walls. **www.mornington.se**

FURTHER AFIELD ÖSTERMALM Mornington Hotel Bromma   🛏 🍴 P 🍴   ⓀⓀⓀ
Norrbyvägen 30, Bromma 168 69 **Tel** *08-507 332 00* **Fax** *08-507 332 05* **Rooms** *217*

This hotel is slightly off the beaten track but only a 15-minute taxi ride to the city centre. As Stockholm's first business sports hotel, it offers a well-equipped gym, table tennis, a sauna from where guests can watch planes take off and land at nearby Bromma airport and an outside climbing wall. **www.mornington.se/bromma**

FURTHER AFIELD ÖSTERMALM Hotel Diplomat   🍴 P 🍴   ⓀⓀⓀⓀ
Strandvägen 7C, 114 56 **Tel** *08-459 68 00* **Fax** *08-459 68 20* **Rooms** *135*   **Map** *2 E4*

This hotel offers every amenity and a renowned standard of service to its guests. In a well-preserved Jugendstil building that dates from 1911, the rooms have typical Swedish decor and elegant bathrooms. Weekend highlights include a "tea house" and the T/Bar's popular brunch. **www.diplomathotel.com**

FURTHER AFIELD ÖSTERMALM Scandic Anglais   🛏 🍴 P 🍴   ⓀⓀⓀⓀ
Humlegårdsgatan 23, 102 44 **Tel** *08-517 340 00* **Fax** *08-517 340 11* **Rooms** *230*

Located in the heart of Östermalm, close to top shops and nightspots, this hotel offers rooms decorated in a modern Scandinavian style. Its bar and restaurant are popular with both locals and tourists alike. Guests can enjoy a "take up" tray of food from the restaurant and drinks in their room. **www.scandichotels.com**

FURTHER AFIELD Ibis Hotel Stockholm Hägersten   🛏 P   ⓀⓀ
Västertorpsvägen 131, Hägersten, 129 44 **Tel** *08-55 63 23 30* **Fax** *08-97 64 27* **Rooms** *190*

Located on the southern approach to Stockholm, near the world's largest IKEA. This hotel was partly renovated in 2008 and offers high standards at reasonable prices, which include free parking. Guests have Internet access and pets are allowed. Approximately 15 km (9 miles) from the city centre. **www.ibishotels.se**

Key to Price Guide *see p280* **Key to Symbols** *see back cover flap*

FURTHER AFIELD Villa Källhagen ▣ ▥   ⓦⓦⓦ
Djurgårdsbrunnsvägen 10, 115 27 **Tel** *08-665 03 00* **Fax** *08-665 03 99* **Rooms** *36*

Elegant establishment with outstanding location on Djurgårdsbrunnsviken Bay. All rooms have a view of the Djurgårdsbrun canal. There are beautiful conference facilities in this historic hotel, which also has a top-class restaurant. In a leafy and quiet residential and embassy area, the hotel makes a peaceful retreat. **www.kallhagen.se**

FURTHER AFIELD Quality Hotel Globe ▥ ▦ ▣ ▥   ⓦⓦⓦⓦ
Arenaslingan 7, 121 26 **Tel** *08-686 63 00* **Fax** *08-686 63 08* **Rooms** *340*

Large hotel near the Globe Arena and a large shopping mall, with women-only rooms and facilities for conferences and special events. Breakfast is served in the Arena Restaurant, one of the hotel's two restaurants. There is also a lounge/bar area. A convenient eight minutes by subway to the city centre. **www.globehotel.se**

EASTERN SVEALAND

ESKILSTUNA City Hotell ▥ ▦ ▣   ⓦⓦ
Järnvägsplan 1, 632 20 **Tel** *016-10 88 50* **Fax** *016-12 42 24* **Rooms** *60*

The City Hotel is over 100 years old and has been beautifully renovated. Its 60 rooms are brimming with old fashioned charm and some feature beautiful stoves from the turn of the century, while other rooms have balconies. Impressive breakfast buffet and coffee and cookies served in the evenings. **www.cityhotell.se**

GRISSLEHAMN Mats Pers Gården ▣   ⓦ
Tomta 291, 760 45 **Tel** *0175-302 25* **Beds** *8*

Open all year round this renovated house from the 17th century is part of an old farm. When checking in guests are likely to be welcomed by dogs, sheep and chickens – whose fresh eggs are served for breakfast each morning. Just south of the idyllic fishing community of Grisslehamn. **www.matspersgarden.com**

KATRINEHOLM Dufweholms Herrgård ▦ ▣ ▥   ⓦⓦⓦ
Herrgårdsvägen 16, 641 92 **Tel** *0150-754 00* **Fax** *0150-754 09* **Rooms** *16*

Dufweholms has been known as the "Manor of Romance" since the 15th century and is ideal for couples. Its 16 non-smoking rooms include eight doubles and two lavish suites Herrskapssviten and Lyxsviten. Unwind and get pampered with a selection of beauty treatments in the hotel's own spa Rosenbadet. **www.dufweholm.se**

NORRTÄLJE Pensionat Granparken ▦ ▣ ▥   ⓦⓦ
Gjuterivägen 10, 761 40 **Tel** *0176-103 54* **Fax** *0176-125 02* **Rooms** *17*

This hotel is located in an idyllic rural setting in Norrtälje less than an hour from Stockholm and exudes old-world charm and a peaceful atmosphere in traditional early 20th-century surroundings. Attractive restaurant offers honest food from local suppliers. Can also cater for conference groups of up to 40 guests. **www.pensionatgranparken.se**

NYKÖPING Clarion Collection Hotel Kompaniet ▦ ▣ ▥   ⓦⓦⓦ
Folkungavägen 1, 611 34 **Tel** *0155-28 80 20* **Fax** *0155-28 16 73* **Rooms** *87*

Located 100 km (62 miles) south of Stockholm, this hotel is well situated alongside a charming river and opposite a beautiful castle. The hotel is just five minutes from the Central Square and shopping district. Guests can go fishing, sailing and swimming nearby. Nice decking area to enjoy an evening drink from the bar. **www.choicehotels.se**

NYNÄSHAMN Skärgårdshotellet ▦ ▣   ⓦⓦ
Kaptensgatan 2, 149 31 **Tel** *08-520 111 20* **Fax** *08-520 105 72* **Rooms** *76*

Set on the hillside above Nynäshamn harbour with breathtaking views of the harbour with its fishing port and small boat marina. When guests check-in they don't get a room number but a pier lot. Rooms are light and comfortable and several have a balcony with views of the island of Bedarön. **www.skargardshotellet.com**

SIGTUNA Sigtuna Stadshotell ▦ ▣ ▥   ⓦⓦⓦⓦ
Stora Nygatan 3, 193 30 **Tel** *08-592 501 00* **Fax** *08-592 515 87* **Rooms** *27*

A distinctive top-class hotel with a blend of medieval, early 20th century and 1950s influences coupled with the latest IT and communication amenities. Rooms are light and airy with quality details and furnishings. The hotel's restaurant is a treat for food lovers, with an exciting menu using local ingredients from the Mälar Valley. **www.sigtunastadshotell.se**

TROSA Bomans Hotel ▥ ▦ ▣ ▥   ⓦⓦⓦ
Hamnen, 619 30 **Tel** *0156-525 00* **Fax** *0156-525 10* **Rooms** *44*

A charming boutique hotel in the small town of Trosa that epitomises high-class Scandinavian style. Imaginative decor and top quality service, with an exciting menu and not one but two in-house sommeliers to help you pick the perfect wine. Every room is filled with personal effects from the Boman family. **www.bomans.se/**

UPPSALA Clarion Hotel Gillet ▥ ▦ ▣ ▥   ⓦⓦ
Dragarbrunnsgatan 23, 753 20 **Tel** *018-68 18 00* **Fax** *018-68 18 18* **Rooms** *161*

A good, value-for-money option located in the heart of Uppsala. Offering everything from free wireless Internet in all rooms to leisure facilities such as an indoor heated pool and a gym, the Clarion Hotel Gillet is a good choice for both business and leisure travellers. Pets are allowed. **www.choice.se**

UPPSALA First Hotel Linné

Skolgatan 45, 750 02 **Tel** *018-10 20 00* **Fax** *018-13 75 97* **Rooms** *116*

Well managed hotel at the edge of the impressive Linnaeus Botanical Garden. Interior design is inspired by the garden, which most rooms overlook. The Orange Bar & Klubb is a lively, hip bar while the First Bistro & Bar serves everything from Swedish fare and bistro favourites to top-class wines and whiskies. **www.firsthotels.com/Linne**

VÄSTERÅS Elite Stadshotellet

Stora torget, 721 03 **Tel** *021-10 28 00* **Fax** *021-10 28 10* **Rooms** *137*

Historic hotel with modern comfort and classic style in central Västerås. The onsite Bishop's Arms is a gastro pub offering good food and drinks in an informal atmosphere. After dinner, unwind with a classic massage or a sauna in the hotel's spa. **www.vasteras.elite.se**

EASTERN GÖTALAND

GLASRIKET STF Grimsnäs Herrgård

Skruv, 360 53 **Tel** *0478-204 00* **Fax** *0478-204 00* **Beds** *35*

Accommodation available in either the main house, which dates back to the 1500s, or the "old store". Guests can cook their own food or for a small fee eat breakfast and dinner in the main house. Cycles can be hired for the day – an ideal way to see the beautiful surrounding countryside. **www.grimsnas.se**

GRÄNNA Hotel Amalias Hus

Brahegatan 2, 563 32 **Tel** *0390-413 23* **Fax** *0390-413 29* **Rooms** *26*

Small and charming hotel once home to Amalia Eriksson who began baking sweets called Polkagrisar to earn a living for herself and her daughter. These sweets are now one of Sweden's most famous souvenirs and her statue can be seen right outside her former home. There is a tiled stove and three-piece suite in every room. **www.amaliashus.se**

GRÄNNA Hotel Gyllene Uttern

Gränna, 563 92 **Tel** *0390-108 00* **Fax** *0390-418 80* **Rooms** *51*

Built in the 1930s by Gyllensuaan, a cavalry captain, this was one of Sweden's first hotels. It is conveniently located just two minutes off the E4 motorway between Stockholm and Malmö. The decor combines a variety of styles – think English castle meets Swedish log cabin, and each room has a lake view. **www.gylleneutternhotelgroup.com**

JÖNKÖPING Elite Stora Hotellet

Hotellplan, 553 20 **Tel** *036-10 00 00* **Fax** *036-215 50 25* **Rooms** *135*

One of Jönköping's most beautiful buildings from the mid 19th-century that has been renovated in traditional Gustavian style. Ideally located close to all main shopping and entertainment hotspots. In the summer the hotel's own pub is a popular place to sit outside and soak up the sun and views over the water. **www.jonkoping.elite.se**

KALMAR Calmar Stadshotell

Stortorget 14, 392 32 **Tel** *0480-49 69 00* **Fax** *0480-49 69 10* **Rooms** *226*

A magnificent Art Nouveau building on the main square (Stortorget) in central Kalmar. This historic hotel has a friendly atmosphere in formal surroundings, with an imposing banquet hall complete with crystal chandeliers. Worth checking out the lobby bar and library, Restaurant Victoria and the pub, Pipes of Scotland. **www.profilhotels.se**

LINKÖPING Scandic Frimurarehotellet

St Larsgatan 14, 582 24 **Tel** *013-495 30 00* **Fax** *013-495 30 11* **Rooms** *207*

This fresh and modern hotel is just a short walk from Linköping's old town and its attractions, and 3 km (2 miles) from Linköping airport. It offers modern, comfortable rooms furnished in Nordic style and a well-equipped gym, spa and pool. A restaurant serves both Swedish and international cuisine. **www.scandichotels.se**

LJUNGBY Hotel Terraza

Stora Torget 1, 341 30 **Tel** *037-21 35 60* **Fax** *037-28 39 78* **Rooms** *95*

The four-star Terraza is conveniently located in the centre of Ljungby and offers all modern amenities, including minibar, hairdryer, in-room wireless Internet access and cable TV. All the rooms are non-smoking and "allergy-friendly". Good food at the En Trappa Upp restaurant and the lively Harry's Pub. **www.terraza.com**

NORRKÖPING Elite Grand Hotel

Tyska torget 2, 600 41 **Tel** *011-36 41 00* **Fax** *011-36 41 01* **Rooms** *205*

One of Norrköping's leading hotels centrally positioned with views over the Motala river and just five minutes walk from the central train station. Stylishly decorated rooms with the latest technology built in. Children will enjoy the playroom open throughout the summer. The hotel's Riverside Restaurant is highly recommended. **www.grandhotel.elite.se**

NORRKÖPING Hotel President

Vattengränden 11, 602 22 **Tel** *011-12 95 20* **Fax** *011-10 07 10* **Rooms** *78*

A modern hotel where function, design and technology combine in a relaxing environment. Will suit business guests and independent travellers searching for high levels of service and comfort. The only hotel in town with DVD players and flat-screen TVs in every room. Films can be borrowed from the reception. **www.profilhotels.se**

NÄSSJÖ Hotell Högland

Esplanaden 4, 571 23 **Tel** *0380-131 00* **Fax** *0380-101 25* **Rooms** *104*

A fun and lively place to stay, with a pub, disco and regular live music acts performing, particularly on Friday and Saturday nights. If guests need to slow down, visit the hotel's impressive spa, where it is possible to soak in a Jacuzzi by candlelight or choose from a range of beauty treatments and massages. **www.hogland.com/**

OSKARSHAMN Best Western Hotel Corallen

Gröndalsgatan 35, 572 35 **Tel** *0491-76 81 81* **Fax** *0491-76 81 80* **Rooms** *75*

The only thing that might disturb your sleep at this hotel is the sound of small fishing boats setting out in the early hours of the morning. Try borrowing one of the hotel's bikes to take in the wonderful views of the archipelago and the nearby national park Blue Maiden. **www.hotelcorallen.se**

SMÅLAND Kosta Boda Art Hotel

Stora Vägen 75, Kosta, 360 52 **Tel** *0478-348 30* **Fax** *0478-348 49* **Rooms** *102*

A stunning designer hotel made of glass and stone, located in the heart of Sweden's Kingdom of Crystal. Much of the decoration in the hotel was created by the Kosta Boda glass designers and there are exhibitions and glass-blowing disfays here. Facilities include a spa, gym and swimming pool. **www.kostabodaarthotel.se**

VADSTENA Vadstena Klosterhotel

Lasarettsgatan 5, 592 24 **Tel** *0143-315 30* **Fax** *0143-136 48* **Rooms** *75*

Comfortable accommodation in a historic environment. During the Middle Ages Vadstena was the location of a catholic monastery for monks and nuns of the Birgittine order. The hotel is largely located in the same medieval buildings that were once the monastery, now adapted to meet the requirements of modern living. **www.klosterhotel.se**

VETLANDA Best Western Vetlanda Stadshotell

Stortorget 5, 574 32 **Tel** *0383-120 90* **Fax** *0383-109 27* **Rooms** *69*

A classic and reasonably priced hotel in Vetlanda. Great choice for those who like the outdoors, with a floodlit ski track, gym, swimming pool, downhill ski slope and golf course in close proximity to the hotel. The wood-panelled restaurant serves dishes with a distinctive Småland influence. **www.vetlandastadshotell.net**

VIMMERBY Hotel Carl IX

Sevedegatan 37, 598 37 **Tel** *0492-12515* **Fax** *0492-15289* **Rooms** *26*

Carl IX is a family-run hotel which in the summer transforms from a business-orientated concept to a family-friendly hotel. Situated on the large central square, shopping and numerous restaurants are just around the corner. Impressive period feature rooms. Astrid Lindgrens Värld amusement park is within walking distance. **www.hotellcarl9.se**

VÄXSJÖ Elite Stadshotellet Växjö

Kungsgatan 6, 351 04 **Tel** *0470-134 00* **Fax** *0470-448 37* **Rooms** *163*

A palatial-looking hotel with classic interiors and period furnishings. Ultra-modern restaurant serves contemporary Swedish cuisine with inspiration from the Småland region. Close to Växjö's train station; car travellers can park in the square right outside the hotel entrance. **www.vaxjo.elite.se**

ÖLAND Halltorps Gästgiveri

Borgholm, 387 92 **Tel** *0485-850 00* **Fax** *0485-850 01* **Rooms** *36*

Charming inn with 25 guest rooms that have each been designed by craftsmen from a different Swedish province. In addition there are beautiful guest rooms in the old mansion, modernized but still in the turn-of-the-century style. On a hot day you can bathe in the cool water from their own well. **www.halltorpsgastgiveri.se**

GOTLAND

BURGSVIK Pensionat Holmhällar

Vamlingbo Austre 980, 623 31 **Tel** *0498-49 80 30* **Fax** *0498-49 80 56* **Rooms** *50*

Holmhällar is located in a pine forest with a long beach only a few hundred metres from the boarding house. Most of this hotel's reservations are repeat business, which speaks highly for the service here. A peaceful place with reasonable prices, personal contact and the most sun hours in Sweden. **www.holmhallar.se**

FÅRÖSUND Fårösunds Fästning by Pontus

Burge, 620 35 **Tel** *0498-22 12 40* **Fax** *0498-22 12 50* **Rooms** *16*

Unique "lifestyle" hotel concept built in a former military complex and owned by renowned Swedish chef Pontus Frithiof. Simply but stylishly designed with natural colours, oak furniture and chalk flooring typical for the region. Open 15 June to 31 August for the public and by request for groups and conferences. **www.farosundsfastning.se**

KLINTEHAMN Pensionat Warfsholm

Varvsholmen, 620 20 **Tel** *0498-24 00 10* **Fax** *0498-24 14 11* **Beds** *180*

A summer hotel open daily during June to August. Located just north of Klintehamn with water on three sides. Hostel-style accommodation in two-, three- or four-bed rooms with access to a shower and toilet. There is also a hostel and some small cabins. **www.warfsholm.se**

LJUGARN Kalkpatronsgården Borgvik Pensionat　　　　🅿 🍴　　　Ⓚ Ⓚ

Katthammarsvik, 620 16 **Tel** *0498-520 87* **Fax** *0498-521 90* **Rooms** *12*

Choose to stay in a fully furnished self-catering apartment with its own entrance, shower, toilet and kitchen; a rustic beach hut beside the sea with shower and kitchen facilities close to hand; or a more conventional guest room in the main building. Restaurant serves a variety of local specialities. **www.borgvik.com**

TOFTA Tofta Strandpensionat　　　　🅿 🍴　　　Ⓚ Ⓚ

Solbacksvägen, 622 66 **Tel** *0498-29 70 60* **Fax** *0498-26 50 09* **Rooms** *77*

Hotel right on the beach in quiet surroundings. Great sea views from the dining room which serves a dish of the day as well as à la carte. During the summer the hotel lays on barbeque evenings on the sun terrace. Some rooms available for guests with pets. Free parking. **www.toftastrand.se**

VISBY Hotell St Clemens　　　　🛗 🅿　　　Ⓚ Ⓚ

Smedjegatan3, 621 55 **Tel** *0498-21 90 00* **Fax** *0498-27 94 43* **Rooms** *32*

The hotel's five buildings are connected by two gardens and built alongside the ruins of the medieval church of St Klemens. Choose between the smallest single room in the Shoemaker's old house with a view over the church ruins or a four-bed room with a sloping ceiling overlooking the Botanical gardens. **www.clemenshotell.se**

VISBY Clarion Hotel Wisby　　　　🛗 🅿 🍴　　　Ⓚ Ⓚ Ⓚ Ⓚ

Strandgatan 6, 621 24 **Tel** *0498-25 75 00* **Fax** *0498-25 75 50* **Rooms** *134*

Guests can experience a medieval atmosphere in a unique city that has been designated a World Heritage Site. In the hotel itself there is a genuine medieval alleyway, pillars dating back to the 13th century and medieval dwellings all carefully restored. A memorable hotel that blends history with functional modern amenities. **www.wisbyhotell.se**

SOUTHERN GÖTALAND

ÄNGELHOLM Hotell Erikslund　　　　📺 🛗 🅿 🍴　　　Ⓚ Ⓚ

Åstorpsvägen15, 262 96 **Tel** *0431-41 57 00* **Fax** *0431-41 5710* **Rooms** *140*

A medium-sized modern accommodation and conference complex complete with two restaurants, a bar and a well-equipped spa and gym. An ideal base for golfers, with 17 courses in north-west Skåne all within easy reach. Reception staffed around-the-clock. **www.hotellerikslund.se**

BÅSTAD Hotel Skansen　　　　📺 🛗 🅿 🍴　　　Ⓚ Ⓚ Ⓚ

Kyrkogatan 2, 269 33 **Tel** *0431-55 81 00* **Fax** *0431-55 81 10* **Rooms** *173*

Parts of the main building of this characterful hotel date back to 1877, and the original wooden beams and brickwork remain. All rooms have en suite bathrooms and DUX beds (a quality Swedish bed maker). One wing is built around an attractive garden. A visit to the luxurious spa is a must. **www.hotelskansen.se**

HELSINGBORG Elite Hotel Mollberg　　　　🛗 🅿 🍴　　　Ⓚ

Stortorget 18, 251 14 **Tel** *042-37 37 00* **Fax** *042-37 37 37* **Rooms** *104*

One of Sweden's oldest hotels has bags of old-world charm with a history dating back to the 14th century. This was once the haunt of kings, counts and barons but now more often business guests enjoying the top-notch amenities. The hotel's restaurant Café le Fil du Rasoir is run by two acclaimed Swedish chefs. **www.elite.se**

KARLSKRONA First Hotel Statt　　　　📺 🛗 🅿 🍴　　　Ⓚ Ⓚ

Ronnebygatan 37–39, 371 33 **Tel** *0455-555 50* **Fax** *0455-169 09* **Rooms** *107*

An elegant hotel on a pedestrian street right in the town centre just minutes away from the sea. For a great night out try the trendy in-house nightclub or if in the mood for singing there's karaoke every Thursday night in the hotel's own pub and restaurant The Fox and Anchor. **www.firsthotels.com/stattkarlskrona**

KRISTIANSTAD First Hotel Christian IV　　　　🛗 🅿 🍴　　　Ⓚ Ⓚ

Västra Boulevarden 15, 291 31 **Tel** *044-20 38 50* **Fax** *044-12 41 40* **Rooms** *86*

Located in Kristianstad's most beautiful building and named after the town's founder the Danish King Christian IV, this hotel is within easy reach by train, bus and car. The impressive hotel lobby with its exquisite vaulted ceilings and contemporary interior design successfully brings back some of the original royal atmosphere. **www.firsthotels.com/christianiv**

LANDSKRONA Hotel Öresund　　　　📺 🛗 🅿 🍴　　　Ⓚ Ⓚ

Selma Lagerlöfsvagen 4, 261 31 **Tel** *0418-47 40 00* **Fax** *0418-47 40 10* **Rooms** *132*

A privately-owned classical hotel with origins dating back to the 18th century. Today it's one of the largest conference and event hotels in the region. Boasts three restaurants where you can choose between à la carte dishes, nutritious lunches and a lavish breakfast buffet. **www.hoteloresund.se**

LUND Grand Hotel　　　　📺 🛗 🅿 🍴　　　Ⓚ Ⓚ

Bantorget 1, 221 04 **Tel** *046-280 61 00* **Fax** *046-280 61 50* **Rooms** *84*

The Grand is a luxurious hotel where tradition, quality and service is paramount. Great importance is placed on food and drink, with diners able to choose from one of the best stocked wine cellars in Sweden, with more than 500 different bottles to choose from. Elegantly furnished rooms exude a sense of class. **www.grandilund.se**

Key to Price Guide *see p280* **Key to Symbols** *see back cover flap*

MALMÖ Elite Hotel Savoy
Norra vallgatan 62, 201 80 **Tel** *040-66 44 800* **Fax** *040-66 44 850* **Rooms** *109*

The Savoy is a modern hotel with an intriguing history dating back to the 14th century. It is well known for its beautiful rooms and suites, each one unique, which have been carefully restored and modern technology subtly installed. The lobby welcomes you with an elegant blend of modern design. **www.savoy.elite.se**

MALMÖ Hotell Plaza
Kasinogatan 6, 200 10 **Tel** *040-33 05 50* **Fax** *040-33 05 51* **Rooms** *48*

A small hotel with friendly staff ready to do their best to make their guests' stay with them comfortable. Limited facilities but a pleasant reception bar with a good selection of bottled beers which can be enjoyed with snacks. Special offers are sometimes available at weekends. **www.hotel-plaza.se**

MALMÖ Hotel Mäster Johan
Mäster Johansgatan 13, 211 21 **Tel** *040-664 64 00* **Fax** *040-664 64 01* **Rooms** *69*

The first class Hotel Mäster Johan is a modern building in the culturally protected part of Malmö known as Gamla Väster. The interior design theme is based on natural materials such as stone, glass and wood. All rooms have plush bathrooms, Bang & Olufsen TVs and luxury Swedish-made beds. A real modern classic. **www.masterjohan.se**

SKANÖR Hotell Gässlingen
Rådhustorget 6, 239 30 **Tel** *040-45 91 00* **Fax** *040-45 91 13* **Rooms** *26*

Hotel Gässlingen stands right next to the white limestone church on the old City Hall Square in Skanör. Very peaceful and picturesque accommodation with light and spacious rooms. Guests staying in rooms facing the West have magnificent views over the strait dividing Denmark and Sweden and the Öresund Bridge. **www.hotel-gasslingen.com**

TRELLEBORG Pensionat Maglarp
Maglarp 3096, 231 93 **Tel** *0410-33 07 04* **Fax** *0410-33 07 66* **Rooms** *26*

Reasonably priced guest house with the ferry harbour of Trelleborg nearby. Both guest rooms and small cottages for hire. Simple standard but fresh, clean and well-run. Pleasant gardens and countryside walks. If interested in golf the nearest course is only a stroll away. **www.pensionatmaglarp.nu**

YSTAD Hotell Continental
Hamngatan 13, 271 43 **Tel** *0411-137 00* **Fax** *0411-125 70* **Rooms** *52*

Sweden's oldest hotel that first opened its doors back in 1829 in the charming medieval town of Ystad, with its 300 half-timbered townhouses. All 52 guest rooms have a private bath or shower, telephone, radio, cable-TV, high speed Internet access and hairdryer and have been extensively refurbished. **www.hotelcontinental-ystad.se**

ÅHUS Hotell Briggen
Lotsg.46, 296 32 **Tel** *044-28 94 93* **Fax** *044-28 94 92* **Rooms** *12*

A seaside location and reasonable prices makes this a good choice for visitors to the wonderfully preserved traditional Swedish village of Åhus. With its central location, there are a number of restaurants and cafés hidden in the winding streets. Rooms are decorated in typically clean Scandinavian style. **www.hotellbriggen.com**

GOTHENBURG

CENTRE City Hotel
Lorensbergsgatan 6, 411 36 **Tel** *031-70 84 000* **Fax** *031-70 84 002* **Rooms** *50*

Quite basic but centrally located hotel parallel to Gothenburg's main high street. Around the corner from the famous Avenue shopping street with many restaurants and stores. The Liseberg amusement park, Ullevi arena and Nordstan – the biggest shopping mall in Northern Europe – are all within walking distance. **www.cityhotelgbg.se**

CENTRE Elite Park Avenue Hotel
Kungsportsavenyn 36–38, 400 15 **Tel** *031-727 10 00* **Fax** *031-727 10 10* **Rooms** *301*

A four-star hotel with an impressive conference and event facility boasting the latest in sound and lighting equipment. Good food selection for all budgets in the Park Aveny Café, Locatelli Restaurant and The Bishop's Arms pub. Classically designed rooms brimming with latest technology such as multimedia TV. **www.parkavenue.elite.se**

CENTRE Hotel Barken Viking
Gullbergskajen, 411 04 **Tel** *031-63 58 00* **Fax** *031-15 00 58* **Rooms** *50*

Hotel Barken Viking is one of the few remaining four-mast barques in the world. She is moored in Gothenburg's Guest Harbour only a stone's throw from the Gothenburg Opera House. An unusual and memorable accommodation with a 24-hour reception and first-class restaurant and bar. Guest parking for a small fee nearby. **www.liseberg.se**

CENTRE Hotel Flora
Grönsakstorget 2, 411 17 **Tel** *031-13 86 16* **Fax** *031-13 24 08* **Rooms** *68*

Ultra stylish and hip design-focused family-run hotel with rooms of a high standard and all with wall-mounted LCD TVs. Close to everything and not far from anything. Licensed bar with indoor and outdoor street pavement seating. Ideal location with a pleasant courtyard with sofas. **www.hotelflora.se**

CENTRE Hotel Gothia Towers

Mässans gata 24, 402 26 **Tel** *031-750 88 00* **Fax** *031-750 88 82* **Rooms** *704*

One of Scandinavia's largest hotels, with 704 rooms and conference facilities for up to 1,500. Offers almost every conceivable amenity, with top-notch restaurants and bars with magnificent views over the city. Modern interior, with furnishings made of Scandinavian woods. Walking distance to most of the city's sights. **www.gothiatowers.com**

CENTRE Hotel Vasa

Viktoriagatan 6, 411 25 **Tel** *031-17 36 30* **Fax** *031-711 95 97* **Rooms** *48*

This family-owned hotel has been fully renovated with additional rooms added. Hotel Vasa is located in the very centre of Gothenburg and dates back to the 19th century. Located close the University, restaurants, coffee shops, museums, shopping and the popular amusement park Liseberg. **www.hotelvasa.se**

CENTRE Scandic Opalen

Engelbrektsgatan 73, 402 23 **Tel** *031-751 53 00* **Fax** *031-751 53 11* **Rooms** *353*

Scandic Opalen is in the heart of Gothenburg close to the Svenska Mässan exhibition centre, Liseberg amusement park and all the main city sights. Don't forget to try out the relaxation area, with Jacuzzi, gym, sauna, solarium and outside decking. **www.scandic-hotels.se/opalen**

CENTRE Vanilj Hotel

Kyrkogatan 38, 411 15 **Tel** *031-711 62 20* **Fax** *031-711 62 30* **Rooms** *32*

Hotel run by three women whose motto is service, charm and personality. Comfortable accommodation at a good price, centrally located close to restaurants, nightlife and the shops. Charming café open every day. Licensed to serve alcohol. Big breakfast buffet served in café. **www.hotelvanilj.se**

CENTRE Eggers Hotell & Restaurang

Drottningtorget, 404 24 **Tel** *031-333 44 40* **Fax** *031-333 44 49* **Rooms** *69*

A listed building and Sweden's third oldest hotel. Built on historic ground in the centre of Gothenburg, this classic hotel offers a mix of early 20th-century charm and modern conveniences. No one room is the same as another, all are tastefully furnished to reflect the historical character of the building. **www.hoteleggers.se**

CENTRE Elite Plaza Hotel

Västra Hamngatan 3, 404 22 **Tel** *031-720 40 00* **Fax** *031-720 40 10* **Rooms** *143*

For many living in Gothenburg, Sveahuset is best known as a centre of learning, having housed archaeological findings until its transformation into a hotel around the turn of the century. Modern art hangs from the walls and contrasts with the classic architecture. Bar, restaurant and its own pub, the Bishop's Arms. **www.gbgplaza.elite.se**

FURTHER AFIELD Novotel Göteborg

Klippan 1, 414 51 **Tel** *031-720 22 00* **Fax** *031-720 22 99* **Rooms** *149*

Hotel with a restaurant and bar with panoramic views of the city. Unusually large rooms makes this a good choice for families. Borrow a bicycle and see the city from the saddle. The hotel has four adult bicycles and two children's bicycles available as well as helmets. **www.novotel.se**

WESTERN GÖTALAND

BORÅS Hotell Sköna Nätter

Box 22133, 504 12 **Tel** *033-10 01 10* **Fax** *033-12 61 27* **Rooms** *63*

A hotel, youth hostel and longer-term accommodation provider all rolled into one. Rooms from singles to family-size can be rented for the night or on a year-round basis. No frills, affordable living a 20-minute walk from Borås town centre with its adventure swimming pool, animal park and shops. **www.borasbostadshotell.se**

FALKENBERG Elite Hotel Strandbaden

Havsbadsallén, 311 42 **Tel** *0346-71 49 00* **Fax** *0346-161 11* **Rooms** *135*

Half of the 135 rooms in this modern hotel face the sea. Located alongside the Skrea Strand in Falkenberg it is one of the west coast of Sweden's most popular conference hotels. Guests are more likely to hear seagulls here than traffic, although Gothenburg is only 50 minutes by car. **www.strandbaden.elite.se**

FJÄLLBACKA Stora Hotellet Fjällbacka

Galärbacken, 450 71 **Tel** *0525-310 03* **Fax** *0525-310 93* **Rooms** *23*

Charming hotel with a marine theme inspired by Klassen, a sea captain who established the hotel in the late 19th century. The 23 rooms are named after people and places from the captain's travels on the high seas – hence the hotel's motto "Around the World in 23 Rooms". Enthralling oceans views. **www.storahotellet-fjallbacka.se**

HALMSTAD Best Western Grand Hotel

Stationsgatan 44, 302 45 **Tel** *035-280 81 00* **Fax** *035-280 81 10* **Rooms** *108*

The Grand Hotel was inaugurated with pomp and splendour in 1905. It remains a first-class hotel with magnificent interior fittings. A good choice for golfers, with Halmstad once being voted the golfing city of Sweden with eight golf courses within easy reach. Good restaurant and attractive lobby bar. **www.grandhotel.nu**

Key to Price Guide *see p280* **Key to Symbols** *see back cover flap*

HALMSTAD Hotel Continental

Kungsgatan 5, 302 45 **Tel** *035-17 63 00* **Fax** *035-12 86 04* **Rooms** *46*

A charming four-star hotel with distinctly feminine touches where owners Jenny and Jeanette have successfully managed to create a welcoming atmosphere in this attractive heritage building. Tasteful decor, with all rooms non-smoking, and a large recreation area that includes a sauna for up to 10 people and a tanning bed. **www.continental-halmstad.se**

KARLSBORG STF Vandrarhem Gula Villan

Ankarvägen 2, 546 30 **Tel** *0505-446 00* **Fax** *0505-446 00* **Rooms** *50 beds*

A pretty youth hostel situated by the water's edge in central Karlsborg. Swimming, fishing, football pitches, golf and tennis courts are all nearby. Rooms cater for one to six people, some doubles with shower and toilet. Prepare and eat meals in the communal kitchen and dining room area. **www.karlsborgsvandrarhem.se**

LIDKÖPING Stadt Lidköping

Gamla Stadens Torg 1, 531 32 **Tel** *0510-220 85* **Fax** *0510-215 32* **Rooms** *67*

Built on the old town square of Lidköping within walking distance to markets, cafés and restaurants, this imposing building dates back to the 17th century. All rooms are fresh and airy, with wooden floors, light furnishings, quality Swedish-made beds and stylish bathrooms. Also offers a nightclub, restaurant and pub. **www.stadtlidkoping.se**

MARIESTAD Hotell Vänerport

Hamngatan 32, 542 30 **Tel** *050-17 71 11* **Fax** *050-17 71 21* **Rooms** *28*

A small hotel that particularly caters for families and believes in high levels of personal service. All 28 rooms have Hästens beds (an exclusive Swedish bed manufacturer) as well as showers and cable TV. A large breakfast buffet is included in the room rate. A must-see is Mariestad's cathedral close by. **www.vanerport.se**

MARSTRAND Båtellet

Kungsplan, 440 30 **Tel** *0303-600 10* **Fax** *0303-606 07* **Rooms** *20*

This spa house built in 1858 was frequently visited by King Oscar II. Today it is a year-round youth hostel with self-catering and conference facilities. With a focus on exercise, guests can choose from dozens of activities including water gymnastics and power yoga, or instead a relaxing massage.

SKARA Stadskällaran Hotell och Restaurang

Skaraborgsgatan 15, 532 30 **Tel** *0511-134 10* **Fax** *0511-121 48* **Rooms** *32*

Centrally located three-star hotel with a homely atmosphere in Skara. All rooms have a TV, shower and toilet. Budget rooms also available without showers, and pets allowed in selected rooms. Restaurant and conference room on-site and free parking. Breakfast buffet included in rate. **www.hotellstadskallern.se**

SKÖVDE Scandic Hotel Billingen

Trädgårdsgatan 10, 541 30 **Tel** *0500-74 50 00* **Fax** *0500-74 50 11* **Rooms** *107*

Hotel Billingen was built in 1888 and has been famous ever since for its beauty. Located next to the train station, the hotel is just around the corner from the town centre. Across the street lies the Culture Centre, housing the library, city museum and Skövde Theatre, where regular shows take place. **www.scandic-hotels.se/billingen**

SMÖGEN Hotell Smögens Havsbad

Hotellgatan 26, 456 51 **Tel** *0523-66 84 50* **Fax** *0523-66 84 55* **Rooms** *73*

One of Sweden's most dramatic and beautiful conference and spa hotels has a spectacular extension that is partly carved into the rock itself. The original wooden building is from the early 1900s while the new extension faces the sea with its huge glass windows and gleaming cedar wood structure. **www.smogenshavsbad.se**

STRÖMSTAD Laholmen Hotell

Laholmen, 452 30 **Tel** *0526-197 00* **Fax** *0526-100 36* **Rooms** *152*

Positioned on a promontory in the harbour, most rooms have superb views across the Koster bay and several have balconies. The conference centre attracts the business crowd while the popular restaurant, Salt, claims to have the best sea views in Strömstad and serves an exciting range of fish dishes. **www.laholmen.se**

TJÖRN Bergabo Hotell & Konferens

Kyrkvägen 22, 471 41 **Tel** *0304-67 70 80* **Fax** *0304-67 70 80* **Rooms** *42*

An hour from Gothenburg lies this scenically positioned hotel and conference centre with views over the sea and Denmark on the far horizon. Established in 1898 it has developed into a modern full-service hotel with rooms, apartments and even small houses to rent, all hugging the rocky coastline. **www.bergabo.com**

TROLLHÄTTAN Albert Kök, Hotell & Konferens

Strömsberg, 461 57 **Tel** *0520-129 90* **Fax** *0520-133 11* **Rooms** *28*

The main building from 1856 stands on a plateau with an expansive view over the waterfalls and the town of Trollhättan below. The kitchen is the first thing to see upon entering and fittingly food plays an important role here. The restaurant has an international reputation for its outstanding culinary creations. **www.alberthotell.se**

ULRICEHAMN Hotell Bogesund

Sturegatan 7, 523 35 **Tel** *0321-154 10* **Fax** *0321-413 10* **Rooms** *48*

In the heart of Ulricehamn with commanding views over the pretty Åsunden lake, this four-star hotel has a growing reputation for attracting the business trade and conferences. All rooms have a shower, toilet and TV. Also houses a pub and restaurant and male and female saunas and a relaxation area. **www.hotellbogesund.se**

VÄNERSBORG Quality Hotel Vänersborg
Nabbensbergsvägen 2, 462 40 **Tel** *0521-57 57 20* **Fax** *0521-609 23* **Rooms** *119*

For guests who like golf this is a good place to stay, with several courses in the near vicinity. This Quality Hotel is minutes from local points of interest like the Vänersborg Museet museum, the Vänersborg Doll Studio & Museum, the Naturskola Nature Center and the Göta Canal. Has an on-site restaurant and bar. **www.choicehotels.com**

VARBERG Best Western Varbergs Stadshotell & Asia Spa
Kungsgatan 24–26, 432 41 **Tel** *0340-69 01 00* **Fax** *0340-69 01 01* **Rooms** *117*

Attractive early-20th-century decor offering comfort and a good standard of technology. The award-winning restaurant is considered one of Halland's finest, with culinary influences taken from around the world. The oriental-style spa offers a range of invigorating massages and beauty treatments. **www.varbergsstadshotell.com**

ÅMÅL Åmåls Stadshotell
Kungsgatan 9, 662 21 **Tel** *0532-616 10* **Fax** *0532-616 19* **Rooms** *29*

In the heart of Åmål beside the beautiful Plantaget park is this exceptionally well-preserved town house that went through a tasteful renovation at the end of the last century. Overlooks the river flowing through the town and has peaceful gardens where food and drinks are served during the summer. **www.amalsstadshotell.se**

WESTERN SVEALAND

ARVIKA Hotel & Spa Oscar Statt
Torggatan 9, 671 31 **Tel** *0570-197 50* **Fax** *0570-197 55* **Rooms** *73*

A town house hotel with a variety of room options, including female-friendly rooms that include extras such as a footbath, makeup pads and a bed canopy. The hotel's restaurant Sofia serves breakfast, lunch and dinner with an international menu offering different price levels. Guests get free entry to a nearby gym. **www.oscarstatt.se**

ASKERSUND Best Western Hotel Norra Vättern
Klockarebacken, 696 30 **Tel** *0583-12010* **Fax** *0583-10094* **Rooms** *61*

A three-star hotel decorated in true Scandinavian style. Positioned on the north shore of Lake Vättern with plenty of scenic walking trails. From the restaurant, diners get a nice view over the harbour in Askersund. Families with young children will enjoy taking a trip over the nearby bridge to Children's Island. **www.norravattern.se**

BORLÄNGE Scandic Borlänge
Stationsgatan 21–23, 784 35 **Tel** *0243-79 90 00* **Fax** *0243-79 90 11* **Rooms** *141*

Conveniently located in the centre of Borlänge, only a 10-minute car journey from the nearest airport. Make sure to do a few laps of the impressive heated indoor swimming pool before letting off steam in the sauna. Cosy restaurant and bar offer a good selection of Swedish fare. **www.scandic-hotels.se/borlange**

FALUN First Hotel Grand Falun
Trotzgatan 9–11, 791 71 **Tel** *023-79 48 80* **Fax** *023-141 43* **Rooms** *151*

With three stars in the Michelin Guide, this modern yet characterful hotel is in the heart of Falun close to the business area. The hotel's popular restaurant, Harry's Pub and impressive spa facilities can all be found under one roof. Standard rooms have a large working area and Internet access. **www.firsthotels.com/grandfalun**

KARLSTAD Elite Stadshotellet Karlstad
Kungsgatan 22, 651 08 **Tel** *054-29 30 00* **Fax** *054-29 30 31* **Rooms** *139*

The Elite Stadshotellet Karlstad is one of the country's most beautiful hotels and is centrally located by the riverside of the River Klarälv. The hotel was completed in 1870 and its 139 rooms have been carefully renovated and individually decorated to maintain the building's original atmosphere. Also has a grand function suite. **www.karlstad.elite.se**

KRISTINEHAMN Park Hotell
Floragatan 2, 681 21 **Tel** *0550-150 60* **Fax** *0550-896 90* **Rooms** *19*

Small but intimate hotel with many rooms overlooking the adjacent park. Located near the train station and only a short walk from the shops and restaurants. Free parking is provided. Every room has been individually decorated and comes equipped with toilet, shower, cable TV and wireless broadband access. **www.parkhotell-kristinehamn.nu**

MORA Best Western Mora Hotell & Spa
Strandgatan 12, 792 30 **Tel** *0250-59 26 50* **Fax** *0250-189 81* **Rooms** *141*

The only four-star hotel in Mora with views towards Siljan, Sweden's sixth largest lake with its long beaches and plenty of walking tracks through the surrounding woods. Spacious spa, sauna, swimming pool and Jacuzzi. Welcoming restaurant and bar with à la carte and bar menu to choose from. **www.morahotell.se**

RÄTTVIK Dala Wärdshus Gärdebygården
Hantverksbyn, 795 36 **Tel** *0248-302 50* **Fax** *0248-306 60* **Rooms** *44*

A charming guest house from the 1890s that has its own beach where guests can enjoy a floating sauna or take a midnight dip. The à la carte meals cooked with local produce are a big hit, so remember to book a table early in the busy summer months. **www.dalawardshus.se**

Key to Price Guide *see p280* **Key to Symbols** *see back cover flap*

SUNNE Quality Hotel Selma Lagerlöf
Ekebyvägen 1, 686 35 **Tel** *0565-68 88 00* **Fax** *0565-68 88 21* **Rooms** *156*

A classic Swedish country-style house that is now a hotel and quality spa on Fryken lake, north of Karlstad. Fifteen of the 156 rooms are disabled accessible and some are also allergy-friendly. Attractive setting, and just a stroll from the first tee of the nearby golf course. **www.choicehotels.se**

TALLBERG Åkerblads Hotell
Sjögattu 2, 793 70 **Tel** *0247-508 00* **Fax** *0247-506 52* **Rooms** *65*

Pretty and romantic country house dating back to medieval times on the shores of Lake Siljan in the old part of the village of Tällberg. Exquisite dining room and a restaurant that has won awards from *Gourmet* magazine 11 years in a row. Impressive wine cellar and home to Sweden's smallest pub. **www.akerblads.se**

ÖREBRO Elite Stora Hotellet
Drottninggatan 1, 701 45 **Tel** *019-15 69 00* **Fax** *019-15 69 50* **Rooms** *133*

The hotel stands opposite the imposing Örebro Castle by the Svartå River. Constructed in 1858 it is one of the country's most historic hotels. The hotel's top-class Slottskällaren restaurant is set in the 14th-century vaults. It also has an English-style pub. Excellent conference facilities. **www.orebro.elite.se**

ÖREBRO First Hotel Örebro
Storgatan 24, 703 61 **Tel** *019-611 73 00* **Fax** *019-10 39 05* **Rooms** *71*

A well-equipped hotel with 46 rooms and staff who believe in personal service. Just a short walk away from the town's landmark castle and the nearby train and bus station. In the summer the hotel's inner courtyard becomes a green oasis of calm. The entire hotel is a smoking-free zone. **www.firsthotels.com/orebro**

SOUTHERN NORRLAND

GÄVLE Scandic CH
Nygatan 45, 803 20 **Tel** *026-495 84 00* **Fax** *026-495 84 11* **Rooms** *220*

The modern Scandic CH in central Gävle is only two minutes' walk from the train station. Wireless Internet access available in all guest rooms. Wind down in the sauna and relaxation area or work out in the well-equipped gym. Just a short walk to Gävle's Stortorget and its 200 shops. **www.scandic-hotels.se/ch**

HIGH COAST STF Vandrarhem Köpmanholmen
Köpmanholmsvägen 2, 893 40 **Tel** *0660-22 34 96* **Rooms** *36*

This STF hostel is open all year round and is situated by the sea in the heart of the High Coast region. Close to great beaches, a national park, Ulvön and Skuleberget (the skull mountain) with its caves and tunnels and opportunities to go rock-climbing. Full-service in the restaurant where breakfast, lunch and dinner is served. **www.stfturist.se**

HIGH COAST Hotell Höga Kusten
Hornöberget, 872 94 **Tel** *0613-72 22 70* **Fax** *0613-72 22 79* **Beds** *36*

Situated on the northern side of the river Ångermanälven in the High Coast. Unrivalled views from the hotel's huge panoramic windows, with the Höga Kusten Bridge serving as a dramatic backdrop. Hotel's interior has been created by several well-known Scandinavian artists and designers. **www.hotellhoga-kusten.se**

HUDIKSVALL First Hotel Statt
Storgatan 36, 824 22 **Tel** *0650-150 60* **Fax** *0650-150 10* **Rooms** *120*

Beautiful 19th-century hotel that has undergone a total renovation with a new relaxation area, two restaurants and live entertainment shows staged several days per week. Hotel is ideally situated in the centre of town, with the railway station close by and Hudiksvall airport within easy reach. **www.firsthotels.com/statthudiksvall**

HÄRNÖSAND First Hotel Stadt
Skeppsbron 9, 871 30 **Tel** *0611-55 44 40* **Fax** *0611-55 44 47* **Rooms** *98*

Family-friendly hotel with children's playroom. Stunning views overlooking the harbour. Just minutes from the famous Smitingen beach, acclaimed as Norrland's finest. Also worth a visit to Sweden's smallest and only white domed church nearby, as well as a walk through Härnösand's 'old town'. **www.firsthotels.com/harnosand**

SOLLEFTEÅ Hotell Hallstaberget
Box 210, 881 25 **Tel** *0620-123 20* **Fax** *0620-164 24* **Rooms** *124*

A high-class hotel located in the High Coast countryside surrounded by ski slopes. The Internet café keeps guests online if needed, and Playstation and X-box consoles can be hired out to keep children amused. Relax after a day skiing or hiking in the Roman-inspired pool with panoramic views. **www.hallstaberget.se**

STORLIEN Storliens Högfjällshotell
Geijerbacken 10, 830 19 **Tel** *0647-701 70* **Fax** *0647-704 46* **Rooms** *192*

Scandinavia's biggest mountain hotel offers a wide range of accommodation from simple singles to elegant suites with open fireplaces. Open year round. Great base for cycle tours and fishing trips in the summer and skiing in the winter. Three-course dinners served in the large dining hall and drinks in the Kopparbaren. **www.storlienfjallen.se**

SUNDSVALL STF Vandrarhem Sundsvall   `P`   Ⓚ

N Stadsberget, 856 40 **Tel** *060-61 21 19* **Beds** *137*

A modern hostel in the quiet, peaceful cultural area of Norra Berget near Sundsvall, which is a gentle 20-minute walk away. Several double rooms with shower and TV. Disabled facilities also available. A basic but tasty breakfast is served between 8am and 10am. A low-cost alternative to the city hotels in attractive countryside. **www.gaffelbyn.se**

SUNDSVALL Elite Hotel Knaust   ⓀⓀ

Storgatan 13, 852 30 **Tel** *060-608 00 00* **Fax** *060-608 00 10* **Rooms** *94*

One of Sweden's most architecturally impressive hotels, with a magnificent central staircase. Built in 1891 and now offering a mix of ultra-modern hotel facilities in a classic setting. All the rooms have been tastefully furnished and have high ceilings. Great selection of draft beers at the hotel's own Bishop's Arms pub. **www.knaust.elite.se**

SVEG Lilla Hotellet   `P` 🍴   Ⓚ

Älvgatan 8, 842 32 **Tel** *0680-102 84* **Fax** *0680-71 81 14* **Rooms** *12*

A basic but comfortable hotel with low-cost rooms and a freshly renovated dining room where guests can eat breakfast. Also operates a café and restaurant specializing in Thai food, filled sandwiches, pies and a wide selection of ice cream. Licensed to serve alcohol. Friendly, personal service. **www.lillahotellet.se**

SÖDERHAMN First Hotel Statt   `P` 🍴   ⓀⓀ

Oxtorgsgatan 17, 826 22 **Tel** *0270-735 70* **Fax** *0270-135 24* **Rooms** *78*

This first-class hotel's restaurant and pub transforms on Friday and Saturday nights into one of Söderhamn's trendiest nightclubs – Varmgarage. Officially the hotel has 78 rooms but there are in fact 79. Room 104 is supposedly haunted by a former worker and the door remains firmly locked to this day. **www.firsthotels.com/stattsoderhamn**

ÅRE Hotel Diplomat   🍴   ⓀⓀ

Åre Torg 1, 830 13 **Tel** *0647-178 00* **Fax** *0647-179 60* **Rooms** *54*

Real mountain lodge feeling in the heart of Åre, close to the ski lifts, shops, restaurants and pulsating after-ski nightlife. But guests don't have to travel far for a great night out – the popular Country Club is located within the hotel itself. Boasts two good restaurants, Bakfickan and Sunes Bar & Kök. **www.diplomathotel.com/?id=1068**

ÅRE Hotell Fjällgården   `P` 🍴   ⓀⓀ

Fjällgårdsvägen 35, 830 13 **Tel** *0647-145 00* **Fax** *0647-145 27* **Rooms** *62*

A ski-in, ski-out hotel overlooking Fjällgården. Tastefully decorated, with a sun terrace and relaxation area and bar built right in the slope. Snow safari trips, heli-skiing and sleigh-dog trips all available in season. In the summer the hotel arranges various themed weeks, including hunting, fishing and golf. **www.fjallgarden.se**

ÖRNSKÖLDSVIK First Hotel Statt   `P` 🍴   ⒦⒦⒦

Lasarettsgatan 2, 891 21 **Tel** *0660-26 55 90* **Fax** *0660-837 91* **Rooms** *115*

Hotel located in the middle of the city centre with one of Sweden's best guest harbours nearby. Close to the university, seaside cabins and traditional houses used to store salt. A short walk from the Paradisbadet adventure pool complex with Jacuzzis, outdoor pools and one of the longest water roller-coasters in Europe. **www.firsthotels.com/Stattornskoldsvik**

ÖSTERSUND Best Western Hotel Gamla Teatern   `P` 🍴   Ⓚ

Thoméegränd 20, 831 34 **Tel** *063-51 16 00* **Fax** *063-13 14 99* **Rooms** *64*

When built in 1883 this was one of Europe's biggest wooden buildings. Transformed into a four-star hotel in 1992 and still retains many of the original interior features, including a stunning chandelier in the hotel's ballroom. Ideally located in the city centre, close to all attractions and shops. **www.gamlateatern.se**

ÖSTERSUND Quality Hotel Östersund   `P` 🍴   ⓀⓀ

Kyrkgatan 70, 831 21 **Tel** *063-57 57 00* **Fax** *063-57 57 11* **Rooms** *126*

Recently undergone a major renovation and added a new trendy restaurant. All rooms feature Jensens beds – known for their quality and comfort – as well as in-room broadband connections. Children's playroom open during the summer and a pleasant bistro and summer pub Casa Margarita serve a good selection of food and drinks. **www.giii.se**

NORTHERN NORRLAND

ABISKO STF Abisko Turiststation   `P` 🍴   ⓀⓀ

Abisko, 98 107 **Tel** *0980-402 00* **Fax** *0980-401 40* **Rooms** *300 beds*

Abisko Turiststation is situated in Abisko National Park and the nearby Aurora Sky Station makes it a great place to stay to see the northern lights. Accommodation is in rooms in the main building or in self-catering chalets and cabins. The hotel restaurant is one of the best in the mountains and offers stunning lake and mountain views. **www.abisko.nu**

DIKANAS Hotell Kittelfjäll   `P` 🍴   Ⓚ

Kittelfjäll, 910 94 **Tel** *0940-810 20* **Fax** *0940-811 34* **Rooms** *27*

In the heart of some of the best – and most demanding – ski slopes, this hotel is a popular destination for thrill-seekers. Through the windows of the Kittelfjäll restaurant are breathtaking views of the surrounding mountains. A party paradise in the winter and popular with hikers in the summer. **www.kittelfjall.com**

Key to Price Guide *see p280* **Key to Symbols** *see back cover flap*

GÄLLIVARE Dundret Resort

Box 82, 982 21 **Tel** *0970-145 60* **Fax** *0970-148 27* **Rooms** *35*

Ski and conference centre in Gällivare. During winter guests can visit a Sami settlement on snow mobiles. From the nearby Dundret's summit it is possible to see an eleventh of the entire surface of Sweden on a clear day. Great spot to see the midnight sun from June to mid July. **www.dundret.se**

HAPARANDA Haparanda Stadshotell

Torget 7, 953 31 **Tel** *0922-614 90* **Fax** *0922-102 23* **Rooms** *89*

Classic hotel in a splendid late 19th-century building, where the Swedish and Russian aristocracy once socialised. Much of the elegance and charm of the building's original character remains, and the game cellar with its vaulted ceiling forms the backdrop for a meal of local specialities such as reindeer, elk, ptarmigan and whitefish. **www.haparandastadshotell.se**

HEMAVAN TARNABY Hemavans Högfjällshotell

Modovägen, 920 66 **Tel** *0954-301 50* **Fax** *0954-303 08* **Rooms** *80*

Great place to stay if wanting to be close to the ski slopes. Described as a huge living room, with a large open fire and soft armchairs to collapse into. Appetising menu in the restaurant with views over the lake and mountain tops. Access to a sauna and hot tub complex next door. **www.hemavan.nu**

JUKKASJÅRVI Jukkasjärvi Icehotel

Jukkasjärvi, 981 91 **Tel** *0980-668 00* **Fax** *0980-668 90* **Rooms** *80 (can vary)*

The world's first and most famous ice hotel is now a major tourist attraction and is situated in the village of Jukkasjärvi. It is covered with a metre-thick layer of ice formed using water taken from the nearby River Torne to create the clearest ice possible. **www.icehotel.com**

KIRUNA Scandic Ferrum

Lars Janssonsgatan 15, 981 31 **Tel** *0980-39 86 00* **Fax** *0980-39 86 11* **Rooms** *171*

A 15-minute car journey from Kiruna airport, this family-friendly hotel has a generally high standard, offering two restaurants and a pub, a sauna, gym and children's playroom. Located in the heart of Kiruna's city centre, near to the famous wooden church. **www.scandic-hotels.se/ferrum**

LULEÅ Elite Stadshotellet

Storgatan 15, 972 32 **Tel** *0920-27 40 00* **Fax** *0920-670 92* **Rooms** *135*

This elegant high-class hotel in the centre of Luleå offers guests all modern comforts. Each room is unique in terms of size and decoration. Of note is the impressive ballroom and the fine-dining restaurant as well as the Bishop's Arms pub next door that serves a wide selection of beers and single malt whiskies. **www.lulea.elite.se**

LYCKSELE Hotell Lappland

Korpberget 1, 921 42 **Tel** *0950-370 00* **Fax** *0950-375 15* **Rooms** *206*

Sprawling conference hotel and exhibition centre, and home to the world's largest Sami tent. One of Sweden's top entertainment venues, with world-class shows and leading Swedish dance band artists regularly performing. Built beside the beautiful Umeälven and within walking distance of the town centre. **www.hotelllappland.se**

PITEÅ Pite Havsbad

Box 815, 941 28 **Tel** *0911-327 00* **Fax** *0911-327 99* **Rooms** *394*

Huge hotel located on the Norrland Riviera with long sandy beaches. With its slogan "365 exotic days a year", the hotel organizes an amazing range of activities and entertainment all year round. As well as good quality hotel accommodation there are also cottages for hire and a campsite. **www.pite-havsbad.se**

SKELLEFTEÅ Quality Hotel Statt

Stationsgatan 8, 931 31 **Tel** *0910-71 10 60* **Fax** *0910-71 10 65* **Rooms** *90*

This four-star hotel was originally built in 1863 but remodelled in 1955 by the architect Anders Tengbom in typical Swedish *funkis* style. All rooms have a dash of retro and wireless Internet. The hotel's nightclub Station 8 is very popular, as is the top quality restaurant Statt. Try the popular lunch buffet. **www.stattskelleftea.se**

UMEÅ Clarion Collection Hotel Uman

Storgatan 52, 903 26 **Tel** *090-12 72 20* **Fax** *090-12 74 20* **Rooms** *89*

A warm welcome awaits at this medium-sized hotel. Emphasis is on making guests feel at home, with free evening paper, endless cups of coffee and home-baked bread. Sauna with free draft beer on tap. Known for its generous breakfast buffet with delicious waffles. Walking distance to the city centre and shops. **www.choicehotels.se**

UMEÅ Scandic Plaza

Storgatan 40, 903 26 **Tel** *090-205 63 00* **Fax** *090-205 63 11* **Rooms** *196*

This top-class hotel contains Umeå's most spectacular sauna, a compound of wood-sheathed rooms on the hotel's panoramic top floor. Each super-heated cubicle provides a view out over the river that flows through the city centre. Close to Umeå airport and a popular conference destination. **www.scandic-hotels.se/plazaumea**

VILHELMINA Hotell Wilhelmina

Volgsjövägen 16, 912 34 **Tel** *0940-554 20* **Fax** *0940-101 56* **Rooms** *64*

Hotel Wilhelmina is situated in southern Lappland with views over Volgsjön. Modern double rooms and relaxation area with a billiard room. Top class food and drink in the restaurant with an à la carte menu, lunch buffet, bar and pub. The railway station is close by. **www.hotellwilhelmina.se**

WHERE TO EAT

Sweden is one of Europe's liveliest and most varied countries for eating out. Swedish cuisine has won many international awards in recent years, and a number of restaurants have been awarded Michelin stars. Many of the best restaurants are relatively small and informal as a number of top chefs have opened their own establishments. Various ethnic styles of cooking are often combined to create

Swedish hot dog

innovative and delicious dishes in what is called "cross-over" cuisine. Traditional Swedish dishes are frequently served at lunchtime and are excellent value for money. There are also plenty of fast-food outlets, pubs, Chinese restaurants, pizzerias and kebab houses offering inexpensive food. Hot-dog stands, providing filling snacks, can be found practically everywhere.

WHERE TO EAT

Sweden has a very wide range of restaurants. The majority are found in the larger cities and towns, but there are a number of good places to eat in the smaller towns. Restaurants and cafés can be found in the larger department stores and shopping malls, as well as at most museums. Along the coast and inland there are many friendly restaurants that open just for summer. Larger towns often have market halls with excellent restaurants and cafés, but they are not open in the evening for dinner.

Open sandwiches with a variety of fillings can be bought at cafés and cake shops, which often serve inexpensive hot dishes at lunchtime as well.

Outdoor cafés spring up on many streets and squares with the arrival of summer, and also in parks and green areas such as Djurgården in Stockholm and Kungsportsavenyn in Gothenburg.

TYPES OF RESTAURANT

Fashionable restaurants usually attract a young clientele, and the trendiest places sometimes have a rather stark decor and extremely high noise levels. If you are looking for somewhere quieter, which also has good service, it is often best to choose an established restaurant. There are many specialist restaurants serving cuisine from abroad, or "cross-over" cooking, which is a combination of styles.

Most restaurants charge roughly the same prices, regardless of quality. If you are looking for somewhere cheaper to eat, there are pizzerias, pubs, kebab houses, sushi bars, fast food chains and cafés to choose from.

Those with a sweet tooth shouldn't miss a visit to one

of the many modern cafés or traditional cake shops which offer delicious Danish pastries, cinnamon buns, cakes and gateaux.

There are few bars as such and the best can be found at the most popular restaurants. Dress is usually informal, even at the more elegant restaurants. Ties are not required but shorts are not acceptable. Since 1 January 2005 smoking has been banned in all bars and restaurants, and this rule must be strictly adhered to.

Inn sign, Gamla Stan

OPENING TIMES

The majority of restaurants open for lunch at 11.30am and close at around 10pm. Dinner is served from 6pm or even earlier. A number of restaurants are closed on Sundays or Mondays. Smaller restaurants may close for their annual holiday during July.

Prices for lunch are often extremely reasonable, even at the more elegant establishments, so lunchtime is an ideal opportunity to enjoy an inexpensive meal at a pleasant restaurant. *Dagens lunch* (Lunch of the Day) is generally not served after 2pm, even if the restaurant is open in the afternoon.

A number of restaurants and pubs serve food right up to midnight or even later, particularly those which provide entertainment, music or a disco. Anyone

Magnificent interior of Café Opera in Stockholm

Outdoor café in Riddarhustorget in Gamla Stan, Stockholm

still hungry during the night can find hot-dog kiosks which stay open very late, sometimes even round the clock.

VEGETARIAN FOOD

Interest in vegetarian food is increasing in Sweden, and this is reflected by the fact that excellent vegetarian cuisine is now served at most restaurants. There are also several completely vegetarian restaurants in the major cities.

BOOKING A TABLE

Reservations should be made for evening meals, but many restaurants do not accept bookings for lunch. If you want to be sure of a table at midday, it is best to arrive at the restaurant before 11.30am or after 1pm, by which time most of the lunchtime clientele will have left.

CHILDREN

All children are welcome in restaurants without exception. They will usually be offered a special children's menu, or half portions from the normal menu. Almost all restaurants have highchairs.

PRICES

Prices of meals in Sweden are very similar. At most places hot dishes cost from about 100 kr, or 200 kr or more at expensive restaurants.

Lunch prices are around 60–70 kr, and that often includes a non-alcoholic drink and coffee. However, the price of beer, wine and other alcoholic drinks can vary considerably. It generally follows that the more expensive restaurant, the higher the price of the wine. The house wine is usually the cheapest, with a bottle normally costing from 150 kr. Beer is cheaper in pubs than in restaurants. Tap water is free of charge, and Sweden's drinking water is of excellent quality.

Tips are always included in the price, but if you want to reward good service you can round up the bill. If the restaurant has a manned cloakroom, the normal price is 10 kr per person. A number of restaurants do not allow guests to take outdoor clothing into the dining room. Credit cards are accepted in virtually every restaurant.

READING THE MENU

Dinner at a Swedish restaurant usually includes a starter (*förrätt*), hot main course (*varmrätt*) and dessert (*efterrätt*). Most offer one or more fixed-price meals with a choice of two or three dishes at a lower price than the à la carte menu. It is perfectly acceptable to have just a starter or main course. At lunchtime most people order only one course. The meal is nearly always served on the plate, but the more elegant restaurants often have dessert or cheese trolleys. Many restaurants have menus in English; if they don't, the waiters and waitresses are usually familiar with English and will be pleased to explain the menu to you.

Some restaurants serve a typical Swedish *smörgåsbord*, usually on Sundays. Some specialize in a fish or shellfish buffet. During December a *Julbord* is usually available. This is similar to the normal *smörgåsbord*, but with a lavish buffet selection of traditional seasonal dishes. You can eat as much as you like at a fixed price, but drinks are not included.

WHAT TO DRINK

Wine and beer are the normal accompaniments to a meal, as well as mineral water. The wine list often features wine from countries outside Europe, along with a house wine. Vintage wines are usually not available at medium-price restaurants.

Many pubs and restaurants offer a wide selection of beers, often with one or more on draught. A few small Swedish breweries make an excellent non-filtered beer. Beer is graded into three classes, with Class I the weakest.

Herring or "home-cooking" is usually washed down with beer, sometimes accompanied by one of the many different flavoured schnapps.

Spirits and wines are more expensive in Swedish restaurants than in most other countries because of the high duty on alcohol and the State retail alcohol monopoly.

Grythyttan, a gastronomic haven with a well-stocked wine cellar which also offers tastings

The Flavours of Stockholm

Thanks to strict regulations, Sweden is one of most unpolluted countries in Europe and produces some of the purest food. Salmon can be caught in the heart of Stockholm, zander and herring are fished from the nearby coastal waters and the lakes and rivers are full of crayfish and other delicacies. Fish is a staple, but other gastronomic treats are also on offer. Wild game, such as grouse, reindeer and elk, is abundant in autumn and winter. The forests are full of berries and mushrooms, and the rich pastures produce superlative dairy produce, including several fine cheeses.

Fresh dill

Fresh anchovies on offer at Östermalmshallen food market

THE SMÖRGÅSBORD

The *smörgåsbord* made its first appearance on Swedish tables sometime in the 18th century, when it consisted of a spread of hot and cold hors d'oeuvres that would be served as a prelude to a grand lunch or dinner. All this was washed down with ice-cold "schnapps" (vodka). Gradually, however, it has grown into a full-scale meal. A traditional *smörgåsbord* will start with a selection of different herring appetizers, followed by a variety of cold dishes such as hard-boiled eggs, meat pies and salads. Then a number of hot dishes are served, including such offerings as meatballs, fried potatoes and Jansson's Temptation (a gratin of potatoes, onions, anchovies and cream). Finally an array of desserts will be placed on the table. Diners help themselves, changing their plates between courses.

Some Swedes will prepare a *smörgåsbord* as a good way of using left-overs. Inventive cooks often improvise a very simple version when unexpected guests arrive, using larder staples, such as eggs, slices of cheese and cooked meats, and tinned or pickled fish.

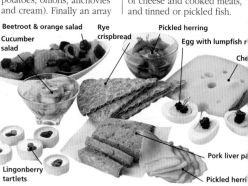

Beetroot & orange salad Rye crispbread Pickled herring
Cucumber salad Egg with lumpfish r
Che
Lingonberry tartlets
Pork liver pa
Pickled herri

Selection of items typically found on a cold *smörgåsbord*

LOCAL DISHES AND SPECIALITIES

A typical Swedish breakfast often includes yoghurt or *filmjölk* (a type of soured milk yoghurt) with cereal. Many Swedes, however, prefer a more savoury start to the day and cheese, ham and even liver paté may be on offer. Bread spread with *kaviar* (a cod's roe paste) is also eaten at breakfast. For lunch, most people reach for something quick and simple to prepare. Salad, perhaps served with a seafood, ham or vegetable quiche, is common and

Lingonberries

pasta is popular too. As well as the main meals, a break for coffee and pastries, known as *fika*, is taken at any time of the day. This strong Swedish tradition is a sociable event as much as an occasion to eat. In the evening, families usually get together for the main meal of the day - dinner, a more elaborate, but still homely, affair.

Gravad Lax, *a salmon fillet, marinated for two days in sugar, salt and dill, is served with a creamy mustard sauce.*

A colourful vegetable stall at Hötorget market

During the Christmas season, many Stockholm restaurants serve a special *smörgåsbord*, known as a Julbord, which will include dishes using nearly every part of the pig, such as various hams, trotters and a special brawn called *sylta*, made from the head.

RUSTIC FARE

The Swedes are very good at using cheap cuts to prepare delicious dishes. Seasoning is usually kept simple with salt, pepper and fresh dill. Such homely fare, known as *husmanskost*, is central to the Swedish diet and regularly features on the menus of many Stockholm restaurants. One favourite is yellow pea soup, traditionally served on Thursdays, accompanied by sausages or lightly salted meat and mustard. This is generally followed by pancakes with jam, washed down with hot *punsch*. Other popular dishes include *pytt i panna* (a hash of meat, onions and potatoes) and meatballs served with lingonberry jam.

A selection of fine fish from Sweden's pristine coastal waters

SWEDEN'S DINING "REVOLUTION"

The turn of the 21st century has witnessed a renaissance of gourmet cooking in Sweden, with people now visiting Stockholm for its food as well as its culture. Traditional dishes, made with the finest – usually organic – ingredients are being given an original, modern twist. Instead of simple meatballs with lingonberries, chefs are increasingly offering delights such as *foie gras* with a spiced mixed berry and apple chutney and turning cheap staples, such as pig's offal, into magnificent, melt-in-the-mouth mousses.

WHAT TO DRINK

Beer Along with vodka, beer is the most popular drink to accompany a *smörgåsbord*. Until recently, little was on offer other than insipid lagers, but a recent beer-making revival has made styles from dark porters to pale ales available, including some interesting fruit beers.

Vodka About 60 types of "schnapps", each flavoured with different herbs and spices, are made in Sweden.

Punsch This sweet arak spirit is often taken with coffee or served hot with pea soup.

Wine A huge variety of fine wines are imported, but are usually very expensive.

Jansson's Temptation *is a dish of layered potato, anchovy and onion with cream, baked until golden.*

Meatballs *made from beef or pork are drenched in a rich meaty sauce and served with lingonberries.*

Apple cake *is a delicious buttery dessert traditionally served piping hot with cold vanilla sauce.*

Choosing a Restaurant

Restaurants have been selected across a wide price range for good value, excellent food and/or their setting. The restaurants are listed area by area, starting with Stockholm. For map references for Stockholm, see the maps on pp112–17. Note that alcohol, particularly wine, is expensive in Sweden.

PRICE CATEGORIES
Average prices for a three-course meal
for one, half a bottle of house wine and
unavoidable charges such as service
and cover.
Ⓚ Under 350 Kr
ⓀⓀ 350–600Kr
ⓀⓀⓀ 600–800Kr
ⓀⓀⓀⓀ Over 800Kr

STOCKHOLM

GAMLA STAN Grill Ruby   ⓀⓀ
Österlånggatan 14, Stockholm, 111 31 **Tel** *08-20 60 15*   **Map** *3 C3*

Wonderful grilled steaks at reasonable prices in a lively but relaxed atmosphere. Grill Ruby also offers a "Late Supper" with a Tex Mex touch from 11pm daily and a special American-style brunch menu on Saturdays. Open daily from 5pm, and from noon on Sundays.

GAMLA STAN Pontus by the Sea   ⓀⓀⓀ
Tullhus 2, Skeppsbron, Stockholm, 111 30 **Tel** *08-20 20 95*   **Map** *3 C3*

Owned by one of Stockholm's star chefs Pontus Frithiof, this restaurant offers a reasonably priced, accessible menu including a large seafood platter and cold meat platter. The food is excellent. In summer diners can sit outside and watch the ships come into port. Closed Monday and Sunday evenings.

GAMLA STAN Pontus!   ⓀⓀⓀⓀ
Brunnsgatan 1, Stockholm, 111 31 **Tel** *08-54 52 73 00*   **Map** *3 C3*

Virtuoso chef Pontus Frithiof creates culinary masterpieces with prices to match. The restaurant is spread over three floors and offers an extensive bar. Other dining options include an oyster and champage bar, as well as an Asian themed bar with dim sum and sushi. Closed Sundays.

CITY Bakfickan   ⓀⓀ
Kungliga Operan, Karl XIIs Torg, Stockholm, 111 86 **Tel** *08-676 58 09* **Map** *2 D4*

A real little gem for its many regular customers, including artists from the nearby opera house, Bakfickan is ideal for those looking for a quick bite to eat. The bar menu consists of Swedish "home-cooked" specials. More complex meals are also available. Closed Sundays.

CITY Ett litet hak   ⓀⓀ
Grev Turegatan 15, Stokholm, 114 46 **Tel** *08-660 13 09*   **Map** *2 E4*

Lively, pleasant local restaurant with trendy Continental cuisine and friendly staff. *Ett litet Hak* means "a tiny bit", which describes the approach precisely. You can enjoy seafood, meat or vegetarian dishes washed down with an ice-cold beer. Open for lunch and dinner. Closed Sundays.

CITY Nalen   ⓀⓀⓀ
Regeringsgatan 74, Stockholm, 111 39 **Tel** *08-50 52 92 01*   **Map** *2 D3*

Formerly the Grand National, this eatery now has the same name as the jazz club around the corner. The menu consisting traditional Swedish cuisine using the best local ingredients such as reindeer, bleak roe and cloudberries. The interior is like a typical Swedish "*krog*" or pub – cosy with old-world charm. Closed Sundays.

CITY Seikoen   ⓀⓀⓀ
Tegelbacken 2, Stockholm, 111 52 **Tel** *08-100 310*   **Map** *1 C5*

One of Stockholm's longest-running Japanese restaurants, set up long before the hordes of other sushi places appeared in the city. The menu includes everything from sushi and tempura to some not-so-Japanese desserts, such as crème brulée and cloudberry cheesecake. Booking recommended. Closed Sundays, two weeks mid-July.

CITY Operakällaren   ⓀⓀⓀⓀ
Operahuset, Karl XII's Torg, Stockholm, 111 86 **Tel** *08-676 58 01*   **Map** *3 B1*

The capital's classic temple of gastronomy. The chefs are young and creative, the dining room with its lavish 19th-century ceiling paintings and the Jugendstil bar are attractions in themselves. While Operakällaren offers fine dining, its next-door neighbour Operabaren provides food at lower prices. Closed Mondays and Sundays.

BLASIEHOLMEN & SKEPPSHOLMEN Atrium in the Nationalmuseum   Ⓚ
Södra Blasieholmshamnen 4, Box 160 17, Stockholm, 10321 **Tel** *08-611 34 30* **Map** *2 E5*

Situated in a unique space in the middle of the Nationalmuseum, chef Patric Karlsson serves a selection of lovely salads and cold meats here. It is always the dish of the day that is particularly tempting, such as *laxpudding* (salmon pudding) or sautéed Baltic herring. The menu changes daily. Closed Mondays.

Key to Symbols *see back cover flap*

BLASIEHOLMEN & SKEPPSHOLMEN Pauli in Dramaten Theatre

Nybroplan 2, Stockholm, 10241 **Tel** *08-665 61 43*   **Map** *2 E4*

A lovely, grand and old-fashioned restaurant on the third floor of this impressive theatre. Traditional *husmanskost* (wholesome home cooking) is served here, such as the delicious Swedish meatballs. George Pauli, a well-known Swedish artist, has decorated the restaurant with portraits of famous actors.

FURTHER AFIELD DJURGÅRDEN Rosendal's Trädgårds Café

Rosendalsterrassen 12, Stockholm, 115 21 **Tel** *08-54 58 12 70*   **Map** *4 F1*

This is an oasis of delicious home-made cooking located in the trendiest botanical garden in Sweden. The cakes and buns are renowned. Visitors can buy a loaf of their wonderful bread from the farm shop, which also stocks superb vegetables, wild flowers and their very own recipe book. A must-visit in Stockholm.

FURTHER AFIELD DJURGÅRDEN Hasselbacken Restaurang

Hazeliusbacken 20, Stockholm, 100 55 **Tel** *08-51 73 43 48*   **Map** *4 F2*

Well-prepared traditional Swedish food served in a finely restored 1850s setting. Their weekend brunch (Sep–Jun) is fantastic. In summer there is an outdoor café, prettily situated next to the Skansen Museum on Djurgården. It has a tendency to be a little touristy, but you will really get a sense of old-time Sweden in this grand building. Open daily.

FURTHER AFIELD DJURGÅRDEN Wärdshuset Ulla Winbladh

Rosendalsvägen 8, Stockholm, 115 21 **Tel** *08-534 89 701*   **Map** *4 F2*

Beautifully located next to the Skansen Museum with an old-fashioned atmosphere and decorated as if out of a Carl Larsson painting. Serves well-prepared classic Swedish cuisine, as well as modern dishes, such as perchpike. The outdoor café is very popular in the summer. Closed Sundays.

FURTHER AFIELD GÄRDET Dell'Attore

Skeppargatan 60, Stockholm, 114 59 **Tel** *08-442 61 18*   **Map** *2 F2*

Dell'Attore means "actors' restaurant" – an apt name for this small, buzzing place decorated from floor to ceiling with photographs of famous actors. It boasts the most delicious pizzas in town for which people join lengthy queues to order. It is advisable to book in advance.

FURTHER AFIELD KUNGSHOLMEN La Famiglia

Alströmergatan 45, Stockholm, 112 47 **Tel** *08-650 63 10*

Particularly popular with children, La Famiglia serves classic Italian cuisine at budget prices in a friendly atmosphere. One dish to try is the excellent shellfish pasta. A good place to take the whole family, as the name suggests. Frank Sinatra even made a special visit here just to try the signature dish, sautéed calves' liver. Open daily.

FURTHER AFIELD KUNGSHOLMEN Tabbouli

Norra Agnegatan 39, Stockholm, 112 29 **Tel** *08-650 25 00*   **Map** *1 A4*

One of the many Lebanese restaurants that have sprung up in Stockholm in recent years, Tabbouli specializes in grilled meats and *meze*, and makes for a refreshing change if you are enjoying an extended stay in Stockholm. The food is good quality and the atmosphere lively Middle-Eastern.

FURTHER AFIELD KUNGSHOLMEN Mäster Anders

Pipersgatan 1, Stockholm, 112 24 **Tel** *08-654 20 01*   **Map** *1 A5*

Specializing in grilled meats and fish, including a delicious chilli bearnaise that leaves a wonderful tingle in the mouth, Mäster Anders also does good traditional Swedish food. The 1913 interior consists of Bentwood chairs, parquet flooring and yellow tiled walls.

FURTHER AFIELD KUNGSHOLMEN Stadshuskällaren

City Hall, Hantverkargatan 1, Stockholm, 112 21 **Tel** *08- 506 322 00*   **Map** *1 B5*

Located in a cellar next to the City Hall where the Nobel Prize ceremony takes place, this restaurant originally opened in 1923 and the decor is typical of that era. They offer a good value lunch menu. For private parties guests can choose from the past Nobel dinner menus served on the Nobel dinner service.

FURTHER AFIELD SÖDERMALM Herman's

Fjällgatan 23B, Stockholm, 116 28 **Tel** *08-643 94 80*

One of Stockholm's most famous and popular vegetarian restaurants, Herman's offers a fantastic buffet of wholesome, home-cooked dishes from a range of cuisines, including Swedish, Asian and Middle Eastern. The all-you-can-eat price includes dessert and coffee refills too. In summer, sit outside and enjoy the views over the waterfront.

FURTHER AFIELD SÖDERMALM Roxy

Nytorget 6, Stockholm, 116 40 **Tel** *08-640 96 55*

Nytorget is a very trendy part of Södermalm and great fun in the summer, when it is bustling with young people. At Roxy the food is mainly Mediterranean and the interior cosy and welcoming. The two girls who own it met up in Barcelona and wanted to recreate the tapas and cava scene in Stockholm. Closed Mondays.

FURTHER AFIELD SÖDERMALM Pelikan

Blekingegatan 40, Stockholm, 116 62 **Tel** *08-556 090 90*

More than 100 years old, this is a Swedish restaurant through and through, with all the staples such as meatballs and *pytt i panna* (Swedish hash). The interior has painted ceilings and wood-panelled walls. Choose beer and schnapps, rather than wine, as they make for perfect accompaniments to the delicious menu.

FURTHER AFIELD SÖDERMALM Ringboms

Hornsgatan 90, Stockholm, 118 21 **Tel** *08-429 92 10*

Gotland is the culinary home of Ringboms, where the home cooking is always a pleasant surprise. With generous portions at low prices and a friendly reception, it serves herrings with almond potatoes, Baltic herrings with honey and mustard sauce, and smoked reindeer with cloudberry and juniper berry sauce.

FURTHER AFIELD VASASTAN Stockholms Matvarufabrik

Idungatan 12, Stockholm, 113 45 **Tel** *08-32 07 04*   **Map** *1 B1*

As its name (Stockholm's Food Factory) indicates, this restaurant serves a wide range of classic dishes from a well-planned menu, which features modern European cuisine. Very friendly, it is considered one of Vasastan's favourite neighbourhood restaurants and the atmosphere buzzes. Closed Sundays.

FURTHER AFIELD VASASTAN Storstad

Odengatan 41, Stockholm, 113 51 **Tel** *08-673 38 00*   **Map** *1 C2*

This is where people go if they want to be seen, and the bar is usually packed. Here diners will find minimalist decor, comfortable seating and courteous staff serving excellent, if a little fanciful, food. Meat and fish are the famed specialities and the dress code is smart and elegant. Closed Sundays.

FURTHER AFIELD VASASTAN Tranan

Karlbergsvägen 14, Stockholm, 113 27 **Tel** *08-527 281 00*   **Map** *1 B2*

A bit off the beaten track, this popular and reliable French bistro-style restaurant serves international cuisine and top-class Swedish home cooking. The menu includes a great choice of fish for starters and a speciality is fillet of beef with sautéed potatoes and horseradish. There's a lively bar downstairs.

FURTHER AFIELD VASASTAN Claes på Hörnet

Surbrunnsgatan 20, Stockholm, 113 48 **Tel** *08-16 51 36*   **Map** *1 C2*

A decadent-looking building with a lovely, old fashioned hotel restaurant serving extremely good Swedish food. It is one of Stockholm's oldest restaurants, dating back to 1731. A plate of herrings, homemade crispbread and cheese is a popular starter. Game and mushrooms feature in season. Closed Sundays.

FURTHER AFIELD VASASTAN Grill

Drottninggatan 89, Stockholm, 113 60 **Tel** *08-31 45 30*   **Map** *1 C3*

A large restaurant and bar that is usually crowded. It mysteriously burned down several years ago and was redecorated in a kitschy style but that hasn't stopped it becoming a favourite local hangout. The grilled meats and special sauces are mouth-watering. Booking recommended. Buffet only on Sundays.

FURTHER AFIELD ÖSTERMALM Beirut Café

Engelbrektsgatan 37, Stockholm, 114 32 **Tel** *08-21 20 25*   **Map** *2 D2*

Stepping into Beirut Café from a sleepy side street is like taking a step into the Middle East. The atmosphere is lively and there's a great choice of Middle Eastern and Lebanese mezze – the artichoke houmus and tabouleh are particularly good. Lebanese wines make a suitable accompaniment. Closed Sundays in summer.

FURTHER AFIELD ÖSTERMALM Teatergrillen

Nybrogatan 3, Stockholm, 114 34 **Tel** *08-54 50 35 65*   **Map** *2 E3*

One of Stockholm's oldest restaurants, Teatergrillen is beautifully old fashioned; for example, diners can order meats from a silver trolley brought to the table, making a refreshing change from the many modern restaurants now in the city. A favourite among celebrities and media workers.

FURTHER AFIELD ÖSTERMALM Gerdas Fiskrestaurang

Östermalms Saluhall, Stockholm, 114 39 **Tel** *08-55 34 04 40*   **Map** *2 E4*

A fun place to visit when looking for good seafood. Located in a lively area close to the Östermalm market (a place where all visiting foodies should go), Gerdas is hugely popular and always busy. Their creamy fish soup is an absolute must. To avoid disappointment, book a table in advance. Closed Sundays.

FURTHER AFIELD ÖSTERMALM Brasserie Godot

Grev Turegatan 36, Stockholm, 114 36 **Tel** *08-660 06 14*   **Map** *2 E3*

The "in" place for eating. The menu has a strong French flavour with such dishes as *moules marinière* (mussels in a creamy sauce) and steak and chips. It attracts lots of young people with its great cocktails and substantial food. However, there are Swedish favourites too, including potato blini with bleak roe and sour cream. Closed Sundays.

FURTHER AFIELD Stallmästaregården

Norrtull, Stockholm, 113 47 **Tel** *08-610 13 01*

A 17th-century inn set in an idyllic location on Brunnsviken Bay. It serves the epitome of Swedish cuisine, which diners can see being prepared on the open kitchen's charcoal grill and rotisserie. Dishes are modern Swedish with a continental European twist. To finish, there's a choice of sumptuous desserts.

FURTHER AFIELD Ulriksdals Wärdshus

Ulriksdals Slottspark, Solna, 170 79 **Tel** *08-85 08 15*

In a magnificent location in a beautiful and historic inn, Wärdshus offers elegant top-class cuisine and fine wines. The world's largest collection of wine was once housed here, until all 600 bottles were taken by burglars in 2006. Famous for its outstanding *smörgåsbord*, especially at Christmas, for which people book their parties a year ahead.

Key to Price Guide *see p298* **Key to Symbols** *see back cover flap*

EASTERN SVEALAND

HÖLÖ Oaxen Skärgårdskrog
*Oaxen, 153 93 **Tel** 08-551 53 105*

Voted among the world's top 50 restaurants producing food that is as visually stunning as it is flavourful. Located on the island of Oaxen, 70 km (43 miles) from Stockholm, it is only open for six months of the year, serving its very modern, international style of cuisine using local produce. Lovely outdoor seating area. Hard to get to but worth it!

JÖNÅKER Wreta Gestgifveri
*Wreta Gård AB, 610 50 **Tel** 0155-720 22*

A restaurant decorated in authentic Gustavian style with a strong sense of nostalgia. The well-composed menu has its roots in the Swedish kitchen and derives inspiration from the rest of the world. Also has a good wine list. In recent years it has won recognition in several well-known Swedish restaurant guides.

NYKÖPING Mickes Skafferi
*Västra Storgatan 29, 611 32 **Tel** 0155-26 99 50*

A small, cosy local pub and restaurant in central Nyköping that retains interior references to the days when it was a hairdressers in the late 1930s. Head chef Gerhard Brandner has created a menu filled with modern takes on Swedish classics, including reindeer calf fillet with chantarelle sauce and pear and lingonberry chutney.

SIGTUNA Sigtuna Stads Hotell
*Stora Nygatan 3, 193 30 **Tel** 08-592 50 100*

Genuine Swedish cuisine in a modern guise served in the picturesque restaurant of this Scandinavian-style designer hotel using local ingredients, many of which are sourced from the rich agricultural district of the Mälar Valley. Occasionally they add spice with international guest chefs. Long and superb wine list with several rare vintages.

SÖDERTÄLJE St Ansgars Källare
*Kaplansgatan 1, 151 72 **Tel** 08-550 32 525*

Classic food served in the brick-lined cellar of one of the town's oldest stone houses. Regarded as one of the better restaurants in Södertälje. Head chef Jonas Isaksson recommends creamy lobster soup and spiced duck breast as part of the restaurant's set two- or three-course lunches. Otherwise go à la carte for many more culinary delights.

TROSA Bomans Hotel & Restaurant
*Östra Hamnplan, 619 30 **Tel** 0156-525 00*

Small but quality menu with a definite Swedish touch. Stina Bowman's meatballs with creamed potatoes and lingonberry sauce are named after one of the founding members of this family-run concern. The beef with truffle, green beans and red wine sauce is delicious.

UPPSALA Lingon
*Svartbäcksgatan 30, 753 32 **Tel** 018-10 12 24*

In a carefully renovated 18th-century building, Lingon has a rustic feel and is full of Swedish charm. Using only organic, locally sourced ingredients, the menu stays fresh and is full of Swedish flavours. The peaceful riverside "Backyard" patio is popular in summer, when there is music and entertainment too. Booking essential on Sundays.

VÄSTERÅS Atrium Restaurang & Bar
*Smedjegatan 6, 722 13 **Tel** 021-12 38 48*

A Greek restaurant complete with roman pillars and art that matches the decor with an exotic menu filled with traditional Greek classics. Try the calamari with saffron aïoli for a starter and the *Paidakia Atrium* (grilled lamb chops with garlic and thyme sauce) for a main course. Some unusual Greek wines are also available.

VÄSTERÅS Bill & Bob's krog
*Stora Torget 5, 722 15 **Tel** 021-41 99 21*

Located in the attractive *bondtorget* (farmers' square) in central Västerås this small restaurant normally holds 50 diners until the summer months when it has a large popular outdoor seating area that adds a further 110 place settings. The menu is largely standard fare but the prices are reasonable and the service is good.

EASTERN GÖTALAND

BORGHOLM Bakfickan, Hotell Borgholm
*Trädgårdsgatan 15, 387 31 **Tel** 0485-770 60*

One of the top restaurants in Sweden where head chef Karin Fransson has built a glowing reputation for inspirational food created from local Swedish ingredients. Both à la carte and set three- or five-course menus are available. Dishes such as lamb fillet with crispy crackling, rosemary gravy and balsamic-cooked vegetables will never disappoint.

JÖNKÖPING Svarta Börsen
Kyrkogatan 4, 553 16 **Tel** *036-71 22 22*

A popular meeting place for players in the Swedish jazz scene where regular performances take place. A cosy, classy restaurant with art on the walls, jazz in the background and good food on the table, such as grilled red char with lemon potatoes and a crayfish butter sauce. Traditional food in a great laid-back atmosphere.

KALMAR Helen & Jörgens
Olof Palmes Gata 2, 392 33 **Tel** *0480-288 30*

Friendly service-minded restaurant with personal style and a menu that makes diners want to come back. The emphasis is towards Mediterranean cooking, but some regional specialities are also included such as Öland chicken cooked in goat's milks with asparagus. They also do a theatre *fika* (coffee and snacks) for those visiting the nearby theatre.

LINKÖPING Stångs Magasin
Södra Stånggatan 1, 582 73 **Tel** *013-31 21 00*

Linköping's trendiest place to eat is located in a 400-year-old warehouse by the beach. The menu is based on modern Swedish food, sometimes with a Mediterranean twist. Terrine of game with crème of wild mushroom and elderberry jelly gives a flavour of their kitchen. Very reasonable prices. Voted best restaurant in the region in the 2009 White Guide.

MOTALA Bryggeriet Rock'n Roll Bar
Prästgatan 3, 591 30 **Tel** *0141-23 39 13*

For diners who like their food served with rock and roll, then this is the place to come. The food is pretty ordinary, with baked potatoes, hamburgers and nachos, but the prices are low and the atmosphere is fun. Live performances several times a week and a buzzing after-work scene. The bar serves a colourful list of cocktails.

VASTERVIK Saltmagasinet
Kulbacken, 593 38 **Tel** *0490-189 35*

A former 17th-century salt warehouse with a large outside seating area with beautiful views over Gamlebyviken. Serves around ten lunch dishes during the summer with an à la carte menu in the evenings. Co-operates with a number of local producers to create food with a distinctly local touch. Large wine list and knowledgeable sommeliers.

VIMMERBY Brygghuset
Åbrovägen 13, 598 86 **Tel** *0492-753 80*

An old English-style pub and restaurant built right next door to the large Åbro brewery. Naturally many of the brewery's beer brands can be ordered from the bar, along with a large selection of wines and whiskies. During the week the pub serves wholesome à la carte lunches. The evening menu is high-class pub grub.

ÖLAND Kvarn Krogen
Eketorpsvägen 1, 380 65 **Tel** *0485-66 13 40*

A memorable restaurant built into a windmill from 1844 that was moved here during World War I. Traditional Swedish fare is the house style, with freshly caught fish directly from the nearby Grönhögens harbour always on the menu. Vegetarian dishes are ever present and the lunch buffets represent excellent value for money.

ÖLAND Guntorps Herrgård
Guntorpsgatan, 387 36 **Tel** *0485-130 00*

Located in a stately grand residence, this hotel restaurant has a kitsch tropical-themed decor that is somewhat at odds with the setting. The à la carte menu features plenty of seafood and meat dishes, and there's a good buffet with Swedish delicacies such as pickled herring, shrimps in dill and local Öland sausages.

ÖLAND Värdshuset Briggen Tre Liljor
Lofta 1463, 387 91 **Tel** *0485-264 20*

A first-class restaurant set in a small country house in a rural setting on Öland that has won numerous awards for its excellent food. Has its roots as a fish and shellfish specialist, but also serves outstanding game and lamb dishes in an à la carte menu full of exciting international flavours.

GOTLAND

VISBY Bakfickan
Stora Torget 1, 621 56 **Tel** *0498-27 18 07*

Charming, simple and cosy restaurant with a focus on fish and shellfish where you can eat outside during the summer. The starter selection of pickled herrings is a Swedish classic, while Bakfickan's fish soup with aïoli is popular. A nicely presented children's menu includes home-cooked meatballs and battered cod fillet with tartar sauce.

VISBY Hamnplan 5
Hamnplan 5, 621 57 **Tel** *0498-21 07 10*

Positioned in the heart of Visby with great views from the terrace over the harbour, this trendy restaurant and nightclub complex is open all year round. Here you can choose from a simple but tasty bar menu or go à la carte. There's something for younger diners from the children's menu.

VISBY 50 Kvadrat
S:t Hansgatan 15, 621 56 **Tel** *0498-27 83 80*

50 Kvadrat presents modern cuisine from Sweden with influences from central Europe and the Mediterranean. Owners Fredrik Malmstedt and Laila Löfkvist have an impressive resumé, having cooked all over the world as well as for members of the Swedish Royal family. For hungry diners, the five-course menu is a good choice.

VISBY Friheten Restaurang
Strandgatan 6, 621 57 **Tel** *0498-24 99 07*

In a fantastic location in the grounds of the Clarion hotel Wisby, this characterful restaurant is open all year round and is a wonderful place to visit after a walk around the island's nearby harbour district. The menu changes with the seasons but there is always a good range of seafood and meat dishes.

SOUTHERN GÖTALAND

BILLEBERGA Farbror Elofs Skafferi
Kvarngården 1, 260 21 **Tel** *0418-43 11 77*

It would take weeks to count the number of pictures, clocks and bric-a-brac hanging from the walls of this charming little restaurant. Little wonder the restaurant owners also have a flea market next door. The chef draws inspiration from Provence, Italy and Sweden, with meat and vegetables coming from the Skåne region.

BRANTEVIK Branteviks Bykrog
Mästergränd 2, 272 38 **Tel** *0414-220 69*

A village restaurant that gets very busy in the summer. Many of the ingredients come from the Österlen region, complemented by game, truffles, oils and spices from other countries to create a menu grounded in Skåne with a French twist. A magnificent wine cellar, with bottles from over 150 producers from around the world.

BROSARP Brösarps Gästgifveri
Albovägen 21, 277 50 **Tel** *0414-736 80*

A 300-year-old roadside tavern that was once the haunt of the local nobility and now a popular retreat for diners searching for wholesome, home-cooked food with a regional flavour. All the food used is bought from the surrounding district, including ducks, chickens, lambs, asparagus and fish. The wild boar is a regional speciality.

GENARP Häckeberga Slott
Häckeberga Slott, 240 13 **Tel** *040-48 04 40*

Visitors are assured of a memorable gastronomic experience in a captivating castle setting. Master Chef Mikael Börjesson gets much of his motivation from the Mediterranean and then adds a regional slant, with game coming from the castle's own grounds. His chocolate work and garnishes rank among Europe's best.

HELSINGBORG Gastro
Södra Storgatan 11, 252 23 **Tel** *042-24 34 70*

Gastro can be counted among the elite restaurants of Sweden, with numerous international awards for its consistently excellent food. Always on the menu and worth trying are Gastro's Swedish delicatessen plates with mustard marinated Baltic herring, sugar-salted salmon, bleak roe and silver eel with eggs royale and Wallenbergers with potato purée.

KARLSKRONA 2 Rum & Kök
Södra Smedjegatan 3, 371 31 **Tel** *0455-104 22*

To dine in Karlskrona's oldest restaurant is an elegant experience surrounded by the unique marine-themed decor that reflects the town's affinity with the sea. The signature meal here is fondue, with seven flavours to choose from, including Cajun and garlic. A very reasonably priced wine list and vegetarian options available.

KRISTIANSTAD Bar-B-Ko
Tivoligatan 4, 291 31 **Tel** *044-21 33 55*

A slightly wacky and fun barbeque restaurant whose tagline "The Place to Meat" sums up nicely what sort of food you get here. Great flamed steaks, lamb racks and spare ribs from the grill, as well as seafood and deer from the oven. Vegetarian meals are always available. Just a stone's throw from the town's Lilla Torg (little square).

KRISTIANSTAD Tomarp Gårdshotell
Helmershusvägen 218, 291 94 **Tel** *044-931 18*

The picturesque Tomarp is a large estate close to the Råbelövs lake. From here chefs at the restaurant source many of their ingredients, making this home-cooking on a grand scale. Whatever is available in season shapes an ever-changing menu. Offers a lunch of the day, an afternoon tea buffet and evening meals.

LANDSKRONA Akropolis Rådhusrestaurang
Rådhustorget 9, 261 31 **Tel** *0418-102 86*

Described as a Greek oasis in the middle of Landskrona, this is a restaurant and bar with a lively crowd. Many of the Greek standards are on the menu, as well as simple meat, fish and pasta dishes. There's a couple of vegetarian suggestions, as well as five plank steaks to choose from.

LUND Gattostretto

Kattesund 6A, 222 23 **Tel** *046-32 07 77*

A cosy restaurant run by an Italian-Swedish couple with a big passion for food. Here you will find real Italian food, including hearty pasta dishes, made with fresh ingredients. The sommelier will guide you through the selection of beers and Italian wines. There is also a fantastic coffee bar where all the pastries are freshly made. Closed Sunday.

LÖDERUP Mötesplats Österlen

Örum 52, 276 40 **Tel** *0411-55 66 88*

This highly acclaimed restaurant comes strongly recommended in all the major gourmet guides. Some of Sweden's best chefs and wine experts compose and update the exciting menu and wine list. Master chef Anders Vendel conjures up some unique taste experiences, presenting meals in a playful, sophisticated way.

MALMÖ Lemongrass

Grynbodgatan 9, 211 33 **Tel** *040-30 69 79*

Asian fusion cooking is served at this in-restaurant, with delicious oriental dishes like creamy curry prawns, szechwan racks of lamb and up to 12 sushi bites. The very sophisticated, sleek interior design conveys a sense of exclusivity, although this is not reflected in the reasonable prices. Three types of Oriental beer to enjoy with your meal.

MALMÖ Årstiderna

Frans Suellsgatan 3, 211 22 **Tel** *040-23 09 10*

Located in the atmospheric vaulted cellars of Jörgen Kock's House, and dating from the early 16th century, is one of Malmö's most exclusive restaurants. Traditional Swedish ingredients are treated with a French touch to create dishes such as cognac-infused lobster soup with a shellfish spring roll. Smart dress. Closed Sundays and public holidays.

MALMÖ Restaurang Kramer Gastronomi

Stortorget 7, 201 21 **Tel** *040-693 54 00*

Enjoy dinner at this fine-dining restaurant overlooking Malmö's Stortorget (main square). The large windows and Nordic-inspired decor make it a light and elegant place to eat. Children are welcome with a kids menu. International cuisine is the theme, with dishes like lobster with browned butter, vanilla and passion fruit.

MALMÖ Salt & Brygga

Sundspromenaden 7, 211 18 **Tel** *040-611 59 40*

The row of award plaques outside the front door of this seaside restaurant pay testament to its food and service. A strong environmental philosophy runs through the entire business, with ingredients sourced locally and organic foods used whenever possible. Healthy and happy place to eat.

MÖLLE Maritime

Bökebolsvägen 11, 260 42 **Tel** *042-36 22 30*

Maritime, the gourmet restaurant of the grand, has made a name for itself with its harmonious menus and well-stocked wine cellar. The beautiful dining room overlooks the harbour and Kullaberg. Naturally, fish and seafood play an important part in the menu. A small but quality selection of dishes to choose from.

RONNEBY Ronneby Brun Hotel & Spa

Brunnsparken, 372 22 **Tel** *0457-750 00*

Top-class entertainers put on a show while you eat at this lively and spacious resort restaurant in Ronneby that can seat up to 600 diners. When the diners take their eyes away from the performance, they'll see a captivating menu centred around local ingredients that change with the seasons.

SIMRISHAMN Måns Byckare

Storgatan 8, 272 31 **Tel** *0414-147 49*

This cosy restaurant and bar in classic style has a varied Swedish-French influenced menu. The lunch buffet is very well priced and popular, with several GI alternatives, including feta cheese salad and chicken fillet in white wine sauce. When the sun is shining sit outside on the pavement and watch the world go by.

TRELLEBORG Tre Lyktor

Flockergatan 1, 231 43 **Tel** *0410-199 93*

Live music acts every Friday and Saturday night make this a fun place to eat out. Essentially this is a British-themed pub, complete with wooden beams and tartan wall paper, but the pub menu is pleasant and value for money and includes meals such as egg and bacon, plank steaks and deep-fried camembert.

YSTAD Steakhouse Bryggeriet

Långgatan 20, 271 43 **Tel** *0411-699 99*

The restaurant is situated around a brewery in Långgatan. A pair of enormous copper boilers tower at the centre of the floor creating a unique interior atmosphere. The half-timbered building dating back to the mid-17th century has a wonderful outdoor serving area. The steaks are a must and are grilled on lava stone grills.

ÅHUS Handelsbaren

Åvägen 4, 296 38 **Tel** *044-24 73 30*

The charismatic owner of this popular summer bar and restaurant is called Stampe, and he's often found behind the bar playing vinyls from his personal collection. There are fewer views in Åhus more beautiful than from the restaurant's wooden decking over the edge of the river. Gets very busy in the high season.

Key to Price Guide *see p298* **Key to Symbols** *see back cover flap*

GOTHENBURG

CENTRE Restaurang Manana
Lasarettsgatan 6, 411 19 **Tel** *031-711 72 90*

Stylishly designed tapas restaurant with a motto of "easy food and happy people". Choose from vegetable, chicken, meat, fish and shellfish dishes as well as some unusual Spanish desserts. Small but good selection of cocktails, wines and beers. The large list of liqueur coffees can round off a meal nicely.

CENTRE Restaurang Wojarski
Skanstorget 7, 411 22 **Tel** *031-13 32 18*

An Eastern European-themed restaurant with food that's a little bit out of the ordinary. Choose from national dishes such as Hungarian goulash soup, Polish *pierogi* (a kind of dumpling) filled with potato, onion and cheese, and *Sremska* (grilled spicy Yugoslavian sausage). The drinks list offers a good assortment of hard-to-find vodkas.

CENTRE Stearin
Tredje Långgatan 8, 413 03 **Tel** *031-14 77 88*

Stearin is a warm and inviting restaurant filled with candlelight. The decor is fairly minimalist with discreet nougat- and lilac tones further adding to the sense of intimacy. The menu is simple and mixes main courses with side dishes. The *råbiffen* (steak tartare) comes highly recommended. Very popular so book ahead.

CENTRE Kock & Vin
Viktoriagatan 12, 411 25 **Tel** *031-701 79 79*

A candle-lit restaurant with an ornate 19th-century ceiling and a modern basement bar. The Michelin-starred Kock & Vin is renowned for its modern Scandinavian cuisine based on the best seasonal ingredients. Dishes might include scallops and oysters with a parsley and cauliflower snow. Smart dress. Closed Mon, Sun, 5 Jul–5 Aug.

CENTRE Restaurang Trägår'n
Nya Allén, 411 38 **Tel** *031-10 20 80*

There may be a nightclub next door but this restaurant is a peaceful oasis of calm. An adventurous à la carte menu is available from May throughout the summer. A popular and reasonably priced lunch buffet is served every weekday consisting of two warm dishes, a vegetarian dish, a selection of salads, bread, coffee and biscuits.

CENTRE Sjöbaren
Haga Nygata 25, 413 01 **Tel** *031-711 97 80*

A small and modern fish and shellfish restaurant in a traditional 1860s building in the attractive Haga district of Gothenburg. Worth trying is the *bouillabaisse* with Atlantic cod and lemon sole and the house speciality Sjöbaren's fish *au gratin* with cod fillet, shrimps and mushrooms served with white wine sauce. Good wine selection.

CENTRE Tvakanten
Kungsportsavenyen 27, 412 56 **Tel** *031-18 21 15*

Relaxed top-end restaurant with food served outside in the summer when the weather permits. Good Swedish fare and great value for money. Order the sesame-fried salmon sashimi with teriyaki and lemon grass reduction and salmon roe or try the beef *rydberg* (diced pan-fried fillet of beef, potatoes and sautéed onions).

CENTRE 28+
Götabergsgatan 28, 411 34 **Tel** *031-20 21 61*

Regarded by many as the city's best restaurant, this Michelin-starred restaurant offers a luxurious menu created by Swedish master chef Hans Boren. The restaurant itself is located in a cellar, and the tiled floor and antique furniture can feel a little cold, but the food is the star here. To accompany it, the wine cellar contains more than 800 labels.

CENTRE Fiskekrogen
Lilla Torget 1, 411 18 **Tel** *031-10 10 05*

Famous fish restaurant run by the charismatic Lars Ahlström, whose knowledge of seafood is unrivalled. Try his small shellfish plateau, with shrimps, langoustines, mussels cooked in wine, accompanying sauces and crisp bread. Also boasts one of the best wine cellars in the country.

CENTRE Restaurang Fond
Götaplatsen, 411 34 **Tel** *031-81 25 80*

Located on Gothenburg's main square this restaurant proudly uses only Swedish ingredients in its dishes and has a very good wine list. In 2001 it was awarded a Michelin star. Large windows mean this is a light and spacious place to eat, decorated in a modern Nordic style. Try the marinated cod cheek and shell fish in frothy cod *bouillon*.

FURTHER AFIELD Sjömagasinet
Klippan 6, 402 41 **Tel** *031-775 59 20*

The Michelin-starred Sjömagasinet is situated in a beautiful building dating from 1775 and has a view over the Älvsborg's bridge and the harbour. Lovers of seafood will be in heaven here. Try the Sjömagasinet's herring platter with matured cheese or the poached oyster filled halibut with cumin hollandaise. Expansive top quality wine list.

WESTERN GÖTALAND

BORÅS Restaurang Oliven

Lilla Brogatan 11, 503 30 **Tel** *033-10 10 65*

Good service and Mediterranean food are the hallmarks of this street corner restaurant with a lovely inner courtyard with seating. Try the *souvlaki chirino* (pork loin on scewers served with deep fried potatoes and tzatsiki) or the *tuna di Medetariano* (charcoal-grilled tuna with prawns and mango salsa) served with the risotto of the day.

HALMSTAD Lilla Helfwetet

Hamngatan 37, 302 44 **Tel** *035-21 04 20*

A modern restaurant, bar and nightclub combined with a lively after-work scene and regular live music. The building's high ceiling gives a real sense of space even when the place is quite crowded. First-rate food and plenty to choose from, with lunch, bar, seafood and à la carte menus.

HALMSTAD Restaurang Akvarell

Tylöhusvägen, 301 16 **Tel** *035-305 00*

Restaurant Akvarell belongs to an elite class of restaurants. The divine food is beautifully presented and complemented by a first-class wine list. Throw in the magnificent sea view from the dining room (in good weather sit on the large sun terrace) and the experience is complete. Has a terrific four-course set menu.

KARLSBORG Idas Brygga

Skepparegatan 9, 546 32 **Tel** *0505-131 11*

This charming award-winning restaurant is built within an old warehouse on the banks of the Göta Canal, with boats and barges floating by the windows a common sight. The menu is varied but with a slight bias towards seafood. Try the local Halstrad fillet of goose or the salmon fillet with dijon cream sauce.

KVÄNUM Bjertorp Slott

Fyrunga Bjertorps Slott, 535 91 **Tel** *0512-30 05 00*

Grand castle dining room dripping with original features. Exclusive atmosphere and high-class food has won this restaurant numerous awards. The menu changes with the seasons but the dedication to local ingredients remains constant. Famous for its wine cellar, and the expert staff can be relied upon to recommend the right wine with every meal.

MARIESTAD Åsgårdens Wärdshus

Järnvägsgatan 2, 548 73 **Tel** *0501-501 06*

A pleasant place to drop in to if looking for some authentic Swedish food. Only open in the summer from June to August, when lunches are served everyday and fixed priced two- or three-course dinners are prepared each evening. Has an appealing homely quality and the staff are very friendly.

MARSTRAND Restaurang Tenan

Rådhusgatan 2, 440 30 **Tel** *0303-603 22*

Found on the bottom floor of the imposing Grand Hotel is the famous Restaurang Tenan with its spacious and sunny veranda. An award-winning West Coast kitchen serves authentic Africana garlic langoustines cooked to the orginal recipe. There's a welcoming bar adjacent to the dining area with a long list of wines and spirits to choose from.

SKÖVDE Husaren

Sta Helenagatan 10, 541 30 **Tel** *0500-41 79 79*

This family-run restaurant is a popular meeting place in Skövde. A recent facelift has given it a trendy look with a splash of retro. A big screen TV makes it the place to be for sporting events and there's regular live music. The menu is small but high quality, with four starters, eight mains and four desserts to choose from.

STRÖMSTAD Pråmen

Söden Hamnen, 452 30 **Tel** *0526-135 09*

In this small town known for its fresh seafood, particularly prawns, where better to enjoy such delicacies than on a restaurant floating in Strömstad's south harbour. Pråmen is a boat restaurant with a stylish minimalist decor. Diners can enjoy reasonably priced fresh fish and other seafood grilled on deck while taking in the sea views. Open May to August.

TROLLHÄTTAN Albert Kök

Strömsberg, 461 57 **Tel** *0520-129 90*

The kitchen and a love of local food forms the centrepiece of this fabulous restaurant. There are stunning views over the waterfalls and the town of Trollhättan below. In season they serve salmon from Vänern, shellfish from the west coast and Mowitz-chicken from the vale of the Göta River.

VÄNERSBORG Restaurang Teatergränd

Kungsgatan 13, 462 33 **Tel** *0521-644 60*

The perfect combination of food and wine at every meal is the goal at Teatergränd – a contemporary and elegant concept owned and operated by two young and ambitious restaurateurs. With more than 90 wines to choose from (30 by the glass) the professional staff are confident diners will find something to match their meal.

Key to Price Guide *see p298* **Key to Symbols** *see back cover flap*

WESTERN SVEALAND

ARVIKA Gate Gästgiveri

Gate Gästgiveri, 671 41 **Tel** *0570-131 20*

A very homely, old-fashioned feel in one of Arvika's oldest houses. Here all the food is home-made with a blend of Swedish and French flavours. Try a starter of cloudberry and blue cheese-filled salmon roll on a bed of lettuce followed by an elk fillet with thyme and red wine sauce. Competitive prices and very personal service.

BORLÄNGE Ulfshyttans Herrgård

Ulvshyttan, 781 96 **Tel** *0243-25 13 00*

This picturesque manor house set in wonderful grounds with views down over Lake Ulvsjön was once frequented by the king of Sweden. Now its inviting restaurant is open to all, with a good range of set-priced menus. The food presentation is attractive and ingredients come from the local community.

FALUN Kopparhatten Cafe & Kök

Engelbrektsgatan 30, 791 60 **Tel** *023-191 69*

At this fresh and modern restaurant they have art from both well-known and obscure artists hanging on the walls for sale. They also believe that food is an art form and pay great detail to presentation on the plate. A nice range of food styles to choose from, including Italian, Mediterranean, tapas and regional dishes.

KARLSTAD Blå Restaurang & Bar

Kungsgatan 14, 652 24 **Tel** *054-10 18 15*

Stylish restaurant with modern decor and nice views over the square. Expert staff serving beautifully presented food with roots in traditional Swedish cuisine but a willingness to experiment with foreign flavours. Try the marinated beetroots, smoked lamb roast, *chevre terrin*, rocket jelly, and pine nut oil.

KRISTINEHAMN Mastmagasinet

Södra Hamngatan 5, 681 31 **Tel** *0550-803 40*

The original 19th-century building this restaurant resides in once housed boats pulled out of the water over winter to stop them being crushed by ice. After a fire ravaged the warehouse in 1994 it was rebuilt with a large decking area where diners can sit and see the boats moored nearby. Food is excellent and artistically presented.

LIDINGO Jernet Bar och Matsal

Stockholmsvägen 56, 181 32 **Tel** *08-731 06 06*

The restaurant is housed in Mora's oldest industrial building dating from the late 19th century. Before eating, have a drink in the busy bar. The extensive menu features international flavours such as steamed Chinese spring rolls or Jernet's tarragon hamburger with cheddar, artichoke salsa, gherkins and oven-baked chips.

RÄTTVIK Jöns Andersgården

Bygatan 16, 795 35 **Tel** *0248-130 15*

This restaurant is a mix of old and new with its timber walls and high ceiling. Diners can enjoy an excellent dinner prepared with meats sourced in the area and locally produced vegetables. There's an excellent selection of wines and beers to accompany your choice of dishes. Relax with a drink in front of the fireplace in the lounge afterwards.

SÄLEN HC Högfjällscenter

Högfjällscenter, 780 67 **Tel** *0280-275 00*

A lively mountain ski resort is home to this trendy restaurant catering for the entire family. Food is served from 6pm every day, with an à la carte, children's buffet and a well priced three-course menu to pick from. Book a table early and get free entry to the nightclub next door, where some of Sweden's top artists regularly perform.

SÄLEN Lammet & Grisen

Lindvallen, 780 67 **Tel** *0280-210 90*

Named Sweden's top wine restaurant in 2007, the huge cellar has room for 3,000 bottles. The large seating area is divided into three rooms, Rioja, Toscana and Bordeaux. Three buffet tables are usually available. Kalix bleak roe with Västerbotten cheese quiche, crème fraîche and finely chopped red onion is a taster of the Swedish-inspired a la carte menu.

TALLBERG Åkerblads Hotell & Gästgiveri

Sjögattu 2, 793 70 **Tel** *0247-508 00*

One can almost sense the history in this restaurant that has belonged to the same family since the 15th century. Head chef Fredrik Svedberg is constantly looking for new ideas and ingredients to add to his already impressive food selection, which includes classic Swedish *husmanskost* (home cooking) and a visually stunning à la carte menu.

ÖREBRO Slottskällaren

Drottninggatan 1, 702 45 **Tel** *019-15 69 60*

There's an intimate atmosphere in this classy restaurant located in the 14th-century cellar vaults beneath the Elite Stora Hotellet. The adjacent veranda is very popular in summer, with stunning views over the river and the majestic Örebro castle. A classic selection of meat and fish dishes are presented, as well as an agreeable wine list.

SOUTHERN NORRLAND

BJASTA Näske Krog   🅥   ⓀⓀ
Norum, 893 91 **Tel** *0660-22 82 38*

Despite the natural setting this restaurant is easily reachable from the E4 motorway that runs lengthways through Sweden. The *dagens lunch* (lunch of the day) is popular, where diners can choose between two to three dishes with all extras included. Open weekdays between 10am and 7pm, and on weekends until 8pm.

GÄVLE Restaurang Matildas   🛉   ⓀⓀ
Timmermansgatan 23, 802 52 **Tel** *026-62 53 49*

Gävle's only classic fine-dining restaurant is well-known locally for its high standards of food and personal service. Although the decor is perhaps a little dated, there's a pleasant atmosphere and an adventurous selection of dishes. Try the fillet of beef with creamy garlic sauce or the very 'un-Swedish' snails fried in garlic.

HÄRNÖSAND Restaurang Royal   🛉 🅥   ⓀⓀ
Strandgatan 12, 871 45 **Tel** *0611-247 07*

One of Härnösand's most popular lunch restaurants that also offers high-class evening service. The à la carte menu is filled with northern Swedish influences such as char and reindeer. The menu changes with the seasons and whatever local produce is available. The lunch menu always includes Swedish traditional cooking and a vegetarian alternative.

HIGH COAST Restaurang Skutskepparn   🛉 🖼   ⓀⓀ
Barsta 270, 870 30 **Tel** *0613-230 90*

The views from this old fisherman's property from the 15th century on the edge of Barsta are spectacular, and during the summer it's an ideal place to sit outside and eat. Freshly caught fish are a speciality of the house, including salmon and whitefish. The different sorts of pickled herring are a must-try Swedish dining experience.

HUDVIKSVALL Restaurang 49   🛉 🖼 🅥   ⓀⓀ
Drottninggatan 17, 824 30 **Tel** *0650-155 50*

Idyllically situated on the shore of Lillfjärden this wooden building from the turn of the century lies in the shadow of the mountain that towers over nearby Hudiksvall. A sterile white and rather sparsely decorated interior. Extensive menu including children's sized portions. Try the locally-inspired Hälsinge cheesecake with blackberry sauce.

SANDVIKEN Högbo Brukshotell   🛉 🍷 🅥   ⓀⓀⓀⓀ
Hans Hiertas Väg 20, 811 22 **Tel** *026-24 52 00*

A bright and airy hotel restaurant that serves an impressive lunch buffet. In the evening, guests and visitors can choose a set three-course meal or go à la carte . The dessert buffet is renowned and has been awarded a prize as Sweden's best hotel dessert. Also listed in Sweden's top 199 *Bästa Bord* (best dining experiences).

STORLIEN Restaurant Flamman   🛉 🍷   ⓀⓀ
Vintergatan 46, 830 19 **Tel** *0647-700 10*

A local institution that has transformed from a waffle kiosk to a disco to a nursery and finally to a restaurant that promises never to close until the last guest wants to leave. The menu is mid-priced and features several fish and meat dishes. A children's menu is also offered. Reasonable selection of drinks available.

SUNDSVALL Brandstation Bar & Matsalar   🛉 🍷 🅥   ⓀⓀⓀ
Köpmangatan 29, 851 06 **Tel** *060-12 39 36*

A charming and cleverly redeveloped restaurant house in the former Sundsvall fire station. Diners sit where the old horse-drawn engines used to be parked while their meals are prepared in the former stables. Pictures of the old station are hung on the exposed brick walls and the wood-panelled bar serves wines from all the leading producers.

SUNDSVALL Sundsvalls Stadshus   🍴 🍷 🅥   ⓀⓀⓀ
Stora Torget, 852 30 **Tel** *060-12 92 60*

A first-class restaurant in the architecturally beautiful town hall in Sundsvall. New owners have created an exciting menu with different national themes from Sweden, Spain, France, Italy and Argentina, as well as a vegetarian menu. Diners can mix different dishes from each menu to get a truly international meal.

ÅRE Villa Tottebo   🍴 🍷 🅥   ⓀⓀⓀ
Parkvägen 1, 830 13 **Tel** *0647-506 20*

Opposite the railway station in Åre is this restaurant that was once a late 19th-century hunting lodge. Upon entering diners are faced with the open kitchen. An open fireplace and contemporary Swedish interior design. Try the flank of reindeer with smoked pork loin flavoured with Västerbotten cheese and blackcurrant sauce.

ÖSTERSUND Innefickan   🍷 🍴 🅥   ⓀⓀ
Postgränd 11, 831 31 **Tel** *063-12 90 99*

Stylish cellar restaurant with a menu that mixes Swedish classics and modern international cooking. High-quality local products are used, mainly from the mountains, farms and forests nearby. For real variety try the reasonably priced five-dish tasting menu (only available if ordered by everyone at your table). Excellent wine list.

Key to Price Guide *see p298* **Key to Symbols** *see back cover flap*

ÖSTERSUND Mikado ⊗⊗⊗

Infanterigatan 12, 831 32 **Tel** *063-209 08*

Remarkably exotic gem of a restaurant in Jämtland that is one of the absolute best Japanese restaurants in Sweden. Located on a former military base camp in Östersund, people come here from all over Sweden for the creative Japanese cuisine. The fondues prepared at the table are a speciality. All meals need to be booked three days ahead.

NORTHERN NORRLAND

BODEN Nordpol Cafe & Restaurang 🍽 V ⊗⊗

Garnisonsgatan 1, 961 75 **Tel** *0921-628 47*

A sports bar concept that has been taken over by two restauranteurs with ambitions to change it into a first-class restaurant. Staple favourites such as their home-made hamburgers and plank steak are mixed in with more unusual alternatives such as chilli shrimp wok and oven-baked salmon. Lunch buffet served on weekdays.

GAMMELSTAD Margaretas Värdshus ⊗⊗

Lulevägen 2, 954 33 **Tel** *0920-25 42 90*

Typical Norbotten restaurant with the emphasis on local cuisine. Lots of old-world charm in this 19th-century building with its traditional tiled stove. Try the whole butter-fried mountain char with almond potatoes. More international fare can be found with dishes such as the house *Châteaubriand* with fresh mushroom and dijon mustard sauce.

HEMAVAN Restaurang Wärdshuset ⊗⊗⊗

Blå Vägen 17, 920 66 **Tel** *0954-305 15*

This 18th-century building is centrally located in Hemavan and is decorated in appropriate period style. Local delicacies include chicken fillet with cep-filled pasta and roasted garlic sauce. The adjacent timbered *stockstugan* (converted grain store built in the 1830s) lays on different themed buffets during the week.

JOKKMOKK Hotel Jokkmokk ▦ 🍽 V ⊗⊗

Solgatan 45, 962 31 **Tel** *0971-777 00*

Here's an opportunity to sample real Norrland food from this restaurant with stunning views over the Talvatis lake. Try regional favourites like *suovas* (smoked reindeer with juniper berry sauce) or the speciality of the house *Jokkmokkspan* (sliced reindeer, potatoes, mushrooms, onion and bacon with cream and lingonberries).

JUKKASJÄRVI Icehotel Restaurang V ⊗⊗⊗⊗

Marknadsvägen 63, 981 91 **Tel** *0980-668 00*

A memorable dining experience in a restaurant that serves up food on plates of ice made from the crystal-clear water of the nearby Torne River. A menu that celebrates Lappish cuisine includes mountain salmon, whiting and grayling, while an abundance of desserts are prepared from cloudberries, blueberries, lingonberries and arctic bramble.

LULEÅ Restaurang Ripan 🍽 V ⊗⊗

Varvsgatan 39, 972 32 **Tel** *0920-168 68*

Local ingredients and flavours form the heart of the menu at this recommended restaurant. Try the cured Artic char, served with Kalix whitefish roe, pickled onion, mild mustard crème and almond potatoe, and the warm cloudberry soup served with almond biscuits and vanilla or coffee ice cream. The restaurant has its own wine guide.

LULEÅ Tallkotten Restaurang 🏃 🍽 V ⊗⊗

Storgatan 15, 972 32 **Tel** *0920-27 40 20*

An Italian restaurant in Luleå with a good range of Mediterranean food, including some notable pasta dishes like *linguini* with scampi, courgette and cherry tomatoes and *Fagottini au gratin* filled with smoked ham and three cheeses. A nice wine list, naturally headlined by Italian producers such as Biondi Santi, Prunotto, Zenato and Sassicaia.

SKELLEFTEÅ Nordanågården 🏃 ▦ V ⊗⊗

Nordanåparken, 931 21 **Tel** *0910-533 50*

This relaxed restaurant is located in a scenic area, and is within walking distance of the town centre. The menu is wide-ranging, featuring homely fare, local specialities and gourmet dishes, which can be enjoyed in the beautifully decorated dining rooms or outside in summer.

UMEÅ Viktor 🍽 V ⊗⊗⊗

Vasagatan 11, 903 29 **Tel** *090-71 11 15*

An outstanding award-winning restaurant that is counted as one of the country's very best. The owners say they never follow a particular food trend – only to use the finest ingredients available. Chef Fredric Andersson has created an exquisite à la carte menu as well as attractively priced three- and four-course menus, including a vegetarian option.

VILHELMINA Hotell Wilhelmina V ⊗⊗⊗

Volgsjövägen 16, 912 34 **Tel** *0940-554 20*

From the distinguished dining room diners get panoramic views over Volgsjön and the Blaikfjället mountain range. Many of the ingredients are gathered from the countryside of southern Lappland and used to produce first-class traditional Swedish fare and an exciting à la carte menu with a regional twist.

SHOPPING IN SWEDEN

Nowadays Sweden is worth visiting for the shopping alone. In all Swedish towns, and even in the big cities, the shops are within easy walking distance of each other. The city centres offer a good range of small, trendy boutiques for fashion and interiors, shops for antiques and curios, luxury international designer outlets and well-stocked department stores. Cameras, mobile phones, furs, children's clothing, toys and Swedish glass

Dala horse
(see p312)

and designer goods are cheaper in Sweden than in many other countries. Those looking for a typical Swedish souvenir could buy a Dala horse or a proper Swedish schnapps glass from one of the factories in the Kingdom of Crystal. Although Lapland is a long way north, Sami handicrafts can be bought in most craft shops, including knives with carved bone handles and silverwork. Leather and fur goods are also good value.

OPENING TIMES

Most shops usually open at 10am and close at 6pm, although many in Stockholm city centre remain open until 7pm. Most shops are open until 2pm on Saturdays, while the major department stores stay open until 5pm. Large stores, shopping malls and some city-centre shops are open on Sundays. Market halls are closed on Sundays and public holidays. Many larger supermarkets are open daily until 8pm.

PAYMENT

All the major credit cards and traveller's cheques are accepted at most Swedish shops. You may be asked for proof of identity. Some larger shops also accept euros *(see p330)*. Goods can be exchanged if you produce the

receipt. Purchases can be made on a sale-or-return basis if this is noted on the receipt.

VALUE ADDED TAX

Value added tax ("MOMS" in Swedish) is charged on all items except daily newspapers. The VAT rate is 25 per cent; but only 12 per cent on food and 6 per cent on books. VAT is always included in the total price.

TAX-FREE SHOPPING

Residents of countries outside the European Union are entitled to a refund of the VAT paid on their purchases. Look for the "Tax-free shopping" sign in shop windows. Keep your receipts and on departure from the EU go to the Global Refund office at the airport or ferry terminal to obtain a 15–18 per cent refund.

Sale-time at an elegant shoe shop in Stockholm

SALES

Twice a year Sweden's shops and department stores have sales with reduced prices on clothing, shoes and other fashion goods. Sales are indicated by the *rea* sign. The year's first sales period starts after Christmas and continues throughout January. The second sales period lasts from late June to the end of July.

SHOPPING CENTRES AND DEPARTMENT STORES

The best-known Swedish superstore internationally is **IKEA**, which has 17 outlets across the country from Sundsvall in the north to Malmö in the south, and has become a popular tourist attraction in its own right. It sells not only furniture, but everything else for the home. The textiles section is particularly good, as well as

NK, Stockholm's most exclusive department store

IKEA's home furnishings stores can be found in many parts of Sweden

the kitchenware and china departments.

Another well-known store is the fashion house **H&M** (Hennes & Mauritz), which has branches in many towns. It stocks the latest fashions at low prices. H&M has its own designers and makes clothing for women, men, teenagers and children. The shops also sell accessories, underwear, perfume and cosmetics.

NK (Nordiska Kompaniet) in Stockholm and Gothenburg is Sweden's leading department store, in which many well-known names in fashion and cosmetics have their own outlets. NK is a practical choice for those in a hurry. It stocks everything from Swedish-designed products, jewellery, handicrafts and souvenirs to cameras, films, books and CDs.

Åhléns, which has stores in many towns and cities, offers most items at good prices.

Opened in the 19th century, but thoroughly modern, **PUB** is a haven for fashionistas.

Åfors glassworks store, Kingdom of Crystal, Småland (see pp152–3)

Almost every large town has its own shopping centre or mall with a standard range of stores such as H&M, Lindex, Kappahl, Twilfit and Dressmann (clothing), Guldfynd (jewellery), Duka (glass and china), Hemtex (textiles), Expert (cameras, stereos, TVs) and Teknikma-gasinet (electronics).

In Stockholm, **Gallerian** on Hamngatan is the largest mall and the prices are lower than in the elegant **Sturegallerian** near Stureplan with its many trendy boutiques.

Nordstan, off Brunnsparken in Gothenburg, is a mall with department stores such as Åhléns and specialist shops.

HansaCompagniet in central Malmö is a modern shopping centre.

A few examples of the larger shopping centres around the country include **Kungspassagen** in Umeå, **Forumgallerian** in Uppsala and **Krämaren** in Örebro.

Most towns have local markets selling flowers, fruit, vegetables and sometimes also handicrafts. Smaller places only have an outdoor market once a week, but in Hötorget in Stockholm, trading carries on every day except Sundays.

WINES AND SPIRITS

The only shops selling alcohol in Sweden are run by Systembolaget, the state monopoly chain. They are open Mon–Fri 10am–6pm and Sat 10am–2pm (except public holiday weekends). The minimum age for buying alcohol at Systembolaget shops is 20 and staff are entitled to ask for proof of age (see also p327).

What to Buy in Sweden

Elk candlestick

The Dala wooden horse must be the most typical Swedish souvenir. But it is facing strong competition from the elk, which has become a symbol for a nation with vast tracts of unspoilt countryside. The Swedes love the great outdoors, so there are plenty of shops selling top-class sporting equipment. Swedish glass and crystal are renowned around the world. Orrefors and Kosta are just two of several glassworks producing both classic and modern glassware. Educational toys in natural materials are a Swedish speciality and so are clogs, which can be found in most shoe shops.

Hand-painted clogs

HANDICRAFTS & DESIGN

Modern Swedish design is a familiar concept worldwide, even for simple everyday items *(see pp24–5)*. Handicrafts have a long tradition in Sweden and contemporary designers often use old crafts such as wrought-iron work, weaving, pottery and woodcarving.

Dala Horse and Cockerel
Originally the brightly painted Dala horses and cockerels were toys carved from left-over fragments of wood. Later the horse became a national symbol, now sold in many variants.

Swedish Glass
Hand-blown sets are made in Småland's glassworks, as well as artistic crystal creations and objects for daily use.

Cheese slicer and knife by Michael Björnstierna

Tray with design by Josef Frank, Svenskt Tenn

Nobel glass carafe from Orrefors by Gunnar Cyrén

Traditional schnapps glasses

Objects for the Home
The larger department stores often commission well-known designers for porcelain, glass, textiles and household items which make highly desirable gifts.

Mama, a humorous clothes hanger

Crux rug by Pia Wallén

Children's Toys
Colourful wooden toys from Brio are worldwide favourites. Educational picture books, games and puzzles are all excellent gifts for children.

OUTDOOR GEAR

Many Swedes enjoy outdoor pursuits such as fishing, hunting, sailing, golf, camping and all types of winter sports, so there are plenty of well-equipped sports shops around. Unique items include Sami handicrafts beautifully made from reindeer horn or skin.

Hand Knits

Caps and gloves with attractive designs, known as lovikka, *are made from a special wool which gives good protection in cold or wet conditions.*

Reindeer Skin Rucksack

Rucksacks have always been popular in Sweden. This exclusive leather model is made in Lapland.

Drinking vessel in carved wood

Sami Handicrafts

A hunting knife with a sheath of reindeer horn, or a kåsa, *a drinking vessel carved in birch, are not only attractive, but useful when out walking in the wild.*

Spinning Reel and Lures

ABU-Garcia makes top-quality fishing tackle, perfect for Sweden's long coastline, countless lakes and rivers with their rich and varied fishing.

SWEDISH DELICACIES

Among the many Swedish goodies are preserves made from wild berries, such as lingonberries (served with meatballs or pancakes) and cloudberries (delicious with whipped cream). Ginger biscuits are for Christmas while crispbread is great year-round, especially with herring.

Lingonberry preserve   **Cloudberry jam**

Pickled Herring

Pickled herring should be enjoyed with new potatoes cooked with dill, chopped chives and sour cream. Versions flavoured with mustard, dill or other herbs or spices are also available.

Swedish schnapps gift-pack miniatures

"Raspberry boat" candy   **Salt liquorice**   **Crispbread**   **Ginger biscuits**

Where to Shop in Sweden

Clothing from all the well-known international fashion houses can be found in Stockholm, Malmö and Gothenburg. If you want something rather different, it is worth seeking out the creations of younger Swedish fashion designers. Swedish interior design is famous for its clean lines, functionalism and the use of pale wood, and the country is a paradise for anyone interested in design. Handicrafts are of a high quality. Leisurewear and sports goods offer excellent value for money.

FASHION

Stockholm's top places for fashion are in the "golden triangle" bounded by Sturep-lan, Nybroplan and Norrmalmstorg. Clothing at more moderate prices can be bought in department centres and shopping centres across the country. **GeKås** in Ullared and **Knalleland** in Borås have become popular attractions due to their very low prices and large number of stores and factory outlets, not least in the "mail-order town" of Borås, with its weaving and textile traditions.

If you are looking for Swedish designers, **NK** in Stockholm and Gothenburg *(see p311)* has a good selection of clothing created by younger designers as well as mainstream Swedish brands. Classic men's clothing of high quality is designed by Oscar Jacobsson, while Stenström shirts are sold in department stores and the more elegant menswear boutiques. **Björn Borg** has his own shops selling men's and women's clothing and underwear, perfume and accessories. The designer **Filippa K** produces smart clothing for fashionable women and men.

DESIGN AND INTERIOR DECORATION

Stockholm, Gothenburg and Malmö have a number of interior decoration shops selling the products of young designers and well-known artists. To see the latest on offer, it is worth visiting **DesignTorget**, which has stores in all three cities displaying designers' work. Stockholm's **R.O.O.M** on Kungsholmen and **Asplund** in

Östermalm, and **Norrgavel** in Stockholm, Gothenburg, Malmö and Lammhult, are just a few of the shops with the most up-to-the-minute selection of products. **Svenskt Tenn** is Stockholm's oldest shop for interiors, with both new and classic designs. **Nordiska Galleriet** in Stockholm has exclusive modern furniture and decorative items, while **Blås & Knåda** on Hornsgatan displays and sells the largest selection of contemporary Swedish ceramics and glass, both objects of art and items for everyday use. **Nordiska Kristall** on Kungsgatan has a wide choice of Swedish glassware, which can also be found in department stores.

MUSIC AND MULTIMEDIA

Many Swedish pop bands now have an international reputation. Exciting new talents continue to find their way into the charts, and the latest products can often be bought in the large record shops before they become available outside Sweden. Apart from pop and rock, Sweden has a long folk-music tradition, as well as many jazz musicians and opera singers. **MEGA Skivakademien** in Stockholm stocks a wide selection of CDs, as do the large department stores.

SPORT AND LEISURE

The Swedes devote a lot of time to outdoor sports and activities. With shops all over the country, **Naturkompaniet** and **Peak Performance** have an exclusive selection of sportswear and equipment. **Stadium** and **Intersport** have a varied choice of sports

clothing and equipment at attractive prices and are also nationwide. Good equipment and exclusive clothing for hunting and fishing can be bought at **Walter Borg** in central Stockholm. **Löplabbet** countrywide specializes in running and jogging.

SOUVENIRS AND HANDICRAFTS

Schnapps glasses, silver jewellery, hand-painted clogs, Sami crafts, hand-knitted garments, candles, Christmas decorations and wrought-iron products can all be bought in department stores and shops specialising in Swedish handicrafts.

At Skansen open-air museum in Stockholm, visitors can shop for handicrafts in attractive little houses.

Nusnäs in Dalarna is the place to buy the original Dala horse, which can be found at **Nils Olsson Hemslöjd AB**.

Yllet in Visby sells hand-spun wool, woollen garments and sheepskin goods.

MARKETS

Small local markets can be found almost everywhere, but a few have become so big that they have attracted international attention.

Jokkmokk's winter market (1st Thu–Sat in Feb) is a major Sami market. Skänninge market (1st Wed–Thu in Aug) is a classic affair dating back to the Middle Ages. The Kivik market (mid-Sep) is like an amusement park. Michaelmas markets are held in central Sweden in autumn.

The bustling flea market in Skärholmen, Stockholm, is the place to find a bargain every day of the week. Entrance fee Sat–Sun, free on other days.

GLASS AND CHINA

Most department stores and gift shops sell glass from Swedish manufacturers. Visitors to the Kingdom of Crystal in Småland have a choice of no fewer than 14 glassworks within a radius of a few miles *(see pp152–3)*. At **Orrefors Kosta Boda Glasbruk**, there are bargains to be had among the everyday glassware and the studio glass. **Reijmyre** in Östergötland is also popular among bargainhunters. For porcelain, the factory shop at **Rörstrand** offers value for money.

SWEDISH DELICACIES

The capital has three market halls – **Östermalmshallen, Hötorgshallen** and **Söderhallarna** – which are a joy to just wander around. Salmon, bleak roe, smoked eel and smoked reindeer meat are all delicious culinary souvenirs. Malmö's **Johan P** and Gothenburg's **Briggen** are also pleasant market halls offering mouth-watering Swedish delicacies.

On the west coast, seafood is a must and whether you are after prawns, crab or autumn's black gold, lobster, it is best purchased at the harbourside when the boats come in. In the north, game of various kinds is the big attraction and you can often find smoked reindeer and reindeer heart in grocery stores, along with fermented Baltic herring and Norrland cloudberry jam.

Swedish crispbread is another delicacy and the bakery in Leksand has a factory shop. Traditional red and white striped candy rock originates from Gränna, which has a large number of shops selling rock.

DIRECTORY

FASHION

Björn Borg
Sergelgatan 12,
Stockholm. **Map** 1 C4.
Tel 08-21 70 40.

Charlotte Göteborg
Drottninggatan 28,
Gothenburg.
Map see p192.
Tel 031-701 75 40.

Dunderdon
Magasinsgatan 5, Gothenburg. **Map** see p192.
Tel 031-734 34 40.

Filippa K
Grev Turegatan 18,
Stockholm. **Map** 2 D4.
Tel 08-545 882 57.

Ge-Kås i Ullared
Danska Vägen, Falkenberg.
Tel 0346-375 00.

Knalleland
Bergslenagatan 45, Borås.
Tel 033-14 03 35.

MQ
Södra Tullgatan 3, Malmö.
Tel 040-12 01 31.
Strömpilsplatsen 1, Umeå.
Tel 090-786 36 80.

Olsén Mode
Södergatan 21, Malmö.
Map see p179.
Tel 040-12 10 50.

DESIGN AND INTERIORS

Asplund
Sibyllegatan 31,
Stockholm. **Map** 2 E3.
Tel 08-662 52 84.

Blås & Knåda
Hornsgatan 26,
Stockholm.
Map 3 A5.
Tel 08-642 77 67.

DesignTorget
Kulturhuset,
Sergels Torg 3, Stockholm.
Map 1 C4.
Tel 08–21 91 50.
Södra Vallgatan 3.
Tel 040-30 70 82.
Vallgatan 14, Gothenburg.
Map see p192.
Tel 031-774 00 17.

Establish
Humlegårdsgatan 14,
Stockholm.
Map 2 E3.
Tel 08-545 853 40.

Nordiska Galleriet
Nybrogatan 11,
Stockholm.
Map 2 E4.
Tel 08-442 83 60.

Nordiska Kristall
Kungsgatan 9,
Stockholm.
Map 2 E4.
Tel 08-10 43 72.

Norrgavel
Birger Jarlsgatan 27,
Stockholm.
Map 2 D3.
Tel 08-545 220 50.
Engelbrektsgatan 20,
Malmö. **Map** see p179.
Tel 040-12 22 46.

R.O.O.M
Alströmergatan 20,
Stockholm.
Tel 08-692 50 00.

Svenskt Tenn
Strandvägen 5, Stockholm.
Map 2 E4.
Tel 08-670 16 00.

MUSIC

Bengans Skivbutik
Stigbergstorget 1,
Gothenburg.
Tel 031-14 33 00.

Mega Skivakademien
Mäster Samuelsgatan 32,
Stockholm.
Map 1 C4.
Tel 08-566 157 00.

SPORT AND LEISURE

Intersport
Björnvägen 1, Umeå.
Tel 090-70 63 63.

Löplabbet
Djäknegatan 2, Malmö.
Tel 040-12 35 70.

Naturkompaniet
Kungsgatan 4A,
Stockholm. **Map** 2 D4.
Tel 08-723 15 81.

Peak Performance
Biblioteksgatan 18,
Stockholm.
Map 2 D4.
Tel 08-611 34 00.
Södergatan 9,
Malmö.
Map see p179.
Tel 040-97 02 20.

Stadium
Fredsgatan 8, Gothenburg.
Map see p192.
Tel 031-711 06 09.

Walter Borg
Kungsgatan 57B,
Stockholm. **Map** 1 C4.
Tel 08-14 38 65.

SOUVENIRS AND HANDICRAFTS

Nils Olsson Hemslöjd AB
Edåkersvägen 17, Nusnäs.
Tel 0250-372 00.

Svensk Hemslöjd
Sveavägen 44, Stockholm.
Map 1 C3.
Tel 08-23 21 15.

Yllet
St Hansgatan 19, Visby.
Tel 0498-21 40 44.

GLASS AND CHINA

Orrefors Kosta Boda Glasbruk
Kosta. **Tel** 0478-345 00.
Orrefors. **Tel** 0481-341 89.

Reijmyre
Rejmyre.
Tel 011-871 84.

Rörstrand (littala)
Lidköping.
Tel 0510-823 46.
Gustavsborg.
Tel 08-570 356 55.

SWEDISH DELICACIES

Briggen
Linnéstaden, Gothenburg.

Hötorgshallen
Hötorget, Stockholm.
Map 1 C4.

Johan P
Saluhallen, Malmö.

Östermalmshallen
Östermalmstorg,
Stockholm.
Map 2 E4.

ENTERTAINMENT IN SWEDEN

The range of cultural events and entertainment in Sweden is large and richly varied. The whole spectrum is covered from outdoor celebrations to mark local customs to top international acts performing in giant arenas. The seasons have an effect on what's on: large city theatres tend to close during the summer and launch their new programmes of plays, opera and dance in late August or early September. Meanwhile, summer reviews, popular comedies and local historical plays are staged across the country. In parks, palace gardens and amusement parks, summer is a particularly eventful time, with artists of every imaginable kind putting on a performance. Added to that are the countless markets, festivals covering film, jazz, music, food, theatre, folklore, and much more besides. Winter brings ski races and skating, indoor fairs and Christmas markets. Nightlife continues all year. There are excellent nightclubs and casinos in the major cities. Jazz clubs and pubs offer a wide range of live music to suit all tastes.

Folk Dancers, Rättvik

SOURCES OF INFORMATION

A reliable source of information is **Sveriges Rese-och Turistråd**'s official tourist and events guide on the Internet. This provides listings for everything from music and sport to seasonal events such as Medieval Week in Visby or the Vasaloppet ski race in Dalarna. The site has links to the websites of Stockholm, Gothenburg and Malmö, but also has details of events across the country.

Daily newspapers and free local papers are an excellent source for regional events such as concerts, theatre performances and nightclubs. The tourist information offices and most hotels also have listings and can often help with advice and booking tickets.

BOOKING TICKETS

Tickets for most events can usually be bought at the box office of the theatre or sports arena in question, but to ensure admission it may be more practical to book in advance, with the help either of the hotel or a tourist information office. Another alternative is to use a booking agency, such as **Biljett Direkt**, which, for a small fee, will take telephone bookings for tickets to stage shows, concerts and sports events. At **Box-office** in Stockholm, tickets can be purchased over the counter for various events in Sweden and beyond, and tickets ordered via the event organizer can be collected. Many tickets are also sold via the gaming agent ATG across the country.

Dalhalla's music stage *(see p241)* in a dramatic quarry near Rättvik

MAJOR ARENAS AND CULTURAL CENTRES

In addition to the long-established, traditional theatres, many towns and cities have more recently built multi-purpose cultural complexes offering a wide spectrum of public events. Often such centres are home to the local theatre company and orchestra.

The major entertainment and event arenas such as **Globen** in Stockholm, the **Malmö Arena** in Malmö and **Scandinavium** in Gothenburg have a huge audience capacity. International rock and pop concerts, charity galas and major sporting events are usually held at these enormous venues.

In the summer, the large outdoor stages, for example at Skansen and Gröna Lund in Stockholm, Liseberg in Gothenburg and Dalhalla, between Rättvik and Mora, attract a wide range of jazz, folk and classical artists alike.

Sea of people at the Philharmonic's annual outdoor concert, Stockholm

THEATRE

Sweden has almost 500 theatres spread across the country. Many are town or county theatres, but there are also private theatres with long traditions and small park and amateur theatres.

Sweden's national theatre is **Kungliga Dramatiska Teatern** *(see p71)*, which has six stages. It regularly mounts international and Swedish classics, including Shakespeare and Strindberg, as well as modern foreign and Swedish works.

Lighter plays and musicals are often performed at **ChinaTeatern** in Stockholm and **Lorensbergsteatern** in Gothenburg. Venues such as **Konsertteatern** in Sundsvall and **Göta Lejon** in Stockholm often stage performances suitable forchildren and families.

CLASSICAL MUSIC, DANCE AND OPERA

World-class music can be heard at **Berwaldhallen** in Stockholm, the home of Sveriges Radios Symfoniorkester and the Radiokören choir, considered one of the internationally leading a cappella ensembles. **Konserthuset** *(see p68)* is the base for Kungliga Filharmoniska Orkestern. The season runs from August to May.

Konserthuset in Gothenburg is home to Göteborgs Symfoniker. Norrköping has the **De Geerhallen** venue and Folkets Park in Sundsvall has **Tonhallen**, one of Sweden's best concert halls.

Classical opera and ballet of the highest quality can be seen at **Kungliga Operan** *(see p66)*. Every season at least

Sundsvalls Teater, an ambitious, go-ahead regional theatre

GöteborgsOperan, with a wide repertoire of opera and musicals

three major ballets delight packed houses. This venue also stages traditional performances of most operas in their original language. During the summer, popular opera performances are held at **Drottningholms Slottsteater** *(see p109)*. All the operas staged here are from the 18th century, with an orchestra of the period.

The spectacular modern **GöteborgsOperan** *(see p196)* is an exciting, internationally-renowned venue for opera, ballet and musicals. Norrlandsoperan in Umeå and Malmö Opera och Musikteater are two of the country's other major venues for opera and ballet.

Dansens Hus in Stockholm, which has taken over the National Theatre's former venue, often hosts top-name dance companies from Sweden and abroad.

FOLK MUSIC

Swedish folk music is enjoying a resurgence in popularity. Skansen in Stockholm *(see p92)* is the prime venue, where musicians and folk dancing troupes perform regularly at traditional events. However, there are local folk groups and regional clubs covering practically every corner of the country. The easiest way of finding out where and how to enjoy Swedish folk music is to check at the local tourist information office or in the local press.

There are a few permanent venues for folk music: **Folkmusikhuset** in Stockholm,

Folkmusikkaféet in Gothenburg and **Folkmusikens Hus** in Rättvik are just some of the places offering a wide programme of performances and information about forthcoming events.

CHURCH MUSIC

Many churches in the cities hold organ recitals at lunchtime, for example Jacobs Kyrka in Stockholm *(see p66)*, where visitors can take a breather in a tranquil setting. Storkyrkan *(see p53)* also holds concerts on Saturday and Sunday afternoons in the spring and autumn. The cathedrals of Uppsala Domkyrka *(see p128)* and Västerås Domkyrka *(see p138)* stage organ recitals every Saturday. Many churches also have a concert programme, particularly in conjunction with major religious festivals.

ROCK AND POP

The largest of the rock and pop venues are **Globen** in Stockholm, the **Malmö Arena** in Malmö and **Scandinavium** in Gothenburg. These attract top international artists, along with the many successful Swedish bands. **Cirkus** in Stockholm is a well-established venue for music and theatre in a beautiful old setting. More modern rock venues include **Münchenbryggeriet** in Stockholm, **Kulturbolaget** in Malmö and **Trädgår'n** in Gothenburg. Around the country there are smaller theatres, students' unions and clubs where groups and artists perform.

Concert in the ruins of Bohus Castle in Kungälv

JAZZ CLUBS

Jazz has enjoyed a renaissance in recent years and the range on offer increases annually. One venue of repute is **Fasching** in Stockholm, with performances almost daily. Another jazz haunt in the capital is **Stampen**, which attracts a rather more mature audience. Gothenburg has **Nefertiti** and in Malmö there is **Jeriko**. Across the country there are jazz clubs holding concerts once a month or so.

Jazz cruises have become popular in the summer. The Stockholm archipelago is plied by *S/S Blidösund*. Cruises are also organized elsewhere in the country, for instance across Lake Vättern and the Åland Sea, on the Dalälven river and out into the Gothenburg archipelago.

MUSIC PUBS

Swedish pub culture has changed enormously and it is becoming increasingly common to follow the Continental pattern of slipping into a bar or pub for a while after work, having a beer and listening to music.

Many pubs have introduced live music – some have folk singers performing on a regular basis, while others have a DJ. The best way of being sure to hear live music is to scan the local press entertainment *(nöjen)* pages.

In Stockholm, the Irish pub **The Dubliner** offers live Irish music. The popular **Engelen**

bar has live music several days a week. Gothenburg's finest pubs include **Sticky Fingers** and Jameson's pub, and Helsingborg has its own English pub, Charles Dickens, where the clientele can enjoy karaoke, live music, singers, bands and various other forms of entertainment.

There are a number of traditional English and Irish-style pubs spread across the country, usually offering a wide range of beer and spirits and serving a selection of bar snacks.

NIGHTCLUBS, CASINOS AND SHOWS

Generally speaking, night-clubs hold traditional disco nights on Friday and Saturday. During the rest of the week the venue is usually hired by various clubs focusing on different styles of music. Almost all the larger towns and cities have one or two nightclubs, but the quality varies, as does the music on offer. In Stockholm,

A traditional folk music festival in Tällberg on Lake Siljan in Dalarna

the majority and the best of the capital's nightclubs are located around Stureplan. At the rear of the Opera House is **Café Opera**, Stockholm's longest-established nightclub, with an international style. The crowd is usually quite mixed – young, trendy types and older, smartly-dressed folks. **Sturecompagniet** is a large club on several floors. At street level there is also a rock bar. Swedish celebrities and visiting foreign stars mingle at top celeb hangout **Spy Bar**, but it can be difficult to get in on certain nights. Other well-known nightclubs include **Crown** in Malmö and **Gutekällaren** in Visby.

A relative newcomer to the entertainment scene is the state-run casino chain **Casino Cosmopol**, which to date has opened branches in Stockholm, Gothenburg, Malmö and Sundsvall.

A combination of good food and top-flight entertainment is on offer at **Hamburger Börs** in Stockholm, with its shows featuring the best Swedish artists. **Wallmans Salonger**, which can be found in Stockholm and Malmö, offers musical entertainment with dinner served by waiters and waitresses who are, in fact, professional performers.

In Gothenburg, **Rondo** is a classic show venue.

FESTIVALS

Countless festivals large and small are organized all across Sweden in the summer. Almost every town has its own festival, some with a specific focus, such as folk, jazz or rock.

Among the most renowned of the local festivals are Göteborgskalaset in Gothenburg, Storsjöyran in Östersund and Gatufesten in Sundsvall.

There are numerous music festivals, the largest of which – for example the Hultsfred Festival – attract huge audiences. Other famous music festivals include the Falun Folk Music Festival, the Sweden Rock Festival in Sölvesborg, the Gotland Chamber Music Festival in Visby, the Stockholm Jazz Festival and the Umeå International Jazz Festival.

The best-known film festivals are the **Gothenburg Film Festival** (Jan/Feb) and the **Stockholm International Film Festival** (Nov), but several other cities and towns hold their own film festivals with a different focus, such as Umeå (Sep).

DIRECTORY

SOURCES OF INFORMATION

Sveriges Rese- och Turistråd
www.visit-sweden.com
Tel 08- 789 10 00.

BOOKING TICKETS

Biljett Direkt
www.ticnet.se
Tel 077-170 70 70.

Box-office
Kungsgatan 38, Stockholm. *Tel 08-10 88 00.*

ARENAS, CULTURAL CENTRES

Globen
Globentorget 2, Stockholm.
Tel 077-131 00 00.

Malmö Arena
Arenagatan 15, Malmö.
Tel 0775-78 00 00.

Scandinavium
Valhallagatan 1, Gothenburg. *Tel 031-81 10 20.*

THEATRE

China Teatern
Berzelii Park, Stockholm.
Tel 08-566 323 50.

Göta Lejon
Götgatan 55, Stockholm.
Tel 08-643 67 00.

Konsertteatern
Köpmangatan 11, Sundsvall. *Tel 060-61 32 62.*

Kungliga Dramatiska Teatern
Nybroplan, Stockholm.
Tel 08-667 06 80.

Lorensbergsteatern
Lorensbergsparken, Gothenburg. *Tel 031-708 62 00.*

CLASSICAL MUSIC, DANCE, OPERA

Berwaldhallen
Dag Hammarskjölds Väg 3, Stockholm.
Tel 08-784 50 00.

Dansens Hus
Barnhusgatan 12–14, Stockholm. **Map** 1 C3.
Tel 08-508 990 90.

De Geerhallen
Dalsgatan 15, Norrköping.
Tel 011-15 50 30.

Drottningholms Slottsteater
Drottningholms Slott, Lovön, W of Stockholm.
Tel 08-660 82 25.

GöteborgsOperan
Christina Nilssons Gata, Gothenburg.
Tel 031-13 13 00.

Konserthuset
Götaplatsen, Gothenburg.
Tel 031-726 53 00.

Konserthuset
Hötorget, Stockholm. **Map** 1 C4. *Tel 08-786 02 00.*

Kungliga Operan
Gustav Adolfs Torg, Stockholm. **Map** 2 D5.
Tel 08-791 43 00.

Tonhallen
Universitetsallén 22, Sundsvall. *Tel 060-19 88 00.*

FOLK MUSIC

Folkmusikens Hus
Dalagatan 7, Rättvik.
Tel 0248-79 70 50.

Folkmusikhuset
Skeppsholmsgården, Stockholm. **Map** 2 E5.
Tel 08-411 99 88.

Folkmusikkaféet
Allégården, Gothenburg.
www.folkmusikkafeet.net

ROCK AND POP

Cirkus
Djurgårdsslätten, Stockholm. *Tel 08-587 987 00.*

Kulturbolaget
Bergsgatan 18, Malmö.
Tel 040-30 20 11.

Münchenbryggeriet
Torkel Knutssonsg 2, Stockholm.
Tel 08-658 20 00.

Trädgår'n
Nya Allén, Gothenburg.
Tel 031-10 20 80.

JAZZ CLUBS

Fasching
Kungsgatan 63, Stockholm. **Map** 1 B4.
Tel 08-534 829 60.

Jeriko
Spångatan 38, Malmö.
Tel 040-611 84 29.

Nefertiti
Hvitfeldtsplatsen 6, Gothenburg.
Tel 031-711 15 33.

Stampen
Stora Nygatan 5, Stockholm. **Map** 3 B4.
Tel 08-20 57 93.

MUSIC PUBS

Engelen
Kornhamnstorg 59 B, Stockholm. **Map** 3 B4.
Tel 08-505 560 90.

Sticky Fingers
Kaserntorget 7, Gothenburg.
Tel 031-701 00 17.

The Dubliner
Smålandsgatan 8, Stockholm.
Map 2 D4.
Tel 08-679 77 07.

NIGHTCLUBS, CASINOS, SHOWS

Café Opera
Operahuset, Stockholm.
Map 3 B1.
Tel 08-676 58 07.

Casino Cosmopol
Kungsgatan 65, Stockholm. **Map** 1 B4.
Tel 08-781 88 00.
Packhusplatsen 7, Gothenburg.
Tel 031-333 55 00.
Slottsgatan 33, Malmö.
Tel 040-664 18 00.
Casinoparken 1, Sundsvall.
Tel 060-14 11 00.

Crown
Amiralsgatan 19, Malmö.
Tel 040-611 80 88.

Gutekällaren
Stora Torget, Visby.
Tel 0498-21 00 43.

Hamburger Börs
Jakobsgatan 6, Stockholm.
Map 2 D5.
Tel 08-787 85 00.

Rondo
Örgrytevägen 5, Gothenburg. *Tel 031-40 02 00.*

Spy Bar
Birger Jarlsgatan 20, Stockholm. **Map** 2 D3.
Tel 08-545 076 55.

Sturecompagniet
Sturegatan 4, Stockholm.
Map 2 D3.
Tel 08-545 076 70.

Wallmans Salonger
Teatergatan 3, Stockholm.
Map 2 E5.
Tel 08-505 560 00.
Generalsgatan 1, Malmö.
Tel 040-749 45.

FESTIVALS

Gothenburg Film Festival
Heurlins Plats 11, Gothenburg.
www.filmfestival.org
Tel 031-339 30 00.

Stockholm International Film Festival
Slupskjulsvägen 36, Stockholm. **Map** 4 E2.
www.filmfestivalen.se
Tel 08 677 50 00.

SPORTS AND OUTDOOR ACTIVITIES

S weden has countryside in abundance and the *"alle-mannsrätt"* (Right to Roam) makes it accessible in a way rarely found elsewhere in the world. No wonder an active outdoor life has become such a staple of the Swedish lifestyle. Constantly rising demand for outdoor activities has led to an increasing range of trails for hiking, canoeing and cycling, and the construction of hundreds of new ski lifts, golf courses and

Recommended cycle trail

guest harbours. There has also been a boom in adventure sports – from challenging hikes in remote mountain regions and sea kayaking in the outer archipelagos to competing in the long-distance Vasaloppet skiing race, the Vansbrosimningen swimming race or the Vätternrundan cycling race, which together make up what is known as the "Swedish Classic". More leisurely pursuits include horse riding and fishing.

GENERAL INFORMATION

In addition to the tourist information offices, there are a number of organizations to assist outdoors enthusiasts. The state-run **Naturvårds-verket** has an excellent website, which also provides useful information about Sweden's 28 national parks. **Friluftsfrämjandet** is a 100-year-old voluntary organization – the backbone of outdoor life for its many activities and operations.

HIKING TRAILS

Although it is possible to pitch a tent almost anywhere, it is often more practical to follow one of the many well-tended hiking trails. There are numerous lowland trails, such as the Skåneleden, which runs south to north through Skåne. Mountain trails proliferate, the

best of which is the renowned Kungsleden stretching 450 km (280 miles) *(see pp274–5)*.

Maps of the trails usually provide information about stopping-off points, attractions, accommodation and services along the way.

The most popular mountain areas have marked trails for day trips and longer hikes with overnight accommodation in huts and at mountain stations. For more than 100 years, **Svenska Turistföreningen (STF)** has been the main provider of services in the mountains in summer and winter.

The mountain trails mainly run through road-free land. There are STF mountain stations at strategic locations from Abisko in Lapland to Grövelsjön in Dalarna. Although out in the wilds, these are relatively easy to access and make an excellent starting point for hiking tours

Walking with poles, a popular form of exercise

in the mountains. The stations have hotel-standard accommodation, restaurants, self-catering kitchens, shops and equipment hire.

Along the trails, there are simple huts in which to stay, with a self-catering kitchen and in some cases provisions for sale. Space cannot be booked in advance, but everyone usually gets a roof over their head. In the summer, STF has special hosts to help with tips and advice.

The trails crossing the high mountains can be extremely demanding for the uninitiated. It is important not to be too ambitious and to have appropriate equipment.

Whatever the time of year, the weather changes quickly, so keep up to date with the forecast, which is usually posted at stations and huts. The summer season for mountain hiking is from about mid-June to mid-September.

A hiker en route to the Sylarna mountain station, Jämtland

One of STF's many huts across the mountains

ENDURANCE TESTS

Competitions for elite athletes and fitness enthusiasts alike have become increasingly popular in Sweden, attracting thousands of participants of all levels. Some enter the "Swedish Classic", in which over one year competitors ski the Vasaloppet *(see p245)* or Engelbrektsloppet (60 km/37 miles), cycle the Vätternrundan (300 km/190 miles), swim the Vansbrosimningen (3 km/2 miles) and run the Lidingöloppet (30 km/19 miles). Other events include the Stockholm Marathon *(see p27)* and the O-ringen in orienteering.

SWIMMING

There are generally no restrictions for anyone wanting to take a dip in lakes, rivers and the sea. However, there is no need to take any risks as there are thousands of public bathing areas where the water quality is checked by the health authorities. Even in the north,

there are plenty of opportunities to swim, for example at Pite Havsbad, where the sunny beaches are known as "The Nordic Riviera" *(see p268)*. In many places, the natural bathing spots are supplemented by water parks and fun pools offering all kinds of watery activities, such as at Skara Sommarland *(see p223)* and Sydpoolen in Södertälje.

Generally, water quality is high in Sweden and even in the cities it is sometimes possible to swim from rocks and beaches. Långholmen in central Stockholm is a favourite spot for a dip. In hot summers, however, poisonous algae sometimes blooms along the coast, so take advice locally on whether swimming is advisable.

Indoor pools are a popular choice. Stockholm has the historic Centralbadet and Sturebadet among others.

The spa and bathing culture has a long tradition in Sweden, particularly in places such as Loka Brunn *(see p139)*, with its modern facilities.

CYCLING

Pedal power is a great way to experience towns and countryside alike. The bicycle has enjoyed something of a renaissance in Sweden and Stockholm in particular has invested heavily in cycle paths and special cycle routes.

Cycling holidays have long been popular on islands with little traffic such as Öland and Gotland. However, there are now cycle trails following minor roads and disused railway lines, often marked by green cycle-trail signs. A wide range of cycling packages are available and there are plenty of places to hire bicycles, tandems and trailers.

There are 30 or so regional cycle trails around the country, which require one or more stopovers to complete the distance. They can often be combined with the extensive Sverigeleden national trail which runs 2,590 km (1,600 miles) from Helsingborg in the south to Karesuando in the far north. The trail is well-signposted and special maps are available.

On the easier routes, 97 per cent of which are paved, those who have the time for a really long cycling holiday can experience Sweden's ever-changing landscape. Information about cycling trails is available from **Svenska Cykelsällskapet**.

Another option for those who fancy pedalling is to take a trolley trip on several railway tracks across the country where rail traffic has ceased.

A cycling trip on Visingsö in Lake Vättern, offering easy routes, fascinating sights and beautiful countryside

Trekkers heading for Storsylen in the Jämtland mountains

WINTER ACTIVITIES

It is no surprise that Swedish skiers have dominated the World Cup at times, both in downhill and cross-country skiing. In winter, much of the country is covered in snow and there is some great skiing to be had.

There is an extensive network of cross-country skiing trails, many of which are floodlit, a necessity during the long dark evenings. It is also possible to ski on snow-covered golf courses or on iced-over lakes and the frozen waters of the archipelagos. The ice is also ideal for skating, an enjoyable experience on a sunny winter's day. Check the safety information first, as things can quickly turn serious if the ice cracks.

Sweden has hundreds of lifts for downhill skiers, which

Snowboarding and skiing are popular in the Swedish mountains

are listed on the website for the skiing organization **SLAO**. **Skistar** deal with reservations for Sweden's two largest ski resorts: Åre, 600 km (370 miles) north of Stockholm, and Sälen, just over 400 km (250 miles) north of the capital. Most people on mountain holidays stay in self-catering cottages or apartments. Accommodation must be booked well in advance, particularly during the high season, and usually for complete weeks (Sun–Sun), weekends (Thu–Sun) or short weeks (Sun–Thu). It is easiest to buy lift passes and hire skis or snowboards at the resort.

GOLF

Swedish golfers have achieved major successes in recent years, particularly in the ladies' events, with Anna Nordqvist leading the way. This golfing phenomenon is partly due to the ambitious junior programme supported by many of the country's golf clubs. Under the umbrella of the **Svenska Golfförbundet**, there are more than 400 golf courses, an extremely high figure in relation to the population size. Although the climate in parts of the country may be considered unsuitable for golf, the courses offer high quality during the summer. Almost all courses are

open to guest players, but demand is great and it can be difficult to find a suitable tee-ing-off time in high season at many clubs. Green fees vary from 150 kr on basic courses to more than 500 kr at exclusive city clubs. You must be a member of a golf club to play as a guest on a Swedish course.

HORSE RIDING

Horse riding is a popular sport in Sweden, and there are almost 1,000 riding clubs. There is a wide range of riding available, from trips for beginners on Icelandic ponies to mountain trekking for those with experience. The tourist offices can provide local contacts.

Trekking on Icelandic ponies

BOATING, CANOEING, WHITE-WATER RAFTING

The long coastline, inviting archipelagos and numerous lakes make exploring the country by water particularly rewarding. There are almost 500 classified guest harbours offering good facilities for sailors. The classification is administered by **Svenska Kryssarklubben**, which is also a good source of information about natural harbours and boating in general. All types of craft from simple rowing boats to large motor boats and yachts can be hired from marinas around the country. **Maringuiden** offers a wealth of useful information.

Although there are no specific requirements for sailing smaller boats, you will need basic knowledge of boating even for a day trip. As a rule, documented qualifications equivalent to the Swedish skipper's certificate *"förar-intyg"* are required for taking out larger boats.

There are great opportunities for canoeing, with almost 20,000 km (12,500 miles) of trails on inland waters and around the archipelagos. The website for **Kanotleder i Sverige** lists 400 tours in Canadian canoes and kayaks, along with canoeing centres and rental sites across the country. For more advanced canoeists, there are plenty of opportunities to try sea kayaks in the outer archipelagos and white-water canoeing on the Norrland rivers. White-water rides are also possible, heading down the rapids in large rubber rafts or up on jetskis.

Rod fishing, often free along Sweden's lengthy coastline

HUNTING AND FISHING

Sweden has more than 300,000 hunters and during the elk hunting season some forest villages are packed. Around 100,000 elks are shot every year. As a guest of land owners and hunting teams, foreign hunters can take part in small game and elk hunts. However, in the latter case, a special elk shooting test is required as well as a hunting permit. Taking your own weapon requires a great deal of bureaucracy, so hiring a weapon is recommended. Details about conditions, hunting times and hunt organizers are available from **Svenska Jägareförbundet**.

A third of all Swedes go fishing at least once a year, and no wonder with access to

the most extensive fishing waters in Europe. There are more than 200 species of saltwater fish on the west coast, some of which also venture into the brackish water of the Baltic Sea. Added to this are around 40 species of freshwater fish in the lakes and rivers.

Rod fishing in coastal waters is often free. In other waters, the necessary fishing permit can be purchased locally. The **Sveafiskekortet** permit is a nationwide option offered by Sveaskog, which administers the national forests and land covering a fifth of the country. Sweden's leading and most traditional salmon fishing waters in Blekinge's Mörrum (*see p187*) are also state-owned.

Salmon and sea trout can even be fished in the heart of Stockholm, where Strömmen has unusually clean water for a city of a million people.

Fishing trips by boat are offered widely. **Sportfiskarna** provides information about sport fishing.

Experiencing the Swedish countryside by canoe

SURVIVAL
GUIDE

PRACTICAL INFORMATION

Sweden is a country of huge distances – it is as far from Malmö in the south to Treriksröset in the north as it is from Malmö to Rome. So, it is worth planning any trip in advance. The local tourist offices publish useful information on the Internet. All types of accommodation from luxury hotels to bed-and-breakfasts can be booked online. Once you have arrived in Sweden, there are more than

Tourist office symbol

300 authorized tourist information offices nationwide which can provide help. The towns all have modern facilities for the traveller, including banking services and emergency medical care, and the public telephone system is first-class. Customs and border controls now apply mainly to travellers from countries outside the EU. For EU citizens and Norwegians, the entry procedure is relatively straightforward.

TOURIST INFORMATION

Sweden has a number of tourist offices abroad, run by **Sveriges Rese- och Turistråd**. An overview of what's on offer for tourists and links to all the local tourist offices can be found at www.visit-sweden.com.

Another user-friendly general website is **Svensk TuristGuide** at www.sverige turism.se. Visitors can click on the map to reach regional tourism organizations and obtain detailed information about accommodation, eating out, attractions and events. Brochures and travel tips can also be requested by e-mail or phone.

In addition to the 300 official tourist information offices, information points open in summer, often attached to larger attractions. Offices with the blue and yellow "i" sign usually offer a broader service than those with the green and white "i".

The hub of Stockholm's tourist information is the **Tourist Centre Stockholm** in Sverigehuset.

PASSPORTS AND CUSTOMS

Citizens of virtually all countries can enter Sweden as tourists without a visa. Norwegians and visitors from European countries which have signed the Schengen agreement do not, in principle, need a passport. However, all airlines require passports for passengers flying from countries outside the Nordic region, so it is always wise to carry your passport.

Different customs regulations apply to travellers from the European Union (EU) and those from other countries. Citizens of EU countries can take an unlimited amount of alcohol and tobacco products into Sweden without having to pay tax, provided they are for personal use. Citizens from non-EU countries can take in 1 litre of spirits or 2 litres of fortified wine, including sparkling wine, 4 litres of wine, 16 litres of beer, 200 cigarettes, or 100 cigarillos, or 50 cigars or 250 g tobacco. But they can only take in goods up to a value of

1,700 Kr in addition to normal travel-related items. To import alcohol, you must be 20 years old, and for tobacco, 18.

Items such as milk, cheese, butter, eggs and potatoes may not be taken into Sweden by private individuals from non-EU countries. Norwegians and EU citizens may only take in a maximum of 15 kg (33 lb) of fish. Visitors from some other countries are permitted to bring in 1 kg (2.2 lb) of fish, but sometimes a certificate from a recognized exporter is required.

Dogs and cats from EU countries can be taken into Sweden, providing they have a veterinary certificate from the animal's home country. The animal must also have an identification marking, as well as an import permit issued by the Swedish Board of Agriculture (available from Swedish embassies).

Tax-free sales in Sweden are permitted only for travellers with a final destination outside the EU.

Tullverket provides up-to-date information in several languages by telephone and on its website.

OPENING HOURS

Most museums and major sights are open between 10am and 6pm all year, and they often have longer opening hours in the summer. Many museums close on Mondays. Some have extended opening hours one evening in the week. Admission to a number of state-run museums is free of charge. Admission charges for other museums

Tourist information office, Stockholm

◁ A ferry bringing summer visitors to the isolated Baltic island of Gotska Sandön, north of Gotland

vary between about 30 and 70 Kr. There is usually a discounted price for children, students and senior citizens. In many places, churches are only open for services, although some have opening hours for visitors.

Stockholm and other cities have special discount cards for tourists. They can be purchased from tourist information offices and many hotels and are valid for one or more days. A family card is usually also available. The card gives free travel on public transport, free or discounted admission to museums and other attractions and events, and may also offer discounts at restaurants and shops.

Discos and nightclubs generally charge an entrance fee of 60–120 kr. Tickets for the theatre, concerts and sporting events can be bought locally, in the cities at special ticket offices, or at the gambling service ATG's outlets via **BiljettDirekt**, www.ticnet.se.

DISABLED VISITORS

In Sweden, public areas have to be accessible for physically or visually disabled people, as well as those suffering from allergies. Sweden is a long away ahead of many other countries in this respect. Wheelchair ramps and spacious toilets for disabled people are fitted in all new buildings.

Disabled car drivers with a disability permit from their home country can park in special areas.

In Stockholm, the Tunnelbana underground network and local trains are adapted for disabled passengers. Buses "kneel" at bus stops to give a reasonable height for passengers to get on or off. Visitors from abroad can

The GöteborgPass, giving free admission to museums

obtain information in English before their stay from **De Handikappades Riksförbund** by telephone or via the Internet. Brochures with information about facilities for disabled visitors at theatres, cinemas, museums and libraries are available from tourist information offices.

ETIQUETTE

Bans on smoking are increasingly common throughout Sweden. Smoking is generally not permitted in public places, including all local transport and queues at bus stops and railway stations. Restaurants and bars are also smoke free.

The Swedes queue patiently, but guard their place jealously. They are usually friendly and pleased to help foreign tourists. The use of first names is the norm and a friendly *"Hej!"* is the common greeting.

Casual clothing is acceptable almost everywhere, including restaurants, particularly in the summer.

Service is always included in restaurant prices, but it is usual to round up the bill by up to 10 per cent for good service.

The logo of Systembolaget, the state-owned liquor store

ALCOHOL

Swedish policy towards alcohol is restrictive. Wines and spirits can be bought only in the relatively few shops of the state monopoly **Systembolaget**. They are open Monday–Friday 10am–6pm, and Saturday 10am– 2pm. The minimum age for buying alcohol in these shops is 20, and young people may be asked to produce proof of their age. In restaurants, the minimum age for buying alcohol is 18. Most restaurants and pubs stop selling alcohol at 1am, but some bars stay

open till 5am. With a maximum permitted blood alcohol level of only 0.2 per mil, drinking is effectively banned for car drivers.

The Swedish custom of *"skåling"* confounds many visitors. To *"skål"*, look the person in the eye, raise your glass, drink, then repeat the eye contact before putting down your glass. If the glasses are full of schnapps, then Swedes like to sing their special schnapps songs.

Personal Security and Health

Police symbol

Sweden is a safe destination compared with most countries in the world. You needn't worry about natural disasters such as earthquakes or hurricanes. Crime does occur, with some cities suffering more than others, but this is rarely a concern for tourists. However, it is important to lock the car and hide valuables when parked. Look out for pickpockets in the summer and avoid the empty, commercial parts of city centres late at night. Sweden has a well-developed network of emergency services which travellers can call on. Rescue services and hospital emergency clinics are highly efficient.

Policeman   Guard

Police car

PROTECTING PROPERTY

Although Sweden is a comparatively safe place, tourists can still run into trouble at times. Especially in the summer months, the many popular events attract bag-snatchers and pick-pockets. In the cities and in crowded public areas visitors should be particularly careful to keep an eye on their property, especially handbags and cameras. Avoid using unmanned cloakrooms at restaurants and museums.

Valuables and personal documents should always be locked in the hotel safe. It is equally important not to leave any valuables in your car; ideally, choose a hotel with its own parking facilities.

There is no need to carry large amounts of cash. All major credit and debit cards are accepted in virtually all shops and restaurants, and cash machines are common, at least in larger places. When

taking out cash, watch out for conmen who may offer to help, but are actually after your money or card.

PERSONAL SAFETY

The Swedish police are generally extremely helpful and speak good English. Police patrolling on foot or in cars are a routine sight in the cities, and mounted police are often in evidence at special events. In the suburbs, however, police can be thin on the ground. Out in the country, the police presence is low. Not all towns have

Mounted police

evening and night police patrols and even fewer have open police stations.

In many places, uniformed security guards have taken over the function of the police. They are a common feature in department stores, at train and Tunnelbana stations and as car patrols.

Stockholm, Gothenburg and Malmö are safe to stroll around on foot. Stockholm's Tunnelbana (underground railway) is efficient and comfortable, as well as being safe at most times. CCTV security systems are installed at some stations, squares, department stores and shops.

Beware the strict rules regarding alcohol, drugs and some medications when driving. A driver is guilty of drunk driving with a blood alcohol level of only 0.2 per mil and gross drunk driving (from 1.0 per mil) is punish-able by imprisonment. The possession of drugs is illegal.

Breaking traffic rules, particularly speed limits, may lead to hefty fines.

For some years it has been illegal to buy sexual services in Sweden so it is the buyer, not the prostitute, who is prosecuted. Street prostitutes are now a very rare sight in the inner cities.

LOST PROPERTY

Lost or stolen property should be reported to the nearest police station. A police report will be needed for any insurance claim. In addition to the police lost property offices (Polisens

Hittegodsexpedition), large towns and cities have lost property offices (Hittegodsavdelning) at railway stations, bus stations and airports. They are often only open during the day and not all of them will give information over the phone. There is usually a good chance of recovering lost goods.

Visitors from abroad should contact their embassy or consulate if they lose their passport.

EMERGENCIES

The emergency telephone number for police, fire or ambulance is **112**. It can be dialled free of charge from all public telephones, but should be used only in emergencies.

HEALTHCARE

No special vaccinations are needed to visit Sweden. Medical assistance is available across the country from doctors and district nurses at the local medical centre open surgeries.

There are duty clinics in the evenings and at weekends, but you must make an appointment by phone. Many hospitals have accident and emergency departments, some of which are privately run. Patients should not report to emergency clinics with minor ailments. First, contact the healthcare information service **Sjukvårdsrådgivningen** for instructions in English. Its staff have up-to-date knowledge about the current situation in the city's hospitals and can assign patients to a suitable hospital or duty doctor. Particularly during the holiday period, it is always advisable to use this central information service, to avoid

unnecessarily long waiting times. For severe toothache, patients can usually receive the help of a local dentist and larger places have special duty dentists.

Citizens of other EU and EEA countries are entitled to emergency medical care at the same low rate as Swedes if they produce a European Health Insurance (EHIC) card and a valid passport or other form of identification. More extensive treatment costs extra so it is advisable to take out separate medical insurance covering specialist care, hospital expenses and repatriation before travelling.

MEDICINES

In Sweden, medicines are only sold at pharmacies. Medicines for minor ailments are available without a prescription, but many medicines which are available over the counter abroad require a prescription in Sweden. There is also a risk that the medication prescribed at home may not be approved in Sweden. It is best to ensure that you pack sufficient medication for the duration of your trip.

Pharmacy staff are well trained and can give good advice. Unfortunately, pharmacies can be hard to find in the countryside and they are not open on Sundays. A limited number of natural remedies are also sold in health food stores.

Pharmacy sign

OUT AND ABOUT

Sweden has a varied landscape and climate and it is important to respect the forces of nature. In the mountains, the weather can change very quickly from still and sunny

DIRECTORY

EMERGENCIES

Ambulance, Police, Fire Brigade, Coastguard, Mountain Rescue *Tel 112.*

HEALTHCARE

Sjukvårdsrådgivningen
Tel 08-32 01 00 (24-hour) or 1177.

EMBASSIES

British Embassy
Skarpögatan 6–8, Stockholm.
Tel 08-671 30 00.

Canadian Embassy
Tegelbacken 4, Stockholm.
Map 1 C5, 3 A2.
Tel 08-453 30 00.

US Embassy
Dag Hammarskjölds Väg 31, Stockholm.
Tel 08-783 53 00.

one moment to fog or a storm the next. If you have the right equipment and follow the rules, a trip in the mountains need not be dangerous. The STF mountain stations offer good advice about safe trails.

Along the coast drowning accidents claim many lives every year. Avoid going out in flimsy craft and boats which are beyond your capabilities. Take advice from local people about the weather.

There is no need to worry about the forest predators – bears, wolves, lynxes and wolverines. They are shy creatures and prefer to avoid people. The same applies to Sweden's only poisonous snake, the adder. However, anyone bitten by a snake should seek medical advice.

Mosquitoes can be a nuisance from June to autumn, especially at dusk, along waterways and in the mountains. Pharmacies stock mosquito repellent. In the archipelagos, there is also a risk of being bitten by ticks, which carry a number of diseases. Ticks should be removed from the skin with tweezers as quickly as possible. If the redness around the bite area persists, consult a doctor.

Ambulance

Banking and Local Currency

Sweden has retained its own currency, the Swedish krona, rather than adopting the euro. A number of shops in major tourist areas will accept euros, but goods are almost exclusively priced in kronor. Visitors can change currency in banks, but better rates of exchange can often be obtained at bureaux de change in the main towns, which have longer opening hours. Automatic cash machines can be found outside most banks and in shopping centres across the country. Credit and debit cards are accepted virtually everywhere, and the larger stores will take traveller's cheques.

Bankomat, the joint cash-machine system of the business banks

BANKS

There are plenty of banks in the towns, all providing a good service. Their opening times vary, but the normal hours are 9.30am–3pm. Some banks stay open until 6pm at least once a week. All banks are closed at weekends and on public holidays, as well as the day before a public holiday.

Svenska Kassaservice, which handles the Swedish post office Posten's cash transactions, has almost 1,000 offices around the country. They are agents for certain banks and accept withdrawals on a debit card.

There are nearly 3,000 automatic cash machines throughout the country. They come in two types: Bankomat machines are the joint system of the business banks, while Uttag machines belong to FöreningsSparbanken. Foreign visitors can use all cash machines provided that they have a bank card with a PIN code that is linked to, for example, Visa or MasterCard. Machines usually have instructions in several languages. The charge for withdrawing cash varies according to the type of card.

CURRENCY EXCHANGE

Various bureaux de change chains are represented in Sweden. Generally they provide a better exchange rate than the banks, and in city centres there is always a bureau de change office close by. Changing money in your hotel is the most expensive option. It is worth checking exchange rates and commission charges, because the differences can be significant. Currency can be changed at international airports from 5.30am, and from 7am at city train stations seven days a week.

DIRECTORY

BANKS

Swedbank
Brunkebergstorg 8. **Map** 3 D4.
Tel 0771-22 11 22.
www.swedbank.se

Handelsbanken
Kungsträdgårdsgatan 2.
Map 4 C1.
Tel 08-701 10 00.
www.handelsbanken.se

Nordea
Hamngatan 12. **Map** 3 D4.
Tel 0771-22 44 88.
From abroad +46 771 22 44 88.
www.nordea.se

S-E-Banken
Sergels Torg 2. **Map** 2 C4.
Tel 0771-365 365.
From abroad +46 771 365 365.
www.seb.se

CREDIT CARDS

American Express
Tel 0771-295 600 (lost cards).
Tel 020-79 51 55 (trav. cheques).

Diners Club
(lost cards and other assistance)
Tel 08-14 68 78.

Eurocard
(lost cards and other assistance)
Tel 08-14 67 67.

MasterCard Global Service
(lost cards and other assistance)
Tel 020-79 13 24.

Visa
(lost cards and other assistance)
Tel 020-79 31 46.

BUREAUX DE CHANGE

FOREX
Service Center
Tel 0200-22 22 20.
www.forex.se

X-change
Tel 08-506 107 00
www.x-change.se

The head office of Handelsbanken on Kungsträdgårdsgatan, Stockholm

Forex bureau de change, situated in large towns and at airports

CREDIT CARDS

All the well-known credit cards, such as **Visa, Diners Club, Eurocard** and **MasterCard,** are accepted across Sweden, but not all places accept American Express because of opposition to the relatively high charges which the retailer has to pay.

Cards can be used not just at larger hotels and restaurants, but at nearly all shops and services. If you pay by credit card, most shops will ask you to produce proof of identity. Some shops also

offer a cash withdrawal service for small amounts in conjunction with purchases.

Cash machines can be used to make withdrawals using an internationally accepted credit card with a PIN code.

TRAVELLER'S CHEQUES

Traveller's cheques are one of the safest ways of carrying large amounts of money. They are not accepted in all shops, but can be changed at banks. It is sensible to keep a receipt showing the serial numbers of the cheques in a separate place. When buying cheques in your home country, it is worth checking the procedure if you lose any of your cheques.

CURRENCY

Sweden's currency is the krona (plural kronor). The krona (abbreviated as SEK or Kr) is divided into 100 öre. The smallest coin is 50 öre and the largest note is 1,000 kronor, which is not used much. If possible, it is advisable not to carry notes of more than 500 Kr.

Although Sweden has not adopted the euro, many shops in tourist areas and border towns will accept payment in euros, but will usually give change in kronor.

20 Kr (Selma Lagerlöf)

Notes
Swedish currency notes are issued in denominations of 20, 50, 100, 500 and 1,000 kronor. They depict famous Swedes, including monarchs, scientists and authors.

50 Kr (Jenny Lind)

100 Kr (Carl von Linné)

500 Kr (King Karl XI)

1000 Kr (King Gustav Vasa)

Coins
Coins are issued in values of 50 öre, and 1, 5 and 10 kronor. The 1 Kr and 10 Kr coins depict Sweden's monarch on the obverse side while the 5 Kr has his monogram on the reverse side. The 50 öre piece incorporates the state "three crowns" symbol.

50 öre

1 krona

5 kronor

10 kronor

Telecommunications, Post and Media

Sweden has a first-class public telephone system. A top-ranking telecommunications industry and high living standards have placed the Swedes among the world's biggest users of telephones. Although the fixed telephone system is well developed, there are now nearly as many mobile phone users as there are people in the country. With the advent of the 3G system allowing video telephony and advanced data services, only a very small percentage of the population does not have coverage. Internet use is widespread, with impressive investment in broadband.

A modern Swedish phone kiosk

MAKING A PHONE CALL

Sweden is divided into 250 dialling code areas. The prefix for international calls from Sweden is 00. Then dial the country code and the phone number without the initial zero of the area code. To dial Sweden from abroad, the country code is 46. For enquiries such as whether your phone will operate in the mountains, call Telia's customer services on 0046 771 99 02 00. For directory enquiries in Sweden, call 118 118. This also provides listings of mobile numbers.

The number of public telephone kiosks has shown a marked decline, as most Swedes have a mobile phone. The remaining public phones are mainly card-operated. They are owned by Telia and are cheapest to use with a Swedish phonecard. These can be bought at newspaper kiosks and in shops, and are available for 50 or 120 units. For a local call, the minimum charge is four units to a landline, with higher charges for calls to mobile phones and international calls. Some credit cards, petrol cards and international phonecards such as Access can be used, but at a higher rate. Instructions on how to use public telephones are also shown in English. It is possible to make reverse-charge (collect) calls within Sweden from all public phones by dialling 2#. The emergency number is 112. Some 020 and 0200 numbers can be called free of charge.

Coin-operated phones are very rare. Should you find one, they also have instructions in English and accept 1 Kr, 5 Kr and 10 Kr coins.

MOBILE PHONES

The Nordic countries have long had the analogue NMT network, which was known for its good coverage. Now the digital GSM network has taken over, offering a broader range of mobile services, and good coverage outside the cities.

Next-generation mobile telephony, 3G, was introduced in 2003 and offers even more advanced services. Coverage has greatly improved in recent years, reaching almost 100 per cent. Having a mobile phone is a good idea even out in the wilderness, but there is no guarantee that you will be able to call for help when you need it.

In most cases, European visitors can use their GSM and 3G phones in Sweden.

FAX, E-MAIL, INTERNET

The majority of hotels, airports, train stations and large shopping centres offer fax, telegram, e-mail and Internet services. There are

USING A CARD TELEPHONE

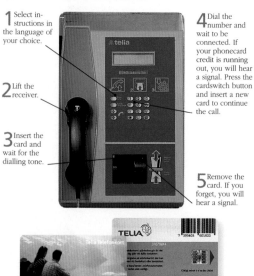

1 Select instructions in the language of your choice.

2 Lift the receiver.

3 Insert the card and wait for the dialling tone.

4 Dial the number and wait to be connected. If your phonecard credit is running out, you will hear a signal. Press the cardswitch button and insert a new card to continue the call.

5 Remove the card. If you forget, you will hear a signal.

Telephone cards
for 50 units.

Internet cafés dotted around the country. Hotels which focus on business travellers may have computers available for use in your room.

Swedish postage stamps

POST

The Swedish postal service has an almost 400-year history, but many Swedes think the service has deteriorated in recent years. Post offices have been closed and replaced by a few large postal centres, mainly for companies. For the general public, there are small service points, primarily in supermarkets and at petrol stations. They have the advantage of longer opening hours in the evenings and at weekends. The disadvantage is a frequent lack of space and services. Cash transactions have also been split off into a special company with its own offices, Svensk Kassaservice *(see p330)*. Perhaps the best service is provided in the really remote areas by mobile postal workers. Stamps can

Yellow postbox for national and international, blue for local mail

be bought at post offices, Pressbyrån kiosks and tourist information offices. The basic postage for a postcard or letter under 20 g within Sweden is 5.50 Kr (non-denominated stamp) or 6 Kr (denominated stamp); for abroad the postage is 12 Kr. Postboxes are painted blue for local letters and yellow for other domestic and international mail. Collection times are shown on the postbox and sometimes take place in the early afternoon. In large towns there are last-minute postboxes, which are emptied in the evenings.

Most international courier services are represented in the cities and special services are also operated by the Swedish post office, Posten.

TV AND RADIO

Most hotels provide a television in the room with both national and foreign channels. The most frequently used are the Swedish SVT1, SVT2, TV3, TV4 and Channel 5, as well as the international CNN, Sky News, BBC and Eurosport channels. SVT1 and 2 are state-run public-service channels. SVT2 and TV4 broadcast local programmes in the morning and evening, including weather forecasts.

There are also a number of local radio stations, broadcasting mainly international and Swedish music. P6, Stockholm International, has English and German-language programmes on 89.6 MHz.

Post office logo

NEWSPAPERS AND MAGAZINES

Major foreign newspapers and magazines can be bought in the cities, at airports and at other transport hubs. Pressbyrån kiosks, tobacconists, department stores

One of the country's many Pressbyrån kiosks

and some tourist information offices stock a limited selection of foreign publications. See the directory below for a range of newsagents.

TRAVEL INFORMATION

Stockholm Arlanda is the busiest of Sweden's international airports, although a number of other airports have international flights, notably Gothenburg's Landvetter and Sturup, near Malmö, in the south. Since summer 2000, Sweden has been linked with Continental Europe by a bridge over the Öresund Strait to Denmark for road and rail traffic. It is now possible to fly to

Aircraft of Scandinavian Airlines (SAS)

Copenhagen and take a short train journey across the bridge to Malmö. There are still a number of car ferry services operating between Denmark and Sweden, as well as across the Baltic Sea from Finland and the Baltic States, and across the North Sea from Norway and Great Britain. In summer, an increasing number of cruise liners call into Swedish ports. Express buses operate services from cities across Europe.

ARRIVAL BY AIR

Most major European cities have direct flights to one of Stockholm's three airports: Arlanda, Skavsta and Bromma. Landvetter near Gothenburg and Sturup outside Malmö also have international traffic. Arlanda is served by around 52 international airlines. It is also possible to fly via Copenhagen in Denmark. The leading Scandinavian airline **SAS** dominates. Other operators include **Lufthansa, British Airways** and **Finnair. Delta Air Lines** operates from the US to Paris with onward flights to Stockholm via Air France; **American Airlines** flies to the UK with onward connections via British Airways or Finnair.

Arlanda is 40 km (25 miles) north of central Stockholm and is also a hub for Swedish domestic flights and charter services. Bromma, situated 7 km (4 miles) from the city centre, may only be used by less environmentally

Arlanda Express linking Arlanda Airport with central Stockholm

damaging aircraft. Skavsta lies 100 km (60 miles) south of Stockholm, near Nyköping. Low-cost airline **Ryanair** flies routes to Skavsta and Gothenburg, from London Gatwick, London Stansted and Glasgow.

GETTING FROM AND TO THE AIRPORT

All the international airports are served by airport buses to the city centre in conjunction with arrivals and

departure times. Stockholm's Arlanda Airport has a "Flygbussarna" bus service, which operates every five minutes at peak times. Journey time is 45 minutes to the City Terminal at Central Station. An onward journey by taxi can be booked on the bus. The taxi ride into town from the airport is quicker, but more expensive. Most taxi firms have a fixed charge to the city centre. Avoid unauthorized taxis and check the fare before departure. The shortest journey time is by the pricier Arlanda Express train, a 20-minute trip to Central Station. Trains depart every 15 min from the two stations, Arlanda South (serving terminals 2, 3 and 4) and Arlanda North (for terminal 5).

AIR FARES

Fare options are many and varied, particularly if you are flexible about departure and arrival dates, or can book well in advance.

Increased competition between the airlines has made it considerably cheaper to fly to Sweden from many European destinations, and now SAS offers low-cost tickets with a no-frills service to meet the competition. It is possible to find return flights from London, Paris or Frankfurt for less than £80. Tour operators often have packages with attractive air fares and accommodation included. Newspaper advertisements and travel companies' websites have details of last-minute deals.

Terminal 5 (International) at Stockholm's Arlanda Airport

Ferry from Finland on the way to its terminal in Stockholm

ARRIVAL BY FERRY

A number of ferry companies operate direct services across the North Sea and the Baltic to Sweden. The large car ferries used on most routes offer plenty of passenger comforts, good food, entertainment and shopping.

From Newcastle in the UK, **DFDS** sails to Gothenburg via Kristiansand in Norway.

Although the Öresund Bridge has reduced ferry traffic from Denmark, the short Helsingør–Helsingborg hop still has several ferries an hour operated by **Scandlines** and **HH-Ferries**. **Stena Line** has the routes Grenå–Varberg and Fredrikshavn–Gothenburg.

The busiest route in terms of passenger numbers is from Finland with regular crossings from Helsinki, Turku and Mariehamn to Stockholm and Kapellskär. Both **Viking Line** and **Silja Line** have terminals in Stockholm at Stadsgården and Värtahamnen respectively. The crossing takes about 15.5 hours from Helsinki and 11 hours from Turku. **RG-Line** operates ferries between Vaasa in Finland and Umeå in northern Sweden. From Estonia, **Tallink** operates the

routes Tallinn– Stockholm and Paldiski– Kapellskär. Tallink also operates between Riga in Latvia and Stockholm.

Polferries has the routes Świnoujście–Ystad and Gdansk–Nynäshamn. **Stena Line** operates the Gdynia–Karlskrona route.

Trelleborg is the major port for traffic from Germany. **TT-Line** goes from Rostock and Travemünde, **Scandlines** from Rostock and Sassnitz. **Stena Line** sails the Kiel–Gothenburg route.

ARRIVAL BY TRAIN OR EXPRESS BUS

There are excellent train links from Continental Europe and Norway and a large network of express bus routes. **Tågplusguiden/ Expressbussguiden** is a good online search service providing an overview of train and long distance bus services.

ARRIVAL BY CAR

Motorists arriving from Denmark can use the spectacular Öresund Bridge between Copenhagen and Malmö *(see p181)*. On the Swedish side, the toll bridge connects with the E6 motorway to the north. Alternatively, there are car ferries.

Car ferries are also the most practical option from Finland and the Baltic States, as driving around the Baltic Sea can take two days.

The borders with Finland and Norway have customs posts which are often unmanned. However, the entry regulations still apply *(see p326)*.

Arrival hall at the Central Station in Stockholm

DIRECTORY

AIRLINES

American Airlines
Tel 1-800-433 7300.
www.aa.com

British Airways
Tel 0770 11 00 20.
www.britishairways.com

Delta Air Lines
Tel 1-800-241 4141.
www.delta.com

Finnair
Tel 0771-78 11 00.
www.finnair.nu

Lufthansa
Tel 0770-111 010.
www.lufthansa.se

Ryanair
Tel 0900-202 02 40.
www.ryanair.com

SAS
Tel 0770-727 727.
www.scandinavian.net

FERRY COMPANIES

DFDS
Tel 031-650 650.
www.dfdsseaways.se

HH-Ferries
Tel 042-19 80 00.
www.hhferries.se

Polferries
Tel 040-12 17 00.
www.polferries.se

RG-Line
Tel 090-185200
www.rgline.com

Scandlines
Tel 042-18 61 00.
www.scandlines.se

Silja Line
Tel 08-22 21 40.

Stena Line
Tel 031-704 00 00.
www.stenaline.se

Tallink
Tel 08-666 60 01.

TT-Line
Tel 0410-562 00.
www.ttline.se

Viking Line
Tel 08-452 40 00.
www.vikingline.se

TRAIN, EXPRESS BUS

Tågplusguiden/ Expressbussguiden
www.resplus.se

Getting Around Sweden

Flying within Sweden has its advantages considering the enormous distances between places, and in many cases the fares are reasonably priced. The high standard of overnight sleeper trains makes long journeys by train a comfortable option. The X2000 Express train running between the major cities often competes well in terms of time and comfort with domestic flights. Elsewhere in the country, buses provide much of the public transport. Travelling by boat offers exciting opportunities to discover Sweden's magnificent archipelagos and waterways.

Skyways, one of many companies offering domestic flights in Sweden

DOMESTIC FLIGHTS

The vast length of Sweden makes domestic flights a convenient option, and deregulation and increased competition in recent years have made prices more reasonable. Of the 45 airports offering scheduled flights, the 17 largest are state-run by **Luftfartsverket**. Its website contains information about the airports, flights and current arrivals and departures.

Stockholm/Arlanda dominates the domestic flight scene, but several companies have chosen to fly from the capital's more centrally located Bromma Airport. Landvetter, outside Gothenburg, and Sturup, outside Malmö, are other major airports.

Flight times are generally short: Stockholm–Gothenburg takes 55 minutes. The longest direct flight, Stockholm–Kiruna, takes 1 hr 50 mins.

SAS is still the leading airline in terms of passenger numbers, but with its 20 destinations, **Skyways** reaches most parts of the country. Other operators include **Malmö Aviation** and **FlyNordic**. Tickets can be bought at travel agents or directly from the airlines. Tickets booked online can generally be paid for with a credit card and collected at the airport. It is worth searching for the lowest prices, particularly if you book a long way in advance. Young people under 26 can buy cheap standby tickets.

Travellers to Malmö could consider flying to Kastrup in Copenhagen, as there is a fast train transfer to central Malmö across the Öresund Bridge.

Larger airports are served by airport buses, which operate in conjunction with arrivals and departures.

Malmbanan line from Kiruna to Narvik in northernmost Norrland

TRAVELLING BY TRAIN

There is a well-developed train network covering parts of Sweden from the Öresund Bridge in the south to Riksgränsen in the north. Stations and services are good by international standards. The trains are run by a number of competing companies. The state-run **SJ** operates most long-distance routes. Other major players include **Connex** and **Tågcompaniet**, which have parts of the lines in Norrland. At county level, train services are run by local train companies in partnership with bus services and in some cases ferry services.

Travel involving different companies and forms of transport is administered by **Samtrafiken**, which is part-owned by each of the transport companies. SJ offers a booking service for Tågplus tickets for English-speaking travellers.

In recent years, airlines have experienced tough competition from the X2000 Express train which links the cities of Copenhagen/Malmö, Gothenburg, Östersund and Falun to Stockholm. The journey time is around 5 hours from Malmö and 3 hours from Gothenburg. The trains offer a business class service similar to that of airlines.

SJ logo

InterCity is the main long-distance alternative to the X2000, offering first- and second-class seats. The overnight sleeper trains are recommended for longer journeys such as Gothenburg–Östersund and Connex routes in northern Norrland. The standard is high and you can often have your own compartment with shower, if you wish. Normal compartments contain three berths, but there are also six-berth compartments. Ticket prices vary considerably depending on the type of train. Discounts are worth searching for.

Tickets can be bought via ATG's outlets around the country and at larger stations. Buying tickets on the train attracts a fee of around 50 kr. Note that seat/berth reservations are necessary for the X2000 and night trains.

The **Inlandsbanan** line operates in summer, offering the opportunity to travel through the Swedish wilderness, forests and mountains. It runs 1,300 km (800 miles) from Kristinehamn on Lake Vänern north to Gällivare in northern Lapland.

TRAVELLING BY BUS

In many places buses are the only public transport available and although services are patchy in rural areas, it is possible to get about. Local timetables are on **Samtrafiken**'s website.

Express buses compete with trains and airlines on longer routes. Journey times are longer, but ticket prices are lower and the buses are modern. See Samtrafiken's Expressbussguiden for routes and times. Some bus companies, such as **Swebus Express**, do not require pre-booking. If one bus is full, another one is laid on.

Many express bus companies arrange special excursions in the tourist season. Contact the tourist information offices for information. Trips are also arranged to the southern Fjällen where there is no train line. **Fjällexpressen** is one of the operators running ski buses from Stockholm and Gothenburg.

Abisko's modest station building on the Malmbanan line

TRAVELLING BY BOAT

Sweden's long coastline, vast lakes and extensive archipelagos make for busy boat services. In addition to the scheduled services, sightseeing trips and tours are offered in summer, occasionally on classic old steamers.

The Dalsland, Strömsholm and Kinda canals attract some charming boats, but the tourist trail to beat them all is the Göta canal *(see pp146–7)*. Sweden's blue ribbon takes you 611 km (380 miles) in a relaxed three days, negotiating 65 locks, the country's three largest lakes and some of Sweden's most attractive scenery.

Boat services to the Baltic Sea's largest island, Gotland, are run by **Destination Gotland**, with its modern high-speed ferries, which take less than three hours on either of the Nynäshamn–Visby or Oskarshamn–Visby routes. In peak summer season, there are up to eight departures a day. Although the ferries can take 500 cars per trip, it can be difficult to get a place for a car during public holidays and other holiday periods if you have not booked in advance.

Gotland's high-speed catamaran service approaching Visby

Road Travel in Sweden

Tourist route sign

Distances within Sweden are huge, and in the rural areas travelling in your own or a rented car is often the only way of getting about. The well-developed road network varies in quality, but the major roads are generally of a good standard. State-run ferries operate a free service in the archipelagos. Although traffic can be heavy in the cities in rush hour, it is never on the same scale as in the UK and on the Continent, and Swedish motorists are generally good-natured. For advice on driving in Stockholm, *see p340.*

Elk on the road, a hazard for motorists in the forests

ROAD STANDARDS

Sweden has an extensive road network, with more than 210,000 km (130,000 miles) open for public use. Almost the same again is not accessible, primarily forestry roads which are closed with a boom. The majority of the public roads are sealed and of a good standard. The exceptions can be found in the forested counties of the northwest, where ice and heavy traffic can make the roads difficult to negotiate.

The national road network comprises *europavägar* ("European motorways"), *riksvägar* (national roads) and *länsvägar* (county roads). Motorways such as the E4 and stretches of the E20 and E6 make up less than 1,200 km (700 miles). With the exception of the Öresund and Svinesund bridges, roads are toll-free.

The three-lane highways require some attention for the uninitiated. The traffic runs in opposite directions along one or two lanes with a wire barrier to separate the flow.

TRAFFIC RULES

Generally, Swedish traffic is comparatively well organized and the majority of motorists follow the rules of the road. Road safety is good, despite occasionally dense traffic and severe weather conditions. The number of road fatalities is around 500 a year, the same level as in the 1940s.

The most common breach of the rules relates to speed limits, despite the presence of speed cameras and radar patrols. The fines are high and there is a risk of losing your licence for serious speeding offences.

The maximum permitted speed on motorways is 110 km/h (68 mph), but the limit is more often 90 km/h (55 mph). On country roads the limit is usually 70 km/h (43 mph) and in built-up areas the limit is 50 km/h (31 mph). The limit is reduced to 30 km/h (19 mph) around all schools and nurseries. Residential areas often have traffic calming measures such

as road narrowing and speed bumps. By law, the driver and all passengers must wear seatbelts. Children up to the age of six must use child seats.

Beware of the strict rules regarding alcohol and driving. A driver is guilty of drink-driving with a blood alcohol level of only 0.2 per mil and gross drink-driving (from 1.0 per mil) is punishable by imprisonment.

Motorists must give way to pedestrians at crossings not controlled by lights. Vehicles must stop at junctions onto major roads, even if there is no Stop sign. At roundabouts, vehicles already on the roundabout always have right of way. Traffic lights with a continuous amber light mean "stop" and there are hefty fines for driving through a red light. Side-lights or dipped headlights must be used even during daylight hours.

Winter tyres must be used from 1 Dec–31 Mar. Studded tyres may be used, but not during the period 1 May– 30 Sep, unless the road conditions require them.

CAR FERRIES

State-run car ferries operate free of charge in the archipelagos and across some of the larger rivers. Some places also have private ferries, which do levy a charge. You rarely need to book, but check the timetable carefully as the ferries may not run late at night unless in emergencies. **Vägverket** can provide information.

Uddevallabron on the E6, one of Sweden's many road bridges

ROAD SIGNS

Swedish road signs mostly follow the European standard, but the country also has some signs of its own. Signs carrying the symbol for elk, reindeer or deer warn drivers that there is a major risk of colliding with wildlife. Thousands of accidents involving animals occur every year and a collision between a car and a full-grown elk is often fatal. The risk is particularly high in the summer around 5am–8am and 10pm–2am, when visibility is poor. Fences along the roadside are no guarantee that animals won't suddenly appear on the road.

Warning sign for elk

As in the rest of Europe, brown signs with white symbols indicate recommended tourist routes, heritage sites, tourist areas and attractions along the road such as a national park or a historic building.

Individual attractions may be indicated by a sign with a white "pretzel" on a blue background.

PARKING

There is usually a charge for parking in towns and built-up areas, especially in the centre of towns and cities. City car parks and on-street parking are often expensive. Sometimes charges apply 24-hours a day and at weekends, too. Many ticket machines accept credit cards and petrol cards, but they may not always work, so it is best to keep a good number of 10 Kr coins to hand.

Diligent traffic wardens hunt out illegally parked cars and the fines can be high, particularly if you have parked illegally in a space reserved for disabled drivers.

Where parking is free during the night, there is sometimes a parking ban on certain days for cleaning, so it is always important to check the signs – otherwise your

car may be towed away. Supermarkets and other large stores often have free parking for a few hours, but be aware that sometimes they require a special parking ticket for your windscreen showing your arrival time.

FUEL AND SERVICES

There are plenty of service stations along the major roads and in built-up areas, but they may be few and far between in rural areas. Although some stations are manned 24-hours a day, drivers are often directed to automatic pumps which take cards and notes. It is sensible to fill up before a night drive. In the event of technical problems, there are few places which can help outside working hours – garages are usually closed in the evenings and at weekends.

Assistancekåren and **Falck** offer emergency roadside assistance. They often have an agreement with motoring organizations and insurance companies abroad.

RENTING A CAR

In addition to the familiar international car hire chains, there are a number of local options, including the petrol companies' extensive rental service. Most places will have some form of car rental.

It is possible to pre-book cars at airports and major train stations, often for one-way rental where you leave the car at your destination. Bookings can be made from abroad via the Internet or by phone. You generally only need a valid driving licence to rent a car, but there may be an age limit of 20, or even 25 for exclusive vehicles. Prices vary considerably, so it is worth shopping around. Special weekend deals are common and considering Sweden's long distances, it is best to opt for offers which include unlimited mileage.

Traffic warden

DIRECTORY

TRAFFIC INFORMATION

Vägverket
Tel 0771-119 119.
www.vv.se

CAR RENTAL

Avis
Tel 0770-82 00 62.
www.avis.com

Europcar
Tel 0770-77 00 50.
www.europcar.com

Hertz
Tel 0771-211 212.
www.hertz.com

OKQ8
Tel 020-850 850.
www.okq8.se

Statoil
Tel 0770-25 25 25.

CAR FERRIES

Vägverket, Färjerederiet
Tel 08-544 415 00.
www.farjerederiet.se

VEHICLE RECOVERY

Assistancekåren
Tel 020-912 912.
www.assistancekaren.se

Falck
Tel 020-38 38 38.

ROAD MAPS

Stanfords, London
Tel 020-7836 1321.
www.stanfords.co.uk

WINTER DRIVING

Road conditions in the winter vary depending on the severity of the weather and the location. Studded tyres are permitted in Sweden and their use is recommended, at least from central Sweden northwards.

Anyone not used to winter driving should not venture out if there is a risk of snow and ice. The major roads are treated with salt, and ploughing is generally good, but even in Skåne in the far south, snow storms can cause traffic chaos and in some years military tracked vehicles have had to be called out.

Getting Around Stockholm

Pedestrians and bicycles

Stockholm is a perfect city for pedestrians. Distances between sights are short, and there is always something interesting to discover among the eye-catching vistas and waterfront scenes. Cycling is popular and there are many cycle lanes throughout the city, although for the visitor a green area such as Djurgården might be more relaxing for a cycle trip. Public transport on buses, trams, underground trains, local trains and ferries is efficient. Apart from Gamla Stan, and during the rush hours, driving a car in Stockholm is relatively easy, although parking can be difficult.

Taking a waterfront stroll along Djurgårdsbrunnsviken

STOCKHOLM ON FOOT

In central Stockholm, walking is the best way to see the sights and get a feel for the place. Road users are more disciplined here than in many other cities. Pedestrians are not allowed to cross a road against a red light, but motorists must stop and give way to pedestrians at zebra crossings without traffic lights.

The clear street signs make it easy to find one's way around, and Stockholmers are always glad to help visitors. There are walking and cycling routes everywhere in the city. Take care not to step out in the cycle lane, which is often marked just with a white line to separate it from the walking lane.

Gamla Stan is a popular area for exploring on foot, and there is always something

to see around Kungsträdgården as well. In good weather, nothing beats Djurgården, with its host of attractions set in beautiful parkland only a short distance from the centre.

There are pleasant waterfront walks along the quays, for example from Stadshuset along Norr Mälarstrand and the Riddarfjärden bay.

Walks with multilingual guides are organized regularly, often with a special theme – history, architecture or parks, for example.

CYCLING

The capital's network of cycle paths is increasing all the time, but you need to be an experienced city cyclist if you want to explore the central area from the saddle. Otherwise Stockholm and its surrounding area are tailor-

made for cycling. There are plenty of places to hire bicycles and mopeds.

DRIVING IN STOCKHOLM

Anyone familiar with driving in large cities will have no problems in Stockholm. It is relatively easy to get about by car, except during the rush hours (7.30am–9.30am, 11.30am–1pm, and 3.30–6pm). Cars are not really necessary in the city centre because of the short distances between sights and excellent public transport. However, a car is an advantage if you want to explore further afield.

Congestion charges were introduced in 2007 to tackle busy traffic and to improve the environment.

The speed limit is usually 50 km/h (31 mph), but near schools it is 30 km/h

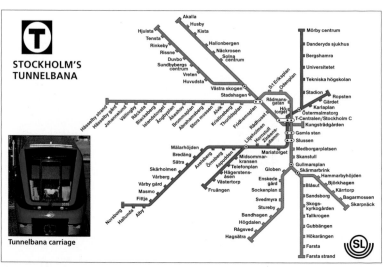

STOCKHOLM'S TUNNELBANA

Tunnelbana carriage

(19 mph). Speeds up to 70 km/h (43 mph) are permitted only on the main roads in and out of the city.

It is often hard to find a parking space. In some areas parking charges apply 24-hours a day, but usually parking is free in the evenings, at night and at weekends. Check for street cleaning times when parking is prohibited.

The city's traffic wardens are diligent. Being wrongly parked could cost you a fine of 450 kr or more. Do not leave valuables in your car, particularly in a car park.

TAXIS

Distances between places in the city centre are short and brief journeys by taxi rarely cost more than 100 Kr. There are usually plenty of taxis available, particularly at taxi ranks and major sights, with the exception of the rush hours. You can also hail an empty taxi, indicated by the illuminated sign on the car roof. The best method is to order a taxi by phone or book one in advance. It is always worth enquiring what the fare is likely to be, as many companies charge a fixed rate. Be careful about using unauthorized taxis without a taxi sign on the outside, or a taxi identity card on display inside, especially at night.

PUBLIC TRANSPORT

All public transport in the county of Stockholm is under the control of **Stockholms Lokaltrafik**, but the actual services are run by several companies. An extensive network of local trains, underground trains, buses and ferries carries hundreds of thousands of commuters in from the suburbs every day.

Red city bus and blue "feeder" bus

In the city centre, the Tunnelbana (T-bana) underground system's green, red and blue lines are the mainstay, supplemented by city buses, a few tramlines and ferry routes.

On regular lines in the Stockholm area there is a choice of tickets: single-trip or 1-, 3-, 7- and 30-day travel cards. It is worth buying a book of ten discount coupons if planning several trips, as the price reduces from 30 kr to 18 kr per ticket. The tickets are valid for one hour from the start of the journey. Single tickets can be bought on departure, while return tickets, books of coupons and travel cards are sold at Pressbyrån outlets and SL and T-bana stations.

The network of red city buses is built around a number of blue "feeder" routes.

Ferry linking Gamla Stan and Djurgården

These run more frequently. Many streets in the city centre have special bus lanes which speed up the traffic. The best routes for sightseeing are 3, 4, 47, 62 and 69.

Run by **Waxholmsbolaget**, public transport in the archipelago is good all year round, with more frequent services from June to August. An excellent way to explore the archipelago is to take the ferries from Strömkajen, which stop off at countless picturesque jetties along the way.

Other recommended trips include Birka, Drottningholm and Mariefred/Gripsholm *(see pp110–11)*. A popular way of getting to Djurgården is on the ferry from Slussen to Allmänna Gränd. SL's one-day and three-day cards are valid on the Djurgården ferry.

(see pp110–11)

DIRECTORY

TRAFFIC INFORMATION

Stockholms Lokaltrafik
Tel 08-600 10 00.
www.sl.se

TAXIS

Taxi Kurir
Tel 08-30 00 00.

Taxi Stockholm
Tel 08-15 00 00.

Taxi 020
Tel 020-20 20 20.

ARCHIPELAGO AND SIGHTSEEING BOATS

Waxholmsbolaget
Strömkajen, Vaxholm, Stavsnäs.
Tel 08-679 58 30.
www.waxholmsbolaget.se

Strömma Kanalbolaget
Nybrokajen, Stadshusbron.
Tel 08-587 140 20.
www.stromma.se

Open Top Tours
Tel 08-1200 4000.
www.opentoptours.com

SIGHTSEEING

A pleasant way of enjoying Stockholm from the water is to take an excursion run by Stockholm Sightseeing (**Strömma Kanalbolaget**). A "Round Kungsholmen" tour departs hourly from the quayside near the City Hall. The "Under Stockholm's Bridges" and "Round Djurgården" tours depart from Strömkajen near the Grand Hotel, and passengers are also picked up from Nybroplan. Tickets can be bought at both these points. A commentary is provided on headsets in several languages. The tours generally run once an hour. Most tours are only available in the summer, but some run until December.

Sightseeing tours by bus include the **Open Top Tours** double-deckers, which run between strategic stops close to attractions in central Stockholm. Passengers can hop on and off along the way.

General Index

Acknowledgments

Streiffert Förlag would like to thank the following staff at Dorling Kindersley:

Publisher
Douglas Amrine

Publishing Managers
Jane Ewart, Anna Streiffert

Senior Editor
Christine Stroyan

Map Co-ordinator
Casper Morris

DTP Manager
Jason Little

Production Controller
Linda Dare

Additional Picture Research
Rachel Barber

Additional Photography
Ian O'Leary

Dorling Kindersley would like to thank all those whose contributions and assistance have made the preparation of this book possible.

Main Contributors

ULF JOHANSSON has produced Swedish guidebooks such as *Sverigeboken* and *Sverigevägvisaren*. He has also been a publisher and year-book editor at the Swedish tourist association Svenska Turistföreningen.

MONA NEPPENSTROM is an editor and travel journalist and has written a large number of Swedish guidebooks, including *Sverigeboken*, *Sverigevägvisaren*, *Turisttoppen* and rail company SJ's travel guide series *Längs spåret*.

KAJ SANDELL wrote the *Eyewitness Stockholm* travel guide. He is a journalist and formerly wrote for Swedish publishers Åhlén & Åkerlunds Förlag and Swedish daily broadsheet *Dagens Nyheter*.

Factchecking
Lena Ahlgren

Proofreader
Stewart J Wild

Index
Helen Peters

Artwork Reference
Svenska Aerobilder AB

Revisions Design and Editorial
Alannah Eames, Anna Freiberger, Amy Harrison, Sonal Modha, Rada Radojicic, Ellen Root, Marta Bescos Sanchez, Kathleen Blankenship Sauret.

Photography Permissions
The publishers would like to thank all those who gave permission to photograph at museums, palaces, churches, restaurants, hotels, stores and other sights too numerous to list individually. Particular thanks go to the Guild of Museum Directors in Stockholm for permitting access to picture archives as well as making additional photographing of objects and exhibitions possible.

Picture Credits
t = top; tl = top left; tlc = top left centre; tc = top centre; trc = top right centre; tr = top right; cla = centre left above; ca = centre above; cra = centre right above; cl = centre left; c = centre; cr = centre right; clb = centre left below; cb = centre below; crb = centre right below; bl = bottom left; bc = bottom centre; br = bottom right; b = bottom.

Works of art have been reproduced with the permission of the following copyright holders:

© ADAGP, Paris and DACS, London 2008: Paradise 1963 Jean Tinguely and Niki de sainte Phalle 49bl, 76clb; © DACS, London: Nils Ferlin KG Bejemark 237c; Concrete Jonas Bohlin 27tr; Noble Glass carafe Gunnar Cyren 314clb; The Dying Dandy Nils Dardel 80bl; The Child's Brain Giorgio De Chirico 81cl; The Dance Carl Eldh 103bc; Selma Lagerlof Carl Eldh 235br; Einar Forseth 102tr; Simon Gate 155tr; statue of Evert Taube Gordon Willy Gordon 62clb; Hans Hedberg 26tr; Visby Wall Hanna Hirsch-Pauli 166tr; Altarpiece in Jukkasjärvi Church Bror Hjort 274c;Märta Måås-Fjetterström 26br; Orpheus Carl Milles 71tl; Poseidon Carl Milles 195cr, 202t; Sigurd Persson 27tl; Crux rug Pia Wallen 314bl; © DACS. London/VAGA, New York 2008: Monogram Robert Rauschenberg 80crb; © Sucession Picasso/DACS, London 2008; Breakfast Outdoors Pablo Picasso 80tr.

Every effort has been made to trace the copyright holders. Dorling Kindersley apologizes for any unintentional omission and would be pleased, in such cases, to add an acknowledgment in future editions.

Commissioned by the publisher, the book's main photographers, Peter Hanneberg, Erik Svensson and Jeppe Wikström, produced the majority of the photographs reproduced in this book. They have also contributed archive pictures which have been listed among the other picture credits. The publisher would like to thank the photographers and all the other individuals, organizations and picture libraries for permission to reproduce their photographs and illustrations:

ALAMY IMAGES: A.P. 97 tr; Marie-Louise Avery 298cl; Brother Luck 9cl; Chad Ehlers 11bl; Peter Forsberg 299c; Nick Haslam 11tr; Leslie Garland Picture Library 9br; Nicholas Pitt 299tl; Rainer Raffalski 11c; Robert Harding Picture Library Ltd/ The Picture Store 10tr; Ray Roberts 10cl; Bjorn Svensson 8tc.

AMAROK AB: Magnus Elander 18t, 18clb.

ARMÉMUSEUM: 266bl. ÁTTJE FJÄLL- OCH SAMEMUSEUM: Jan Gustavsson 22tr.

CORBIS: Kevin Schafer 8br; Zefa/ Fridmar Damm 10br.

DANSMUSEUM:64tr. DROTTNINGHOLMS SLOTTSTEATER: Bengt Wanselius 109tr, 109bc.

ETNOGRAFISKA MUSEET: Bo Gabrielsson 93c.

FJÄRILS & FÅGELHUSET: 97cl.

GETTY IMAGES: Stone/ Ted Wood 8cl. GREAT SHOTS: Peter Gerdehag 118–119. GUNNEBO SLOTT:225tl.

GÖTEBORGS KONSTMUSEUM: *Karin and Kersti*, Carl Larsson 237b.

HSB MALMÖ 2006: Ole Jais 181lbr. PETER HANNEBERG: 2–3c, 4t, 17t, 18cla, 18cra, 19tc, 19cl, 19br, 21cr, 22tl, 22b, 23cb, 123b, 161bc, 161br, 246, 247b, 248c,

258bl, 259tr, 262, 263b, 268c, 269br, 270–271, 274ca, 275cb, 318b, 320b, 321t, 321b, 324–325. CHRISTER HÄGG: *East Indiaman Wasa*, Jacob Hägg 198b. IMS BILDBYRÅ: 43tl. JÖNKÖPINGS LÄNS MUSEUM: *Bianca Maria in Among Elves and Trolls*, John Bauer 23bl.

KOSTA BODA:Ann Wåhlström 25b; Ulrika Hydman Vallien 152b; Kjell Engman 153bc. KUNGLIGA BIBLIOTEKET: 36br, 70b. KUNGLIGA HUSGERÅDSKAMMAREN: Alexis Daflos 4b, 56tr, 56clb, 57tr, 107tc; 106cl, 106bl, 107bl, 108tr, 108clb; *The Triumph of Karl XI*, Jacques Foucquet 37tl; 46b; Håkan Lind 54cra, 54crb, 54br; 54tl, 55tc, 55cr, 56cla, 107cr; 135c. KUNGLIGA MYNTKABINETTET: 51crb; Jan Eve Olsson 52cl, 69tr. KUNGLIGA OPERAN: Mats Bäcker 64bc, 67tl, 67c. KÄLLEMO AB: 25c. LIVRUSTKAMMAREN : 37bl, 41br; Göran Schmidt 41cla, 51tl; Nina Heins 52bl.

MALMÖ TURISM: Oskar Falck 181cl; Mårten Swemark 179tl; MEDELHAVSMUSEET: Ove Kaneberg 64cla. METRIA KIRUNA: 8cr. MODERNA MUSEET: 78br, 78bl; Per Anders Allsten 78bc. MUSEUM TRE KRONOR: 56br. MUSIKMUSEUM: Nina Heins 70cra.

NATIONALMUSEUM: 24clb; *Flowers on the Windowsill*, Carl Larsson 24–25c; *Gustav Vasa*, Cornelius Arendtz 30; *Ansgar Preaches Christianity*, Georg Pauli 32bl; *Stockholm Bloodbath*, Dionysius Padt-Brügge 33t; *The Entry of King Gustav Vasa of Sweden into Stockholm, 1523*, Carl Larsson 34t; *Portrait of Erik XIV*, Steven van der Meulen 34c; *The Fire at the Royal Palace 7th May 1697*, Johan Fredrik Höckert 35tr; *Portrait of Queen Kristina*, David Beck 35cl; *The Death of Gustav II Adolf of Sweden at the Battle of Lutzen*, Carl Wahlbom 36bl; *The Crossing of the Belt*, Johan Philip Lemke 36–37c; *Karl X Gustav*, Sébastien Bourdon 37cr; *Bringing Home the Body of King Karl XII of Sweden*, Gustaf Cederström 37br; *King Gustav III of Sweden*, Lorens Pasch d.y. 38tl; *Portrait of the Bernadotte Family*, Fredrik Westin 38crb; *The Coronation of Gustav III*, Carl Gustav Pilo 40cla; *The Battle at Svensksund*, J T Schoultz 40clb; *A Noisy Dinner*, Johan Tobias Sergel 40bc; *Conversation at Drottningholm*, Pehr Hilleström 40–41c; *The Murder of Gustav III*, A W Küssner 41tr; *Bacchanal on Andros*, Peter Paul Rubens 47tl; 55br; *The Conspiracy of the Batavians under Claudius Civilis*, Rembrant 80cla; *Amor and Psyche* (1787) Johan Tobias Sergel 80clb; 80bc;

Lamino Chair (1955) Yngve Ekstrom photo Hans Thorwid 81c;*The Love Lesson*, Antoine Watteau 80tr; *The Lady with the Veil*, Alexander Roslin 81tl; *Karl XIV Johan's Visit to Berga*, A C Wetterling 146t; *Valdemar Atterdag Plunders Visby 1361*, Carl Gustaf Hellqvist 167b. NATURHISTORISKA RIKSMUSEET: Staffan Waerndt 96c. NORDISKA MUSEET: Birgit Brånvall 88tr; Mats Landin 47tr; 88cl; Sören Hallgren 88bc; *Snowstorm at Sea*, August Strindberg 89cra; 89tr; *The Proposal*, Knut Ekwall 89tl.

PARKEN ZOO I ESKILSTUNA AB: 135bc. POSTMUSEUM: 59crb. PRESSENS BILD: 5tr, 6–7c, 10, 11b, 16t, 23tr, 2, 27b, 43cr; Hans T. Dahlskog 43br; 54bl; Jan Delden 68br; Gunnar Seijbold 71tl; 87tl; Axel Malmström 99tr; 105br, 120t, 206, 259b, 310cr, 311tr, 316cr, 322tl.

REDERI AB GÖTA KANAL:147cra. LAILA REPPEN: 20–21c. RIKSANTIKVARIEÄMBETET: 3c.

SJÖHISTORISKA MUSEET: 94c. SKANSEN: Marie Andersson 92c. SKOGSKYRKOGÅRDEN:105c. SKYWAYS: Jonas Kosunen 336t.INGALILL SNITT: 20t. STATENS HISTORISKA MUSEUM: 84cla, 84clb, 84bl, 84br, 85tc, 85ca, 85cb, 85br, 85bl, 130b. STENINGE SLOTT: 130t.STOCKHOLMS AUKTIONSVERK: 41bl. STOCKHOLMS STADSBYGGNADSKONTOR: 95c. STOCKHOLMS STADSHUS: Jan Asplund 100br, 101tl. STOCKHOLMS STADSMUSEUM: 32t; *Tre Kronor Palace*, Govert Camphuysen 36cl; *Newspaper Readers*, J A Cronstedt 39tl; *The Regicide Anckarström Punished in Front of the House of Nobility*, 41cr; 42bl, 43clb. STRINDBERGSMUSEET: Per Bergström 69bc. SVENSKA AKADEMIEN: Leif Jansson 40tr. ROLF SØRENSEN: 18bl, 19bl.

THIELSKA GALLERIET: *Hornsgatan*, Eugène Jansson 93tr. LARS TUFVESSON: Lars Tufvesson 181b.

VASALOPPSMUSEET: 244t, 244cla, 244cra, 244bl. VASAMUSEET: Hans Hammarskiöld 47br, 90tr, 90cla, 90bl, 90br, 91tc, 91cra; 91crb, 91bl. VIN & SPRITHISTORISKA MUSEET: 98c.

CLAES WESTLIN: 24cla. JEPPE WIKSTRÖM: 26b, 27t, 29b, 44-45, 48, 52tr, 62, 64clb, 65crb, 65bl, 68tl, 72, 76br, 77ca, 82, 83t, 86t, 87tr, 97br, 99tl, 99b, 100bl, 102t, 103t, 103cl, 103b, 104tl, 110cr, 110cra, 111tl, 111br, 276–277, 290b, 316bl, 335t, 334t.

ÖSTASIATISKA MUSEET: Erik Cornelius 76bl; Karl Zetterstrom 74cla.

JACKET: Front - AWL IMAGES: Peter Adams. Back - ALAMY IMAGES: Jon Arnold Images Ltd/Doug Pearson tl; PVstock.com clb; Sola/parasola.net bl; DORLING KINDERSLEY: Peter Hannenberg cla. Spine - AWL IMAGES: Peter Adams t.

Phrase Book

When reading the imitated pronunciation, stress the part which is underlined. Pronounce each syllable as if it formed part of an English word, and you will be understood sufficiently well. Remember the points below, and your pronunciation will be even closer to the correct Swedish.

ai:	as in 'fair' or 'stair'
ea:	as in 'ear' or 'hear'
eu:	like the sound in 'dew'
EW:	try to say 'ee' with your lips rounded
oo:	as in 'book' or 'soot'
OO:	as in 'spoon' or 'groom'
r:	should be strongly pronounced

Swedish Alphabetical Order
In the list below we have followed Swedish alphabetical order. The following letters are listed after z: å, ä, ö.

You
There are two words for 'you': 'du' and 'ni'. 'Ni' is the polite form; 'du' is the familiar form. It is not impolite to address a complete stranger with the familiar form.

In an Emergency

Help!	Hjälp!	yelp
Stop!	Stanna!	stanna!
Call a doctor!	Ring efter en doktor!	ring efter ehn doktor
Call an ambulance!	Ring efter en ambulans!	ring efter ehn ambewlanss
Call the police!	Ring polisen!	ring poleesen
Call the fire brigade!	Ring efter brandkåren!	ring efter brandkawren
Where is the nearest telephone?	Var finns närmaste telefon?	vahr finnss nairmasteh-telefawn
Where is the nearest hospital?	Var finns närmaste sjukhus?	vahr finnss-nairmasteh shewkhews

Communication Essentials

Yes	Ja	yah
No	Nej	nay
Please (offering)	Varsågod	vahrshawgOOd
Thank you	Tack	tack
Excuse me	Ursäkta	ewrshekta
Hello	Hej	hay
Goodbye	Hej då/adjö	haydaw/ahyur
Good night	God natt	goonatt
Morning	Morgon	morron
Afternoon	Eftermiddag	eftermiddahg
Evening	Kväll	kvell
Yesterday	Igår	ee gawr
Today	Idag	ee dahg
Tomorrow	I morgon	ee morron
Here	Här	hair
There	Där	dair
What?	Vad?	vah
When?	När?	nair
Why?	Varför?	vahrfurr
Where?	Var?	vahr

Useful Phrases

How are you?	Hur mår du?	hewr mawr dew
Very well, thank you.	Mycket bra, tack.	mewkeh brah, tack
Pleased to meet you.	Trevligt att träffas.	treavlit att traiffas
See you soon.	Vi ses snart.	vee seas snahrt
That's fine.	Det går bra.	dea gawr brah
Where is/are ...?	Var finns ...?	vahr finnss...
How far is it to ...?	Hur långt är det till	hewr lawngt ea dea till
Which way to ...?	Hur kommer jag till ...?	hewr kommer yah till ...
Do you speak English?	Talar du/ni engelska?	tahlar dew/nee engelska
I don't understand	Jag förstår inte.	yah furshtawr inteh
Could you speak more slowly, please?	Kan du/ni tala långsammare, tack.	kan dew/nee tahla lawng-ssamareh tack
I'm sorry.	Förlåt.	furrlawt

Useful Words

big	stor	stOOr
small	liten	leeten
hot	varm	varrm
cold	kall	kall
good	bra	brah
bad	dålig	dawleeg
enough	tillräcklig	tillraikleeg
open	öppen	urpen
closed	stängd	staingd
left	vänster	vainster
right	höger	hurger
straight on	rakt fram	rahkt fram
near	nära	naira
far	långt	lawngt
up/over	upp/över	EWp/urver
down/under	ner/under	near/ewnder
early	tidig	teedee
late	sen	sehn
entrance	ingång	ingawng
exit	utgång	ewtgawng
toilet	toalett	too-alett
more	mer	mehr
less	mindre	meendre

Shopping

How much is this?	Hur mycket kostar den här?	hewr mewkeh kostar dehn hair
I would like ...	Jag skulle vilja ...	yah skewleh vilya
Do you have?	Har du/ni ...?	hahr dew/nee...
I'm just looking	Jag ser mig bara omkring	yah sear may bahra omkring
Do you take? credit cards	Tar du/ni kreditkort?	tahr dew/nee kredeetkoort
What time? do you open	När öppnar ni?	nair urpnar nee
What time do you close?	När stänger ni?	nair stainger nee
This one.	den här	dehn hair
That one.	den där	dehn dair
expensive	dyr	dewr
cheap	billig	billig
size (clothes)	storlek	stOOrlek
white	vit	veet
black	svart	svart
red	röd	rurd
yellow	gul	gewl
green	grön	grurn
blue	blå	blaw
antique shop	antikaffär	anteek-affair
bakery	bageri	babgeree
bank	bank	bank
book shop	bokhandel	bOOkhandel
butcher	slaktare	slaktareb
cake shop	konditori	konditoree
chemist	apotek	apoteak
fishmonger	fiskaffär	fisk-affair
grocer	speceriaffär	spesseree-affair
hairdresser	frisör	frissurr
market	marknad	marrknad
newsagent	tidningskiosk	teednings-cheeosk
post office	postkontor	posstkontOOr
shoe shop	skoaffär	skOO-affair
supermarket	snabbköp	snabbchurp
tobacconist's	tobaksaffär	tOObaks-affair
travel agency	resebyrå	reasseh-bEWraw

Sightseeing

art gallery	konstgalleri	konnst-galleree
church	kyrka	chewrka
garden	trädgård	traidgawrd
house	hus	hews
library	bibliotek	beebleeotek
museum	museum	mewseum
square	torg	tohrj
street	gata	gahta
tourist information office	turistinformationskontor	turrest-informashOOns-kontOOr
town hall	stadshus	statsheus
closed for holiday	stängt för semester	staingt furr semester
bus station	busstation	beuss-stashOOn
railway station	järnvägsstation	yairnvaigs-stashOOn

Staying in a Hotel

Do you have any vacancies?	Har ni några lediga rum?	hahr nee negra leadiga rewm
double room with double bed	dubbelrum med dubbelsäng	doobelrewm med doobel-seng